Eugenic Nation

T0355557

AMERICAN CROSSROADS

Edited by Earl Lewis, George Lipsitz, George Sánchez, Dana Takagi, Laura Briggs, and Nikhil Pal Singh

Eugenic Nation

*Faults and Frontiers of Better Breeding in
Modern America*

SECOND EDITION

Alexandra Minna Stern

UNIVERSITY OF CALIFORNIA PRESS

University of California Press, one of the most
distinguished university presses in the United States,
enriches lives around the world by advancing scholarship
in the humanities, social sciences, and natural sciences. Its
activities are supported by the UC Press Foundation and
by philanthropic contributions from individuals and
institutions. For more information, visit www.ucpress.edu.

University of California Press
Oakland, California

Library of Congress Cataloging-in-Publication Data

Stern, Alexandra.
  Eugenic nation : faults and frontiers of better breeding
in modern America / Alexandra Minna Stern.—Second
edition.
     p. cm.
  Includes bibliographical references and index.
  ISBN 978-0-520-28506-4 (pbk : alk. paper)
  ISBN 978-0-520-96065-7 (ebook)
  1. Eugenics—United States—History. 2. Eugenics—
California—History. I. Title. II. Series: American
crossroads; 17.
  HQ755.5.U5S84 2016
  363.9′209794—dc23
                                         2015018767

25   24   23   22   21   20   19   18   17   16
10   9   8   7   6   5   4   3   2   1

Contents

Illustrations

Preface to the Second Edition

In July 2013 the Sacramento-based Center for Investigative Reporting (CIR) released an article alleging that 150 female inmates in California state prisons had been sterilized without proper authorization between 2006 and 2010.[1] The outcome of more than one year of investigative journalism, this article exposed a broken and unjust system of reproductive health services in California women's prisons. Senator Hannah-Beth Jackson, Democrat from Santa Barbara and vice-chairwoman of the Legislative Women's Caucus, was one of the first lawmakers to respond to these revelations. She evinced dismay that such reproductive abuse could have transpired in the twenty-first century. Jackson lambasted the federal Receiver's Office for failing to maintain medical standards of care in California prisons: "Pressuring a vulnerable population—including at least one instance of a patient under sedation, to undergo these extreme procedures erodes the ban on eugenics. In our view, such practice violates Constitutional protections against cruel and unusual punishment; protections that you were appointed to enforce."[2] In the same breath, Jackson requested an investigation by the California state auditor.

A comprehensive audit was issued one year later. Corroborating and expanding on the CIR's findings, it confirmed that 144 women had been sterilized between fiscal years 2005–6 and 2012–13 without adherence to required protocol and that "deficiencies in the informed consent process" had occurred in 39 of these cases.[3] Some of the irregularities included inadequate counseling about sterilization and its lasting consequences, missing physician signatures on consent forms, neglect of the mandated waiting period, and destruction of medical records in violation of records retention policies. After the release of the audit, Jackson, with ample support from other legislators and the guidance of Justice Now, a prisoners' rights group, drafted legislation (SB 1135) to ban sterilizations in state prisons except in extreme cases when a patient's life is in danger or when there is a demonstrated medical need that cannot be met with alternative procedures. This legislation moved easily from committee to the floor, where it received unanimous approval (77 ayes and 0 noes), and finally to the desk of Governor Jerry Brown, who signed it in September 2014.[4]

The CIR's coverage of this story, and the additional information that emerged during the legislative process, unmasked a carceral environment characterized by a haphazard mixture of disregard and undue pressure, coupled with inconsistent supervision that allowed medical staff to act with little procedural accountability. Particularly disturbing were the prejudices expressed by Dr. James Heinrich, a physician who performed many of the tubal ligations. He indifferently explained to a reporter that the money spent sterilizing inmates was negligible "compared to what you save in welfare paying for these unwanted children— as they procreated more."[5] This callous attitude about the reproductive lives of institutionalized women, the majority of whom were low income and women of color, was not new to California. In the 1930s, at the height of eugenic sterilization, superintendents of California state homes and hospitals repeatedly discussed the need to reduce the economic burden of "defectives" and their progeny through reproductive surgery. In the late 1960s the University of Southern California/Los Angeles County General Hospital obstetrician who oversaw more than one hundred nonconsensual postpartum tubal ligations of Mexican-origin women purportedly spoke to his staff about "how low we can cut the birth rate of the Negro and Mexican populations in Los Angeles County."[6]

Looking back over more than one century, we can map three overlapping chapters of sterilization abuse. Most dramatically from the late 1900s to the early 1950s, about twenty thousand people in state homes and hospitals were sterilized. By the 1960s, as approaches to mental health and disability evolved, sterilization fell into disfavor and annual rates dropped to the single digits. Yet sterilization abuse appeared in another domain. Newly available federal programs that could finance tubal ligations in public facilities converged with readily circulating stereotypes of women of color, above all Mexican-origin women, as hyperbreeders.[7] This potent combination set the stage for the sterilization abuse that occurred in the late 1960s and early 1970s in the University of Southern California/Los Angeles County General Hospital, which in turn triggered two lawsuits and street protests. In tandem with similar cases throughout the country, rising awareness of sterilization abuse among women of color, low-income women, and female minors paved the way for the development of federal and medical guidelines to ensure against such violations in the future.

What happened in California women's prisons in the early 2000s represents a contemporary link in the chain of a history of reproductive injustice in public facilities and demonstrates that the hard-won safeguards developed by the 1980s could buckle under the weight of a troubled prison system. In 2006, after countless cases of mistreatment and abhorrent neglect, a district court judge placed the delivery of inmate health care in California under federal receivership. In the words of the judge, "The harm already done in this case to California's inmate population could not be more grave, and the threat of future injury and death is virtually guaranteed without drastic action."[8] This court order, ironically, helped to usher in the Gender Responsive Strategies Commission, established to address the needs of female inmates. Despite a promising name and in breach of both California law and federal law, this commission loosened policies around sterilization.[9] In a crisis-ridden and overcrowded prison system with multitudinous administrative problems, the results of this policy relaxation and reorientation were extreme. Prison officials pursued sterilization lackadaisically, and Heinrich was contracted to provide obstetrical services despite a long trail of "medical controversies and expensive malpractice settlements both inside and outside prison walls."[10] In addition to carrying out many of the unauthorized tubal ligations, Heinrich was investigated by the Receiver's Office after two pregnancies ended in infant deaths. In one case he administered the wrong medicine; in the other he failed to identify a common bacterial infection. At Valley State, many of the inmates described Heinrich as creepy, spooky, and inappropriate. According staff members, he was unhygienic, often eating popcorn, cheese, and crackers while carrying out vaginal examinations. Some inmates recounted instances in which he pressured them into tubal ligations, telling them they already had enough children.[11]

As distasteful as Heinrich was, he was not an aberration but the acute manifestation of a system that undervalued the reproductive and maternal lives of incarcerated women. The prison staff and administration at Valley State and the California Institution for Women in Corona, the two institutions where sterilizations took place, appear to have either consciously pursued or irresponsibly ignored a high volume of tubal ligations among inmates. Crystal Nguyen, a former inmate who worked in the infirmary at Valley State in 2007, told the CIR that she frequently overheard "medical staff asking inmates who had served multiple prison terms to agree to be sterilized." Nguyen was shocked by these exchanges: "Do they think they're animals, and they don't want them to breed anymore?"[12]

According to the state audit, 94 (65 percent) of the 144 women sterilized at Valley State and the Corona facility were women of color (black, Hispanic, Mexican, or other, using the audit's terminology). The majority, 101 (70 percent), were in prison for the first time; only 13 (9 percent) had been incarcerated for the third time.[13] These figures are reflective of California's overall prison profile, in which African American women, who make up approximately 7 percent of the state's female population, constitute 30 percent of the female prison population, and Latinas constitute 27 percent. The majority of female prisoners in California institutions have been imprisoned for nonviolent offenses, most often drug related.[14] The skyrocketing rates of incarceration in California, and around the country, followed the implementation of mandatory sentencing laws in the 1980s. For example, from 1982 to 2000, California's prison population grew almost 500 percent, and approximately two-thirds of those incarcerated were African Americans and Latinos.[15] From 1986 to 1998, female incarceration in California shot up 305 percent.[16] These decades of neoliberal restructuring saw a flurry of prison construction. For example, the state built twice as many prisons, twenty-three, between 1985 and 2005 as it had over the 130 preceding years (between 1852 and 1984), when twelve prisons were constructed.[17]

The upsurge of California's prison population was related to another dynamic—the deinstitutionalization of state homes and hospitals. From the 1910s to the 1960s, these institutions housed a heterogeneous mix of patients that today we would recognize as ranging from people with serious psychiatric disorders to people punished for transgressing sexual norms, from people with a spectrum of intellectual disabilities to people charged with minor offenses such as truancy and petty crime. The deinstitutionalization of the 1970s and 1980s involved the release of most of these patients to developmental centers, family care networks, or sometimes the streets. As places such as the Sonoma State Home and Stockton State Hospital were shuttering their doors, left abandoned

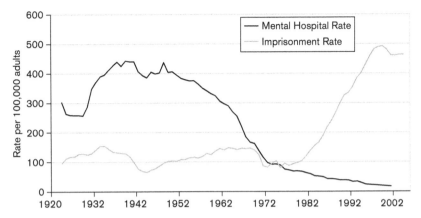

FIGURE I. Deinstitutionalization of California mental hospitals and feebleminded homes and the concomitant rise of incarceration, 1922–2005. This process of transinstitutionalization accelerated rapidly starting in 1975. Source: Prepared by researcher Nicole Novak using data from Bernard Harcourt, "An Institutionalization Effect: The Impact of Mental Hospitalization and Imprisonment on Homicide in the United States, 1934–2001," ICPSR34986-vi, Inter-university Consortium for Political and Social Research, Ann Arbor, MI.

or converted to limited-term treatment facilities, prisons were appearing throughout the state, usually in the distant rural, semisuburban areas that had been chosen for the asylums of yesteryear. Valley State, built in 1995 and located in Chowchilla, a small city in the San Joaquin Valley, was one of these new facilities and exemplifies the new era of institutionalization in California.

This dynamic is most aptly described, not in terms of book-ended patterns of deinstitutionalization and concomitant escalating incarceration, but as a process of transinstitutionalization that started in the 1970s and was consolidated by the 1990s.[18] Figure 1 demonstrates the overlap between declining population rates in California's feebleminded homes and mental hospitals and the state's rising prison population.

Although the populations we would have found in Sonoma or Stockton in the 1930s do not correspond identically to populations today at Valley State or Corona, there are striking similarities, including elevated numbers of racial minorities, people with limited education, youth committed for minor offenses, and a substantial number of inmates diagnosed with mental illness.[19] Moreover, both then and now, sterilization abuse was facilitated by a staggering lack of oversight and the cultivation of institutional milieus where administrators and medical directors could dictate the terms for reproductive surgery with little worry about scrutiny.

The similarities between the homes and hospitals of the first half of the twentieth century and the prisons that appeared starting in the 1970s are demonstrated by historical analysis using a novel and recently available resource. In 2007, while visiting the Department of State Hospitals in Sacramento, I discovered nineteen microfilm reels containing eighteen thousand sterilization recommendations and supplemental documents for the period 1921 to 1952. Several years later, after digitizing these materials, receiving institutional review board approval, and setting up an interdisciplinary team capable of qualitative and quantitative data entry and analysis, we are beginning to generate findings about patterns and experiences of sterilization in California state institutions during the height of the eugenics era. Chapter 4, written for this revised second edition, is based principally on these new data. It demonstrates that racial and gender bias undergirded eugenic sterilization and explores the contradictions of a system that foregrounded consent even though it was not a legal requirement. Because parole or release from an institution was contingent on sterilization, patients and families could find themselves in an excruciating bind, making an impossible choice between either accepting reproductive surgery to leave the institution or insisting on bodily autonomy by objecting to the procedure even though that meant forfeiture of the opportunity to be discharged. This voluminous set of sterilization records shows that superintendents regularly took advantage of legal prerogatives to override resistance to sterilization, which was most vigorously mounted by Mexican-origin parents whose children were placed in state facilities.

Perhaps the new law prohibiting sterilization in California prisons will fulfill its proscription. But even if it does, we can now map more than one hundred years of episodic sterilization abuse in the Golden State. This extended history has ramifications for the pursuit of reproductive justice and offers compelling evidence for why sterilization safeguards are still needed in the twenty-first century.[20] Yet overreacting to California's prisons sterilizations, as appalling as they are, has the potential to counterproductively limit the reproductive freedom of marginalized women who seek tubal ligations as a preferred mode of birth control.[21] Cumbersome paperwork and mandated waiting periods for sterilization are a significant issue, especially for Latinas who face multiple obstacles to obtaining access to other options such as long-acting reversible contraception.[22] Recent hysteria over "anchor babies" or children born to undocumented Mexican and Central American women on US soil who acquire *jus soli* citizenship evokes and rekindles eugenic anxieties about the supposed fecundity of Latinas, whose reproductive bodies yet again become targets of concern and control.[23]

Compulsory sterilization was a critical and integral component of eugenics in twentieth-century California; and eugenic assumptions about parental fitness and worth were conspicuous in Valley State and Corona when tubal ligations were performed improperly and sometimes coercively on female prisoners. Nevertheless, eugenics is not a necessary ingredient of sterilization abuse. Nor does eugenics always pivot around policies and practices of reproductive regulation. As *Eugenic Nation* shows, theories of better breeding in the United States affected many other domains, including immigration, education, and environmentalism, in explicit and implicit ways that reverberate into the present.

. . .

Niels Hooper and his team at the University of California Press made this second edition possible, and I thank them for working with me so smoothly toward publication. I remain indebted to the many colleagues, archivists, and friends who were integral to the first edition of *Eugenic Nation*. Added to that long list one decade later are the wide range of people who assisted with the creation of the eugenic sterilization data set and offered incisive commentary on the quantitative and qualitative dimensions of the new research. Natalie Lira, Kate O'Connor, Nicole Novak, and Emma Maniere have been deeply committed to this project from the beginning, and I could not have asked for a more dedicated and intelligent group of students to serve as the core of my team. I am particularly grateful to Natalie Lira, who took the lead in designing the data capture instrument and whose scholarship has expanded my understanding of the intersections of Latina/o studies, disability studies, and reproductive politics. I am very lucky to count as my trusted faculty collaborators Sharon Kardia and Sioban Harlow from the University of Michigan's School of Public Health, who generously offered biostatistical and epidemiological expertise and much-coveted lab space.

The Departments of American Culture, Obstetrics and Gynecology, History, and Women's Studies have served as distinct and complementary academic homes where I could nurture innovative and interdisciplinary approaches to studying reproductive health and social justice. Among many wonderful colleagues I would like to acknowledge Lisa

Harris, Ed Goldman, Tim Johnson, Maria Cotera, Amy Sara Carroll, June Howard, Anthony Mora, Lisa Nakamura, Ruby Tapia, Donna Ainsworth, and Will Glover for their ongoing interest in this project. The dynamic communities of the University of Michigan's Science, Technology, and Society program and Latina/o Studies program have shaped the interpretation and analysis of my new research. In particular, I would like to thank Gabrielle Hecht, Paul Edwards, Joel Howell, John Carson, Shobita Parthasarathy, Marty Pernick, and Perrin Selcer. I have also benefited from insightful conversations with David Wallace, Jennifer Robertson, Celeste Brusati, Sidonie Smith, Patrick Tonks, Stephen Modell, Toby Citrin, and Justin Joque. These discussions have ranged from tackling the technical aspects of the eugenic sterilization data set and companion digital archive to contemplating their relevance to contemporary health policy.

I am fortunate to have a wide network of colleagues and friends whom I trust to hold my feet to the fire, especially when reading chapter drafts. Nathaniel Comfort, Paul Lombardo, Erika Dyck, Terri Koreck, Marcy Darnovsky, Katie Wataha, Kate O'Connor, Devon Stillwell, and Marion Schmidt each took time away from busy semesters and jobs to give me astute feedback. In addition, I am grateful to the many colleagues who gave me tips or suggestions as this project evolved: Janet Golden, Johanna Schoen, Miroslava Chávez-Garcia, Terence Keel, Troy Duster, Nayan Shah, Susan Schweik, Emily Beitiks, Catherine Kudlick, Randall Hansen, Rob Wilson, Corey Johnson, Gerri Ondrizek, Milton Reynolds, Osagie Obasogie, Jessica Cussins, Natalia Molina, Rickie Solinger, Elena Gutiérrez, Ernie Chávez, Amanda Alexander, Gilberto Hochman, Marcos Cueto, Gabriela Soto Laveaga, Loretta Ross, Sara McClelland, Jacqueline Wernimont, Sarah Gualtieri, and the late and much-loved Maria Elena Martínez.

My father, Andrew, always has been a great supporter of my research and interests, and I am ever grateful to him. My partner, Terri, and daughter, Sofia, make life enjoyable every day, and I thank them profusely for putting up with the many hours I hide away in my office working on projects, including this book.

Abbreviations

ABA	American Breeders' Association
AES	American Eugenics Society
AIFR	American Institute of Family Relations
ASHA	American Social Hygiene Association
CBJR	California Bureau of Juvenile Research
CCC	Commonwealth Club of California
CIR	Center for Investigative Reporting (Sacramento)
CSUS	California State University at Sacramento
CVS	chorionic villus sampling
ERO	Eugenics Record Office
ESNC	Eugenics Society of Northern California
HBF	Human Betterment Foundation
HEW	US Department of Health, Education and Welfare
INS	US Immigration and Naturalization Service
IQ	Intelligence Quotient
JTA	Johnson Temperament Analysis Test
M-F Test	Male-Female Test
NAACP	National Association for the Advancement of Colored People
NIPT	noninvasive prenatal testing

OEO	Office of Economic Opportunity
PPIE	Panama-Pacific International Exposition
SNCC	Student Nonviolent Coordinating Committee
SNCRB	Second National Conference on Race Betterment
UNESCO	United Nations Educational, Scientific and Cultural Organization
USPHS	US Public Health Service
ZPG	Zero Population Growth

Introduction

At a ceremony held in Oregon's capitol building in December 2002, Governor John Kitzhaber stood before an overflowing crowd and apologized for the more than 2,600 sterilizations performed in that state between 1917 and 1983.[1] Since the summer, Kitzhaber had been under mounting pressure from a vocal coalition of mental health advocates, disability rights groups, and sterilization victims to express public remorse for what he referred to at the December event as the "misdeeds that resulted from widespread misconceptions, ignorance and bigotry."[2]

Kitzhaber's apology was the second in a series initiated by Virginia's governor, Mark Warner, who in May 2002 deemed his commonwealth's sterilization program "a shameful effort in which state government should never have been involved."[3] The governors of North Carolina, South Carolina, and California followed suit, delivering similar statements of regret over the next twelve months. Tangible and symbolic gestures usually accompanied these apologies. In Virginia, for example, two of the approximately eight thousand people sterilized between 1924 and the 1970s unveiled a highway marker recognizing the injustice suffered by Carrie Buck. The first person affected by Virginia's sterilization law, Buck was the plaintiff in *Buck v. Bell*, the infamous 1927 US Supreme Court case in which the justices overwhelmingly upheld the constitutionality of involuntary sterilization. In Oregon, acknowledging that a "great wrong" had been done "in accordance with eugenics," Kitzhaber designated December 10 as Human Rights Day, a day on which henceforth "we will affirm the value of every human being."[4] North Carolina's governor, Mike Easley, approved compensation, in the form of health care and education benefits, to any living resident of the 7,600 sterilized by the state between 1929 and 1974. Although it took some years to formalize Easley's proposal, in 2010 North Carolina created the Office of Justice for Sterilization Victims, and in 2014 it began to issue checks in the amount of $20,000 to victims whose sterilizations could be verified as performed by the Eugenics Board of North Carolina.[5]

These five states represent a fraction of the thirty-two that had sterilization laws on the books at some point in the twentieth century; nevertheless, their actions are noteworthy. For many victims, these apologies and monetary compensation assuaged the pain and indignity they had endured after forced operations. As public utterances predicated on an awareness of the past, the governors' statements helped to foster valuable historical research into the personal stories of those sterilized and the activities of the responsible health and welfare agencies. They also sparked important bioethical discussions in legislative, university, and community forums about the potential for medical abuse and miscommunication, particularly with regard to genetic and reproductive technologies.

Yet these apologies can close rather than open retrospective windows, and they raise serious questions about how we remember—and forget—eugenics. By drawing a fairly stark line between an ugly and benighted chapter of pseudoscience in which misguided authorities were ensnared by Nazi-inspired ideas of racial hygiene and a much savvier and sagacious present in which such mistakes will not be repeated, the apologies can create a specious sense of security, even hubris. As admonitions against future medical coercion or exploitation, such statements are well-meaning reminders at best and, in a post–Cold War global era defined by a dense traffic of restitutive and contritional pronouncements, vacuous truisms at worst.[6] Most worrisome from a historian's perspective, they can make it more difficult to extract eugenics from the shadow of Nazism. Without doubt, familiarity with German racial hygiene is imperative to grasp the international and philosophical milieu in which eugenics arose and to understand how medical abuse can converge with dictatorial politics to produce genocide.[7] The atrocities of the Final Solution should never be minimized. Nonetheless, the looming presence of the Holocaust in our collective memory, into which context the apologies must be placed, has helped to privilege renditions and narratives of eugenics in America that, ultimately, flatten and simplify the historical terrain.[8] *Eugenic Nation* seeks to explore continuities, permutations, and ramifications of better breeding in the United States that have been obscured; in so doing, it proposes a revised chronology, decenters the vantage point from which the story is often told, and excavates a set of topics that have rarely received more than a passing nod.

There are several reasons to challenge the prevailing historical understanding of eugenics and its underlying assumptions about time, place, and thematic relevance. First, the declension narrative of Nazism is so potent and seductive that it has often served as the principal lens through which much US scholarship has framed eugenics. There is a deep emotional charge to associating any practice or person with Nazism, and in the writing of history the recitation of such connections can stand in for careful analysis of historical contingencies and can verge on sensationalism. Of course, it is vital to document the parallels between the United States and Germany and to acknowledge the shared historical trajectories of these two countries.[9] Several prominent US eugenicists corresponded regularly with their German counterparts, eugenic and lay periodicals applauded the passage in the 1930s of Nazi marriage and sterilization laws (which were partly derived from American models), and at least two eugenicists received honorary degrees from German universities during the rise of fascism.[10] By the eve of Hitler's defeat, leading US scientists, journalists, and politicians had positioned themselves against Nazi-style doctrines of racial superiority and noted anthropologists were jettisoning biological determinism and embracing cultural explanations of human difference.[11] In 1952, a United Nations Educational, Scientific and Cultural Organization (UNESCO) committee that included well-known American geneticists issued a far-reaching statement on the falsity of the "race concept."[12]

Given that eugenics in the United States is frequently aligned with scientific racism, the fall of Nazism and the abandonment of overt racial categories by many postwar eugenicists have encouraged the view that eugenics disappeared, or at least languished, in the 1940s. Hereditarianism, however, did not perish after World War II; it was repackaged. Exhibiting more flexibility than their predecessors, postwar eugenicists partly accepted the role of extrinsic factors and incorporated tenets from demography, sex research, psychoanalysis, and anthropology into their repertoires. Guided by experiments in endocrinology and human genetics that were examining hormonal function, sex selection, and chromosomal patterns, and increasingly attentive to theories of polygenic disease causation and genetic susceptibility, most postwar eugenicists let environmental precipitants in the door without, however, relinquishing the ultimate primacy of heredity.[13]

Eager to sever any association with state coercion, eugenicists in the postwar period shifted their scope in two directions. In the first direction, they began to place greater emphasis on individual choice and private decision making, often under the emergent rubric of medical genetics. This was the case with genetic counseling, which was launched at a handful of heredity clinics and university-based human genetics departments in the 1940s. Using family pedigree charts and armed with fledgling knowledge of the biochemistry of a variety of genetic diseases, genetic counselors advised couples on the probability that their off-spring would carry deleterious or lethal traits.[14] They publicly disdained earlier eugenicists' fixation on race and instead believed that the universal gene pool could be improved through judicious mating and a personal reluctance to propagate defects.[15] The individual was also the focus for practitioners of constitutional medicine and biotypology, specialties that mixed physiology, psychology, and anthropometry in a quest to identify omnipresent human types that corresponded not to racial classifications but to binaries such as hyperkinetic and hypokinetic, introvert and extrovert, endomorph and ectomorph.[16]

If genetic counselors and biotypologists headed in the first direction, population experts headed in the second. After World War II, as the United States became a global superpower, a core group of eugenicists merged their interest in salvaging and retooling eugenics with the export of Western-led modernization to the Third World. This resulted in organizations such as the neo-Malthusian International Planned Parenthood Foundation and the Population Council, founded in 1948 and 1952, respectively, which pursued family planning and birth control abroad.[17] Wary of totalitarianism, most postwar eugenicists distanced themselves from arguments about the need to subordinate individual rights to the national collectivity and moved simultaneously into the domains of marriage, the family, and the geopolitics of international development.[18]

Thus efforts to encourage better breeding continued in the United States, primarily through family planning, population control, and genetic and marital counseling. At the same time, a few organizations, such as the Pioneer Fund, formed in 1937, forged ahead undaunted with studies aimed at furnishing a scientific basis for racial discrimination.[19] In addition, as content analyses of the most widely assigned biology textbooks demonstrate, eugenic explanations of social behavior were heartily endorsed in classrooms around the country into the 1960s.[20] During the 1940s and 1950s, there were heated debates about "good" versus "bad" eugenics—the latter usually equated with "pseudoscience"—but the term itself did not fall into general disrepute until the 1970s.[21] Indeed, the American Eugenics Society (AES) did not feel compelled to change its name to the Society for the Study of Social Biology until 1973 (although its directors clarified that this did "not coincide with any change of its interests and policies").[22] Last, the stringent immigration and sterilization laws passed decades earlier remained in force, affecting the ethnic and demographic composition of the United States and the lives of thousands of patients and inmates in state institutions.[23]

The second reason to challenge the prevailing historical understanding of eugenics is that until recently eugenics historiography, like much of the history of medicine, has been quite East Coast–centric. For the most part, scholars have explored eugenics from the vantage point of organizations, such as the Eugenics Record Office (ERO) and the AES, and individuals, such as Charles B. Davenport and Madison Grant, all based on the Atlantic seaboard. For the first generation of historians delving into eugenics, archival repositories such as the American Philosophical Society Library—which houses the papers of the ERO and Davenport—were the logical place to start, and the books and articles resulting from this research laid down a solid foundation for future work.[24] With New York, Washington, D.C., and Boston as epicenters, most students of eugenics developed a narrative that tacitly made the East Coast its geographical reference point and then projected that interpretation across the rest of the country, often with only remote interest in regional variations. Certain seminal events, such as the creation of the ERO in 1910 and its closing in 1940, or the sparsely attended Third International Eugenics Congress, held in New York in 1932, became salient signposts. However, historical records of eugenics in the South, Midwest, and West reveal alternative chronologies that do not fit with these East Coast temporal markers. For example, in 1907, the state of Indiana stood at the vanguard, ushering in the country's first sterilization law. Seven years later, John Harvey Kellogg, in the cereal capital of Battle Creek, Michigan, incorporated the first sizable eugenics organization, the Race Betterment Foundation.[25] We also see that, in the 1930s, as the ERO was coming under fire, several southern states passed sterilization laws for the first time, the number of sterilizations performed nationwide increased markedly, and several groups on the West

Coast, such as the California Division of the AES and the American Institute of Family Relations (AIFR), expanded their activities.[26]

Over the past decade, studies focused on Vermont, Virginia, North Carolina, Minnesota, Indiana, and Oregon have underscored the multidimensional presence of eugenics from coast to coast.[27] They have demonstrated the longevity of hereditarianism across the arc of the twentieth century and have detailed the range of alliances that eugenicists forged with socialists, free-love advocates, feminists, horticulturists, pediatricians, obstetricians, public health advocates, philanthropists, industrialists, and a motley cast of politicians and legislators. Further, it is now impossible to disregard the global reach of eugenics, which thrived in places as diverse as Norway, Japan, China, Argentina, and Canada.[28] Eugenics was a worldwide phenomenon; what its heterogeneous adherents shared was faith in the application of biology and medicine to the perceived problems of modern society. And in many countries, such as Mexico, Chile, and France, eugenics grew in popularity not in the 1910s and 1920s but from the 1930s to the 1950s, inspiring socialist education campaigns, the professionalization of social work, and the construction of planned housing communities for fecund working-class families.[29] Once situated in this multiregional and transnational panorama, the timetable and topography of eugenics in the United States appear more elongated and striated than previously imagined.

In particular, by turning our gaze thousands of miles west, away from the headquarters of the ERO, we encounter a history that was both paradigmatic of large-scale national trends and particular to the region. It is surprising that the American West has been largely overlooked, given that California performed twenty thousand sterilizations, one-third of the total performed in the country; that Oregon created a State Eugenics Board in 1917; and that the impact of restrictive immigration laws designed to shield America from polluting "germ plasm" reverberated with great intensity along the Mexican border. In addition, the "West" spawned metaphors and myths for the initial generation of American eugenicists, who updated the Manifest Destiny doctrines of the 1840s with a twentieth-century medical and scientific vocabulary to expound on the noble westward march of Anglo-Saxons and Nordics.[30]

From the perspective of the American West, conventional assumptions no longer hold; in their place materialize novel subjects and avenues of inquiry. For example, the Second National Conference on Race Betterment, held at the Panama-Pacific International Exposition in 1915, needs to be understood not just as part of an ascendant eugenics movement that had one foot on the West Coast but also in terms of the circulation of tropical medicine from the Panama Canal and the Philippines to San Francisco. A closer look at the implementation of medical inspections and immigration regulations along the Mexican border illustrates the eugenic dimensions of the Border Patrol, which was formed in 1924 to help enforce the Johnson-Reed Immigration Act and regulate Mexican immigration. The affinity between eugenic and environmentalist ideas about the purity and preservation of nature can be captured by reviewing the origins of the interpretative parks movement and the Save-the-Redwoods League, both of which were generously supported by Charles M. Goethe, the Sacramento businessman who launched the Eugenics Society of Northern California.[31] In California, eugenics was promoted by state agencies, most notably the Department of Institutions, which oversaw sterilization in public institutions and the rollout of psychometric and IQ testing and carried out deportation drives that removed foreign nationals from state homes and hospitals on the basis of an intertwined logic of cost savings and biological betterment. Last but certainly not least, the AIFR, founded in 1930 by Paul Popenoe, an ardent sterilization proponent, not only shows the concerns of eugenicists in the rapidly expanding city of Los Angeles before and after World War II but also illuminates the eugenic designs behind the personality, marital compatibility, and sexual function tests that were formulated during the Cold War era.

A third reason to challenge the prevailing historical understanding of eugenics is that, as feminist scholars have shown, placing gender and sexuality at the center of the analysis reconfigures the history of eugenics, demanding substantial temporal and thematic revisions and delineating a story that is at once more ordinary and more complex.[32] For example, when the reproductive and erotic body is highlighted, an uninterrupted line can be drawn from the sterilization laws passed by state legislatures in the 1910s that targeted "morons" and the "feebleminded" to the sexual surgeries performed by federal agencies on poor female welfare recipients during the 1960s.[33] As the twentieth century progressed, and following the simplification and routinization of the salpingectomy (removal of one or both fallopian tubes, which still entailed greater risks and longer convalescence than the vasectomy) in the 1930s, more operations began to be performed on women than men.[34]

This transition indicates that the forced sterilization of women in the United States was interwoven with the enlargement of the welfare state, the denigration of dependent and single mothers, and the perceived burden of "illegitimate" children.[35] This was certainly the case in North Carolina, where sterilizations of African American women deemed "unfit" and incapable of proper parenting rose in the 1950s and 1960s.[36] For more than fifty years, involuntary sterilizations were motivated by a shifting mix of anxieties about sexual deviance and the promiscuity of teenage girls, fears of biological deterioration, and a discourse of institutional cost saving.

In addition to urging a reevaluation of sterilization practices, foregrounding sexuality and gender complicates many of the conceptual retaining walls that have circumscribed eugenics and other social and cultural phenomena. For example, the records of North Carolina's Eugenics Board show that while black women were being disproportionately sterilized in the 1950s and 1960s, some of them, intent on obtaining birth control, actually filed applications for the operation.[37]

Although only about 6 percent (468) of the 8,000 total sterilizations in North Carolina were requested, the insistence of a vocal minority on obtaining approval for the procedure reveals the extent to which the battle for reproductive control was framed by eugenic categories and priorities. Feminist scholars have recognized this symbiotic relationship for quite some time and have shown how male physicians gradually took over birth control, how eugenicists appropriated the agenda of family planning, and how the women's movement struggled to reverse these trends in the 1960s and 1970s.[38] All too often, however, these issues are distilled into a thumbnail sketch of the hot-button figure of Margaret Sanger, who has been alternately described as a die-hard eugenicist with virulent race and class prejudices or as a true if misguided feminist who cultivated strategic alliances with eugenicists but did not fully accept the implications of their ideas.[39]

A tendency to depict eugenics in black and white has elided uncomfortable nuances. For instance, according to one scholar, the majority of women in Puerto Rico (mostly middle or working class) who underwent sterilization had a positive or neutral assessment of the procedure, which was their preferred contraceptive option.[40] Yet it is common for scholarship on twentieth-century Puerto Rico to ignore this feminist attitude toward sterilization as well as the vibrancy of the early feminist movement, which fought for reproductive autonomy, and to instead echo condemnations of the scientific experts who pushed "la operación" as a "remedy" for a purported overpopulation problem. Although the experiences of Puerto Ricans who underwent surgery in New York City hospitals may have had more in common with those of African American and

Native American women who spoke out against forced tubal ligations in the 1960s and 1970s, much of the history of sterilization needs to be considered a fractious interplay between diverse feminist groups, those sterilized, physicians, the welfare bureaucracy, and eugenicists.

Finally, if attention to gender and sexuality has illustrated some of the gray areas of reproductive politics, it also sheds light on how everyday eugenics played out, above all, among white middle-class Americans.[41] After World War II, as eugenicists turned toward genetic and marital counseling, their target populations changed.[42] Instead of tallying the "undesirable" and the "feebleminded," they began to devote greater attention to married heterosexual couples, who they hoped would amply procreate. Although some historians juxtapose these two approaches as "positive" (fostering the reproduction of the "fit") and "negative" (impeding the reproduction of, and even euthanizing, the "unfit"), such a distinction implies that they can be easily disentangled. In California, however, the most vocal champions of "positive" eugenics, Popenoe and Goethe, who used that term to explain their interests and the organizations they founded, were also the most heavily invested in "negative" campaigns such as compulsory sterilization and unyielding immigration restriction. Rather than accepting such descriptors transparently, it is crucial to historicize their rhetorical function and be cognizant of their explanatory limitations. Scholars have also relied on the terminology of "mainline" and "reform" to characterize, respectively, the racist eugenicists of the 1920s, such as Harry H. Laughlin, and their more moderate successors, such as Frederick Osborn, the longtime president of the AES who foregrounded population planning and demography.[43] Yet once gender is factored into the equation, these lines too become blurred.

Beneath the surface of the distinction between "mainline" and "reform" lay a significant continuity in twentieth-century hereditarianism. In the 1940s and 1950s, many eugenicists traded in their previous interest in determining the biological differences between discrete racial groups for a fascination with the male-female dichotomy, which was envisioned as stretching along a continuum of overlapping gradations of personality, temperament, and compatibility. The disarticulation and transposition of "race" onto gender and sexuality was an integral component of the midcentury "shift from the categorical to the scalar" and was central to the perpetuation of a hereditarian and evolutionist vision of civilization and its discontents in the United States.[44] This reconfiguration helped spur national alarm over homosexuality (manly women and effeminate men), frigid wives, and sexual dysfunction and contributed to the pronatalist zeal of the "baby boom."[45] The racial panics of the 1920s reemerged as the sexual conformity of the 1950s, even as institutional racism and the racialized baggage of social Darwinism perdured, the latter often embedded in population and family planning or psychotherapeutic constructs of gender and sex.

Through these temporal, spatial, and topical lenses, systematic opposition to eugenics occurred not in the 1930s and 1940s but during the civil rights era, when its two principal legislative achievements, sterilization laws and national origins immigration quotas, were dismantled through a combination of grassroots mobilization and legislative action. By the 1960s and 1970s, there was increasing uneasiness and anger, in streets and assembly halls, about the lingering and persistent ramifications of hereditarianism on specific groups, such as poor African American women who were being unwittingly sterilized, Mexican American youths whose life options were restricted by the results of intelligence testing and vocational tracking, and middle-class white women who were eager to finally wrest birth control out of the hands of male family planners.[46]

Furthermore, the patriarchal culture, gender imbalances, and racial prejudices of the medical establishment were coming under attack from many sides.[47] A sea change was under way, as evidenced by the media and congressional uproar over revelations that the US Public Health Service had conducted an unethical and harmful syphilis study on poor rural blacks in Macon County, Alabama, for more than forty years.[48] The 1973 hearings on the now notorious Tuskegee study catalyzed the formulation of informed consent protocols, which nations had been urged to adopt after the Nuremberg Trials, and bolstered the claim that racial minorities had been pawns, not beneficiaries, in the advancement of American medicine and science. The protest movements of the 1960s and 1970s—ranging from desegregation, black power, Chicano nationalism, and second-wave feminism to gay liberation—arose in part as an assault on the decades-long effects of eugenics-based policies and rationales. Certainly, the 1960s should not be reduced to a revolt against eugenics, but this tumultuous era cannot be comprehended outside the troubled history of hereditarianism in the United States.

Eugenics is an elusive word. It has had divergent connotations and has galvanized disparate projects across the world.[49] As the preceding pages suggest, the transformation of eugenics over time necessitates defining it in contextual, not absolute, terms. However, this does not imply a lack of precision. When Sir Francis Galton, the British statistician and cousin of Charles Darwin, coined the term in 1883, he combined the Greek *eu* (good or well) with the root of *genesis* (to come into being, be born) and added the modifying suffix *-ics*.[50] After trying out various formulations, in *Essays in Eugenics,* published in 1909, Galton wrote that eugenics was "the science which deals with all influences that improve the inborn qualities of a race; also with those that develop them to the utmost advantage."[51] If "science" encompasses both theory and practice, knowledge and skill, and "race" comprises the human species, interpretations that correspond to Galton's description of eugenics as a kind of interventionist religion and his emphasis on the betterment of all human "specimens" and "stock," then *eugenics* can simply be defined as better breeding. Indeed, in 1911 Davenport reiterated this definition of *eugenics* as "the science of the improvement of the human race by better breeding."[52] Of course, the operative word is *better*, the significance of which was, and continues to be, the source of the intense politicization of eugenics. Who decides what potential progenitor or offspring is "better," and who has the leverage to enforce such preferences? What is the rationale for selection, and who, ostensibly, in the short and long term, will benefit or suffer? What if members of a given society disagree on who and what is superior or inferior, normal or abnormal? What roles should the state and the individual be allowed or encouraged to play in the development and enforcement of eugenic programs? What restrictions, if any, should be placed on commercial access to genetic technologies and information, particularly those that enable certain people and groups potentially to buy eugenic enhancement while others are left behind? Nestled in Galton's foundational definition are the perplexing questions that have haunted attempts at better breeding for more than a century.

Whether today or at the height of the Cold War or in the late 1800s, both supporters and detractors have linked eugenics to anxieties about biological deterioration and hopes for genetic optimization. Over time, these oscillating concerns have continuously, albeit unevenly, affected our understandings of race, sexuality, reproduction, and nature. For example, in the 1980s, some scholars expressed worry that the development of genetic tests for diseases such as Tay-Sachs and sickle-cell anemia had the potential to revive the associations between particular racial groups and biological defects that had been so popular in the 1920s and 1930s. One sociologist suggested that instead of overtly guiding medical and public policies, these stereotypes were now being insidiously and sometimes inadvertently furthered by genetic screening programs that allowed eugenics to enter through the back door.[53] Several decades earlier, Hermann J. Muller, a Nobel Prize–winning geneticist with socialist leanings, proposed artificial insemination and the establishment of sperm banks stocked with superior "germinal material" as the ideal route to genetic perfectibility. He was confident that his plan was compatible with the values of a democratic society, since the donations from "persons of unusual moral courage, progressive spirit, and eagerness to serve mankind" would be voluntary.[54] Although Muller asserted that his scheme of artificial insemination was a far cry from the controlled procreation of a Hitler or Mussolini, his assumption that women would happily serve as the wombs of such superlative progeny was offensive to many Americans, especially feminists struggling to win greater reproductive freedom.

These two examples illustrate how medical or social programs designed to encourage the breeding of some people and not others have incited anticipation, trepidation, and controversy in the United States. It is exceedingly difficult, if not impossible, to discuss the motivations for and implications of genetic testing and "genius" sperm banks without grappling with bioethical dilemmas and revisiting the legacy of eugenics. Over the past decades, with the launching of the Human Genome Project and the ramifications of the decoding of the human genome for genetics and reproduction, these issues have become more salient than ever before. One of the greatest ironies of our contemporary era is that sensitivity to the discrimination and abuse promoted by eugenics, understood mainly in terms of state coercion and violative bodily intrusion, has made many scientists and legislators wary of regulation, a position that has only boosted the commercialization of reproductive and clinical genetics. Even with the bioethical concepts of autonomy, choice, consent, and beneficence codified into medical practice and research, American society is characterized by wide discrepancies in genetic health access and literacy that can easily turn one person's perfection into another person's defectiveness. One biologist has suggested that, if driven solely by market demand, Americans' tendency to choose the "best" for their children could eventually translate into two branches of *Homo sapiens:* a wealthy genetic elite that would replicate itself through designer babies and a medically underserved genetic underclass.[55] Although such futuristic specters of the survival of the richest and fittest may be overblown, the ubiquity of such scenarios in books and on television underscores the value of exploring how eugenics has been and continues to be conceived in modern historical memory. Eugenics has left discernible imprints on race relations, the immigrant experience, marriage patterns, sexual expression, contraceptive use, standardized testing, and even parks and recreation systems. A fruitful way to begin to track the broad social reach and the continuities and shifts in better breeding is by returning to the context in which eugenics emerged more than one hundred years ago.

In the late 1800s, far-reaching processes of industrialization, urbanization, immigration, imperialism, and secularization were remaking national, cultural, and economic landscapes across the globe. It was a period of technological innovations, from the railroad to the telegraph; of medical discoveries, from X-rays to microbes; and of the birth of new interpretive human sciences, such as sociology and psychology. But accompanying Progress (with a capital P) were such perceived social ills as sprawling urban tenements, malnourished children, disease outbreaks, environmental degradation, class conflict, and racial strife. As assorted elites in various countries sought to make sense of a world in flux, they increasingly turned not to religion but to science, which offered authority, rationality, and explanatory power. Evolutionism, physical anthropology, and bacteriology could help diagnose, ameliorate, and perhaps even perfect society.

If there was one word to which reformers gravitated to express their predicament, it was *degeneration*, a term imbued with both scientific and moral meaning.[56] A concern with degeneration was sparked in part by Darwinism and the ascendance of monogenesis, which posited that humans were much closer to animals, specifically primates, than polygenesis had suggested.[57] Not only was reversion to a more primitive state possible, according to the hierarchies formulated by physical anthropologists, but it was already embodied by types further down on the evolutionary ladder. The turn of the twentieth century was the heyday of racial taxonomies that placed whites and Europeans at the apex of civilization, blacks and Africans on the bottom rungs, and nearly everyone else in the suboptimal middle position of hybridity and mongrelization.[58] In the United States, the solidification of these racial hierarchies was integral to the entrenchment of Jim Crow segregation after Reconstruction and the rise of Sinophobia and anti-Asian discrimination, and it helped rationalize colonial ventures in Latin America and the Pacific. Furthermore, doctrines of racial decline coincided with the advent of modern contraception and a decline in fertility in parts of western Europe and the United States, both of which prompted some reformers to worry that the flagging birthrate of the "fit" was being outpaced by the rampant propagation of the "unfit." In the United

States, degenerationism translated into alarm about immigrant invasions and miscegenation and admonitions against "race suicide," which President Theodore Roosevelt, for one, was convinced was jeopardizing America's vitality and global stature.[59]

Eugenics was sown in the soil of degenerationism. From the outset, it had strong affinities with contemporaneous notions of racial decadence and spoke much the same language as the burgeoning disciplines of sociology, anthropology, and sexology. However, the coalescence of organized eugenics movements required the convergence of the competing and complementary hypotheses in plant and animal biology that gave rise to modern genetics. One of the initial catalysts was the neo-Lamarckian theory of the inheritance of acquired characteristics, which posited that environmental forces, both favorable and unfavorable, could alter human heredity and be transmitted down the familial line. Formulated by the French naturalist Jean Baptiste de Lamarck in the early nineteenth century, this version of natural selection stressed the role of external stimuli in either improving or damaging hereditary material. On the one hand, neo-Lamarckism promoted optimism in reformers who hoped that cleaning up urban decay and instituting public and personal hygiene could produce more vigorous "stock." On the other hand, it also made reformers skeptical about their ability to impede the likely and natural regression of humans back down the evolutionary scale. Neo-Lamarckism provided the basis for eugenics movements in "Latin" countries such as France, Romania, Argentina, and Mexico. Following neo-Lamarckism, for example, Mexican and Brazilian eugenicists supported public health measures and prohibition campaigns that they believed would offset the permanent destruction inflicted on the national "race" by overwork, alcoholism, tuberculosis, and syphilis.[60]

At the same time that neo-Lamarckism was alternately fueling hope and dismay, another concept of heredity was on the horizon. Linked to the studies of Galton, the German cytologist August Weismann, and the rediscovery of the hybridization experiments of the Austrian monk Gregor Mendel, this theory claimed that hereditary material was transmitted from generation to generation with absolutely no modification. As this doctrine of strict hereditarianism was being formulated, Galton embarked on the inquiries into the biographies of famous men that would convince him that musical, intellectual, and other traits were not learned but innate.[61] Emboldened by his conclusions, Galton began to espouse eugenics, organized projects to stimulate breeding among the upper classes, and calibrated anthropometric and biometric techniques to measure and correlate the physique, psychology, and physiology of a cross section of British families. While Galton gathered biometric data on "hereditary geniuses," Weismann refuted neo-Lamarckism from the perspective of cell biology. Weismann contended that the human body contained two distinct kinds of cells—germ and somatic. In the 1880s, he had first asserted that germ cells were located in the gonads and produced sperm and eggs and that all other bodily tissues were composed of somatic cells. Moreover, he claimed that hereditary material was fixed in the germ cells, which determined the arrangement and expression of the somatic cells but were never reciprocally affected by them. By disputing the theory of the inheritance of acquired characteristics, Weismann challenged the environmental reform impulse of neo-Lamarckism and infused hereditarianism with a heavy dose of fatalism.[62]

Despite Weismann's principles, however, it was not until 1900, when scientists rediscovered the results of Mendel's experiments, that neo-Lamarckism gradually lost its tenacious hold.[63] Working with pea plants in an Austrian monastery in the 1860s, Mendel had painstakingly elucidated the patterns underlying the transmission of hereditary material from parent to offspring.[64] Most important, he had postulated that to be expressed in the next generation, some hereditary factors needed to be passed on by both parents whereas others required only one progenitor. He had labeled these traits, respectively, recessive and dominant and then had calculated his well-known 3:1 ratio, which he had replicated in thousands of garden experiments with smooth, wrinkled, long, and short peas.[65] Along with these postulates, Mendel's laws of segregation and independent assortment—which stated that during the formation of gametes the germ cells disaggregated and then recombined independently, producing different variations—rapidly gained currency among scientists.[66]

After 1900, Mendelianism became the basis of modern genetics. In subsequent decades, Weismann's germ and somatic cells were renamed genotype and phenotype by the Danish geneticist Wilhelm Johannsen; chromosomes were identified as the locus of the gene; the workings of sexual selection were determined; and certain diseases caused by dominant genes, such as Huntington's disease, and by recessive genes, such as phenylketonuria (PKU), were identified.[67] In 1953, James Watson and Francis Crick proposed that genetic material was contained in DNA (deoxyribonucleic acid), structured as a double helix consisting of paired combinations of four nucleic acids held together by hydrogen bonds. By this time, the field of genetics had expanded beyond Mendel's original formulas into highly involved and technical laboratory experiments crossbreeding mice, flies, and worms and a complicated universe of acronyms and cryptic scientific notations. Geneticists were mapping the metabolic pathways of dozens of genetic diseases and discovering masking effects (epistasis) and patterns of incomplete dominance and codominance. Moreover, the intersection of genetics with new technologies of medical imaging (such as X-ray crystallography) and the techniques of molecular biology and biochemistry (such as karyotype analysis and eventually electrophoresis) was generating voluminous information about plant and animal genomes.[68]

In the United States, eugenics was informed principally by Mendelianism. Although neo-Lamarckism held some sway in the first decade of the century, especially among idealist Progressives, by the onset of World War I the emphasis was on strict hereditarianism.[69] This was evident in the family pedigree studies, which relied on Mendelian ratios to delineate the transmission of bad "unit characters" or genes that might cause criminality, alcoholism, or feeblemindedness from generation to generation. These studies often profiled poor rural white families through morality tales in which irresponsible and degenerate offspring recklessly reproduced more of their kind. In rare exceptions, a family member chose the respectable path of childlessness or, when fortunate enough to have been born with a majority of good genes, sought out vigorous mates.[70] During the 1920s, it was the application of Mendelianism to humans, and above all the corollary that specific racial and degenerate types had distinct "unit characters," that propelled eugenic campaigns for sterilization, interracial marriage bans, and immigration restriction. If surgical operations and marriage laws would protect the nation from the feebleminded and defective from within, then tight immigration laws would do the same from without.

Eugenics achieved its greatest national visibility in the 1920s, when it was virtually synonymous with biological racism and modern degenerationism. Furthermore, it was during this decade that eugenicists achieved two critical victories: *Buck v. Bell,* the US Supreme Court case that upheld the constitutionality of Virginia's sterilization law (1927), and the Johnson-Reed Immigration Act (1924), which set a quota of 2 percent on all immigrants from southern and eastern Europe based on the 1890 census and closed the gates to practically all newcomers from Asia. Instead of constituting a decrescendo, however, these triumphs worked to naturalize eugenics into the body politic and into state, federal, and county institutions and laws. Thus ultimately eugenics had a broader reach in the 1930s and 1940s because the precepts of its initial generation of adherents regarding defective "unit characters" had been codified into law. Notably, spurred by *Buck v. Bell* and the economic pressures of the Depression, sterilizations peaked in the United States from 1935 to 1945, even as many eugenicists admitted that sexual surgeries could do little, in the short or long run, to curtail the spread of deleterious recessive genes, which were transmitted heterozygously and often remained unexpressed.[71]

Historical definitions of American eugenics are grounded in the close association of hereditarianism with biological racism that developed in the 1920s and became even stronger in the 1940s as the brutal extremes of Nazi racial hygiene and extermination campaigns were recognized. For the most part, our understanding of eugenics remains trapped in the vortex of the interwar period, even though revamped eugenic projects prospered into the 1960s. After World War II, many eugenicists embarked on the task of redefinition. Osborn, who led the charge of "reform" eugenics, blamed postwar discomfort with "eugenics" on Hitler, who had "prostituted" the term and was responsible for the American public's eagerness to "drop the word from its vocabulary."[72] To renew hereditarianism and demonstrate its applicability, Osborn returned to Galton. In his book *The Future of Human Heredity,* Osborn invoked Galton's vision of eugenics and reiterated the British statistician's call for a systematic plan of study and education. Echoing Galton, Osborn wrote, "The improvement of the race should be man's highest aspiration toward which all men should work."[73] In the postwar period this would entail initiating policies to reduce "defects and abnormalities that have a genetic origin," modifying familial and environmental factors to ensure that children's natural abilities would flourish, and encouraging couples to visit heredity clinics to make genetically informed and rational decisions about reproduction. Even as Osborn promoted genetic counseling, the optimization of intelligence, and medical genetics—all in the name of enhancing the gene pool— he and his contemporaries, especially in population planning, did not condemn, and often quietly endorsed, sterilization, which they viewed as an integral, if sometimes mismanaged, facet of a comprehensive eugenics program.[74] From the perspective of its postwar crusaders, eugenics could emerge unscathed from the horrors of the Final Solution if the original intent of Galton's definition was honored and made to conform to principles of democracy and individualism.

Eugenic Nation foregrounds Galton's definition of eugenics because of its historical provenance, staying power, and flexibility. It can serve as a compass to explore changes and continuities in American eugenics over the twentieth century. As recently as 1994, Richard Herrnstein and Charles Murray, authors of *The Bell Curve,* justified their arguments about race and intelligence by emphasizing the validity of Galtonian biometrics and eugenics.[75] Over and over again, Galton was (and is) the point of departure for eugenicists seeking to redefine their science, for scholars narrating the past, and for philosophers delving into bioethics. Guided by this definition, *Eugenic Nation* approaches eugenics in the United States as a multifaceted set of programs aimed at better breeding that have straddled many social, spatial, and temporal divides. At times I use *hereditarianism* interchangeably with *eugenics,* both for the purposes of word variation and to describe ideas and practices based on the primacy of heredity over cultural or behavioral explanations. *Eugenic Nation* seeks to push the bounds of what has been considered eugenics, not to vilify but to raise questions about the extent to which medicine, biology, and the hereditarian impulse have shaped modern society.

In 1905, Lewis S. Terman, a freshly minted graduate of Clark University with a PhD in psychology, accepted a job as principal of San Bernardino High School. Like many before and after him, Terman was motivated by more than professional opportunity; he hoped that the aridity of Southern California would cure him of a chronic tubercular infection.[76] The relocation not only rejuvenated him but also set him on the path to becoming one of the most prominent psychologists of the twentieth century. After a few years in the Southland, Terman moved to Stanford University, where he devoted himself to the nascent discipline of psychometrics and set out to redesign the mental test invented by Alfred Binet in France in the early 1900s, an undertaking that resulted in the Stanford-Binet intelligence test. Just over a decade later, he and his protégés had administered intelligence tests to thousands of children, had helped to introduce mental testing in dozens of school districts, and had set up the California Bureau of Juvenile Research to study the cognitive aptitudes of the state's youngest generation.

Terman was pivotal to the national eugenics movement; he was a longtime member of the AES who maintained an undying belief that inferior or superior intelligence was determined principally by genetics. Tracing his trajectory illuminates the meteoric rise of standardized testing and demonstrates how correlations between race and intelligence became embedded in statistical methods.[77] The numerical classifications for feeblemindedness, moronity, and idiocy and the expected average intelligence quotients (IQs) of different racial groups that he detailed in *The Measurement of Intelligence,* published in 1916, dominated psychometrics for years.[78] The eugenicists and nativists who championed the 1924 Johnson-Reed Immigration Act and encouraged the feeble-minded threshold (usually an IQ of 70 or below) for compulsory sterilization relied chiefly on Terman's scales.

Terman was very much a creature of the American West. He was one of hundreds of entrepreneurial easterners and midwesterners suffering from respiratory ailments who sought relief in the dry climates of Denver, Los Angeles, and El Paso.[79] He arrived in California just as the young universities of Stanford, the University of California at Berkeley, and the California Institute of Technology (Caltech) were achieving prestige and renown. Like other transplanted men of science and letters at the cusp of the twentieth century, such as David Starr Jordan and Luther Burbank, Terman embraced eugenics as a means to build a new social and racial order in postconquest and post–Gold Rush California. He cofounded the Eugenics Section of the Commonwealth Club of California and belonged to the Human Betterment Foundation and the California Division of the AES. His psychometric rankings and the surveys conducted by the California Bureau of Juvenile Research (which designated itself the "Western representative" of the ERO) fostered the channeling of immigrant, especially Mexican, schoolchildren into vocational tracks and the manual trades. Moreover, in the 1930s, when Terman began to evince agnosticism about the causal links between race, intelligence, and heredity and started instead to probe norms of gender and sexuality, he collaborated with Popenoe to calibrate his M-F (Male-Female) Test at the AIFR.[80] Terman's career, which stretched into his work on "gifted children" in California schools in the 1960s, constituted a critical facet of eugenics in the United States. It is also a revealing sliver of the history of science and medicine in the American West.

Recently, historians have started delving into the intriguing ways that agribusiness, public health, and physics shaped the American West.[81] In general, this scholarship fits under the rubric of "New Western" history, an analytical and thematic turn initiated in the 1980s that sought to chase away the lingering ghost of Frederick Jackson Turner and open up a more textured interpretive landscape. "New Western" historians rejected the main tenets of Turner's "frontier thesis," which asserted that the United States, distinguished from Europe by its ethos of individualism and democratic values, had been born out of the struggle between barbarism and civilization that unfolded in the sequential frontiers of the trans-Mississippi wilderness.[82] Practitioners of ethnic, gender, and environmental studies spearheaded this revisionism and sought to repopulate the West with a panoply of historical actors that had been all but erased in heroic and masculinist narratives of westward expansion and the settlement of vacant lands by intrepid pioneers. "New Western" historians contended that the Turnerian model of virgin territories and apocryphal yeomen left no room for women, immigrants, or minorities and, moreover, that violence, conquest, and colonization stood at the center of the incorporation of the West into the continental United States.[83]

Initially "New Western" historians embarked on recovery efforts, seeking to give voice to subjects whose stories had been silenced or ignored. Through careful reconstruction, scholars began to bring to life the experiences of women and minorities, expose the fraught dynamics of gender, race, and class, and demonstrate how subaltern identities were forged in the postcolonial and multicultural context of the American West.[84] If one of the "New Western" history's aspirations was to explore the American West as a multiracial region like no other, then scholars swiftly realized that many routes to understanding ethnicity and race passed through the realms of science and medicine.[85] For instance, much of the impetus behind the anti-Asian agitation that gripped San Francisco and the West Coast starting in the 1870s may have been based in white working-class resentment at the perceived encroachment of "coolie labor," but the animus and ridicule directed at Chinese immigrants almost always drew on images of contagion and constitutional malaise. Again and again, West Coast nativists graphically portrayed Chinese men as effeminate, enervated, and spotted with suppurating pustules or ugly lesions.[86] Medicine and public health molded the adaptation of Asian immigrants to the West, from the health inspections and psychological exams they endured on Angel Island to the antiprostitution and antivice campaigns waged by Progressives in Chinatowns and the public hygiene angles of the Americanization campaigns that were promoted from inside and outside Chinese, Japanese, and Filipino communities.[87]

In a similar vein, Mexicans were simultaneously racialized and medicalized, sometimes in competing directions. Whereas eugenicists claimed that Mexicans needed to be placed under an exclusionary immigration quota because they constituted a mongrel—half South European and half Amerindian—"race," agricultural growers contended that this same biological composition endowed Mexican laborers with remarkable "stooping abilities" and the capacity to work long hours in the fields.[88]

From 1917 until the late 1930s, Mexicans entering the United States along the southern border were subjected to aggressive disinfection rituals that were based on exaggerated, nearly hysterical, perceptions of them as dirty and diseased.[89] Mexicans were commonly associated with typhus, plague, and smallpox in the 1920s, and Mexican women were stereotyped as hyperbreeders whose sprawling broods of depraved children threatened to drain public resources.[90] Furthermore, more than in any other region of the country, the racialized public health measures implemented in the American West were initially devised and assayed in US colonies. From the 1890s on, the cities, towns, and inhabitants of the Philippines, Cuba, Puerto Rico, Hawai'i, and the Panama Canal functioned as laboratories for the elaboration of modern modalities of epidemiological surveillance and disease control that in short order were transposed to San Francisco's Chinatown and El Paso's Chihuahuita barrio.[91]

Colonialism also circulated back to the American West in the racial taxonomies that informed miscegenation statutes, which forbade unions between whites and persons of color, as identified by a hodgepodge of classifications including mulatto, Malay, Mongolian, and Negro. It was in the West, not the South, that miscegenation laws "reached their most elaborate, even labyrinthine, development, covering the broadest list of racial categories."[92] First enacted in early America in the 1660s and in the West in the mid- to late 1800s, these legal edicts were undergirded by segregationist ideas that resonated with the eugenic racism of the 1920s.[93] They were not overturned until after World War II, when the California Supreme Court declared the state's miscegenation law unconstitutional in *Pérez v. Lippold* (1948) and the US Supreme Court issued a similar verdict on the federal level in *Loving v. Virginia* (1967).[94] A related genre of segregation was ensured by laws that decreed as "violable the marriages of idiots and the insane" and "restricted marriage among the unfit of various types, including the feebleminded and persons afflicted with venereal disease."[95] Taken together, these laws sought racially and medically to manage courtship, love, and sexuality by policing the boundaries of the intimate.

Eugenic ideas about biological purity and reproductive control resonated strongly in the American West and were espoused by many transplanted white professionals, such as Terman, who emphasized medical and scientific approaches to crafting a new biopolitical order. Starting at the turn of the twentieth century, eugenicists strove to manage racial, ethnic, and class interactions and categories through marriage, sterilization, and alien land laws. However, if eugenics was propelled by the racial and classificatory imperatives of elite settlers, it also flourished because of the region's particular investment in agriculture and nature. For example, contemporaneous with Mendel, Burbank, the whimsical "plant wizard," was also experimenting in his Santa Rosa garden. Through inventive hybridization techniques, Burbank produced the Shasta daisy, the Humboldt blackberry, and what we today call the Russet potato. At the same time, he believed that the "human plant" could be improved through propitious mating, cleanliness, fresh air, and exercise, a conviction that led him to help establish one of the country's first eugenics groups.[96] In 1906, after receiving a request from Davenport, Burbank agreed to serve as a founding member of the Eugenics Section of the American Breeders' Association, which published the influential *Journal of Heredity* and acted as a precursor to the ERO and the AES.

Burbank was accompanied by Jordan, the president of Stanford University. Whereas Burbank came to eugenics through horticulture, Jordan arrived through his dual interests in animal biology and environmentalism. An ichthyologist, Jordan converted to Darwin's theories of evolution after studying the marine life of the Pacific Slope in the late nineteenth century.[97] In 1891, the same year that he accepted Leland Stanford's offer to run his new private university in Palo Alto, Jordan, an avid mountaineer, cofounded the Sierra Club with John Muir. Jordan adamantly believed that some species needed to be protected and preserved while others should be eliminated or excluded. He applied this logic to plant, animals, and people alike. In addition, for Jordan there was a eugenic connection between nature conservation and pacifism. Jordan opposed US entry into World War I because he thought that war was dysgenic: it stole the nation's healthiest and fittest men, leaving the rest to breed lesser offspring.[98] From his base in Northern California, Jordan became one of the most prominent Progressives and eugenicists in the early twentieth century and played a pivotal role in the formation of the ERO in 1910. According to Davenport, it was largely owing to Jordan's stature and persuasion that Mrs. E.H. Harriman, after receiving personal correspondence from the Stanford biologist explaining the country's need for a dedicated eugenics organization, decided to finance the ERO.

The sex and gender contours of American eugenics are also delineated by illuminating patterns in the American West. For example, in 1917, after the passionate lobbying of the suffragist and feminist physician Bethenia Owens-Adair, Oregon's governor signed a law sanctioning the sterilization of the feebleminded in state institutions. When this statute was ruled unconstitutional in 1921, the Oregon legislature reworded the law, making consent or a court order a prerequisite for surgery, and passed an amended version in 1923. By the Great Depression, as states became increasingly worried about the costs of incarceration, and release in exchange for sterilization became customary, officials began to promote operations with much enthusiasm.[99] The experiences of Oregon and Washington, where substantial numbers of those targeted for sterilization were classified as "sexual deviants"—often men caught in flagrante delicto with other men—demonstrate how eugenic practices often operated as methods of sexual regulation.[100] Furthermore, they suggest important avenues for future research into the intersections of medicine, sexuality, and the state.

Finally, the American West served as auspicious terrain for the development of eugenics during the postwar period. It was geographically removed from the criticism that some agencies and individuals heaped on the ERO and other East Coast organizations starting in the 1930s, and by that time hereditarianism had infused key institutions and organizations. For instance, the California Division of the AES, founded in 1929, remained active into the 1940s, helping to fortify an extensive nexus of psychologists, physicians, and scientists who remained engaged in eugenically inspired projects into the 1960s. Terman, Goethe, and Popenoe corresponded with one another during the midcentury, expressing their mutual support for family planning, managed parenthood, and confidence in psychometric tests as valid tools for categorizing human traits. Furthermore, it was at the AIFR that postwar eugenics burrowed intimately into the prosaic worlds of thousands of Californians and millions of Americans and sought to reinforce the conformist norms of the "happy days" of the 1950s.

Eugenic Nation proceeds chronologically and thematically. Chapter 1 begins in 1915 at the Panama-Pacific International Exposition, where West Coast eugenics initially coalesced under the aegis of the Race Betterment Foundation. In this chapter, I describe the context in which advocates of race betterment from across the country united in the cosmopolitan city of San Francisco to articulate a vision of human improvement for the twentieth century. Many of the actors who star in this chapter—Jordan, Popenoe, Claude C. Pierce, and Terman—reappear later. One of the striking features of race betterment at the Exposition is the extent to which it was shaped by colonial medicine, particularly tropical medicine as implemented in the Philippines, Cuba, Puerto Rico, and the Panama Canal. Furthermore, the racial imperatives behind colonial medicine, and concepts and practices such as quarantine and prophylaxis, not only informed eugenics but also became entwined in the American public health mentality.

Chapter 2 draws more connections between colonial medicine and eugenics, this time along the US-Mexican border, where a protracted quarantine scrutinized, and simultaneously racialized, the bodies of Mexican immigrants. Against the backdrop of an unusual and disturbing public health regime not seen anywhere else in the United States (not on Ellis or Angel Islands or along the Canadian border), the US Border Patrol began policing the binational boundary line. I argue that the Border Patrol, like the Johnson-Reed Immigration Act to which it was attached, should be seen as the product of a negotiation between capitalist growers and nativist restrictionists and that in this sense it was part of the eugenic puzzle of the 1920s. In addition, the mandate of the Border Patrol to protect the white American family from intrusion and contamination was strongly influenced by ideas of racial purity.

In chapter 3, *Eugenic Nation* moves back to California for an in-depth exploration of the unfolding of the eugenics movement in that westernmost state from 1900 to the 1940s. Beyond painting a picture of the organizational and individual network that mobilized California's dynamic eugenics movement, I seek to demonstrate how hereditarian initiatives were literally instituted by the state, through agencies affiliated with the Department of Institutions. California was home to an interwoven tripartite system in which the sterilization program, antialien deportation policies, and psychometric research aimed mainly at children and adolescents worked in concert to create one of the most activist eugenics movements in the country and even the world.

Chapter 4, written for the revised edition, builds on the most recent scholarship on eugenics, race, and reproduction in California and uses newly discovered historical sources to explore patterns and experiences of eugenic sterilization in state institutions. California was by far the most aggressive sterilizer of any state, performing approximately one-third of the sixty thousand operations that occurred nationwide in the twentieth century. From 1909, the year California passed the country's third eugenic sterilization law, until 1979, when this statute was repealed, twenty thousand inmates and patients in state hospitals and homes were sterilized on the basis of diagnoses that included but were not limited to feeblemindedness, idiocy, dementia praecox, and psychosis. Combining quantitative and qualitative analysis and focused on the period 1935–44 when sterilizations reached their apogee, this chapter mobilizes a data set of eight thousand sterilization recommendations to highlight salient trends such as elevated rates of the sterilization of Spanish-surnamed patients, a pronounced pattern of the sterilization of adolescent female Latinas who were classified as feebleminded and sexually promiscuous, and the greater likelihood that inmates in psychiatric rather than feebleminded homes would refuse and protest sterilization. In addition, this chapter examines personal experiences as gleaned through the bureaucratic format of sterilization recommendations. Even in the monotonous institutional forms there are glimmers of the personal trajectories and struggles of those the state deemed unfit to reproduce. This chapter describes a small but vocal minority of inmates that protested sterilization by appealing to the head of the Department of Mental Hygiene; it also contextualizes the resistance of Mexican-origin families who objected to the sterilization of their kin for religious, familial, and moral reasons. Finally, this chapter delves into the thorny issue of consent. According to the state's own law, consent from family, kin, or patient was not necessary. Despite this, the state went to great lengths to produce thousands of forms and acquire signatures—of family members, superintendents, court guardians, and other key actors—in order to formalize and institutionally insulate the process of sterilization. This dynamic itself sheds light on the ambiguous status of sterilization as a legally mandated procedure and raises questions about how to define coercion historically and with relevance to reproductive justice in the twenty-first century.

Chapter 5 moves from sterilization and reproduction to the relationship between nature-making and eugenics in California, beginning at Vollmer Peak in Berkeley, named after the iconoclastic eugenicist and criminologist August Vollmer. From there the chapter examines, through the portal of the redwood tree and the Save-the-Redwoods League, the deep affinities between conservationist arguments about species survival and early twentieth-century fears of "race suicide." One of the overarching arguments of this chapter is that narratives of western conquest and colonization, and, more broadly, the mythology of the American West, were infused with eugenic notions of regeneration and the possibility of racial perfection. This chapter dissects such tropes in the writings of Burbank and Jordan. It also seeks to show how eugenics was inscribed on the California landscape by its role in shaping park systems and, quite concretely, in dedicatory plaques and memorial groves. The section on place-names focuses on the fascinating and disquieting biography of

Goethe, an avid conservationist who was largely responsible for introducing the naturalist ranger into the national park system.

Chapter 6 continues probing the history of eugenics in California by describing the founding and mission of the AIFR. Established in 1930 by Popenoe, the AIFR had become the country's premier marriage counseling center by World War II, sponsoring a family-centric eugenics that resonated powerfully with the sex-gender dictates of midcentury America. The AIFR offers a compelling window onto the remaking of eugenics during the Cold War and illustrates how planned parenthood, mate selection, and marital advice were implemented and affected the attitudes, behavior, and uncertainties of Americans. Furthermore, analyzing the AIFR's operating principles with regard to sex, gender, and the family sheds light on the layered transition from the discrete racial typologies of the 1920s to the variance continua of the 1950s. The trajectory of Popenoe and the AIFR reveals—not linearly, neatly, or completely—how the eugenic racism of the 1920s became the hereditarian sexism of the 1950s.

Eugenic Nation's final chapter reassesses the extent to which the protest and liberation movements of the 1960s and 1970s challenged the legacy and longevity of eugenics in the United States. This chapter provides a brief overview of the criticisms leveled at eugenics from the early decades of the twentieth century to midcentury and argues that the sustained attacks of the 1960s were of a different order of magnitude. Not only were some racial groups, such as Mexican Americans on the West Coast and African Americans in the South, fighting stereotypes that had long been buttressed by doctrines of biological inferiority and superiority, but a heterogeneous group of activists were assailing eugenic landmarks. In 1970, for example, Media Women, a loose contingent of radical feminists, stormed into the offices of *Ladies' Home Journal* with a long list of demands, one of which was the cessation of the column "Can This Marriage Be Saved," penned for almost two decades by Popenoe. Furthermore, starting in the mid-1960s and cresting in the early 1970s, civil rights and feminist organizations denounced the federally funded involuntary sterilizations of poor and minority women. In Los Angeles in 1975, ten Chicanas filed suit against the Los Angeles County/University of Southern California Hospital for tubal ligations performed on them without their consent. The calls for sexual and bodily liberation that were integral to the radicalism of the 1960s should be reevaluated in light of a protracted century of hereditarianism.

A revised conclusion explores the relevance of this history today, especially in light of the 2013 revelations about unauthorized sterilizations in California's women's prisons. Although the past has not repeated, patterns of reproductive injustice enacted on women of color have continued. If eugenics can be used as a framework to understand harmful reproductive control in prisons and more broadly in the criminal legal system, it can also be used to critically evaluate the intentions and outcomes of new kinds of genetic technologies, particularly prenatal tests geared to identifying an increasing number of chromosomal and genetic anomalies. This chapter explores the eugenic resonances and potential outcomes of emerging genetic technologies, which owe their more recent development and dissemination not to the state but to an intense wave of biotech commercialization.

Rather than imply that eugenics was totalizing and all-encompassing, the title *Eugenic Nation* was chosen to express the extent to which the United States was (and continues to be) shaped by the faults and frontiers of better breeding projects, often in ways that are so naturalized that they are not readily apparent. Additionally, *Eugenic Nation* narrates a regional story about the American West, above all about California, that had a profound and dialectical impact on the national level. Starting in the early 1900s, California eugenicists simultaneously applied concepts of heredity to the Pacific Slope and molded the broad and assorted agenda of American eugenics. Instead of either confining this to a regional story about medicine, race, and sexuality in the American West or magnifying its conclusions outward in a fashion that sacrifices some of the fine-grainedness of place, *Eugenic Nation* seeks to articulate these two geographical and conceptual scales.

CHAPTER 1

Race Betterment and Tropical Medicine in Imperial San Francisco

At six o'clock on the morning of February 20, 1915, San Francisco was engulfed by a cacophony of sounds. To signal the opening of the Panama-Pacific International Exposition (PPIE), the fire department rang its bells and whistles, automobilists honked their horns, policemen banged on trolley poles, and, just in case anyone was still asleep, the fife-and-drum corps paraded through the streets.[1] A few hours later, under a bright sky, an entourage of politicians and merchants headed by Mayor James Rolph Jr. and Governor Hiram Johnson led a two-and-a-half-mile-long procession from Van Ness Avenue and Broadway to the marina. At the vanguard of this parade was a small cavalry, followed by six carriages of pioneers, "men that had seen the city grow from a few shacks at the edge of a cove that has long since disappeared."[2] These dignitaries congregated at the Tower of Jewels, beneath a ceiling that depicted the heroic saga of the Panamanian isthmus, from the voyages of the Spanish conquistadors to the US Canal Commission.[3] The president of the fair's board of directors, Charles C. Moore, along with a local rabbi and minister, welcomed the crowd and congratulated the city on its marvelous achievement. Unable to attend, President Woodrow Wilson sent Franklin K. Lane, the secretary of the Interior. Deeply impressed by what he saw, Lane intoned to the crowd, "The seas are now but a highway before the doors of the nations," and connected the benevolence of US imperialism to the unstoppable march of westward expansion: "The greatest adventure is before us, the gigantic adventure of an advancing democracy, strong, virile, and kindly, and in that advance we shall be true to the indestructible spirit of the American Pioneer."[4] The fair did not officially commence, however, until President Wilson, three thousand miles away, pressed a golden key linked to an aerial tower in Tuckerton, New Jersey, whose radio waves sparked the top of the Tower of Jewels, tripped a galvanometer, and closed a relay, swinging open the doors of the Palace of Machinery, where a massive diesel engine started to rotate. Minutes later, Moore notified President Wilson via telegraph that the first world's fair to begin wirelessly was under way.[5]

A grand extravaganza that had been envisioned before the devastating earthquake of 1906 and for which planning had begun in 1910, the PPIE was organized to commemorate the completion of the Panama Canal, a project directed by the United States and finished in 1914. Held near Fort Mason in San Francisco, the fair covered 635 acres, a substantial portion of which had been leased from the military.[6] After passing through its turnstiles, visitors entered a vast "city of domes," filled with courts, palaces, towers, pavilions, and concessions, whose epic proportions and evocative style had been designed by architects such as Louis Christian Mullgardt and Bernard Maybeck.[7] An event extolling the myriad technological advances that imbued the twentieth century with the promise of perfection, the PPIE unfolded, sometimes discordantly, as brutal trench warfare killed thousands in Europe. When the exposition closed ten months later, on December 4, with lavish festivities that included a concert by the Philippine Constabulary Band, the reading of a toast sent by President Wilson, the sounding of bugles, and evening fireworks, nearly nineteen million people had passed through the PPIE's turnstiles.[8]

For the fair's coordinators and local elites, the staging of the PPIE in their westernmost city was no coincidence but rather the culmination of the inexorable and forward march of progress. As one of many promotional pamphlets declared, "California marks the limit of the geographical progress of civilization. For unnumbered centuries the course of empire has been steadily to the west."[9] In keeping with the theme of the advancement of civilization, the PPIE prominently showcased recent developments in agriculture, manufacturing, science, technology, architecture, and the arts. One subject that received an enormous amount of time and space was health and disease, especially the areas of race betterment and tropical medicine. Indeed, the fair's official poster, the "Thirteenth Labor of Hercules," symbolized the intertwined significance of these two concerns and provided an iconography for the apotheosis of empire, race, and sanitary intervention that crowned San Francisco as the Jewel of the Pacific. The poster features a muscular man in his physical prime, seen from the back, as he forces apart Panama's Culebra Cut; the PPIE's iridescent lights shimmer at the Canal's vanishing point.[10] If this figure embodied sheer masculine might, it was also a metaphor for the success of tropical medicine, which strove to rid the world's hot and humid regions of insect- and waterborne diseases in order to make them hospitable for Europeans and European Americans. With its veneration of the extraordinary white body, the poster reflected the racial hierarchies of Victorian anthropology and social Darwinism that had saturated international expositions since the late 1800s and helped ideologically to justify colonial ventures across the globe. The "Thirteenth Labor of Hercules" glorified sanitary engineering in the tropics at a time when the underlying tenets of race and disease were being reconfigured in light of new theories of human heredity and health.

The PPIE occurred at a transitory moment, as biology and medicine were becoming beholden to reductionism and new perspectives on disease identification and causation. Environmental explanations of human degeneracy and sickness, influenced by neo-Lamarckian doctrines of the inheritance of acquired traits and miasmatic principles of contagion, still dominated in some corners. They were being supplanted, however, by less flexible theories of germs and genes that demanded exact diagnoses and targeted solutions. On the one hand, for more than a decade, tropical medicine, which combined bacteriology, parasitology, and entomology, had concentrated on isolating and attempting to eradicate the etiologic agents of infections caused by microbes, helminthes, and protozoa, as well as intermediary disease vectors, such as mosquitoes, flies, and lice.[11] On the other hand, biology and the incipient field of genetics were increasingly dependent on Mendelian theories of hereditary transmission and "upward causation" models of molecular interaction.[12] Concomitantly, clinical medicine saw the enthroning of organ-based specialties and the beginnings of subspecialization. The PPIE took place in the midst of this trend toward reductionism, as more malleable conceptions of health and disease were buckling under the power of the microscope to make visible what was hidden to the human eye, the impulse toward quantification, and the elaboration of specific prophylactic measures for specific conditions.

Tropical medicine and race betterment differed in terms of their objects of analysis and the consequences of their hygienic therapies:

public health authorities could achieve their goal of ending a plague outbreak by destroying the culpable carriers, rodents, yet eugenicists rarely saw any immediate or even desired results from their attempts at manipulation. Nevertheless, both fields emerged during a reconstellation of the diagnostic, therapeutic, and heuristic role of medicine in modern society. Furthermore, what connected the two was an often-shared vocabulary of racial degeneracy and fitness. Thus, in one seamless sentence, scientists at the fair could applaud activities ranging from rat poisoning to better babies contests. Either way, the potential impact of deleterious germs and genes could be contained or controlled. More often than not, the accompanying corollary was a belief in the constitutional and mental superiority of Anglos and Caucasians and the limited reasoning abilities and foul habits of virtually all other racialized groups.[13]

The proximity of race betterment and tropical medicine at the PPIE belies the separation that some scholars have erected between eugenics and public health, contrasting them as incompatible, insofar as the former emphasized the propagation of the "fittest" and the elimination of those deemed degenerate, while the latter strove to save and extend lives by bringing the advantages of health to all. Instead, as the PPIE demonstrates, the early twentieth century was a period in which diverse and seemingly contradictory initiatives could mingle under the Progressive banners of improvement, efficiency, and hygiene, with all being motivated by the idea that the application of wide-ranging scientific knowledge could optimize American society. Thus in the 1910s public health and eugenics crusaders alike moved with little or no friction between calls for school vaccinations, for the teaching of "scientific motherhood" to women, for classification of human intelligence, for immigration restriction, for the promotion of the sterilization and segregation of the "unfit," and for the passage of marriage laws. Later in the century, academic professionalization and heightened specialization—whether in the laboratory, clinic, or office—would create more defined niches for these various kinds of initiatives.

It was during this transitional moment, in the context of a spectacular tribute to San Francisco's place in the US imperial cartography and under the spell of racial hierarchies, that California's burgeoning eugenics movement coalesced, acquiring a multifaceted agenda and the potential for attracting a broad social membership. At meetings convened during the PPIE, a heterogeneous group of sanitary experts, zoologists, horticulturalists, medical superintendents, psychologists, child advocates, and anthropologists established a social network that would influence eugenics on the national level in the years to come. Furthermore, the exposition provided an arena where well-known Progressives such as David Starr Jordan, Luther Burbank, and Paul Popenoe articulated a hereditarian vision apposite to California, a vision that in short order would become a formidable force in the state's laws, landscapes, institutions, and politics.

COLONIAL CIRCUITS

Like the World's Columbian Exposition, held in Chicago in 1893, the PPIE was made possible by industrial and urban expansion that stretched far beyond San Francisco into the resource-rich hinterlands of California and the American West.[14] The fair's water was supplied via aqueducts from remote watersheds, its electricity was generated by recently built regional networks of hydropower, and much of its raw building material, such as lumber, was felled or extracted in distant forests and fields and then shipped on freight trains along serpentine tracks from the North, South, and East.[15] The overlapping grids of infrastructure that fed San Francisco, helping to make it the most populous city in the US West by 1900, took shape rapidly in the second half of the nineteenth century, propelled by conquest, statehood, and the Gold Rush. In addition, the establishment and fortification of military bases around San Francisco Bay, which was part and parcel of the heightened US navalism of the 1890s, was a critical dimension of this growth.[16] In the eyes of elite San Franciscans, military preparedness, geographical location, and an indomitable spirit made the city the obvious gateway to the Pacific, particularly to the Philippines, where California financiers pictured untouched gold mines and the lucrative cultivation of export crops. During the 1890s, San Francisco publications regularly beat the drum for an empire launched from California shores.[17] A 1900 editorial in *Overland Monthly* titled "The Subjugation of Inferior Races," for instance, energetically embraced the colonization of the Philippines as part of a new "national policy" that followed "along the line of British domination" and necessitated "the gradual subjugation of these weaker groups of people by the stronger and more highly civilized powers."[18]

By the early twentieth century, San Francisco's coming prominence was being linked not only to accentuated militarism and colonial desires but also to revived calls for a Central American canal, which would augment trade on the West Coast and extend the geopolitical reach of the United States. Without a navigable passage across the isthmus in the

mid-nineteenth century, thousands of gold seekers had perished, primarily because of epidemic scourges and unforgiving territory, en route to
California from the Gulf Coast via Panama. Moreover, when sum-
moned to war in 1898, the battleship *Oregon,* fabricated in San Francisco's shipyards, had no choice but to proceed fourteen thousand miles
around Cape Horn, a voyage that took more than two months.[19] The
existence of a Central American canal would forever do away with such
obstacles and usher in a technologically modern century.

The construction of the Panama Canal unfolded against the backdrop of the Spanish-American War and the installation of American
colonial rule in Cuba, Puerto Rico, the Philippines, Guam, and Hawai'i.
Through a series of adroit and manipulative political maneuvers, orchestrated by President Theodore Roosevelt, Panama seceded from Colombia and the Canal Zone was transferred from the French to the United
States.[20] In 1903, after the signing and congressional ratification of the
Hay-Bunau-Varilla Treaty, the Isthmian Canal Commission was formed
to govern the Canal Zone "in perpetuity" and to oversee the gargantuan
assignment of carving a waterway through the rocky, bug-infested jun-
gle.[21] For the next decade, as tens of thousands of West Indian, European, and American laborers excavated more than 230 billion cubic
yards, blasted massive boulders, and built dams and locks, the United
States attempted to run its newly obtained "unorganized possession"
meticulously and methodically. In many ways, the Canal Zone functioned as a laboratory of US colonialism. The daily routines of work and
leisure, and their attendant racial and class demarcations, were rigidly
scripted and policed.[22] Interlaced with militaristic and moralistic surveillance were rigorously implemented measures of disease prophylaxis that
tracked the movement of all living organisms—humans, insects, and
rodents. After the waterway opened, many isthmian sanitary engineers
returned to the continental United States, bringing the techniques they
had honed in Panama to bear on public health ventures; their initial stop
was San Francisco.

THE DREAM OF A "CITY BEAUTIFUL"
AND THE NIGHTMARE OF PLAGUE

As soon as the first ditch was dredged in Panama, the San Francisco
businessman Reuben B. Hale launched a campaign claiming that his
city would be the ideal home for a major exhibition to mark the completion of the canal. The city's merchant associations, along with the

Society for the Improvement and Adornment of San Francisco and the California Promotion Society, were persuaded by Hale and endorsed his recommendation. Vexed by aspersions cast on their city from the East Coast, the local elite had become enamored of the "City Beautiful" movement. Eager to imitate the best of Washington, D.C., and New York City, while pointing up San Francisco's captivating topography, the city's business leaders asked the eminent urban planner Daniel Burnham to draft a blueprint for an awe-inspiring metropolis.[23] Burnham drew up an "imperial city" that boasted an acropolis atop Twin Peaks, "colonnaded shelters and temple-like edifices, courts and terraces," nine arterial boulevards radiating outward from the civic center, wide steps that cascaded down hillsides, and elegant and sweeping parkways.[24] The prospects for this Romanesque dreamscape were crushed, however, by bitter infighting among merchants and politicians and, more calamitously, by the deadly earthquake that rocked the Bay Area and set the city aflame in 1906.

Nonetheless, for many elite San Franciscans, with destruction came the possibility of renewal. Immediately after the earthquake, Hale, Charles C. Moore, the owner of prosperous hydroelectric enterprises and president of the Chamber of Commerce, and William H. Crocker, the son of Charles Crocker and one of the "big four" barons of the transcontinental railroad, redoubled their commitment to hosting a world's fair. Even if Burnham's "City Beautiful" had become financially and politically unfeasible amid the rubble, the splendor of San Francisco could still materialize and be revealed to all at the PPIE. Thus, in 1909, at a dinner convened by Hale at the Bohemian Club, about twenty businessmen reiterated their intentions and formed a board of directors. Moore was named president, and by 1910, despite fierce competition from San Diego and New Orleans, he had secured congressional approval for the exposition.[25]

The PPIE quickly became the medium for rebuilding a more magnificent San Francisco, which would rise like a phoenix from the ashes and prove that the city deserved to stand at the apex of an empire that straddled two oceans and controlled the world's most heavily trafficked waterway. The PPIE managers were keenly aware that their success was contingent on portraying an image of San Francisco as ordered and virtuous. This entailed debunking San Francisco's reputation as a sybaritic haven teeming with "flagrant houses of prostitution," especially in the Barbary Coast and Tenderloin districts. Given the city's history of lax enforcement of regulations on prostitution, alcohol consumption, and gambling, especially in comparison with Los Angeles, this was a tall order for PPIE organizers, who were under relentless pressure from antivice groups to "clean up" the city.[26] In addition, it meant demonstrating that San Francisco was salubrious and free of disease. Having served as chairman of the executive committee of the Citizens' Health Committee in 1908, Moore was well versed in the idioms and methods of disease control.[27]

In 1907 bubonic plague had reappeared in San Francisco, taking the lives of several dozen white residents. In response, the mayor, worried about an impending quarantine against the city, founded the Citizens' Health Committee. Composed of civic leaders and medical officers, this committee was charged with eradicating bubonic plague in San Francisco. The mayor and local officials were eager to reverse the negative attention the city had attracted in 1900, when a bungled quarantine had demonized Chinese immigrants by sealing off Chinatown and scapegoating its residents.[28] This incident not only was motivated by Sinophobia and racialist associations of the Chinese with contagion but also revealed a profound lack of coordination between municipal, state, and federal health agencies.

With firm resolution and guided by the latest medical findings about the etiology and epizootic transmission of plague, the Citizens' Health Committee set out to kill each and every rat in the city, even if that meant house-by-house fumigation and the placing of poison and traps along every block.[29] In contrast to the earlier outbreak, health officials knew that they would prevail only if citizens were disabused of the misconception that plague was solely an "Oriental disease" exclusive to Chinatown.[30] Thus the committee embarked on a massive educational campaign that strove to teach all San Franciscans about the essential roles of the rat and the flea in the spread of Yersinia pestis. Week after week, public health workers scoured every street, residence, shop, wharf, and factory in the city: "Wherever plague was found in rat or man, a horde of rat catchers descended on that place and trapped every rat for four blocks around to prevent the hunted animals from carrying the infection any farther."[31]

One year later, this offensive had succeeded. The fumbling between different agencies that had characterized the 1900 debacle had been replaced by a much more streamlined approach in which federal sanitary officers, affiliated with the US Public Health Service (USPHS), were in the lead, clearly vested with more clout than their municipal and state counterparts. Although anti-Asian sentiment was still pervasive, the fact that Chinatown accounted for only two cases attenuated the intensity of medicalized Sinophobia in San Francisco, at least with respect to plague.[32] In addition, the success of the campaign underscored the increasing importance of the laboratory in the precise identification of bacilli. In this case, USPHS facilities near the Presidio and on Angel Island received and tested a steady stream of dead rats, more than one million of which were killed from 1908 to 1909.

To a great extent, this concerted antiplague effort functioned as a dress rehearsal for the PPIE and helped elevate health and disease to the top of the exposition's list of concerns. Many of the key players in the two ventures were the same. Moore, for example, presided over both undertakings, convincing local merchants and organizations to donate money, buy bonds, and pay special taxes to fund each of them.[33] Furthermore, the USPHS officers who directed plague eradication—John Hurley, William Rucker, and, most important, the surgeon general, Rupert Blue—were the medical men contacted when sanitary arrangements for the fair began.[34] Finally, just as the Citizens' Health Committee's activities were coming to a close, Frank Morton Todd, the author of its official report, *Eradicating Plague from San Francisco,* began to compile the hundreds of boxes of materials he would use to write five hefty tomes on the PPIE.[35]

RACIALISM ON DISPLAY

To tour the carefully ordered universe of the PPIE was to experience, on a reduced scale, the grandeur of Burnham's "City Beautiful," marked less, however, by the classical and Beaux Arts styles that the Chicago architect favored and more by a Mediterranean eclecticism that mixed Oriental, Moorish, Greek, and Spanish Revival forms. Seeking to convey the natural landscape of California, the painter James Guerin had decided on a pastel color scheme for the PPIE that mirrored "the hues of the sky and the bay, of the mountains, varying from deep green to tawny yellow, and of the morning and evening light."[36] Visitors remarked that this palette, when suffused by indirect lighting in the evening, lent the fairgrounds an ethereal luminosity.[37]

The aim of the built environment of the PPIE, like that of the Columbian Exposition of 1893 and the St. Louis Exposition of 1904, was to embody allegorically the mythos of the American Century. In San Francisco, the terminus of the US West and the springboard to the Pacific, this meant the presence of artifacts such as *Fountain of Energy,* a strong male mounted on horseback with his arms spread out and crowned by figurines of "Fame" and "Valor." Referred to by its creator as the *Victor of the Canal*, this sculpture symbolized "the vigor and daring of our mighty nation, which carried to a successful ending a gigantic task abandoned by another great republic."[38] Many other monuments, large and small, such as *Adventurous Bowman*, *Energy*, and *Earth*, sought to portray the telos of universal progress that the United States had harnessed for the benefit of all humankind by constructing the canal across the Panamanian isthmus. The trope of hemispheric harmony was also seen in murals such as *Atlantic and Pacific* and *Gateway*, which pictured the two halves of the world meeting at the Panama Canal in a swirl of commerce and human communion.

This tale, however, was one with clear-cut winners and losers. According to many sources, the most popular sculpture, *The End of the Trail* by James Earle Fraser, located in the Court of Flowers, showed an exhausted Indian hunched over a feeble horse—a pathetic figure who was all but defeated by westward expansion and European American settlement. Paired with *The End of the Trail* was *American Pioneer*, housed in the opposite Court of Palms, which provided the inspiration for Secretary of the Interior Lane's opening remarks. Seated astride a horse and alertly holding a rifle, *American Pioneer* personified not the cowboy outlaw found in dime novels of the "Wild West" but a dignified man of reason who was "very typical of the white man and the victorious march of his civilization."[39] The broader cultural and geographical implications of these two faces of the "survival of the fittest" were reinforced by the juxtaposition of two sculptured groups, *Nations of the East* and *Nations of the West*, in the Court of the Universe. The latter centered on a wholesome, fair-skinned, and sprightly prairie girl, called "Mother of Tomorrow," poised in front of an oxen-drawn wagon, and flanked by white boys, a French American trapper, a totem-bearing Alaskan woman, and Americans of Latin, German, Italian, and English descent, as well as a "squaw with a papoose" and an "Indian chief on his pony."[40] Instead of a wagon, at the center of the *Nations of the East* stood an ostentatiously ornamented elephant, ridden by an Arab prince who was accompanied by a mounted sheik, an Egyptian atop a camel, an Arab falconer with a bird, a Tibetan lama, a Muslim, and two black slaves.[41] If the Nations of the East were associated with exoticism, servitude, idolatry, and the excesses of royalty, their Western counterparts personified enterprise, ingenuity, and inter-American solidarity. In the words of the exposition's official chronicler, the *Nations of the West*

statue "was rough and real, and it was also hopeful, buoyant, and progressive. . . . This group expressed the thrusting heave of western ambi-
tion and progress."[42]

As was the case with earlier international expositions, the doctrines of
racial and cultural difference expressed by the PPIE's art and architecture
also shaped the experiences and encounters of fairgoers. Broadly speaking, the PPIE was wracked by tensions between inclusion, in the name of
international fellowship and trade, which its managers hoped to encourage, and exclusion, as dictated by hierarchies of race, ethnicity, and
nation. In some ways, the PPIE broke with convention. For example, in
contrast to previous fairs, the PPIE unreservedly welcomed white middle-class female reformers and did not relegate their participation to a
separate women's building. California's elite women, having gained the
vote in 1911, were exceedingly involved in the exposition. Under the
leadership of Mrs. Phoebe Apperson Hearst and Mrs. Frederick G. San-
born, two of the city's most active reformers, the Woman's Board par-
took in many aspects of the fair, hosting lectures, teas, and conferences.[43]
Partially owing to their insistence, the PPIE was the stage for vocal peace
demonstrations that condemned war as wholesale "organized murder."[44]
Throughout the entire fair, a sizable contingent of learned women assev-
erated that their maternal instincts and political conscience compelled
them to struggle against US entry into World War I, as well as for child
welfare, national suffrage, and Progressive legislation.[45]

Spaces comparable to that carved out by elite women were not similarly occupied by racial and ethnic minorities. In a city and state whose
restrictive anti-Chinese ordinances and laws supplied templates for the
federal Chinese Exclusion Act (1882), the drawing of boundaries by
European Americans, whether against or around *californianos*, Mexicans, Chinese, Japanese, and Filipinos, was integral to the fractious settlement and remaking of urban and rural California. Despite proclamations
of universal belonging, the PPIE continued this legacy.[46] African American visitors, for example, complained bitterly to fair managers about
employment discrimination, and their request that black veterans of the
Spanish-American War be hired alongside white guards fell on deaf ears.[47]
A lawyer writing on behalf of the Colored Non-Partisan Leagues of California was incensed that African American fairgoers were often barred
from centrally located restaurants and were forced to "trudge, and starve
while they trudge, mile after mile until they come to some 'Jim Crow
snack house' or 'chit'lin' [chitterling] den."[48] On the surface, the PPIE
managers responded that no color lines were being demarcated. How-

ever, an internal letter, in which a PPIE attorney told Moore that he was confident that "a few tactful words will quiet the fears of these 'wards of the nation'" reveals the degree of condescension faced by black fairgoers.[49] In addition to these criticisms, nearly a dozen Chinese groups, including the Chinese commissioner general, the owner of the Oriental Hotel, and the Chinese Six Companies, sent a flurry of letters to PPIE offices denouncing the "Underground Chinatown" concession, located on the "Joy Zone," the fair's entertainment area. They vociferously objected to what they perceived as a degrading caricature of their culture, represented by a subterranean opium den and an enslaved prostitute. Under pressure to maintain positive diplomatic relations with China in light of the broadened American economic mission in Asia, this concession was temporarily suppressed and eventually replaced with the only slightly less offensively named "Underground Slumming."[50] In short, celebrating the forging of an empire, shored up by doctrines of racial superiority, was incompatible with the rhetoric of universalism or internationalism. Ultimately, racialism was on display at the PPIE, whether through overt discrimination on the fairgrounds, the fetishized display of "primitive" artifacts collected from the Navajo, the Chippewa, and the Ainu, or the maintenance of "native villages" that featured "live" Indians dancing or making handicrafts.[51]

TROPICAL MEDICINE COMES HOME

One of the most popular attractions in the Joy Zone was a model of the Panama Canal with motorized carts that transported people across a five-acre simulacrum of the isthmus. On their journey, phonographic records designed and tested by Thomas Edison broadcasted lectures describing the tremendous feat of building the canal. So impressed was Major F. C. Boggs, chief of the Washington Office of the Panama Canal, that he stated that within half an hour this ride could "impart to anyone a more complete knowledge of the Canal than a visit of several days to the waterway itself."[52] Functioning as an interactive testament to the American possession of the Canal Zone, this concession implied that only the acumen and industry of US engineers could have tamed an unruly region that had vanquished earlier attempts by the French. Pivotal to this story of the American mastery of the tropics was the sanitary regime instituted by Colonel William C. Gorgas, the medical chief of the Isthmian Canal Commission from 1904 to 1914.[53] Like many officers who served in the Spanish-American War, Gorgas had spent much of the 1880s and 1890s in the West, in his case Texas and South Dakota, where he simultaneously pursued frontier medicine and territorial administration.

Armed with knowledge of bacteriology and parasitology, health officers stationed in the Panama Canal Zone, affiliated with the US military and the USPHS, sought to stamp out the pernicious ailments that had doomed the dream of a canal across the isthmus in the nineteenth century. Their achievements in the Canal Zone involved replicating the extensive campaigns against both insect- and waterborne diseases waged in Cuba and the Philippines during the Spanish-American War.[54] It was in Havana, as Yellow Jack overpowered the American troops, that Gorgas inaugurated an effective system of epidemiological surveillance and mosquito eradication, reducing cases of yellow fever from fourteen hundred in 1900 to zero by the close of the following year.[55] Gorgas relied—for a good while quite reluctantly—on the prescient observations of the Cuban physician Carlos Finlay, the research results of the US Army physician Walter Reed, and the experiments of the British scientist Ronald Ross, which demonstrated that yellow fever was transmitted by the *Aëdes aegypti* (then called *Stegomyia fasciata*) mosquito and malaria by the *Anopheles* mosquito. He imposed a totalizing system that divided Havana into sanitary districts, each overseen by a medical team that kept a detailed inventory of file cards on the status of every house and water source as a potential breeding spot for mosquitoes.[56] After these data were compiled, Gorgas's brigades drained, oiled, or capped all wells, cisterns, and ponds and fumigated homes, often burning bedding and clothing. This novel strategy worked. Within three months yellow fever and malaria had diminished markedly, and nine months later they had all but vanished.[57]

The lessons learned in Havana informed Gorgas's approach in Panama, a more extensive and challenging terrain. Once in the Canal Zone, Gorgas mounted a frontal assault on mosquitoes, which were numerous enough to thicken the air at night.[58] His careful review of the procedures carried out by the French in the 1880s revealed that their dependence on miasmic principles of disease transmission via filth or "noxious gases" had cultivated an environment ripe for mosquito breeding. For example, at the French-built Ancon Hospital, crockery dishes filled with water were placed beside plants and flowers to ward off ants, thus creating a propitious home for mosquito larvae.[59] Because the French effort to reproduce the Suez Canal in Central America took place before the medical breakthroughs of Louis Pasteur and Robert Koch, and because it instead relied on beliefs that many tropical ailments were caused by "bad air" or moral depravity, the conditions were ripe for the loss of an estimated twenty thousand lives.[60] Two decades later, emboldened by his Havana campaign and eventually granted substantial financial resources, Gorgas implemented markedly different and efficacious techniques in Panama. He designated twenty-five sanitary districts, each assigned an inspector with a team of twenty to one hundred men.[61] Dozens of sanitary workers initiated drainage projects, conducted house-to-house inspections and fumigation, constructed mosquito coverings and netting, applied kerosene, sulfur, and alcohol to kill mosquitoes and larvae, and cleared and lined ditches and water channels. In 1906, during one month at the height of Gorgas's antimosquito assault in Panama City, an average of forty-seven men worked long hours cleaning the streets and collecting garbage, while close to a dozen men captured rats and watered the ground to diminish the dust. The *Stegomyia* brigade inspected nearly ten thousand houses, identifying and destroying larvae in 1,785.[62]

Many early twentieth-century commentators averred that the engineering and manual construction of the canal could succeed only because American health officers had managed to turn Panama from a "pest-hole" and "ancient plague spot" into one of the "most healthful spots in the world."[63] As one source stated, "Colonel Gorgas realized that it was necessary to immediately revolutionize the sanitary conditions of the Canal Zone and that until this was done it would be impossible to proceed with the work with any degree of dispatch."[64] Beyond proving the unmatched scientific skills of the United States, this transformation affirmed that because insects and germs were the cause of tropical diseases rather than heat and humidity the tropics could be made habitable for whites.[65] In the words of a Boston physician, who spoke before the Massachusetts History Society in 1911 after touring the Canal Zone and interviewing Gorgas, Panama demonstrated that "the white man can live and work in any part of the tropics and maintain good health," adding that "the settling of the tropics by the Caucasian will date from the completion of the Panama Canal."[66] Once seen as resulting from pestilential emanations, tropical diseases began to be understood as infections caused by tiny microbes that, with the appropriate laboratory and medical equipment, could be managed through a militarized brand of surveillance, record keeping, and coordinated extermination.

The formation and implementation of tropical medicine in the colonies bolstered the confidence of the Americans, who attributed their newfound vigor and mobility to their resilient racial makeup and the recalcitrance of certain ailments to the unhygienic customs of "primitive" peoples lower down on the evolutionary ladder who did little or nothing to control pathogens.[67] In the Canal Zone, this translated into a self-fulfilling prophecy because it was the quarters and districts of the whites, engineers and laborers, where mosquitoes were most vigorously attacked. Eradication methods often followed a colonial logic of immunity, where European Americans believed that they required prophylaxis because of a presumed lack of exposure to tropical diseases, while assuming that darker-skinned laborers had usually already acquired resistance, particularly to yellow fever. The sad irony, of course, was both that such theories of racial immunity oversimplified the complexity of disease ecologies and diasporas, and that many times the arrival of European Americans instigated the very conditions that gave rise to epidemics, thus determining the contours and even inventing the field of tropical medicine. In the Canal Zone, the homes of West Indian workers were not systematically screened, standing water was often left untouched in their neighborhoods, and treatment for other, equally deadly diseases, such as pneumonia or dysentery, was given only haphazardly. Thus, in the appendices at the back of President Theodore Roosevelt's glowing 1906 report on Panama and the wonderful results of the health crusade, the mortality figures actually revealed that "the white worker and his family were indeed faring extremely well; otherwise, for the vast black majority, the picture was alarming." From January to October 1906, for instance, 17 whites died per 1,000, as opposed to 59 blacks per 1,000. This meant that West Indians were dying three times as fast as whites. Furthermore, from 1904 to 1910, pneumonia killed at least 25 percent of the silver roll workers, who primarily hailed from Jamaica, Barbados, and Colombia.[68] If "it was no longer a whiteman's graveyard," it was only slightly "less deadly than it ever had been" for blacks.[69]

The message—of American prowess, medical might, and white superiority—pervaded the PPIE and was frequently applied to the westward settlers who had remade California and catapulted San Francisco to global prominence. In his address titled "The Physician as Pioneer," the president-elect of the American Academy of Medicine, Dr. Woods Hutchinson, credited the colonization of the Mississippi Valley to the discovery of quinine, which had stymied malaria, and then told his audience that for progress to proceed apace in the current "age of the insect," the stringent sanitary regime imposed and perfected by Gorgas in the Canal Zone was the sine qua non.[70] From opening to closing day, a chorus acclaiming Gorgas and American colonial sanitation could be heard at the PPIE. As the exposition's official handbook proclaimed: "The completion of this herculean task marks an epoch in the history of the world. A gigantic battle against floods and torrents, pestilence and swamps, tropical rivers, jungles and rock-ribbed mountains has been fought—and won!"[71]

THE MANY FRONTIERS OF CLAUDE C. PIERCE

The colonial circuits that linked public health and sanitation in Cuba, the Philippines, and the Canal Zone to the PPIE were busy highways, certainly traveled by Gorgas, but perhaps by no one more than Claude C. Pierce. Born in Tennessee in 1878, Pierce received his degree from Chattanooga Medical College and joined the USPHS in the lower ranks in 1900 after serving in the Spanish-American War. In 1904 he was sent to Panama, where he worked his way up from assistant to senior surgeon, acting first as a quarantine officer and then, starting in 1913, as the superintendent of Colon Hospital.[72] For more than a decade, Pierce fought typhoid, plague, and yellow fever in the Canal Zone. In 1915, he brought this experience in tropical medicine to San Francisco, where he served as chief sanitary officer for the duration of the PPIE.

As a uniformed health officer fresh from the occupation of Panama, Pierce, and his USPHS colleagues, treated the fairgrounds much like a zone under martial law. For instance, when the USPHS arrived on the scene months before opening day, one of its preliminary tasks was to carry out a comprehensive medical census of all persons on the premises according to age, sex, and occupation, evaluate them for hookworm and trachoma, and, if necessary (as mandated by a recently passed USPHS regulation), vaccinate them against smallpox.[73] Once the exposition had begun, Pierce and his underlings surveyed the buildings, scrutinized concession stands, hung antispitting signs on buildings, and assessed the public bathrooms, all the while searching for vermin, locating pools of standing water, and regularly testing the drinking supply for bacteria. For example, for the month of April, Pierce reported that he applied borax to fertilized soil to discourage fly breeding, turned off and oiled water fountains to destroy mosquito larvae, inspected in total 244 concessions and structures, and reinspected the Joy Zone, avenues, and stockyards more than six hundred times, ultimately pinpointing 125 problems that needed fixing.[74] When he found sick individuals, he sent them to the Exposition Hospital, which was run by the USPHS and operated as both a critical care center and an exhibit. It boasted four wards, an operating room, an anesthetizing room, a waiting room, an X-ray machine, a laboratory, electric massage machines, urine and blood analysis kits, two spiffy Cadillac ambulances, and personnel close to fifteen, including several attending physicians and nurses, technicians, orderlies, and a maid.[75] While the PPIE was being built, the Exposition Hospital tended to injured workers, and from the day the first brick was laid to the last day of demolition, more than seven thousand people were treated or hospitalized, sometimes repeatedly, by the USPHS.[76] The Exposition Hospital also fostered the circulation of modern medical thought at its library, where professionals could peruse a collection of more than one thousand books or borrow from a stereopticon archive of eight thousand lantern slides, many produced during health campaigns in the field.[77]

This demonstration hospital was accompanied by USPHS exhibits, six of which won medals, including one gold medal and one grand prize, from the PPIE's international jury committee.[78] These didactic displays detailed the organization and mission of the USPHS, illustrated epidemiological patterns and surveillance techniques, and even featured a habitat of living breeding mosquitoes.[79] Pierce oversaw all of the USPHS exhibits, the largest of which covered 5,250 square feet in the Palace of Liberal Arts and aimed to present in a "popular and comprehensive way, easily understood by the general public, the latest methods of preventing the common communicable diseases."[80] It highlighted more than a dozen conditions, including typhoid, tuberculosis, rabies, Rocky Mountain spotted fever, and syphilis. Through morality tales (of negligent "silent" carriers, which echoed the melodrama of Typhoid Mary) and positive examples (of wharves properly guarded against rats and securely muzzled rabid dogs), the USPHS instructed its viewers in the basics of bacteriology and made the concealed universe of germs visible through magnified drawings of microorganisms and the anthropomorphism of creatures such as the liver fluke and the whip worm.[81]

Aside from the USPHS sites, fairgoers could tour many other booths that emphasized public health and hygiene (figure 2). In the Palace of Education, the state of New York outlined its sewage disposal system, Baltimore portrayed its methods of water filtration, and the US Children's Bureau foregrounded the virtues of scientific motherhood and pasteurized milk while its contracted physicians examined children and dispensed free child-rearing advice to parents. Throughout the fair, visitors could not witness these medical advances without reference to their colonial

MODELS ILLUSTRATING METHODS FOR THE DISPOSAL OF EXCRETA

MODEL OF A RAT-PROOF VESSEL

MODEL OF A RAT-PROOF HOUSE

FIGURE 2. Demonstration models for controlling plague, from the US Public Health Service exhibit, directed by Claude C. Pierce, at the Panama-Pacific International Exposition, San Francisco, 1915. Source: W. C. Rucker and C. C. Pierce, *United States Public Health Service Exhibit at the Panama-Pacific International Exposition, San Francisco, 1915.* Suppl. no. 27, USPHS Reports (Washington, DC: Government Printing Office, 1915).

connections. For example, not far from the tables on which babies were weighed and measured by the Children's Bureau stood the award-winning Rockefeller exhibit on hookworm transmission, a display sent by the "republic of Cuba" on tropical medicine that underscored "diseases peculiar to the tropics of the Western Hemisphere," and the Philippine Bureau of Health's installation, which aspired to show "the progress made in health conservation and sanitation since the advent of the Americans."[82]

If medical knowledge was absorbed by fairgoers as they walked the palaces, it was articulated and discussed at the more than thirty meetings grouped together during the "Medical and Hygiene Period" in the last two weeks of June. So vast were the numbers, so many the lectures, and so distinguished the figures who journeyed to San Francisco for the occasion that Todd referred to it as "the greatest period of medical conventions in the world's history."[83] That the priorities of tropical medicine dominated these meetings was to be expected at an exposition devoted to the Panama Canal and in a city preoccupied with the specter of plague. As soon as PPIE managers started to map out the event schedule, they began to contact preeminent physicians, asking for their input and collaboration. In 1912, for example, James A. Barr, in charge of conventions and conferences, wrote to Dr. William F. Snow, then director of California's board of health, to request his help in guaranteeing that medical groups sign up for the exposition. Barr began his entreaty: "Tropical diseases are already far too common in San Francisco, and California. With the opening of the Panama Canal we shall have a flood of immigration from Southern Europe, and other parts of the world, bringing all sorts of diseases into our midst. In fact, the opening of the Canal is certain to bring many sanitary problems to the front in San Francisco, and California generally."[84] It was this kind of anxiety, which constituted the flip side of unbridled optimism about scientific advancement, that had prompted Moore to obtain a pledge from Surgeon General Rupert Blue, his ally from the 1908–9 plague eradication campaign, that the USPHS would strictly oversee all sanitary matters at the PPIE. For many physicians and observers, acquiring overseas possessions entailed the tropicalization of the United States, a prospect that in turn demanded full-scale prophylaxis against vectors of ailments such as hookworm and yellow fever and, by extension, those deemed most likely to harbor them. Like the many fin-de-siècle anti-imperialists (and cautious imperialists) who feared the incorporation of the "mongrel races" into the body politic, physicians worried about the epidemiological ramifications of colonialism.

Among the organizations in attendance during the "Medical and Hygiene Period" were the Spanish American War Nurses, the Pan-American Medical Congress, the American Medical Association, the Medical Association of the Isthmian Canal Zone, the American Society for Tropical Medicine, and the American Social Hygiene Association, each of which helped put tropical medicine center stage during the last two weeks of June.[85] For instance, Victor C. Vaughan, dean of the University of Michigan Medical School, who had joined forces with Reed and other medical officers during the Spanish-American War to fight typhoid fever, called to order the American Medical Association meeting, which adjourned with the election of Blue as incoming president.[86] According to Helen Dare, a popular *San Francisco Chronicle* columnist, the American Medical Association meeting was one of the "most interesting, important and vital to public welfare" at the fair and provided an opportunity to recognize that the "greatest achievement of modern civilization," the building of the canal, would have been impossible without the great strides in medical science made by the Americans, especially Gorgas in his brilliant war against mosquitoes.[87]

Blue also took part in the conference of the American Society for Tropical Medicine, which Gorgas had cofounded five years after the annexation of Cuba, Puerto Rico, and the Philippines. Invoking the narrative of medico-military conquest that bridged the Panama Canal and the PPIE, the society's secretary, John M. Swan, stated that the exposition was

> planned to commemorate the connection of the Atlantic Ocean with the Pacific Ocean across the isthmus of Panama. We must not forget that the French would have constructed this canal had it not been for mosquitoes, malaria, and yellow fever. The low forms of life which are responsible for the development of these diseases in the human body and their transmission from man to man are indifferent to race, creed, or social position. It is solely because the sanitary department of the canal commission has made it possible for non-immune men to work without the dangers of acquiring infections of this type that the task has been accomplished.[88]

The scientific skill of the United States was also touted at the Pan-American Medical Congress, where its president, Dr. Charles L. Reed, delivered a lengthy address praising the hemispheric security ensured by the 1823 Monroe Doctrine and "the combined genius of American medical scientists, Latin and Anglican," in quelling tropical diseases, above all yellow fever, in the Canal Zone.[89]

Nonetheless, behind such declarations of the overarching magnanimity of the United States and its egalitarian leadership in a global quest against indiscriminate microscopic enemies lay worries about vulnerability and contagion that were entangled with the racialism of the era. In many ways, associations between particular racial groups and diseases were counterintuitive. If bacteriology had shown anything, it was that microbes and their vectors happily transgressed all social and national lines and that, as San Francisco's plague eradication campaign demonstrated, the extirpation of germs necessitated broad-based campaigns in which everyone participated and cooperated. Tropical medicine, however, was deeply connected to the production of colonial and racial difference, so much so that, in the transition from miasmatic to germ theories of transmission, assumptions of the backwardness and pathology of colonized peoples remained largely intact, now seen as the result of unclean habits and even genetic propensity for infection or immunity rather than climate or environment.[90] It is not surprising that at the PPIE, where doctrines of racial superiority and inferiority were ubiquitous—expressed and encountered in murals, statues, concessions, and de facto segregation—a white supremacist interpretation ultimately won the day. For instance, as Reed's lecture ultimately disclosed, his understanding of Pan-American medical progress was based not on a common cause among hemispheric equals but rather on the enlightened effects of "Aryan blood" in American lands.[91] Moreover, for Reed and many of his colleagues, the ultimate goal of the "practical application" of new scientific knowledge was the "betterment of human efficiency through the physical and, consequently, the mental development of the race."[92] Indeed, the biases of tropical medicine, which were already tethered to social Darwinism and Victorian anthropology, insinuated themselves into the race betterment movement during its incipient formation, eventually leaving imprints on eugenics, especially in the American West.

This relationship between tropical medicine and race betterment had layered repercussions in the continental United States, affecting how immigrants often negatively experienced health, illness, and even daily life. In the 1920s, for example, on the basis of the supposition that particular ethnic, racial, or national groups were more likely to be afflicted with certain conditions, fecal samples were routinely demanded of the Chinese who landed at Angel Island to screen for hookworm and other parasites.[93] More directly, the week after the PPIE ended, Pierce was ordered to Laredo, Texas, to investigate several incidents of typhus fever on the border, an inquiry that eventually led to the imposition of a harsh quarantine against Mexico that lasted more than two decades and perpetuated stereotypes of Mexicans as dirty and lousy.[94] Pierce was instrumental in fusing tropical medicine and race betterment and implementing colonial strategies of disease control and containment throughout the American West.[95] Guided by more than a decade of experience in quarantine and sanitation in Panama, he diligently set up and assiduously directed the USPHS exhibits, scrupulously assessed the grounds for any signs of germs or disease, and shared his epidemiological and experimental knowledge with other practitioners.[96] Undoubtedly, Pierce performed an important public health function at the fair and helped keep potential outbreaks in check. Yet his sanitation work was permeated by developing ideas of eugenics and human difference. For example, in August 1915, Stanford's chancellor, David Starr Jordan, the horticulturist Luther Burbank, and Pierce were the guests of honor at a luncheon hosted by the Race Betterment Foundation.[97] The fact that Pierce availed himself of this opportunity to lecture on typhoid fever and the proper disposal of human excreta suggests the affinity between race betterment and tropical medicine at the PPIE.[98]

"OF THE GREATEST IMPORTANCE TO HUMANITY"

On most afternoons during the fair, at 3:00 p.m. in Theater No. 1 at the Palace of Education Dr. A. J. Read could be found holding forth on topics such as "Heredity and Environment" and "Diet and Health."[99] When he was done, Read walked back to his headquarters at the Race Betterment booth, where he was "in almost constant attendance to give information and advice."[100] This exhibit, which won a bronze medal for "illustrating evidences and causes of race degeneration and methods and agencies of race betterment," made eugenics a daily feature of the PPIE.[101] According to Read, it attracted more than one thousand visitors each day, many of whom returned twice and some of whom returned even six or eight times.[102] It comprised six booths that displayed medical equipment, charts detailing the degenerative effects of alcohol and "race poisons," rules of healthy living and eating, a list of eugenics organizations, and an assortment of instruments used by physicians to gauge the physiological and biological capacity of humans from conception to adulthood.[103] Among the latter was the "New Laughlin Gyotometer" for determining "various hereditary results from parent combinations," which had probably been devised by the superintendent of the Eugenics Record Office, Harry H. Laughlin.[104] To relieve fatigue and stress, visitors could sit in two battery-operated vibrating chairs typical of the electrotherapy and hydrotherapy offered at John Harvey Kellogg's Battle

Creek Sanitarium.[105] Todd wrote that this display "caught the eye of every visitor." Echoing PPIE motifs, its statues were "large plaster casts of Atlas, and Venus, and of Apollo, Belvedere type, to advertise the human race at its best, and get that race interested in its glorious past and possible future."[106]

The presence of this exhibit and of eugenics at the PPIE was a result of the deliberate planning of its managers. In February 1913, James A. Barr, head of conventions and congresses, contacted David Starr Jordan to ask him to help arrange for a major eugenics gathering at the exposition and expressed a willingness to cover the travel costs of some of the participants.[107] Aware that the first international eugenics conference had been held in London in 1912, Barr was interested in holding its successor at the PPIE: "I am still hoping against hope that we may yet be able to bring the International Congress on Eugenics to California in 1915."[108] Although this never materialized, by calling upon Jordan and communicating with other national figures, Barr was able to fill the PPIE's calendar with race betterment events.

Barr's ambitions were shared by Alvin E. Pope, chief of the section on "the Social Economy," which concentrated on "human improvement" in all its guises. For Barr, the two pillars of social economy were "prevention" and "efficiency," which he strove to bring to life at the fair to illuminate the "greatest achievement of the centuries—the Panama Canal— a completion made possible by the rigid application of the discoveries in hygiene."[109] Pope determined to have eugenics play a commanding role at the exposition, arguing that the "exhibits in Eugenics and in Sex and Mental Hygiene" would render the PPIE "absolutely unique" among world's fairs and related events.[110] For him, showing graphs and dioramas of hereditary disease transmission, social biology, and the menace of the feebleminded was "of the greatest importance to humanity."[111]

Both Barr and Pope succeeded in making eugenics matter at the PPIE. Race betterment was a staple concern at the meetings of the American Association for the Advancement of Science and the National Educational Association, where the Stanford psychologist Lewis Terman, his Harvard colleague Robert M. Yerkes, and the psychiatrist Aaron Rosanoff discussed abnormality, intelligence testing, and mental hygiene.[112] They were joined by Henry H. Goddard, who in addition to being the author of the influential book *The Kallikak Family: A Study in the Heredity of Feeble-Mindedness* had several years earlier personally carried a copy of the Frenchman Alfred Binet's mental test across the Atlantic in order to translate it and administer it at the New Jersey Vineland

Training School.[113] Eugenicists also dominated the annual gathering of the American Genetic Association (previously the American Breeders' Association), where about three hundred people attended sessions "devoted to promoting knowledge of the laws of heredity and environment and their application to the improvement of plants, animals, and peoples."[114] On the day before the beginning of the Second National Conference on Race Betterment (SNCRB), the American Genetic Association's Eugenics Section convened. As Paul Popenoe, secretary pro tem of the association and the editor of its *Journal of Heredity*, noted, talks were delivered on the intersection of eugenics and sociology, how to foster a eugenic conscience, the need for broadened sterilization laws, and the medical inspection of immigrants at California ports of entry.[115] In his talk "The Long Cost of War," Jordan propounded the moral and biological costs of military engagement, a message that he repeated at the International Purity Congress, where "he pointed out that the 8,000,000 men who are reported as killed, wounded or missing in Europe are the flower of their country's manhood, and that the degenerate and unfit are left behind to repopulate the warring nations."[116]

Of all the eugenics events, however, the SNCRB was the largest and most important. In 1913, Jordan, Kellogg, and Charles B. Davenport, head of the Eugenics Record Office, had started to exchange letters about the feasibility of arranging a second international eugenics congress in San Francisco.[117] When it became clear that financial considerations and the shadow cast by war in Europe would foreclose this option, Kellogg, fresh on the heels of the First National Conference on Race Betterment, held in his hometown of Battle Creek, Michigan, in 1914, decided that the PPIE would be the ideal site for his organization's next meeting. Jordan pledged his support and, along with more than a dozen others, including Read, Burbank, and A. W. Hoisholt, who was medical superintendent at the Napa State Hospital, he joined the SNCRB's California Committee.[118] Through Jordan, Kellogg hired Herbert R. Stolz, an assistant professor of hygiene at Stanford University, to coordinate the conference.[119] At Kellogg's request, Popenoe assembled a photographic exhibit for the race betterment booths (figure 3).[120] August 4 to 8 was the fair's official Race Betterment Week, when educators, biologists, physicians, and social workers assembled with the intent of launching "a progressive battle for bettering our race."[121]

Over these five days, hundreds of people crowded into the Inside Inn to hear race betterment lectures, and, according to Kellogg, more than three thousand people turned out for the final session at the Oakland

FIGURE 3. Entrance to the Race Betterment Exhibit, sponsored by the Race Betterment Foundation and designed by Paul Popenoe, at the Panama-Pacific International Exposition, San Francisco, 1915. Source: *Official Proceedings of the Second National Conference on Race Betterment* (Battle Creek, MI: Race Betterment Foundation, 1915).

Civic Center, which was capped off by "Redemption, a Masque of Race Betterment," a theatrical tale about the morality and science of eugenic mating.[122] Pierce, as mentioned, presented on typhoid fever. Jordan spoke yet again on the dysgenic consequences of war, contending that only pacifism could protect the "germ plasm" of the country's healthiest and most cherished element, young men of fighting age: "A continual killing off at the upper end and a continual breeding from the lower end, lets a Nation down."[123] Burbank, the cultivator of the Shasta daisy and the Paradox walnut, applied his practical knowledge of plant biology to the problem of race betterment, which, he asserted, depended on a two-pronged strategy: "one by favorable environment which brings individuals up to their best possibilities; the other ten thousand times more important and effective—selection of the best individuals through a series of generations."[124] Hoisholt, who, as a member of the State Commission in Lunacy, had championed California's 1909 sterilization law, insisted that the insane should be rehabilitated, not punished. Like many Progressives, he believed that mental patients were best handled by medical, not correctional officers, and that depriving so-called morons, idiots, and the feebleminded of their reproductive capacity benefited both the individual and society.[125] Calls for sterilization and the elimination of the "unfit" were also voiced by Popenoe, who decried any attempts to impede natural selection, which he thought was appropriately leading to the extinction of decadent races such as the American Indian. Instead, in the name of civilization and progress, he implored scientists to identify those that were a "burden to the race" as well as the social and medical measures to stimulate race betterment. In his talk "Natural Selection in Man," Popenoe adumbrated his future advocacy of better breeding, which he would promote in the 1920s after returning to California and embarking on a comprehensive survey of sterilization in state institutions.[126]

Just as insecurity over racial contagion simmered below the surface of tropical medicine, not far beneath the optimism of race betterment lay uncertainty about the United States during a period of unprecedented immigration, urbanization, corporatization, and industrialization. In the preface to the *Official Proceedings* of the SNCRB, for example, readers were warned of the "the rapid increase of race degeneracy, especially in recent times," and the terrible need to rid the country of millions of degenerates.[127] Kellogg's answer to the impending threat was the birth of a "real aristocracy made up of Apollos and Venuses and their fortunate progeny."[128] He calculated that the United States was already suffering under the burden of five hundred thousand lunatics, eighty thousand criminals, one hundred thousand paupers, ninety thousand idiots, and ninety thousand epileptics, and he cited statistics proffered by Davenport and Laughlin that mental defectives constituted at least 10 percent of the population.[129] To save the nation from ruin, Kellogg enumerated twelve measures for race betterment, which included a thoroughgoing health survey to be conducted in every community every five years, free medical dispensaries for the afflicted, the inspection of schools and schoolchildren, health education, prohibition of the sale of alcohol and tobacco, strict marriage laws in each state, and the establishment of experiment stations where experts could devote their energies to investigating the laws of heredity in plants, animals, and humans. His final recommendation was to start a eugenics registry that would take into account three constituencies: those interested in eugenics, those who met eugenic standards, and children born of eugenic standards.[130] For Kellogg, the eugenics registry was essential to the "creation of a new and superior human race" based on Mendelian principles. He made it the hallmark of the SNCRB and was proud of the fact that

Davenport, although absent from the conference, had agreed to sit on the registry's board of directors.[131]

In part, the pessimism about the future that marked the SNCRB reflected the mounting acceptance of Mendelian and Weismannian theories of heredity among eugenicists. Neo-Lamarckian explanations of degeneracy were popular in the United States among many Progressives at the turn of the twentieth century.[132] Indeed, Kellogg's original dual strategy of "euthenics" or personal and public hygiene combined with "eugenics" or race hygiene typified the race betterment agenda in the early 1900s. By 1915, however, "euthenics," which had been in much greater evidence at the 1914 Race Betterment Congress in Battle Creek, began to be seen by many prominent eugenicists as soft, ineffective, and scientifically unsound.[133] It is partly because of such interpretations that Kellogg has been ignored in the eugenics scholarship. While he maintained close friendships with many of the country's most notorious eugenicists such as Davenport, many saw his enthusiasm for vegetarianism, electric baths, enemas, and bran consumption as futile and fanciful. Some commentators at the PPIE in 1915 viewed Kellogg's clamors for a "eugenic aristocracy" as preposterous, and his eugenics registry was also mocked: "That is to say, America can be saved from extinction and insanity by employing a vast army of medical registrars and inspectors, as though to adopt such a policy would not of itself be an evidence of mental deficiency."[134] Dare, the *San Francisco Chronicle* columnist, believed that Kellogg, along with other purists, sought nothing more than to purge society of its entertaining diversity. She wrote acerbically, "When we all are raised to an admirable—but undiverting—level of physical, mental and moral perfection (through the indefatigable efforts of purity leagues, prohibition parties, eugenic societies, anti-swearing, anti-kissing, anti-corset, standing-up-straight, don't-wear-a-hat, vegetarian, fruitarian, granarian, let-your-hair-grow-long, back-to-nature, esperanto, volapuk, mind-your-step organizations), won't our excellent sameness rather pall on us?"[135]

But Kellogg's ideas of race betterment and human improvement persisted for decades, even if the Race Betterment Foundation was soon overshadowed by other eugenic organizations and "euthenics" was relegated to the realms of body culture and therapeutic self-help. Moreover, at the PPIE Kellogg and his foundation functioned as handmaidens, helping to crystallize a eugenics movement that privileged surgical sterilization, marriage laws, immigration restriction, and ever more elaborate ways of counting and classifying the fit and the unfit. The talks by

Popenoe, Jordan, Hoisholt, and Kellogg fostered this metamorphosis. Even Burbank, who had long upheld a belief in the neo-Lamarckian inheritance of acquired traits, was careful to state that heredity was "ten thousand times" more important than environment. The SNCRB was crucial to the formation of a network of heterogeneous reformers, many of whom would lead the eugenics charge in the 1920s. Furthermore, the tenets around which the eugenics movement coalesced in San Francisco in 1915 would have profound effects in the decades to come. The SNCRB consolidated the ties between California eugenicists, not just among an older generation, which included Jordan and Burbank, but also among a young cohort of crusaders, such as Popenoe and Terman, who would direct the state's main eugenics societies from the 1920s until as late as the 1960s.

Kellogg was supremely pleased with the SNCRB, writing to Davenport soon after that the conference had received more press coverage than any other except for the American Association for the Advancement of Science. Seeking to impress on Davenport the advances made for their shared cause, he wrote, "Your efforts in behalf of eugenics are certainly beginning to bear fruit. The public are beginning to understand better and appreciate more."[136] Kellogg profusely thanked Jordan for his leadership on the California Committee, crediting him for much of the SNCRB's success.[137] To repay him, Kellogg extended an invitation to Jordan to spend one month at the Battle Creek Sanitarium. Although subsequent meetings kept Jordan at the PPIE for the rest of the year, he did accept Kellogg's medical advice, which led to a diagnosis of pronounced diabetes and auricular fibrillation and a lifelong supply of soybean biscuits, carbonates, and yeast extract.[138]

The PPIE closed on December 4, 1915, repeating the fanfare with which it had opened 288 days earlier.[139] By this time it had become clear that the war in Europe would not abate anytime soon. Despite the admonitions of Jordan and the Woman's Board, the United States was mobilizing and training troops across the Southwest in preparation for action on the European Front. The PPIE was the last of the great colonial fairs; the next exposition in the United States would not be held until 1933, in Chicago. Two more, in New York City and on San Francisco's Treasure Island, would follow in 1939.[140] The world's fairs of the 1930s were a different genre—homages to modernist architecture and industrial science that incorporated the wonders of new forms of mass media, such as radio and film. After World War II, the pace of international expositions slowed considerably. Television and movies had helped to bring entertainment into the home, and airplane travel made it possible for many more Americans to visit the "exotic" places they might have caught glimpses of at world's fairs fifty years before.

Even if the PPIE represented a culmination of the spectacles inaugurated with the Philadelphia Centennial in 1876, the seeds that were planted in San Francisco in 1915 with respect to health, medicine, and eugenics would sprout in the decades to come. Key figures from the PPIE, such as Pierce and Popenoe, would be instrumental in shaping the racial and sexual order of the American West, Pierce along the US-Mexican border and Popenoe, briefly, on the border and in much more sustained fashion in Southern California. The nucleus of California's eugenics movement converged at the PPIE, mostly at the SNCRB but at other venues as well. Terman advanced his new version of the Stanford-Binet test at a joint meeting of the American Psychological Association and the American Association for the Advancement of Science.[141] Charles M. Goethe, a Sacramento philanthropist who attended a Playground and Recreation Congress at the fair and was an admirer of Jordan, cofounded the Eugenics Section of the Commonwealth Club of California in 1925 and the Eugenics Society of Northern California in 1933.[142]

Moreover, the PPIE fostered the cross-fertilization of tropical medicine and race betterment at a critical moment of transition in modern medicine in American society. Both were fostered by similar racial doctrines and supported by shifting notions of race, germs, and genes rooted in the identification and illumination of specific disease etiologies that demanded expert intervention and prophylaxis, whether by sanitary brigade or surgical sterilization. Over time, tropical medicine and race betterment would veer apart and become linked to differing scientific and medical agendas. In San Francisco in 1915, however, the theories of race, disease, and degeneracy that infused both domains were still sufficiently in formation to closely intermingle. In any case, they had proven their centrality to narratives about the triumph of the Panama Canal and the promise of American empire in the West and the Pacific.

CHAPTER 2

Quarantine and Eugenic Gatekeeping on the US-Mexican Border

In March 1916, Mexicans living in the twin cities of Laredo–Nuevo Laredo on the Texas-Mexican border began to complain loudly to their local consul. They were outraged that the US Public Health Service had started to brand their arms, in permanent ink, with the word *admitted* after they had been bathed and physically examined at Laredo's international footbridge. Angered as well, the Mexican consul sent a letter to the USPHS asserting that "the American sanitary and immigration authorities are acting against all principles of respect, justice, and humanity, by stamping Mexican citizens, who are looking for work, with indelible ink."[1] The USPHS medical inspector in charge of operations in Laredo, H. J. Hamilton, disagreed, responding that this measure was neither a violation of rights nor an assault on dignity but an action carried out "for their own benefit."[2] According to Hamilton, the ink branding was necessary to defend Texas from the lice, smallpox, and other germs usually carried by "Mexican paupers," and in a letter to the US surgeon general in anticipation of denunciations in the Mexican press he described it as a "very good plan" that would help to deter "future illegal entry."[3] Invoking the authority of the governor of Texas and the state's quarantine laws, Hamilton further contended that aside from introducing infectious diseases into cities and towns, Mexicans were a severe drain on the state's charity and welfare institutions. Justifying the actions of the USPHS as a form of benevolent paternalism, he added that by being so marked, clean and admissible Mexicans were differentiated from the great numbers of anonymous ailing immigrants that circulated along the border. Within days, this exchange between the Mexican consul and Laredo's medical inspector had been forwarded to the Mexican Secretariat of Foreign Relations and the US Department of Treasury. In a final missive, an official from the US Immigration Service explained to the Mexican consul that the stamp, which he denied contained indelible ink, was employed in lieu of highly impractical identification cards and suggested that it effectively shielded Mexicans from the harassment of Texas Rangers.[4]

Hidden away in the papers of the Secretariat of Foreign Relations in Mexico City, this small incident encapsulates many of the conflicts and complexities that characterized the Mexican-US borderlands in the first half of the twentieth century. On the one hand, this confrontation illustrates the centrality of medicalization to the solidification of the border and to the atmosphere of heightening tension that shaped Mexican-Anglo relations. In this instance, the arms of Mexican border crossers were literally imprinted with proof of cleanliness. In the eyes of the USPHS, bearing the word *admitted* converted Mexicans from the status of undesirable and questionable outsiders to that of quasi-citizens with—albeit temporary—constitutional and legal protection. In a related sense, the branding scandal demonstrates the extent to which the borderlands were becoming militarized in the early twentieth century. Seeking to bolster their authority as federal bodies, the Immigration Service and the Public Health Service argued that Mexicans marked as admissible by the United States would be safeguarded from the depredations of local vigilantes. Through modern forms of policing, enumeration, and classification, the USPHS and the US Immigration and Naturalization Service (INS) sought to civilize the "wild West" by bringing order and administration to a barbarous frontier still teeming with outlaws. The practice of stamping the arms of Mexicans that began in Laredo in 1916 presaged historical patterns that would unfold rapidly in the Southwest. Within one year, Mexicans crossing into the United States would be subjected to a much more harrowing rite of medicalization; within ten years, the US Border Patrol would be formed and would start to implement strategies of surveillance, detection, and interception that continue to this day. In tandem, these two trends—medicalization and militarization—worked to create a regime of eugenic gatekeeping on the US-Mexican border that aimed to ensure the putative purity of the "American" family and nation while generating long-lasting stereotypes of Mexicans as filthy, lousy, and prone to irresponsible breeding.[5]

THE 1917 TYPHUS QUARANTINE

Less than a year after the Laredo incident, the US government and the USPHS launched a quarantine, targeted at the eradication of typhus fever, along the entire length of the US-Mexican border. For more than twenty years, border crossers and their baggage were subjected to rigorous procedures of disinfection and fumigation. The quarantine hardened the boundary line between Mexico and the United States, facilitated the creation of the Border Patrol, and fostered scientific and popular prejudices about the biological inferiority of Mexicans. As with many of the important dimensions of the history of medicine, race, and power in the American West, several of the principal protagonists of this drama had been active participants in eugenics and public health meetings at San Francisco's Panama-Pacific International Exposition.

Indeed, the USPHS's senior surgeon who instituted the quarantine, Claude C. Pierce, had served as chief sanitary officer at the fair. When the PPIE ended, the USPHS instructed Pierce to report to Laredo, Texas, to assess the likelihood of a serious typhus outbreak.[6] Just as he had done when he implemented prophylactic measures in San Francisco, Pierce brought the racial presumptions of the tropical medicine that he had practiced for more than a decade in the Panama Canal to the US-Mexican border.[7] When Pierce arrived, a process of medicalization had already been under way in the borderlands for the preceding three decades. Antedating the United States, which was slower than many countries to adhere to the tenets of germ theory, the Mexican health service had established quarantine and fumigation plants in border cities and towns such as Ciudad Juárez, Nuevo Laredo, and Piedras Negras in the early 1890s.[8] Sanitary agents in these facilities were responsible for sterilizing immigrants and animals and for fumigating baggage entering Mexico. Although the USPHS stationed inspectors at various points along the two-thousand-mile border at about the same time, routines mirroring those in effect in Mexico were not standardized until the 1910s.

At the turn of the century, a lack of epidemics and a fluid interconnected economy of peoples, industries, and culture allowed for relatively easy passage through border stations in places such as El Paso and Laredo. During this era, in fact, immigration and public health officials were primarily interested not in Mexicans but in the Chinese, Syrians, and Greeks who apparently avoided Ellis Island by using the border as a "back door" into the United States.[9] Documents of the INS and local oral histories show that until the first decade of the twentieth century

Mexicans regularly came into the United States unquestioned. For this reason, Greeks and Syrians often sought to learn enough basic Spanish to enter as *mexicanos*.[10]

As the twentieth century progressed, however, and Mexicans began to settle in the United States—often making a seasonal visit into permanent residence—the situation along the border began to change. With the USPHS in a growth phase and with the generalized expansion of epidemiological surveillance, US border cities began sporadically to enforce quarantines, usually for yellow fever and smallpox, against their southern neighbors.[11] As nativist alarm over rising numbers of newcomers, especially southern and eastern Europeans, fueled the formulation of stricter immigration laws, USPHS officials became more aware of the porosity of the Mexican and Canadian borders. This transition was also catalyzed by the Mexican Revolution, which began in the northern states of Coahuila and Chihuahua in 1910. As the uprising spread and as Emiliano Zapata and Pancho Villa led thousands into armed struggle against the Mexican government, the USPHS and immigration officials began to express great trepidation about the increasing circulation of insurgents, refugees, and temporary laborers in the twin cities of El Paso–Juárez and Laredo–Nuevo Laredo. When news of a typhus epidemic in Mexico's interior surfaced in 1915 and several cases of the fever appeared in 1915 in Laredo, the USPHS dispatched Pierce to the border. Reaching Laredo a few days before Christmas, Pierce met with Hamilton and local physicians, who reviewed the history of a family (a mother and two sons) taken ill with typhus earlier that month and the measures enacted to quell the disease. They explained that the patients were kept in isolation, that they were bathed with kerosene, that their hair was cropped, and that the family's "shack and all its contents" as well as an adjoining structure were burned to the ground to destroy all potential vermin.[12] Hamilton showed Pierce how the baggage of persons entering the United States was sulfur fumigated at the international bridge, and, revealing Mexico's superior medical infrastructure—the product of a centralized attempt to modernize the country during the decades-long dictatorship of Porfirio Díaz—that immigrants suspected of infection were deloused, with the permission of local authorities, at a Nuevo Laredo plant outfitted with a French steam chamber and boiler.[13] After gathering information about the situation in Laredo, Pierce traveled to El Paso, where he began to refurbish the city's disinfection plant, spending approximately six thousand dollars remodeling and furnishing it with up-to-date fumigation and bathing equipment.[14]

After more than one year of preparing the plant, observing USPHS activities along the border, and receiving steady news of typhus fever in Mexico's interior, Pierce announced on January 23, 1917, that the moment had arrived for an "iron-clad quarantine" against everybody entering the United States from Mexico.[15] Although fewer than five fatal cases of typhus fever had been reported in El Paso in the previous two months, one of these had taken the life of El Paso's city physician, Dr. W. C. Kluttz.[16] This death caused quite a stir among the Anglo elite, who were very invested in projecting an image of El Paso as a dynamic frontier city and "a great health center for the Southwest."[17] This loss was compounded two weeks later by the withdrawal from northern Mexico of General John J. Pershing, who after nine months of an elusive quest had failed to capture the Mexican revolutionary Pancho Villa.[18]

This time, the draconian actions of the USPHS provoked even angrier protest than that seen in Laredo the previous March. The morning the quarantine was enforced, Carmelita Torres, forty-seven years of age and most likely a domestic employed by an El Paso family, spearheaded a demonstration of about two hundred "Juarez women, incensed at the American quarantine regulations," at the Santa Fe Street Bridge, which was shut down almost the entire day: "From the time street cars began to run until the middle of the afternoon thousands of Mexicans thronged the Juarez side of the river and pushed out to the tollgate on the bridge. Women ringleaders of the mob hurled stones at American civilians, both on the bridge and on the streets of Juarez."[19] The women were irate at the prospect of being forced into kerosene showers and had heard rumors that American soldiers were "photographing the women while bathing and making the pictures public."[20] The following day the "bath riots" continued as several men joined the fray and, "armed with empty bottles, rocks and sticks," "rushed the American troops, customs, immigration and quarantine officers."[21]

By the end of the week the commotion subsided, and Mexicans as well as all other immigrants seeking entry through El Paso found themselves subjected to a medical inspection that differed in significant ways from procedures being carried out concurrently at Ellis and Angel Islands.[22] In a special report featuring photographs of four different points at the quarantine plant—the station for the sterilization of clothes, the entryway alongside the bridge where Mexicans waited to be deloused, the yard, and the women's shower room—Pierce described how medical inspectors scrutinized and cleansed the multitudinous bodies seeking to cross the international bridge (figure 4). Stating definitively that "all

FIGURE 4. Mexicans waiting to be disinfected at the El Paso street bridge, 1917. Source: File 1248, Records of the US Public Health Service, Record Group 90, National Archives and Records Administration.

persons coming to El Paso from Mexico, considered as likely to be vermin infested, are sent through this plant for disinfection," Pierce explained that upon entering the building the bodies were segregated by sex and stripped naked.[23] While their clothing was being chemically scoured, a laundering that lasted about thirty minutes, each scalp was examined by a "male or female attendant, as the sex requires," for lice, the vectors of typhus fever.[24] If lice were found, it was common procedure at the time, especially in the case of schoolchildren for "the hair of the men or boys [to be] clipped with No. oo clippers, the hair dropping on a newspaper, which [was] then rolled up and burned. Women with head lice [had] a mixture of equal parts of kerosene and vinegar applied to the head and hair for half an hour with a towel covering the head."[25] Attendants then directed border crossers into sex-segregated showers, where they were sprayed with a mixture of soap, kerosene, and water; after this, they were vaccinated for smallpox if this was deemed necessary (figure 5). At the end of these ablutionary rites, sterilized clothing was returned to its owners, who received a signed certificate with the heading "United States Public Health Service, Mexican Border Quaran-

FIGURE 5. Mexican man being administered the smallpox vaccination by a public health official at the El Paso immigration station, 1917. Source: File 1248, Records of the US Public Health Service, Record Group 90, National Archives and Records Administration.

tine," verifying that they had "been deloused, bathed, vaccinated, clothing and baggage disinfected."[26] The passage was not complete, however, for the immigrant still faced a general medical examination, occasionally a psychological profile, and questioning about visa or citizenship status.[27] Shortly after its unveiling in El Paso, the quarantine was implemented in the Arizona towns of Naco, Nogales, Douglas, and Tucson, and in Texas in Laredo, Eagle Pass, Rio Grande City, Brownsville, and Hidalgo, although only Eagle Pass and Laredo had fully functional disinfection stations.[28]

In June 1917, after approximately four months of quarantine, Pierce could finally confirm that no new cases of typhus fever had occurred along the Mexican border.[29] Out of thirty-one cases recorded in the United States as a whole during this period, the total number of fatalities was three, all in El Paso.[30] This figure of three shrinks in comparison, though, when juxtaposed against its accompanying statistics: 792,629 bodies inspected, 60,295 deloused, 27,537 vaccinated for smallpox, 373 excluded on account of illness or for refusing disinfection, and 11 retained for observation. According to Pierce, the USPHS inspected 37,774 bodies per week, or 5,392 per day.[31] Considering that most entrants came through El Paso, we can divide the latter figure in half to arrive at what is surely a conservative estimate: 2,696 bodies inspected each day at the Santa Fe Street Bridge, with a schedule that began at 7:00 a.m. and ended at 7:00 p.m., 225 per hour, or about 75 per physician each hour.[32] These figures surpass those calculated for Ellis Island during the same time period, even given that quarantine and inspection were separate processes. On the East and West Coasts, disinfection and vaccination were performed by steamship companies and state health officials responsible for examining passengers before disembarkation; these procedures had developed during the nineteenth century and became codified into law with the 1893 National Quarantine Act and subsequent immigration acts.[33] In fiscal year 1917, for example, with reduced European entry due to World War I, 129,000 immigrants, or 350 per day, were scrutinized by approximately twenty physicians as they passed through Ellis Island.[34] Given the limited infrastructural capacity of the Santa Fe Street plant in comparison to Ellis Island, the figure of 225 bodies per hour reveals the fervor that characterized the quarantine. Even more striking is the fact that strip showers were compulsory and integrated into the general examination. According to Pierce's numbers, 410 immigrants per day, or 34 per hour, were deloused at Mexican border ports. If delousing seldom occurred at Ellis Island, on the southern border it constituted the threshold of entry for hundreds of people each day.

Over the next two decades, the sanitation plants along the border were enlarged and further equipped, and despite the disappearance of any typhus threat the quarantine became more widespread and demanding. In 1923, US secretary of labor James J. Davis, who was worried about lax enforcement of immigration laws along the Mexican border, asked for reports from the field about immigrant processing. He received letters from the Arizona stations of Ajo, San Fernando, Nogales, Naco, and Douglas and the Texas ports of El Paso, Presidio, Eagle Pass, Brownsville, Del Rio, and Laredo, all of which mentioned, usually in some detail, medical inspection.[35] For instance, El Paso's acting assistant surgeon, Irving McNeil, meticulously described the modus operandi at the Santa Fe Street Bridge. Noting that 90 percent of all arrivals required chemical showering because of their physical appearance and perceived status as lower-class laborers, he wrote: "The line inspection for the Immigration Service is governed by the regulations covering the medical inspection of aliens prepared under the direction of the Surgeon General, with certain modifications at this port, on account of the fact that the arriving alien who goes through the bathhouse at the disinfecting plant is previously thoroughly inspected while naked, by a trained and experienced attendant, male or female, as the case may be, and, if necessary, by a medical officer as well." McNeil reiterated the same litany of showers, steaming, and vaccinations that Pierce had recited six years earlier, stressing the routinization of weekly disinfection and the renewal of quarantine cards. He wrote, "The working classes from the neighboring Mexican cities known as 'locals' are required to pass through the disinfecting plant once a week. A bath certificate is issued to these and taken up at the expiration of a week, a new one being issued after each disinfection."[36] In another letter to Davis, the Santa Fe Street Bridge's inspector in charge, Will E. Soult, provided additional details about the thoroughness of the medical examiner, who was not content to stand "at a distance noting and certifying obvious defects," and described a procedure of streamlined efficiency: "The aliens are formed into single file, spaced about twelve feet apart, with head coverings removed and required to pass singly with hands upraised, nails to the front, before the Medical Examiner, who stations himself, with back to light, about twelve feet in front of and facing the line of approaching aliens."[37]

Antityphus delousing and fumigation were institutionalized along the US-Mexican border from 1917 to the eve of World War II. By the late 1920s, for instance, El Paso had a new cyanide room for treating baggage and a full-time staff of fourteen that included two supervising surgeons and ten inspectors in charge of vaccinating immigrants, routing them into the baths, assisting with laboratory work, and running the boilers and steam machines.[38] In 1926, a revamped quarantine plant was built at Laredo's international footbridge, allowing for delousing of more than five hundred border crossers per day.[39] By the early 1930s, many of the smaller border ports had received dry air sterilizers and additional personnel. This was a system characterized by clear-cut class distinctions from the outset, as most middle- and upper-class Mexicans were able to bypass disinfection because they were familiar to inspectors, arrived on the train via first class, were well coiffed and dressed, or could furnish a doctor's waiver. Conversely, the majority of Mexican laborers, whether they hailed from the interior or commuted daily across the border, were required to undergo sterilization on a weekly basis and carry a card noting the date of their next shower. Although the intensity and pace varied from port to port and were periodically affected by attempts to control minor outbreaks of other diseases, these requirements for entry were enforced in the large border cities as well as small towns such as Terlingua and Roma.

El Paso's disinfection plant did not cease operations until 1938, when medical inspectors decided that a combination of factors made mass sterilization unwarranted.[40] An increase in commercial aviation meant that more visa entrants and visitors now arrived at airports, not border stations. Moreover, starting in the 1920s, doctors contracted and authorized by the USPHS and the INS had begun to perform medical exams in the immigrant's country of origin.[41] Finally, by the 1940s, antibiotics and greater access to vaccines and antitoxins had wiped out many of the contagious diseases such as measles and diphtheria that had terrified doctors and patients at the turn of the twentieth century. Nonetheless, pedestrians, streetcar passengers, and drivers were still checked for smallpox. They were vaccinated if they appeared healthy but lacked visible scarification and were deported if they appeared to be pocky or feverish.[42] By the early 1940s, Laredo and Eagle Pass appear to have followed El Paso's example, discontinuing substantial portions of their stations and often transforming them into venereal disease treatment clinics for the US Army.[43] When the Bracero Program, launched to transport seasonal laborers from Mexico's interior to American industries and farms during an upsurge of war-driven industrialization, began in 1942, the USPHS returned to more systematic delousing. Now, however, instead of passing through kerosene and vinegar showers at border ports, Mexicans were dusted with DDT as they departed from the Bracero recruitment centers in Mexico. Two years into the Bracero Program, El Paso's medical officer informed the surgeon general that "the use of DDT powder as a preventive of body lice [was] effective to a large extent."[44]

The extreme nature of the extended quarantine along the US-Mexican border is thrown into relief by examining the Canadian border, which was quiescent during the same period. One of the most important reasons for this discrepancy was the racialized lens through which USPHS officials stationed along the two borders viewed and categorized those who crossed from one country to the next. In 1928, for example, the physician who had worked at Port Huron, Michigan, for more than twenty years wrote that the great majority of the bodies he processed consisted "of the more desirable northern or western European."[45] Just two years earlier, John W. Tappan, El Paso's chief inspector in the 1920s, published an article in the *Journal of the American Medical Association* in which he wrote, "Conditions differ from those on the Canadian border. We have here to contend with an alien race: one with a different language, different customs, different moral standards and different diseases."[46]

MEDICAL RITES AND RACIAL EXCLUSIONS

The border quarantine helped solidify a boundary line that had previously been much more nebulous and, in doing so, helped racialize Mexicans as outsiders and demarcate Mexico as a distant geographical entity despite topographic and climatic similarity. It not only intensified racial tensions in the borderlands but also catalyzed anti-Mexican sentiment on a national level and fueled nativist efforts to ban all immigration from the Southern Hemisphere. To a great extent, the pathologization of Mexicans represented an extension of the association of immigrants with disease into new racial and metaphorical terrain. While those disparaged as "other" have been depicted as ill, depraved, or untouchable since before the lazarettos of the Middle Ages, in the United States the linking of foreigners with sickness entered a more pronounced stage in the late nineteenth century when Chinese immigrants began to be associated with physical weakness, parasitic ailments, and bubonic plague.[47] By the early twentieth century, this xenophobic logic was being applied to eastern European, Jewish, and Middle Eastern immigrants, all of whom were explicitly targeted by nativists in the 1920s. Fears of a diseased, feebleminded, and dysgenic "immigrant menace" peaked in the 1920s when Harry H. Laughlin, the superintendent of the Eugenics Record Office, was appointed "Expert Eugenical Agent" of the Committee on Immigration and Naturalization in 1921 by Seattle's Republican representative, Albert Johnson.[48] Laughlin, Johnson, and the East Texas congressman John C. Box—all members of the American Eugenics Society—collaborated with political allies to secure passage of the Johnson-Reed Immigration Act, which stipulated a 2 percent quota per nation based on the 1890 census. Passed in 1924, this legislation, also known as the National Origins Act, was biased heavily against southern and eastern Europeans and debarred nearly all immigration from Asia.[49]

Despite its stringency, the Johnson-Reed Immigration Act did not place the Western Hemisphere under the quota system. In conjunction with the pull of long-standing family networks in the Southwest, labor demands that could not now be met by European and Asian migrants, and the push of ongoing civil unrest in Mexico, this provision spurred immigration from Mexico, which rose substantially in the 1920s, from somewhere around 500,000 in 1910 to 1.5 million or more in 1930.[50] As Mexicans came to the United States, sometimes settling in big cities beyond the Southwest such as Chicago and St. Louis, eugenicists redirected their gaze from the coasts to the southern border. In the latter half of the 1920s, calls to ban Mexican immigration began to be expressed in congressional chambers, scientific and popular journals, and books on the future of the American nation.[51] Reflecting the conflation of germs and genes, the image and description of Mexicans as filthy, lousy carriers that had been inspired by the border quarantine merged with eugenic arguments about the bad hereditary "stock" of immigrants. Indeed, it was not unusual for restrictionists to frame their anti-Mexican sentiment around the dangers of lice and typhus.

Charles M. Goethe, for example, a Sacramento real estate broker, clamored loudly for an end to Mexican entry into the United States. In the 1920s he traveled to the Arizona border to survey health and social conditions. As a member of the national council of the widely distributed journal *Survey Graphic,* Goethe had probably read the steady stream of articles that it had published about Mexico and the typhus quarantine in 1916 and 1917.[52] Soon after his return from Arizona, Goethe founded the Immigration Study Commission, with the aim of determining the extent of the mestizo peril to the American "seed stock."[53] Given a platform to disseminate his views in *Eugenics,* the monthly journal of the American Eugenics Society, Goethe concluded that Mexicans were scruffy and contagious: "Eugenically, as low-powered as the Negro, the [Mexican] peon is, from a sanitation standpoint, a menace. He not only does not understand health rules: being a superstitious savage, he resists them."[54] Profiling a young couple who chose to go "south of the Rio Grande, where so much of the Medieval persisted," for their honeymoon, Goethe then used the imagined tragedy that befell them to insist upon closure of the "back door" to Mexican immigrants. Three nights after the couple's arrival at a tropical spot overflowing with bougainvillea, "The young bride lay tossing with an alarming temperature. Outside her bedroom door the doctor told the almost frantic bridegroom 'It *is* typhus fever.' 'But it cannot be,' the bridegroom objected. 'We have been only in the cleanest hotels. See how scrupulously neat our quarters are, tiled floor and all.' 'Yes,' replied the physician; 'but peon servants like this chambermaid, Mercedes Ramirez, are only too often contagion carriers.'"[55] Reprinted as a broadside for free distribution, Goethe's article depicted Mexicans as apparently healthy yet lethal carriers of deadly germs.[56] If allowed to defile the United States, here represented by a recently married couple at the sacred moment when procreation might begin, the propagation of the "American" family would be doomed.

Such graphic associations were also staples of the eugenic and nativist vocabulary of Laughlin, who during the 1920s authored studies asserting that the country's "melting pot" was being contaminated by bad "germ plasm." As he became increasingly preoccupied with definitions of whiteness predicated on family lineage and Mendelian fractions in the late 1920s, Laughlin offered to undertake a trip to the border on behalf of the so-called Citizens Committee, which had been formed by Box in the wake of rising Mexican immigration. Laughlin requested money from the Carnegie Institution, which was then financing the Eugenics Record Office, to travel to Texas to "find out the relative amount of race-crossing between American men and Mexican women and between Mexican men and American women."[57] During the course of his investigation, Laughlin obtained two confidential questionnaires that had been sent to Box. Both respondents were El Pasoans, and one identified himself as a physician with a local practice of thirty years.[58] Furnishing in-depth answers to all the questions, this informant responded to the query "What contagious diseases have they?" by stating: "Tuberculosis mainly, tho smallpox is constantly bobbing up here along the border and a constant fight by health authorities is the result. We have had typhus fever on more than one occasion, brought directly from Mexico. They bring disease into American families but Americans must use them because there are no others, and besides, they work cheap. The 'Mexican situation' has been a problem for the El Paso County Medical Society for years. Instead of solving the matter, we are getting worse."[59] Laughlin interwove these claims about the diseased nature of Mexicans with warnings about the low scores obtained by Mexican schoolchildren on intelligence tests to press for Mexican exclusion. His proposals and ruminations served as fodder for the bills proposed by Box throughout the 1920s to restrict immigration from the Western Hemisphere to a 2 to 3 percent quota. Although these attempts did not succeed, Goethe, Laughlin, Box, and other eugenicists did manage to formulate an alternative solution to the "Mexican problem": the US Border Patrol.

The quarantine had other important consequences. Although ostensibly a provisional measure instituted to combat a temporary health crisis, it became the status quo on the border, lasting until World War II. It contributed to the culture of segregation, suspicion, and violence that took shape in the Southwest and California during the first half of the twentieth century. In the popular memory of El Paso residents, the experience of the border as a strict and forbidding line dividing Mexico from the United States was connected intimately to the implementation of the quarantine and the bodily assault of disinfection and the medical exam. Although the voice of the "auburn-haired Amazon," Carmelita Torres, who led the "bath riots," is irretrievable, in oral histories conducted by the University of Texas at El Paso, border residents identified disinfection as a moment of bodily desecration.[60]

For example, one Mexican woman, remembering her husband's accounts of the quarantine, told an interviewer, "The only thing they did [in the immigration building] was bathe them [the immigrants]. . . . They bathed them and took off their clothes, which were washed somewhere else and returned all wrinkled." All this, as Señora X recalled, was because "they thought [Mexicans] were bringing microbes or something like that over from Mexico."[61] For José Burciaga, who came to El Paso in 1907 and crossed frequently, the quarantine transformed the bridge into an obstacle and the boundary line into a construct verified and enacted upon the body itself. Noting that the disinfection plant was located right next to the bridge, Burciaga told his interviewer: "You see, when someone entered they doused him with something. What a nightmare! And then there was more: men, women, they shaved everyone. . . . They bathed everyone, and after the bath they doused you with cryolite [sodium aluminum fluoride], comprised of some sort of substance, it was strong."[62] Felix López Urdiales, who resided in Juárez, stopped crossing into the United States in the 1920s in part because of his distaste for the quarantine. He recalled that the plant, which included "some baths, some showers, and a boiler," was underneath the bridge. Remarking that his steamed clothing was always returned wrinkled, López remembered that habitual crossers were required to undergo disinfection every week in order to renew their quarantine cards and that at his workplace this weekly requirement would cost them a half-day's pay.[63]

For some Mexican immigrants who ventured outside the Southwest in search of opportunity, the quarantine framed their migration stories. This is aptly captured by a fictionalized account of the journey of "José," one of many informants interviewed by a prominent group of sociologists who launched a survey of race relations in 1925. José began the tale of his passage from Mexico to Pennsylvania with his arrival at the Santa Fe Street Bridge. After he crossed the bridge, the immigration officers "led me first to the Disinfecting Plant. It did me no good to tell them that I had taken a bath a few minutes before in Juarez; I had to take the bath anyway, and meanwhile they took my clothing to disinfect. I made a bundle and tied it with my belt, then they put it in an oven very hot; from there it came out ready to put on again, except that my belt being of leather was wrinkled by the heat." After being photographed, José and the other Mexicans in line were vaccinated and then marched to a medical inspector who looked "at our eyes and fingernails and head."[64] For many Mexicans who entered the United States at official stations, the quarantine was an unforgettable passage into the strict racial order of the United States. Moreover, the preceding oral histories and statistics from the INS suggest that the severity of the disinfection procedure encouraged many to avoid designated points of entry. By the early 1920s, instead of undergoing baths, sterilization, and fumigation at El Paso's Santa Fe Street Bridge or Laredo's international footbridge, many border crossers opted to head for isolated spots along the river or desert.

It is quite telling that one of the immediate precursors to the Border Patrol was a unit created by the USPHS called the Mounted Quarantine Guard. Formed in Laredo in 1921, this guard was in charge of monitoring 150-mile-long stretches of the Rio Grande for "illegals," vaccinating immigrants for smallpox if they lacked signs of scarification, and bringing seemingly dirty and sick Mexican immigrants to quarantine plants for kerosene baths. According to one official, these guards were instructed "in quarantine work and in fact have done work at the Station in order to gain this knowledge that is: how to vaccinate, how to examine [for] vermin; for ringworm of the nails, Trachoma etc. in other words how to give a general quarantine examination."[65] The journal entries written by the two mounted quarantine guards stationed in Laredo in 1921 detail this dual mission of surveillance and disinfection. On August 22, 1921, for example, Alvis C. Taylor, a river guard, wrote that he "scouted San Antonio road from 9:30 am till 3:00 pm and apprehended 3 wet feet [who were then] delivered to immigration, bathed and deported."[66] The following month, the same guard noted that he reported to the "footbridge at 7:10 am, left for San Antonio road 8:40 a.m. with Martin [his coworker]," and "stopped 3 Mexicans," who were promptly "vaccinated and given the same preliminary medical inspection."[67] The journals reveal that up to twenty immigrants at a time were vaccinated by guards on patrol, and in fiscal year 1923 the Mounted Quarantine Guard intercepted and transported to Laredo's international footbridge 1,120 "alien Mexicans," along with a handful of Italians, Spaniards, Cubans, Greeks, and other immigrants.[68]

After the creation of the Border Patrol, the Mounted Quarantine Guard was phased out. During its brief existence, however, this unit, like the disinfection process itself, helped to mark Mexicans as outsiders who could be admitted to the United States only if sanitized by the methods of modern science. The Border Patrol buttressed and intensified the racial dynamics of boundary maintenance. Engaged in strategies of bodily pursuit that complemented those of the USPHS, the Border Patrol strove to uphold immigration laws that determined inadmissibility on the basis of national provenance, physical condition, financial status, moral standing, and occupation. Rather than raising an impenetrable shield between the United States and Mexico, however, the Border Patrol functioned as a gatekeeper that allowed or denied entry depending on the country's economic, political, and ideological climate as well as on patrolmen's personal predilections and local customs.

PROTECTING THE AMERICAN FAMILY

The installation of the Border Patrol at ports stretching from Galveston to Calexico and from Nogales to Los Angeles constituted a continuation of patterns of militarization that dated back to the seventeenth century, when the Spanish empire had erected presidios and garrisons along its northern frontier. This spatial configuration, which came to be known as the "line of defense" (*linea de defensa*), was part of Spanish attempts to control raids by "hostile" Indians and, beginning in the late eighteenth century, to offset the increasing encroachment of the French, Anglo-American, and Russian empires into the area and its embryonic trading circuits.[69]

After Mexico gained its independence in 1821, the region was beset by both legal and illegal Anglo colonizers responding to Mexico's enticing offers of land in return for conversion to Catholicism. Secessionist movements in Texas and the US invasion of Mexico in 1846, which sparked the Mexican-American War, unleashed more bellicosity. After the signing of the Treaty of Guadalupe of Hidalgo granted the United States most of the present-day Southwest in 1848, militarization was further bolstered by the activities of US cavalry and army regulars (many posted at old trading forts), who waged guerrilla warfare against Indians. Augmenting this climate were the Mexican *rurales,* who hunted down Indians and defended the property of rich northern *hacendados,* as well as border raiders seeking either to extirpate Anglo capitalists and land speculators or to overthrow the autocratic government of Porfirio Díaz.[70] In 1904, the Bureau of Immigration (the INS's precursor) installed its first cadre of mounted inspectors on both the Canadian and Mexican lines. Commissioned with debarring primarily Chinese and southern Europeans, the arrival of these inspectors—many of whom had seen duty in the Spanish-American War—should be seen as an overlapping part of a longer chronology of militarization in the contested postcolonial space of the US-Mexican borderlands.[71]

During the first two decades of the twentieth century, both the mounted inspectors and the Texas Rangers monitored the boundary line. Officially formed in 1873, although with roots reaching to the 1830s, the Rangers were a group of Anglo "mobile troubleshooters" known for frequently taking the law into their own hands and aggressively pursuing "frontier justice."[72] First formed to run Apaches and Comanches either back into Mexico or into the rapidly expanding reservation system, in the early twentieth century the Rangers turned their attention to working-class Mexicans and Mexican Americans. As Anglo farmers and merchants gradually gained control of land in the Southwest, they shifted their focus from the supposed depredations of "hostile" Indians to the perceived abuses committed by Mexican "outlaws" against their private property. From 1915 to 1917, during the height of the Mexican Revolution and the transition to commercialized agriculture, the Rangers were instrumental in the emergence of a new capitalist order and helped incite what scholars have called a "race war" in Texas's Rio Grande Valley.[73] Hundreds of Mexicans were killed, and many protested to Mexican consuls in border cities about the Rangers' brutalities. In the 1910s, both the Rangers and immigrant inspectors were regularly accused by border residents of violence and vigilantism, and the records of the Mexican Secretariat of Foreign Relations, the INS, and the USPHS all contain numerous complaints of mistreatment, especially of women.[74]

When the Border Patrol was established, federal officials desired a national and professional police unit that would eschew the hooliganism of the Texas Rangers but be nonetheless capable of efficacious control. Added to a congressional appropriations bill that was part of the Johnson-Reed Immigration Act, the Border Patrol was officially established on May 28, 1924.[75] Its creation was motivated by the same eugenic arguments that pegged the quotas of the Johnson-Reed Immigration Act to the 1890 census. Unable to secure a ban on Mexican immigration, eugenicists such as Johnson, Laughlin, and Box essentially compromised with southwestern growers, who vehemently opposed any federal interference with their seasonal labor supply.

With a starting budget of $1 million, this "additional land-border patrol" was formed to defend the "long, wide-open stretches of unguarded border between the ports where inadmissible aliens could readily enter the United States."[76] A year after its formation, the Border Patrol was given the power to arrest, without warrant, any "alien" suspected of entering the country illegally or violating federal law, and to board and search vessels used to transport "aliens" or material contraband.[77] In 1925 the Border Patrol was granted an initial force of 472. After nearly doubling to 875 men five years later, with the hiring constraints of the Great Depression, the patrol still had fewer than 1,000 employees in 1934.[78]

Created during a decade characterized by purity campaigns against alcohol, venereal disease, and prostitution, the Border Patrol embodied the era's fixation on boundary maintenance. Its preferred image was one of reform, efficiency, and technological prowess. Notably, whereas only a common badge had identified previous immigration inspectors and the Texas Rangers, standardized military uniforms and a federal badge exteriorized the Border Patrol's sweeping authority. With its powers of search, seizure, and arrest, the Border Patrol also possessed official police prerogatives that its predecessor agencies had lacked. As Johnson clarified in a 1926 congressional hearing: "Our border patrolman arrests when he sees a violation of the law exactly like the policeman. He also has the right to serve any warrant that has been issued, exactly as a police officer may do, or as a marshal or deputy. This is the way we made that law work."[79]

Entrusted with maintaining the "first line of defense" against an "army of aliens," the Border Patrol played a critical role in the delimitation of the northern and southern boundaries.[80] In a fashion akin to that of the USPHS, the Patrol helped racialize the United States by enforcing the stringent quotas of the Johnson-Reed Immigration Act and by transforming Mexican Americans and border-crossing Mexican laborers who had migrated back and forth for years into "illegal aliens" and suspected criminals. In part, this was the outcome of the application of visa requirements, literacy tests, head taxes, and other administrative protocol to Mexicans, who had previously been waived from such demands, and of punitive immigration laws such that illegal entry became a misdemeanor (or, if repeated, a felony).[81] Not surprisingly, the Border Patrol's execution of these laws led to a steep climb in deportations. In 1920, 2,762 people were expelled from the United States; in 1925, this figure had quadrupled to 9,495; and in 1930, it had climbed to 38,796.[82] Mexicans bore the brunt of accelerating deportations, at rates higher than all Europeans combined: from 1,751 in 1925 to more than 15,000 in 1929, figures that do not include the 8,000 to 10,000 Mexicans expelled voluntarily each year after 1927.[83] In addition, the nebulous legal status of Mexicans made them particularly vulnerable to deportation. Mexicans could be categorized as nonresident aliens (usually migrating across the border for seasonal labor with the intent of returning), commuters recognizable to immigration inspectors or carrying documentation, or American citizens certified by a passport or other identification. If they lacked papers or looked "suspicious" to patrolmen, Mexicans could easily be classified as "aliens" subject to removal. Once combined with low morale, a high turnover rate, and uneven knowledge of immigration law among patrolmen, the slipperiness of Mexicans' legal status helped promote an environment of suspicion and uncertainty in the borderlands, in which the Border Patrol arbitrarily used and often abused its authority.[84]

When out scouting, the Border Patrol relied on new technologies to enhance its surveillance capabilities. Defending the border, for example, meant not just guarding the one-dimensional line that stretched from the Gulf to the Pacific Coast but also developing a "defense in depth" model that conceived of the landscape as a series of interlocking zones and entry as a journey that terminated only at the immigrant's final destination.[85] As the founders of Texas's Marfa Sector wrote, "To accomplish its mission the Border Patrol is strategically deployed over a wide area to achieve maximum coverage," an arrangement that allowed for close linkages between headquarters and patrolmen via "short wave radio and other means of communication."[86] This mental mapping, which elongated the boundary line in adjoining sections from El Paso all the way to Los Angeles, extended a racialized logic and practice of surveillance into the borderlands at large. It was this cartographical vision that enabled patrolmen to move swiftly from the border into interior cities—such as San Antonio, Albuquerque, and Los Angeles— and to deport Mexicans in large numbers during the repatriation campaigns of 1929 and 1930 and Operation Wetback in 1954.

If these modalities of spatial control were seen as state-of-the-art, patrolmen also honed practices of detection that they viewed as similar to the ancestral skills of Native Americans. Describing the techniques patrolmen used to pursue and apprehend "aliens," the INS deputy commissioner wrote in 1934, "There is one angle to the work of the Border Patrol which links it with the Indian fighters of the early days. The science of tracking is constantly called into use by inspectors. Broken reeds on a river bank may tell the plain story of the landing of a smuggler's boat."[87] By developing an instinctual connection to the southwestern topography, its flora and fauna, inhabitants, and weather patterns, patrolmen revived and perfected their latent primordial capacities for hunting and capture. Many patrolmen referred to this mode of perception as a "sixth" or "super" sense and claimed that they had learned it, either directly or derivatively, from southwestern Indians.[88] In one book dedicated entirely to the topic, an ex-patrolman profiled one of California Imperial Valley's "greatest trackers." Once a dude rancher, an Apache fighter, and a reservation range rider, Fred D'Albini led Border Patrol tracking efforts on the Arizona and California borderlands in the 1920s and 1930s. D'Albini claimed that his mentor had been a Papago Indian. According to D'Albini, to be an effective tracker "you have to have good eyes" to read clues such as gum wrappers, barely discernible footprints, and trampled vegetation.[89] Illustrating the assumptions about the comportment of nonwhite bodies that underpinned the perception of the first generation of patrolmen, D'Albini averred that a fugitive's nationality could usually be ascertained because "a Mexican always walks heavy on the outside of his feet. When he walks, he puts his foot down on the heel first and then rolls off it—Indians will do that too. Whites and blacks ordinarily put their feet down flat."[90]

By appropriating the primordial "sixth sense" of Papagos or Apaches, the Border Patrol simultaneously symbolically erased the presence of living Indians in the borderlands and tied the maintenance of the nation's boundaries to a powerful story of origins. In this sense, it shared much with the Boy Scouts and the Seton Indians, organizations founded in the early twentieth century to mold young boys into maturity through scouting, nature study, wilderness trips, and survival games.[91] By "playing Indian," patrolmen brought out the childlike, natural, and intuitive sides of themselves, which could then be harnessed in the name of border control.

If the mythology of the Border Patrol revolved around renditions of the past that romanticized the Vanishing Indian, it was also driven by myopic visions of the nation's racial and demographic future. Like the eugenicist Goethe, who told the morality tale about the mating of a US couple that ended disastrously because of their typhus-ridden Mexican maid, patrolmen and their superiors were charged with protecting the "American" family and nation from potential contamination from alien outsiders. As one military expert said when presenting his plan for an enlarged Border Patrol to Congress in 1926, "Undesirable aliens often become public charges and must be cared for by our pauper institutions and insane asylums. . . . Many are a further menace to the health of the communities in which they settle."[92] For many patrolmen this meant embracing the heroic image of the lone ranger who risked his life against all odds to save others. Many recruits were attracted to the Border Patrol because they viewed it as another incarnation of the rough-and-tumble Texas Rangers or the Rough Riders that Teddy Roosevelt had led up Cuba's San Juan Hill during the Spanish-American War. In this sense, if the USPHS and Pierce, in particular, can be interpreted as bringing colonial medicine from island and isthmus to the US-Mexican border, then many of the Border Patrol's first members should be seen as embodying a cowboys-and-Indians primitive masculinity born out of imperial conflict and conquest in the US West.[93] The so-called grandfather of the Border Patrol, Jefferson Davis Milton, one of the original Texas Rangers, epitomized this macho persona. After chasing Apaches, Milton resigned from the Rangers in the 1880s to work as a deputy sheriff, a customs inspector, El Paso's chief of police, and a Wells Fargo messenger. In 1904 he joined the Immigration Bureau, was presented with a badge, and soon became known in the lore as the "one man Border Patrolman." Personifying gritty ruggedness and bravado, Milton "was known throughout the great Southwest for his many feats of derring-do" and was recognized by his admirers as a "real *hombre*."[94]

While this legacy attracted a mix of cowpunchers, ranch hands, war veterans, and civil servants to the Border Patrol, it also troubled many of the agency's officers, especially those concerned with presenting an image of sober professionalism. As soon as the Patrol was established, both immigration officers in the field and their superiors in Washington embarked on a campaign to shift the authority of surveillance from the local to the federal level. Clifford Perkins, who helped to design the organizational scheme of the Border Patrol and wrote a memoir about his career, directed attempts to temper the unruliness of many patrolmen.[95] Responding in part to denunciations that trigger-happy patrolmen were arbitrarily arresting Mexican American citizens and unlawfully entering homes, Perkins traveled from El Paso headquarters in the late 1920s to take stock of the Laredo and San Antonio branches. In these districts, a large percentage of patrolmen were ex-Rangers.[96] Perkins explained that the professionalization of such men was a trying and sometimes unsuccessful endeavor: "It took considerable indoctrinating to convince some of the inspectors they were not chasing outlaws, and we never did get it out of the heads of all of them, for we had to discharge several for being too rough."[97] Nonetheless, Perkins asserted that through repeated inculcation of the need for hierarchy, self-discipline, and adherence to the agency's motto "Honor First," he was eventually able to turn coarse frontiersman into well-mannered soldiers. From the Border Patrol's inception, this makeover was linked to practicing marksmanship and daily calisthenics. In 1934, when the Border Patrol Academy was established in El Paso, more involved screening and preparation of recruits was put in place.[98] Perkins boasted that it required just two years of his leadership in El Paso for the district patrol to become a "healthy, coordinated outfit" that inspired "a considerable amount of public confidence." He claimed that close to a decade after its formation, "The officers were well trained and disciplined; they could be counted on in any tight spot they encountered; generally, they reflected the efforts expended to set up a model of the nationwide, responsible division of the Immigration Service we hoped the Patrol would become."[99]

This trend toward professionalization meant that by the 1930s the exaltation of the patrolman as cowboy-ranger was being overshadowed by the veneration of a tamer type of male hero, the compassionate yet brawny protector. This reorientation fit well with eugenic concerns about the need to enforce immigration laws in order to guarantee the proper boundaries of the nation and the intactness of the white American family. Converging with the nascent discourse of the welfare state, which stigmatized dependency and valorized propagation only of the fit, immigration officials and patrolmen began to cast their activities of seizure, arrest, and deportation in paternalistic terms. It is striking that INS deputy commissioner I. F. Wixon chose to conclude his 1934 instructive tract, "The Mission of the Border Patrol," by proclaiming compassion for the "honest, industrious alien whose only offense has been his illegal entry into the United States." Despite this benevolent gesture, however, Wixon went on to claim that although such an "alien" might seem quite innocent, his integration into the country would necessarily lead to disruption and familial disintegration. Speaking hypothetically, Wixon proposed the following scenario: "In the natural course of events, he marries an American citizen, establishes a home, becomes the father of American-born children. Then comes his arrest on deportation charges."[100] Once excluded, this "alien" would be forced to abandon his wife and children, who, in turn, would have no choice but to turn to the largesse of the federal government. In this vision, human sympathy and defense of the nation's borders were one and the same. It was imperative to debar such interlopers before "they had sunk their roots into this country and given hostages to fortune in the shape of American-born wives and children who would be the main sufferers in the almost inevitable event of their ultimate defection and deportation."[101] By the 1930s the logic of paternal surveillance at play during the Laredo branding incident had developed into one of the core operating principles of the Border Patrol.

The degree to which familial metaphors were mobilized to express the links between patriotism, gender, and race is illustrated by the writings of Anglo border women who corresponded with the Border Patrol. For example, the sister of a patrolman who had been killed in a smuggling shoot-out along the Rio Grande penned the agency a letter in 1929. Referring to the Border Patrol as "the boys," she thanked her brother's compatriots for their fraternalism and told them that she could be found praying every night for the "God-fearing men who for the sake of civilization leave your happy homes and loved ones day and night, rain or shine, and go down to that terrible river, trying to uphold and enforce the laws of our country." Asking God to watch over all the patrolmen, she implored "the boys" to "think of your fathers and mothers, wives and babies, and homes" and to act carefully.[102] Similar analogies between patriarchy at home and manliness on "the line" were echoed by Mary Kidder Rak, the wife of an Arizona rancher, in her two popular books on the Border Patrol.[103]

By the decade of the Great Depression, the racial division that was emergent in 1900 had hardened into an uneven but pervasive version of Jim Crow segregation in the US-Mexican borderlands. In many parts of the Southwest and California, this process of social differentiation involved more than just a binary division. It revolved around shifting exclusionary dynamics and hierarchies among whites, African Americans, Mexicans, and the Chinese, who faced harsh Sinophobia on both sides of the US-Mexican border.[104] Increasingly, it also involved pronounced animosity between middle-class and professional Mexican Americans and more recent working-class arrivals from Mexico.[105]

From the 1910s to the 1940s, the USPHS and the Border Patrol promoted and shaped this multilayered process of racialization in the US-Mexican borderlands. By making admissibility into the United States dependent on standards of health and cleanliness, the USPHS merged medicalization with the politics of social and racial labeling. This pattern was clearly under way in incipient form in 1916 when Laredo's

Mexicans discovered that passage across a previously open space had become contingent upon a physical examination and the ink-stamping of their arms. When the typhus quarantine was inaugurated the following year, medicalization along the border became systematic and streamlined. For more than two decades, the quarantine and its accompanying procedures of disinfection and vaccination discursively linked Mexicans with disease and pathology. Nativists and eugenicists repeatedly mobilized the stereotypes that spiraled out of the border context in the 1920s and 1930s in an effort to curtail immigration from the South. Furthermore, the quarantine also left its mark, as the external borders of nation became intimate frontiers for Mexican border crossers whose memories of unidirectional or circular migration came to include humiliation as their naked bodies were showered with chemicals, their hair was sheared, and their baggage was fumigated and often ruined.[106]

Vivid medicalized associations insinuated themselves into campaigns to enact immigration quotas for the Southern Hemisphere and into proclamations about the Mexican menace. For example, reformers intent on controlling vice on the US side by policing prostitution and upholding Prohibition regularly availed themselves of adjectives such as *dirty*, *lousy*, and *infected* to describe Mexican border towns and their inhabitants. In the 1920s, US calls for border closings, which typically followed drunken and violent incidents involving Americans who sought out the illicit across the national line, reveled in this language, a trend that Mexicans noted with displeasure. The implementation of closures along a string of ports of entry on the California-Mexico boundary led to stinging rebukes from Chambers of Commerce on the Mexican side. In 1929, the Tijuana chamber expressed dismay about the justifications frequently used for such actions, writing to President Herbert Hoover that we "do not consider ourselves an inferior race whose contact means danger at night hours nor as a body afflicted with an infectious plague."[107]

If the quarantine concentrated on the boundary line, then the tracking and monitoring of the Border Patrol extended the border into the US interior. Preceded by the Spanish militarists who guarded the presidios, the Texas Rangers who hounded the Comanches and Apaches, and the first immigration "line riders" stationed on the border in early 1900, the Border Patrol emerged out of both local and national concerns. On the one hand, it was a response to the growing numbers of immigrants who started circumventing designated ports of entry, in part to avoid the quarantine. On the other, the Border Patrol must be situated within the debates over immigration restriction that gripped the United States in the 1920s and resulted in the passage of the Johnson-Reed Immigration Act in 1924. From multiple angles, the Border Patrol can be understood as a facet of a larger eugenic movement rooted in anxieties about biological purity and attendant to contracting and shifting categories of race.[108] Perhaps somewhat unexpectedly, it is not the Border Patrol's initial incarnation as a uniformed extension of the Texas Rangers but its more professionalized image as a federal police agency that illuminates some of its most striking affinities with eugenic ideas about racial purity and the protection of America.

Indeed, patrolmen, even as they enacted the racist scripts that helped turn Mexicans into illegal aliens, also liked to cast themselves as empathetic protectors who disliked and decried the mistreatment of women and the separation of families. The Border Patrol embraced the image of the benevolent patriarch who guarded the body politic. This more restrained and upstanding masculinity was part of the gendered persona of the patrolmen that cohered in the 1930s and 1940s and that sought to maintain boundaries that were at once national, biological, and social. In this sense, the Border Patrol influenced the country's demographic composition and shaped understandings of the legitimate American family during a moment when the welfare state was expanding and the category of whiteness was coming to include previously denigrated ethnic whites and to exclude Mexicans and Asians.[109] Moreover, the eugenic impulse behind the formation of the Border Patrol, which harbored particular enmity toward Mexicans, had a far-reaching impact beyond the border region and affected health and welfare agencies and health care access throughout the American West. Working in tandem, medicalization and militarization helped congeal formulaic associations of Mexicans as illegal, alien, and diseased that continue to have profound reverberations for Mexican and Chicana/o communities as well as for contemporary immigration and border control debates.[110]

CHAPTER 3

Instituting Eugenics in California

From 1935 to 1941, readers of the *Los Angeles Times* could open their Sunday magazines to the column "Social Eugenics," written by the veteran arts and society contributor Fred Hogue.[1] An enthusiast of the American Eugenics Society (AES), Hogue attended the meetings of its California Division, often held at the Los Angeles Public Library, which he then summarized for his audience. He also frequently cited the publications of the Human Betterment Foundation (HBF), organized by the Pasadena citrus magnate Ezra S. Gosney to promote surgical sterilization, and commended the marriage and mate counseling offered by Paul Popenoe and Roswell M. Johnson, authors of *Applied Eugenics,* at the American Institute of Family Relations (AIFR) in central Los Angeles. Although by 1940 Hogue was criticizing the "war hysteria" and imperialist ambitions gripping Nazi Germany, he never maligned Adolph Hitler's program of racial hygiene, and in 1936 he had applauded "the movement in Germany and other Nordic countries of Europe for the elimination of the reproduction of the unfit."[2] That Hogue's feature found a home in the *Los Angeles Times* was not surprising, given that the newspaper's owner, Harry Chandler, was a charter member of the HBF who published a defense of Nazi policies in 1935.[3]

At once sensationalistic, folksy, and doctrinaire, "Social Eugenics" dwelt on the topics of population, birth control, venereal disease, marital exams, and, above all, sterilization. Reflecting the viewpoint of an influential sector of elite Californians that embraced eugenics as the best solution to the state's perceived problems, Hogue saw sterilization as a "protection, not a punishment."[4] Not only would it save the state thousands of dollars by preventing the birth of defective children and allowing the release of inmates in overflowing mental institutions, but most important, it would enable society to shield "itself against the reproduction of the physically and mentally underprivileged, against the continued pollution of the human bloodstream."[5] Without such targeted intervention, Western civilization would collapse, just as Carthage had fallen centuries earlier.[6]

Hogue encouraged his readers to be competent breeders who considered the "fate of those yet unborn," and he proffered advice to correspondents worried about the transmission of hereditary blemishes down the family line.[7] However, he believed that ultimately it was the "constitutional right" and the moral responsibility of the state, not the individual, to safeguard the public welfare by breaking "the chain of hereditary degeneracy."[8] To this end, Hogue advocated the broadening of California's sterilization law to permit operations on people identified as feebleminded or otherwise unfit beyond the walls of state hospitals or asylums.[9] In particular, he supported legislation drafted in 1935 and 1937 to establish a State Board of Eugenics and to expand the applicability of the sterilization law beyond the purview of mental hospitals and feebleminded homes to encompass prisons, correctional schools, reformatories, and detention camps.[10] These proposed bills sought to grant superintendents, wardens, and directors of all such institutions the discretion to file a petition to sterilize any patient or inmate, who, once released, appeared likely to "procreate a child or children" with "a tendency to serious physical, mental, or nervous disease or deficiency."[11] These draft laws also required only written notification to the patient or next of kin, who was allowed thirty days to appeal the order. Seeking to insulate surgeons and state officials against litigation, these bills left virtually no room for civil or criminal liability and, furthermore, mandated that the Eugenics Board's records be sealed from "public inspection."[12]

Although these bills failed, their proponents were not fringe renegades out of touch with the times but rather prominent doctors, philanthropists, journalists, academicians, and administrators who wished to extend the reach of an extensive eugenics agenda that dated back to the turn of the century.[13] Indeed, the sweep and scope of these attempted statutes illustrate the extent to which ideas about the dangers and costs of hereditary degeneracy pervaded California government and culture. Even with this legislative setback, the number of sterilizations rose markedly in the state in the mid- to late 1930s, peaking in 1940, when, according to available records, 967 men and women at nine institutions underwent reproductive surgery.[14] In absolute terms, California far outpaced the rest of the country, performing approximately twenty thousand sterilizations—or one-third of sixty thousand total nationwide—from 1909 to the 1960s.[15] California stood at the vanguard of the national eugenics movement. Although hereditarianism certainly flourished elsewhere, its roots ran exceptionally deep in the Golden State.[16] When European Americans such as the horticulturalist Luther Burbank and the doctor Joseph P. Widney migrated to California from the East in the late 1800s, they sought to settle the land and order society according to the principles of selective propagation and race betterment. By the 1910s, a dynamic network of scientists, reformers, and professionals were consolidating and launching eugenics projects and endeavoring to make hereditarianism integral to state priorities and practices. Eugenicists shaped modern California—its geography, inhabitants, and institutions—through agricultural experimentation, nature and wildlife preservation, medical intervention, psychological surveys, municipal and state legislation, and infant and maternal welfare.

In contrast to their counterparts in other states who imitated broader trends, California eugenicists were players on the national scene from the outset. For instance, the Santa Rosa "plant wizard" Burbank and the Stanford president David Starr Jordan were members of the first eugenics body in the United States, the Eugenics Committee of the American Breeders' Association. Established in 1906 under the direction of Charles B. Davenport, a biologist at the Carnegie Institution's Station for Experimental Evolution in Cold Spring Harbor, New York, the Eugenics Committee was chaired by Jordan and included Alexander Graham Bell and the physical anthropologist Alès Hrdlicka. Formed to "investigate and report on heredity in the human race, and emphasize the value of superior blood and the menace to society of inferior blood," this committee organized sections to study the hereditary etiology of insanity, criminality, eye defects, and many other conditions.[17]

The Eugenics Committee of the American Breeders' Association served as the nucleus for the Eugenics Record Office (ERO). Attached to the Cold Spring Harbor Station and funded by Mrs. E. H. Harriman, the widow of the wealthy railroad baron, the ERO sponsored inquiries into feeblemindedness, family ancestry, and genetic diseases. According to Davenport, the ERO owed much to the reputation of Jordan. When Mrs. Harriman contacted Davenport, seeking an "opinion as to the desirability of the proposed work of studying extensively and intensively the blood lines in the country, both those that have resulted in criminality, imbecility, and poverty and those in which our most effective men have arisen," he immediately requested Jordan's assistance.[18] Jordan, in turn, sent a letter to Mrs. Harriman stressing the enormous value of her potential donation, a missive that roused her to action: "Owing very largely to your letter, in which I gather you spoke some kind personal words, Mrs. Harriman has decided to begin work at once instead of waiting until the first of January as was her original intention."[19] The ERO eventually absorbed the Eugenics Committee and served as the springboard for the AES in the 1920s. This pattern of California eugenicists facilitating national developments while pursuing projects peculiar to the Pacific Slope recurred throughout the twentieth century.

Initially, eugenics resonated with the concerns of California Progressives, whose shared faith in scientific solutions to societal problems often overshadowed discrepant political opinions and approaches.[20] For example, to John R. Haynes, a physician and one of Los Angeles's most outspoken reformers, sterilization, the construction of colonies for the feebleminded, and direct municipal control of resources such as water and electricity were interrelated social endeavors best guided by the laws of physiology and biology. With well-placed adherents such as Haynes and Jordan spearheading eugenics, the movement gained momentum in the 1910s. In the 1920s and 1930s, the radius of eugenics widened, with the founding of, in chronological order, the Eugenics Section of the Commonwealth Club of California (CCC), the HBF, the California Division of the AES, the AIFR, and the Eugenics Society of Northern California.

Eugenics prospered in California for several reasons. First, for many of the European American settlers who streamed into the Pacific West starting in the late 1800s, the act of civilizing what they saw as fertile yet underutilized terrain meant applying modern science, above all, the maxims of heredity and biology, to graft a new polis onto the Spanish and Mexican past. This was most visible in agricultural enterprises, such as large-scale citriculture, but also in other arenas where a premium was placed on selective breeding, such as the better baby contests held at state fairs and monetary inducements for the fit to have more children.[21] Second, there was a strong affinity between the doctrines of Manifest Destiny and nativism that seized California during and after the Gold Rush and eugenic racism. Sinophobia and discrimination against Latin Americans and American Indians, which permeated California from the

1860s to the 1880s, offered propitious ground for scientific racism, targeted principally at Mexicans and Filipinos, to materialize in the 1920s and 1930s.[22] Third, unlike other Western states, such as Oregon or Washington, which also passed sterilization laws, California possessed a dense and multilayered matrix of educational organizations, civic groups, business associations, medical societies, and philanthropies that subscribed to eugenic philosophies. Furthermore, at key points in this nexus stood powerful figures, such as Fred O. Butler, the medical superintendent of the Sonoma State Home; Lewis Terman, one of the foremost popularizers of intelligence testing; Paul Popenoe, the AIFR's director and *Ladies' Home Journal* columnist; and John R. and Dora Haynes, who endowed Los Angeles's first private foundation in 1926 to foster research aimed at the "social betterment of mankind."[23] Although not always in agreement, these individuals and organizations collaborated to make California home to a dynamic eugenics movement. Their efforts were significantly enhanced by the State Department of Institutions, which implemented anti-immigrant policies, intelligence testing, and mass sterilization.

SCIENTIFIC RACISM AND EUGENIC EXCLUSIONS

From his plant nursery, Burbank, who had abandoned Massachusetts for the Mediterranean climes of Sonoma County, espoused an optimistic neo-Lamarckian view of the harmonious outcome of race mixing and open immigration that countered much eugenic thinking at the time. Almost always, xenophobia, most vehemently aimed at Mexican and Asian immigrants, was the explicit or implicit corollary of the eugenic construal of the state's problems. Nativism was no stranger to California, having migrated westward with many of the European Americans who colonized the Pacific Slope. At best, California nativism was a paradoxical brand of racial discrimination, applied by recent East Coast and Midwest transplants to peoples with generations-long connections to the region.

By the eve of the US invasion of Mexico in 1846, white supremacy was poised to become a staple of the postconquest political and legal regime. In 1851, one year after the state entered the Union, a law was passed that taxed any quantity of placer gold mined by foreign nationals. In the 1870s and 1880s, San Francisco was home to the Workingmen's Party, whose virulently Sinophobic platform set the stage for the federal Chinese Exclusion Act of 1882. White mobs repeatedly attacked

Chinese communities, burning down homes and business, and rallying to drive the "Yellow Peril" out of town. Additionally, like other Western states, California passed an antimiscegenation statute in 1850 that forbade unions between whites and "negroes and mulattoes," adding "Mongolians" to the list in 1880.[24] By the 1890s, the *californiano* and Mexican grip on power at the local and state levels, which had proved quite resilient from the 1850s to the 1880s, had become much more tenuous and was under relentless assault from European American entrepreneurs, lawyers, and politicians.[25]

At the turn of the century, California nativism was infused with budding eugenic notions of biological difference and racial capacity. More often than not, fears about the impending hereditary contamination brought on by racial or immigrant groups were couched in fiscal terms: not only would bad genes defile the "germ plasm," but also the demands placed on the state by "defectives" would drastically deplete resources. Following this logic, the state's principal reform agency, the Department of Institutions, implemented exclusionary racial policies. Originally formed in 1896 as the Commission in Lunacy, this department (renamed the Department of Institutions in 1920) created the Office of the Deportation Agent in 1915, whose responsibility was to expel foreigners and nonresidents confined in state asylums and mental hospitals, a practice that had begun *sub silentio* as early as 1905. The deportation agent was partisan to the perception, popular at the time, that California had become the "the greatest sanitarium in America," luring the mentally and physically ill from far and wide.[26] This sentiment was accentuated by worries that the farther one ventured into the Western frontier, the greater the likelihood of a disordered mind.[27] In the early 1920s, the deportation agent bemoaned a 120 percent surge in arrivals and blamed ignorant and parochial doctors in the East and Midwest for prompting an exodus of hundreds of the infirm to the Pacific.[28] Over a span of about twenty-five years, the Department of Institutions delivered more than eight thousand nonresidents across state lines and, working with federal immigration authorities, repatriated more than two thousand foreign nationals—predominantly to Mexico, the Philippines, and China.[29]

The year deportations officially began, the Department of Institutions' sister agency, the Board of Charities and Corrections, announced that the county hospitals were suffering from a "foreign problem," notably a "Mexican problem," because Mexicans constituted 4.8 percent of the twelve thousand patients treated in 1914.[30] In the eyes of the Department of Institutions, Mexicans cost the state money and, worse, were ungrateful for any care they received: "The Mexican does not make a good eleemosynary charge. He will not work and is sullen and surly."[31] From 1915 to the late 1920s, the deportation agent consistently repatriated Mexicans at the highest rate. Between 1926 and 1928, Mexicans made up 47 percent of those deported, chiefly from Southern California, where "the problem of caring for the defective, delinquent and destitute of Mexico" was "most acute."[32] During the Depression, when thousands of Mexicans returned across the border under intense pressure and often force, Filipinos and Chinese surged to the top of the banished list. For instance, the deportation agent sent back seventy-six Filipinos in 1930 and fifty-eight in 1938.[33] The deportation agent also ousted scores of poor European Americans who hailed from the East and South, particularly "Okies" who had fled the Dust Bowl in search of jobs in California's fields and factories. It was common practice to place deportees on trains with attendants to chaperone them and their clinical histories, ultimately delivering them to destinations as scattered as Parsons, Kansas, and Little Rock, Arkansas. Departing patients left California with the clothes on their backs and negligible amounts of personal property. For example, of 21 patients deported from Norwalk in November 1937, one man left with 12 cents, his pocket book and two plates of false teeth; another man possessed no cash but one rosary. Many deportees returned to next of kin in previous places of residence with nothing more than a coat.[34] Los Angeles replicated the exclusionary techniques of the Department of Institutions in the 1930s, when the mayor set up a Committee on Indigent Alien Transients to bar Mexicans, African Americans, and Okies from entering the city.[35] Fiscal justifications for such policies loomed large (figure 6). In 1942, for example, the Department of Institutions calculated that the deportation of 10,359 nonresidents and foreign nationals over the previous three decades had resulted in an estimated net savings of more than $12 million.[36]

If the Department of Institutions sometimes emphasized financial over eugenic reasoning, justifications for expulsion based on the menace of race degeneracy were touted in other quarters. During the 1910s and 1920s, the CCC, an exclusive fraternal society founded in San Francisco in 1903 to "investigate and discuss problems affecting the welfare of the Commonwealth and to aid in their solution," served as a hub for Pacific Coast nativism.[37] In its Immigration Section, initiated in 1913, members clamored for more stringent immigration restriction, labeling the Japanese and Mexicans as dysgenic. In 1920, after being briefed by this section, the CCC endorsed California's second Alien Land Law, which

TABLE No. 5. SHOWING THE FINANCIAL BENEFITS DERIVED BY THE STATE THROUGH THE EFFORTS OF THE DEPARTMENT OF INSTITUTIONS

Year		Aliens deported and nonresidents returned	Per capita cost of maintenance	Savings based on cost of maintenance	Per capita cost for construction, furnishing, etc.	Savings based on cost of construction, etc.	Total based on cost of maintenance construction, etc.	Expense of deportation	Net savings to the state
1905		10	$156 37	$1,563 70	$550 00	$5,500 00	$7,063 70	$1,200 00	$5,863 70
1906		15	150 35	2,255 25	550 00	8,250 00	10,505 25	1,200 00	9,305 25
1907		8	163 32	1,298 56	550 00	4,400 00	5,698 56	1,200 00	4,498 56
1908		15	165 08	2,476 20	550 00	8,250 00	10,726 20	1,200 00	9,526 20
1909		27	163 03	4,401 81	750 00	20,250 00	24,651 81	1,200 00	23,451 81
1910		63	180 02	11,341 26	750 00	47,250 00	58,591 26	1,200 00	57,391 26
1911		63	176 50	11,119 50	750 00	47,250 00	58,369 50	1,200 00	57,169 50
1912		44	167 70	7,378 80	750 00	33,000 00	40,378 80	1,200 00	39,178 80
1913		39	177 24	4,912 36	750 00	29,250 00	34,162 36	1,200 00	32,962 36
1914		146	189 47	27,662 62	750 00	109,500 00	137,162 62	12,925 00	124,237 62
1915		27	189 59	5,118 93	750 00	20,250 00	25,368 93	1,200 00	24,168 93
1916		175	183 52	32,116 00	750 00	131,250 00	163,366 00	18,700 00	144,666 00
1917		123	198 87	24,461 01	750 00	92,250 00	116,711 01	13,500 00	103,211 01
1918		201	222 09	44,640 09	1,000 00	201,000 00	245,640 09	12,600 00	233,040 09
1919		144	257 40	37,065 60	1,000 00	144,000 00	181,065 60	12,600 00	168,465 60
1920		304	289 54	88,020 16	1,000 00	304,000 00	392,020 16	20,700 00	371,320 16
1921		198	303 20	60,033 60	750 00	148,500 00	208,533 60	20,700 00	187,833 60
1922		266	277 47	72,807 02	750 00	199,500 00	272,307 02	29,210 00	243,097 02
1923	Insane	236	280 00	66,080 00	750 00	177,000 00	259,738 64	24,680 00	235,058 64
	Delinquents	12	638 22	7,638 64	750 00	9,000 00			
1924	Insane	293	259 63	76,071 59	750 00	219,750 00	489,929 51	36,880 00	453,049 51
	Delinquents	148	561 54	83,107 92	750 00	111,000 00			
1925	Insane	308	263 00	81,004 00	850 00	261,800 00	647,685 52	43,621 99	604,063 53
	Delinquents	214	574 68	122,981 52	850 00	181,900 00			
1926	Insane	296	254 81	75,423 76	850 00	251,600 00	582,378 12	36,231 90	546,146 22
	Delinquents	177	592 68	104,904 36	850 00	150,450 00			
1927	Insane	241	251 35	60,575 35	850 00	204,850 00	606,323 40	45,101 88	561,221 52
	Delinquents	235	600 63	141,148 05	850 00	199,750 00			
1928	Insane	223	254 64	56,784 72	850 00	189,550 00	484,115 52	33,251 14	450,884 38
	Delinquents	160	636 13	101,780 80	850 00	136,000 00			
1929	Insane	180	250 89	45,160 20	850 00	153,000 00	428,671 68	29,761 44	398,910 24
	Delinquents	152	666 49	101,311 48	850 00	129,200 00			
1930	Insane	225	258 04	58,059 00	850 00	191,250 00	506,320 16	41,929 97	464,390 19
	Delinquents	166	698 26	115,911 16	850 00	141,100 00			
Totals		5,134		*$1,736,635 02		$4,260,850 00	$5,997,485 02	$444,398 32	$5,553,091 70

* This column merely shows the saving for one year. A conservative estimate of the average institutional life of an insane person is ten years, and that of the delinquents is 18 months. On this basis we estimate the next saving to the State on maintenance at §10,302,124.57.

FIGURE 6. Calculation of cumulative costs saved by deportations from state institutions, from the California Department of Institutions' *Biennial Report*, 1930. Source: California State Department of Institutions, *Fifth Biennial Report of the Department of Institutions for the Year Ending June 30, 1930* (Sacramento: California State Printing Office, 1930).

stripped Japanese farmers of their land by making ownership contingent on American citizenship, a legal status that virtually none could attain.[38]

In the mid-1920s, the Immigration Section turned its attention to the "Mexican problem" when the Berkeley professor Samuel J. Holmes and the Sacramento realtor Charles M. Goethe began to press for a quota akin to the 2 percent cap placed on southern Europeans and Asians in the Johnson-Reed Immigration Act. A zoologist by training, Holmes taught eugenics at the University of California, produced a family pedigree inventory of Berkeley undergraduates, and espoused the idea of monetary incentives for white female students and faculty wives to produce more children.[39] In an article titled "Perils of the Mexican Invasion," Holmes assailed Mexicans as undemocratic, mentally retarded, and wildly procreative carriers of plague, typhus, and hookworm. Enjoining his readers to back extreme limits on immigration from the south, he identified Mexicans as the "least assimilable" of the "foreign stocks" and urged that it was imperative to "exclude all people who do not measure up to the average level of our own American stock."[40] For Holmes, the racial hybridity of Mexicans, who "may be anything from a descendent of pure Castilian stock to an Indian peon without a trace of Caucasian blood," rendered them unfit for inclusion in the American body politic.[41] Many of Holmes's CCC associates shared this perspective, voting overwhelming in club polls for a ban on Mexican entry, stricter enforcement of deportation laws, and a national registry of "aliens."[42]

The growing stature of hereditarianism among CCC members inspired Goethe, who frequently harangued members of the Immigration Section on the dangers of bad "germ plasm," to propose a Eugenics Section in 1924. In a letter written to the Board of Governors, Goethe praised the activities of CCC nativists and submitted the question, "What next in race improvement?"[43] Goethe opined that a Eugenics Section would provide the ideal forum in which to discuss how to combat the underbreeding of the "fit" and the overbreeding of the "unfit," what Teddy Roosevelt had termed "race suicide" two decades earlier. Goethe thought the section could evaluate strategies for the elimination "from our population by preventing their reproduction, of the, say, perhaps 2 per cent thereof who are notoriously unfit to propagate."[44] Holmes, who had already conferred with Goethe about establishing a eugenics group in Northern California, agreed to preside over the section, which Terman, Haynes, and Jordan also joined.[45] Holmes was upbeat that the section would mature into a "center of influence" in California, a hope reiterated by Goethe, who prophesied in 1925, "With the work of Dr. Holmes you have now a section on Eugenics that is going to have a profound influence. It is developing into the one great center of eugenic thought here in the West, just as they have in the East the Galton Society and the Eugenic Research Society and the Eugenic Society of America [sic]."[46]

Holmes swiftly pinpointed California's two overriding eugenic issues: the "restriction of the propagation of defectives," and "immigration, especially from Mexico." Holmes was of the opinion that "from the standpoint of the future inheritance of the people of our State, there are few matters of greater importance than those presented by the rapid increase of migrants across the Mexican border."[47] Meeting at times with the Immigration Section, CCC eugenicists pushed to shut the gates to Mexicans, Filipinos, and the Japanese. Echoing the Department of Institutions, they reprimanded Mexicans for abusing public aid. In 1928, for example, Stuart Ward presented the results of a three-year survey of Mexicans in California.[48] Complaining about the more than ten thousand legal and illegal immigrants crossing the border each week, Ward conceded that Mexicans made good parents and agricultural laborers because they could withstand "the intense heat of the Imperial Valley which the white man cannot endure." Despite these virtues, however, Mexicans were rarely endowed with IQs over 85, came from a "mongrel" nation, and exploited free clinics.[49] In another meeting, the invited speaker charged that Mexicans in Los Angeles availed themselves of 78 percent of the county's charity.[50]

Gaining in intensity in the 1920s, scientific racism was bluntly expressed by some of the state's most prominent Progressives. In 1925, for instance, Jordan wrote to Davenport that Mexicans were to blame for California's waning tourist economy, as they bring "with them bubonic plague, small pox, and typhus fever. While these diseases do not touch the clean living part of the south, they have still kept the health officers very busy, and probably diminished by half the chief crop of Southern California, winter tourists."[51] Three years later, on the letterhead of the Immigration Study Commission he had formed to raise alarm about the dangers of entrants from the Western Hemisphere, Goethe wrote, "The intelligent Mexican of white stock does not come here. The peon, who is an Amerind, has an average intelligence quotient of only 60."[52] In short order, dispatches such as these, sent by Jordan, Goethe, Holmes, and other Californians, found their way into the country's flagship eugenics journal, *Eugenical News,* and by the late 1920s Pacific Coast nativism had become a national affair: "The Mexican peon does more than bring into the United States smallpox. With his numerous offspring he tends to dilute our old American blood. Thus he is giving us a new color problem."[53]

From the 1910s to the 1930s, the Deportation Agent, the Eugenics Section of the CCC, and nativists with university credentials vilified Mexicans as defective, diseased, and overly fecund and urged that they be barred from the state, even as industry and agribusiness thrived precisely because of their labor. California eugenicists crafted an intransigent and tenacious xenophobia that resurfaced throughout the twentieth century, most notably with Proposition 187, which sought to deny public services, including medical care and education, to "illegal aliens."[54] Passed by a majority of California voters in 1994, this proposition was ruled unconstitutional in 1998 for overstepping the bounds of state authority.[55]

PSYCHOMETRICS AND JUVENILE RESEARCH

The same year that the deportation agent began his rounds, the Department of Institutions created the California Bureau of Juvenile Research (CBJR). The first unit in the country devoted exclusively to research into the "causes and consequences of delinquency and mental deficiency" among children and adolescents, the CBJR functioned until 1941, when it was discontinued and replaced by the California Youth Authority.[56] From 1916 to 1938 the CBJR published the *Journal of Delinquency* (renamed the *Journal of Juvenile Research* in 1928).[57] Headquartered at the Whittier State School, a facility for boys younger than age sixteen, the CBJR, which treated the state's correctional homes, schools, prisons, and detention halls as its domain, pioneered the introduction of psychometrics into the arena of juvenile welfare. For many bureau psychologists and *Journal* contributors, the answer to delinquency was rehabilitation, through the inculcation of discipline and the acquisition of skills suitable to one's cognitive level, as weighed by psychometric exams. At the Department of Institutions' three homes—Whittier, the Ventura Home for Girls, and the Preston School of Industry—rehabilitation was linked, for boys, to mastering a trade; for girls, to achieving proficiency in sewing and home economics; and for immigrant children, to "Americanization" exercises.[58]

The creation of the CBJR reflected an increasing national preoccupation with children and young adults, as illustrated by the formation of separate juvenile courts and justice systems, which began in Chicago (Cook County) in 1899 and was soon replicated across the country. By the early twentieth century, California maintained several such institutions, including the Los Angeles Juvenile Court, founded in 1909.[59] Children, especially adolescents, were gaining an autonomous identity in the fields of pediatric medicine, developmental psychology, and evolutionary science, and they frequently served as the projection screen for adults' unease about the present malaise and future cohesion of modern society.[60] In the case of young women, reformers' anxieties revolved principally around reproduction and sexuality; it was common for girls who rejected chastity and middle-class gender norms to be labeled wayward or immoral. For boys, worries generally centered on perceived incorrigible or antisocial tendencies that might impede their employment prospects or tempt them to break the law. In California, where physicians had long anguished over steep rates of institutionalization and insanity, the mental and physical well-being of the youngest generation was of paramount importance.[61]

Terman and his protégés paved the way for the CBJR in the early 1910s. From his base at Stanford, Terman set out in 1910 to revise the Binet-Simon mental test, newly minted by Alfred Binet and his apprentice Theodore Simon in France. Unlike Binet, however, who regarded intelligence as too complex to be captured by a number alone, Terman thought that intelligence was quantifiable and innate, a tenet that prompted the German psychologist William Stern to invent the concept of the intelligence quotient in 1912.[62] This belief, namely that intelligence was hereditary and immutable, was buttressed by simplistic Mendelian theories of ratios and genes, which posited a one-to-one correlation between "unit characters" and mental, emotional, and physiognomic traits. It merged comfortably with hierarchical evolutionary schemes that posited that each "race" was a biological group with distinct attributes and faculties.[63] In his 1916 book *The Measurement of Intelligence,* Terman outlined just such a formulation, expounding on the scientific accuracy of IQ tests and their ability to impartially identify delinquent, retarded, diseased, and otherwise unfit individuals.[64] Exhibiting an undying faith in numbers, Terman devised a quantitative scale that categorized test takers as idiots, imbeciles, morons, borderline deficients, feebleminded, dull normal, normal, superior, very superior, or geniuses.[65] The IQs of morons fell between 51 and 70, geniuses topped the charts at 140 or higher, and people of average IQ deviated not more than 10 points on either side of 100. Following a self-fulfilling logic of racial aptitude, Terman's "Normal Curve" located the IQs of Mexicans, Indians, and "negroes" in the borderline range of 71 to 90, with Mexicans hovering between borderline deficiency and somewhat more able groups "usually classed as normal but dull."[66]

In order to recalibrate the Binet-Simon for use in the United States to gauge the extent of the "menace of feeblemindedness" in California, Terman began to administer hundreds of exams throughout the state.[67] In 1911 he studied four hundred children in a school near Stanford; in 1912 he focused on the small coastal town of San Luis Obispo; and in 1914 he and his graduate student J. Harold Williams brought their testing booklets to Whittier.[68] In 1914, Stanford's education department, under Terman's direction, received a substantial endowment from the Buckel Foundation for the "psychological and pedagogical study of backward and mentally defective children."[69] These funds enabled Williams to conduct a survey at Whittier with Terman's revamped Binet-Simon, the Stanford-Binet. Williams examined 150 "delinquent boys," in order to ascertain their IQs and cluster them into four categories: "definitely feebleminded," "borderline," "dull normal," or "normal or above." Only 25 percent were determined to be "normal or above," an outcome that delivered proof of the "plainly seen" correlation between delinquency and defective heredity and that provoked apprehension about the mental vigor of California's youth.[70]

This study, along with several others, compelled Whittier's superintendent, Fred C. Nelles, to back a bill requesting the foundation of the CBJR, which was approved in 1915 and expanded and clarified in 1917.[71] Williams was appointed the director, and Whittier the home, for a "department for the clinical diagnosis of inmates of the school and other state institutions, and to inquire into the causes and consequences of delinquency and mental deficiency, and related problems."[72] With Davenport's blessing, the CBJR was designated "the official Western Representative of the Eugenics Record Office" and was licensed to employ the ERO's diagnostic and classificatory methods.[73] Shortly after a visit from the ERO's superintendent, Harry H. Laughlin, to Whittier in 1913, the Department of Institutions arranged for the installation of ERO-trained field workers in California's homes and hospitals.[74] In 1915 the "exceptionally successful" Karl M. Cowdery arrived at Whittier to apply what he had learned at the ERO, and in 1918 Mildred S. Covert followed in his footsteps, becoming a bureau field worker.[75]

As the CBJR grew, it continued to rely on the ERO for personnel and forms and reciprocated by sending copies of all of its case histories to Cold Spring Harbor for review and archiving.[76] In 1920, the bureau started to educate "a limited number of persons for field-work" in accordance with the ERO model, and the following year it published the *Whittier Social Case History Manual,* which drew from Davenport's *Trait Book* and Laughlin's *How to Make a Eugenical Family History.*[77] In keeping with the eugenic nomenclature of the era, bureau psychologists assigned alphabetic "unit characters"—*A* for alcoholic, *F* for feebleminded, and *W* for wanderer—encasing them in squares or circles (depending on the relative's gender) as they traced back the familial lineage of the child in question.[78] For instance, in the case of an eleven-year-old male truant, Williams first traced the youngster's paternal side, finding wanderlust and tuberculosis, and then his mother's lineage, which revealed excitability, alcoholism, and immorality, and then assessed his subject's "inferior mentality." Having received an IQ score of 82, or dull normal, this boy was judged incapable of advancing "beyond a routine or semi-skilled worker or artisan," and Williams recommended that his "evident tendency to wanderlust [should] be recognized in his vocational placement by providing employment which would give some outlet to this inherent trait."[79]

In 1921, Covert completed Social Case History no. 351, a twenty-page evaluation of a fifteen-year-old Mexican male truant who had been declared a ward of the court and committed to Whittier. Classifying him as a moron, Covert then reviewed his proclivity for bad behavior and purported lack of interest in school, underscoring his "inferior mentality" and "low intelligence." On the basis of her impressions from meeting this boy's parents, who lived in a poor section of San Diego and supported seven children with income from a tamale stand, Covert concluded that the mother and, at a minimum, two siblings were feebleminded. Even though this boy had exhibited foresight and volition by asking to "learn some trade while in Whittier State School so that he can be self-supporting when released," Covert closed the report by highlighting his inauspicious heredity and offered that, if kept under "close supervision," he could do adequately in the manual trades.[80] It is possible that this Mexican boy, with an IQ of 67, was moved to a mental hospital, given that minors with IQs of 70 or below (and hence, at the very least labeled feebleminded) were frequently institutionalized. In 1925, the CBJR's director proudly proclaimed that the percentage of feebleminded boys housed at Whittier had plummeted from 28 in 1914 to 2 in 1924 because of increased transfer rates to the Sonoma State Home and the Pacific Colony.[81] Once so interned, these young inmates were prime candidates for sterilization, done with or without parental consent, a procedure that the *Journal* countenanced from its first to its final issue.[82] Indeed, most CBJR psychologists viewed reproductive surgery as a mandatory precondition for release from a state institution.[83]

In addition to its pivotal role in the state's juvenile facilities, the CBJR was instrumental in the explosion of IQ testing in California classrooms in the 1920s.[84] The bureau propelled the rapid expansion of psychometric testing that became pervasive in the Los Angeles public schools, which had recently acquired a Division of Psychology and Educational Research.[85] This district administered the National Intelligence Test, a cousin of the Stanford-Binet, to more than eighty thousand pupils in 219 elementary schools, approximately half of the total enrollment of the city.[86] The mushrooming of IQ testing coincided with the influx of roughly three hundred thousand Mexicans to the Southwest between 1910 and 1930, many fleeing the chaos of revolution and civil war.[87] Upon arriving in California, these newcomers and their children, if attending school, encountered an environment where segregation had been intensified by scientific racism and intelligence testing.

Psychometrics, as pursued by the CBJR, carried forward the nativist and exclusionary policies of education boards that dated back to the 1850s.[88] Starting in the late nineteenth century, African American, Chinese, and Japanese schoolchildren faced de jure segregation in public education; in response, these communities waged protracted legal battles on the municipal and state levels.[89] Mexicans, who were considered white according to census and juridical standards, were instead subjected to a pervasive and insidious de facto segregation that was often framed by eugenic arguments about mental and procreative fitness. In Southern California in particular, separate schools were part of a broader dynamic of spatial division between European Americans and Mexicans, as the former moved to the burgeoning suburbs and the latter constructed communities in urban barrios near the factories where they worked.[90] The first "Mexican" school was established in Santa Ana in 1912, and by the 1920s more had sprouted in Pasadena, Ontario, Riverside, and the San Fernando Valley.[91] When not instituting divided classrooms in urban Los Angeles, the school board "manipulated attendance zones to produce segregation" in the 1920s and 1930s.[92] IQ testing offered a putatively scientific reason for this two-tiered system and vindicated the channeling of Mexican children into vocational instruction.[93] Every psychometric study that corroborated Terman's claims about Mexican retardation worked to reinforce educational segregation in California.

One of the CBJR's inaugural surveys helped set the tone. In the 1920s, as part of an effort to standardize the Stanford-Binet, bureau psychologists undertook an extensive and multiphased study of hundreds of boys at various sites, arriving at a mean IQ of 69.4 for Mexicans (although this figure rose to 74.6 for American-born Mexicans). Whites, on the other hand, averaged 83.6, the Chinese 74, and "Negro" children 79.2.[94] For all but the white boys, who appeared to become smarter by the year, these numbers were mirrored in study after study.[95] Analogous scores were extracted again and again by CBJR psychologists and ERO field workers in almost every institution holding children—public schools, orphanages, the juvenile court, and specialty clinics. For the most part, their investigations found that IQs varied dramatically between racial groups and that, with few exceptions, Mexicans always fared the worst.

Kimball Young, another of Terman's disciples, started to test Mexicans in the early 1920s, completing a dissertation that compared a cross section of twelve-year-old students in central and Northern California. Young tacitly colored "Americans" as white and described a competence ladder in which Mexicans were fixed at the bottom rungs, followed by the Portuguese, and finally, Italians, who most closely approximated "Americans." Along the lines of eugenicists such as Madison Grant and Carl C. Brigham, author of *A Study of American Intelligence,* Young presumed parity between the degree of Nordic blood and intrinsic intelligence. Relying on a "Latin" versus "American" dichotomy, he proclaimed that the IQ of the former reached only 83, with that of Mexicans slightly less.[96] Young was convinced that mental ability was transmitted in a strict Mendelian manner from parent to offspring and dismissed English literacy as a factor in test comprehension. Instead, he claimed that a lack of racial homogeneity and distance from Nordic or Alpine stock doomed Mexicans to a permanently reduced IQ: "Biologists and anthropologists both look with little favor on a violent mixture of races so divergent as some of these elements are." Young disparaged Mexicans as an "unfortunate hybrid race, and for good measure reminded readers that "although hybridization might produce an occasional genius, the overall tendency is downwards, this miscegenation means race suicide."[97]

Psychometricians gleaned matching scores from classrooms across California and the Southwest. In one survey of orphan children given the revised Binet-Simon, the psychologist obtained an IQ of 77 for "Spanish-Mexican" girls, twenty points below other racial groups, and surmised that she had discerned a pronounced racial variation.[98] In a study of 341 girls at Ventura, using the Stanford-Binet, Julia Mathews arrived at the figure of 68 for the average IQ of Mexican girls, which was 13 points below their white counterparts and 4 below their black counterparts. Additionally, she reported that her scores mirrored those gathered for Mexican boys at Whittier and Preston.[99] One study in Roswell, New Mexico, using a version of the Binet, calculated an IQ of 89 for Mexicans and 105 for whites.[100] A five-year survey of one thousand young Mexicans in Texas, New Mexico, and Colorado produced a mean IQ of 78.1 and confirmed that "the retardation of the Mexican children is very high."[101] Other studies, many of them done by students of Terman and Norman Fenton, the CBJR's director from 1928 to 1941, generated similar results. From San Jose to San Antonio, psychometricians consistently recorded scores for Mexicans in the 70 to 90 range, usually right around 80, exactly the borderline zone described by Terman in *The Measurement of Intelligence*. When psychometricians did not encapsulate intelligence with a number, they still frequently categorized Mexicans as mentally inferior by one or more years to whites, a divergence that was explicated through racial composition: "Not more than 20 to 25 percent of Mexican germ plasm is white and this includes, of course, that in the mestizos as well as that in the pure whites."[102]

The implications of these findings for Mexicans were far-reaching. Eugenicists and restrictionists who wished to exclude Mexicans from the United States and tried to set exceedingly low quotas for them constantly invoked the magic numbers of IQ and referred to psychometric surveys. In a pamphlet titled *What Will Your Greatgrandchildren Face?* Goethe inveighed against "low-power" immigration from Latin America, a region that had produced none of the world's 7,955 "men of genius."[103] Comments about the "dullness," the lower "animal capacities," and the retardation of Mexican immigrants saturated the statements given by Thomas Jenkins, Roy L. Garis, and the East Texas congressman John C. Box at immigration hearings during the push for quotas in the late 1920s and early 1930s.[104] In sum, eugenicists rallied around differential IQ scores to urge a lockdown on the southern border.

Furthermore, scores from mental tests were mobilized to condone segregation and the channeling of Mexican children into vocational training, unskilled labor, and agricultural occupations. Thomas R. Garth, a psychometrician who concentrated on evaluating Mexican competence, concluded in 1926 that Mexicans would do well in mining, steel working, and farm work.[105] Don T. Delmet, the superintendent of schools in Norwalk, California, echoed Garth. After administering intelligence tests to students ages six to twelve, he concluded that Mexicans' mental backwardness constrained their occupational opportunities. He recommended that young Mexicans enroll in English classes, manual training, domestic arts, music, and social studies, and he asked vocational counselors working with Mexicans to "take into consideration their social background and future economic status."[106]

If educators did not employ IQ scores to cast Mexicans as dull or borderline, criminologists brandished them to demonstrate that Mexicans possessed innate tendencies toward vagrancy and malefaction. At a 1924 crime symposium convened by August Vollmer, an interim chief of the Los Angeles Police Department who traveled in eugenic circles, most of the presenters defined criminality as a product of defective heredity and identified Mexicans as the greatest offenders.[107] An examination of arrests of Mexicans in the 1920s induced one participant to emphasize that "the Mexican whom we find in Los Angeles is, as a class, of relatively low mentality; he is probably best fitted for work demanding ability of an inferior grade."[108] Even with the criticism of the cultural biases of IQ tests articulated in the 1930s by some psychologists who started statistically controlling for the variables of language, poverty, and acculturation, stereotypes of Mexican boys as prone to malfeasance remained common to the point of ubiquity in Southern California.[109]

It is no coincidence that the 1946 class action lawsuit *Méndez v. Westminster* was filed by parents whose children were forced to attend separate schools in Orange County, a district where the CBJR's IQ testing program had provided the rationale for constructing Mexican-only classrooms and tracking of Mexicans into industrial education beginning in the late 1910s.[110] In this case, the court ruled that the segregation of Mexicans in the public school system was unconstitutional—a conclusion based, ironically, on the fact that Mexicans were technically classified as white and hence were not subject to the laws that affected Japanese, Chinese, and Indian students. Nevertheless, this verdict prompted Governor Earl Warren to sign legislation overturning segregation in California in 1947.

STERILIZATION: "PROTECTION, NOT PENALTY"

In 1909, two years after Indiana and a few weeks after the state of Washington, California passed the third sterilization bill in the nation.[111] Envisioned by F. W. Hatch, the secretary of the State Commission in Lunacy, this legislation granted the medical superintendents of asylums and prisons the authority to "asexualize" a patient or inmate if such action would improve his or her "physical, mental, or moral condition."[112] The law was expanded in 1913, when it was repealed and replaced, and was updated in 1917, when clauses were added to shield physicians against legal retaliation and to foreground a eugenic, rather than penal, rationale for surgery.[113] The 1917 amendment, for example, reworded the description of a diagnosis warranting surgery from "hereditary insanity or incurable chronic mania or dementia" to a "mental disease which may have been inherited and is likely to be transmitted to descendants."[114] More encompassing than its predecessors, the 1917 act targeted inmates afflicted with "various grades of feeblemindedness" and "perversion or marked departures from normal mentality or from disease of a syphilitic nature."[115] Performed sporadically at the outset, operations began to climb in the late 1910s, and by 1921, 2,248 people—more than 80 percent of all cases nationwide—had been sterilized, mostly at the Sonoma and Stockton hospitals.[116]

The state's aggressive attempts to control the procreation of committed persons deemed insane, feebleminded, or otherwise unfit, as well as the clinical and ideological contributions of several ardent medical superintendents to sterilization procedures and policies, make California stand out when compared to the rest of the country. In New Jersey and Iowa, for instance, sterilization laws were declared unconstitutional in the 1910s, judged to be "cruel and unusual punishment" or in violation of equal protection and due process.[117] This impelled some states to draft legislation that avoided punitive terminology, a tactic that underpinned the approbation of revised or original sterilization laws in the 1920s. During the Great Depression, the strain of shrinking state budgets and the vindication of eugenic justifications for sterilization in *Buck v. Bell,* the 1927 Supreme Court decision upholding Virginia's statute, spurred additional sterilization legislation, especially in the South.[118] In 1932, twenty-seven states had laws on the books, and the number of operations nationwide peaked at just over 3,900.[119] In 1937 Georgia passed the last of the sterilization statutes, bringing the total number of state laws to thirty-two.[120] Puerto Rico, a US colony, also approved sterilization legislation that same year. Significantly, California's statute—although reworked over the decades—remained on the books from 1909 until it was repealed by the state legislature in 1979.

California's sterilization program had a very forceful contingent of champions from the 1910s into the 1950s. During the first half of the twentieth century, physicians, reformers, psychologists, and some patients and their parents looked favorably at reproductive surgery as a procedure that could raise the fitness of society, potentially cure the sterilized individual, and result in early parole. As with the other two facets of eugenics in California, scientific racism and intelligence testing, the Department of Institutions supplied most of the administrative scaffold- ing for the state's sterilization program. At the same time, it gave profes- sional sterilization crusaders more legitimacy, imbuing their mission with the aura of officialdom. As was the case with related health and reform initiatives, a handful of influential advocates played a decisive role in advancing the cause. These proponents launched investigations into the prevalence, effects, and impact of reproductive surgery and marshaled their findings, which were wrapped in the mantle of medical authority, to widen the ambit of the law and its application. Although many eugeni- cists dedicated themselves to this campaign, John R. Haynes and Paul Popenoe were critical to bringing sterilization into the mainstream.

Haynes epitomized the Progressive Era's idealization of science and efficiency. A member of the AES, the HBF, and the Eugenics Section of the CCC, Haynes had been trained as a physician at the University of Pennsylvania. In 1887 he decided to relocate to semiarid Los Angeles to relieve his chronic bronchitis. After less than one decade of treating patients and pursuing a lucrative career in real estate, he had become one of the city's leading physicians, practicing and teaching surgery and gyne- cology at hospitals and universities, and eventually setting up a bustling clinic in downtown Los Angeles.[121] Haynes brought his understanding of the human sciences to bear on Southern Californian politics and culture. Viewing the municipal body as an organism that needed regulation to reach equilibrium, in the early 1900s he created the Direct Legislation League. Fueled by his efforts, initiative, referendum, and recall measures were incorporated into the city and later the state charter. At one point Haynes described society as a colony of siphonophores (free-swimming hydrozoans with discrete functions) that was "now federated and on the road to integration."[122] He believed that through the oversight of eugen- icists and other scientifically enlightened experts, society could become "organized for well-being" and could escape the destructive and pur- poseless drifting that had gone on for eons.[123] Weaving a cosmology from German physiology and the sociology of Herbert Spencer and Émile Durkheim, Haynes envisaged a regulated and streamlined Los Angeles. In this urban wonderland the monopolistic control exercised by the Southern Pacific Railroad and the *Los Angeles Times* would be broken up, the municipality would control resources through boards elected by informed citizens, and the enforcement of labor laws would lessen antag- onisms between workers and capitalists. He fought for these changes on the Los Angeles Civil Service Commission and, for many years, the Water and Power Board. Haynes's unique blend of socialist leanings, nativism, and civic philanthropy, which may seem contradictory at first blush, was actually quite consistent with his eugenic creed and his intellectual reliance on physiological doctrines of homeostasis.

A devout Malthusian who equated overpopulation with social disorder, Haynes passionately backed California's sterilization law, declaring in the 1910s "that no patient should be discharged from the state insane asylum without being sterilized."[124] He also countenanced birth control, acting as treasurer of the Los Angeles Mothers' Clinic Association and the Los Angeles Chapter of the American Birth Control League. Working alongside her husband, Dora Haynes pursued a parallel agenda of maternal and infant care through the Friday Morning Club, the city's premier group of European American female reformers.[125] But Haynes did much more than orchestrate municipal housekeeping. During his thirteen-year appointment to the State Board of Charities and Corrections, he laid the foundation for broadening eugenic sterilization and institutionalization in California.

In 1916, on the letterhead of the Board of Charities and Corrections, Haynes sent out 517 questionnaires to asylums, reformatories, and homes in nearly every state. Gathering information in anticipation of a welfare conference, Haynes asked superintendents how many sterilization procedures they had performed, their opinions of the surgery, and whether they considered feebleminded patients released without surgery to be a hazard to society. He received about 275 responses. Given the contested status of sterilization statutes in the courts, the majority of physicians noted that they were unable to answer thoroughly the questions because either their state lacked such a law or it had been overturned. Many, however, longed for such programs and endorsed their therapeutic, moral, and eugenic value. For example, J. Percy Wade, of the Spring Grove State Hospital in Maryland, told Haynes, "I think the sterilization of a certain class of the insane and feebleminded, particularly the Moron type and the defective delinquent of the female sex, would be a great benefit to the patients themselves, to the happiness of their families if any exists, and to the community at large, not only from a moral, but a financial standpoint."[126] And G. A. Smith, of the Central Islip State Hospital on Long Island, who regretted the cumbersomeness of New York's law, declared, "Personally, I am very much in favor of the sterilization of certain defectives, especially cases of dementia praecox, epileptics, chronic alcoholics, and subnormal mental individuals. I believe this procedure would be to the best interests of society and that every inmate as indicated above should be sterilized before discharged."[127] Almost all of Haynes's California respondents praised sterilization, which they were confident would lead eventually to the elimination of deleterious germ plasm from the populace. John A. Reily, the medical superintendent at the Department of Institutions' Patton Hospital in San Bernardino, declared that "the primary benefit from sterilization" was "the ultimate results in improving the standard of the human race," adding that the occasional denial of the pleasures of parenthood was a "small consideration as compared with the vast benefits accruing to society in the prevention of the propagation of the unfit."[128]

This survey unequivocally convinced Haynes of the pressing need for broader provisions in California and the comprehensive legalization of sterilization throughout the country. In October 1918, Haynes incorporated the replies into a report titled "Care of the Insane," in which he insisted that Americans "make it our business to awaken the people to a realization of the fact that it is as foolish to permit human defectives to reproduce themselves as to permit defective domestic animals to beget offspring. The whole stream of human life is being constantly polluted by the admixture of the tainted blood of the extremely defective."[129] As he traversed California lecturing to welfare, correctional, and medical groups, Haynes repeatedly marshaled his data to praise the state's sterilization program and campaign for its extension into untapped institutional and extrainstitutional domains.[130]

During the 1920s, Haynes became more and more dismayed with what he perceived to be a marked upsurge of mental incompetents in California. Beholden to rudimentary Mendelian theories of hereditary transmission, he wrote, "It is a fact obvious to every intelligent observer, whether layman or specialist, that feeble-bodied parents beget feeble-bodied children; and that feeble-minded parents beget feeble-minded children."[131] Haynes was especially worried about morons, whose mental functioning surpassed that of imbeciles and idiots and who possessed sufficient interpersonal skills and curiosity to pursue sexual relations and engage in other untoward behavior. If not sterilized, morons—above all, moron girls—would bring into the world the next "generation of feeble-minded."[132] To contain this risk, Haynes urged the founding of a hospital expressly for morons, and, largely owing to this lobbying, an act was approved in 1917 authorizing the building of the Pacific Colony. In spite of a rocky start in the early 1920s, the colony was fully operational by 1927 and in 1930 housed 528 patients, mostly transferred from county and state homes. About 20 percent of these 528, or 107, had been sterilized; of these, 64 percent, or 69, were female.[133] These operations were part of a marked increase in sterilization in the 1920s. Whereas fewer than 1,000 operations had been carried out between 1909 and 1920, over 6,000 had been performed by 1929.[134] These developments bolstered Haynes's eugenic convictions, and, ever conscious of the looming specter of lawsuits against fellow physicians who performed surgeries, in 1922 he tried "to set up a $100,000 defense fund for state hospital directors who might be sued if sterilizing patients was ruled illegal."[135]

If Haynes's 1916 survey put sterilization center stage in California, then the study by Popenoe, commissioned by the HBF a decade later, did the same for a much larger national and international audience. The HBF was the brainchild of Ezra S. Gosney, a lawyer who had worked for the St. Joseph and Council Bluffs Railways in Missouri during the 1880s and had moved to the dry climate of northern Arizona in 1888 to recover from malaria. There he organized the Arizona Wool Growers' Association, acting as its president for ten years. His familiarity with the livestock industry attuned Gosney to nascent doctrines of selective breeding.[136] When he relocated to Pasadena in the early twentieth century, Gosney purchased more than three hundred acres of prime land, where he planted more than twenty-four thousand lemon trees as well as oranges and juice grapes.[137] Selling his products through the Sierra Madre–Lamanda Citrus Association, which was affiliated with the monopolistic California Fruit Growers Exchange, Gosney grew rich off Southern California's bountiful citrus industry. With his substantial holdings, Gosney would have earned about $70,000 annually, or forty times the average per capita income in the United States at the time.[138]

Already aware of the writings of Davenport and other eugenicists, Gosney became very enthusiastic about a book called *Eugenical Sterilization in the United States* and decided to travel to Cold Spring Harbor to confer with Laughlin, its author. Keen to invest in a eugenics organization, Gosney asked Laughlin for guidance, and shortly after their reunion Gosney received a memorandum that Laughlin had written expressly for him. Laughlin trusted that his "Plan for Practical Work in Family-Stock Betterment" would "be of some service," assuring Gosney, "I should be very glad if, after further discussion, I could aid in any manner in perfecting a practical outline for the consummation of your work in family-stock betterment."[139] This ambitious proposal recommended that Gosney assemble a board of representatives from the fields of genetics, law, business, and education and that he hire able researchers and a clerical staff. Laughlin told Gosney that the group would need to stay abreast of current research in eugenics, encourage legislation by drafting bills, and oversee the administration of existing laws.

Gosney was temporarily stalled by a freeze, which damaged his crops, and by bad weather in 1924. Nevertheless, the following year he reported to Laughlin that he was still eager to embark on the project: "This is just a line to say that I hope to get a start in the work discussed with you in the very near future. The plan outlined by you seemed sound and I am now getting in closer touch with a few prominent men who will be valuable in a small committee or council to direct the work."[140] Seeking a well-known scientist, Gosney asked several eugenicists who, in their estimation, would be the finest candidate to carry out the foundation's research.[141] This quest led him to Paul Popenoe, who had spoken at the Second National Conference on Race Betterment in San Francisco in 1915. Raised in California, Popenoe had studied biology at Occidental College and Stanford University, had worked as an editor at a Pasadena newspaper, had managed the *Journal of Heredity*, had served as an army health officer on the US-Mexican border during World War I, and most recently had been executive secretary of the American Social Hygiene Association. Like Gosney, Popenoe also held vast fruit acreage, in his case date palms, which he cultivated at his family's Coachella ranch according to lessons learned through his own experiments with the species.[142]

Without delay Popenoe drafted a blueprint for a "race-hygiene foundation."[143] Providing more detail than Laughlin, Popenoe proposed public lectures; the screening of motion pictures; closer contact with newspapers and magazines; collaboration with civic, infant welfare, and women's groups; the creation of programs in high schools and colleges; the stocking of local libraries with eugenic materials; the mounting of museum exhibits; the sponsorship of annual physical examinations at the YMCA; and the installation of psychometric laboratories in police departments and courts. As his lecture on race betterment at the Panama-Pacific International Exposition in 1915 had illustrated, Popenoe believed that charity had furthered the survival of the unfit and that the moment to put an end to the propagation of defectives had long since arrived. Convinced that extreme measures were necessary, Popenoe opined, "The first project taken up might well be sterilization, for which the data exist in California to an unusual extent. A thoroughgoing and impartial investigation, which would doubtless occupy at least a year or two, should serve to reveal what the actual results have been from the four or five thousand operations already performed."[144]

Gosney wholeheartedly agreed and resolved to underwrite the inquiry.[145] By spring 1926, Gosney and Popenoe had visited five state institutions to procure access to medical records, a hurdle overcome by the patronage of the Department of Institutions, whose director sent instructions to the medical superintendents at Norwalk, Patton, Stockton, Napa, and Sonoma to accommodate these two eugenic investigators: "Mr. Gosney is a man of considerable wealth, as I understand it, and is desirous of using some of his money for the purpose of disseminating proper information regarding this matter, to the end that all of the states of the Union will enact sterilization laws and carry on the work the same as we are here in California." He continued, "I would ask that you give him and Mr. Popenoe whatever assistance you can along such lines as you feel would be proper."[146]

For about two years, Popenoe gathered statistics, demographic profiles, and clinical case histories, regularly updating Gosney on his progress. While on the road, he consolidated and enlarged California's network of eugenicists by speaking before civic clubs, meeting with the likes of Goethe, Holmes, and Jordan, and consulting with the juvenile courts.[147] Popenoe was warmly welcomed at all the state institutions. At Stockton, he was impressed with the zeal of physician Margaret Smyth, who, he noted, had "sterilized more women than any other surgeon in the world, no doubt," and at Mendocino he was pleased that such a small facility managed to handle about two operations a week.[148] At Sonoma, medical superintendent Butler unreservedly put all the hospital's records at Popenoe's disposal.[149] In charge of Sonoma for more than thirty years, Butler was a vociferous sterilization campaigner, who recommended that "all defectives who are capable of propagating, especially the hereditary class," "be asexualized before leaving the institution" and who was adamant that discharge be contingent on surgery.[150]

Popenoe's research culminated in dozens of papers, which he presented as lectures around the state and the country; articles, appearing in periodicals such as the *Journal of Social Hygiene, Journal of Heredity, Journal of Applied Psychology, Journal of the American Medical Association, American Sociological Review,* and *American Journal of Obstetrics and Gynecology*; and a book, *Sterilization for Human Betterment,* which he coauthored with Gosney.[151] This treatise was a glowing appraisal of sterilization as a surgical solution for the serious troubles facing the nation. Holding California up as the paragon, Gosney and

Popenoe sought to dispel misrepresentations of sterilization as damaging to sexual pleasure and individual morale, or as a viable excuse employed by young women to enter prostitution. Above all, *Sterilization for Human Betterment* strove to impress upon readers the imperviousness of eugenic logic and the immense urgency of the task at hand. Contending that at least 5 percent of the American population were borderline or feebleminded, and that hundreds of thousands more were affected by devastating mental and physical diseases rooted in bad heredity, they cast the elimination of defectives yet unborn as one of the final saving hopes for modern civilization and the human race. Eager to rid sterilization of any punitive connotations and to disassociate it from castration, Gosney and Popenoe clarified that "eugenic sterilization of the hereditary defective is a protection, not a penalty, and should never be made a part of any penal statute."[152]

During the 1930s, Popenoe was America's sterilization guru, and his message was not one of moderation. In 1937, repeating Butler's calls for more extramural operations, Popenoe penned a short piece for *Eugenical News* sketching what he limned as the overarching trends in human sterilization. Like his writings for the HBF, this was part journalistic fact-finding and part wish list. Popenoe described a general move toward sterilization for "social as well as eugenic indications," evaluation of the entire (not only committed) population for potential surgical intervention, the targeting of recessive carriers of undesirable traits, the inclusion of criminals, and exceptions for religious objectors (as long as they paid for their own institutional segregation).[153] This article was informed by a follow-up study that Popenoe had just completed with the CBJR's director, Fenton, in which they assessed national developments and drew attention to a Nebraska statute that entailed the registration of all the feebleminded in the state and was predicated on overtly social, not hereditary, considerations.[154] By this point, Popenoe's vision, and the state's sterilization program, had inspired Nazi Germany, whose 1933 Law on Preventing Hereditarily Ill Progeny was partially modeled on California's statute. During the 1930s, the Third Reich and the Golden State maintained strong ties. In 1934, the HBF's hometown, Pasadena, hosted a "Public Health and Eugenics in New Germany" exhibit, and throughout the decade California and German eugenicists traded ideas, statistics, and protocols and complimented each other's escalating sterilization programs.[155]

Besides disseminating his findings in the United States and abroad, Popenoe collaborated with Gosney to further better breeding in California.

In 1928, Gosney incorporated the HBF, whose charter members included Terman, Goethe, and Jordan, as well as many other local physicians and reformers. In 1929, the HBF helped to spawn the AIFR and the California Division of the AES, both headed by Popenoe. The HBF dictated the agenda of the Eugenics Section of the CCC starting in 1930, when it turned from Mexican immigration to the "elimination of the unfit" and set out to uncover "what steps might be taken to stem the rising tide of idiots, imbeciles, epileptics, cretins and the like who are burdens to themselves and relatives and the State."[156] Section members listened to lectures by medical superintendents, such as Butler and Smyth, who persuaded them of the myriad benefits of reproductive surgery.[157] Taking direction from the HBF, this section backed the 1935 and 1937 draft bills to establish a State Eugenics Board and spread sterilization to all state facilities. By that point, the HBF was aware of the over six hundred vasectomies performed on inmates in San Quentin by medical superintendent Dr. Leo Stanley. These operations pushed the limits of the law, which stipulated that, to be sterilized, inmates had to have been convicted twice for a sexual offense or three times for any other kind of offense. To navigate around these obstacles, Stanley contended that inmates had volunteered and furthermore could be classified as feebleminded.[158] Surely aware that Stanley was flouting the law, Gosney and the HBF expressed concerns about his "over-enthusiastic" approach.[159] From the HBF's perspective, the broadening of the state's sterilization program into prisons and other state facilities would assuage such anxieties and would shield superintendents like Stanley from any legal attack.

The HBF also promoted sterilization in private doctors' offices around California. In the 1920s it maintained rosters of sterilizations carried out by eugenically minded obstetricians and gynecologists and affiliated with county clinics and in private practice. These numbers rivaled those in the smaller state institutions. During this decade, doctors at the Pasadena, Hollywood, Angelus, Methodist, and County General hospitals in Los Angeles as well as other facilities in Santa Barbara and Oakland sterilized over one thousand women, according to most of the patient records with the consent of the patient or her husband or both.[160] These records end in the late 1920s; it is quite conceivable the rate of these private operations rose in tandem with the quickening pace of sterilizations in state institutions the 1930s and 1940s.

Even without the passage of new laws or the efforts of private physicians, California's sterilization program had become the most aggressive in the country. From the early 1900s into the 1950s, thousands of people were subjected to compulsory sterilization. The state's program flourished in a bureaucratic and political culture of institutional insularity that sharply curtailed the possibility of oversight in mental hospitals or feebleminded homes. At the same time, civically and medically active eugenic organizations played an instrumental role in legitimizing sterilization as a panacea for many of the Golden State's perceived social problems.

Eugenics flourished in California from 1900 into the 1940s, during which time an influential web of individuals and groups endorsed, financed, and directed eugenic projects. These included physicians such as Haynes in Los Angeles, businessmen such as Goethe in Sacramento, and biologists such as Jordan in Palo Alto, all of whom infused hereditarianism into state, city, and county concerns and policies. Eugenics also bolstered doctrines of white supremacy and Manifest Destiny that dated back to the 1840s, providing new and seemingly modern grounds for racial segregation and stereotypes. Particularly novel was the way in which eugenicists linked biological inferiority to the abuse of state resources, a connection reinforced by the deportation agent and during the exclusionary purge of the Great Depression. Finally, the implementation of eugenic programs would not have reached such extremes in California without the active involvement of the Department of Institutions, which led the country in the expulsion of foreigners and undesirables, the development of large-scale intelligence testing, and the sterilization of those deemed unfit.

Many groups, including immigrant and working-class European Americans, especially young girls classified as immoral or delinquent, African Americans, and Asian Americans, were affected by the eugenics movement in the first several decades of the twentieth century. Yet Mexicans and Mexican Americans bore the brunt of eugenic racism. It was Mexicans who most perturbed the quota seekers of the Eugenics Section of the CCC and who were transported en masse across the southern border. The implementation of IQ testing programs provided a rationale for racial segregation and a two-tracked school system, helping to lay the foundation for deep educational inequities that were not overcome by psychologists' intensifying focus on cultural and linguistic variables in the 1930s and 1940s. Furthermore, Mexicans, and more generally Spanish-surnamed patients, at state institutions were sterilized at disproportionate rates. For example, at Pacific Colony, an institution envisioned by Haynes as the answer to growing menace of "morons," Spanish-surnamed patients—most of whom were of Mexican origin—

were 2.4 times more likely to be sterilized than the general patient population.

Even as California had its own homegrown movement, it supplied national leadership, presaging many of the trends that would reconfigure hereditarianism in the second half of the century. Starting in the 1940s, for example, Popenoe helped to reorient eugenics away from public and legislative arenas and into the intimate domain of domesticity and the family, as the AIFR counseled thousands of people on their career, marital, and reproductive choices using revamped theories of human heredity and personality. Powerful tropes of Mexican inferiority continued to guide eugenicists' beliefs and were evident when young Americanized Mexican boys were derided as mentally incompetent and Mexican women were caricatured as hyperbreeders dependent on welfare handouts and medical care. For these and many other reasons, California's eugenic genealogies demand a reperiodization of the overarching history of American eugenics and disrupt the rise-and-fall narrative that has interpreted the 1940s as a time when hereditarianism evaporated in response to the heinousness of Nazism.

CHAPTER 4

"I Like to Keep My Body Whole"

Reconsidering Eugenic Sterilization in California

In 1924 Hector Rivas was admitted to the Stockton State Hospital, an institution for the mentally ill, because of his "strange and unusual behavior." Rivas had been piling up rocks "on the railroad tracks" and carrying them around in his pockets. More troubling, he muttered to himself and "says he is Jesus Christ."[1] A native of Mexico, Rivas was forty-six years old and lived in a rural county near Lake Tahoe. Like many patients at Stockton, he was diagnosed with manic-depressive insanity, in his case depressed phase.[2] Adhering to the language in California's revised 1917 sterilization law, Stockton's medical superintendent recommended that Rivas be "operated on for the purpose of sterilization as he would likely transmit to descendants."[3] Per the policy in place at the time, the superintendent, the director of institutions, and the secretary of the state board of health approved Rivas's sterilization, which almost surely was performed.

Twelve years later, Martina Suárez was committed to the Sonoma State Home, a facility designated for patients classified as feeble-minded. Suárez was sixteen and had completed a seventh-grade education. Fred O. Butler, the long-serving medical superintendent, recommended sterilization based on her IQ of 60, which placed Suárez in the middle moron category. However, her parents objected to the operation. To overcome this obstacle Butler wrote to the director of institutions to explain why such action was warranted: the parents were "low grade Mexicans" living in a common-law union, each with children from previous relationships, and dependent on the Catholic Welfare Bureau. Butler requested pro forma permission to operate "above the parent's consent," on the grounds that Suárez was "suffering from a mental disease which is likely to be transmitted to posterity." She was sterilized eight days later on November 12, 1936.[4]

In 1947, Thomas Rogers, a Protestant clergyman, arrived to Patton State Hospital, one of the larger institutions for the mentally ill. Originally from Ohio, Rogers was more educated than many patients, with four years of college. Apparently his wife, with whom he had two small children (ages two and three), had committed him to Patton because of dementia praecox, catatonic type. One month after arriving to Patton, the box was checked indicating that Rogers should be sterilized because of a "mental disease which may have been inherited and is likely to be transmitted to descendants."[5] His wife consented to the operation, but Rogers did not. Despite his presumed catatonic state, Rogers possessed enough composure and energy to send a handwritten objection to the Department of Institutions, now called the Department of Mental Hygiene. All indications are that his plea succeeded. Rogers's name does not appear on the lists of surgical sterilizations at Patton in that or any subsequent year.

At the outset of the next decade, in 1950, Vernon Jones, a fourteen-year-old African American boy, was placed in Pacific Colony. Originally from Texas, Jones had completed fifth grade. His family history was tragic; his father had been killed and his mother ostensibly had psychological problems including three nervous breakdowns and at least two marital separations. Jones came from a large, blended family, with six half-siblings. Evidently he had been abused, receiving "injuries to head during childhood" that seemed to partially explain his classification as a moron with an IQ of 58. Jones had many run-ins with the law and was dubbed a "mentally deficient, incorrigible runaway little Negro boy charged with petty thefts."[6] His mother offered consent for the operation, and it is likely that Jones was sterilized within the year.[7]

These four snapshots from California homes and hospitals across the decades from the 1920s to the 1950s illustrate variations in sterilization experiences based on gender, age, ethnicity, diagnosis, institution, and family situation. These differences were related to manifold and interlocking legal, social, and medical factors. California carried out twenty thousand sterilizations during this extended period, and over the years the wording and application of the law changed, administrative procedures were revised and updated, and state institutions shifted in tandem with the approaches of the superintendent in charge. Analysis of sterilization patterns in state homes and hospitals from the 1920s to the 1950s reveals racial, gender, and disability discrimination, evolving mental health and medical practices, and the complex dynamics of decentralized public institutions characterized by insularity and their own idiosyncrasies.

Since the unearthing in 2007 of nineteen microfilm reels stored in a file cabinet in the offices of what is now the Department of State Hospitals, scholars have access to an extraordinarily valuable resource that can illuminate the macro and micro dimensions of eugenic sterilization in California. Sometime in the 1950s, one of the statisticians in the Department of Mental Hygiene decided to use the increasingly popular technology of microfilm to preserve about eighteen thousand sterilization recommendations that had been sent from institutional superintendents to headquarters in Sacramento. In addition to the recommendations, he microfilmed thousands of accompanying interdepartmental letters, lists of performed operations, consent forms, discharge sheets, and correspondence, all told comprising about thirty thousand individual documents. In 2012, my team of researchers at the University of Michigan digitized the content of these reels and embarked on the process of creating a data set, using REDCap, a HIPAA (Health Insurance Portability and Accountability Act)-compliant data capture system designed for quantitative and qualitative analysis. We identified 212 unique variables, such as age, gender, diagnosis, and parental status, that could be coded. In addition to nationality and race (when noted), we used Spanish surname to identify the ethnicity of Latin American–origin patients, most of whom were of Mexican ancestry. As of the writing of this chapter in June 2015 we have entered seventeen thousand of the eighteen thousand records and have completed statistical analysis of a subset of eight thousand records that span the decade from 1935 to 1944.

Reconsidering California eugenics with this novel resource helps account for the Golden State's leading role in sterilizations nationwide and underscores several defining dimensions of the state's program. First, sterilizations occurred during an era and in institutions strongly influenced by medical paternalism. Health experts, from the personnel on site to agency directors in Sacramento, wielded inordinate power over the reproductive lives of patients. For example, the law explicitly stated that superintendents, in consultation with the director of the Department of Institutions, could "cause a person to be sterilized" even if approval was not forthcoming from the patient, family member, or guardian.[8] Compared with sterilization programs in other states, such as Indiana or Oregon, there was little room for appeal or resistance. Nevertheless, patients and their families opened wedges in the system, and by the late 1940s the supremacy of superintendents was faltering. Second, when we take the analysis to the granular level and examine the interpersonal and interactional dynamics of thousands of cases of sterilization, the rationales for the procedure grow more heterogeneous. Over the course of four decades, as medical techniques advanced, and as successive superintendents directed the state's nine different institutions, the implicit and explicit reasons for sterilization shifted and included, sometimes simultaneously, hereditarian, therapeutic, punitive, economic, and pragmatic rationales. Some superintendents believed that the principal motivation of sterilization was to improve a patient's psychiatric condition; others recommended reproductive surgery because of a concern about the financial burden of any future children of patients deemed feebleminded; and others unreservedly advocated the operation as a preventive measure to ensure that the "unfit" would not beget more of their kind. Sterilization also served as a method of punishment, meted out by superintendents to children and wards of the state deemed incorrigible, unruly, and incapable of recovery or rehabilitation. Third, preliminary statistical analysis reveals elevated rates of the sterilization of Spanish-surnamed patients, most of Mexican origin. Given the anti-Mexican dimension that was pervasive in eugenic organizations and rhetoric in California, this is not surprising. Yet seeing the disarticulation of families and the denigration of Mexican reproductive bodies through the lens of institutional sterilization accentuates how scientific racism was put into medical practice. The profound implications of sterilization as an act of bodily desecration that infringed on legal rights, familial integrity, and religious beliefs was not lost on Mexican-origin patients and their parents, who waged the most vocal resistance to California's sterilization regime.

Some scholars split hairs about whether sterilizations performed in institutions in California can be defined as eugenic. The answer to this question is an unequivocal yes. Sterilizations in California's homes and hospitals were made possible in legal and administrative terms by state laws, which from 1909 until full-fledged repeal in 1979 were firmly rooted in eugenic theories of hereditary improvement. Moreover, as this book and a growing body of scholarship suggests, eugenics encompassed more than strict hereditary control, extending into strategies of reproductive regulation such as institutional segregation (as in Illinois or New York, which had no sterilization statutes), patriarchal containment of women who transgressed gender and sexual norms, and remedial vasectomies on men classed as homosexual who posed little threat of unrestrained procreation.[9] Furthermore, patients and families that accepted sterilization as a therapeutic procedure or as a condition for release did so under the parameters of eugenic policies. The minority of patients who perhaps sought out sterilizations because they desired permanent birth control during a period when contraception was illegal might have been exercising a constrained form of reproductive autonomy. This does not make these sterilizations any less eugenic; it does, however, complicate our understanding of the slippery intersections between the desire for reproductive freedom and the imposition of reproductive control—or choice and coercion, in one scholar's poignant phrasing.[10]

STERILIZATION BY THE NUMBERS

In the first half of the twentieth century, thirty-two states passed eugenic sterilization laws, and according to official statistics about sixty thousand operations occurred, overwhelmingly in institutional settings. California carried out twenty thousand, or one-third, of this national total. This leadership can be explained partially by the high volume of activity in four institutions: Patton, Stockton, Sonoma, and Pacific Colony. The former two were hospitals for the mentally ill, whose patients were committed primarily for dementia praecox (60 percent at Patton, 64 percent at Stockton) and secondarily for manic depressive anxiety (11 percent at Patton, 15 percent at Stockton). Although men and women were classified as dementia praecox in equal numbers, during the period 1935 to 1944 there was a striking gender disparity in rates of manic-depressive diagnosis, with 72 percent of these cases attributed to women. *Dementia praecox*, a term popularized by the German psychiatrist Emil Kraepelin, was associated with a progressive and inexorable mental deterioration that often included delusions and hallucinations. Over the course of the twentieth century it was supplanted by *schizophrenia*, which sought to describe the split-mindedness of this disease. In contrast, manic-depressive insanity was characterized by phases of relative stability punctuated by extreme conditions of mental depression or exaltation.[11]

Reviewing the symptoms associated with these conditions shows minimal conformity and instead a wide array of conduct and behaviors that might have led to commitment. These could have included stopping cars, as was the case with twenty-seven-year-old Ricardo García, a Spaniard who was committed to Stockton in 1924 because of his erratic and seemingly paranoid behavior. García had been stopping cars and kneeling down to pray on public highways, and he complained of "pains in his head which can only be cured by charms of a Spanish woman."[12] According to clinical notes, many patients in the mental hospitals experienced auditory sensations or heard voices that induced feelings ranging from righteousness to persecution, carried out seemingly delusional acts of violence against people or property, or participated in non-normative sexual activities such as excessive masturbation or the pursuit of same-sex encounters.

In comparison to institutions for the mentally ill such as Patton and Stockton, patients at Sonoma and Pacific Colony, homes for the feebleminded, might be given a psychiatric diagnosis, but the foremost classification was feeblemindedness, as represented by IQ and mental grade, which was subtyped into "idiot" (0–25), "imbecile" (26–50), "moron" (51–70), and "borderline" (71–84). At some point along the journey to commitment—in the juvenile court, at the sending reformatory, or once in the institution—a patient's IQ was assigned by an expert drawing on test scores or mental assessment, and she or he was then branded with that numeric and diagnostic marker.[13]

To gain a deeper understanding of patterns in and across institutions, we analyzed coded data from the decade 1935–44, when operations peaked. In total, 7,989 documented sterilizations were performed in nine institutions during this busy decade, or roughly the same number of sterilizations as occurred in Virginia (8,000) and North Carolina (7,600) during the entirety of their sterilization programs.[14] The peak year was 1940, with 967 operations, followed by 949 in 1938 and 936 in 1935. In 1942 sterilizations began to decrease, to 737, and the following year they decreased to 530. Sterilizations then steadily declined until 1951, after which they dropped considerably.

California maintained seven mental hospitals (Patton, Stockton, Agnews, Norwalk, Camarillo, Mendocino, and Napa) and two feebleminded homes (Sonoma and Pacific Colony).[15] Sonoma was the most active sterilizer between 1935 and 1944, carrying out 2,005 operations, followed by Patton with 1,859, Stockton with 1,256, and Pacific Colony with 1,003. Figure 7 illustrates the differences in sterilization rates from 1935 to 1944 across institutions and includes a background bar graph of total rates.

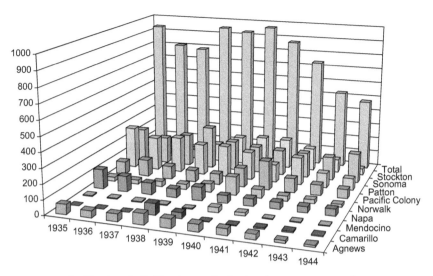

FIGURE 7. Sterilizations in California state institutions by year, 1935–44. Source: Prepared from Eugenic Sterilization Data Set, California Department of State Hospitals, Sacramento, by author and researcher Kate O'Connor.

The divergence among facilities can be demonstrated by comparing occurrences during the year 1938, when Sonoma carried out 289 operations, nearly 6 per week, while Norwalk performed 36 and Mendocino just 6. By a large amount, Sonoma and Patton were the most active. According to retrospective data compiled in the early 2000s, between 1909 and 1950 these two institutions sterilized a total of 10,115 people—5,530 at Sonoma and 4,585 at Patton.[16]

Taking into account the five most common diagnoses of patients sterilized between 1935 and 1944, figure 8 illustrates the differences between the mental hospitals and the feebleminded homes and confirms that the vast majority of those sterilized were classified as dementia praecox and feebleminded. These diagnoses corresponded with superintendents' differing perspectives on the social purpose and medical value of sterilization. In general, superintendents at mental hospitals like Stockton and Patton were more likely to view sterilization as both a procedure for hereditarian improvement and an intervention with therapeutic benefits.[17]

The quantity of sterilizations at Patton cannot be explained by sheer population size. For example, in the peak year of 1940 Patton housed 3,913 patients, fewer than Stockton (4,389) and only slightly more than Napa (3,574) and Agnews (3,552).[18] Nor can higher rates be explained

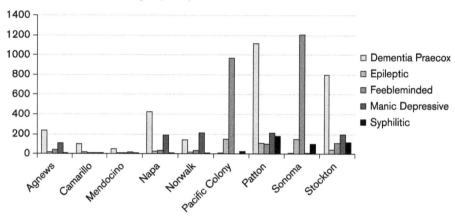

FIGURE 8. Numbers of patients in various diagnostic categories in California state institutions, including the five most common diagnoses in all nine institutions, 1935–44. Source: Prepared from Eugenic Sterilization Data Set, California Department of State Hospitals, Sacramento, by author and researcher Kate O'Connor.

primarily by the problem of overcrowding. As a precondition for discharge or parole, sterilization could function as a release valve for institutions. However, the crisis of excess patients was extreme across all institutions, including those that performed many sterilizations and those that performed only a few. Between 1910 and 1955 the total resident population in all mental hospitals increased more than fivefold, from 6,864 to 36,403.[19] In absolute terms, Patton's population growth, from 1,372 in 1910 to 4,128 in 1950, was in sync with this overall trend.[20] In the 1930s, Patton did report an excess population upwards of 50 percent; in 1939, for instance, Patton held 3,843 patients despite a certified capacity of 2,983.[21] Yet in 1950, Patton's excess of 888 patients (with a total of 4,128 patients) was 27.3 percent. This fell below the surpluses of 38.1 percent reported at Agnews and 31.4 percent at Norwalk but exceeded the overcommitments of 15 percent at Stockton and 2.8 percent at Napa. In 1950, the two feebleminded homes, Sonoma and Pacific Colony, also reported excess populations, respectively, of 33.3 percent and 19.3 percent. In the 1930s and 1940s, Sonoma's overcrowding constantly was higher than 25 percent, and its staff frequently bemoaned this issue as they eagerly awaited the pledged construction of additional state facilities.[22]

Undoubtedly overcrowding, which affected most institutions around the country during the Depression era, encouraged higher sterilization rates in the 1930s and 1940s but does not fully account for them. Instead, these rates generally correlated with the attitudes of superintendents and reflected the milieus they fostered in the totalizing institutions they oversaw. For example, beginning with the passage of the inaugural law in 1909, superintendents at Patton were outspoken advocates of reproductive surgery for both therapeutic and eugenic purposes, and this two-pronged approach helped make that institution the most aggressive sterilizer of all. In 1916, Patton superintendent Dr. John A. Reily wrote in response to a survey sponsored by the California Department of Charities and Corrections that the aim of sterilization was to improve "the standard of the human race," adding that the occasional denial of the pleasures of parenthood was a "small consideration as compared with the vast benefits accruing to society in the prevention of the propagation of the unfit."[23] Ten years later, Dr. G. M. Webster echoed his predecessor: "We are trying, in so far as possible, to sterilize every male and female who enters the hospital during active sexual life," not only to relieve the patient's "present mental condition" and avert future attacks, but also to limit "as far as possible the birth of the unfit into the world."[24]

Similar although more muted patterns were at play at Stockton, where Dr. Fred P. Clark was superintendent from 1906 to 1929. Clark championed sterilization for its eugenic and therapeutic value, contending that vasectomy could result in the mental and physical improvement of male patients.[25] In 1924, the year Hector Rivas was sterilized at Stockton, Clark applauded the "law permitting the sterilization of the insane" as "one of the best things that has been done to prevent the unfit from reproducing their kind."[26] Dr. Margaret Smyth, who became superintendent upon Clark's death in 1929, continued this trend during her seventeen-year tenure at Stockton. As one of a handful of superintendents who traveled in eugenic circles, networking and delivering lectures, she received positive feedback about the priorities she promoted at Stockton.[27] In 1938 Smyth wrote glowingly about California's sterilization program, affirming that the state's laws were being applied "without racial or political implications and with a minimum of difficulty."[28] The counterexample to Stockton and Patton is Agnews, where Dr. Leonard Stocking was much more cautious: performing very few sterilizations, chiefly because he did not "think direct benefit to the patient is to be expected unless it may be in cases where the mental trouble follows and recurs with pregnancy or childbirth."[29] Stocking's reluctance is evident in the official statistics, which show comparatively fewer operations performed at Agnews during Stocking's superintendence and their twofold increase after his retirement.[30]

The zeal for the "surgical solution" at Patton and Stockton helped ensure that California's mental hospitals performed more total sterilizations (approximately twelve thousand) than its feebleminded homes (approximately eight thousand) over the course of the twentieth century. In absolute terms, there were more operations in mental hospitals because they housed an average of five times as many patients as the feebleminded homes. For example, in 1940, California's mental hospitals held 22,953, compared to 4,076 in Sonoma and Pacific Colony combined.[31] Given this, it is all the more striking that the two feebleminded homes, Sonoma and Pacific Colony, carried out eight thousand operations in the twentieth century. These numbers can be attributed to the ardent impulse to prevent people with intellectual disabilities from procreating, a motive exemplified by Fred O. Butler, who served as Sonoma's superintendent from 1918 to 1949.[32] Over these three decades he proudly oversaw approximately four thousand surgeries, one thousand of which he purportedly did himself.[33] In line with California eugenicists who strove to expand the purview of sterilization, Butler was convinced that combating the menace of mental deficiency required reaching beyond state institutions. He made strides toward that goal by turning Sonoma into something of a revolving operating room. Working with juvenile courts and reformers in Northern California, he tried to ensure that teenage girls identified as unruly, promiscuous, and mentally defective by caseworkers and county officials were transferred temporarily to Sonoma for salpingectomy. Paul Popenoe took note of this in 1926 during a site visit conducted for the Pasadena-based Human Betterment Foundation: "It appears that something like 25% of the girls who have been sterilized were sent up here solely" for surgery. "They are kept only a few months—long enough to operate and install a little discipline in them; and then returned home."[34] According to Butler, "sterilization only" cases made up 21 percent of Sonoma's load, and it was routine for persons categorized as "retardates" (possessing an IQ of 80 or below) to be surgically fixed and released in under a month's time.[35]

Butler's concern about women and girls categorized as social problems is borne out by the numbers. From 1909 to 1950, for example, 55 percent of those sterilized at Sonoma were women.[36] Moreover, Sonoma and its sister institution Pacific Colony were instrumental to two overlapping longitudinal trends related to gender and diagnosis. At the outset of the state's sterilization program, more men than women were sterilized. To some extent, this reflected the relative safety and simplicity of vasectomy, which involves small incisions to sever the vas deferens. For example, at all institutions from 1909 to 1934, 5,267 men as compared to 4,843 women underwent the procedure: that is, men made up 52 percent of those sterilized and women 48 percent. By the 1940s, in part because of advances in speed and safety of surgical techniques for salpingectomy (which entails removal of the Fallopian tube), female sterilizations began to outpace those of men by what would become a growing margin. For example, from 1934 to 1960, 4,939 women were sterilized as compared to 4,085 men: that is, women now made up 55 percent of those sterilized.[37] Nationwide, by the 1930s female rates of sterilization were surpassing male rates. However, the comparatively early start of California's sterilization program meant that women would not substantially outpace men in annual or aggregate numbers until the 1940s.

This gendered transition mapped onto rising rates of sterilization in the feebleminded homes starting in the 1930s. Initially, the majority of operations occurred in mental hospitals, affecting more men than women. However, this pattern started to level off in the 1930s and soon began a minor reversal. Preliminary analysis of sterilization data from Pacific Colony, matched with individual-level census data from the 1940 US Census, demonstrates the disproportionate sterilization of women, who had a 20 percent greater risk of reproductive surgery when compared to men. Young people also were more likely to be sterilized; individuals under eighteen years of age had 3.3 times the risk of being sterilized as compared to those over eighteen. Finally, patients with Spanish surnames had 2.4 times the risk of being sterilized as compared to non-Spanish-surnamed patients. Our analysis also shows that those with middle-level IQs (morons) were more likely to be sterilized than those in the lower ranges (idiots and imbeciles). In multiple regression models, female gender, Spanish surname, and age younger than eighteen each remained associated with a higher likelihood of sterilization, so that the group most likely to be sterilized would be Spanish-surnamed women under age eighteen.[38] These findings from Pacific Colony underscore the racial and gender biases of sterilization, as well as the anxieties about "morons," who preoccupied eugenicists precisely because they could "pass" and function in society while still threatening future generations with their deleterious heredity.[39]

RACISM AND RESISTANCE: TRENDS
AMONG MEXICAN-ORIGIN PATIENTS

Spanish-surnamed individuals constituted an elevated proportion of sterilized patients at both feebleminded homes and mental hospitals, particularly at the four most active facilities. Figure 9 illustrates percentages of sterilized patients who had a Spanish surname. The highest percentages of Spanish-surnamed patients could be found at Pacific Colony, where 29 percent of those sterilized were Spanish-surnamed, followed by Sonoma with 21 percent, Patton with 14 percent, and Agnews with 13 percent. For all institutions the average percentage of sterilized patients who had a Spanish surname was 16 percent. In and of itself, this figure emphasizes the extent to which Mexican-origin persons, who made up the majority of Spanish-surnamed patients, were overrepresented, given that between 1910 and 1940 they never made up more than 6.5 percent of the state population according to census figures.[40]

Across institutions, Mexican-origin sterilized patients, both male and female, tended to be younger than the overall population. For example, the mean age of non-Spanish-surnamed sterilized patients in all institutions from 1935 to 1944 was twenty-six (the median was twenty-five), whereas the mean for sterilized Spanish-surnamed patients was twenty-three (the median was nineteen). This pattern was particularly pronounced at the feebleminded homes, such as Pacific Colony, where the mean age of sterilized Spanish-surnamed patients was eighteen (the median was seventeen). Reflective of this pattern was seventeen-year-old Dolores Chávez, who was committed to Pacific Colony in 1941. Chávez had been a ward of the Ventura Juvenile Court and was classified as a middle moron with an IQ of 56.[41] Her father, deported years earlier to Mexico, was deceased, as was her mother. At some point, she had been placed in the care of a female guardian, perhaps an extended family member, also of Mexican origin. Chávez was tagged as a truant and a "behavior problem," and her home was disparaged as unfit. Figure 10 is the sterilization recommendation for this girl. In the 1920s and early 1930s, sterilization recommendations were processed as letters, sometimes accompanied by additional communications and modified consent forms. In 1936 the Department of Institutions adopted the "787" form, which streamlined the process. Staff could simply type onto the form, filling in the sections on personal, family, and clinical history, and checking a box under "Legal Provisions" that included phrasing from the state's sterilization law. As with many Mexican-origin families, Chávez's next of kin, in this case her guardian, refused consent. Exercising the legal prerogative to make the final determination, Pacific Colony's superintendent proceeded to authorize the operation on the grounds of Chávez's purported mental deficiency, and two weeks later she was sterilized.[42]

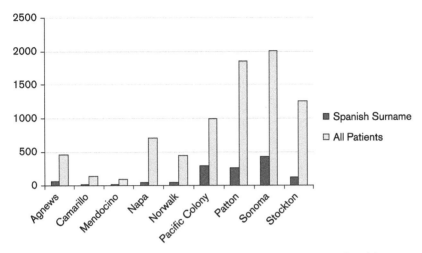

FIGURE 9. Percentage of sterilized patients with a Spanish surname in each California state institution, demonstrating higher proportions of Spanish-surnamed patients in Sonoma, Patton, and Pacific Colony, 1935–44. Source: Prepared from Eugenic Sterilization Data Set, California Department of State Hospitals, Sacramento, by author and researcher Kate O'Connor.

In contrast to several other states, California's law offered next to no room for appeal or objection. This, however, did not deter hundreds of Mexican-origin families, who resisted the sterilization of their children more intensely than any other group.[43] In 1937, for example, the mother of Carlos Vásquez "refused two letters of consent" that Sonoma had sent to her home. Seeking to overcome this hindrance, Butler dispatched a letter to the director of the Department of Institutions in which he described Vásquez as a "run-away and a menace to society" who had been remanded to the court for petty and grand theft. Butler impugned the mother, labeling the boy's parentage "a low grade Mexican type" and requesting permission to proceed with the operation, which was carried out the following year.[44]

Many parents declined consent in written correspondence. However they also lobbied officials who had been involved in their child's commitment. In 1931, Butler recommended the vasectomy of Juan Romero, who had arrived to Sonoma from the Preston School of Industry, so that he would never "reproduce his kind, for we know from experience that individuals of his mentality should never bear off-spring, as they are usually defective in some manner."[45] One of Mr. Romero's three sons, Javier, had already been sterilized, and in the same communication Butler reminded him that Sonoma was still awaiting approval for

*Recommendation and approval for Vasectomy or Salpingectomy
for the Purpose of Sterilization*

Name

Institution ___ PACIFIC COLONY - Spadra

PERSONAL HISTORY   Hospital Case No. 2671

Age 17 yrs. Nativity California Religion Baptist Education 7th grade - special classes

Marital status Single Sex Female No. of children None Ages

FAMILY HISTORY (for additional space use reverse side): Father deported to Mexico, now dead. Mother was promiscuous, had three illegitimate children by three different men, now dead. One brother court ward, attempted to attack an eight year old cousin. Home was unfit.

CLINICAL HISTORY (for additional space use reverse side): Mentally deficient girl, truant, behavior problems.

Date admitted June 16, 1941 ___ Present diagnosis Mental deficiency-Middle Moron level; familial type.

Attacks (previous, and diagnosis of each):

LEGAL PROVISIONS (compliance with)

This form is submitted in accordance with section 6624 of the Welfare and Institutions Code of the State of California.

1. Legally signed and prepared commitment papers {are} on file at this institution.

2. This patient is afflicted with:

   ☐ Mental disease which may have been inherited and is likely to be transmitted to descendants.
   ☒ Feeble-mindedness, in any of its various grades (specify grade) Middle Moron grade, I. Q. 56
   ☐ Perversion or marked departures from normal mentality.
   ☐ Disease of a syphilitic nature.

Written consent {not given} by Parents dead, no known guardian; girl is ward of Juvenile Court of Ventura

under date of ___ copy of which is attached hereto.
(If consent not given, submit separate letter giving circumstances)

After careful consideration of the case of ___ by the members of the Medical Staff of this institution, it is their belief that this patient is suffering from the affliction above noted and it is their recommendation that the operation for the purpose of sterilization be performed, with which opinion and recommendation I concur and do hereby request your approval.

[Date] November 5, 1941

Approved and authorization for an operation for sterilization granted this 7th day of November 1941.

FIGURE 10. Sterilization recommendation made in 1941 for a seventeen-year-old Mexican-origin girl at Pacific Colony who was a ward of the Juvenile Court of Ventura and was classified with an IQ of 56 (middle moron grade). Source: Eugenic Sterilization Data Set, California Department of State Hospitals, Sacramento, used in accordance with the California Committee for the Protection of Human Subjects under 12–04–0166.

his third son, Pablo. Butler asserted that having three boys in one family who ended up in correctional facilities was evidence of "a hereditary thread" and that any grandchildren born of these boys would certainly be defective.[46] Attempting to reverse this planned course of action, Mr. Romero went to talk to the health officer at the San Francisco Detention Hospital who had initiated his son's institutional odyssey. According to the health officer, Mr. Romero was "violently opposed" to sterilization and rebuffed the classification of his son as feebleminded. Like Carlos Vásquez's mother, Romero's father was belittled, described as "an ignorant, unintelligent Spanish man." Authorities found it "impossible to convince him of the value of the operation for sterilization either for his son's protection or for that of society."[47] Six months after this letter exchange Butler convened a conference on this case and decided that the presence of three defectives in one family and the thirteen burglaries attributed to Romero warranted his sterilization.[48]

In addition to challenging authorities that endorsed sterilization, Mexican-origin families sought intervention from community allies. In 1936, Celia Ramírez was recommended for sterilization at Pacific Colony. She had been classed as a high moron with an IQ of 68 and had a long case history that involved repeated running away and institutional escapes. Ramírez's record suggest that she was gang-raped at age nine by five men, including her uncle. Despite clinical detection of venereal disease, her account of this sexual violence was deemed to be "without foundations" by juvenile authorities. Ramírez's protracted and pained trajectory involved various stints in the court and in homes including Pacific Colony. Both separately and together her father and mother "opposed sterilization on religious grounds." They contacted the Mexican Consulate in Los Angeles, which in turn wrote to Sacramento "verifying the parents' objections to sterilization and stating that the Consul had taken the liberty of informing the mother that such operation would not take place without her consent."[49] It is possible the Mexican's consul's actions stalled Ramírez's sterilization, as there is no record of her name in the lists of patients sterilized at Pacific Colony in 1936 and succeeding years.

The Catholic Church also played a role in protesting sterilization. In 1942, the father of Ignacio Domínguez, a fifteen-year-old boy diagnosed with a borderline IQ of 75, responded negatively to Butler's request for sterilization through the intermediary of his priest. Domínguez was under the watch of the Santa Barbara Police Department's Probation Office because he had been found intoxicated in a local pool hall, had been party to a knife fight, and had been "involved with a local gang of

marauding Mexicans."[50] According to Butler, Domínguez's parents were
divorced, feebleminded, and unable to care for their many children,
several of whom were at a local reformatory. Disregarding the priest's
objections to Domínguez's sterilization, Butler requested permission
from Sacramento, which was granted, and this boy was sterilized the
following year.[51]

Most dramatically, Mexican-origin families took to the courts, filing
what appear to be the only constitutional challenges to California's sterilization law.[52] In 1930, sixteen-year-old Concepción Ruíz, through her
guardian, sued in district court for $150,000 damages for the salpingec-
tomy performed "against her wishes and in spite of protest" at Sonoma
the previous year. Her attorneys argued that Ruíz's Fourteenth Amendment rights to due process had been violated.[53] There is no indication
that Ruíz won her suit or that any legal precedent was set. Nine years
later Sara Rosas García, a widow with nine children, filed a Writ of Prohibition in the second appellate district to prevent the Pacific Colony
superintendent from sterilizing her eldest daughter, Andrea. Represented
by David C. Marcus, a Jewish American lawyer with ties to the Mexican
Consulate and the NAACP (National Association for the Advancement
of Colored People), García put forth a compelling criticism of the proposed sterilization as an infringement on the equal protection clause of
the Fourteenth Amendment and on due process given that there was no
mechanism for patient appeal. Marcus averred that the surgery would
be performed against the "wishes and desires" of García's daughter and
that the law gave "no remedy or method of redress" for the "irreparable
damage" she would suffer. Although García's writ was denied in a 2 to
1 decision, Judge J. White, who was sympathetic to Marcus's argument,
excoriated the existing law in a terse dissent. White wrote that the granting "of such power should be accompanied by requirements of notice
and hearing at which the patient might be afforded an opportunity to
defend against the proposed operation. To clothe legislative agencies
with this plenary power, withholding as it does any opportunity for a
hearing or any opportunity for recourse to the courts, to my mind par-
takes of the essence of slavery and outrages constitutional guaranties."[54]
Despite this legal contest, records indicate that Garcia's daughter was
sterilized at Pacific Colony in 1941.[55]

Mexican-origin parents were not the only ones who fought sterilization. In 1937, the Italian father of a sixteen-year-old girl housed at Sonoma refused consent. His daughter had been committed because she

had stolen from friends and neighbors and "once from an oil or service station." Yet this girl with a registered IQ of 75, or borderline grade, had "very good scholastic standing." Thus Butler saw her as a prime candidate for house parole where "she might receive further schooling on the outside." Butler wrote to Sacramento asking that this girl be "sterilized over and above the father's objections" so that she could be released and "receive further schooling on the outside."[56] Butler's petition was granted, and the salpingectomy performed in 1938.[57]

Parental resistance to sterilization was a persistent feature of California's sterilization regime. By far, this pattern was most pronounced among Mexican-origin families, who exhibited an unwillingness to abide by the strictures of institutionalization for religious, moral, and cultural reasons. This pattern of pushback comprised more than several hundred solitary episodes of refusal and can be interpreted as a hitherto obscured dimension of mid-twentieth-century ethnic and civil rights mobilization around family dignity and bodily autonomy.[58] The strident rejection by so many Mexican-origin families of the assumptions and justifications of the state's sterilization regime underlines the heightened racial hostility that permeated eugenics in California. Although all patients were labeled as mentally deficient or insane, only Mexican-origin parents were so consistently derided as "low grade," or "inferior stock" in formulations that condemned both their biological and social capacity to parent. Mexican-origin parents were struggling against an inimical system that sought to disarticulate families, many of which were already coping with the strain of seasonal migration and poverty. The stakes were high as parents sought to make an impossible choice between familial separation through long-term institutionalization or the prospect of reproductive surgery foreclosing the possibility of future generations.

THE HARD AND SOFT EDGES OF CONSENT

The majority of patients and families did not object to sterilization but signed on the line consenting to reproductive surgery. Even though the law did not require consent, superintendents nevertheless put a great effort into obtaining signatures from the patient and from parents, spouses, and guardians. This practice speaks more to officials' concerns about liability and professional standards than to a compelling interest in the agency of patients. Because of its asymmetries, the microdynamic of consent offers a window through which to examine the nuances of acceptance, acquiescence, and refusal among institutionalized patients and their families.

Some patients signed recommendation forms themselves. Thus far, we have identified sixty-seven instances of self-consent in the 1935 to 1944 period. One such self-consenter was a twenty-five-year-old Canadian man who voluntarily committed himself to Stockton in 1935 for dementia praecox, hebephrenic type, and then of his own avail agreed to sterilization.[59] Figure 11 is the Sterilization Recommendation for this young man. The reasons why his signature appears on the form cannot be deciphered satisfactorily even with sensitized, subaltern readings of sterilization forms as administrative documents that contained and elided human subjectivity to construct a diagnosis. We can speculate that, given the dual-purpose approach to sterilization embraced by superintendents at Stockton, this man might have accepted surgery as an intervention aimed to quell his reported sexual perversions and pathologized same-sex desires.[60]

More often than the patient her- or himself, a parent or spouse offered her or his signature. In 1939 Rhonda Johnson, a white twenty-six-year-old mother of three, arrived at Patton. According to her file, Rhonda qualified for salpingectomy under the law on three counts: she was classified as dementia praecox, catatonic type; she tested positive for gonorrhea; and she was ranked as an imbecile with an IQ of 46. The clinical notes indicated that Johnson "got drunk, left home," and "associated with other men." Her husband provided written consent for the operation just three days after her commitment, and one month later she was sterilized.[61] Bertha González's mother approved her sterilization. González, a nineteen-year-old Mexican American woman, was placed in Pacific Colony in 1950.[62] She had a third-grade education and had taken some "special development classes." Forms indicate that she was married and had a one-year-old child. González's IQ score was 35, in the imbecile range, and her overall diagnosis was "mental deficiency-familial type." The brief family history suggests what González had suffered. Her father was a violent alcoholic who had been jailed for ninety days for attacking her. Apparently she was "beyond control of her mother" and her three siblings were "none too bright."[63] Against the backdrop of these compounded troubles, her mother endorsed sterilization, which took place about one month after being recommended.[64]

These operations occurred during the height of medical paternalism in the United States, when parents and patients relied heavily on the expertise and recommendations of physicians. It is likely that many family consenters, lacking alternative possibilities for care or treatment,

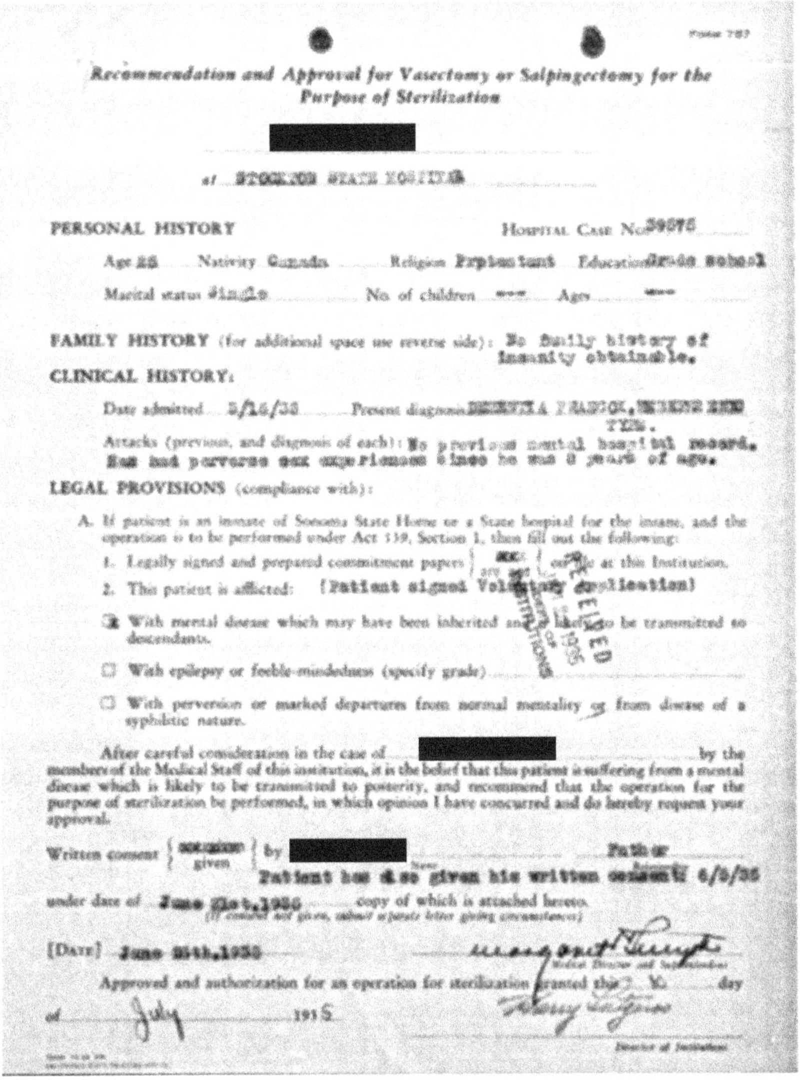

Recommendation and Approval for Vasectomy or Salpingectomy for the Purpose of Sterilization

at STOCKTON STATE HOSPITAL

PERSONAL HISTORY   HOSPITAL CASE No. 59075

Age 25   Nativity Canada   Religion Protestant   Education Grade school

Marital status Single   No. of children ---   Ages ---

FAMILY HISTORY (for additional space use reverse side): No family history of
insanity obtainable.

CLINICAL HISTORY:

Date admitted 5/16/35   Present diagnosis DEMENTIA PRAECOX, MIXED TYPE.

Attacks (previous, and diagnosis of each): No previous mental hospital record.
Has had perverse sex experiences since he was 8 years of age.

LEGAL PROVISIONS (compliance with):

A. If patient is an inmate of Sonoma State Home or a State hospital for the insane, and the operation is to be performed under Act 539, Section 1, then fill out the following:

1. Legally signed and prepared commitment papers   are   on file at this Institution.

2. This patient is afflicted: (Patient signed Voluntary application)

☒ With mental disease which may have been inherited and is likely to be transmitted to descendants.

☐ With epilepsy or feeble-mindedness (specify grade)

☐ With perversion or marked departures from normal mentality or from disease of a syphilitic nature.

After careful consideration in the case of _____ by the members of the Medical Staff of this institution, it is the belief that this patient is suffering from a mental disease which is likely to be transmitted to posterity, and recommend that the operation for the purpose of sterilization be performed, in which opinion I have concurred and do hereby request your approval.

Written consent { not given / given } by _____   Father

Patient has also given his written consent 6/6/35

under date of June 21st,1935   copy of which is attached hereto.

[DATE] June 24th,1935

Approved and authorization for an operation for sterilization granted this __ day

of July 1935

FIGURE 11. Sterilization recommendation made in 1935 for a man of Canadian origin at Stockton State Hospital identified as a sexual delinquent who "has had perverse sex experiences since he was 8 years of age." Source: Eugenic Sterilization Data Set, California Department of State Hospitals, Sacramento, used in accordance with the California Committee for the Protection of Human Subjects under 12–04–0166.

were doing what they thought was best and most prudent for their dependents and loved ones. Indeed, many parents were eager to have their children with disabilities committed to state homes because they could not manage financially or emotionally and they wished to devote more attention to their "normal" children. In March 1952, a father who worked as a pilot flying between San Diego and Oakland airports wrote to Governor Warren, pleading that Pacific Colony accept their older boy, five-year-old Thomas, who was "mentally and physically under developed since birth" and in need of "constant medical care" that neither he nor his wife could provide.[65] Pacific Colony responded to his impassioned plea, informing him that his son was "number fourteen on the urgent list of San Diego children awaiting admission to the Nursery B Cottage." Officials sympathized with his situation, stating that "at the present time we have over 2800 such patients awaiting admission and every effort is being made to meet this end" and alerting him that additional state homes were slated for construction. We do not know if his son ever was admitted to Pacific Colony.[66]

From today's vantage point, the consent process followed in California would not pass ethical or legal muster. It lacked core elements of bona fide informed consent. First, the diagnoses assigned by the institutions themselves, which classified patients with low mental grade or insanity of some sort, would have disqualified patients from having the necessary capacity to understand the information provided about the operation and its consequences or to make an informed decision based on that information. Second, although California authorities painted the picture of a voluntary consent process, by definition voluntariness—a core tenet of informed consent—cannot be conditional. From the 1920s to the 1950s, sterilization was a precondition of release and was held over the heads of patients and their families. Third, superintendents relied heavily on a system of surrogate decision making, whereby a designated family member or guardian was assumed to be acting in the best interest of the child or patient judged incompetent of possessing autonomous judgment. Not only do doubts arise about whose autonomy is actuated in this model, but eugenic sterilization was predicated on a formula in which the best interest of society superseded that of the individual in the name of human improvement. Thus California's sterilization system was based on implicit and explicit conditional and coercive features that severely restricted the autonomy and options of patients and their kin.[67]

The contingency of sterilization is exemplified by the case of a father who wanted his adopted son released but was not willing to acquiesce to sterilization for religious reasons. This father wrote to the director of mental hygiene in 1947, explaining that his son was in Pacific Colony because he was a truant who would not attend school, not because he had ever gotten in any serious trouble. His file shows that the boy, diagnosed with an IQ of 68, was sent there from the Los Angeles Superior Court, whose evaluation generally concurred with the father's: the boy "was a problem in his home and in school although he had not actually become a delinquent."[68] A veteran, the father remarked, "I fought in World War II and I wonder if that's the sort of thing I fought for."[69] In its correspondence, the Department of Mental Hygiene reminded the father that the "law now authorizes sterilization with or without consent of the patient or responsible relatives." However, he also was reassured that his son's case would follow "a definite procedure which culminates in the case being reviewed in headquarters."[70] Records indicate that the father's petitions resulted in a half-victory: this boy's sterilization was postponed, but without the surgery he remained in Pacific Colony while his father awaited his return.

The vacuity of the consent process comes into stark relief in instances of surrogate decision making where parents or guardians with limited literacy signed with an "X" on the instruction of institutional staff. In 1944, a thirteen-year-old Spanish-surnamed girl was committed to Pacific Colony for "mental deficiency" and was placed in the "high imbecile grade," with an IQ of 43. This girl had been sexually abused by her stepfather; the family was described as having "low moral background" and a "low standard of living." At the courthouse in San Bernardino, an X was placed on the consent line of a makeshift sterilization form, and "Grandmother's mark" was written by one of the witnesses in cursive.[71] In another case, an X was offered by or for the mother of a twenty-six-year-old Italian American woman with a tested borderline IQ of 75 who was committed to Sonoma in 1935. On the margins of the index card–sized consent form are the words "I don't know how to write but I should make a cross showing my signature," a phrase that probably was read to her by the Sonoma official with whom the mother interacted.[72] Two problematic elements converged in surrogate signatures: the limited ability of the consenting family member to understand the surgery and its consequences, especially since little to no explanation was provided, and the assumption that the patients, because of IQ scores and other prejudicially derived characteristics, did not possess the capacity to comprehend or decide.

In the late 1940s, fissure lines appeared in the pillars of the state's sterilization program, partially in response to changes implemented by

Dr. Dora Shaw Heffner, who in 1943 became the head of the Department of Institutions under Governor Earl Warren. Like her predecessors, Heffner countenanced sterilization, but, seeking a more scientifically informed and democratic approach to institutional care, she created some latitude for patient communication and appeal. Starting in the mid-1940s, at least at Patton, patients slated for sterilization began to receive typeset memos, printed in English and Spanish, clarifying that the director of the Department of Institutions had authorized sterilization; if the patient wished to object, she or he needed to send a letter to Heffner within the next ten days. The ward physician and attendants would furnish paper and pen to patients who wished to pursue this option.[73] The memo clarified that the operation did not affect sex function but was solely for the purpose of ending the ability to procreate. The microfilm reels contain approximately fifty such written appeals from patients at Patton. The penmanship and grammar of these letters vary, but they all convey strong objections to reproductive surgery. In 1947, a twenty-seven-year-old mother of two, diagnosed with dementia praecox, hebephrenic type, expressed her disagreement with her husband's consent: "I do object to this strenuously, kindly permit me to explain my reasons against it." She explained that she and her husband were unhappy, "sexually and otherwise," and that her in-laws had committed her to Patton. She thought her husband had approved sterilization because although he "evidently still loves me and is hurt," he nonetheless was naturally "seeking a kind of revenge." She believed she could remarry and might be happy again. She concluded, "My religion also causes me to object to sterilization. I have no venereal disease and there is no insanity in my family's background and I am young enough to remarry and have a normal, happy life with children."[74] In spite of clearly articulating her opposition, Heffner endorsed the sterilization that she underwent two weeks after writing this letter.[75]

A perfunctory yet very poignant letter was penned by Thomas Rogers, a pseudonym for the clergyman introduced at the beginning of this chapter whose wife had approved his vasectomy. She probably did not realize that her husband would take advantage of a newly available avenue of appeal. But on March 11, 1947, Rogers sat down to write a letter to Heffner in capital block print.[76] His letter is shown in Figure 12. It succinctly states, "Inasmuch as I am religiously opposed to sterilization, I am submitting this as a protest against any such action."[77]

Unlike the petition of the young mother discussed above, Rogers's petition appears to have succeeded. It was taken seriously enough to prompt a reply from Heffner's medical deputy director. Writing to Patton's

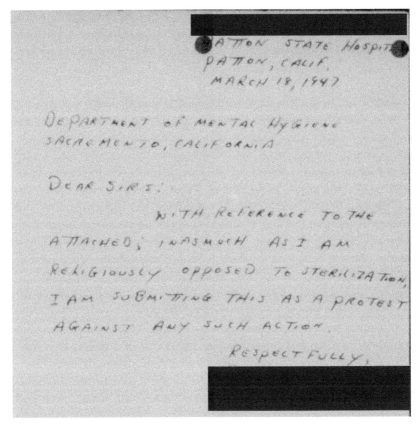

FIGURE 12. Letter written in 1947 by an inmate at Patton State Hospital who opposed his sterilization on religious grounds. Source: Eugenic Sterilization Data Set, California Department of State Hospitals, Sacramento, used in accordance with the California Committee for the Protection of Human Subjects under 12–04–0166.

superintendent, he noted that the patient was a clergyman who disagreed on "religious grounds." This official gave the superintendent permission to perform Rogers's operation without any further communication with Sacramento. However, he asked that it be deferred, in hopes that Rogers, once his mental state had improved, would be "amenable to reason on this subject" and would acquiesce to the surgery.[78]

A similar outcome occurred with Karen Wright, the mother of two young children, diagnosed with dementia praecox, simple type, who hailed from Washington State. In a 1946 missive to Heffner she pleaded: "I like to keep my body whole. I feel insulted by the whole thing," adding, "I don't think that I am insane either."[79] Referring to this letter, and to information gleaned from her case file, Heffner cautioned Patton's super-intendent, "It would seem from her letter that a sterilization at this time would cause a psychic trauma." Heffner added that since the patient was divorced, "Nothing would be lost by deferring this sterilization to a more appropriate time."[80] Heffner clarified that sterilization and discharge should be revisited when this patient's mental attitude had improved.

A few currents merged to allow for a reprieve for these two patients at Patton. In the case of Rogers, as an educated white man and clergy-man, the tenor of the correspondence suggests that he was treated with some respect and as a person eventually capable of coming to reason to consent to sterilization. In the case of Wright, emergent theories of men-tal illness, which encompassed psychoanalytic understandings of trauma, worked in her favor, as did her status as a divorcée unlikely to have any children in the near future. As new somatic therapies, such as insulin coma and convulsive therapy, and antipsychotic drugs such as chlorpromazine were introduced in Patton and the other mental hospi-tals, sterilization gradually was being abandoned as a viable therapy for mental illness, a transition that benefited Wright.[81]

It was not only white middle-class patients at Patton who managed to stall their own sterilizations. In 1950, the family of a twenty-one-year-old African American woman, Gladys Marshall, originally from Glen-dora, Mississippi, wrote to Pacific Colony. Marshall had been commit-ted three years earlier, sent from San Diego County, which had "expressed fear that she would produce feebleminded children." Although she was briefly married, Marshall's two children apparently were born out of wedlock, and her IQ, as tested at Pacific Colony, was 42 (imbecile) (it had tested at 55 in San Diego). Marshall's mother wanted her daughter released but without reproductive surgery, which Pacific Colony staff strongly recommended for Marshall on the grounds that she was "alco-holic, incorrigible, mentally deficient; interested in men." The staff felt that "releasing supervision of the girl without sterilization would not be justified." Without consent to sterilization, Marshall's parents were not able to bring her home on furlough. The parents emphatically did not want their daughter in Pacific Colony, but they were unwilling to agree to sterilization as a quid pro quo for release. Seeking assistance, Mar-shall's mother contacted the NAACP, who in turn retained an attorney to represent the family. Faced with this legal action, Pacific Colony's superintendent, George Tarjan, backed down, stating, "The operation cannot be performed because of lack of consent."[82] It appears that the family won the day, as Marshall's name does not appear in the lists of those sterilized at Pacific Colony in those years. This concession, however, meant that Marshall was not released from Pacific Colony.

Rumblings of change were under way starting in the late 1940s, inside state institutions and in the broader arena of mental health. In 1949, the conclusions of the "Report on the Governor's Conference on Mental Health" suggested that the state's mental hygiene system needed to be transformed from a model of custodial care to one of treatment, from an investment in bricks and mortar buildings to trained personnel, and from rural asylums to more urban institutions located near medical schools and research centers.[83] These shifts presaged revisions to the state's sterilization laws in the early 1950s, when successful senate (1951) and assembly (1953) bills deleted any references to syphilis (long since understood as bacterial rather than hereditary in etiology) and sexual perversion; removed references to "the feebleminded," "idiots," and "fools," terms seen as archaic; and instated patient and next-of-kin notification as well as channels for legal appeal at the county court level.[84] The Roman Catholic bishops of California, who opposed the existing law in its entirety, and the Department of Mental Hygiene, now striving to modernize the nomenclature for people classified as mentally ill and retarded, backed this update.[85] Approved by Governor Warren, these legislative amendments reflected his administration's commitment to revamping California's mental health and public health programs.[86]

The revisions had an immediate impact, turning the sterilization recommendation process from a formality into a more demanding exercise. This change is captured in the numbers. From 255 operations in 1951, the number dropped to 51 in 1952, and by the mid-1950s it hovered around 20, even as three new hospitals and homes opened.[87] For example, at Sonoma, only 4 operations were performed in fiscal year 1952–53 and only 1 was performed in 1953–54. The superintendent at the time, Butler's successor, noted the "conspicuous drop" in the number of surgeries, which he attributed to factors including the revamped law.[88]

At the same time as the sterilization law was rewritten, psychiatry was moving into the mainstream, and the mix of patients in mental hospitals such as Patton and Stockton started to encompass people with nonpsychotic and less severe conditions such as psychoneuroses or personality trait disturbances. In 1952, the American Psychiatric Association issued the first edition of the *Diagnostic and Statistical Manual of Mental Disorders (DSM-I)*, which both standardized psychiatric nosology and incorporated psychodynamic and psychoanalytic theories.[89] Heffner's concern about the "psychic trauma" that might befall Karen

Wright, the mother institutionalized at Patton who wanted to keep her "body whole," is indicative of this emerging trend.

Mental health attitudes toward what was now referred to as mental retardation, and no longer feeblemindedness, were undergoing an analogous metamorphosis. As a Sonoma physician explained in 1956, mental retardation was "as much a social and psychological problem as it is a medical one."[90] In a shift propelled in part by a generation of middle-class parents skeptical of doctors' assumptions that their children required institutionalization, mental retardation ceased to be viewed as a hereditary stigma that must be eradicated and instead began to be understood as a condition that required thoughtful conversation among experts and families. The founding of the National Association of Retarded Children in 1950 signaled this shift, as did the publication of best-selling memoirs by well-known authors such as Pearl Buck and Dale Evans Rogers about the value and joy of their children with intellectual disabilities.[91] Most prominently, in 1962 Eunice Shriver, President John F. Kennedy's sister, published "Hope for Retarded Children" in the *Saturday Evening Post*. Frankly discussing her sister Rosemary's diagnosis of mental retardation, Eunice Shriver wrote, "Like diabetes, deafness, polio or any other misfortune, mental retardation can happen in any family. It has happened in the families of the poor and the rich, of governors, senators, Nobel prizewinners, doctors, lawyers, writers, men of genius, presidents of corporations—the President of the United States."[92]

In the 1960s and 1970s, the rejection of labels of *retarded* or *insane* was hastened by muckrakers who exposed the abysmal conditions and overcrowding at state institutions. Increasingly, Americans were challenging the farce of public custodial "care" and questioning the inflexible demarcation between normal and abnormal, abled and disabled. Many Americans were shocked to learn that people with physical and intellectual disabilities had served as subjects in myriad medical experiments, including an infamous case in which hundreds of children at the Willowbrook State School in Staten Island, New York, were deliberately infected with hepatitis.[93]

The glaring absence of either institutional oversight or legal recourse for patients from 1909 to the late 1940s helps explain California's comparatively high sterilization rates. During these decades superintendents acted with great impunity, aided by a geography of isolated institutions and legal statutes that afforded remarkable protection. In this scenario institutional peculiarities thrived, and California's sterilization program unfolded unevenly across the state's nine institutions. There were clear differences among the mental hospitals and the feebleminded homes as well as among superintendents depending on their beliefs about the therapeutic, eugenic, or punitive purpose and value of reproductive surgery. Nevertheless, one preponderant pattern was an unforgiving racial antagonism toward Spanish-surnamed, primarily Mexican-origin, patients and their families, which was expressed both in ethnic derision and in disproportionate rates of sterilization. This racialized dynamic set the stage for the resistance of Mexican-origin patients and families inside and outside the walls of the institutions.

With the benefit of the digitized archive of sterilization documents, a picture begins to coalesce—of institutional paternalism, the pretense of a consent process, and multiple instances of speaking back to compulsory sterilization. Ultimately, the acts of Reverend Thomas Rogers, who wrote a short letter expressing his objection to sterilization, Sara Rosas Garcia, who appeared before the second appellate court, the parents of Celia Ramírez, who sought the Mexican consul's intervention, and the family of Gladys Marshall, who retained an attorney through the NAACP, served as pressure points on a system that faced more organized assaults in subsequent years. Indeed, this quieter and largely forgotten resistance adumbrated the activism of the 1960s and 1970s, when the antipsychiatry, feminist, and gay and lesbian rights movements rejected the paternalism of midcentury medicine and institutions; the disability movement expanded that critique to upend assumptions about the physical and intellectual limitations of people deemed "retarded"; and the Chicana/o movement, aligned with ethnic and racial justice struggles, upbraided the stereotypes of inferiority, criminality, and delinquency that were staple ingredients of midcentury eugenic racism.

In 1979, California's sterilization law was unanimously repealed by a generation of lawmakers astonished that the Golden State still had such a statute on the books. And by 1986, the reproductive control of earlier decades had become anathema; the law now stipulated that people with disabilities could be sterilized only at the request of a conservator or guardian after a court process and that "the right to choice over procreation is fundamental and may not be denied to any individual on the basis of disability. Persons with developmental disabilities should be provided with services to enable them to live more independent lives, including assistance and training that might obviate the need for sterilization."[94]

Despite these noble intentions, the sterilization of vulnerable populations in state institutions did not end in California with the erosion of the eugenics era. Starting in the 1980s, the overlapping trends of deinstitutionalization and skyrocketing incarceration led to a process of transinstitutionalization, whereby the same kinds of people deemed "social problems" and "menaces" to society, especially those convicted of minor offenses or with mental health problems, who in the 1930s might have been committed to Patton or Sonoma, were incarcerated in San Quentin or Valley State Prison. At the outset of the twenty-first century, a generalized crisis in California's mismanaged prison system made possible yet another episode of reproductive injustice in state institutions.

CHAPTER 5

California's Eugenic Landscapes

The extent to which certain places dominate the California
imagination is apprehended, even by Californians, only
dimly. Deriving not only from the landscape but from the
claiming of it, from the romance of emigration, the radical
abandonment of established attachments, this imagination
remains obdurately symbolic, tending to locate lessons in
what the rest of the country perceives only as scenery.

—Joan Didion, "Girl of the Golden West"

Atop a steep ridge lined with eucalyptus and pines in the hills above
Berkeley, California, sits Vollmer Peak, named for August Vollmer, an
eclectic eugenicist and one of the most innovative reformers in modern
policing.[1] What was formerly known as Baldy Peak was christened in
honor of Vollmer in 1940, after New Deal and relief projects had transformed the face of much of California and the Southwest.[2] Thanks to
the toil of thousands of young workers attached to the Civilian Conservation Corps and the State Emergency Relief Administration, hundreds
of parks, gardens, recreation facilities, and historical monuments were
constructed during the Great Depression.[3] In the East Bay, one centerpiece of public works was the East Bay Regional Park District, which
consisted of ten thousand acres of woodlands acquired through a public
bond initiative from the Municipal Utility District.[4] In the November
1934 election, the residents of seven East Bay cities voted for the park
and elected five Regional Park Board directors, charged with oversight
and administration.[5] Two of the "leading citizens" on the board were
Charles Lee Tilden, for whom the park is now named, and Vollmer.

Born to German parents in New Orleans in 1876, Vollmer moved
with his family to Berkeley in the late 1890s. A founder of Berkeley's
volunteer fire department, Vollmer became town marshal soon after

returning from duty in the Spanish-American War. In 1905 he organized his patrol into the Berkeley Police Department, serving as its chief until 1932. After retiring from the force, Vollmer was appointed professor of police administration in the political science department at the University of California at Berkeley, where he established the School of Criminology. A prolific author of books and articles on crime control and the criminal personality, Vollmer was in great demand on the lecture circuit and was active in dozens of local and national organizations.[6] Throughout his long career, Vollmer emphasized the need to professionalize police agencies and do away with the vigilantism and Old Boys' personalism that had characterized many law-and-order squads in the nineteenth century, especially in the American West. Above all, this meant reliance on scientific methods: "Criminology will be on solid ground when it follows in the footsteps of medical science."[7] For Vollmer, objective observation, laboratory science, and clinical diagnosis provided civilized solutions for the rehabilitation of criminals that were a far cry from the shackles and corporeal punishments of yesteryear. Vollmer's philosophy was strongly rooted in hereditarian and evolutionary theories, and he insisted that the starting point for an evaluation of a criminal's mind-set and motivations should be his or her genetic and constitutional makeup. Vollmer made a place for extrinsic factors, which could discourage or encourage positive or negative dispositions, above all "during the early and formative years of the individual's life," but ultimately exerted little influence.[8] Using the example of an orange tree, he explained, "Environment plays an important role in developing all of the potentialities of the tree, but that is all that environment can do. It can add nothing to the tree that was not there at the beginning of its existence." Extending this analogy to humans, Vollmer continued, "A constitutionally defective individual will always be defective," adding, "As a general rule, brilliant and talented persons usually are descendants of people of superior qualities while the stupid and insane are descendants of dull or defective forbears."[9]

To infuse science and medicine into policing, in Berkeley and the other locales across the Americas (Los Angeles, San Diego, Kansas City, Detroit, and Havana) where he revamped police departments, Vollmer introduced an array of new technologies and procedures, such as integrated radio communications, an identification records system, mobile patrols, sophisticated laboratories, and mandatory fingerprinting.[10] Taken with anthropometrics and biometrics, Vollmer commissioned a physiologist at the University of California at Berkeley to design the country's first polygraph or "lie-detector" apparatus.[11] He was also keen on intelligence testing, which he thought could both accurately identify feebleminded and delinquent adolescents and grade the ability of police recruits. Under his watch, the Berkeley Police Department began to administer the army's Alpha and Beta tests to screen policemen and women in the late 1910s.[12] In Vollmer's estimation, the coordinated implementation of these original tactics constituted the cutting edge of the modern fight against crime. If there was one key word for Vollmer's philosophy, it was *prevention*, a concept he understood principally in medical terms: "Crime should be combated by preventive measures in the same manner that diseases are fought by professional health officials."[13] Just as a particular vaccine could inoculate a person against a particular infection, a scientifically informed and calculated intervention administered at the appropriate time and place could reduce crime and deter criminals.

When he was elected to the park board in 1934, Vollmer brought his ideas about hereditary potentialities to bear on the mission and purpose of the East Bay Regional Park District.[14] Like many other proponents of expanded recreation, Vollmer subscribed to arguments about humans' evolutionary need for open space and access to wilderness. Such notions began to gain currency during the Progressive Era as urban reformers emphasized how playgrounds and recreation could improve the physical and psychological well-being of American children, and conservationists began to push for managed park systems.[15] During the New Deal, the environmentalist agenda was given a boost by Franklin Delano Roosevelt's relief agencies, such as the Civilian Conservation Corps, which employed more than two million Americans to carve out and enlarge nearly one thousand parks across the country.[16] The corps itself reflected popular attitudes about the invigorating effects of nature contact and the anticipation that assigning demoralized, jobless, and often malnourished young men to parks and wilderness projects would bolster both their virility and national fitness.[17]

By the mid-twentieth century, access to recreation and nature areas was seen as a crucial component of maintaining a balanced and harmonious society. In 1941, for example, a National Park Service report outlined the drawbacks of the modern exile from nature, which risked turning Americans into automatons and severing man's (the relationship to nature was almost always expressed in androcentric terms) bond to his primitive self, a predicament "which can be alleviated only by making it possible for him to escape at frequent intervals from his urban habitat to the open country."[18] Many reformers contended that, besides these salutary effects, parks could stem juvenile delinquency by keeping in check the dormant antisocial tendencies of overstimulated city youth. These concerns, coupled with the desire to take advantage of federal funds and workers, underpinned the construction of Tilden Park. So too did Vollmer's scientific and biological approaches to criminality and crime prevention. In his campaign report, Vollmer declared that the East Bay had less recreational acreage per capita than any other community and that urban sprawl had "now reached practically to the hilltops and no play space [was] left."[19] The provision of nature areas, hiking trails, rifle ranges, camping grounds, and botanical gardens would stimulate health and diminish crime: "Delinquency thrives where there is no super-vised recreation. The National Crime Commission says that if we paid one half the amount for recreation that we do for jails we would not have half as many criminals."[20]

Vollmer has been forgotten in the literature on eugenics; he does not fit the expected mold, and he devoted scant energy to high-profile issues such as sterilization and immigration restriction. Nonetheless, his story is one path along the variegated terrain of hereditarianism in the twen-tieth century. He sat on the advisory councils of the American Eugenics Society (AES) and the Euthanasia Society of America and was a member of the National Committee of Mental Hygiene and the National Society for the Legalization of Euthanasia.[21] Vollmer backed the legalization of birth control and the voluntary suicide of the infirm and incompetent. However, as a criminologist with a humanitarian agenda, he strongly opposed the death penalty. Disdainful of doctrines of racial superiority, Vollmer championed desegregation as well as free speech. He took part in Berkeley's Inter-Racial Committee, founded in the early 1940s, and during that same period refused to censor socialist discussion groups at the local YMCA.[22] His life ended at his own hands, when, at the age of seventy-nine, suffering from Parkinson's disease and diagnosed with cancer, he fatally shot himself with his service revolver in his Berkeley home.[23]

A NATURAL ALLIANCE?

Eugenicists profoundly shaped California's landscapes. Their approaches to the environment encompassed the entire spectrum, from preserva-tionists fiercely intent on forever insulating the wonders of nature from intrusion, to parks and recreation enthusiasts who wanted to build roads, lookouts, and concessions to make the outdoors more accessible if not commercially profitable.[24] What united them was the extent to which they comprehended California's biota and topography through a framework of selective breeding, one in which specific species and organisms were elevated, chosen, and revered over others. In a more general sense, they viewed exposure to nature as a method of containing the worst and actualizing the best of humans' evolutionary and hereditary predispositions. Almost always their vision at once mirrored and extended into the world of plants and animals the Pacific West's brand of nativism and racial exclusion. There were exceptions, such as Vollmer, whose ecumenical hereditarianism—based not on assumptions about the inherent capacities of certain races but on the principle that genetic assets and defects were universally distributed among the human population—anticipated later understandings of the interplay between nature and nurture.

There are many histories of human intervention embedded in California's landscapes: the patchwork of missions first forged by indentured Indians in the eighteenth and nineteenth centuries and refurbished by the Works Progress Administration during the Great Depression, the vast fields of agribusiness cultivated by migrant laborers in the central and southern valleys, the suburbs creeping further and further into the desert, and all the aqueducts dredged and paved over the past hundred years, to name just a few. After the fact, the human beings who imagined, orchestrated, and physically built these geographies are frequently rendered invisible.[25] Instead, what is perceived is the sheer beauty of the topography or the concrete results of arduous labor, such as bridges, skyscrapers, and highways. This phenomenon is even more pronounced for parks and wilderness areas, which exist in large part because of modern myths of virgin lands, untouched forests, and the sacred quality of nature free from people. This helps explain why much of the story of eugenicists remains hidden in California's everyday landscapes. Its invisibility is even more striking considering that eugenicists intentionally inscribed the geography with an exultant historical narrative of westward expansion and progress that culminated in California with their entrance as saviors and victors.

California was the cradle of the modern environmental movement. In 1892 John Muir and more than one hundred kindred Yosemite lovers founded the Sierra Club; the Sempervirens Club for the defense of central coast redwoods followed in 1900, and the Save-the-Redwoods League in 1918. From the outset, eugenic guidelines of selective breeding and species endangerment were central to these three organizations, especially the Save-the-Redwoods League.[26] Indeed, hikers passing through the Madison Grant Forest and Elk Refuge in Prairie Creek Redwoods State Park or climbing Mount Jordan in Sequoia National Park might be surprised to learn that they are enjoying places named in honor of two of the most prominent eugenicists in the first half of the twentieth century.[27]

Men such as these promoted nature-making in California in three key ways. First, they founded, directed, and financed environmental organizations, thus facilitating the legislative and fiscal involvement of governmental agencies in land appropriation and management. For instance, about fifteen years before they joined the country's first eugenics body, the Eugenics Committee of the American Breeders' Association, Jordan and the horticulturist Luther Burbank were charter members of the Sierra Club. Eugenicists were also behind some of the initiatives that produced shelters, playgrounds, parks, and arboretums across the state.[28] The Sacramento real estate tycoon Charles M. Goethe, who established the Eugenics Society of Northern California (ESNC), enabled Stephen Mather, the inaugural director of the National Park Service, to launch the interpretive parks program in Yosemite in 1920 and gave more than $2 million to the Save-the-Redwoods League for memorial groves and related projects.[29] Others who resided on the East Coast, such as Henry Fairfield Osborn and Madison Grant, lent energy, time, and their prestige to California's environmental groups and campaigns.

Second, California eugenicists interwove hereditarian and evolutionary tenets and motifs into the narratives they crafted about the Pacific West and the westward expansion of empire as the crucible of the American nation. As part of the rush of European American settlers who sought to order and appropriate postcolonial California, eugenicists fabricated origins stories about the exceptionalism of the West. They frequently invoked the trope of the Garden of Eden, now being harvested anew by a superior class of colonist.[30] These narratives evoked the evolutionism of Frederick Jackson Turner's "frontier thesis" and the "agrarian myth" of "simple, rural people coming into a western country . . . and creating there a peaceful, productive life."[31] Burbank, for instance, expressed buoyant optimism about the potential for the innovative hybridization of fruits, flowers, and people in a region rich with Spanish, Mexican, Russian, French, and, most recently, Anglo-Saxon heritages. In a complementary fashion, eugenicists also conceived of the West as a savage frontier where men afflicted by neurasthenia and the deleterious effects of urbanization and industrialization could be restored through mountaineering, bareback riding, and communing with the primeval forest.[32] At the turn of the twentieth century, this was often tied to fantasies of a tribe of white supermen marching westward to the ocean, carrying the banner of civilization. Joseph P. Widney, a Los Angeles physician, propounded the Aryanization of the entirety of the Pacific Coast, and for Teddy Roosevelt, staving off "race suicide" involved remasculinizing and toughening up the country's flaccid men in the badlands and borderlands. Commonly, these narratives about "winning the West" or the "conquest of a continent" traced the forging of the American republic back thousands of years, from the dawn of *Homo sapiens* to the gradual global dominance of Nordics and finally to the dire urgency of ensuring the perpetuation of "pioneer stock."[33]

Third, California eugenicists literally left their mark on the landscape by naming it, in a manner akin to European colonizers, starting with Christopher Columbus, who staked a claim to the New World through "ceremonies of possession" and rituals of proclamation.[34] Comparable patterns unfolded centuries later, when expeditions, such as Lewis and Clark's, started to fan out across the American West. Scientists classified flora and fauna while surveyors plotted the terrain, attaching their surnames to plants and places and alternately erasing and raiding Native American tribal lexicons.[35] The landscape of the American West is a nomenclatural testament to the numerous rites of possession realized by the naturalists and explorers affiliated with the Army's Corps of Topographical Engineers, the Mexican Boundary Survey, and other expeditions.[36] As scientists eminently concerned with the natural universe, eugenicists followed in the footprints of these forerunners: they named varieties of flowers and vegetables, expanded botanical and zoological taxonomies, and left their names for posterity on memorial plaques and eponymous markers.[37]

REDWOODS AND RACE SUICIDE

In 1918, three men at the core of the American eugenics movement, John C. Merriam, Henry Fairfield Osborn, and Madison Grant, founded the Save-the-Redwoods League.[38] Merriam was a paleontologist at the University of California at Berkeley who in the early 1900s had catalogued vertebrate and invertebrate fossils and unearthed evidence of the Pacific Coast's prehistoric past.[39] After serving as dean of the paleontology department, Merriam moved to Washington, D.C., in 1920 to head the

Carnegie Institution, which was the chief sponsor of the Eugenics Record Office from 1917 until its unceremonious closing in 1940. Osborn, a comparative anatomist, was president of New York's American Museum of Natural History and a member of the Galton Society and similar organizations. A year earlier he had written the preface for the second edition of Madison Grant's popular book *The Passing of the Great Race,* praising the author's thesis that history was best interpreted as a violent competition among races and that the brightest hope for human civilization lay with the "Anglo-Saxon branch of the Nordic race," a strain of "human stock" characterized by its "unanimity of heart, mind, and action."[40] As Grant explained in his tome, barring drastic action, the "great race" that had conquered America would soon be extinct, obliterated by its inferiors, such as immigrant laborers, who were "breeding out their masters and killing by filth and by crowding as effectively as by the sword."[41] A seasoned outdoorsman, Grant was also president of the Boone and Crockett Club, a fraternal game hunting society (motto: "Promote manly sport with the rifle") established by Teddy Roosevelt in 1887.[42] All three had long been enraptured by California's towering redwoods, particularly the *Sequoia sempervirens,* which for millions of years had covered vast portions of the Northern Hemisphere but was now limited to a narrow band of foggy coast that snaked from Big Sur to the Oregon border.[43]

The impetus for the Save-the-Redwoods League had originated the previous summer when the trio made a pilgrimage from San Francisco to Humboldt County in search of "a forest wall reported to have mystery and charm unique among the living works of creation."[44] Encountering a cluster of trees that stretched more than three hundred feet toward the sky, they were awestruck by the trees' scale, the kaleidoscopic patterns of sun and shade, and the statuesque elegance of the "evergreen" *sempervirens.* Grant sensed that he was seeing one of the "most magnificent forests in the world," and Merriam saw "a fragment of the garden of Eden, coming to us directly from the hand of the Creator."[45] Aware that logging was fast encroaching on this site, that very night they decided to rescue the splendid giants. From a hotel in Arcata, they composed a letter to Governor William D. Stephens "urging that the legislature take some action to acquire the finest of these redwood forests."[46] Within a year, with the backing of scientists and politicians from both coasts, they had formed the Save-the-Redwoods League, which immediately began to coordinate the purchase of a patchwork of forestlands from private owners with matching funds from donors and the California State Park Commission.

The Save-the-Redwoods League's initial roster consisted mainly of affluent European American Protestant and professional men, two-thirds of whom lived in California and one-third on the Atlantic sea-board.[47] Many were natural scientists, landscape architects, or engineers, and a few were lawyers, bankers, independent entrepreneurs, and real estate agents. In addition to Grant, Merriam, and Osborn, several league councilors—including Charles M. Goethe and Vernon Kellogg—belonged to local and national eugenics organizations, while many others—such as Harold Bryant, the educational director of the California Fish and Game Commission; Benjamin Ide Wheeler, the president of the University of California; Newton Drury, a businessman who eventually became director of the National Park Service; and fellow travelers William Kent, Joseph D. Grant, and George Lorimer—endorsed eugenically driven immigration restriction and the dreams of Aryan and Nordic supremacy that crested to popularity in the 1920s.

For redwood savers, the *sempervirens* was a potent symbol of looming destruction, possible regeneration, and the fate of the American West. Several decades earlier, in "Song of the Redwood-Tree," Walt Whitman had conveyed bittersweet nostalgia over the impending ruin of the redwood, which, like the Indian and other inhabitants of the West, was destined to succumb to the march of civilization ("Our term, our term has come") and be vanquished at the hands of a "superber race" and "an empire new."[48] Eager to turn the tide against the unregulated felling of these majestic trees, in 1900 a coalition of scientists, surveyors, and female reformers organized the Sempervirens Club to guard the dense groves in the Santa Cruz mountains from the ax and sawmill.[49] The club took its name from the *Sequoia sempervirens,* which was taller and scarcer than its wider, shorter, and older distant relative, the *Sequoia gigantea,* often referred to as the Big Tree.[50] In 1902 the club, with the help of the Native Sons and Native Daughters of California, the Sierra Club, and the American Association for the Advancement of Science, purchased nearly four thousand acres in Big Basin to create California's first bona fide Redwood Park.[51] Over the next decade, the Sempervirens Club devoted itself to enlarging Big Basin and safeguarding the redwoods in the Santa Cruz vicinity. By the 1910s, however, Grant, Merriam, and Osborn had determined that saving California's redwoods was a much bigger task that warranted a more powerful organization.

If Whitman had depicted the vanishing of the redwood as one of the inevitable costs of progress, then Grant and his colleagues saw defending the *sempervirens* from extinction as a battle that had to be won for scientific, spiritual, and racial reasons. For Grant and other conservationists, the redwood—its stateliness, grandeur, and persever-ance—represented the "great race." Like Anglo-Saxon America, which was being engulfed by hordes of defectives and mongrels and menaced by the excessive breeding of undesirables, the redwood was imperiled by a similar process of "race suicide" from rampant logging, urban encroachment, and human ignorance. Analogies between the redwood and the Anglo-Saxon race abounded at the turn of the century. Muir had called the Big Trees of Calaveras County "the noblest of a noble race," and Merriam called them the survivors of a "splendid race."[52] In a tract dedicated to the genus *Sequoia,* one author wrote, "The great white race which dominates the world today had made its entrance on the stage of history when the Grizzly Giant began its existence."[53] Sav-ing the redwoods meant more than just protecting a tree; it was a meta-phor for defending race purity and ensuring the survival of white Amer-ica. With proper measures of preservation and prophylaxis, the resilient redwoods, like the Anglo-Saxon race, would revive and prosper: "*Sequoia sempervirens*—the immortal Sequoia—is far from being a battered remnant. . . . [It] is a beautiful, cheerful, and indomitable tree. Burned and hacked and butchered, it sprouts up again with a vitality truly amazing."[54]

Wilderness is the greatest of contradictions: we can enter and relish it only because we have construed it as untamed and untrampled.[55] Since the late nineteenth century, efforts at preservation and conservation have been based primarily on the idea that nature must remain unimpaired by human interference. This stimulated the creation of Yellowstone, the nation's first national park, in 1872, and organizations such as the Wil-derness Society, founded by Aldo Leopold and Robert Sterling Yard in 1935.[56] Certainly, trees, streams, geologic formations, and meadows abloom with spring lupine all exist, but the concept of pristine wilder-ness was part of the ideology of settlement and conquest that European Americans brought to the American West.[57] Even though Native Ameri-cans had interacted for centuries with the western landscape—burning controlled fires, for instance, to ensure the longevity of mature oak trees—many European Americans insisted that what eventually became Yosemite and Big Basin were unspoiled territories that they alone had discovered and were compelled to defend, at times with army scouts.[58]

Up until the mid-1800s, when the United States was still largely rural, it was not unusual for writers to portray nature as bewildering and forbidding. By the end of the century, however, as urbanization and colonization rolled westward across the United States, wilderness gradually began to be cast as sacrosanct. By the close of the nineteenth century, John Muir and many of his contemporaries were describing mountains and forests through an empyrean poetry of canopies, sanctuaries, and cathedrals. Of Yosemite, Muir rhapsodized, "Benevolent, solemn, fateful, pervaded with divine light, every landscape glows like a countenance hallowed in eternal repose; and every one of its living creatures, clad in flesh and leaves, and every crystal of its rocks, whether on the surface shining in the sun or buried miles deep in what we call darkness, is throbbing and pulsing with the heartbeats of God."[59] Other preservationists, especially redwood savers, were similarly effusive. Joseph D. Grant, a close friend but no relation of Madison Grant, enthused about his journey through the Dyerville and Bull Creek Flats: "Standing in the radiance of this filtered sunlight, slanting down in long shafts like angel paths in the Primitives' pictures, it was impossible not to think of the forest as a cathedral. . . . Overhead, fan-vaulting, and an exquisite tracery of branches against a heaven of intense blue. More glorious to me than any Gothic fane, more inspiring to awe and devotion!"[60] These embellished paeans imbued tree saving with transcendental meaning and imagined the wilderness as a temple apart from the mundane.

Redwood preservation was one stratum of the bedrock of the modern environmental movement, and its logic informed later generations of environmentalists who linked nature protection to the need to safeguard the most precious human "stock" from annihilation. After World War II, for example, a segment of environmentalists rearticulated "race suicide" within the parameters of postwar theories of developmentalism and modernization.[61] They turned toward neo-Malthusian arguments about zero population growth and pushed for immigration restriction and mandatory birth control, including the implementation of sterilization programs in less developed countries. Now the burden of saving nature was tied to the regulation of reproduction, child spacing, and the adoption of the nuclear family model.[62] A leading proponent of this trend was Fairfield Osborn, the son of one of the three Save-the-Redwoods League founders (Henry Fairfield Osborn) and the author of *Our Plundered Planet,* an immensely popular book that painted a grim portrait of the fate of Earth and the human species.

In 1948, the same year *Our Plundered Planet* appeared, Fairfield Osborn was invited to speak at a commemoration dinner at the Fairmont Hotel in San Francisco. Hosted by the Save-the-Redwoods League, this event was convened to dedicate the Madison Grant Forest and Elk Refuge, a tract of more than sixteen hundred acres in Humboldt County that had been obtained from two lumber companies. Madison Grant's name was already on display in Northern California's forests. In 1929, he and Joseph D. Grant had donated $10,000 each to jointly create a grove in Del Norte Coast State Park; after Madison Grant's death in 1937, his brother used family monies to pay for the casting of a bronze tablet for the site. In 1931, the tallest known redwood in Northern California, not far from the magical spot that had transfixed the trio in 1917, was consecrated the Founders Tree for Madison Grant, Merriam, and Osborn.[63] Another honor was conferred on Madison Grant posthumously when the Grant estate, John D. Rockefeller Jr., Archer M. Huntington, the New York Zoological Society, the National Audubon Society, the National Wildlife Association, and the Boone and Crockett Club all made sizable contributions for the acquisition—matched by the league and the California State Parks Commission—of the forest and elk refuge.[64] According to the league, this refuge paid tribute to Madison Grant's life as a "conservationist, author and anthropologist" and, moreover, was intended to save from harm the "last remaining band of Roosevelt Elk in California."[65] For the league, this addition symbolized the "climax of the entire preservation program in this superb region, the last forest wilderness of large extent on the western side of the Park."[66] In his address, Fairfield Osborn told the audience that his two supreme idols were his father and Madison Grant, a "man of extraordinary vision." He then detailed California's population boom with numbers and statistics, lamenting Americans' ignorance about the evils of unprecedented population growth and skeptically questioning the prospects for "the long-term preservation of our national life."[67] Through men like Osborn junior, the preservationist agenda of the first generation of redwoods savers was repackaged in terms of overpopulation and its frightening consequences.[68]

If faith in science and technology made Fairfield Osborn's catastrophism unpalatable to some at the start of the Cold War, his predictions resonated with the pessimism of the 1960s and 1970s as societal upheaval, political turmoil, defeat in Vietnam, and mounting cognizance of environmental degradation rocked the country. Paul Ehrlich's *The Population Bomb*, published in 1968 by the Sierra Club through Ballantine Books, reiterated many of Osborn's jeremiads and made population growth "a major focus for groups interested in linking the problem of resource limits to the growing concern about 'quality of life.'"[69]

Ehrlich proposed pegging tax rates to family size, levying taxes on basic staples for children such as diapers, and sterilizing all men in India who had fathered three or more children. This book had an enormous impact, selling more than one million copies in less than two years and going through twenty-two printings. It also catalyzed the formation of Zero Population Growth (ZPG), a group based at Stanford University, where Ehrlich was a professor of biology. ZPG mushroomed to more than thirty-three thousand members and 380 chapters by the early 1970s.[70] It strove to attain replacement-level fertility rates in the United States, a goal shared by allies in the Sierra Club, Planned Parenthood, and the Audubon Society.[71] With a strong presence in California, ZPG relied on decades-old stereotypes of Mexicans and Mexican Americans as diseased hyperbreeders and demonized Spanish speakers and undocumented immigrants. This animus intensified in 1978 when John Tanton, a Sierra Clubber and "English only" advocate, founded the Federation for American Immigration Reform to press for stricter immigration laws and border control. By the late 1970s, population control, particularly in the Southwest and California, had fused with "efforts to control the flow of Mexican migrants."[72]

In the 1950s, some leaders, such as David Brower, tried to challenge the elitism and racial exclusivity of mainstream environmentalism.[73] For the most part, such attempts fell on deaf ears; it was not until the late 1970s and early 1980s, when a more racially and economically diverse group of grassroots activists began to address issues such as soil contamination and toxic waste dumping, usually in or surrounding urban communities, that the color and scope of American environmentalism changed.[74] Today distinctions are often made between the conservation and preservation endeavors of the past and the contemporary environmental justice movement. Nonetheless, the alliance between eugenic racism and environmentalism, which seemed quite natural to the founders of both movements, continues to flicker on and off in the twenty-first century in the xenophobic platforms endorsed by the population section of the Sierra Club, and sometimes in the rhetoric employed to campaign for greenbelts, no- or slow-growth policies, and strict zoning codes.

ORIGIN STORIES

For redwood savers, theirs was an epic crusade unfolding in epoch time. European Americans "brought a very particular concept of time, and their place in it, to their understanding of the trees, in the process weaving a tale of conquest, domination of outsiders, and, ultimately, of racial supremacy."[75] This usually involved tracing the genesis of the redwood back to antiquity, following its evolution, protracted destruction, and Lazarus-like fight for resurrection to the moment that enlightened white knights arrived at the antediluvian forests of the West Coast. This story pivoted on the depiction of the redwood as timeless and immortal specimens whose wanton decimation bordered on blasphemy and crimes against evolution. On a tour of California in 1903, Teddy Roosevelt declared to his audience at Stanford University, "I feel most emphatically that we should not turn a tree which was old when the first Egyptian conqueror penetrated to the valley of the Euphrates, which it has taken so many thousands of years to build up, and which can be put to better use, to shingles."[76] Madison Grant and fellow preservationists viewed the redwood as a portal to a past buried in fossils: "Sequoias were flourishing when dinosaurs roamed the earth."[77] Gazing down from on high over eons of time, redwoods had "witnessed, if not the birth of man, at least man's development from the lowest estate. It has seen the rise and fall of civilization."[78] David Starr Jordan wrote that the redwood forests constituted "the oldest living plant representatives of an earlier geologic era."[79] From the paleontological perspective, Merriam viewed the redwoods as a "living link in history" that "connect us as by handtouch with all the centuries they have known. The time they represent is not merely an unrelated, severed past; it is something upon which the present rests, and from which living currents still seem to move."[80] By claiming intimate and expert knowledge of the geologic and scientific lifespan of the redwood, which they adorned with spiritual sentiment, preservationists inserted themselves as key figures into the unfolding dramaturgy of the settlement of the American West.

The sequoia was a common protagonist in tales of conquest and colonization in California. Furthermore, redwood savers often grafted these historical chronologies onto nature by affixing date markers and plaques to redwood logs and rounds.[81] Once a tree's age had been ascertained by counting growth rings, preservationists plotted "great moments" of Western civilization on these concentric calendars, whose diameters could reach ten feet. The earliest event was placed at the eye of the round and the most recent at its perimeter. On one Santa Cruz redwood slice, for example, the passage from antiquity to the present was distilled down to the birth of Christ, Mayan civilization, the coronation of Charlemagne, Marco Polo, Columbus's discovery of America, the Declaration of Independence, Lincoln's Gettysburg Address, and the day that very tree was felled.[82]

The origin stories of California eugenicists extended beyond the redwood, however, incorporating broader themes of the rational exploitation of land, soil, and natural resources in pursuit of a Pacific paradise. More often than not, these narratives of racial regeneration countenanced white supremacy. Such was the case with Joseph P. Widney, an Ohio-born physician who arrived in Los Angeles in the 1860s by way of Panama. The second president of the University of Southern California and founder of the Los Angeles County Medical Association, Widney was an indefatigable booster of the Southland. In *Race Life and the Aryan Peoples,* published in 1907, Widney chronicled a Wagnerian saga. Molded by his stint as a military surgeon during the Apache Wars, Widney saw Anglo colonization west of the Mississippi as a triumphant procession that had begun centuries ago in Eurasia. From this distant region, the Aryan began his journey to the New World and eventually to Los Angeles, which, he argued, would become the world capital of white domination.[83] According to Widney, it was "not by chance but through the working of purely natural laws, and laws which are general in scope, not special, that the Teuton and not the Latin was to control the New World."[84] In a California freed from the vestiges of Spain and Mexico, the drama of the survival of the fittest would reach its ineluctable conclusion, giving birth to a hardier American race that far surpassed its ancestors. Widney advocated his views for at least thirty years. For example, in 1935, then in his nineties, he wrote *The Three Americas,* reasserting his previous predictions of Aryan ascendancy.[85] Three years later, he submitted to the Los Angeles City Planning Commission a plan that visualized that metropolis as the "greatest health resort of the world" and petitioned for the "building of a hundred miles of mountain-slope sanitariums, facing out upon the broad slope of the desert."[86]

Other California eugenicists, such as Burbank, painted a much more inclusive picture of racial regeneration. When Burbank followed his brother, moving from Massachusetts to Santa Rosa in 1875, he brought with him knowledge of Darwin's theories of variation and selection, experience in horticultural experimentation, and unbridled enthusiasm about the fecundity and lushness of Northern California.[87] After working in several local nurseries, Burbank quickly developed prune and plum varieties capable of unparalleled crop yield. By the 1890s he had set up his own garden; it was there that he produced the Shasta daisy, the Burbank rose, the Paradox walnut, and the Humboldt blackberry-raspberry by tailoring new methods of cross-fertilization and hybridization. His fame grew, especially after Hugo de Vries, the Dutch botanist who had independently rediscovered and confirmed Gregor Mendel's laws of heredity, visited Burbank in the early 1900s and dubbed him the "plant wizard."[88]

To many European American settlers, Burbank's robust hybrids symbolized the metamorphosis of fertile soil and vegetation—disparaged as fallow during the Spanish and Mexican eras—into resplendence. Burbank himself was often lauded as the ideal settler.[89] In 1929, Ray Lyman Wilbur, the president of Stanford University and a member of the AES, called Burbank to mind when he described the exemplary colonist as someone "who could make an investment, who could work with his neighbors, who could develop ten acres so intensively that they would produce as much as one hundred acres elsewhere."[90] Burbank was central to the development of large-scale crops in California, a role buttressed by his appointment as dean of the College of Agriculture at the University of California and his receipt of a prestigious grant from the Carnegie Foundation, both in 1905. For California's agricultural entrepreneurs, no industry put land to a better utilitarian purpose than the citrus industry, which "became a model more or less for the whole Pacific slope."[91] Burbank contributed to these efforts in 1914 when he joined a committee entrusted with choosing a site for the Citrus Experiment Station in Riverside.[92] This station promoted the modern cultivation of the California navel orange, aiding growers by supplying fertilizers and recommending premium rootstocks.[93] Many of the scientists affiliated with the Citrus Experiment Station, including Burbank and Thomas Hunt, Burbank's successor as dean of the College of Agriculture, tied racial progress to the manipulation of nature and the judicious crossing of diverse plant species.[94]

In his writings about his journey westward, Burbank folded a sense of the sublime, reminiscent of Muir, into a narrative of biological renaissance that foresaw the materialization of a superlative hybrid race. Like many other European Americans who came to California in the late nineteenth century, Burbank was taken with the varied landscape, the temperate climate, and the austere beauty of the Sierra Nevada. After surveying Santa Rosa, he wrote to his relatives in Massachusetts, "I firmly believe from what I have seen . . . that it is the chosen spot of all this earth as far as nature is concerned, and the people are far better than the average. The air is so sweet it is a pleasure to drink it in. The sunshine is pure and soft, the mountains which gird the valley are very lovely. . . . I cannot describe it. I almost have to cry for joy when I look upon the lovely valley from the hillsides."[95] Burbank credited his peculiar hereditary makeup, which contained a strain that "responded so instantly to the repeated call of California," for spurring him, a "small, wiry, active young man" with deep roots in New England, to pack up and head west.[96]

Compared to most other American eugenicists of his era, Burbank's philosophy was atypical. Deeply influenced by his hands-on hybridization experiments, Burbank supported the theory of the inheritance of acquired characteristics formulated by the French naturalist Jean Baptiste de Lamarck. Following Lamarck, Burbank believed that a living creature could inherit traits from its environment and, moreover, that these traits could become intrinsic to the organism. From his perspective, the best characters from each "race" could be consciously amalgamated into a tougher, stronger type.[97] For these reasons Burbank, unlike almost all the prominent American eugenicists that succeeded him, was ebullient about racial mixing and open to immigration. In his most well-known text, *The Training of the Human Plant,* he wrote, "I think it is fair to say [that it] is the grandest opportunity ever presented of developing the finest race the world has ever known out of the vast mingling of races brought here by immigration."[98] With its salubrious climate, California—where the "North, powerful, virile, aggressive," could be "blended with the luxurious, ease-loving, more tempestuous South"—was the perfect laboratory for the gestation of "a magnificent race, far superior to any preceding it."[99] Burbank's caveat was that experts needed to watch over this experiment, much as he supervised the cultivation of new varieties of flowers and vegetables in his orchard.

One of Burbank's close colleagues, David Starr Jordan, an ichthyologist, the first president of Stanford University, and a leading eugenicist, also authored publications about the glory of California's landscape and its hale denizens. In the late nineteenth century, Jordan came to appreciate the complex "niche" ecology of the state's topography and speciation when he participated in scientific expeditions along the Pacific Coast and its inland waterways. During these trips, he helped identify about four hundred shore fishes (particularly trout and salmon), many of which were being discovered and named by European American biologists.[100] In *California and the Californians,* first published as a syndicated column in the *Atlantic Monthly,* Jordan introduced readers to the majesty of the mountains and the abundance of the coastal plains, which he connected to the innate superiority of Californians. He wrote, "Men live longer there, and, if unwasted by dissipation, strength of body is better conserved," adding that, "other things being equal,"

California's children were "larger, stronger, and better formed than their Eastern cousins of the same age."[101] This perception was reinforced by a trip that Jordan took to his hometown in western New York in the 1910s, where he found that many of the "young men who were full of energy and vigor" had "gone West."[102] And in his two-volume autobiography, *The Days of Man,* Jordan traced his own robust lineage back to his New England Puritan ancestry and metamorphosis into a "Californiac."[103] In response to easterners' criticism of San Francisco's dissolute tendencies, Jordan defended California and its cosmopolitan city by stressing its wealth, optimism, and, above all, sturdy racial stock: "In my judgment the essential source of Californianism lies in heredity. The Californian of today is of the type of his father of fifty years ago. The Argonauts of '49 were buoyant, self-reliant, adequate, reckless, thoroughly individualistic, capable of all adjustments, careless of conventions, eager to enjoy life and action. And we, their sons, with all admixture of other blood and of other temperament are still made in their image. It is blood which tells."[104]

With its vast wilds, California was the place to pursue what Teddy Roosevelt called the "strenuous life," a regimen that Jordan heartily embraced. He instituted mandatory physical education for the students at Stanford and spent much of his leisure time mountaineering in the Sierras, where, "with sweat pouring down his face, straps biting into his shoulders, a long road ahead, Jordan acted out his moral vision of biological struggle and physical conquest."[105] Like Madison Grant and Merriam, Jordan was an avid preservationist. He was a charter member of the Sierra Club, helped organize the Sempervirens Club, and belonged to the Save-the-Redwoods League. Jordan was so smitten with the *sempervirens* that in 1892, when Stanford enrolled its inaugural class, he chose the coastal redwood as the university's official seal, a logo still sported on sweatshirts and bumper stickers.[106]

In contrast to his friend Burbank, Jordan envisioned an exclusionary utopia, one in which certain "blood" was better and purer. Informed by Victorian anthropology, Jordan's early writings placed Anglo-Saxons at the apex of a racial hierarchy, a prejudice fortified in the 1920s by his acceptance of Mendelian theories of the fixed inheritance of unitary traits. In the coauthored volume *Footnotes to Evolution,* Jordan outlined his views on Mendelianism, explicating the mechanics of heredity through the fictional character of Richard Roe. Jordan underlined the validity of the conclusions reached by Galton, Mendel, and Weismann and dismissed any neo-Lamarckian principles, averring that Roe (just like any other person) would be a direct product of his "germ cells."[107] In a chapter on degeneration that excoriated paupers, defectives, and constitutional weaklings, Jordan exhibited his social Darwinian creed: "The strong races were born of hard times, they have fought for all they have had, and the strength of those they have conquered has entered into their wills. They have been selected by competition and sifted by the elements. They have risen through struggle and they have gained through mutual help, and by the power of the human will have made the earth their own."[108] Conversely, the lesser "races," many of whom hailed from tropical countries, the Southern Hemisphere, and the once-great cities and towns of a deteriorating Europe, were most accurately defined as parasites that enfeebled society and milked its precious biological and material resources. Like many other eugenicists, he maintained that "the dangers of foreign immigration lie in the overflow to our shores of hereditary unfitness. The causes that lead to degeneration have long been at work among the poor of Europe."[109] Jordan saw the peopling of California through this nativist lens. He advocated the restriction of South European and Asian immigrants, asserting that "only the Saxon and the Goth know the meaning of freedom," and during the 1920s he complained bitterly about Mexican immigrants.[110] In a letter to Charles B. Davenport, he lamented that the American "germ plasm" was under assault from "the Mexican peon, who for the most part can never be fit for citizenship," and was "giving our stock a far worse dilution than ever came from Europe."[111] For these reasons, he joined Goethe, the Berkeley zoologist Samuel J. Holmes, and the restrictionist congressmen John C. Box and Albert Johnson in demanding tighter border controls and national origins quotas for Mexicans.

Whether taking the neo-Lamarckian or Mendelian route, California eugenicists penned narratives that touted the region's superior species and biological versatility, the protection of ancient wilderness, and the rationally managed utilization of the soil. More often than not, these revolved explicitly around celebration of the cultural and scientific conquest of the West by the fabled "races" of the Anglo-Saxons and Nordics and condemnation of the inferior "stock" of immigrants, especially Mexicans. By writing evocatively and extensively about geology, vegetation, plant breeding, and redwoods and heralding their privileged place in California's landscapes, eugenicists naturalized notions of racial difference and interlaced another thread into the mythology of the Pacific West as Garden of Eden and the frontier of American opportunity.

WHAT'S IN A NAME?

On July 11, 1966, the *San Francisco Chronicle* paid homage to "America's Grand Old Man of the conservation movement," Charles Matthias Goethe.[112] At the age of ninety-one and after months of failing health, the inveterate Sacramento resident had passed away. The *Chronicle* acclaimed the steady stream of missives from Goethe about biology, ornithology, botany, and geology that had "graced this newspaper for a half-century" and fondly remembered one letter in which he had explained the "remarkable survival mechanism of alligators."[113] On the same day the *Sacramento Bee* ran front-page coverage of the death of its native son, extolling his venerable career as a "philanthropist, author, scientist, civic leader, and world traveler" and highlighting his outstanding devotion to nature preservation.[114] The *Bee,* which had been a friendly home for Goethe's wide-ranging editorials for decades, quoted from the condolence messages that "poured into Sacramento from throughout the world and abroad."[115] Recognizing a "great loss to California and the nation," Governor Edmund G. Brown eulogized: "This marvelous man dedicated most of the waking moments of his life to the betterment of mankind. The results of his efforts are evident throughout the length and breadth of this land."[116]

Over the preceding fifty years, Goethe had built up his reputation as a renowned conservationist, rising to enough prominence to be designated "Honorary Chief Naturalist" by the National Park Service.[117] He belonged to dozens of environmental organizations such as the Sierra Club and the Audubon Society, donated thousands of dollars to naturalist projects, helped introduce the interpretative parks movement, and funded plant biology and genetics research. Goethe's passion and zeal were rooted in an eccentric and multipronged eugenic philosophy that integrated nature preservation, immigration restriction, and selective breeding. Goethe invested in what he understood as the comprehensive betterment of the biota, a grand goal that could be attained through the enlightened management of the earth's multitudinous and interrelated species, particularly those he deemed hardy, supple, and righteous. As a young man, Goethe coined two adages that became his lifelong mantras: "Learn to read the trailside as a book," and "Reduce biological illiteracy."[118] The former applied directly to his conservationism. In addition to reading about plants, animals, and rocks in the library, Goethe was convinced that people should learn about evolution in nature's laboratory. The latter slogan took this a step further to patterns of human reproduction and fitness, which Goethe thought could be grasped only by mastering biology and the health sciences, and above all the laws of heredity.

If Goethe's brand of eugenics was a product of his idiosyncratic intellect, it was also framed by his self-identification as a child of the American West. In his memoir *Seeking to Serve*, Goethe credited his interest in eugenics to his boyhood amazement at California's fascinating flora and fauna, which his mother had nourished by teaching him about Darwin and showing him how to press and catalogue wild flowers.[119] Like his contemporaries, Goethe predicated the Arcadian fulfillment of California on the persistence and propagation of the "white pioneer stock," which, through rough-and-tumble frontiering, had proven its indomitable and remarkable fiber. He compared the European American migrants who had settled in the arid and montane American West to the rugged cacti of the desert and the Egyptian Bedouins, all of which thrived in extreme elements. For Goethe, California's frontier "race," like a well-bred racehorse or delphinium, was a superlative biological strain whose purity demanded defense.[120] Ever aware of himself as an actor in this drama, Goethe wrote that he and his wife "were of Covered Wagon stock" and that the overland journeys of the late nineteenth century had "meant further severe selection of stocks, already winnowed by Mother Nature to eliminate weaklings."[121] Goethe viewed his personal trajectory, political and ideological battles, as well as the fate of California and the world, through the prism of his eugenic cosmology. He certainly persuaded many of the uprightness of his cause, although the extent to which his colossal wealth or the chance of being touched by his philanthropy motivated his allies will never be known.

Goethe's grandparents had come to California from Germany via Australia in the 1870s. Looking for business opportunities, Goethe's family settled on the state capital, Sacramento, where Charles was born in 1875. Arriving during a period of rapid regional economic development, his father gradually became quite well off through a mix of real estate, agriculture, and banking.[122] By the first decade of the 1900s, Charles was well assimilated into the family business, working as a solicitor, clerk, and bookkeeper, and on the road to fashioning a lucrative career of his own.[123] Goethe completed high school in Sacramento, and although he did not earn a bachelor's degree he passed the California bar examination in 1900.[124] Always an exceedingly disciplined man, Goethe was vigilant about diet and exercise and followed a rigid daily schedule. It was not unusual for his diary to contain entries in which he chastised himself for falling short of his own exacting standards.[125] Into his nineties, Goethe arose before six in the morning to "arrange dictation before his secretaries arrived" punctually at seven, and he organized his activities with clockwork precision.[126]

In 1903, Goethe married Mary Glide, a daughter of one of the area's wealthiest families. According to his diaries, it took nine frustrating attempts before Mary consented to become his wife. Apparently, "Mimi," as Charles affectionately called her, was hesitant for two reasons. First, she wanted to be absolutely sure that Charles was not hungry for the Glide family money. Twice during their courtship Mimi told Charles that she had been disinherited, at one point insisting that she would wed him only on the condition that her financial resources were channeled into human betterment and not wasted on profligate luxury, a request that Charles easily endorsed. Second, it is likely that Mimi stalled because of her infertility, alluded to in Charles's diaries. After a melodramatic (but scantly detailed) confession from Mimi, Goethe consoled himself: "It takes a great deal of courage to do what you're doing. Your mother who loves you dearly has told you that the one thing you have been willing to sacrifice is the one thing that *all* men demand—that is the pleasure of marriage" (his emphasis). He expressed remorse that he would fail to give his "eldest son the proud title—a title of a family that made its influence felt throughout the Fatherland."[127] The Goethes never had any children, an absence that they attempted to compensate for by backing youth programs and junior scientists and by supporting, most likely with monetary incentives, those they deemed eugenically fit to produce more offspring.

By the 1920s, Goethe was running several ranches and had diversified into Sacramento real estate, from which he turned a high profit by selling inexpensive subdivided plots through mortgages and installment plans.[128] During the Great Depression, Goethe invested his proceeds in the stock market, purchasing gilt-edged and blue-ribbon stocks. Additionally, Mary's liquid assets and the profits she accrued from various agricultural enterprises and oil wells, even with a lawsuit that diminished the inheritance she received from her mother, augmented the couple's income.[129] By the end of World War II, Goethe had become an exceptionally prosperous man, with sizable savings, a bulging stock portfolio, and considerable property holdings, as well as lucrative beet and citrus orchards. When Mary passed away in 1946, her estate was valued at nearly $1.5 million. Charles invested this fortune shrewdly, which, in conjunction with his other ventures, resulted in a total net worth of $24 million at the time of his death.[130]

Although Goethe was not able to bestow his illustrious German family name on a son or daughter, he did leave his inscriptions on the landscape of Northern California. A fervent redwood saver, Goethe spearheaded the purchase and designation of three memorial redwood groves—the Jedediah Smith Grove, the Mary Glide Goethe Grove, and the Drury Brothers Grove—and was directly involved in the establishment of the Luther Burbank Grove, the Aubrey Drury Grove, the Madison Grant Grove, and the Madison Grant Forest and Elk Refuge. He endowed scholarships in his and his wife's name and sponsored honorary titles so that the California Historical Society could enshrine those he admired, such as the Stanford psychologist Lewis Terman.[131] In turn, many sites bear his name. There is a plaque acknowledging the vital role of the Goethes in initiating the naturalist ranger program at Fallen Leaf Lake near Lake Tahoe.[132] Sacramento is home to the Charles M. Goethe Middle School and the Charles M. Goethe Park, which was approved by the county board of supervisors and contains another plaque honoring the Goethes, subsidized by the Save the American River Association and the Audubon Society.[133] In 1959, California State University at Sacramento (CSUS) founded the Goethe Arboretum, and five years later it decided to name the campus's main science building after its famous benefactor.[134] At the California Academy of Sciences, in San Francisco's Golden Gate Park, where the Goethes assisted in the construction of the Morrison planetarium, there is a Goethe room. In 1964, Sacramento's mayor decreed March 28 "Dr. Charles M. Goethe Day" in acknowledgment of one of the city's "most outstanding citizens."[135] Finally, in 1977, the Save-the Redwoods League posthumously honored their steadfast patron's "magnanimous support" by naming the Charles M. Goethe Memorial Grove in the Prairie Creek Redwoods.[136]

Goethe himself recognized the consequence of place-names and often ruminated on their historical and expressive significance. For him, they were onomastic clues to California's vibrant pioneer past, which, if carefully scrutinized, could illuminate the "selection of the fittest" at play. In one of his books, *What's in a Name?*, Goethe traced the etymology of Gold Rush town names, such as Whiskeytown, One-Horse Town, and Flea Valley, to the wave of enterprising Anglos and Nordics who began to populate the Pacific Slope in the mid-nineteenth century. In answer to the rhetorical question "What's in a name?" Goethe responded, "Imagination, contemplation, discussion, some agitation, then finally Selection, Decision."[137] For him, to take stock of the crusty, haphazard, and playful names of these hard-scrabble towns was to unravel the making of a

"Male-Land" of intrepid colonists, who, as "products of ten generations of Frontier's Life most severe selection, could have had the stamina, the courage, the lust for wandering, the invention, the alertness, the daring, the imagination, the resourcefulness to complete the Conquest of our Continent."[138] Adhering to the "race extinction" rationale of redwood saving, Goethe claimed that these ghost towns-in-waiting needed to be preserved in deference to "those blue-eyed, blonde empire-building Nordics" who had settled California.[139]

From the outset of his participation in social, civic, and political programs, Goethe was astutely interested in how space and the environment could best serve the aim of human betterment. Around 1910, after having reviewed urban development in Europe, Goethe began to advise the Sacramento Chamber of Commerce on city planning.[140] In 1911, the Goethes underwrote Sacramento's first supervised playground, and shortly thereafter they embarked on a multi-city trip through Asia, Africa, and Europe to explore the possibilities of exporting American-style playgrounds abroad.[141] The Goethes were instrumental in introducing the Boy Scouts to the region, financed the Sacramento orphanage, and helped found the Alta Sanitarium.[142] It was through these kinds of endeavors, which sometimes included field trips into the Sierra foothills, and after an inspiring tour through the European Alps, that Charles formed the California Nature Study League in 1918.[143] He was so animated about the prospects for nature study, which he hoped would teach children to "read the trailside like a book" and "reduce biological illiteracy," that one year later he and Mimi launched what would soon be termed the interpretative parks movement.[144]

In 1919, the Goethes were spending the summer at a resort on Fallen Leaf Lake near Lake Tahoe. They were sponsoring two naturalists, Harold C. Bryant, the educational director of the California Fish and Game Commission, and Loye Holmes Miller, from the University of California at Los Angeles, to direct nature study groups and walks. For several years, Bryant had run a biology program for youngsters in the Bay Area, leading them into the Berkeley Hills or Marin County to "see the wild flowers and the birds and the trees and everything along a trailside."[145] At some point during their stay, the Goethes persuaded the owners of the various lake resorts to invite their guests to one of the educational evening sessions offered by Bryant and Miller.[146] Serendipitously, that same night Stephen Mather happened to have stopped at Fallen Leaf Lake while en route to Sacramento.[147] Mather was the inaugural director of the National Park Service, which was formed in 1916 and embodied the federalization of the conservationist impulse. The Park Service's mission differed in moderate degree from the Save-the-Redwoods League, which was devoted first and foremost to the preservation of designated species and areas. Instead, as a conservationist agency, the Park Service was entrusted with a seemingly contradictory task: both wilderness stewardship, as defined by the nature-as-pristine axiom, and transformation of the nation's parks into usable and accessible recreation grounds. This paradox was encapsulated in the Park Service's mission statement, namely, that the parks be "maintained in absolutely unimpaired form for the use of future generations" and that they be "set aside for the use, observation, health, and pleasure of the people."[148]

As he was walking to the hostel to register, Mather "passed the crowded auditorium" and was dazzled by Miller's wild birdcalls.[149] So absorbed by the spectacle that he missed dinner, Mather approached Bryant about introducing nature lore into the parks under the auspices of the Park Service; the next year Bryant and Miller, with ongoing support from Goethe, transferred the "Tahoe Laboratory" to Yosemite.[150] The program was an immediate success. In 1922, the Yosemite Educational Department was formed. Two years later the fire-resistant Yosemite Museum, which operated as a training facility for naturalists, was built thanks to a Rockefeller Foundation grant, and *Yosemite Nature Notes,* which adopted Goethe's motto to "Learn to Read the Trailside as a Book," began circulation.[151] The message of *Yosemite Nature Notes* tapped deeply into legends of mountain men and daring white settlers. Describing the Yosemite Museum, *Nature Notes* enticed the public with "Here you will learn the full story of the Park—what tools were used by the great Sculptor in carving this mighty granite-walled gorge; who lived here before the white man came; how the Days of Gold led to Yosemite's discovery; how the pioneers prepared the way for you; and how the birds and mammals and trees and flowers live together in congenial communities waiting to make your acquaintance."[152] In 1930, nature study attained national stature when Bryant relocated to Washington, D.C., to head the Park Service's newly created Research and Education Unit. Thus was the American nature ranger born and, with him (and later her), the interpretive methods—nature loops, historical trails, guided trips, wildflower displays, wildlife exhibits, campfire lectures, museums, and informative ranger stations—that have greatly enriched this country's parks system.[153]

At the same time that Goethe was underwriting federal naturalists, he was also becoming increasingly vocal in congressional debates over immigration restriction. Eager to apply his catchphrase of reducing biological illiteracy to people as well as plants, in the early 1920s Goethe formed the Immigration Study Commission. Its aim was to investigate the influx of "low-powers" to California, especially Mexicans and South Europeans, whom Goethe alleged were endangering the state's pioneer heritage.[154] Goethe sent editorials to newspapers throughout the Southwest, warning of the scraggly masses from the south that were stealing jobs from Americans and contaminating the national "germ plasm."[155] Again and again Goethe sounded the alarm of race suicide. In his usual blunt style, his 1927 submission to the *Santa Cruz Sentinel* alleged, "The Anglo-Saxon birth rate is low. Peons multiply like rabbits. . . . If race strains remains absolutely pure, and if an old American-Nordic family averages 3 children while an incoming Mexican peon family averages 7, by the fifth generation, the proportion of white Nordics to Mexican peons descended from these two families would be as 243 to 16,807."[156] Speaking an uncensored idiom of raciology and regularly relying on numbers and calculations to demonstrate what eugenicists called "differential fecundity," Goethe pressed for passage of the Box Bill and the implementation of strict immigration caps on Mexicans as well as the "Zambo-negro group extending from the Caribbean through Brazil."[157] When Goethe was not publicly railing against Mexican immigrants, he was erecting racial boundaries in Sacramento through his real estate policies. In a 1926 letter to Stuart Ward, who also belonged to the Eugenics Committee of the Commonwealth Club of California, Goethe remarked that since the Johnson-Reed Immigration Act had gone into effect, he was making fewer sales to eastern and southern Europeans. Appearing in their stead, however, were Mexicans, whom he shunned; because of their inferior intelligence, troublesomeness, and delinquency, he "instructed [his] brokers to make no more sales to them."[158]

Through the Immigration Study Commission, the Eugenics Section of the Commonwealth Club of California, regular monthly checks to immigration restriction leagues, and a great deal of letter writing, by the 1920s Goethe had situated himself as a magnet in American eugenics. He was a member of key organizations and corresponded with Jordan, whom he had first met aboard a train in Japan in 1911, Davenport, Terman, Holmes, Laughlin, Paul Popenoe, Ezra Gosney, and Ellsworth Huntington, among others.[159] His commitment to eugenics deepened over the ensuing years. In addition to belonging to the AES and the Human Betterment Foundation and sitting on the board of the American Institute of Family Relations, in 1935 and 1936 Goethe acted as president of the Eugenics Research Association, which was affiliated with the Eugenics Record Office.[160] In his 1936 presidential address, Goethe praised America's immigration and sterilization laws, likening them to related legislation in Germany, whose sterilization program seemed to him to be "administered wisely, and without racial cruelty."[161] The subsequent year, Goethe expounded on one of the themes highlighted in his eugenic pamphlets, the extinction of the Inca high castes, forewarning against such an agonizing imperial collapse in the United States. To avoid a "similar, even though longer-drawn out destruction of our high-powered," he espoused tighter immigration control, especially along the southern border, and applauded the Nordic nations that were sterilizing the "markedly social inadequate, such as those insane, blind, criminal by inheritance."[162]

Despite the existence of dynamic eugenics groups in California in the 1930s, Goethe was not satisfied with the fight against "biological illiteracy" in Sacramento and environs. Thus, in 1933, he and Eugene H. Pitts, a Sacramento physician who was also a member of the Eugenics Research Association, cofounded the ESNC, with the stated goal of promoting "positive" eugenics.[163] Although Pitts served as president and delivered radio lectures on behalf of the society during its formative stage, by the 1940s the ESNC had become wholly Goethe's pet project and was headquartered at his office in the Capital National Bank building.[164] For approximately twenty years, the ESNC broadcasted its existence through the dissemination of nearly one hundred imaginative, disturbing, and bizarre pamphlets, almost all of which were written by Goethe and expressed his unique eugenic vision. In these pocket-size booklets, Goethe merged mystical stories of superior species, such as the egret—the ESNC's mascot and symbol of the "near-extinct's comeback"—with clamors for population and family planning, tirades against ethnic and racial groups, and exalted tales of magnificent and robust ancient civilizations.[165] Goethe estimated that he spent close to $1 million producing and distributing his pamphlets, which he was proud to send, along with hundreds of books and journals, to individuals and libraries across the country.[166] In an oral history interview conducted two months before his death, Goethe stated that one of the reasons for so many pamphlets was to ensure a continuous supply for librarians, key figures in the quest to "reduce biological illiteracy."[167]

Nature conservation, immigration restriction, and better breeding continued to dominate Goethe's agenda in the postwar era, and after

Mimi's unexpected death he threw himself deeply into writing, churning out six books between 1946 and 1955.[168] In the positively reviewed *War Profits and Better Babies,* Goethe linked his fascination with urban planning and fertility to a glowing endorsement of the Ungemach Gardens in Strasburg, France.[169] This eugenic family experiment was designed in the 1920s, financed with profits the French had garnered during World War II, and consisted of 120 houses available only to "young married couples in good health, desiring to have children and raise them under favorable conditions of hygiene and morality."[170] Two year later, Goethe published *Geogardening,* a tract with ninety-one vignettes about the nurturing of plants ranging from narcissus to oleander to fuchsias, aimed at raising public awareness of the linkages between nature and eugenics.[171] In addition to his pamphlets and books, Goethe wrote dozens of letters each month to librarians, educators, conservationists, biologists, and legislators. In the 1950s, for example, he wrote to select congressmen urging that the Walter-McCarran and subsequent immigration acts retain national origins quotas. He received replies from senators including Robert F. Kennedy, Richard Nixon, Barry Goldwater, and Strom Thurmond, who told Goethe that he appreciated his comments and concurred with his opinion: "I am also opposed to opening up our immigration flood gates."[172]

Starting in the late 1940s, Goethe, often in remembrance of his "sweetheart" and their companionship (which he regularly referred to as "we-two" and "us-two"), turned his attention to memorial redwood groves, vowing to bankroll several through the Save-the-Redwoods League in the coming years and in his will.[173] Most important, he envisioned and paid for the Mary Glide Goethe Grove and the Jedediah Smith Grove.[174] The former had originally been commissioned for Mary's mother and nephew, but after his beloved was gone Charles opted to dedicate it solely to her.[175] In 1952, it was situated in a 160-acre plot in the Prairie Creek Redwoods.[176] The Jedediah Smith Grove, located in Mill Creek State Redwoods Park in Del Norte County, represented Goethe's love of California history, place-naming, and nature parables. According to Goethe, while on a hiking expedition that passed by the Smith River (named for Jedediah in 1851), he and Mimi became intrigued with the mountain man of "superhuman courage" who had trekked through the American West and Northern California in the 1820s.[177] For Goethe, Smith was the quintessential white pioneer—a fur trapper, botanist, and nature aficionado—whose death in a Comanche raid had earned him near martyrdom status.[178] In the late 1940s, Goethe suggested to Aubrey Drury, the president of the Save-the-Redwoods League (and Newton's brother), that a grove commemorate this "great pathfinder and explorer, who was the first white man to cross the Sierra Nevada."[179] Goethe wrote the epigraph for the plaque, which was replicated almost verbatim and attached to the smooth face of a boulder surrounded by ferns and oxalis that he and a park superintendent had personally chosen.[180] To this day it reads: "To Jedediah Smith, referred to as 'Bible-Toter,' first white man to cross from the Mississippi to the Pacific, thus starting the train of events which made California the 31st star in our flag. This Grove on the Smith River (which he discovered in 1828) dedicated to his memory by Mr. and Mrs. C.M. Goethe of Sacramento and by the State of California."[181] About ten years after the installation of the plaque, Aubrey Drury assured his friend that "indeed Jed Smith [has been] rescued from oblivion."[182] Through this act of place-naming Goethe literally wrote history onto nature and naturalized a particular rendition of history, memorializing the story of a vacant land, pregnant with promise, discovered, civilized, and ushered into the present by white pioneer stock on whose perpetuation California now depended.[183] Goethe also facilitated the founding of the Luther Burbank Grove and was the primary donor to the Drury Brothers Grove, which adjoined his wife's in the Prairie Creek Redwoods.[184]

In March 1961, Goethe's name was similarly etched in bronze when CSUS unveiled the C.M. Goethe Arboretum. Comprising seven acres on the fringe of the campus, the arboretum was established in 1959 as an outdoor laboratory for students in the biological sciences and to beautify the grounds.[185] It was administered by a society headed by Dr. Albert Delisle, one of the faculty members whose research on plant and animal evolution had been funded by Goethe.[186] In order to recognize Goethe's generosity, Guy West, CSUS's president, and Rodger Bishton, a close confidante who shared Goethe's faith in eugenics and had received a fellowship from him for a project on "gifted children," decided to imitate the tradition practiced at parks and museums across the Redwood Empire.[187] With assistance from the Save-the-Redwoods League, they acquired a "good size redwood log," about five feet in diameter, cut from a 602-year-old Mendocino county tree, for a dedicatory marker.[188]

On the day the arboretum was officially dedicated, high-level administrators, faculty, and Sacramentans took part in the ceremony, reading notes of congratulation (figure 13). Dr. William J. Van Der Berg, chairman of the college advisory board, lauded Goethe's eugenic efforts "to

FIGURE 13. Dedication of Charles M. Goethe Arboretum at California State University, Sacramento, March 25, 1961. Pictured in front of a 602-year-old redwood round, found in Mendocino County, are (from left) Warner L. Marsh, president of the C.M. Goethe Arboretum Society, and Dr. William J. Van Den Berg and Guy A. West, chair and president respectively of California State University, Sacramento. Photo from Charles M. Goethe Papers, courtesy of the Department of Special Collections and University Archives, California State University, Sacramento.

increase the number of sound minds and bodies, and cut the chain of defective humans who crowd our institutions."[189] If you visit the arboretum today, below the round you will find a bronze tablet, which reads: "ERECTED IN HONOR OF CHARLES M. GOETHE GOOD FRIEND OF MAN AND NATURE AND PRESERVER OF THE BEST IN BOTH THROUGH GENEROUS CONTRIBUTIONS OF HIS TIME, HIS TALENTS, AND MATERIAL RESOURCES."[190] Below the round sits a time line, "A Sierran Redwood's Reflections on the Second Millennium," which lists about fifty salient events in the making of the modern world (figure 14). It begins at the center with the Viking Leif Ericsson's arrival in America via Nova Scotia, followed by, just to mention a few, the First and Second Crusades, the publication of *The Canterbury Tales,* Galileo's scientific discoveries, Malthus's *Essay on the Principle of Population,* the opening of the Suez Canal, the building of the Eiffel Tower, World War I, the outlawing of the Communist Party in the United States, the first human heart transplant, and the landing of man on the moon. The last two entries are

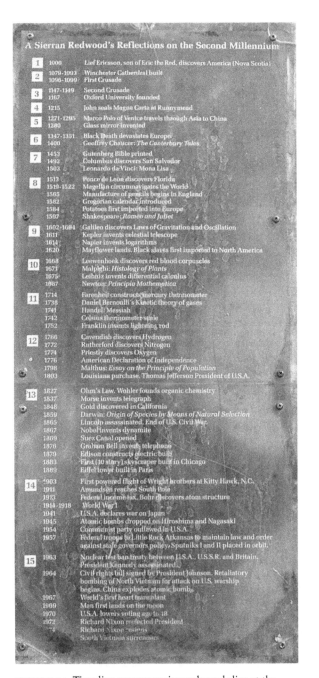

FIGURE 14. Time line accompanying redwood slice at the Charles M. Goethe Arboretum. Photo courtesy of Andrew Stern.

1974 and 1975, Nixon's resignation and the fall of South Vietnam, respectively, indicating an origins story that tapered off less than a decade after Goethe's death, as the university's commitment to the arboretum dissipated.[191]

Once Goethe's will was executed, it became clear that his engagement with eugenic projects would continue into the next century. He had carefully planned his bequest to a mix of individuals and civic, scientific, and environmental groups, many focused exclusively on eugenics or human genetics.[192] For example, Goethe gave a little over $25,000 each to the American Genetic Association, the American Institute of Family Relations, the Association for Voluntary Sterilization, and the Population Reference Bureau.[193] Goethe was "generous beyond words" to the Save-the-Redwoods League, which received more than $80,000 in liquid assets and an interest-bearing endowment.[194] He also bequeathed substantial monies to the Dight Institute at the University of Minnesota, one of the country's first genetic counseling centers.[195] However, Goethe reserved his biggest prize, more than $650,000, for CSUS, which had already benefited from multiple donations. There were disbursements to sustain the arboretum, produce a nature study manual, support the research of certain professors, such as Bishton, and fund students and projects in biology, eugenics, and population genetics.[196] CSUS also became the repository for Goethe's library and "letters and documents related to biology, eugenics and history" (much of which later disappeared under clouded circumstances), and the proprietor of his Julia Morgan home on T Street, which Goethe requested be turned into "a recreation center for children and the aged, for a branch library and for a health museum, for a eugenics museum and a children's museum or kindred purposes."[197]

Goethe was famous when he died. At an extravaganza for his ninetieth birthday in 1965, Lyndon B. Johnson called Goethe "an American whose life has been so richly dedicated to the service of humanity," accolades repeated by the likes of the Supreme Court chief justice Earl Warren, the secretary of the Interior Stewart Udall, and the National Park Service director George B. Hartzog Jr. as well as the presidents of the Nature Conservancy and the Audubon Society.[198] Goethe's loyal comrade Bishton, who arranged the event, prepared an elegantly bound program, profiling his mentor as a man devoted to human welfare, an inquisitive scientist, a conservationist, an educator, a friend of youth, and a church and civic leader, who had presciently grasped "long before most physicians . . . the relation of genetics to disease prevention."[199]

Hundreds gave to the Goethe gift fund, and even more sent words of appreciation.

Even with so many friends in high places, Goethe realized that many saw his views as extreme. For instance in the 1940s, Carey McWilliams, writing in *The Nation,* publicly denounced Goethe as the bigoted originator of the virulently anti-Japanese Home Front Commandos.[200] And in 1949, during a period when many American eugenicists were fighting marginalization, Maurice A. Bigelow, executive secretary of the AES, griped to Popenoe about Goethe's pamphlets. Granting that "much of his pamphlet is interesting reading if you read it as you would the Readers Digest," he nonetheless asserted that many of Goethe's vignettes "had no connection to eugenics," were causing confusion and, because of their "wide-spread distribution," were "much more dangerous than the Eugenics Publishing Company of New York."[201] Goethe often grumbled about censorship and alleged that too many environmentalists had been co-opted by "hyphenates," and "for selfish reasons, were advocating world hybridization."[202] If Goethe had been a magnet of American eugenics in the 1920s and 1930s, by the midcentury he was beginning to repel. Nevertheless, until his dying day, it seems, Goethe had many sincere fans, although the possibility of being named in his will probably meant that some acquaintances treated him covetously with esteem if not obsequiousness.

For many of the European Americans who migrated to the Pacific West starting in the late nineteenth century, to colonize California was to lay stake to its landscapes, through manipulation of the soil, the revealing and preservation of wilderness, and the construction of parks and playgrounds. The quest to establish a new social order was premised on assumptions about the naturalness of male authority and the innate superiority of certain classes of species over others. Fears of extinction could simultaneously pertain to redwoods and Anglo-Saxon pioneers: both needed shielding and safeguarding and awaited biological regeneration based on the principles of scientific and hereditarian management. Enamored of California's brilliant topography and fascinating ecology, eugenicists such as Jordan, Merriam, and Goethe sought to remake their chosen state from the ground up. They inscribed their names and priorities onto California's geography and at the same time invented and legitimized certain versions of the Golden State's historical memory, lending their expert knowledge, professional authority, and financial resources. Their presence is apparent on plaques and maps, in forest groves and refuges, atop mountains, and among the pantheons of founders and firsts that circulate in textbooks and brochures.

There was no one way that eugenicists shaped California's landscapes. As August Vollmer illustrates, xenophobia was not a requirement for the melding of hereditarian convictions and parks advocacy. However, there is no denying that the apparition of eugenics at the heart of American environmentalism has never been completely laid to rest and that it still revisits periodically during debates over urban sprawl, immigration, and overpopulation. Probably tree sitters who spend months if not years living in old-growth redwoods to spare them from chainsaws and writing impassioned poetry about the wisdom of the sequoia would be disconcerted if not aghast to learn that, close to a century later, their epiphanies closely echo those of the founders' trio. And what about naturalist rangers? In 1964 Newton Drury, the director of the National Park Service in the 1940s, impressed on an interviewer, "I don't think you can minimize the importance of C.M. Goethe in this whole program of nature conservation. There's no question that he had a great effect on Stephen Mather and Madison Grant and some of the pioneers, both in the formation of the National Park Service and of the Save-the-Redwoods League."[203] Yet for Goethe strict immigration quotas, involuntary sterilization, population planning, Nordic domination, and nature conservation were one and the same; he brazenly conflated them through analogies that would make most contemporary biologists shudder. In the late 1940s, he pondered: "Perhaps the greatest national gains from a really completed National Park system interlocks [sic] with State Parks' chains, can be expected in the accelerated building of a eugenically-better nation. This would include gradual elimination of imbeciles, those insane through inheritance, carriers of congenital diseases, such as Huntington's chorea, haemophilia. This would further reverse the tragic decline of the leadership type's birthrate."[204] Very few, if any, other eugenicists or philanthropists for that matter would ever so cavalierly connect the outbreeding of bad genes to wilderness management. In analyzing Goethe's legacy, it is tempting to compartmentalize the good, the bad, and the ugly. However, only exploring his life on its own inimitable terms can provide insight into the alliance between eugenics and environmentalism in twentieth-century California.

CHAPTER 6

Centering Eugenics on the Family

In 1945, Mr. and Mrs. C came to the offices of the American Institute of Family Relations (AIFR), located not far from central Hollywood on Sunset Boulevard. The couple and their two young daughters had recently moved to Southern California from Indianapolis and were on the verge of divorce. Mrs. C had confessed to her husband that she had an unconsummated infatuation with a male coworker, a "sinful" relationship for which she was wracked with guilt. Given their circumstances, Mr. and Mrs. C decided to seek marital counseling at the AIFR, which had been offering such services for fifteen years. Mrs. C explained to the counselor that she didn't "like the feeling of being just" a wife whose "whole being [was] submerged in [her] home life or children."[1] She added that she felt "something [was] eating away at [her] all the time," that her husband no longer sexually excited her and that she did not respect or admire him. Mrs. C wanted to avoid divorce, however, in order to "keep the home together because of the children."[2] For his part, Mr. C was happy with his new job in Los Angeles and did not want the marriage to end despite his wife's transgressions.

After an initial intake session, for which Mrs. C wrote an autobiographical statement, the AIFR counselor administered the Johnson Temperament Analysis Test (JTA), an instrument designed scientifically to measure temperament, which was defined as a principally innate although complex human characteristic. Consisting of 182 questions, the JTA assessed overall personality and compatibility on the basis of nine oppositional pairs: Nervous-Composed, Depressive–Gay Hearted, Active-Quiet, Cordial-Cold, Sympathetic–"Hard Boiled," Subjective-Objective, Aggressive-Submissive, Critical-Appreciative, and Self-Mastery–Impulsive.[3] The results were then plotted along a spectrum with four gradations—white, light gray, medium gray, and dark gray—that indicated, respectively, "improvement urgent," "improvement desirable," "acceptable," and "excellent." The test relied on several modes of statistical and graphical representation, including numbers and averages, percentiles and deviation zones, and lines (blue for women, red for men) that expressed each individual's itemized profile.

While Mr. C's scores revealed a generally balanced temperament punctuated only by exaggerated aggressiveness (ninety-fifth percentile on the Aggressive-Submissive axis), Mrs. C's results were much more troubling. Scoring above the ninety-fifth percentile in nervousness and subjectivity (improvement urgent) and below the fifteenth percentile in coldness and impulsivity (improvement desirable), Mrs. C was diagnosed with "masculine protest." The counselor assigned to Mrs. C was concerned that her client was becoming "more and more resentful of spending her day in housework" and noted that her "heart [was] not in it."[4] To encourage her to accept homemaking as a respectable profession on which her family depended, Mrs. C was given *What Every Woman Wants* and *Emotional Questions,* just two of the AIFR's dozens of pamphlets devoted to marriage, sexuality, and gender norms.

One month later, Mrs. C returned to the AIFR. This time, she explained how much she wanted her husband, who ignored her and spent his evenings and weekends listening to the radio and smoking cigarettes, to change. The counselor, however, "worked with her from the point of view that we couldn't do anything with the husband at the moment, it was his problem, but we could do a lot toward changing her attitude to build up something constructive." When asked to write up a list of actions that she could take to better the marriage, Mrs. C came up with seven ideas, including devoting more time to her husband in the morning, trying to be "more submissive," overlooking "a lot of the little things that irritate me," taking "more interest in the house," and being more entertaining and fun-loving when they were out on the town.[5] The counselor also recommended that Mrs. C find a satisfying "ego outlet," such as volunteering at a local church or taking up a recreational hobby.

The JTA, in conjunction with three marital counseling sessions, had determined that Mrs. C needed to confront her "masculine protest" through a self-willed readjustment to wifehood and a deliberate embrace of femininity. Although we do not know what happened to Mrs. C, if she became more "feminine," identified an "ego outlet," or perhaps even ended up leaving her husband, we do know that between 1930 and 1970 thousands of people were similarly advised at the AIFR and that starting in 1941, when Roswell H. Johnson unveiled his first prototype, the JTA became the centerpiece of the institute's marriage counseling and personality evaluation. It was one of an expanding battery of tests that stretched psychometrics beyond intelligence into the domains of aptitude, personality, and vocation.[6] Its underlying logic reflected and fostered the postwar revision of eugenics, as the door of strict hereditarianism opened up enough to let in various psychogenic and psychoanalytic explanations of human development and deviance.

BIOTYPES AND POPULATIONS

By the 1940s, as the cultural anthropology espoused by Margaret Mead, Ruth Benedict, Franz Boas, and others began to predominate in many intellectual arenas and as the public slowly became aware of the brutality of the Final Solution, many eugenicists revamped their thinking. They began consciously to distance themselves from overt hierarchies and rankings, and particularly to reject as simplistic and anachronistic those predicated on race or class. As Frederick Osborn, the president of the American Eugenics Society (AES), wrote in 1946, "The ten years, 1930 to 1940, marked a major change in eugenic thinking. Before 1930 eugenics had a racial and social class bias." Now he and his colleagues contended that the differences between individuals far outweighed "any differences which might be discovered between the averages of the larger racial or social groups."[7]

In addition, by this time most eugenicists had conceded that earlier attempts to stamp out hereditary traits defined as recessive or latent, including alcoholism, immorality, and the catchall of feeblemindedness, had been proven futile by the Hardy-Weinberg equilibrium principle, which demonstrated that the overwhelming tendency of gene frequencies and ratios was to remain constant from one generation to the next. Hence, targeted interventions, such as sterilization, could not breed out defects; even if viable, these techniques would show results only after thousands of years of regulated procreation.[8] Increasingly and sometimes begrudgingly, eugenicists traded in "unit characters" for polygenic inheritance and genetic predispositions. Accompanying this realignment was a heightened interest in the manipulation and management of human heredity through population control. Against the backdrop of postwar internationalism, the hardening of geopolitical boundaries, and rising fears of nuclear annihilation, eugenicists forged relationships with organizations such as the Population Council, the Population Reference Bureau, and Planned Parenthood. Many eugenicists viewed population control as a vehicle for modernization, the introduction of liberal democracy, and, if properly pursued, world peace.[9] As Guy Irving Burch, the director of the Population Reference Bureau and the AES, explained in 1945, "Uncontrolled human reproduction not only favors the survival and the multiplication of the least gifted members of society; it menaces and in the long run will destroy human liberties and any chance for a world at peace."[10] Under the banner of population control, eugenicists established birth control clinics, distributed devices such as foams, jellies, and the IUD, and set up oral contraceptive trials in countries and colonies, including India and Puerto Rico, where they forged what were often tenuous and fraught alliances with a heterogeneous mix of feminists, nationalists, and modernist reformers.[11]

Rather than thoroughly annul earlier presumptions about racial capacities and endowments, however, this shift refocused eugenicists' scales of analysis in two countervailing yet corresponding directions: at once outward toward a global framework and inward toward the family and its constituent parts. Race was no longer understood as a singular trait or a person's blood, but rather in terms of aggregated yet somewhat fluid population subdivisions that had been constituted through fairly endogenous patterns of language, geography, and interbreeding.[12] Now, guided more by Malthus than Mendel, many eugenicists tended to blame racialized population subdivisions, principally those in the Third World, for resource depletion, skyrocketing fertility, and environmental degradation; more and more, the advocacy of sterilization was linked to the goal of population reduction, rather than to a recessive carrier rationale.[13]

In keeping with this transformation, one of the most salient developments in postwar eugenics was the advent of biotypology, which sought to classify humans scientifically as composite organisms beyond the strictures of pure races. Replacing categorical pyramids with gradated spectrums, biotypologists used an array of instruments, such as spirometers, stethoscopes, Rorschach inkblots, blood sampling kits, ergographs, dream analysis, and personality and temperament tests, to measure human capacities and variations.[14] Starting in the 1930s, scientists who remained committed to the primacy of heredity but wanted to reenvision human differentiation and allow greater latitude for psychological, hormonal, and environmental factors were attracted to biotypology and constitutional holism. This was most definitely the case at the AIFR, where counselors regularly labeled clients as biotypes—endomorphs/ectomorphs, hypokinetic/hyperkinetic, and extroverted/introverted—in order to treat their marital and sexual problems. As was the case with population subdivisions, racial and evolutionary conceits lingered, though often submerged, sometimes masquerading as gender and sexual maladjustment.[15]

Some scholars have suggested that this should be seen as a transition from "negative" to "positive" or from "mainline" to "reform" eugenics.[16] Such interpretations, however, fail to capture many aspects of better breeding during the postwar period. First, "negative" practices—such as marriage restrictions, immigration quotas, and compulsory sterilizations—did not disappear during this period. Although rarely enforced in some states, laws forbidding interracial unions were not overturned on the federal level until *Loving v. Virginia* in 1967, national origins quotas were not replaced with the family reunification model until the Hart-Celler Act of 1965, and sterilization statutes were not repealed by state legislatures until the 1970s and 1980s. By the time that anthropologists and geneticists had begun to refute many aspects of "negative" eugenics, its attendant measures had been naturalized into federal, state, and even municipal institutions and were underpinning postwar norms of conformity. Furthermore, sterilization operations peaked nationwide from the late 1930s to the early 1940s and in some states, such as North Carolina and Virginia, escalated into the 1950s and 1960s.[17] Thus "positive" eugenics, which concentrated on encouraging those deemed fit to reproduce in higher numbers, worked in tandem with the existing "negative" eugenics of medicalized exclusions. Second, as they gravitated toward family planning and biotypology, "reform" eugenicists often began to locate the marrow of human differentiation not in racial distinctions, as previously understood, but in sex and gender. This was a Faustian transposition: as race moved progressively into the terrain of culture, sex and gender in turn became more tightly wedded to biology. From this perspective, "reform" eugenics retained and even extended the rigidity of "mainline" eugenics. To a great extent, the racism of the 1920s was rearticulated into the sexism of the 1950s. Moreover, for many American eugenicists this reorientation was linked to a diminishing interest in the abnormal and a pronounced interest in those considered normal and fit, mainly the white middle class, whose numbers increased in urban and suburban areas of the country after World War II.[18]

The AIFR and its director, Paul Popenoe, exemplified and propelled these changes, promoting a family-centric eugenics that rested on and demanded sex and gender uniformity. For Popenoe the male-female difference transcended all others and was the "greatest that can exist between two normal human beings."[19] It was a distinction based on evolution, nature, and genetics that was essential to the interconnected health and survival of the family, the nation, and Western civilization, and it had to be preserved at all costs in modern society, where it was under assault from forces of hedonism, commercialism, and decadence. By including a broad range of characteristics under the labels of masculinity and femininity and then considering their interactions, largely through the biotypological binary of extroversion-introversion, Popenoe engendered a layered eugenics, one that paid heed to psychogenic, physiological, polygenic, and behavioral variables.

Popenoe's more moderate eugenics was in tune with the sexual liberalism of the Cold War and, as such, contained divergent tendencies that would come into open conflict in the late 1960s. By World War II, the middle classes had greater access to contraception, marriage was idealized as a mutual emotional and sexual partnership, and women's erotic pleasure had become a valid topic for discussion in many quarters. These developments were circumscribed, however, by the tyranny of sex-gender norms, particularly the double standard expected of women and deep-seated paranoia about homosexuality and sexual deviance.[20] Some feminist historians have anchored the Cold War cult of male expertise and the prominence of marriage and sex counseling to Freudian pathologies of "penis envy" and "frigidity."[21] Although sexual liberalism owed a great debt to Freud and his American protégés, biological determinism affected the postwar sex-gender system in significant yet overlooked ways. The veneration of maternity and parenthood and the pronatalism advocated by Popenoe and his contemporaries set the stage for the "baby boom," which lasted from 1946 to 1964.[22] Moreover, marital counseling, which affected the lives of thousands of women and men in North America and was a bête noire of second-wave feminism, became a household fixture largely because of Popenoe's efforts to make a rather rudimentary version of sex biology integral to mating, marriage, and procreation.

FROM DATES TO MARRIAGE

The AIFR represented the culmination of Popenoe's career as a plant breeder, social hygienist, and eugenicist and was an enterprise that dominated his adult life. In the early 1900s, when Popenoe was a teenager, his father moved the family from Topeka to Santa Monica to start West India Gardens, a subtropical nursery that supposedly introduced the profitable "fuerte avocado" to California.[23] Once the family was settled, Popenoe enrolled in Occidental College, and two years later, with the encouragement of several professors, he transferred to Stanford University, where he studied under David Starr Jordan. This apprenticeship with California's foremost eugenicist was formative for Popenoe, who wrote a term paper for his mentor on the relationship between heredity and alcoholism that helped crystallize his belief in the authority of Mendelian, not Lamarckian, theories of genetic transmission.[24]

As with many of his contemporaries, Popenoe's path to eugenics involved a sustained engagement with plant breeding.[25] Upon returning to the Southland from Palo Alto in 1908, Popenoe, a skilled writer, was hired by the *Pasadena Star,* where he was promoted up the ranks from cub to managing reporter. In 1911 the city of Pasadena sent Popenoe to Europe to conduct a study of government, politics, and economic conditions. After gathering data on a dozen cities including London, Paris, Antwerp, and Berlin, Popenoe continued his journey to North Africa and the Middle East in order to fulfill his father's request to return with some promising date palms for cultivation. The following spring, Popenoe deposited one thousand carefully handpicked offshoots of Algerian Deglet Noors in Thermal, a small town in the Coachella Valley, supplying some of the seeds for the large-scale date industry that would flourish in the area now known as Palm Springs.[26] With this modest addition to the assorted species being grown by West India Gardens, Popenoe began his fascination with the origins, genetics, and transplantation of Arabian date palms. Several months later he was in the Persian Gulf searching for varieties likely to thrive in the arid American West and within short order had loaded a barge, this time with more than fifteen thousand specimens. While closely monitoring the slow progress of his offshoots across the Atlantic to the port of Galveston, from which they would be transported overland to California, Popenoe wrote *Date Growing in the Old World and the New,* in which he examined the selection, pollination, and harvesting of dates.[27] This project led him to the Washington, D.C., headquarters of the Bureau of Plant Industry to consult with David Fairchild, the son-in-law of Alexander Graham Bell and an influential member of the American Breeders' Association (ABA), then the hub of America's nascent eugenics movement.

Impressed with the young Popenoe, Fairchild asked him to become the editor of the ABA's journal and in that capacity to recast and extend its focus from plants and livestock to people and from horticulture and animal husbandry to eugenics. As Popenoe explained in a letter to his parents, "The idea is to show that plants and animals obey the same laws of heredity, and that these laws are the ones which govern Homo Sapiens, as well."[28] Popenoe accepted the post, and his proposed title for the ABA's updated publication, the *Journal of Heredity*, was chosen over two alternatives (*Breeding and Eugenics* and *Heredity and Breeding*). With Popenoe in charge, the *Journal of Heredity* began to print articles on the topics that preoccupied most eugenicists of the day: feeblemindedness, the inferior stock of immigrants, the need for marriage and sterilization laws, and the transmission of undesirable traits (such as polydactylism or criminality) down the family line according to Mendelian ratios. From 1914 to 1917, Popenoe was the editor of the *Journal of Heredity*. He maintained his interest in fruit horticulture and was particularly intrigued by the taxonomy and evolution of the date palm.[29] This was a passion that he shared with his brother, Wilson, with whom he had traveled in the Middle East and who also worked for Fairchild, as an agricultural explorer stationed mainly in the South American tropics.[30] At the same time, Popenoe was becoming immersed in the burgeoning movement of race betterment. Besides fraternizing with Fairchild's circle and lecturing on human heredity to civic groups such as the YMCA, Popenoe began to befriend prominent American eugenicists. In 1914, for instance, he attended the inaugural conference of the Race Betterment Foundation, held in Battle Creek, Michigan, under the auspices of John Harvey Kellogg, and visited the Eugenics Record Office (ERO) in Cold Spring Harbor, New York, where he toured the facilities and lunched with its superintendent, Harry H. Laughlin.[31] In the fall of that year, Kellogg asked Popenoe to collect photos for the Second National Race Betterment Conference, scheduled to take place in San Francisco at the Panama-Pacific International Exposition the following summer.[32] In addition to contributing to the race betterment exhibit, Popenoe delivered a paper at the world's fair titled "Natural Selection in Man," which laid out his hard-line hereditarianism and emphasized the importance of eliminating the unfit lest they defile the "germ plasm" and drain precious financial resources.[33] In 1918, Popenoe and his steadfast collaborator Roswell Johnson expounded on these ideas and underscored the need for higher birthrates among the fit in *Applied Eugenics,* an immensely popular text that the duo updated for a second edition in 1933.[34]

Shortly after the United States entered World War I, Popenoe left the *Journal of Heredity* for the military, recruited by the American Social Hygiene Association (ASHA) and the Army Sanitary Corps to serve as a first lieutenant. During his absence, his younger brother Herbert, who had come to eugenics by way of psychology and statistics, took his place at the *Journal of Heredity.*[35] For twelve months, Popenoe patrolled the US-Mexican border for venereal diseases, shutting down red-light districts, saloons, and gambling houses and prosecuting offenders under the National Defense Act.[36] At the war's conclusion, he moved to New York City to act as ASHA's executive secretary.[37] It was there that Popenoe, now thirty-two, met and married Betty Lee Stankovitch, a dancer and nursery school teacher thirteen years his junior. Despite a solid future at ASHA and various job prospects on the East Coast, Popenoe could not resist the lure of California. Eager to return to the land of his youth and try his hand at date palm cultivation, in the summer of 1920 Popenoe resigned from his position and by September of that year was back in Coachella, this time accompanied by Betty.[38] Popenoe romanticized California, and above all the inland valley, where he and his betrothed could enjoy a simple and rigorous "outdoor" life. In letters he penned to "the sweet-lipped daughter of the desert, the incomparable companion of the date-palms, the lovely Lady Betty," while preparing for their cross-country relocation, Popenoe described the beauty of the landscape—its snow-capped mountains, fields of yellow flowers, luscious orange groves, and palo verde trees.[39] He envisioned a desert paradise where he and Betty could remake themselves and commune with one another: "You and I must have a complete change of environment, where we can live primarily in each other."[40]

Once in Coachella, the couple began married life in a shack that Popenoe had constructed and for their honeymoon traversed the northern rim of the desert on horseback, toting their camping gear in saddle packs.[41] Relying on his father's agricultural networks and guided by the lucrative example of West India Gardens, Popenoe purchased a ranch, conveniently situated across the road from a preexisting date-packing house, which boasted eighty acres, six wells, and three pumping stations. Within several years, he was producing a half million dates annually, as well as Malaga grapes and Bermuda onions.[42] According to a remembrance written by one of Popenoe's four sons, David, the move to California was not restorative but "wrenching" for Betty, who suffered from the "social isolation, the intense heat, the inadequate housing, the sandstorms, the scorpions, and the need to carry a pistol to kill rattlesnakes."[43]

As his crops yielded fruit, Popenoe read and wrote voraciously about human heredity. Perhaps motivated by the tensions that he and Betty confronted as newlyweds in Coachella, by 1926 Popenoe had published three books related to the family, reproduction, and marriage, all three of which adumbrated the mission of the AIFR.[44] Nor did he lose contact with the eugenicists he had met in the 1910s. In 1924 Popenoe even entertained the possibility of spending half the year at the Battle Creek Sanitarium to assist Kellogg with projects for the Race Betterment Foundation.[45] Although this never transpired, two years later Ezra S. Gosney, the wealthy Pasadena philanthropist and citrus grower, asked Popenoe to help him set up a eugenics organization in Southern California. Popenoe responded by drafting a blueprint for a "race-hygiene foundation," which, with added input from Laughlin, resulted in the formation of the Human Betterment Foundation (HBF). As an initial venture, Popenoe and Gosney carried out a systematic inquiry into the results of California's sterilization law. This legislation, initially passed in 1909, affected patients in state institutions, more than twenty thousand of whom were sterilized between 1909 and 1979. Eager to augment the scope and ambit of this law, Popenoe traveled about the state gathering extensive data at each of California's hospitals about the benefits of reproductive surgery, eventually coauthoring *Sterilization for Human Betterment: A Summary of Results of 6,000 Operations in California, 1909–1929* and touting sterilization as a surgical solution for both patients and the general population.[46]

Galvanized by his sterilization investigation, Popenoe became the Southland's very own eugenic dynamo. In 1929 he was instrumental in establishing the Southern California Branch of the AES, which he hoped could serve as "an excellent vehicle for educational and legislative action, in cooperation with the existing eugenics section of the Commonwealth Club in San Francisco."[47] Its aims were to promote eugenic education on the elementary school, high school, and college levels, broaden the scope of the state's sterilization law, and sponsor "fitter families" contests.[48] After formal approval by the AES as a regional office, the branch was incorporated in November 1929. It convened gatherings at the University of Southern California and the Los Angeles

Public Library that brought together physicians, psychologists, and educators, many of whom held positions at local universities and colleges.[49] Until the 1940s this branch, renamed the California Division in 1935, organized monthly lectures and produced broadsheets with alerts and factoids about Mexican immigration, genetic diseases, premarital exams, sterilization policies, the activities of sister organizations abroad, and family and population planning.[50]

Despite the activities of the HBF, the California Division of the AES, and the Eugenics Section of the Commonwealth Club of California, Popenoe felt that one arena remained almost totally neglected: the propagation and nurturance of eugenic families and marriages. Not only were educational resources few and far between, but there were no centers for scientific and objective guidance. As Popenoe, ever the pragmatist, was fond of saying, "If your automobile broke down, you knew where to go for help," but if your marriage collapsed, there was almost nowhere to turn.[51] To rectify this situation, Popenoe decided to establish a clearinghouse "where anyone with a problem in family relations could go and get access to all of the existing information that would make for success."[52] On February 4, 1930, with Gosney's financial backing, Popenoe opened the institute, which he directed, with few interruptions, for more than forty years. The *Los Angeles Times* announced the founding of the AIFR on its cover page, notifying readers that it had "started operations with the idea in mind that a few cold, unadorned and scientific facts thrown out to those floundering in the sea of domestic difficulties may prevent many a shipwreck or rescue some of the perishing."[53] For Popenoe, Southern California, with its booming population and plentiful temptations, was the ideal home for the AIFR.[54] According to David Popenoe, it was unlikely that his father "would have taken up the profession of marriage counseling had he remained in the Midwest, away from 'the Hollywood scene' where the need for such counseling was constantly staring one in the face."[55] Indeed, Popenoe repeatedly expressed dismay over Hollywood's chronic culture of divorce, at several points offering advice and administering the JTA to some of the biggest female stars of the silver screen, such as Susan Hayward during her acrimonious divorce from Jess Barker.[56]

Popenoe modeled the AIFR on the clinics formed in Germany in the 1920s to assess the eugenic and mental fitness of potential spouses, stating that its intention was to "bring all the resources of modern science to the promotion of successful family life."[57] Like other marriage experts of the day, such as Ben Lindsey and Theodore H. Van Der Velde,

Popenoe championed "companionate marriage" and spoke frankly about female sexual desire, which he believed was central to harmonious childbearing unions. In contrast to other counselors, however, Popenoe placed heredity at the center of his marriage philosophy; it was the core from which concentric rings of human relations—psychological, medical, sociological, legal, and religious—radiated outward. Upon its founding, Popenoe declared that the institute was "the only place in the United States which deals with these questions of individual heredity as a business, and not casually or incidentally."[58] He defined heredity not as the total sum of the individual but as the inborn potentialities that delimited a person's baseline capacity. Popenoe taught AIFR counselors that genetic makeup was as hard to annihilate as gravity and that the only effective strategy was to "redirect or sidestep" undesirable traits.[59]

Popenoe envisioned the AIFR as a eugenic endeavor that would make Americans not "merely family-minded, but discriminatingly family-minded."[60] In the chapter on heredity in the institute's training manual, for example, Popenoe included a long section on the role of the marriage counselor, who was "in a particularly favorable position to give advice that will have eugenic value."[61] At the most basic level, creating eugenic families meant impeding the unfit, the feebleminded and grossly defective, from reproducing, primarily through sterilization, which Popenoe already supported through the HBF and his collaboration with the California Department of Institutions.[62] However, for the vast majority of Americans who were neither in state institutions nor subject to sterilization statutes, what was needed was sensible guidance about the suitability of marriage and procreation.[63] One of the AIFR's goals was to offer such direction, and the refrain usually repeated to its white middle-class clientele was to breed, ideally more than the replacement level of two children per couple. This responsibility of creating fit families fell squarely on women: "The wife who refuses to bear a child when health and eugenic considerations are favorable, and when her husband wants children, is refusing to meet a very important expectation in marriage."[64] Popenoe defined the AIFR's eugenic program as "humane, far-reaching, and constructive," warned counselors of the far-reaching social forces working against it, and declared, "Only a complete reorientation of American society along eugenic lines can prevent a catastrophe."[65]

The AIFR did not signify Popenoe's abandonment of "negative" for "positive" eugenics. While preparing to launch his syndicated column "Can This Marriage Be Saved?," for example, Popenoe was praising the virtues of sterilization, and his articles on the topic were being reprinted in the German journal *Archiv für Soziale Hygiene und Demographie*.[66] As he outlined in 1940, the institute's objective was to contribute "something to the spread of negative eugenics" even as it offered more to "positive eugenics than is to be had today from any other source."[67] Like his peers in the 1940s, Popenoe ceased to speak the discredited idiom of nativism and degenerationism and began, more and more, to communicate in the language of family planning, biotypology, psychology, and medical genetics. For example, although he cautioned against racial intermarriages because of possible "disharmony in the offspring" and "social handicaps," the topic received less than one page in the AIFR training manual.[68] Insofar as it privileged human heredity, the AIFR was a predecessor of the genetic counseling programs that appeared on the American landscape in the 1940s, the first two launched at the University of Michigan and the University of Minnesota. Marriage and genetic counselors alike relied on ERO-inspired pedigree charts to ascertain the probability that offspring might inherit a "deleterious trait" associated with autosomal recessive inheritance, frequently addressed queries related to interracial unions and child paternity, and took cues from the client-centered therapy of Carl Rogers.[69]

That Popenoe viewed the AIFR as partly a heredity clinic is demonstrated by his happily agreeing to become the forwarding address for marital queries sent to the ERO after its closure in 1940.[70] Popenoe also maintained a sizable file on genetic counseling, kept abreast of procedures at the University of Minnesota's Dight Institute, and in the mid-1950s corresponded with the AES about writing an essay on the role of heredity counseling in marriage advice.[71] Following World War II, however, the paths of the AIFR and genetic counseling veered apart, as the former moved more solidly into personality testing and family and sex psychology, while the latter became intermeshed with clinical genetics and attached to the laboratory, especially after the indicators for several chromosomal and metabolic disorders, such as Down syndrome and phenylketonuria (PKU), were identified.[72] Additionally, while genetic counselors ostensibly valued the autonomous decision making of their patients, the AIFR pursued a diametrically opposed strategy; its experts were in the business of doling out specific instructions that their clients were expected to follow.

Ultimately, the AIFR encompassed much more than a heredity clinic, employing myriad techniques to investigate and mold marriage, reproduction, and sexuality. Its diverse staff of medical and social science professionals contributed to the institute's comprehensive and flexible diagnostic approach, which could range from dispelling parents' fear that they might transmit epilepsy to their children to suggestions on handling intrusive in-laws.[73] Institute psychologists, for example, administered an array of tests to gauge gender comportment, emotional maturity, sexual attitudes, and extroversion-introversion.[74] AIFR physicians participated in client evaluation. Dr. John Vruwink, a gynecologist who also belonged to the HBF, screened women for diseases, with a keen eye out for syphilis, at onsite clinics. And social workers and statisticians used the latest demographic methods to track and weigh variables related to marriage, divorce, and sex relations.[75] With more than forty active personnel by the mid-1930s, the influence of the AIFR reverberated across Southern California's social services matrix, from the juvenile courts to women's groups such as the Friday Morning Club, the County Health Department, churches, hospitals, the police, and schools.[76] The institute's seminars, such as "Thinking about Marriage" and "Modern Marriage and the Modern Family," were aimed at local professionals, while its six- to twelve-month correspondence courses versed clergymen, high school principals, and leaders of youth groups in the basics of premarital and marital counseling.[77]

After two years of activity, Popenoe reported that the institute had aided scores of couples with the trials of family adjustment, inadequate finances, and child welfare, as well as "impotence, frigidity, homosexuality, and all sorts of worries growing out of sexual behavior."[78] Each year, more and more clients came through the AIFR's doors. Such was the momentum that Popenoe sold his ranch in 1934, and he and Betty moved to Altadena around the same time, so that he could devote undivided attention to the institute's daily management. During its inaugural decade, the AIFR's staff lectured in two hundred colleges and universities, advised thousands of clients, led nearly one hundred all-day conferences, and reached an estimated twenty million people through an ever-growing list of newspaper and magazine articles.[79] In 1941 alone, 2,763 people were seen at the institute's office while 3,695 corresponded with its counselors.[80] By this point, Popenoe and AIFR personnel were issuing a host of pamphlets with titles such as *Building Sex into Your Life,* publishing the monthly bulletin *Family Life,* and contributing regularly to health, social work, and religious journals.

RECONSTITUTING THE FAMILY

By the time the United States declared war on Japan, the AIFR was on firm footing, and its director, who could be saluted as Dr. Popenoe, thanks to an honorary degree from Occidental College, was solidifying his reputation as a national marriage expert. If the AIFR had acted as a salve for the spousal strife and high divorce and desertion rates that marked the Great Depression, then in Popenoe's opinion the possibilities after the war were unbounded.[81] Popenoe viewed the reincorporation of thousands of returning soldiers as an opportunity to bolster marriage, boost reproduction, and enforce strict gender norms. In *Be It Ever So Jumbled There's No Place Like Home,* a 1945 booklet distributed by the YMCA's Army and Navy Department, Popenoe unveiled a plan of action for sweethearts reuniting after Armistice Day whose deepest desire was a productive partnership, a prospect for which they were woefully unprepared. Popenoe told young Americans that to succeed marriage must be "organized, deliberately and intelligently," and toward that end he exhorted all couples to submit to a battery of temperament and personality tests to measure their compatibility.[82] More than the scientific management of matrimony was required, however; secure postwar marriages were contingent on the acceptance and embodiment of stark gender roles, or, in his words, "better sex differentiation, to use a biological term; that is, the man will be more masculine, the woman more feminine."[83] While men would have to realize that breadwinning alone was the route to confidence and prowess, women would need to direct their abilities into cooking, child rearing, and cleaning and to find wholesome "ego outlets." Above all, this implied the redomestication and deskilling of women, many of whom had come to relish the independence of working in the factory or office during wartime.

This was the message that awaited thousands of AIFR clients, composed preponderantly of white, middle-class migrants who had moved in droves to Southern California to fill white- and blue-collar jobs and purchase federally subsidized homes in sprawling suburban subdivisions.[84] They streamed into the AIFR in record numbers; by the 1950s the institute was open for business from 9:00 a.m. to 9:00 p.m., Monday through Saturday, and its average caseload was 15,000 one-hour consultations per year or about 350 per week.[85] In 1954 alone, AIFR counselors gave close to 14,000 consultations to 4,197 individual clients.[86] For the multitude that, for geographical reasons, were unable to seek assistance in person, the institute offered correspondence counseling for a fee of fifteen to twenty-five dollars. Popenoe, who was already being heard on the radio waves, now became a television personality, initially alongside the AIFR's counseling director, Roswell Johnson, in a weekly advice show, and then on *Divorce Hearing,* a forum where couples presented their disputes for resolution, and for a fourteen-year stretch on the much-loved *Art Linkletter's House Party*.[87] Americans were also exposed to Popenoe's creed in the film *Modern Marriage,* which was screened in three thousand theaters and which the institute helped to produce.[88]

If Popenoe is remembered today, it is probably for his newspaper and magazine series, which ran in North America continuously from the late 1940s to the early 1970s. In 1936, Popenoe started discussing the possibility of a syndicated feature with the National Newspaper Service, imagining something that would "cover the general field of the relations between the sexes both before and after marriage, bringing in relevant material from the fields of biology, sociology, and psychology; and including some heredity and eugenics (non-controversial phases) and some mental hygiene."[89] This project was postponed by the war, but in 1947 "Modern Marriage" debuted in the *St. Louis Dispatch* and was quickly picked up by the *Cincinnati Times Star,* the *Hollywood Citizen News,* and the *Indianapolis News,* and within months by dozens more. Under varying titles, this series ran until Popenoe bid an upbeat farewell to his readers in 1972.[90] In 1953, "Can this Marriage Be Saved?" commenced in *Ladies' Home Journal* and was met with much applause.[91] That same year Popenoe and Dorothy Cameron Disney, an editor at the *Journal,* coauthored a book compilation of these columns, which contained an introduction by Popenoe summarizing the history and aims of the AIFR and chapters with instructive vignettes about fixing rocky marriages.[92]

Letters poured in to the institute's mailbox from women and men across the United States and Canada who had listened to *Art Linkletter's House Party,* perused "Can This Marriage Be Saved?," or happened upon one of the AIFR's pamphlets. These ranged from perfunctory notes of thanks and requests for more information to lengthy confessions, often from those who had never before dared to share their secrets of adultery, transvestism, sibling incest, and children born out of wedlock. Most readers were delighted with Popenoe's brief and accessible columns, which one even deemed far superior to Ann Landers.[93] Women and, to a lesser extent, men showered Popenoe with thanks for his sage counsel, which they judged to be sane, practical, and just plain commonsense. In 1959, for example, Mrs. T from Stockton, California, wrote, "I read your column every evening, and think what you advise people to do about their difficulties is human and very sensible. So very simple that we wonder why they themselves had not thought of it."[94]

Hundreds asked for copies of the pamphlets *Success in Marriage, Family Teamwork,* and *The Battle of the Budget* and filled out the AIFR's scorecards, designed to calculate if a man was a perfect husband, a woman was a perfect wife, or a person was truly a mature adult. Devoted fans, such as Mrs. S from Indiana, sincerely appreciated these tools: "Thank you so much for all the help and encouragement your column has given me. Your self-rating scales have helped me to improve in several ways as well as helping me better understand the faults of others."[95] These journalistic endeavors, which narrated under pseudonyms the trials and tribulations of many couples that had sought help at the AIFR, solidified Popenoe's standing as "Mr. Marriage."

The AIFR flourished in the 1950s because its mission resonated with the culture and ideology of the Cold War and above all with the doctrine of containment, which applied not only to the Soviet Union and China but also to gender and the family. In the United States, fighting communism abroad and shoring up internal security at home were linked to the idealization of motherhood and reproduction and to the sexual regulation of women's bodies.[96] Furthermore, if the AIFR prospered in this climate, it also contributed substantially to it. The institute was staunchly committed to the reconstitution of the American family from the inside out. Its pursuit of this objective was one piece of the puzzle of postwar eugenics. Indeed, Popenoe linked marital counseling to population policy through the rubric of planned parenthood; he published articles outlining the virtues of population planning and in 1952 presented a paper on the vital social function of the marriage counselor at the Third International Conference on Planned Parenthood in Bombay.[97] However, for Popenoe the most effective way to influence reproduction and the family was not to do fieldwork or attend congresses in foreign countries but to teach fit Americans that breeding was the key to human satisfaction and advancement: "There must be identification of having children with personal happiness, an elevation of the family and children to a higher place in the multiple scale of values characteristic of a high level of civilization."[98]

At the AIFR, reaching this "higher level" began with clear-cut sex differentiation. The initial step in assessing clients was gauging the degree to which their gender identity and comportment corresponded to their anatomical sex.[99] A proximate correspondence between sex and gender equaled normality, while distance and deviation indicated conditions stretching from minor and fixable gender distortion to nearly fatal gender pathology. According to Popenoe, sex differentiation had "characterized the species for many millions of years" and was "pretty firmly embedded in the constitution of every human being—even though not invariable."[100] Sex distinction was deep and carried profound ramifications: "Men and women differ in every cell of their bodies, having a different combination of chromosomes—those little 'strings of beads' in the cell which are the carriers of heredity."[101] Defined as innate, with minimal leeway for adjustment, sex differentiation affected genetic inheritance, basal metabolism, constitutional vitality, anatomical form, physiological functionality, glandular composition, emotional equipment, and intellectual endowment.[102] In this constellation, the average man, compared to the average woman, was more active, venturesome, aggressive, consistent, nomadic, businesslike, secular, rational, high-minded, and courageous. Women, conversely, were modest, submissive, romantic, sincere, religious, vindictive, "catty," drawn to trivia, and affectionately demonstrative.[103]

Popenoe believed this intrinsically complementary dichotomy was under assault by nefarious modern trends, particularly the anomie of urban living and the higher education of women, which decreased birthrates of the fit. His answer to this predicament was a return to, and a reinvention of, fecund marriages structured by appropriate sex-gender roles: "Men and women were made for marriage, biologically and psychologically."[104] Making marriages work, however, was a burden that fell largely on wives. Even though Popenoe claimed that the sexes balanced one another, the AIFR's marriage counseling program viewed the woman as much more malleable than the man, a condition rooted in her procreative capacity. Popenoe wrote that the female was an "intermediate between the baby and the adult man in her anatomy and her physiology."[105] Whereas a boy matured uneventfully into a man, a girl, at the onset of puberty, became trapped in a state of arrested development, only passing "on to the physical maturity which makes her more like a man" at menopause.[106] The complications for girls arose with puberty, when new reproductive imperatives not only shut down any budding athleticism but also resulted in a lessening of intelligence. In arguing for the deep-seated effects of puberty on girls, Popenoe referred to a study conducted by Terman in which their average IQ dropped 13 points (as opposed to a decline of 3 for the boys) during this phase. The "girl, who probably inherits just as much intellectual capacity as her brother, has to lose part of this as the price she pays for motherhood—or at least, for specialization which will permit motherhood."[107] Women, such as Mrs. C, who refused to accept their sex destiny had most likely gotten "off track" during childhood; instead of readily relinquishing their smarts and sports ability to the hormonal demands of ovulation and menstruation, they had become deluded into thinking they were on a par with men. At the AIFR, this phenomenon was regularly diagnosed as "masculine protest," a condition unique to what Popenoe called the "Machine Age": "Primitive women seem to have no such inferiority complex—it is only the well-educated woman who is ashamed of her sex."[108] Women were perpetual juveniles, and this protracted adolescence, which lasted from the first to the last menses, made them more open to alteration through self-help and modification. This stance reflected the insinuation of Freudian theories of arrested development and female infantilism into a model that privileged biological explanations.[109] In brief, because of women's physiology and biology, it was much easier to change women than men. For this reason, Popenoe contended that when marital conflicts arose, the wife would have to "make more of the larger adjustments."[110] In a 1952 article written for general physicians, Popenoe explained that marriage counseling was about "re-educating one or both partners" but also claimed that "when marital conflicts arise, it is usually the wife who comes to the physician for help and advice" (figure 15).[111]

The corollary of this sex-gender logic was the presumed "greater aggressiveness of the male," which "often gets out of bounds and becomes a nuisance, but if it had not existed, the race would never have survived."[112] Once naturalized as a male attribute, aggressiveness became anathema in women and mandatory for men.[113] Wives were portrayed as engaging in the most egregious form of gender distortion when they nagged, pushed, or were too forceful. Bossy wives, for example, hurt the egos of their husbands, who, even if they apparently enjoyed being the passive partner, deep down craved to prove their supremacy. It was a patent fact: "A man who does not see himself in the age-old role of hunter, fighter, and protector of the home becomes dissatisfied."[114] At the AIFR, wives learned that making more money than their spouses was an aberration that most husbands could not tolerate, and they were warned at all costs to avoid competing with their husbands lest they diminish their manhood: "If she is wise, she will let Ray run his own business while she turns her energy and enthusiasm, her real ability, into some other channel."[115] To substantiate such assertions, Popenoe often quoted a national AIFR survey of three thousand respondents that had shown that the least happy marriages were the ones in which the wives dominated. Only 47 percent of such unions were content, as compared to 61 percent of those where the man was

*When marital conflicts arise, it is usually the wife
who comes to the physician for help and advice.*

FIGURE 15. Woman entering the American Institute of Family Relations office when it
was on Sunset Boulevard. Source: Photograph in article by Paul Popenoe, "Marriage
Counseling," *General Practitioner* 6, no. 4 (1952): 53–60. Photograph is from page 53.

dominant and 87 percent of those that qualified as "cooperative part-
nerships."[116] In pamphlets such as *Smart Wives Don't Have to Nag* and
Boss Him and Lose Him, AIFR counselors clarified through marital
fables why female aggressiveness was detrimental and how to effectively
combat it.[117]

If this biological reductionism faulted aggressiveness in women, it
granted men a wide margin for violent behavior since their sex destiny
was posited, in a quite primatological fashion, to be hard-wired and virtually unchangeable. Male aggressiveness was "widespread in evolution" and could be traced to man's primal role as warrior and fierce
guardian of the tribe.[118] Over and over again Popenoe painted men as

innately prone to outbursts and anger, and, furthermore, linked this to the sexual domination of women. As he conjectured, "Suppose that husband and wife have had a violent quarrel, as may happen in almost any family. The husband's aggressiveness is aroused by the quarrel, and, as a result, he is then ready for and desirous of intercourse. But the wife's aggressiveness, which has also been aroused by the quarrel, makes her quite unfitted for the submissiveness that is a part of her role in intercourse."[119] Perhaps the most damning accusation that could be leveled at Popenoe and the AIFR was the extent to which they condoned or ignored husbands' emotional and physical abuse of their wives. In letters responding to women who complained bitterly about their misery at the hands of hostile husbands, Popenoe, following clearly delineated AIFR protocol, never recommended divorce (although separation was sometimes an option).[120] In one instance, where the wife stated that she was frequently beaten, the "counselor then pointed out how much her nagging was undermining her husband, making it impossible for him to show love for her. She admitted that she had egged him into beating her."[121]

Women were admonished for being too aggressive and belittling their spouses. In contrast, men were sometimes encouraged to embrace their masculinity by being more aggressive. In 1940, for example, Mr. R wrote to Popenoe about his confusion regarding a young woman whom he had been dating and with whom he shared the hobbies of music, poetry, and sports. This young woman had kissed Mr. R passionately two times but lately had been giving him the cold shoulder. He declared gushingly that he worshipped her but that because he did not want to hurt her feelings he was hesitant to ask her directly if her attention was genuine. Popenoe candidly told Mr. R that he was too passive and that if he was prepared to marry her he needed to be "aggressive, insistent, insuring her that you could not live without her any longer."[122] On rare occasions, men, usually military officers home from the war whose rigid disciplinary tactics were disrupting the household, were encouraged to temper themselves by finding physical and social outlets.[123]

Through the lens of an ordinary and family-centric eugenics, the AIFR's clients were first analyzed according to the dictates of this sex-gender hereditarianism. Biology should be destiny, and if it was not, then behavior—which was understood in terms of what we today call gender or gender identity—was expected to change, usually through self-help and therapeutic exercises based on psychosexual and psychoanalytic theories of human personality and relations.[124] The concepts of gender and gender identity began to be adopted during the Cold War era as a majority of scientists interested in the etiology of polymorphous sexualities abandoned biological for psychological explanations.[125] It should be recognized, however, that postwar eugenicists, who pursued a more plastic hereditarianism and wielded the diagnostic tools of personality tests, contributed to the decoupling of sex and gender by inventing new kinds of gender distortion and pathology and new techniques to measure them.

If the sex-gender system stood at the foundation of the AIFR's marriage counseling, then the binary of extroversion-introversion was well ensconced on the ground floor. Besides the "difference between male and female," this was the "greatest that can exist between two 'normal' human beings," and distinguishing extroversion-introversion variance according to likes, dislikes, metabolism, temperament, and body build was a crucial component of the AIFR's client evaluation. According to Popenoe, extroversion-introversion was "largely inborn and seen in the cradle," and he often warned marriage counselors that they ignored it at their peril.[126] Drawing from the psychologists Alfred Adler and Terman, Popenoe stated that the introvert had "his attention turned on himself" and was found "more frequently in the asthenic body-build, a slender physique sometimes called the linear type because the characteristic lines are vertical."[127] Conversely, the extrovert was more interested in external circumstances and "more likely to be of the lateral type, characteristic lines being horizontal."[128] The extrovert was boisterous, uninhibited, and closer to a "primary type of personality," akin to a "wild animal," while the "secondary type," the introvert, was more fastidious, shy, and detail oriented.[129] As examples of introverts, who were more likely to be engineers, artists, and planners, Popenoe listed Charles Lindbergh, Henry Ford, Woodrow Wilson, and Adolf Hitler. On the other roster, which included "men of action," administrators, entertainers, and sheriffs, were Huey P. Long, Will Rogers, and Dwight Eisenhower.[130] These two biotypes were determined by the resistance of the neural synapses, which in introverts was low, implying that nervous impulses tended to be captured in the brain and not made manifest. The synapses of extroverts, on the other hand, put up "a high resistance to the circulation of an idea, hence it tends to branch off and express itself in action, instead of remaining in the closed circuit of thought processes."[131]

In the AIFR's framework, women were more likely to be introverts and, in turn, were more complicated and problematic than their opposites. Introverts were also more likely to be unhappy in marriage, repressed, and neurasthenic, whereas extroverts were predisposed to hysteria and mania. Like females, introverts were easier to change: "You can turn an introvert out, to some extent; you can't turn an extravert in."[132] And it was the introvert who required more expert care, in order to be "pushed out and socialized."[133] Extroverted women were often characterized as having too much "ego drive" and were instructed to become more submissive and deferential. In one case, JTA tests determined that the wife was an introvert and her husband a near polar opposite. Even though this husband was generally disengaged from social life, except for his obsession with baseball, the wife was instructed to "take him 'as is'—he's an extravert and she can't change that." To save the marriage, she was advised to "*act* as if she enjoyed the game" of baseball and take responsibility for enriching "their common life with other activities that he finds enjoyable and profitable."[134]

The AIFR's ideas about sex-gender distinctions and constitutional types reached thousands via the radio, television, and the printed lay media. Through these venues, and by promoting eugenic marriage through education, training, and directive counseling, the AIFR fostered the internalization of sex and gender norms and helped popularize biotypological understandings of human difference. Unlike other postwar eugenicists, who preached in the pages of professional journals and books about family relations, reproduction, and eugenic marriages, the institute's activities had an immediate impact and left a lasting imprint on the intimate lives of thousands, if not millions, of Americans. One of the hallmarks of the Popenoe's family-centric eugenics was that it encouraged Americans to absorb dominant norms by engaging in self-scrutiny and self-measurement. Seemingly impartial instruments, such as personality tests, were offered as the most reliable way for a client to take stock of her or his malaise and problems. Perhaps it was the enticement of revealing and realizing oneself simply by responding to true-false or multiple-choice personality profiles that made Popenoe and the AIFR so appealing to Americans during the Atomic Age. Through reflecting on his performance on self-rating scorecards, a person could see "himself, as in a mirror, through his own eyes. He is not taking somebody else's word—he has described his own personality."[135]

THE GENDER OF TEMPERAMENT

When Mrs. C was asked to change her attitude and behavior in order to defuse her "masculine protest," she was just one of hundreds of women who were expected to perform the lion's share of alteration indicated by the results of the JTA. Taken as a microcosm of the values inherent in the AIFR's marriage counseling, the JTA illuminates the operating principles and biases of the family-centric eugenics of the postwar period. As a psychometric and statistical instrument, the JTA rewarded strict gender conformity; women and men who strayed from the reproductive and biological function of their sex were transgressing and required reconditioning, which could come in the form of one-on-one therapy, self-improvement exercises, and physical regimes. Mirroring the AIFR's philosophy, the JTA's statistical assumptions and assessment protocols allowed men much greater deviation than women. The internal architecture of the JTA was profoundly asymmetrical: although masculinity was implicitly valued as normal and normative, women were harshly criticized for even minimally overstepping the boundaries of expected femininity.

That the JTA was fixed in the male-female binary was not surprising. In the 1930s, when Terman, who belonged to the HBF and worked closely with the California Bureau of Juvenile Research, began to formulate his Male-Female (M-F) Test, he was in regular contact with the AIFR. Having abandoned the racial assumptions underlining his recalibration of the Binet-Simon into the Stanford-Binet intelligence test, Terman, in tandem with other eugenicists in the 1930s, turned to sex and gender in the hopes of pinpointing some of the fundamental determinants of personality and temperament.[136] In particular, he was concerned to develop a psychometric tool that could ascertain the etiology of homosexuality, which he believed was caused by a knotty combination of genetic, psychological, social, and endocrine factors. After administering the M-F Test to more than 130 men from prison and the general population, Terman suggested that passive male homosexuals were true biological inverts while their active counterparts were not. This conclusion reflected the kind of sex-gender hereditarianism that was being consolidated at the AIFR, which often clandestinely incorporated Freudian speculations about human sexuality. Moreover, it implied that more masculine active male homosexuals, who tended toward bisexuality, not "true inversion," were much more amenable to gender reform.[137] In 1937, Johnson, the AIFR's counseling director, wrote to Terman and asked him for copies of the M-F Test form in order to "put the invert test in the routine for all male homosexuals," and to integrate the test into their evaluation of "marital maladjustment."[138] Returning the favor, that same year the AIFR provided Terman access to eight hundred subjects for his Marital Happiness Survey, which he conducted utilizing the M-F scale and which found that marital contentment hinged on well-delineated gender comportment. Through its circular reasoning, and by fostering the "rigid standards of masculinity and femininity," the M-F Test and its offshoots helped consolidate the family values that characterized the Cold War era.[139]

Despite its merits, the AIFR deemed the M-F Test too specific to gauge the totality of human personality and consequently of limited value for comprehensive marriage counseling.[140] Thus, in the late 1930s, Johnson began to craft an instrument that could capture the nuances of temperament, which he conceived as encompassing the breadth of human personality and, although multifarious in origins and expression, as rooted principally in heredity. In a diagram of concentric circles that Johnson prepared in 1950 to illustrate the "factors producing temperament," he located genes dead center, followed sequentially by the intrauterine environment, birth injuries, infancy, childhood, and finally, nutrition, accidents, and disease. In the words of Popenoe, temperament was "probably 60% inherited or the product of deep-seated early conditioning."[141] An understanding of temperament as inherent, in contrast to "character," which was seen as more fungible, had cohered at the close of the nineteenth century as the disciplines of sociology and psychology generated novel techniques for rationalizing emotion and quantifying intimacy.[142] In the first three decades of the twentieth century, Mendelian eugenics continued to buttress the notion that temperament was biologically fixed. For instance, one of the first tests, the Downey Will–Temperament Test, viewed temperament as innate and permanent.[143] In the 1930s, however, as part of a general assault on biological reductionism, Boas and Mead and others began to assert that temperament and other aspects of personality were culturally constructed, varied across time and place, and could not be easily captured as a singular inherited trait.[144] In order to incorporate environmental and psychogenic variables, many scientists turned toward constitutional holism and biotypology in their quest to calculate temperament. Some physicians used primarily anthropometric and physiological instruments that measured lung capacity, visual acuity, and thorax-to-limb ratios, whereas others, predominantly psychologists, employed written and drawing tests. Some scientists began to lend greater faith to psychometric tools because of expanding distrust of the readability of the human body, which, despite being probed and measured in many laboratories, could be stubbornly elusive when it came to explaining confounding subjects such as manly homosexuals and feminine lesbians.[145] The AIFR fell in the psychometric group, actively seeking out tools scientifically to measure the mental, emotional, and psychic traits of their clients, information that they believed was critical to curing ailing marriages and stimulating procreation. Soon after its founding in 1930, institute psychologists were administering the M-F Test, the Willoughby Emotional Maturity Scale, the Humm-Wadsworth Temperament Scale, the Kent-Rosanoff Test, the Bernreuter Personality Inventory, the Neymann-Kohlstedt Scale for introversion-extroversion, the A-S Reaction Study for ascendance-submission, Guildford's S.T.D.C.R. Test, and the Rorschach Inkblot.[146] Their "main dependence," however, was on the JTA.[147]

When he designed the JTA, Johnson chose nine oppositional traits that, once plotted on a variance spectrum, revealed an individual's unique temperament. The test taker responded to a long list of one-sentence questions, usually tagged to one adjective, including whether or not she or he was forgiving, a regular exerciser, neat and orderly, organized, openly affectionate, optimistic, lenient, reflective, likely to carry a grudge, slow to complain, often depressed, empathetic, or emphatic.[148] Once tallied, the results mapped fairly neatly onto either the masculinity-femininity or the extroversion-introversion continuum. Dominant-Submissive, for example, resonated with sex-gender norms, whereas Active Social–Quiet and Expressive-Inhibited correlated with extroversion-introversion. To identify clear-cut personality types, AIFR counselors were given instructional sheets on trait and cross-trait interpretation. If a client was classified as highly nervous, he was told to watch his diet, take vitamins, relax, and have his thyroid checked. High activity was seen as desirable, especially if paired with high self-mastery and low nervousness. Following the injunction to push introverts out, cordiality was defined as "one of the most valuable traits, and one of the easiest to cultivate."[149] High subjectivity was more problematic and, if matched with high aggressiveness, could translate into a paranoid personality. The two most damaging traits, if high or poorly combined, were aggressiveness and criticalness. The former was beneficial for leaders, such as "military officers and responsible executives," but was potentially combustible when found in subordinates such as wives, and could wreak havoc in certain marriages. For such cases, AIFR counselors concentrated on diverting "the aggressiveness into channels that are less harmful or even helpful," which could mean physical activities such as boxing. Criticalness was similarly described. For women, an "improvement desirable" or "improvement urgent" score on the Aggressive and Critical axes translated into diagnoses of badgering, ego-damaging, and unpleasantly

FIGURE 16. Paul Popenoe pointing at a placard of the Johnson
Temperament Analysis Test showing an example of test results.
Photo courtesy of the Paul Popenoe Collection, Box 177, Folder 16,
American Heritage Center, University of Wyoming.

forceful wives. Another telling trait was self-mastery, which determined
if a person was "systematic, responsible, dependable, able to plan in
advance." Those with low self-mastery percentiles were "impulsive,
impatient, likely to fly off the handle."[150] AIFR counselors were taught
which trait combinations were highly problematic, such as low Active/
low Cordial/low Aggressive, which suggested ill health and weak vitality.[151] Furthermore, sex-gender presumptions were reinforced when the
JTA was calculated, as men and women were scored with two different
stencils and raw-score-to-percentile calculators.

The JTA stood at the center of the AIFR's marriage counseling (figure
16). From 1941 to 1962, at least seventy thousand people were

administered this test at the institute.[152] Additionally, it was part of the AIFR's business strategy, mobilized to ensure that clients would return. On a sheet titled "Clients will come back for a second time if . . . ," the scenarios listed were "You leave part of his story in the air," "You emphasize the need of time" (from one week to one year for thorough counseling), and "You promise report on JTA."[153] It was also the premier tool called into action when assessing clients who contacted the AIFR from afar. In 1954, Popenoe announced the institute's "Marriage Readiness Service," in the *Ladies' Home Journal,* which sought to prepare women nearing or over the age of thirty to find a mate before they were relegated to spinsterhood. Dozens of women wrote letters to the AIFR to take advantage of this opportunity, which for a fee included a personality assessment based on the JTA, a supplemental written questionnaire, relevant pamphlets, and four personalized letters written by an institute counselor.[154] Within less than six months, sixty young women had participated in the Marriage Readiness Service.[155]

One of these was a twenty-seven-year-old Canadian who wrote to Popenoe, care of the *Journal,* "Last night I read with avid interest the story of 'Marcia Carter' and the Marriage Readiness Course. This morning I came in at 7:00 to write to you." She identified completely with Marcia's story—"I am 27 and more than anything else in the world I long for a good husband, a home, and children but I can't seem to achieve it. As each year goes by I become more afraid, more lonely, more heart-hungry, wondering desperately what is wrong"—and added, "I am quite nice looking and try to dress nicely. I like housework, can sew, mend, knit, have pleasant good taste." She closed her letter asking, "Can you, can you possibly help me?"[156] Mrs. Leslie F. Kimmell, of the AIFR's public relations department, immediately dispatched a letter to this young woman, informing her that she could certainly do the service by mail. After taking the JTA, this young woman was diagnosed as hypercritical, depressive, and cold, as well as aggressive, and was sent counseling sheets to begin to work on her deficiencies.[157]

Another client, a twenty-eight-year-old advertising agent with a successful career in Chicago, participated in the Marriage Readiness Service. Miss M had serious problems: "Your score on Aggressive is also unusually high—you scored higher than 92% of all women." Given her unbalanced temperament, it would be nearly impossible for Miss M to locate a "man aggressive enough that you could create a mutually satisfying relationship with him." Mrs. Gene Benton, one of the institute's many certified female counselors, explained Miss M's problem as a form of gender distortion. This young woman needed to begin to emulate her intrinsic sex-gender identity: "Our desire for an aggressive male is deep, biologically rooted in centuries of evolution where the only survivors, the only producers of offspring, were those clever enough, fleet enough, or strong enough to protect their females during the young-bearing period." To improve her chances of finding a man, Miss M was instructed to channel her aggressiveness into feminine behavior and, furthermore, to self-scrutinize: "From time to time when you are with a man, note what you are doing that you feel is aggressive."[158]

In addition to hyperaggressiveness among women, the JTA often diagnosed frigidity, alerted by "improvement urgent" or "improvement desirable" on the Cordial-Cold axis. Mrs. P, for example, an "uninhibited" and handsome woman, with "strong-looking, capable and expressive hands," sought expertise at the AIFR in 1952, where she was determined to be suffering from "possible frigidity."[159] Mrs. P was depicted as unmaternal, prone to puerile crushes, and reaching orgasm on very rare occasion. Once her JTA confirmed frigidity, she was given several AIFR pamphlets.[160] Frigidity was found in another woman, a twenty-eight-year-old from Washington, who completed the Marriage Readiness Service.[161] Her counselor encouraged her to celebrate sexual desire and view it as a physical and reproductive communion between two biological mates: "This is the deep, strong urge, so strong that only with the most powerful distortions can we possibly block or change it. This is the drive that insures the survival of the human race."[162] From the AIFR's standpoint, frigidity was perhaps the most egregious form of gender distortion. It destabilized male-female relationships and jeopardized the perpetuation of the middle-class family.[163]

The AIFR implored women diagnosed with masculine protest and frigidity to embark on a course of self-transformation and reeducation involving therapeutic and behavioral techniques or sometimes simply to feign enjoyment for the sake of the marriage. Ideally, wives would be rewarded with more affection from their husbands and a richer sex life. Given his advocacy of incipient family values, we might expect that Popenoe's gender conservatism would steer him away from frankly discussing sexuality and pleasure. But this was far from the case; he was a tireless advocate of the female orgasm and eroticism, as long as it occurred vaginally on the traditional marriage bed.[164] He encouraged husbands to learn what aroused their wives, avert premature ejaculation, and slow down the sex act if that was what fulfilled their spouses. Popenoe claimed that all this could be accomplished in the missionary position, which allowed for the natural aggressiveness of the male and the passivity of the female. Like other marriage counselors, many influenced by Freud, Popenoe insisted that an authentic and mature female orgasm could be obtained only vaginally. He associated the clitoris with infantilism, fear of men, hatred of the penis, and perhaps even homosexuality. It was of secondary importance: "Both husband and wife may be well instructed to leave the clitoris alone, contrary to the advice given in many manuals."[165]

For the most part, frigidity could be cured or managed through psychological counseling and attitudinal modifications. Sometimes, however, medical intervention was necessary. In 1954, Dr. Arnold Kegel, a Los Angeles physiologist, joined the AIFR as a consulting scientist for a "cooperative project" and began to aid the AIFR in "gaining a deeper understanding of 'frigidity' and new techniques for aiding the wife to help herself."[166] The institute referred one thousand patients to Kegel, who probed the strength of their vaginal contractions in millimeters with the perineometer, an instrument he had developed with this purpose in mind.[167] His focus was on the "innermost, softer portion of the muscle," the middle third of the vagina, which had been neglected as an erogenous zone. After his hands-on examination and calculations, Kegel prescribed exercises, known to many who grew up in the 1950s and 1960s as "Kegels," to build up the muscle by " 'pulling up' on it as if the flow of urine were being shut off."[168] The frigid wife could engage in her Kegels "even while she is engaged in some of her housework."[169] According to an article in *Family Life,* many of Kegel's patients reported that after following his training they found coitus no longer painful and dreaded but supremely gratifying.[170]

In spite of a difficult period in the early 1960s when the institute's Board of Trustees hired a director whose lack of management skills caused a precipitous decline in consultations and mutiny among the staff, the AIFR was afloat forty years after its birth.[171] Popenoe was still penning his syndicated series, now called "Your Family and You." The institute ran four satellite clinics—in Redondo Beach, Orange County, Riverside County, and East Los Angeles, the latter bilingual, with a large Mexican clientele. Hundreds of marriage counselors were being educated, and one thousand clients per week, on average, sought guidance at the institute.

Within several years, however, the AIFR would disappear from the Los Angeles landscape. In the mid-1970s, Popenoe retired to Florida to be near one of his brothers, and in 1979 he died. The new directors relocated the AIFR to North Hollywood, near the San Fernando Valley, and soon after that the institute was absorbed by another counseling institution.[172] In some senses, the AIFR died with the man who had founded it, but not before it came under attack, first and foremost from the very generation whose parents had probably heeded, or at least scanned, the words of "Mr. Marriage." As his son David put it, by the late 1960s, his father's message was one that "people no longer wanted to hear."[173]

Yet for more than forty years the AIFR successfully conveyed this message, introducing ideas about heredity, fitness, marital compatibility, and personality to Americans who came of age between the Great Depression and the 1960s. By expanding eugenics and focusing it securely on the family, sexuality, and reproduction, Popenoe and the AIFR recrafted aspects of better breeding in the postwar period. Through its extensive marriage counseling enterprise, the AIFR promoted a sex-gender system that was based primarily on simplistic theories of biological determinism but was also influenced by dominant paradigms in psychiatry, psychometrics, endocrinology, and sex research. In particular, the introversion-extroversion dichotomy, with its embedded assumptions about the differences between male and female constitutions and the distribution of universal biotypes across population groups, epitomized the AIFR's philosophy. Moreover, if the institute strove to spread the gospel of family, marriage, and normalcy, this vision strongly appealed to tens of thousands of American men and women who eagerly sought out and applied the tools of self-assessment and self-discovery developed by the AIFR's cadre of experts. It is important to emphasize that many of these concepts of human differentiation, especially with regard to sex and gender, are still recognized if not accepted today.

Indeed, one of the striking ironies of the AIFR is that by legitimizing the erotic expression and physical pleasure of women, albeit married women, through studies and counseling, and by constructing concepts of gender identity and embodiment, it laid the groundwork and began to articulate the vocabulary of the sexual revolutions of the 1960s and 1970s. Needless to say, Popenoe derided these movements as a grave threat to the family-nation-civilization triumvirate. Starting in the late 1960s, as male experts and scientific authority began to come under attack by feminists and antipsychiatry activists, Popenoe found more and more affinity with Christian conservatives, who shared his convictions about the sanctity of marriage and strict sex-gender norms. Thus at least one current of postwar eugenics streamed into incipient family

values campaigns and can partially account for the echoes of "race suicide" arguments voiced by the Moral Majority in the 1980s and some
evangelical Christians to this day. In another historical twist, it was
through these channels that the JTA, an instrument initially based on
understandings of human heredity and evolution, migrated into funda-
mentalist ministries, where its successor, the Taylor-Johnson Temperament Test or T-JTA, is a preferred tool for premarital counseling.[174]

CHAPTER 7

Contesting Hereditarianism

Reassessing the 1960s

In 1965, the May Second Committee, a radical student organization at California State University at Sacramento (CSUS), began disseminating a leaflet titled "Sacramento State's Own Doctor Strangelove." This mimeograph demanded that the university administration refrain from bestowing the name "C. M. Goethe" on the campus's new science building, which was under construction. Asking, "Who is C. M. Goethe?" the students responded angrily that he was a Nazi sympathizer who had instituted racial segregation in Sacramento and had trumpeted bigotry and eugenics. At the conclusion of their six-page single-spaced indictment, which vilified Goethe as a coldhearted capitalist who funded biased genetics research at CSUS and bought off the administration and faculty with his philanthropy, the May Second Committee declared:

THE NAMING OF THE NEW SCIENCE BUILDING AFTER C. M. GOETHE WOULD BE A MOCKERY AND A BLASPHEMY AGAINST SCIENCE. IDEAS SUCH AS GOETHE'S ARE SCIENTIFICALLY, HISTORICALLY, AND MORALLY BANKRUPT; AND EVEN THOUGH HE IS NOT FINANCIALLY BANKRUPT, HE AND HIS MONEY SHOULD BE BANISHED FROM INFLUENCE. [Capitals in the original.][1]

In a subsequent flyer, they charged that "Goethe's programs and attitude of Nordic superiority are akin to fascism and are therefore incompatible with scientific or democratic institutions."[2] In response to this rebuke of one of the CSUS's "founding fathers," the administration insisted that the May Second Committee cease to disseminate their leaflets. The students, in turn, upbraided the university for what they interpreted to be a censorial violation of their right to free speech. The May Second Committee situated the administration's actions and their fight over the science building in the context of a youth rebellion against the status quo that was gaining momentum by the day: "All over the country, students are coming into conflict with a power structure inside and outside the colleges which supports, tacitly or otherwise, those racists and reactionaries who would perpetuate the oppression of Black Americans."[3]

Despite the May Second Committee's condemnation, the Committee on Gifts and Public Affairs of the California State College Board of Trustees, which had unanimously agreed to immortalize Goethe's name on the $4.7 million structure about a month earlier, remained committed to their original plan, which included a lavish banquet for their donor's ninetieth birthday.[4] Over the past several decades, Goethe had given CSUS money for student fellowships, genetics research, and library collections, as well as unrestricted gifts, and upon his death the following year he would leave the university a bequest of more than $650,000 as well as his historic Julia Morgan–designed home.[5] From the perspective of CSUS trustees, they were attaching the name of a magnanimous benefactor to an edifice designed to teach the knowledge that Goethe most revered—science, especially plant and animal biology—to college-bound Californians. For many students, however, anything touched by Goethe or his appellation was tainted. How could CSUS name its newest building, one dedicated to the objective pursuit of science, after a man who had founded the Eugenics Society of Northern California, harangued against immigration and overpopulation, and expressed an unabashed belief in white supremacy?

Two years later, once the science building was ready to be unveiled, a group of concerned faculty introduced a resolution in the Academic Senate to ensure that the structure would not carry Goethe's name, proposing that no campus buildings be named after individuals and that any exception to this policy require approval from both the senate and the president. This action reflected the faculty's general dissatisfaction with the top-down management style of the CSUS administration and desire to democratize academic governance. However, the policy change also had a very specific aim; as one professor in the Academic Senate stated, "The faculty knew what Goethe stood for."[6] In the end, under pressure from students and professors, the administration sheepishly backed down and dropped the issue.[7] Just two years after the May Second Committee's initial denunciations, its concerns had moved from the fringe to the center.[8] By this time, Goethe had been dead for more than a year and the country was entering the maelstrom of 1968, a year marked by street violence, antiwar agitation, and political assassinations. In brief, Goethe's name was never engraved on what today appears on the CSUS map simply as Science Hall, and this minor hullabaloo was all but forgotten. However, when the May Second Committee and some CSUS faculty threw themselves into this battle, they were contesting the legacy of eugenics in Sacramento and California. In this sense, the incident was neither isolated nor insignificant.

The protest and liberation movements of the 1960s and 1970s arose out of multiple and sometimes competing currents—the intensification of the struggle against segregation in the South, the coming of age of a generation of idealistic college students unsettled by the dangers and alienation of the nuclear age, the mounting dissatisfaction of middle-class women with the limits of Cold War family and gender roles, and the emergence of a militant brand of ethnic nationalism and racial pride. The background of these developments was the Vietnam War, which began in the 1950s as a gradual attempt to contain communism in Indochina and by the mid-1960s had escalated into a protracted military engagement that would take more than fifty thousand American lives and kill millions of Vietnamese. As disapproval and ire over US involvement in Vietnam grew, protest intensified and many Americans became convinced that their country needed to be thoroughly transformed; by the late 1960s, antiestablishment revolt was at its zenith across America and the globe.[9]

One facet of this long decade that has remained persistently "hidden in plain view" is the extent to which eugenics and its accumulated effects came under sustained popular assault.[10] On the one hand, more than five decades of eugenic policies—which ranged from immigration laws to racial and spatial boundaries, sterilization statutes, and marriage laws—were dismantled or overturned. On the other hand, second-wave white feminists, radical women of color, gay and lesbian liberationists, and disability rights activists sought to upend the reconceived hereditarianism that had hardened during the Cold War. One of the motifs of the 1960s—the reclamation and liberation of the reproductive and sexual body—was part of a collective repudiation of assorted hereditarian theories, especially as espoused on high from experts. Skeptics might rebut that reinterpreting this period as a broad-based contestation of hereditarianism is an exercise in historical exaggeration, given that so many other kinds of social, economic, and cultural injustices were questioned if not assailed during the decade. But although this complex historical period should certainly not be reduced to a firestorm of protest against eugenics, it is nearly impossible to explore the intersections of race, reproduction, sexuality, and gender—all of which were flashpoints of the 1960s—without reckoning with eugenics, whether it persisted as residual scientific racism or was reconceived in new forms of the postwar era.

EUGENICS AND ITS CRITICS

Eugenics was never short on critics, nor were its adherents strangers to discord and recrimination. A diverse lot, eugenicists disagreed, often sharply, among themselves. Some were beholden to doctrines of free love and anarchism, others believed in state-managed utopias.[11] There were eugenicists who found answers in competing and often clashing doctrines of neo-Lamarckism, Mendelianism, biometrics, and, later, biotypology and population policy. In the 1920s Herbert S. Jennings, a professor of zoology at Johns Hopkins University, resigned from the American Eugenics Society, disgusted with the race and class prejudices of his colleagues. An early advocate of the importance of nurture in development, Jennings was impatient with leading eugenicists who stubbornly clung to the theory of singular unit characters despite substantial proof that most human traits were polygenic.[12] Jennings was particularly offended by Harry H. Laughlin, the superintendent of the Eugenics Record Office, who was appointed "Expert Eugenical Agent" of the Committee on Immigration and Naturalization, which convened the hearings on the Johnson-Reed Immigration Act. In his testimony before this committee, Laughlin, loaded with statistics and graphs, convinced his receptive audience that southern and eastern European immigrants were degenerate "stock" that must be stopped at the gates; his data became ammunition for the national origins quotas that were enacted in the late 1920s and not rescinded until 1965.[13] Later in that decade, John C. Merriam, president of the Carnegie Institution, which was supporting the Eugenics Record Office, complained bitterly to Charles B. Davenport about the invective of Laughlin's noisy nativism. Over the 1930s, animosity toward Laughlin would increase and would be instrumental in spurring the Carnegie Foundation's defunding, and the subsequent closure, of the Eugenics Record Office. There were also rancorous backstage skirmishes, revealed in private correspondence between Laughlin and Davenport, about whether *Eugenical News,*

Eugenics (1928–31), or the short-lived *People* (1931) should be the flagship journal of organized eugenics.[14]

Several decades later, Frederick Osborn, who sought to remake eugenics during the postwar period, stepped down from the Pioneer Fund. Established in 1937 to launch initiatives for "gifted" children and to conduct "study and research into the problems of heredity and eugenics in the human race," the Pioneer Fund was the brainchild of Laughlin and the wealthy Colonel Wickliffe Draper.[15] By the mid-1950s, Osborn, the fund's first secretary, had clashed too many times with Draper over the mission of the organization, which the colonel envisioned as a vehicle for protecting racial purity and which Osborn wanted to steer down the less controversial avenues of population planning and demography. Under Osborn's leadership, critical stocktaking was not uncommon; for him, this was part of making eugenics relevant to liberal democracy. In 1962, for example, while he was managing editor, *Eugenics Quarterly* (which succeeded *Eugenical News* in 1954) published an article questioning the therapeutic and institutional benefits of sterilization. After locating fifty patients who had been discharged from California's Pacific State Hospital (previously the Pacific Colony) between 1949 and 1958, the two researchers interviewed them about their feelings about the procedure, which had been performed as a prerequisite for release. Sixty-eight percent stated that, in retrospect, they disapproved of the operation, while less than 20 percent approved. Moreover, there were noteworthy gender discrepancies: 35 percent of men viewed their sterilizations favorably, compared to only 9 percent of the women. Some patients stated that it was difficult for them to pass as "normal" after sterilization, and others bore the surgery as a stigma of a "degraded" or "reduced" status.[16]

Besides the wrangling within organized eugenics, there was public disapprobation. In 1922, the journalist Walter Lippmann criticized the army's intelligence tests, the Alpha and Beta, as well as Lewis Terman's revision of the Binet-Simon, the Stanford-Binet. Although he believed that mental tests could be effective in vocational placement, Lippmann contended that the assumptions undergirding the ubiquitous and blindly trusted IQ tests of the day—namely, that "intelligence" was unchangeable, that it could be easily quantified, and that a pencil-and-paper test could actually measure such an entity, even if it did exist—were preposterous.[17] Several years later eugenics was mocked, this time in *Arrowsmith*, a sardonic novel by Sinclair Lewis about scientific research, doctoring, and the limits of male heroism.[18] In charge of the public health

department in an Iowa town while its permanent director is out cam-
paigning for Congress, the book's protagonist, Martin Arrowsmith,
learns the true heritage of the "Eugenic Family" on display at the Health
Fair. According to official accounts, this family's pedigree is pristine: the
parents and their five children neither smoke, drink, spit on pavements,
nor use foul language. A few days into the fair, however, a police officer
divulges that the crew is none other than the "Holton Gang." The parents are unmarried and living in sin, only one of their kids is their own,
and they have been recently imprisoned for bootlegging liquor and running confidence scams. What is more, at high noon on closing day,
"when the Eugenic Family was giving a demonstration of perfect vigor,
their youngest blossom had an epileptic fit."[19]

The 1930s witnessed more disputation. Sometimes this entailed
eugenicists recanting previously held positions. For instance, Carl C.
Brigham, who devised the prototype for today's Scholastic Achievement
Test (SAT), rejected the correlations between "race" and mental ability
that he had proposed earlier, in which Nordics, Alpines, and Mediter-
raneans towered above all other groups. In addition he stated that the
army Alpha and Beta tests had been useless for measuring recruits
because of sloppy sampling and because "the tests had measured familiarity with American language and culture, not innate intelligence."[20]
Also during this decade, Mary Conway Kohler, a graduate of Stanford
Law School, was appointed as a referee of the San Francisco Juvenile
Court, where she heard the cases of delinquent girls and directed the
Mothers' Aid Program. While at Stanford, Kohler had worked as a
research assistant for Terman and had become well versed in IQ testing
and critical of its ingrained biases. She insisted that these psychometric
instruments were incapable of identifying delinquents or accurately
gauging intelligence, and, once in the court, she strove to terminate their
diagnostic use. As a juvenile referee, Kohler was charged with sending
girls who scored 75 or below on IQ tests, and hence were classified as
feebleminded, to the Sonoma State Hospital for internment and probable sterilization. She avoided submitting female juveniles to such a fate
and spoke out against compulsory salpingectomies, which were regularly performed without patient or parental consent. Kohler was a
vociferous critic of Terman, whom she disliked personally and profes-
sionally. She was appalled by the imperatives to "purify the race" that
were so often voiced during the Great Depression, and she blamed California's prosterilization climate on Popenoe's propaganda and his pan-
icked warnings about the impending deterioration of civilization.[21]

Similar doubts emerged from some pockets of the medical establishment. In 1936, a committee formed by the American Neurological Association and directed by the Boston psychiatrist Abraham Myerson released a stinging report on eugenic sterilization: "There is at present no sound scientific basis for sterilization on account of immorality or character defect. Human conduct and character are matters of too complex a nature . . . to permit any definite conclusions to be drawn concerning the part which heredity plays in their genesis."[22]

And in the 1940s and 1950s many earlier bedfellows—scientists and social scientists—bid a lasting farewell to eugenics, assigning it to the dustbin of history.[23] In 1941, Ashley Montagu, then an anatomist at Hahnemann Medical College in Philadelphia, asserted that the anthropological concept of race was "meaningless," a position that became generally accepted by geneticists.[24] He was soon just one in a chorus that included the prominent geneticists L. C. Dunn and Theodosius Dobzhansky, coauthors of the canonical refutation of eugenic racism, *Heredity, Race, and Society*. In this tract, published in 1946, Dunn and Dobzhansky appreciated the biological variation of humankind, stressed the importance of environment in the development of individuals and the species, and disabused their readers of the notion of "pure races," stating, "Mankind has always been, and still is, a mongrel lot."[25] Dunn and Dobzhansky played a crucial role in aligning human genetics with theories of population maps and gene frequencies and were among the international luminaries who formulated UNESCO (United Nations Educational, Scientific and Cultural Organization) influential statements on race.[26] Written in the powerful language of postwar humanism, these revisionist documents were central to the definitions of universal rights that solidified during the Cold War and were put to the test later in the century.[27]

What happened in the 1960s and 1970s, however, was of a very different order of magnitude. Americans from diverse backgrounds began to challenge hereditarian doctrines, as they had been implemented on the ground over the previous fifty years. Eugenics—in its various permutations—helped build the structures of exclusion and discrimination that, if not toppled, were shaken at their foundation in the 1960s. The social movements of this era need to be reassessed in light of the longevity of hereditarianism across the twentieth century, not only because most eugenic laws enacted in the 1920s and 1930s were not repealed or pronounced unconstitutional on the legislative and judicial level until the 1960s and 1970s, but also because of the accreted effects of hereditarianism on several generations of Americans. The 1920s witnessed the consolidation of "Caucasian" as a racial category that encompassed European Americans who hitherto had been distinguished according to minor distinctions of nationality and language. This phase of racial reordering involved the stark separation of whites from nonwhites, who, like African Americans, remained relegated to second-class citizenship or, like Mexican Americans and Asian Americans, were deemed essentially foreign and inassimilable.[28] Eugenic typologies, based largely on simplistic interpretations of Mendelian unit characters, played a crucial role in cementing this racial regime, which far outlasted the scientific suppositions on which it was based.[29]

The civil rights struggles that began in the 1940s were galvanized by what African Americans and people of color perceived as a gaping and hypocritical disjuncture between the nation's promise of equality and the harsh reality of racism, particularly as endured during World War II.[30] Civil rights and student organizations were concerned with many interlocking issues including housing, employment, transportation, and voting rights. Challenging such institutions often implied ridding the American landscape of the remnants and reinventions of eugenics. For example, *Méndez v. Westminster*, a class action suit against a Southern Californian school district that had served as a laboratory for the California Bureau for Juvenile Research's IQ testing programs, can be understood partially as an attempt to rectify the ramifications of eugenic racism in California's public education system.[31] Even though segregation was ruled unconstitutional in this instance and the "separate but equal" law was overturned by the US Supreme Court in 1954 in the twin cases of *Hernández v. Texas* and *Brown v. Board of Education*, these decisions did not fundamentally alter many of the underlying tenets of racial classification in American society. To some extent, racial ideologies were supported, not undermined, by the turn to population and family planning, which shored up "culture of poverty" and family pathology models of race and social difference, especially with regard to reproduction and parenthood. Furthermore, when hereditarianism was rearticulated along the lines of sex, gender, and biotypology during the Cold War, it became integral to what second-wave feminists and reproductive rights activists identified as some of the most offensive dimensions of modern sexism: marriage counseling, a pronatalism driven by confining gender norms, and virtually no authority or ability to either definitively choose or reject available means of birth control.

Mexican Americans launched their civil rights struggle during World War II, forming organizations such as the American G.I. Forum and the

Mexican American Political Association, in addition to working hand in hand with the National Association for the Advancement of Colored People (NAACP). In the 1940s, a decade marked by rising concern over juvenile delinquency in American cities, these coalitions fought against stereotypes of Mexicans, especially Americanized male adolescents, as either mentally deficient or criminally prone. These characterizations were deeply engrained in the language and practice of sterilization, which Mexican families contested from inside and outside the walls of state institutions. Such depictions circulated with intensity in Southern California during the 1943 Sleepy Lagoon Trial, in which twenty-four Mexican-origin boys were indicted for the alleged murder of one man. An influential report produced for the trial by the Los Angeles Sheriff's Office argued that Mexicans committed disproportionate crimes because of their racial status as unstable and volatile mestizos, a biological fact that Mexican American community organizations and their allies were "loathe to admit."[32] In a letter forwarding this report to Walter White at the NAACP, a representative from the Pan American Council on Democracy, which supported the Sleepy Lagoon Defense Committee, decried the permissibility of such reasoning in the courtroom: "It will shock you. Never to our knowledge has there been a more unvarnished exposition of Hitler's theory of race supremacy in this country."[33]

Given that Los Angeles was a critical hub of American eugenics in the 1940s, it is not surprising that the caricatures of Mexicans as diseased and degenerate that were common in the 1920s and 1930s persisted after the war. Moreover, even when updated, such portrayals still often relied on notions of bad or corrupted breeding. Emory Bogardus, a professor of sociology at the University of Southern California, a member of the American Eugenics Society (1927–35), and a trustee of the American Institute of Family Relations (AIFR), wrote prolifically on the predicament of Mexicans and Mexican Americans at midcentury. Like many other postwar eugenicists, by the 1940s Bogardus was averse to blanket assertions that Mexican youth were "descended from 'bad' ancestry" and genetically wired to become criminals: such claims "ran counter to anthropological knowledge." But even though Bogardus recognized the debilitating socioeconomic circumstances faced by many Mexicans, he still referred to heredity, suggesting that the children of Mexican migrants, especially if poor, were most likely born "subnormal" and that their low IQs were probably the result of inbreeding.[34]

Not until the 1960s and 1970s, with the self-identification of a new generation who called themselves Chicana/os, were the underpinnings of such stereotypes systematically challenged. A crucial piece of this critique concentrated on the implications of the ongoing use of IQ and aptitude tests to classify and track Mexican students. In the 1930s, the Mexican American educator George I. Sánchez, who was trained in educational psychology and served as president of the League of United Latin American Citizens from 1941 to 1942, inveighed against strict hereditarianism and race psychology and criticized IQ tests, both the National Intelligence Test and the Stanford-Binet, for their many drawbacks.[35] Nevertheless, he did not recommend that IQ tests be relinquished; instead he suggested that they be cautiously employed as barometers of social and linguistic assimilation.[36] In the 1970s, Chicanos pushed Sánchez's analysis a few steps further. This decade saw a flurry of counterstudies that denied the validity of IQ and aptitude tests even after language, class, and educational access were taken into consideration and traced how psychometrics had demoted and diminished Chicanos for decades.[37] For example, in 1970 in the third issue of the journal *El Grito*, published in Berkeley, an editorial applauded a recent court decision that mandated bilingual testing in California and stated simply, "For generations the intelligence testing of Mexican-American children has caused untold harm." In looking back to the origins of the label *mentally retarded*, the editor pinpointed a 1923 study that had set the precedent for racial discrimination by advancing "the definite notion that Mexican and Indian children suffered from a severe case of 'bad blood.'"[38] To begin to address the vast educational discrepancies in the American West, one Chicana scholar recommended "a change in the whole approach to testing and the evaluation of IQ tests," while another was more skeptical about such pedagogical reform: "There is also the alternative of doing away with I.Q. testing altogether."[39]

In 1968, Mexicans made up 40 percent of those tracked into programs for the "mentally handicapped" in California even though they constituted only 14 percent of the state's elementary and secondary students.[40] Not surprisingly, the Los Angeles school system, which had been a stronghold of eugenically inspired research into the 1940s, was one of the first targets of emboldened young Chicanos. In the spring of 1968, thousands of high school students affiliated with United Mexican American Students stormed out of their classrooms in East Los Angeles in a chain reaction of "blowouts" demanding curriculum revisions, reduced class size, expanded bilingual programs, Mexican American teachers, and, in short, more community jurisdiction over primary and secondary education. While marching to the school board to present their grievances, these young protesters shouted, "Chicano Power!" and carried signs exclaiming, "Education, not Eradication," and "We are not 'Dirty Mexicans.'"[41]

More broadly, Chicana/os swept back through the twentieth century, cataloguing the myriad ways scientific and social scientific theories had contributed to representations of them as lazy, stupid, childish, and inclined toward drug addiction and thievery.[42] This analysis was accompanied by the creation of mental health categories and services that Chicano/as defined from within their own communities.[43] In general, the (re) assertion of ethnic and racial identity during the 1960s was often expressed in terms of gaining ownership and control over one's own body as an aesthetic, psychic, and physical entity.[44] Health and healing often figured prominently in this politics of corporeal reappropriation. For example, the Black Panthers, the Chicano Brown Berets, and the Puerto Rican Young Lords all opened up community health centers in places such as Los Angeles, Oakland, and New York City.[45] Along these lines, Chicano activists convened a conference in New Mexico in 1972 to begin to address the particular needs of Mexican-origin patients in the United States.[46] The previous year, Chicano health practitioners—physicians, nurses, and medical students—founded the National Chicano Health Organization to promote culturally sensitive care and devise strategies to increase the number of Mexican American practitioners.[47] On a more fundamental level, this was a period in which medical authority, interpreted as patriarchal and repressive, came under attack from many quarters including ethnic nationalists, feminists, and gay and lesbian liberationists, as well as some radicalized medical students and nurses.[48] For example, in the early 1970s disabled college students, intent on disentangling themselves from what they perceived as infantilized and constrictive relationships with doctors, psychologists, and other experts, spearheaded the independent living movement, establishing their first center in Berkeley in 1972.[49]

LIBERATING THE SEXUAL BODY

When Paul Popenoe read *The Feminine Mystique* in 1963, he may have recognized as familiar the universe of housewives, mothers, and caretakers described by Betty Friedan.[50] After all, that claustrophobic universe was what Popenoe and the American Institute of Family Relations had been recommending for the past thirty years: wives channeling their "ego outlets" into wholesome hobbies, marriage at a younger and younger age, nuclear families with daughters enrolled in the Brownie Troops and sons in the Boy Scouts, and an implicit recognition of deep-seated and unalterable differences between women and men. Where Popenoe saw a harmonious utopia that would guarantee the survival of the human species and civilization, however, Friedan witnessed a nightmare—an unspeakable emptiness gnawing away at middle-class American women, who were ensnared in a relentless cycle of empty daily routines. After ruminating on the "problem that had no name," Friedan began to see in "a strange new light" what was behind the baby boom: female frigidity, despondency, depression, and the many "character pathologies and sexual problems being reported by the doctors."[51] Although focused on white suburban housewives, The Feminine Mystique opened a wedge for the articulation of the resentment and dissatisfaction of millions of American women and began to craft a language for second-wave feminism.

Friedan blamed the circumscribed and unfulfilled life of the housewife largely on Freudian theories, which insisted on reading women's problems, frustrations, and neuroses as psychosexual maladies, not as the result of the suffocation of human potential through enforced motherhood, marriage, and child rearing.[52] Like Friedan, most second-wave feminists held up Freud as the effigy that needed to be burned. Yet when they denounced the expectations of femininity that they found so oppressive and degrading, they were also denouncing the pronatalism, family planning, and mate selection that had been promoted by eugenicists since the 1940s. Reading the incendiary and evocative tracts of second-wave feminists, it is hard not to see Paul Popenoe, "Mr. Marriage," standing right beside Freud as an as yet unacknowledged accomplice.

For more than forty years, Popenoe and the AIFR, which he founded and directed, had translated family-centric eugenics into daily counseling, influencing the lives of thousands of Americans. Through AIFR pamphlets and Popenoe's syndicated columns—above all his long-running "Can This Marriage Be Saved?" which appeared in the Ladies' Home Journal—women were taught that "biologically the individual was made for marriage" and that women's evolutionary and social calling was to listen to their husbands, try anything to keep the marriage together, and even tolerate emotional and physical abuse.[53] Popenoe, and other eugenicists who expounded on the centrality of family and marriage in the pages of Eugenics Quarterly and similar publications, merged demographic imperatives, psychoanalytic terminology, and a rudimentary form of sex-gender hereditarianism to turn out a version of better breeding that resonated powerfully with the Cold War apotheosis of home and hearth. This reconfigured eugenics helped prepare the stage for the profamily climate of the 1950s, a story borne out by the numbers. From a low of 18.4 per 1,000 in the 1930s, for example, births increased to a high of 25.3 per 1,000 in 1957, and the average number of children per family rose from 2.4 to 3.2. Additionally, the rate for third children doubled, and the rate for fourth children tripled. The divorce rate plummeted, and by the mid-1950s the average age at marriage for men was twenty-two and for women was twenty.[54]

When Friedan issued her clarion call, she intended to subvert the strictures of domesticity, the veneration of women as mothers and helpmates, and the application of Freudian notions of "penis envy," clitoral infantilism, and vaginal frigidity to the lives and bodies of middle-class American women.[55] She was also, however, dissecting the crude biologism that continued to inform dominant ideas about gender difference and acceptable gender behavior. Shortly after it was published, Popenoe reviewed *The Feminine Mystique;* he dismissed its "shrill and excited tone," calling it a "Jeremiad, with little supporting evidence." Popenoe was particularly irked by Friedan's assertion that a woman could attain self-fulfillment only by transcending her reproductive function as breeder. For Popenoe, this message could only lead to the race suicide of white middle-class America: "It is obvious that, in general, the home must be given first place in the life of both men and women—otherwise the survival of a nation is endangered. Beyond that, it is imperative that the ablest women, who can create the best homes, also bear and rear a fair proportion of the nation's children—otherwise leadership will gradually die out." Popenoe's answer to the malaise-afflicted housewife profiled by Friedan was to find enjoyable hobbies and make her home "the center, not the periphery, of her life." *The Feminine Mystique*, he concluded, should be read as an indirect cry for help from women who needed to become more "efficient as homemakers."[56]

The divergence between Popenoe and Friedan foreshadowed the conflicts that would surface later in the decade as second-wave feminists began to attack marital counseling, the concepts of frigidity and the vaginal orgasm, and personality testing. Since the 1940s, male medical or psychological experts, who were now enemy number one, had championed all of these. Although second-wave feminists lashed out at the entire enterprise of marital advice, first and foremost as featured in women's magazines, they reserved special wrath for Popenoe. Since 1953, Popenoe had offered practical advice for distraught wives (and a few husbands) in "Can This Marriage Be Saved?" which drew from actual cases of AIFR clients. The column presented scenarios of conflict and miscommunication between spouses, which were resolved through some form of self-scrutiny or self-assessment, in which the troubled individual, invariably the wife, grasped how she could repair the marriage and improve as a person. One of the defining moments of women's liberation was March 18, 1970, when Media Women, a loosely knit coalition of feminist collectives, staged a sit-in at *Ladies' Home Journal.* Outraged at the *Journal's* depiction of women as merely wives, consumers, and sex objects, more than one hundred feminists marched into the magazine's headquarters and occupied the offices of its editor, John Mack Carter. They brought with them a detailed list of demands, ranging from the hiring of a female editor in chief, to free day care, substantial raises for all staff, and the removal of all exploitative and degrading advertising. In addition, they insisted that the *Journal* "cease to publish the advice column 'Can This Marriage Be Saved?'"[57] In her memoir, which traces the overlaps and tensions between second-wave feminism and lesbian liberation, Karla Jay, who participated in the Media Women action, explains one of the reasons *Ladies' Home Journal* was singled out: "The magazine featured advice columns, including one entitled 'Can This Marriage Be Saved?' It was patently offensive: No matter how brutal or demeaning the circumstances a woman faced in her marriage, she was advised to stick with it, be more compliant, and become more caring. Sometimes the columnist proffered advice on making a woman's husband a bit nicer, but women were generally expected to make any necessary adjustments themselves. The obvious question '*Should* this marriage be saved?' was never raised."[58]

In *It Ain't Me Babe,* a short-lived magazine produced by one of the hundreds of feminist groups that sprouted up across the country in the late 1960s, an author who identified herself simply as Gina derided the paternalism of the *Ladies' Home Journal* in general and "Can This Marriage Be Saved?" in particular. She dissected one of Popenoe's marital fables, in which Tessa, a wife with two small children, was reduced to begging for sex and affection from her aloof husband, Tom, a successful businessman. One night, when Tessa and Tom were finally making love, the phone rang, interrupting them and leaving "Tessa on the brink of orgasm" as Tom rushed out the door to pursue a lucrative deal. Gina ridiculed Popenoe's suggestion that Tessa should recognize that her agitation stemmed from her own insecurity and that she could attain greater happiness only by showering Tom with more love and encouragement, which, as an exemplary breadwinner, he rightly deserved. Gina deemed this kind of advice so blatantly demeaning as to stimulate the "ire of women who seek freedom and full personhood."[59]

If second-wave feminists excoriated marital counseling, they also radically reinterpreted one of its standard diagnoses: frigidity. During the Cold War era of domesticity, women who shunned men, rejected their sexual advances, were uninterested in procreation, and failed to achieve vaginal orgasm were labeled frigid. At the AIFR, marriage counseling headquarters USA, the condition of frigidity had been ascertained since the early 1940s through the administration of temperament tests. If a woman's score on the Johnson Temperament Analysis Test placed her in deviation zones for traits such as Cold (as opposed to Cordial) or Critical (as opposed to Appreciative), she was deemed frigid, perhaps a man-hater, and was coached either to absorb the lessons of self-help manuals or to perform vaginal contraction exercises. For women's liberationists, frigidity and the vaginal orgasm were two of the most destructive myths perpetuated by the phallocentric advice industry. In her groundbreaking 1968 essay "The Myth of the Vaginal Orgasm," Anne Koedt, informed by the sex research of Alfred Kinsey and Masters and Johnson, recentered female sexuality on the clitoris. For Koedt, the fixation on the vagina was a result of women being "defined sexually in terms of what pleases men." She implored women to take charge of their own biology and "redefine our own sexuality. We must discard the 'normal' concepts of sex and create new guidelines which take into account mutual sexual enjoyment."[60]

Second-wave feminism converged on the clitoris, which was reclaimed as the primary site of erotic and sexual pleasure and as an organ that detached female sexuality from the imperatives of reproduction.[61] It also signified women's biological difference from men, which became a source of celebration and identity-making. When they repudiated marriage counseling, whether in its psychoanalytic or hereditarian renditions, second-wave feminists paradoxically reaffirmed the notion that women were intrinsically unlike men. However, it was precisely because psychology and sex research had so badly misconstrued this distinction, shackling it to a misogynistic biology, that women needed to formulate new methods and theories to apprehend womanhood in all its complexity.[62] In her classic essay "Kinder, Küche, Kirche as Scientific Law: Psychology Constructs the Female," Naomi Weisstein, then a postdoctoral student and activist in Chicago, deplored the ignorance of male psychologists, who, she claimed, knew absolutely nothing about women and for years had explicated female maladies through androcentric theories and techniques. Although Weisstein's critique is usually read as an indictment of Freudianism, she leveled biting criticism at biological theories of sex differentiation, which underlay, sometimes tacitly, scientific psychology. She was offended by the projection of primate behavior onto humans, a "patently irrelevant" reverse anthropomorphism that anticipated and rewarded greater male aggressiveness.[63] Weisstein also debunked experimental psychology as performed in the laboratory and declared, "Personality tests never yield consistent predictions."[64] *Our Bodies, Ourselves,* published in its first edition (under the title *Women and Their Bodies*) by the forerunner to the Boston Women's Health Book Collective in 1970, was also emblematic of the cult of female distinctiveness.[65] It was one of the most visible examples of feminist health activism, which emerged across the country in communities large and small in the late 1960s, taking up the issues of abortion, pregnancy and childbirth, contraception, sexuality, rape, mental health, and menopause, and disputing the terms of the traditional female patient–male doctor relationship.[66] Through health collectives, publications written for and by women, and accompanying forms of sexual and erotic exploration, the body "came to symbolize the new citizen of the sixties revolutions: it was a body freed from the effects of racism, classism, technology, and sexual repression."[67]

The unfettered body also occupied center stage for gay liberationists, who had no choice but to construct their identity in opposition to scientific and medical depictions of deviancy and abnormality. Psychologists and physicians disagreed intensely about the etiology of homosexuality; some linked it to genetic predisposition, others to coddling mothers and "penis envy." At the AIFR, Popenoe was so perturbed by homosexuality that, starting in the 1950s, he began to collect relatively obscure homophile pamphlets such as the *Mattachine Review* and *One.* He believed that, like women's liberationists, homosexuals were a menace to civilization and, if allowed to "recruit" and proliferate, would destroy the modern family. His closed system of sex-gender hereditarianism could contain neither, and the AIFR found homosexuality much more enigmatic to diagnose and treat than frigidity or masculine protest. From the outset the institute's counseling director, Roswell H. Johnson, thought it crucial to devise tests capable of identifying "passive male homosexuals" and traded letters with Terman on how best to develop such instruments. After over a decade of psychometric studies and observation, Johnson concluded that homosexuality was the consequence of a "variety of factors" including a constitutional inclination, which might stem "direct from the gene" or from an "environmental physical-chemical effort." Even though he conceded that homosexuality could be "eugenically useful in sterilizing many dysgenics," Johnson asserted that the threat posed, particularly by "endogenous" or unrepentant homosexuals, was grave enough to warrant internment in an isolation colony. Over the years, he devoted a great deal of psychometric attention to the detection of homosexuality and after World War II claimed that he had finally figured out a secret formula to detect it with the Minnesota Multiphasic Personality Inventory.[68]

Predispositional explanations for homosexuality diminished the possibility of efficacious treatment, while psychoanalytical causation veered too deeply into Freudian territory for Popenoe and the AIFR to fully endorse.[69] Thus they straddled the fence and, depending on the counselor in question, viewed homosexuality writ large as detrimental to the survival of the human race while at the same time evaluating possible strategies for reconditioning and "cure," which they assumed would be most promising for bisexuals or "ambi-verts."[70] In 1972, for example, Popenoe wrote to Barry Tanner at the Center for Behavior Change in Atlanta, Georgia, asking him to describe how he used electroshock therapy and to recommend equipment and treatment protocols.[71] Although it is unclear whether the AIFR employed shock therapy, Popenoe spent much of the 1960s and 1970s excoriating the "homosexual revolution." In 1962 he wrote that it "should be regarded as an intolerable evil that should not exist in a sound Society," and in 1967 he claimed that it deprived "the individual of the possibility of the fullest satisfaction of his nature."

On the eve of 1973, Popenoe stated that, analogous to women's liberation, the increasing visibility of homosexuals was menacing society: "The race is purified continually by the fact that the next generation is produced by family-minded persons, not by the enemies of family life. It is when the latter become too numerous, that the race is threatened."[72] By this point, Popenoe probably realized that gay and lesbian activists were very close to winning the deletion of the classification of homosexuality as a mental disorder from the American Psychiatric Association's *Diagnostic and Statistical Manual,* an emendation that occurred after explosive demonstrations and an internal vote in 1973.[73]

As gay and lesbian activists assailed well-known psychiatrists such as Charles Socarides and Irving Bieber, who claimed that homosexuality was a psychopathology that warranted extensive therapy and the rechanneling of sexual desire, they also lambasted Popenoe and the stance of the AIFR.[74] In 1971 Popenoe and four other institute staff participated in a radio discussion about homosexuality on KABC in Los Angeles. After this broadcast, in which Popenoe referred to same-sex desire as an illness that was "usually found in civilizations that are decaying," he received a letter from an incensed member of the Los Angeles Gay Community Alliance.[75] This activist attacked Popenoe for backing "hypocritical anti-sex laws" and for the circulation of the AIFR's pamphlet *Are Homosexuals Necessary?* Invoking Alfred Kinsey's theory of a continuum stretching from heterosexual to homosexual and replete with healthy variation, this young Angeleno stated that there were many people "in between." He mocked Popenoe's contention that homosexuality was a disease and rejected the premise that heterosexuality was innate, natural, or normal: "Perhaps you do not really understand the basic nature of human sexuality. We are not dogs, cats, or rats. Unlike those animals, sexual behavior in man is learned rather than instinctive. We have no basic heterosexual drive."[76] Like feminists, many gay and lesbian activists cast their struggle in terms of the negative emotional and psychological effects of doctrines of psychosexual development and misplaced "object choice." Their rage, however, was also vented against Popenoe and other anointed medical gurus, who operated outside prominent psychoanalytic circuits but nonetheless profoundly influenced postwar attitudes about sex, gender, and the family.[77]

STERILIZATION REDUX: *MADRIGAL V. QUILLIGAN*

Close to fifteen years after students protested the naming of the CSUS science building, another group confronted the lingering presence of eugenics in California. This time it was legislators, who expunged the state's seventy-year-old sterilization statute from the official record. Assemblyman Art Torres, chairman of the Health Committee, spearheaded this political action. In a letter to Governor Edmund G. Brown urging him to sign the repeal, Torres asserted that the sterilization law was "outdated" and that the criteria used to authorize an operation—particularly the clause regarding the genetic origins of mental disease and the phrase "having a marked departure from normal mentality"—had "no meaning in modern medical terminology."[78] Backed by the Department of Developmental Services and the California Association for the Retarded, this bill was approved unanimously in the assembly and the senate in committee and on the floor in August 1979.[79]

Torres learned that California's sterilization law was still on the books when, in the mid-1970s, several residents of his predominantly Latino Los Angeles district sued the Women's Hospital at the University of Southern California/Los Angeles County General Hospital (hereinafter County Hospital) for nonconsensual sterilizations.[80] The plaintiffs in this class action suit, *Madrigal v. Quilligan,* were working-class Mexican-origin women who had been coerced into postpartum tubal ligations minutes or hours after delivering via cesarean section. In contrast to the operations carried out at state institutions beginning in 1909, these procedures were supported by federal agencies that began to disperse funds in conjunction with the family planning initiatives of the War on Poverty launched by Lyndon B. Johnson in 1964.

For the most part, *Madrigal v. Quilligan* has been understood in light of the thousands of incidents of compulsory sterilizations reported in the United States from the late 1960s to the mid-1970s. And certainly, the experiences of the Mexican-origin women who were operated upon by County Hospital physicians mirror those of the African American, Puerto Rican, and Native American women who came forward with comparable stories during the same years. Nevertheless, *Madrigal v. Quilligan* has not been situated as an important link on a longer chain of eugenics and reproductive injustice in California that reaches back to the 1900s and forward to the twenty-first century. This episode can illuminate continuity and change, in terms of both the sterilization of poor women and Mexicans, male and female, and the longevity and potency of prosterilization arguments predicated on the protection of the public health and state resources.

A series of overlapping developments created the milieu for widespread sterilization abuse in the late 1960s. First, there was increased availability of and access to birth control. For example, by 1970 North Carolina, Virginia, Oregon, and Georgia had passed voluntary sterilization laws, and Washington, D.C., and New York had legalized abortion.[81] Quite simply, more women were using birth control, especially after the IUD and the Pill came on the market in the 1960s; voluntary sterilization rates rose in tandem so that in 1973 sterilization was the most common method of birth control by Americans in the thirty to forty-four age bracket.[82] Second, partly in response to feminist demands, in 1969 the American College of Obstetricians and Surgeons dropped its age-parity stipulation, which required that a woman's age multiplied by the number of her children equal 120 in order for her to qualify for voluntary sterilization. The following year, the College also retracted the proviso that a woman needed to consult two doctors and a psychiatrist before procuring surgery.[83] Third, federal funding for birth control and family planning rose markedly in the late 1960s, most decisively with the passage of the Family Planning Services and Population Research Act in 1970 and the creation of the Office of Economic Opportunity (OEO), which was commissioned with introducing contraception and related education programs to millions of underserved women. Whereas in 1965 about 450,000 women had access to family planning projects, by 1975 this number had jumped to 3.8 million.[84] In 1971, after heated debate over the degree to which the federal government should intrude into personal and bodily privacy (often disputed not by the Left but by libertarian-leaning conservatives such as the OEO's director, Donald Rumsfeld), the OEO incorporated sterilization into its medical armamentarium. Concurrently, Medicaid was authorized to reimburse up to 90 percent for a sterilization procedure.[85] Factoring in the operations backed by Medicaid and the US Department of Health, Education and Welfare (HEW) before the OEO's decision, between the late 1960s and 1974, when federal guidelines were formally enacted, approximately one hundred thousand sterilizations were carried out annually.[86] In theory, the advent of family planning resources and reproductive health clinics could provide millions of American women and men with heretofore scarce or nonexistent medical services. And many women took advantage of newly available OEO grants. In Pittsburgh, for example, African American women petitioned and received funds to set up a birth control clinic, a move that infuriated male black nationalists, who joined forces with the Catholic Church in a failed attempt to block its establishment.[87]

The increasing access to contraception, however, overwhelmingly benefited middle-class white women.[88] Against the injunction to define themselves primarily as breeders, mainstream feminists framed their struggle for reproductive and sexual autonomy in terms of the right not to have a child, focusing principally on abortion and elevating its federal legalization to their utmost goal.[89] While many women of color and working-class women also clamored for greater reproductive control, they often found themselves combating the reverse perception, namely, that they were destructive overbreeders whose procreative tendencies needed to be managed.[90] Given that the family planning model was underpinned by the populationist paradigm and the nuclear ideal of two to three children per couple, a substantial influx of resources into birth control services and the absence of standardized consent protocols made an environment ripe for coercion.

One of the most well-known cases was that of the Relf sisters, ages twelve and fourteen, who were sterilized without consent in 1973 in Alabama, in OEO-financed operations overseen by the Montgomery Community Action Committee. When the Southern Poverty Law Center sued on their behalf, it was revealed that their mother, who could not read, had unwittingly authorized the procedures. Believing she was authorizing birth control for her daughters, in the form of Depo-Provera injections, she signed an "X" on what was actually a sterilization release form.[91] By the time the Relfs and their legal counsel held a press conference in 1973, African American and Native American women from across the South and Southwest were coming forward with parallel allegations.[92] When *Relf v. Weinberger* was heard in federal district court, Judge Gerhard Gesell concluded that "an indefinite number of poor people have been improperly coerced into accepting a sterilization operation under the threat that variously supported welfare benefits would be withdrawn unless they submitted," and added that "the dividing line between family planning and eugenics is murky."[93] He also estimated that over the past several years, 100,000 to 150,000 low-income women had been sterilized under the auspices of federal programs.[94]

Along with African American women, who constituted 43 percent of all federally funded sterilization patients according to a 1973 survey, Native Americans were heavily affected by this aspect of the War on Poverty.[95] For example, one study commissioned by the Government Accounting Office found that between 1973 and 1976 the Indian Health Service, usually with HEW backing, sterilized more than 3,400 Native American women in the states of New Mexico, Arizona, Oklahoma, and South Dakota.[96] In the late 1970s, spokespeople for several Native American tribes claimed that somewhere between 20 and 50 percent of women of childbearing age in their communities had been sterilized without their consent.[97] Although Puerto Rican women, especially those on the island, had sought out and used sterilization as a reliable and practical form of contraception for several decades, they began to report nonconsensual surgeries. In New York City the vast majority of women sterilized at public hospitals were Puerto Rican, a predicament that spurred Dr. Helen Rodrigues-Triaz to cofound the Committee to End Sterilization Abuse in 1975.[98] During the same period, the Young Lords in New York City, strongly influenced by Puerto Rican feminists, simultaneously waged campaigns against forced sterilization and for augmented birth control and abortion services, which they saw as two complementary sides of reproductive control.[99]

If the surge of HEW-supported sterilizations was facilitated by a set of factors specific to the late 1960s, it was also enabled by the existence of state sterilization laws and the ongoing utilization of the psychometric labels *feebleminded* and *mentally defective*.[100] From the 1920s to the 1970s, the rationale for sterilization had gradually but never entirely shifted from one based on the transmission of faulty genes down the family line to one centered more and more on the purported negative consequences of unfit parenthood, dysfunctional families, and over-population. Nevertheless, there was one constant refrain throughout the twentieth century: reproductive surgery could serve as a techno-surgical fix that, in whatever instance, would save the state money, impede irresponsible parents from having more children, and boost the well-being of society.[101] In some states, this translated into the criminalization of illegitimacy, whereby unmarried mothers were extorted into sterilization with the threat of terminated welfare support or forced to submit to an operation to avoid incarceration.[102] In North Carolina, for example, Nial Cox, an eighteen-year-old unwed black mother, was forcibly sterilized in 1965 after her mother was told that unless Nial submitted to surgery she would cease to receive welfare assistance for Nial's siblings. North Carolina's Eugenics Board heard Nial's case, judged her to be feebleminded, and sent her to the operating table. Nial also held a press conference in 1973 to draw attention to her plight and filed a legal suit through the American Civil Liberties Union.[103] The previous year, in Mississippi, the house had passed a bill (HB 180) that pronounced a woman who gave birth to a second illegitimate child a felon punishable by either one to five years in prison (depending on the total number of children) or reproductive surgery.[104] The Student Non-violent Coordinating Committee (SNCC) promptly issued a pamphlet condemning HB 180, which was clearly aimed at poor and African American women, as a "program of officially supported and sanctioned genocide."[105] SNCC was instrumental in putting this bill, and corresponding legislative attempts, on the civil rights agenda and in the national spotlight. Once under attack from many sides, the Mississippi Senate relented, although a less stringent bill that made "unmarried parenthood a crime" did become law.[106] During the same period, Fannie Lou Hamer traveled the South, attacking the unwitting sterilization of black women—many of them underage—at Indianola's Sunflower City Hospital in the name of public health and welfare protection. For civil disobedience and black power activists, "Mississippi appendectomies" became an electrifying cry of 1960s activism.[107]

The plaintiffs in *Madrigal v. Quilligan* were neither welfare recipients nor on trial for illegitimacy; instead, they were working-class migrant women sterilized in a county hospital where obstetric residents were pressured to meet a quota of tubal ligations to adequately complete their training, and the physicians at the top of the chain of command held racially slanted ideas about population control. In 1973, appalled by the unethical medical behavior he had witnessed during his residency at County Hospital, Dr. Bernard Rosenfeld coauthored a Health Research Group report on sterilization abuse. He and his collaborators identified three hospitals, each of which had been heavily swayed by family planning and overpopulation concerns and had received HEW monies, as the gravest offenders: County Hospital, Boston City Hospital, and Baltimore City Hospital. At County Hospital, Rosenfeld documented a 742 percent increase in elective hysterectomies, a 470 percent increase in elective tubal ligations, and a 151 percent increase in postdelivery tubal ligations.[108] Moreover, he described a situation in which there was "little evidence of informed consent by the patient" and in which doctors were "selling" sterilizations "in a manner not unlike many other deceptive marketing practices."[109] According to Rosenfeld, County Hospital obstetricians instructed residents to strong-arm patients who were at the peak of labor into tubal ligations, often packaging the operation as an opportunity to gain needed surgical experience ("Remember everyone you get to get her tubes tied means two tubes for some resident or intern").[110]

Cognizant of what was transpiring at County Hospital, Los Angeles Chicanas began to organize and investigate, eventually locating 140 women who claimed that they had been forcibly sterilized in medically unnecessary surgeries.[111] As with Puerto Ricans on the East Coast, the sterilization cases galvanized Chicana feminists, who distinguished themselves from both white feminists, whose quest for abortion rights often made them oblivious to reproductive abuse, and male Chicano nationalists, who frequently described birth control as either superfluous to race and class or, more stridently, as treason against the perpetuation of the Chicano family and nation.[112] Chicanas mobilized demonstrations against County Hospital and formed the Committee to Stop Forced Sterilization, which linked sterilization to federal antipoverty programs, the greed of big international corporations, and the oppression of poor people worldwide, declaring, "We believe that the purpose of birth control is to given [sic] women more choice about how we will live our lives" (figure 17).[113]

FIGURE 17. Protest in Los Angeles against forced sterilizations at Los Angeles County–USC Medical Center, 1974. Copyright © 1974. Los Angeles Times. Reprinted with permission.

The *Madrigal v. Quilligan* trial, which in the end pitted the ten sterilized women against County Hospital obstetricians, began in May 1978. Four years earlier, some of the same plaintiffs had been involved in *Andrade v. Los Angeles County,* a civil suit that sought $6 million in damages.[114] In both cases, plaintiffs charged that their civil and constitutional rights to bear children had been violated and that between 1971 and 1974 they had been forcibly sterilized by obstetricians at County Hospital—specifically, that they had signed consent forms under duress, hours or minutes before or after labor, or had never been informed, or had been misinformed, that their tubes would be "tied."[115] Antonia Hernández and Charles Nabarette of the Los Angeles Center for Law and Justice represented the plaintiffs in *Madrigal v. Quilligan,* all of whom were low-income monolingual Spanish speakers who had migrated to California in their teens from rural areas in Mexico in search of economic opportunity or to join relatives. Although they varied in age, occupation, and number of children, their stories were strikingly similar. All of them had been approached about sterilization after having been in labor for several hours and had endured complicated and difficult deliveries, which were ultimately performed by cesarean section.[116] Their lawyers asserted that "these women were in such a state of mind that any consent which they may have signed was not informed" and that in three cases no consent was obtained.[117] Rebecca Figueroa was falsely given the impression that she was submitting to a reversible procedure. Elena Orozco was told that her hernia would be repaired only if she agreed to be sterilized, which she refused repeatedly "until almost the very last minute when she was taken to be delivered."[118] At no point after being admitted to County Hospital in 1973 did Guadalupe Acosta sign a consent form.[119] Dolores Madrigal did so after a medical assistant told her that her husband had already offered his signature, a deliberate falsehood. The women's accusations were supported by the affidavits of seven additional women, one of whom stated that a County Hospital doctor had told her after her cesarean that "I had too many children" and that "having future children would be dangerous for me."[120] Another was pressured by a doctor who told her that birth control pills and contraceptive foam were unreliable methods of birth control and that only sterilization was guaranteed to be effective; en route to the operating room, "confused and tired," and "frightened by what the doctor had told me," she signed a release handed to her by a Spanish-speaking nurse.[121] And yet another woman who provided a supporting affidavit was led to believe that she had offered her signature for the cesarean, not for a tubal ligation.[122]

Despite commanding and corroborated testimony about sterilization abuse at County Hospital, the judge ruled against the plaintiffs and for the defendants, who, he determined, had acted in good faith and had intended no harm. During the hearing several patterns emerged that presaged the final outcome. First, only one key witness, Karen Benker, spoke out against the doctors. Then a medical student and technician, Benker related an entrenched system of forced sterilization based on stereotypes of Mexicans as hyperbreeders and Mexican women as welfare mothers in waiting. She recalled conversations in which Dr. Edward James Quilligan, the lead defendant and the head of obstetrics and gynecology at County Hospital since 1969, stated that "poor minority women in L.A. County were having too many babies; that it was a strain on society; and that it was good that they be sterilized."[123] She also testified that he boasted about receiving a federal grant for a substantial sum that he intended to use to show, in his words, "how low we can cut the birth rate of the Negro and Mexican populations in Los Angeles County."[124] According to Benker, sterilizations were particularly pushed on women with two or more children who underwent C-sections. Facing the animosity of the judge, Benker's testimony was curtailed and then drowned out by the voices of the preponderantly male experts heard in the courtroom.

Second, the anthropologist Carlos Vélez-Ibañez, who threw himself into the case and sought with much passion and professionalism to make a compelling argument on behalf of the women, did so in a manner that ended up partially reinscribing problematic stereotypes of Mexican women. Drawing primarily from structural anthropology, Vélez contended that the essence of Mexican women's identity, particularly this "subgroup" of working-class *mestizas* from rural backgrounds, was motherhood. Not only that, the plaintiffs were naturally predisposed to want a large brood of children, so forced sterilization even after the fifth or sixth child was an affront to the ingrained values of Mexicans and constituted a violent kind of "cultural sterilization."[125] Vélez's character study of poor rural Mexican women helped emphasize national and cultural differences, an issue that distracted attention from the plaintiffs' most promising argument: that the legal standards for informed consent had not been met and that the abrogation of individual, civil, and constitutional rights outweighed the medical judgment of the doctors.

Finally, Hernández and Nabarette waived the option of a jury trial, a decision that placed the adjudication in the hands of one man, Judge Jesse Curtis. Although Curtis recognized that the women had "suffered severe emotional and physical stress because of these operations," he refused to blame County Hospital physicians for what he called "a break-down in communication between the patients and the doctors."[126] At the conclusion of a two-and-a-half-week trial that produced a transcript of more than 1,500 pages, Curtis ruled that he had found "no evidence of concerted or conspiratorial action" and stated that he had been persuaded by the defendant physicians' claim that they "would not perform the operation unless they were certain in their own mind that the patient understood the nature of the operation and was requesting the procedure."[127] Although Curtis did not explicitly endorse the neo-Malthusianism expressed by the physicians, he conveyed that it was not objectionable if a physician believed that a tubal ligation could improve a perceived overpopulation problem, as long as said physician did not try to "overpower the will of his patients."[128] Curtis described the case as a "clash of cultures" and in a damning reversal invoked Vélez's arguments about Mexican culture to suggest that if the plaintiffs had not been inclined toward wanting such large families, then their postpartum sterilizations would never have resulted in a class action lawsuit.

Less than two weeks after the ruling, the Center for Law and Justice announced that it would appeal and harshly criticized the court's neglect of Benker's testimony as well as that of an obstetrician called as an expert witness who contended that a woman in labor could never give what qualified as genuine informed consent.[129] Even though this legal action seems to have fizzled out, *Madrigal v. Quilligan* did have major consequences for the elaboration of sterilization stipulations, especially by securing a clause that consent forms be bilingual.[130] Now under many watchful eyes, County Hospital began to comply with federal sterilization guidelines, which included a seventy-two-hour waiting period between consent and operation, a near moratorium on steriliza-tion of persons younger than twenty-one, and a written and signed statement of consent, preceded by a clear explanation that welfare ben-efits would not be terminated if the patient declined the procedure. These guidelines had officially taken effect in 1974, although persistent violations and inconsistencies in hospitals across the country spurred more than fifty organizations to meet in Washington, D.C., in 1977 to push for stricter enforcement and oversight by HEW, and noncompli-ance was repeatedly reported at many hospitals into the 1980s.[131]

The sterilization of Mexican-origin women in Los Angeles unfolded alongside related abuse throughout the South and Southwest in the early 1970s and cannot be comprehended without attention to the con-fluence of forces—enlarged federal family planning initiatives, a county hospital with residents eager for obstetric training, the penetration of population planning into federal policy and some medical fields, and the rising availability and use of contraceptive methods—that facili-tated these forced operations. Nevertheless, the rationale used to dis-parage these women, indeed to deprive them of their human rights, had a much older provenance. As early as the 1920s, California eugenicists such as Goethe, David Starr Jordan, and Samuel J. Holmes claimed that Mexicans were irresponsible breeders, flooded over the border in "hordes," and undeservingly sapped fiscal resources. In 1935, for exam-ple, Goethe wrote to Laughlin, "It is this high birthrate that makes Mexican peon immigration such a menace. Peons multiply like rab-bits."[132] In editorials, pamphlets, and personal correspondence, promi-nent eugenicists foregrounded the "Mexican problem" as a danger to every facet of the state's health. The sterilizations at County Hospital were not under the purview of the Department of Institutions, like the twenty thousand that occurred from 1909 into the 1960s, but they can-not be extracted from the history of sterilization in California, particularly because they occurred in Los Angeles, which after the dissolution of the Eugenics Section of the Commonwealth Club of California in 1935 overtook San Francisco as the Pacific West's eugenic epicenter.[133] Los Angeles was home to several prominent groups, such as the Human Betterment Foundation, the California Division of the American Eugenics Society, and the AIFR, that were active into the 1950s and 1960s and that included as members several physicians affiliated with the University of Southern California hospitals.

With the repeal of state sterilization statutes, the end of national origins quotas, and the overturning of marriage bans, Americans exited an era of eugenics in which the state played a principal role in instituting and upholding hereditarian ideas and practices. From the early twentieth century to the 1960s, key state agencies, usually working in concert with private organizations and individuals, often made better breeding a guiding principle of social and health programs. There were differing permutations of eugenics across the country, depending on regional variations in race relations, gender dynamics, environmental policy, professional networks, and patterns of state governance and administration. The 1960s and 1970s saw the popular contestation of a eugenic nation through street protests, legislative reform, and lawsuits. Activists condemned practices they associated with racism, sexism, oppression, and exploitation and regularly expressed their moral outrage with terms such as *imperialism, fascism,* and *genocide.* References to and representations of Hitler, Nazis, and extermination were ubiquitous during the 1960s, expressed in the maxim "Question authority." This discourse resonated powerfully in a country with profound medical inequities, where medical and human subject abuse was not uncommon, and where the field of reproductive health was imbued with tenets of selective breeding.

Just as the transformations of the 1960s helped usher us out of an era of coercion, many of the keywords and conceptual frameworks we have employed since to understand eugenics in America originated during this decade. Quite ironically, the discursive bundling of eugenics, biological determinism, and scientific racism with Nazism and the Holocaust, which coalesced in American historical memory in the 1970s, has often helped obfuscate the long chronology of better breeding across the twentieth century.[134] It has made it more difficult to capture nuances, appreciate gray areas, and analyze the complicated interactions of various social actors.

In the end, there are many more stories to be told about how Americans challenged, embraced, and adapted hereditarianism. Eugenics took hold in states as diverse as Indiana, Vermont, and Virginia, providing a scientific framework to interpret and address perceived social problems. More than just a concern of elites, better breeding was often popular among working-class and middle-class Americans. In rural parts of the country many people extrapolated from the experience of crop cultivation and animal husbandry to human improvement. In the 1920s, for example, parents flocked to better babies contests to compare their children to their neighbors' and to learn scientific motherhood. In midcentury, women in Puerto Rico, Minnesota, and North Carolina solicited sterilizations through eugenics boards because they wanted permanent birth control, even when that meant being labeled feebleminded or mentally retarded. Although this book has concentrated on how European Americans and those who considered themselves to be white or Anglo pursued eugenics, African Americans intent on racial uplift and "righteous propagation" cultivated their own oppositional forms of better breeding.[135] In short, many more aspects of eugenics in modern America remain to be explored. Uncovering additional aspects of hereditarianism can enhance our understanding of subjects and processes as varied as the family, the state, sexuality, and race relations, especially in the period after 1940, when eugenics movements declined, continued forward, or splintered in competing directions. Finally, further excavating this history can raise new and challenging questions and concerns related to the ethical and social implications of genetic and reproductive technologies in the twenty-first century.

Conclusion

In February 2015 Virginia became the second state to establish a compensation plan for living victims of a forced sterilization program.[1] Virginia's general assembly and Governor Terry McAuliffe approved a $400,000 budget designed to pay out $25,000 to victims of a program that had sterilized roughly eight thousand people between 1924 and 1979.[2] This compensation package comes two years after North Carolina made history as the first state to authorize monetary reparations, allocating $10 million for one-time payments to the living victims of the 7,600 sterilized between 1929 and 1974.[3] At the twelve-month mark of this program about 220 people had each received checks for $20,000, although some victims frustratingly did not qualify because their operations—labeled eugenic sterilizations by physicians at the time of surgery—were not administered by the official North Carolina Eugenics Board.[4]

The reparations in North Carolina and Virginia are the culmination of years-long advocacy by victims, mental health advocates, legislators, and scholars who fought for additional restorative gestures following the apologies issued for eugenic practices and mass sterilization in the early 2000s by a previous cohort of governors and lawmakers. In 2002, Virginia spearheaded a wave of gubernatorial apologies and legislative acknowledgments that soon spread to North Carolina, South Carolina, Oregon, California, and Indiana.[5] This accumulating recognition of the wrongs carried out in the name of eugenics under the aegis of states and their health and welfare agencies heightened awareness of the history of eugenics in these and other states (thirty-two total) that had passed sterilization laws in the twentieth century. For example, reporters at the *Winston-Salem Journal* worked with civil rights advocates, community activists, and academicians to uncover personal stories and historical materials that became part of a 2002 series on North Carolina's sterilization program. Entitled "Against Their Will" and eventually published as a book compilation, these articles elucidate the racial and gendered logic that guided North Carolina's program, which sterilized African American women at intensifying rates in the 1950s and 1960s.[6] Several years later in Indiana, historians, bioethicists, and legislators organized an exhibit, a conference, and several publications around the centennial of the 1907 passage of the Hoosier state's sterilization law, the first such legislation in the world.[7] These commemorative endeavors included the installation of a historical plaque recognizing the 2,500 people sterilized in state homes and hospitals in Indiana between 1907 and 1974.[8] In Alberta—one of the two Canadian provinces with a eugenic sterilization program—a university-community team launched a dynamic project exploring the eugenic past and its ramifications for the present, above all for people with disabilities. Anchored to the question "What sorts of people should there be?" and supported by the Social Sciences and Humanities Research Council of Canada, the Living Archives on Eugenics in Western Canada is informed and enriched by collaboration among scholars and community activists. Its Web platform includes an impressive collection of resources such as video testimonies of sterilization victims and time lines and encyclopedia entries written by specialists. Users can immerse themselves in autobiographical narratives of forced sterilization in Alberta and connect this critical facet of North American eugenics to global histories and patterns.[9]

California has been home to similar activities. In March 2003 following a senate hearing in the state capitol, Governor Gray Davis apologized for the state's sterilization program. Speaking for the "people of California," Davis conveyed his message to the "victims and their families of this past injustice," lamenting, "Our hearts are heavy for the pain caused by eugenics. It was a sad and regrettable chapter—one that must never be repeated."[10] Soon California's attorney general issued a separate apology, and the state senate passed a resolution expressing "profound regret over the state's past role in the eugenics movement and the injustice done to thousands of California men and women."[11]

Since that flurry of political activity, advocates and academicians have organized virtual and in-person meetings to discuss the relevance and importance of remembering California's eugenic past and evaluating its implications and echoes today.[12] While gratified by gubernatorial and legislative statements that acknowledge how eugenic sterilization trampled on human rights and reproductive autonomy, some of us involved in these events took pause. For the most part, these headline-grabbing apologies painted a stark boundary between our enlightened and ethically informed present and a benighted past in which "pseudoscientific" theories with Nazi origins misguided health and political leaders. This kind of rhetoric relies on and reinforces a certain brand of hubris that can induce complacency around contemporary issues of social justice, reproduction, and genetics. The 2013 revelations about the 144 unauthorized sterilizations performed on female inmates in California prisons from 2006 to 2010 proved the fragility of conceits drawn from historical interpretation. Tucking the past away in a neat package can also hinder a deeper appreciation of the complexity of eugenics, particularly of those gray areas where hereditarianism overlapped with dimensions of public health and medicine, such as infectious disease management or infant and maternal care, that have been much less controversial.

Over the past decade, there has been periodic and sometimes intense reflection among scholars and advocates and in the media on California's eugenic past. During this entire time there also has been one persistent and glaring absence: living sterilization victims who can accept apologies or tell their stories, let alone clamor for compensation. Whereas in Virginia, Oregon, and North Carolina sterilization victims unveiled plaques, recounted their experiences to reporters, or participated in the establishment of agencies such as North Carolina's Office of Justice for Sterilization Victims, in California there has been a void.[13] Even after concerted attempts by legislators, journalists, and scholars to locate sterilization victims through press announcements and official channels, only one person, the late Charlie Follett, ever ventured into the public spotlight. Sterilized at the Sonoma State Home in 1945 at the age of fifteen, Follett felt that he was entitled to compensation for his suffering and humiliation, describing his life as "miserable." All indications are that Follett was destitute after leaving Sonoma; he lived for many years out of his battered Cadillac in the small town of Lodi and died without even a penny for his own burial.[14]

I have learned about a handful of patients who were sterilized in state institutions through relatives who tracked me down upon learning about my research. Of this modest group of six, almost all were curious about an aunt or uncle sent to Sonoma, Pacific Colony, or Stockton whose life story is shrouded in obscurity and limited to patchy information and partial recollection. I was able to locate most of these patients by checking the digitized sterilization forms and data set. However, California law permits only conservators to access patient information. Thus I could not divulge anything to the relatives who contacted me. They had telling clues about the circumstances that led to their family member's institutional commitment, and historical memory would benefit from assembling the puzzle pieces they offered with data points in official documents. However, in accordance with Health Insurance Portability and Accountability Act (HIPAA) regulations, and with conflicting feelings of obligation and frustration, I directed them to the Department of State Hospitals' Legal Department to pursue their genealogical quests.

How is it possible that in California, where more than twenty thousand sterilizations were performed, there is nobody willing or able to tell her or his story? The answer lies mainly in timing. In several states, persons classified as mentally retarded or unfit to bear or rear children were sterilized, sometimes at increasing rates, into the 1960s. Yet California's program slowed considerably in the early 1950s. Today none of the fifty patients interviewed in the 1960s by UCLA psychiatrist Robert Edgerton for a study about the psychological and emotional impact of sterilization at Pacific Colony are still alive.[15] Moreover, whether because of shame, apathy, or stigma, no living victims in California have expressed any interest in remembering their sterilizations aloud and in public. This simple act could attach a human face to the statistics and draw attention to the lasting, often harrowing, consequences of forced reproductive surgery. In light of recent developments in Virginia and North Carolina, it might spur the California legislature to consider compensation.

Given these limitations, and with slight possibility of reparations for sterilization victims, how can we encourage California to recognize, and never forget, its paramount role in the history of eugenics and sterilization?

First and foremost, we can reconstruct in broad strokes and elucidate in detail stories and patterns of sterilization in state institutions. In my case, this has been facilitated by uncovering materials like the microfilms with thousands of pages of sterilization documents. Preliminary quantitative analysis of the data set we have constructed from these historical records shows discernible ethnic, gender, and age bias. In at least one institution, Pacific Colony, Spanish-surnamed females under eighteen years of age were at the greatest risk of sterilization. Population-level data can show significant associations among a large set of variables, and further analysis will expand our grasp of social patterns and longitudinal trends. Yet each patient committed to a state home or hospital and recommended for sterilization was a human being deserving of dignity and rights that were violated by state laws and institutional practices. By foregrounding social justice, work with the sterilization records that aims to recover marginalized and elided stories and make them accessible in traditional and digital formats can help heal and restore even if pseudonyms suppress the historical subjectivity contained in actual names.[16] Writing sterilization experiences back into history can happen at the scholarly level as well as in K-12 education. The 2011 passage of the FAIR (Fair, Accurate, Inclusive, and Respectful) Education Act in California, which mandates the incorporation of disability and lesbian/gay/bisexual/trans/questioning (LGBTQ) history into public school curricula, offers an entry point for informing young people about this problematic aspect of California's past.[17] My team of researchers is prototyping a digital archive that links storytelling to data visualization, with the objective of producing of an interactive online resource that will be of value to students and other researchers and that can restore historical knowledge to the communities most harmed by eugenic sterilization.

Confronting historical amnesia involves a good dose of retrospective reflection; it also prompts us to tease out the insinuation and reach of eugenic ideas and practices today. From several perspectives, eugenics is more than a residue that can be effortlessly wiped away. For example, twenty-first-century anti-immigrant vitriol, whether involving anxieties about anchor babies, birthright citizenship, or unaccompanied minors from Central America crossing the US-Mexican border, draws heavily on resilient stereotypes of biological inferiority that arose and became consolidated during the eugenic racism of the 1920s and 1930s.[18]

Continuities are also visible when we trace rationales of hereditary disease prevention from the sterilization programs of the 1930s to the development of prenatal testing in the 1970s. From the vantage point of some disability studies scholarship, eugenic selection never ended, it just acquired more sophisticated methods of detection and more precise diagnostic categories. Amniocentesis, the breakout form of prenatal diagnostic testing, was propelled forward in the 1970s and 1980s by the entwined rationales of genetic disease prevention and cost savings.[19] It soon was supplemented by another diagnostic tool, chorionic villus sampling (CVS), and a steady stream of genetic screening technologies designed to calculate the probability that a fetus had chromosomal anomalies, spina bifida, neural tube defects, and other genetic conditions. When prenatal testing was introduced in the 1970s and 1980s, eugenic presumptions about normality and health were palpable in the language and images employed to describe the potential lives of people with physical and intellectual disabilities. For example, genetic counselors tended to present Down syndrome and inherited disabilities as problems to be avoided or bad news to be delivered to expectant parents awaiting test results.[20] Although the logic of disease prevention still undergirds prenatal testing, over the past two decades genetic counseling approaches have changed substantially. Buoyed by hard-won civil rights victories for people with disabilities, most notably the 1990 Americans with Disabilities Act (ADA), as well as the mainstreaming of a segment of children with disabilities into schools, genetic counselors have revised how they communicate with and provide support to parents who are considering prenatal testing or receiving test results.[21]

Nevertheless, in the 1990s, as genetic counselors were becoming sensitized to disability issues, the landscape of genomic medicine was undergoing a transformation exemplified by the Human Genome Project. Underwritten by federal scientific agencies, the Project embarked on the ambitious goal of decoding the human genome, a task started in 1990 and completed ahead of schedule in 2003, in large part because of concurrent rivaling efforts by Celera Genomics, a private company that developed an innovative and faster technique of genome sequencing. Unlike Human Genome Project scientists, who adhered to President Bill Clinton's declarations that the human genome could not be patented, Celera initially sought proprietary control of over six thousand genes.[22] Eventually Celera relented on its patent requests. Nonetheless, this episode is emblematic of the migration, during the 1990s and 2000s, of much of genomic medicine into the commercial domain, where there is little regulation or red tape to slow down research and development.

Prenatal diagnosis and genetic screening programs emerged in the 1970s in the milieu of university hospitals, specialty clinics, and public health departments. During this decade, the National Institutes of Health's National Institute of Child Health and Human Development (NICHD) funded nine prenatal clinics affiliated with prominent hospitals across the country to create an amniocentesis registry that conducted the first blind control study of the safety and effectiveness of the procedure. This collaborative group studied the experiences of 1,040 women who had undergone amniocentesis. After reviewing maternal complications, fetal loss, newborn evaluations, and the status of one-year-old infants of mothers in the study sample, the group concluded that the "results of this study provide evidence, for the first time, that midtrimester amniocentesis, despite its potential risks, is a safe procedure."[23] Following this stamp of validation, amniocentesis started to become a routinized feature of prenatal care. In this same period, health departments and community organizations initiated the first wave of Tay-Sachs and sickle-cell anemia screening programs. Both prenatal diagnosis and genetic screening programs carried presumptions about disability prevention and racial and ethnic susceptibility toward certain genetic conditions, but they were motivated by an interest in expanding reproductive and genetic health services to underserved populations.[24]

Today it's a brave new commercialized world. Genetic companies such as Sequenom or Natura are at the forefront of the development and marketing of the latest addition to the prenatal armamentarium: noninvasive prenatal tests (NIPT), which examine fetal cells in maternal blood to ascertain if a woman is carrying a fetus with one of the three most common trisomies (21, 18, and 13). Unlike amniocentesis, which involves extraction of amniotic fluid with a fine needle and carries minimal but extant risk, NIPT can be performed with a blood draw. Companies assure consumers that this ease is matched with same degree of accuracy, but given the newness of this technology and limited product regulation it is difficult to confirm these assertions. Indeed, critics have evinced concern that the rapid rollout of NIPT and its glossy advertising have drowned out professional medical guidelines that recommend against its use in routine prenatal care and clarify that it does not deliver clear-cut diagnoses but instead offers risk calculations. In addition, observers have criticized NIPT for producing too many false positives, which can prompt women to unnecessarily undergo more invasive diagnostic procedures like amniocentesis or CVS. In some instances, women have predicated a decision to terminate a pregnancy solely on NIPT results.[25] An in-depth report by the New England Center for Investigative Reporting determined that manufacturers of NIPT are failing to properly educate consumers, with ramifications that are troublesome for patients and society as a whole: the "companies selling the most popular of these screens do not make it clear enough to patients and doctors that the results of their tests are not reliable enough to make a diagnosis."[26] Whether we are looking back at the early days of amniocentesis, when it was securely tied to arguments about the need to reduce the medical and economic costs of having children with disabilities, or critically evaluating our contemporary moment, when NIPT evokes questions about the ability of genetic companies to transparently and ethically market the new shiny products they are eager to sell, there is no denying that prenatal tests have real-life and philosophical ramifications for those of us concerned both with consumer rights and with omnipresent ableism in American society.

Reproductive and genetic technologies need not be construed as antagonistic to the aims of reproductive rights and justice. There is a place and need for these services, which expand procreative and reproductive options, enabling straight couples with infertility struggles and LGBTQ couples and single people to parent and create families. Indeed, these technologies often are in the crosshairs of struggles over women's reproductive health and bodies. In a majority of states, reproductive rights are being curtailed by legislation that enacts various requirements to restrict abortion access, shutting down clinics that provide a wide range of reproductive health services. Since 2011, 204 antiabortion measures have passed on the state level; in 2013 alone, twenty-two states passed 70 such laws. Throwing down the gauntlet to *Roe v. Wade* through a state-by-state strategy, the antiabortion movement is successfully creating a patchwork nation in which a small number of unaffected states offer the full range of reproductive health services, including abortion, and a majority offer next to none.[27]

In a few states, these restrictions are tied to prenatal testing results under the guise of protecting fetal rights. In 2014 North Dakota introduced a law that bans women who discover a fetal anomaly from obtaining an abortion. In early 2015 Republican legislators in Ohio put forth a bill prohibiting abortion specifically in cases where trisomy 21, or Down syndrome, is detected in the fetus.[28] Such developments are part of a strategy to chip away abortion rights that is equally detrimental to reproductive rights and disability rights and is less about protecting the unborn than about reasserting state control over the procreative and reproductive autonomy of all women. Such disregard for and deprivation of liberty was at the core of eugenic sterilization.

Awareness of the history of eugenics keeps us alert when assessing the values underlying contemporary genetic medicine and technologies.[29] It can help us trace one of the most enduring forces in human genetics: reductionism, which was central to the simplistic theories of inheritance favored by eugenicists and which still casts a spell on scientists and observers intent on identifying genes for complex conditions such as obesity, sexual identity, or intelligence.[30] This pursuit becomes particularly pernicious when the search for single-gene causation focuses on medical conditions associated with particular racial and ethnic groups.[31] Even if potentially beneficial drugs are developed as part of such efforts, this dynamic can easily obscure and undercut explanations of racial health disparities that prioritize social determinants.[32]

Revisiting *Eugenic Nation* ten years later leaves me with a perplexing question: How can California be home simultaneously to extreme patterns of incarceration and sterilization and to the unbridled development of commercialized genomics, much of which is based in Silicon Valley? The response to this loaded question is complex and multilayered but is inextricably linked to the state's peculiar brand of progressivism, which advances multiracial, multicultural, and disability rights agendas while punishing and warehousing thousands of low-income people, people of color, and minor offenders, many suffering from mental illness. Geographically and figuratively California is a state where entrepreneurs offer new technologies that promise people more control over their genetic and reproductive futures while others are irrevocably deprived of such opportunities. Although the terms of such countervailing patterns and the social groups they affect have changed over the years, the exalted aspirations of genetic and social enhancement have resonated and continue to resonate profoundly in the Golden State.

Notes

PREFACE TO THE SECOND EDITION

1. Corey G. Johnson, "Female Inmates Sterilized in California Prisons without Approval," Center for Investigative Reporting, July 7, 2013, http://cironline .org/reports/female-inmates-sterilized-california-prisons-without-approval-4917.

2. Corey G. Johnson, "Lawmakers Call for Investigation into Sterilization of Female Inmates," Center for Investigative Reporting, July 10, 2013, http:// cironline.org/reports/lawmakers-call-investigation-sterilization-female-inmates-4961.

3. California State Auditor, "Sterilization of Female Inmates: Some Inmates Were Sterilized Unlawfully, and the Safeguards Designed to Limit Occurrence of the Procedure Failed," Report 2013–120, June 2014, Sacramento, CA.

4. "California Governor Signs Inmate Sterilization Ban," Reuters, September 25, 2014, www.reuters.com/article/2014/09/26/us-usa-california-prisons-idUSKC NoHL07720140926; "History of SB 1135," n.d., http://leginfo.legislature.ca.gov /faces/billNavClient.xhtml;jsessionid=2ccf80445 1d89d5c5834f82b9c3a.

5. Quoted in C. Johnson, "Female Inmates Sterilized."

6. "Madrigal v. Quilligan," CV 74–2057-JWC, Report's Transcript of Proceedings, Tuesday, May 30, 1978, Carlos G. Vélez-Ibañez Papers, Sterilization Archive, Item 5, Chicano Studies Research Library, University of California at Los Angeles.

7. See Elena R. Gutiérrez, *Fertile Matters: The Politics of Mexican-Origin Women's Reproduction* (Austin: University of Texas Press, 2008).

8. Quoted in Tim Stelloh, "California's Great Prison Experiment," *Nation*, July 5, 2013, www.thenation.com/article/174680/californias-great-prison-experiment#.

9. Cynthia Chandler, "The Gender-Responsive Prison Expansion Movement," in *Interrupted Life: Experiences of Incarcerated Women in the United*

States, ed. Rickie Solinger et al. (Berkeley: University of California Press, 2010), 332–37.

10. Quoted in Corey G. Johnson, "Calif. Prison Doctor Linked to Sterilizations No Stranger to Controversy," Center for Investigative Reporting, February 13, 2014, http://cironline.org/reports/calif-prison-doctor-linked-sterilizations-no-stranger-controversy-5859.

11. Johnson, "Female Inmates Sterilized" and "Calif. Prison Doctor." Also see Rachel Roth and Sara L. Ainsworth, "'If They Hand You a Paper, You Sign It': A Call to End the Sterilization of Women in Prison," *Hastings Women's Law Journal* 26, no. 7 (Winter 2015), https://litigation-essentials.lexisnexis.com /webcd/app?action=DocumentDisplay&crawlid=1&doctype=cite&docid=26+ Hastings+Women%27s+L.J.+7&srctype=smi&srcid=3B15&key=7ff27794b45 b9a4a98ef8086ef3a9a64.

12. Quoted in Johnson, "Female Inmates Sterilized."

13. California State Auditor, "Sterilization of Female Inmates," 37–38.

14. California Coalition for Women Prisoners, "Critical Statistics," updated March 2007, accessed February 13, 2015, www.womenprisoners.org/resources /critical_statistics.html.

15. Ruth Wilson Gilmore, *Golden Gulag: Prisons, Surplus, Crisis, and Opposition in Globalizing California* (Berkeley: University of California Press, 2007), 7.

16. California Coalition for Women Prisoners, "Critical Statistics."

17. Gilmore, *Golden Gulag*, 7. On rethinking mass incarceration in postwar America, see Heather Ann Thompson, "Why Mass Incarceration Matters: Rethinking Crisis, Decline, and Transformation in Postwar American History," *Journal of American History* 97, no. 3 (2010): 703–34.

18. See Dominic A. Sisti, Andrea G. Segal, and Ezekiel J. Emanuel, "Improving Long-Term Psychiatric Care: Bring Back the Asylum," *Journal of the American Medical Association* 313, no. 3 (2015): 243–44.

19. See Michael A. Rembis, "The New Asylums: Madness and Mass Incarceration in the Neoliberal Era," in *Disability Incarcerated: Imprisonment and Disability in the United States and Canada*, ed. Liat-Ben Moshe, Chris Chapman, and Allison C. Carey (New York: Palgrave Macmillan, 2014), 139–59.

20. Deborah Reid, "Reproductive Justice Advocates: Don't Roll Back Sterilization Consent Rules," RH Reality Check, April 2, 2014, http://rhrealitycheck .org/article/2014/04/02/reproductive-justice-advocates-dont-roll-back-sterilization-consent-rules/.

21. Sonya Borrero, Nikki Zite, and Mitchell D. Creinin, "Federally Funded Sterilization: Time to Rethink Policy?" *American Journal of Public Health* 102, no. 10 (2012): 1822–25.

22. Joseph E. Potter et al., "Frustrated Demand for Sterilization among Low-Income Latinas in El Paso, Texas," *Perspectives on Sexual and Reproductive Health* 44, no. 4 (2012): 228–35; Karl White et al., "Knowledge and Attitudes about Long-Acting Reversible Contraception among Latina Women Who Desire Sterilization," *Women's Health Issues* 23, no. 4 (2014): 257–63.

23. See Carmen R. Lugo-Lugo and Mary K. Bloodsworth-Lugo, "'Anchor/ Terror Babies' and Latina Bodies: Immigration Rhetoric in the 21st Century and

the Feminization of Terrorism," *Journal of Interdisciplinary Feminist Thought* 8, no. 1 (2014), http://digitalcommons.salve.edu/jift/vol8/iss1/1/?utm_source =digitalcommons.salve.edu%2Fjift%2Fvol8%2Fiss1%2F1&utm_medium =PDF&utm_campaign=PDFCoverPages; and Priscilla Huang, "Anchor Babies, Over-breeders, the Population Bomb: The Reemergence of Nativism and Anti-population Control in Anti-immigration Policies," *Harvard Law and Policy Review* 2 (2008): 385–406.

INTRODUCTION

1. Laurence M. Cruz, "Eugenics Yields Dark Past," *Statesman Journal* (Salem, OR), December 1, 2002, and "Governor Apologizes for Eugenics," *Statesman Journal,* December 3, 2002; Randi Bjornstad, "Sterilization Apology Offered in Oregon," *Register-Guard* (Salem, OR), December 3, 2002.

2. "Full Text of State's Apology Regarding Eugenics," *Statesman Journal* (Salem, OR), December 3, 2002.

3. Peter Hardin, "Apology for Eugenics Set: Warner Action Makes Virginia First State to Denounce Movement," *Richmond Times-Dispatch,* May 2, 2002; William Branigin, "Virginia Apologizes to the Victims of Sterilizations," *Washington Post,* May 3, 2002.

4. "Full Text."

5. Eric Mennel, "Payments Start for N.C. Eugenics Victims, But Many Won't Qualify," NPR, October 31, 2014, www.npr.org/blogs/health/2014/10/31 /360355784/payments-start-for-n-c-eugenics-victims-but-many-wont-qualify.

6. See Elazar Barkan, *The Guilt of Nations: Restitution and Negotiating Historical Injustices* (Baltimore: Johns Hopkins University Press, 2001).

7. See Hannah Arendt, *The Origins of Totalitarianism* (1951; repr., New York: Harcourt, Brace, 1973).

8. See Peter Novick, *The Holocaust in American Life* (Boston: Houghton Mifflin, 1999).

9. See Stefan Kühl, *The Nazi Connection: Eugenics, American Racism, and German National Socialism* (Oxford: Oxford University Press, 1994).

10. See Edwin Black, *War against the Weak: Eugenics and America's Campaign to Create a Master Race* (New York: Four Walls Eight Windows, 2003); and Elazar Barkan, *The Retreat of Scientific Racism: Changing Concepts of Race in Britain and the United States between the World Wars* (New York: Cambridge University Press, 1992). On German eugenics, see Robert Proctor, *Racial Hygiene: Medicine under the Nazis* (Cambridge, MA: Harvard University Press, 1988); and Paul Weindling, *Health, Race, and German Politics between National Unification and Nazism, 1870–1945* (Cambridge: Cambridge University Press, 1989).

11. See George W. Stocking, *Race, Culture, and Evolution: Essays in the History of Anthropology* (Chicago: University of Chicago Press, 1982).

12. See Barkan, *Retreat of Scientific Racism;* L. C. Dunn and Th. Dobzhansky, *Heredity, Race, and Society* (New York: Mentor Books, 1946); and United Nations Educational, Scientific and Cultural Organization, *The Race Concept: Results of an Inquiry* (Paris: UNESCO, 1952).

13. See Daniel J. Kevles, *In the Name of Eugenics: Genetics and the Uses of Human Heredity*, rev. ed. (Cambridge, MA: Harvard University Press, 1995); and Adele E. Clarke, *Disciplining Reproduction: Modernity, American Life Sciences, and "the Problems of Sex"* (Berkeley: University of California Press, 1998).

14. See Molly Ladd-Taylor, "'A Kind of Genetic Social Work': Sheldon Reed and the Origins of Genetic Counseling," in *Women, Health, and Nation: Canada and the United States since 1945*, ed. Georgina Feldberg et al. (Montreal: McGill-Queen's University Press, 2003), 67–83; Diane B. Paul, *The Politics of Heredity: Essays on Eugenics, Biomedicine, and the Nature-Nurture Debate* (Albany: State University of New York Press, 1998); and Alexandra Minna Stern, *Telling Genes: The Story of Genetic Counseling in America* (Baltimore: Johns Hopkins University Press, 2012).

15. Genetic counselors were aware, however, that conveying information about the likelihood of transmitting identified genetic diseases sometimes would encourage couples to have more children in order to ensure the eventual production of "normal" offspring. As Diane Paul has noted, this is antithetical to a eugenic standpoint, which would discourage the proliferation of defects, especially those carried recessively and not phenotypically expressed. Genetic counselors, though, were confident that most of their middle-class clients would make sensible decisions for the sake of both their families' future and the gene pool. See D. Paul, *Politics of Heredity*, 133–56.

16. See Sarah W. Tracy, "An Evolving Science of Man: The Transformation and Demise of American Constitutional Medicine, 1920–1950," in *Greater Than the Parts: Holism in Biomedicine, 1920–1950*, ed. Christopher Lawrence and George Weisz (New York: Oxford University Press, 1998), 161–88, and "George Draper and American Constitutional Medicine, 1916–1946: Reinventing the Sick Man," *Bulletin of the History of Medicine* 66, no. 1 (Spring 1992): 53–89; and Alexandra Minna Stern, "From Mestizophilia to Biotypology: Racialization and Science in Mexico, 1920–1960," in *Race and Nation in Modern Latin America*, ed. Nancy Applebaum, Anne S. MacPherson, and Karin Alejandra Rosemblatt (Chapel Hill: University of North Carolina Press, 2003), 187–210.

17. The English Eugenics Society served as the London headquarters of the International Planned Parenthood Foundation. See Linda Gordon, *Woman's Body, Woman's Right: Birth Control in America*, rev. ed. (New York: Penguin Books, 1990), chap. 13.

18. See D. Paul, *Politics of Heredity*; Kevles, *In the Name*; Celeste Michelle Condit, *The Meanings of the Gene: Public Debates about Human Heredity* (Madison: University of Wisconsin Press, 1999).

19. See William H. Tucker, *The Funding of Scientific Racism: Wickliffe Draper and the Pioneer Fund* (Urbana: University of Illinois Press, 2002).

20. See Steven Selden, *Inheriting Shame: The Story of Eugenics and Racism in America* (New York: Teacher's College, Columbia University, 1999); and Diane B. Paul, *Controlling Human Heredity: 1865 to the Present* (Atlantic Highlands, NJ: Humanities Press, 1995).

21. See D. Paul, *Politics of Heredity*, 4.

22. See Society for the Study of Social Biology, "A New Name—Society for the Study of Social Biology (formerly the American Eugenics Society)," *Social Biology* 20, no. 1 (1973): 1.

23. See Philip R. Reilly, *The Surgical Solution: A History of Involuntary Sterilization in the United States* (Baltimore: Johns Hopkins University Press, 1991); and Julius Paul, "The Return of Punitive Sterilization Proposals: Current Attacks on Illegitimacy and the AFDC Program," *Law and Society Review* 3, no. 1 (1968): 77–106.

24. See Kenneth M. Ludmerer, *Genetics and American Society: A Historical Appraisal* (Baltimore: Johns Hopkins University Press, 1972); Mark H. Haller, *Eugenics: Hereditarian Attitudes in American Thought* (New Brunswick, NJ: Rutgers University Press, 1963); and Garland E. Allen, "The Eugenics Record Office at Cold Spring Harbor, 1910–1940," *Osiris*, 2nd. ser., 2 (1986): 225–64, and "The Misuse of Biological Hierarchies: The American Eugenics Movement, 1900–1940," *History and Philosophy of the Life Sciences* 5, no. 2 (1983): 105–28.

25. See Race Betterment Foundation, *Race Betterment Exhibit* (Battle Creek, MI: n.p., 1915); and Brian C. Wilson, *Dr. John Harvey Kellogg and the Religion of Biologic Living* (Bloomington: Indiana University Press, 2014).

26. See Edward J. Larson, *Sex, Race, and Science: Eugenics in the Deep South* (Baltimore: Johns Hopkins University Press, 1995).

27. See Nancy L. Gallagher, *Breeding Better Vermonters: The Eugenics Project in the Green Mountain State* (Hanover, NH: University Press of New England, 1999); Lisa Linquist Dorr, "Arm in Arm: Gender, Eugenics, and Virginia's Racial Integrity Acts of the 1920s," *Journal of Women's History* 11, no. 1 (Spring 1999): 143–66; Gregory Michael Dorr, *Segregation's Science: Hereditarian Thought in Virginia, 1785 to the Present* (Chapel Hill: University of North Carolina Press, in press); Johanna Schoen, *Choice and Coercion: Birth Control, Sterilization, and Abortion in Public Health and Welfare* (Chapel Hill: University of North Carolina Press, 2005); Katherine Castles, "Quiet Eugenics: Sterilization in North Carolina's Institutions for the Mentally Retarded, 1945–1965," *Journal of Southern History* 68, no. 4 (November 2002): 849–78; Molly Ladd-Taylor, "The 'Sociological Advantages' of Sterilization: Fiscal Policies and Feeble-Minded Women in Interwar Minnesota," in *Mental Retardation in America: A Historical Reader,* ed. Steven Noll and James W. Trent Jr. (New York: New York University Press, 2004), 281–99; Mark A. Largent, "'The Greatest Curse of the Race': Eugenic Sterilization in Oregon, 1909–1983," *Oregon Historical Quarterly* 103, no. 2 (2002): 188–209; and Alexandra Minna Stern, "Making Better Babies: Public Health and Race Betterment in Indiana, 1920–1935," *American Journal of Public Health* 92, no. 5 (2002): 742–52.

28. See Gunnar Broberg and Nils Roll-Hansen, *Eugenics and the Welfare State: Sterilization Policy in Denmark, Sweden, Norway and Finland* (East Lansing: Michigan State University Press, 1996); Jennifer Robertson, "Japan's First Cyborg? Miss Nippon, Eugenics, and Wartime Technologies of Beauty, Body, and Blood," *Body and Society* 7, no. 1 (2001): 1–34; Frank Dikötter, *Imperfect Conceptions: Medical Knowledge, Birth Defects, and Eugenics in China* (New York: Columbia University Press, 1998); Mark B. Adams, ed., *The Wellborn Sci-*

ence: Eugenics in Germany, France, Brazil, and Russia (New York: Oxford University Press, 1990); Nancy Leys Stepan, *"The Hour of Eugenics": Race, Gender, and Nation in Latin America* (Ithaca, NY: Cornell University Press, 1991); Angus McLaren, *Our Own Master Race: Eugenics in Canada, 1885–1945* (Toronto: McClelland and Stewart, 1990); and Richard Cleminson, "Eugenics by Names or by Nature? The Spanish Anarchist Sex Reform of the 1930s," *History of European Ideas* 18, no. 5 (1994): 729–40. There are many other excellent articles and books on Romania, India, and Brazil, to name just a few.

29. See Stern, "From Mestizophilia to Biotypology"; Karin Alejandra Rosemblatt, "Sexuality and Biopower in Chile and Latin America," *Political Power and Social Theory* 15 (2001): 315–72; and William H. Schneider, *Quality and Quantity: The Quest for Biological Regeneration in Twentieth-Century France* (New York: Cambridge University Press, 1990).

30. For example, see Madison Grant, *The Conquest of a Continent; or, The Expansion of Races in America* (New York: Charles Scribner's Sons, 1933).

31. Charles M. Goethe, *Seeking to Serve* (Sacramento, CA: Keystone Press, 1949), 137.

32. See Wendy Kline, *Building a Better Race: Gender, Sexuality, and Eugenics from the Turn of the Century to the Baby Boom* (Berkeley: University of California Press, 2001); Laura Briggs, *Reproducing Empire: Race, Sex, Science, and U.S. Imperialism in Puerto Rico* (Berkeley: University of California Press, 2002); Nancy Ordover, *American Eugenics: Race, Queer Anatomy, and the Science of Nationalism* (Minneapolis: University of Minnesota Press, 2003); and Molly Ladd-Taylor, "Saving Babies and Sterilizing Mothers: Eugenics and Welfare Politics in the Interwar United States," *Social Politics* 4 (1997): 136–53.

33. See Thomas M. Shapiro, *Population Control Politics: Women, Sterilization, and Reproductive Choice* (Philadelphia: Temple University Press, 1985); and Betsy Hartmann, *Reproductive Rights and Wrongs: The Global Politics of Population Control*, rev. ed. (Boston: South End Press, 1995).

34. See Reilly, *Surgical Solution*; Kline, *Building a Better Race*.

35. See Rickie Solinger, *Wake Up Little Susie: Single Pregnancy and Race before Roe v. Wade*, 2nd. ed. (New York: Routledge, 2000). Similar patterns developed in Sweden and Norway. See Broberg and Roll-Hansen, *Eugenics*.

36. See Castles, "Quiet Eugenics."

37. See Schoen, *Choice and Coercion*.

38. See L. Gordon, *Woman's Body, Woman's Right*.

39. See Ordover, *American Eugenics*; and Carole R. McCann, *Birth Control Politics in the United States, 1916–1945* (Ithaca, NY: Cornell University Press, 1994).

40. See Briggs, *Reproducing Empire*.

41. See Kline, *Building a Better Race*; Molly Ladd-Taylor, "Eugenics, Sterilisation and Modern Marriage in the USA: The Strange Career of Paul Popenoe," *Gender and History* 13, no. 2 (2001): 298–327.

42. See Kline, *Building a Better Race*.

43. See Carole McCann, "Birth Control, Eugenics, and the Foundations of Demography," unpublished manuscript, University of Maryland, Baltimore County.

44. See Joanne Meyerowitz, *How Sex Changed: A History of Transsexuality in the United States* (Cambridge, MA: Harvard University Press, 2002), 29. On the transition from discrete categories to continua, also see Hamilton Cravens, *The Triumph of Evolution: The Heredity-Environment Controversy, 1900–1941* (Baltimore: Johns Hopkins University Press, 1988).

45. See Kline, *Building a Better Race*; Elaine Tyler May, *Homeward Bound: American Families in the Cold War Era* (New York: Basic Books, 1988); Jennifer Terry, *An American Obsession: Science, Medicine, and Homosexuality in Modern Society* (Chicago: University of Chicago Press, 1999); and Stephanie Coontz, *The Way We Never Were: American Families and the Nostalgia Trap* (New York: Basic Books, 1992).

46. See Dorothy Roberts, *Killing the Black Body: Race, Reproduction, and the Meaning of Liberty* (New York: Vintage Books, 1997); Elena Rebéca Gutiérrez, "The Racial Politics of Reproduction: The Social Construction of Mexican-Origin Women's Fertility" (PhD diss., University of Michigan, 1999); Ian F. Haney López, *Racism on Trial: The Chicano Fight for Justice* (Cambridge, MA: Belknap Press of Harvard University Press, 2003); L. Gordon, *Woman's Body, Woman's Right*; McCann, *Birth Control Politics*; and Solinger, *Wake Up Little Susie*.

47. Naomi Rogers, "'Caution: The AMA May Be Dangerous to Your Health': The Student Health Organizations (SHO) and American Medicine, 1965–1970," *Radical History Review* 80 (2001): 5–34; Sheryl Burt Ruzek, *The Women's Health Movement: Feminist Alternatives to Medical Control* (New York: Praeger, 1978); Sandra Morgen, *Into Our Own Hands: The Women's Health Movement in the United States, 1969–1990* (New Brunswick, NJ: Rutgers University Press, 2002).

48. See James H. Jones, *Bad Blood: The Tuskegee Syphilis Experiment*, rev. ed. (New York: Free Press, 1992); and Susan M. Reverby, ed., *Tuskegee's Truths: Rethinking the Tuskegee Syphilis Study* (Chapel Hill: University of North Carolina Press, 2000).

49. See D. Paul, *Controlling Human Heredity*; Kevles, *In the Name*; Frank Dikötter, "Race Culture: Recent Perspectives on the History of Eugenics," *American Historical Review* 103, no. 2 (1998): 467–78; and Martin S. Pernick, *The Black Stork: Eugenics and the Death of "Defective" Babies in American Medicine and Motion Pictures since 1915* (New York: Oxford University Press, 1996).

50. See D. Paul, *Politics of Heredity*; and M. Adams, *Wellborn Science*.

51. Francis Galton, *Essays in Eugenics* (London: Eugenics Education Society, 1909), 35.

52. Charles B. Davenport, *Heredity in Relation to Eugenics* (New York: Henry Holt, 1911), 1.

53. See Troy Duster, *Backdoor to Eugenics* (New York: Routledge, 2003).

54. See Hermann J. Muller, "Better Genes for Tomorrow," in *The Population Crisis: Implications and Plans for Action*, ed. Larry K. Y. Ng and Stuart Mudd (Bloomington: Indiana University Press, 1965), 246; and Kevles, *In the Name*, chap. 12.

55. Lee M. Silver, *Remaking Eden: How Genetic Engineering and Cloning Will Transform the American Family* (New York: Avon Books, 1997).

56. See J. Edward Chamberlain and Sander L. Gilman, eds., *Degeneration: The Dark Side of Progress* (New York: Columbia University Press, 1985); Daniel Pick, *Faces of Degeneration: A European Disorder, c. 1848–1918* (Cambridge: Cambridge University Press, 1989); and Robert A. Nye, "The Rise and Fall of the Eugenics Empire: Recent Perspectives on the Impact of Biomedical Thought in Modern Society," *Historical Journal* 36, no. 3 (1993): 687–700.

57. See Jan Breman, ed., *Imperial Monkey Business: Racial Supremacy in Social Darwinist Theory and Colonial Practice* (Amsterdam: V.U. University Press, 1990).

58. On hybridity, see Robert J.C. Young, *Colonial Desire: Hybridity in Theory, Culture, and Race* (New York: Routledge, 1995).

59. See Gail Bederman, *Manliness and Civilization: A Cultural History of Gender and Race in the United States, 1880–1917* (Chicago: University of Chicago Press, 1995); and Tom Lutz, *American Nervousness, 1903: An Anecdotal History* (Ithaca, NY: Cornell University Press, 1991).

60. Stepan, *"Hour of Eugenics."*

61. D. Paul, *Controlling Human Heredity,* chap. 2.

62. Ibid., 41.

63. See Jan Sapp, "The Struggle for Authority in the Field of Heredity, 1900–1932: New Perspectives on the Rise of Genetics," *Journal of the History of Biology* 16, no. 3 (1983): 311–42.

64. His results were published in 1866; see Gregor Mendel, "Experiments in Plant Hybridization," in *Classic Papers in Genetics,* ed. James Peters (Englewood Cliffs, NJ: Prentice Hall, 1959), 1–20.

65. See Kevles, *In the Name,* chap. 3.

66. Ibid.

67. See ibid.; and Robert F. Weir, Susan C. Lawrence, and Evan Fales, eds., *Genes and Human Self-Knowledge: Historical and Philosophical Reflections on Modern Genetics* (Iowa City: University of Iowa Press, 1994).

68. See James D. Watson, *The Double Helix: A Personal Account of the Discovery of the Structure of DNA* (New York: Atheneum, 1968).

69. Kathy Cooke convincingly argues that scholars have dismissed the role of environment too readily and that World War I was the watershed in the transition to strict Mendelianism. See Kathy J. Cooke, "The Limits of Heredity: Nature and Nurture in American Eugenics before 1915," *Journal of the History of Biology* 31, no. 2 (1998): 263–78; and Peter J. Bowler, *The Eclipse of Darwinism: Anti-Darwinian Evolution Theories in the Decades around 1900* (Baltimore: Johns Hopkins University Press, 1983).

70. On the family studies, see Nicole Hahn Rafter, ed., *White Trash: The Eugenic Family Studies, 1877–1919* (Boston: Northeastern University Press, 1988).

71. See D. Paul, *Politics of Heredity,* chap. 7.

72. See Frederick Osborn, *The Future of Human Heredity: An Introduction to Eugenics in Modern Society* (New York: Weybright and Talley, 1968), 86.

73. Ibid., 84.

74. Ibid., 92–94. Also see Frederick Osborn, *Preface to Eugenics,* rev. ed. (New York: Harper, 1951), chap. 2; and Alan F. Guttmacher, "The Place of Sterilization," in Ng and Mudd, *Population Crisis,* 201–6.

75. Richard J. Herrnstein and Charles Murray, *The Bell Curve: Intelligence and Class Structure in American Life* (New York: Free Press, 1994).

76. See Paul Davis Chapman, *Schools as Sorters: Lewis M. Terman, Applied Psychology, and the Intelligence Testing Movement, 1890–1930* (New York: New York University Press, 1988).

77. See ibid.; and Stephen Jay Gould, *The Mismeasure of Man,* 2nd ed. (New York: W. W. Norton, 1996).

78. Lewis M. Terman, *The Measurement of Intelligence: An Explanation of and a Complete Guide for the Use of the Stanford Revision and Extension of the Binet-Simon Intelligence Scale* (New York: Houghton Mifflin, 1916).

79. On health seeking and the myth of the curative West, see Sheila M. Rothman, *Living in the Shadow of Death: Tuberculosis and the Social Experience of Illness in America* (Baltimore: Johns Hopkins University Press, 1995).

80. See Kline, *Building a Better Race,* for a discussion of Terman's M-F Test at the American Institute of Family Relations. For the national role, see Michael Kimmel, *Manhood in America: A Cultural History* (New York: Free Press, 1996).

81. See, for example, Stephen Tchudi, ed., *Science, Values, and the American West* (Reno: Nevada Humanities Committee, 1997); Rebecca S. Lowen, *Creating the Cold War University: The Transformation of Stanford* (Berkeley: University of California Press, 1997); Steven Stoll, *The Fruits of Natural Advantage: Making the Industrial Countryside in California* (Berkeley: University of California Press, 1998); Matt Garcia, *A World of Its Own: Race, Labor, and Citrus in the Making of Greater Los Angeles, 1900–1970* (Chapel Hill: University of North Carolina Press, 2002); Douglas Cazaux Sackman, "Inside the Skin of Nature: Science and the Quest for the Golden Orange," in Tchudi, *Science, Values,* 117–45; and Kevin Fernlund, ed., *The Cold War American West, 1945–1989* (Albuquerque: University of New Mexico Press, 1998).

82. Volumes have been written on Frederick Jackson Turner. An imaginative retrospective is Kerwin Lee Klein, *Frontiers of Historical Imagination: Narrating the European Conquest of Native America, 1890–1990* (Berkeley: University of California Press, 1997).

83. See Patricia Nelson Limerick, *The Legacy of Conquest: The Unbroken Past of the American West* (New York: W. W. Norton, 1987); Patricia Nelson Limerick, Clyde A. Milner II, and Charles E. Rankin, eds., *Trails: Toward a New Western History* (Lawrence: University of Kansas Press, 1991); and William Cronon, George Miles, and Jay Gitlin, eds., *Under an Open Sky: Rethinking America's Western Past* (New York: W. W. Norton, 1992).

84. See Elizabeth Jameson and Susan Armitage, eds., *Writing the Range: Race, Class, and Culture in the Women's West* (Norman: University of Oklahoma Press, 1997); David G. Gutiérrez, "Significant to Whom? Mexican Americans and the History of the American West," *Western Historical Quarterly* 24, no. 4 (1993): 519–37; Neil Foley, *The White Scourge: Mexicans, Blacks, and Poor Whites in Texas Cotton Culture* (Berkeley: University of California Press,

1997); Lisbeth Haas, *Conquests and Historical Identities in California, 1769–1936* (Berkeley: University of California Press, 1995); Sarah Deutsch, "Landscape of Enclaves: Race Relations in the West, 1865–1990," in Cronon, Miles, and Gitlin, *Under an Open Sky,* 110–31, and *No Separate Refuge: Culture, Class, and Gender on an Anglo-Hispanic Frontier in the American Southwest, 1880–1940* (New York: Oxford University Press, 1987); Judy Yung, *Unbound Feet: A Social History of Chinese Women in San Francisco* (Berkeley: University of California Press, 1995); and Sucheng Chan, ed., *Entry Denied: Exclusion and the Chinese Community in America, 1882–1943* (Philadelphia: Temple University Press, 1991).

85. See Limerick, *Legacy of Conquest;* Deutsch, "Landscape of Enclaves."

86. See Nayan Shah, *Contagious Divides: Epidemics and Race in San Francisco's Chinatown* (Berkeley: University of California Press, 2001); and Charles J. McClain, *In Search of Equality: The Chinese Struggle against Discrimination in Nineteenth-Century America* (Berkeley: University of California Press, 1994).

87. See Howard Markel, *When Germs Travel: Six Major Epidemics That Have Invaded America since 1900 and the Fears They Have Unleashed* (New York: Pantheon, 2004); Alan M. Kraut, *Silent Travelers: Germs, Genes, and the "Immigrant Menace"* (Baltimore: Johns Hopkins University Press, 1995); Shah, *Contagious Divides;* and Peggy Pascoe, *Relations of Rescue: The Search for Female Moral Authority in the American West, 1874–1939* (New York: Oxford University Press, 1990).

88. See David G. Gutiérrez, *Walls and Mirrors: Mexican Americans, Mexican Immigrants, and the Politics of Ethnicity* (Berkeley: University of California Press, 1995).

89. See Alexandra Minna Stern, "Buildings, Boundaries, and Blood: Medicalization and Nation-Building on the U.S.-Mexico Border, 1910–1930," *Hispanic American Historical Review* 79, no. 1 (1999): 41–81.

90. See William Deverell, "Plague in Los Angeles, 1924: Ethnicity and Typicality," in *Over the Edge: Remapping the American West,* ed. Valerie J. Matsumoto and Blake Allmendinger (Berkeley: University of California Press, 1999), 172–200; and E. Gutiérrez, "Racial Politics of Reproduction."

91. On the connected histories of the US West and imperialism, see Peggy Pascoe, "Democracy, Citizenship, and Race: The West in the Twentieth Century," in *Perspectives on Modern America: Making Sense of the Twentieth Century,* ed. Harvard Sitkoff (New York: Oxford University Press, 2001), 227–46. On colonial medicine, see Warwick Anderson, "'Where Every Prospect Pleases and Only Man Is Vile': Laboratory Medicine as Colonial Discourse," in *Discrepant Histories: Translocal Essays on Filipino Cultures,* ed. Vicente L. Rafael (Philadelphia: Temple University Press, 1995), 83–112. On the postcolonial turn toward conceiving of metropolis and colony in one analytical framework, see Frederick Cooper and Ann Laura Stoler, eds., *Tensions of Empire: Colonial Cultures in a Bourgeois World* (Berkeley: University of California Press, 1997).

92. For a comprehensive and critical history on racial marriage laws, see Peggy Pascoe, *What Comes Naturally: Miscegenation Law and the Making of Race in America* (Oxford: Oxford University Press, 2009).

93. See Peggy Pascoe, "Race, Gender, and the Privileges of Property: On the Significance of Miscegenation Law in the U.S. West," in Matsumoto and All-mendinger, *Over the Edge*, 215–30, and "Miscegenation Law, Court Cases, and Ideologies of 'Race' in Twentieth-Century America," *Journal of American History* 83, no. 1 (1996): 44–69.

94. On the latter, see Paul A. Lombardo, "Miscegenation, Eugenics, and Racism: Historical Footnotes to *Loving v. Virginia*," *University of California, Davis Law Review* 21, no. 421 (1988): 421–52.

95. Kevles, *In the Name*, 99.

96. See Luther Burbank, *The Training of the Human Plant* (New York: Century, 1922).

97. See Michael L. Smith, *Pacific Visions: California Scientists and the Environment, 1850–1915* (New Haven, CT: Yale University Press, 1987).

98. See David Starr Jordan, *The Blood of the Nation: A Study of the Decay of Races through the Survival of the Unfit* (Boston: American Unitarian Association, 1910).

99. See Largent, "'Greatest Curse.'"

100. See Peter Boag, *Same-Sex Affairs: Constructing and Controlling Homosexuality in the Pacific Northwest* (Berkeley: University of California Press, 2003).

1. RACE BETTERMENT AND TROPICAL MEDICINE IN IMPERIAL SAN FRANCISCO

1. Frank Morton Todd, *The Story of the Exposition: Being the Official History of the International Celebration Held at San Francisco in 1915 to Commemorate the Discovery of the Pacific Ocean and the Construction of the Panama Canal* (New York: G.P. Putnam's Sons, 1921), 2:264.

2. Ibid., 2:265.

3. See John D. Barry, *The City of Domes* (San Francisco: John J. Newbegin, 1915), 42.

4. Quoted in Todd, *Story of the Exposition*, 2:270.

5. Ibid., 272; Gray Brechin, *Imperial San Francisco: Urban Power, Earthly Ruin* (Berkeley: University of California Press, 1999), 245–49.

6. In terms of acreage, the PPIE was the third-largest exposition held in the United States. The exposition at Chicago (1893) was slightly bigger and that at St. Louis (1904) almost twice the size.

7. See Barry, *City of Domes*.

8. Todd, *Story of the Exposition*, 5:159, 225–30; Donna Ewald and Peter Clute, *San Francisco Invites the World: The Panama-Pacific International Exposition of 1915* (San Francisco: Chronicle Books, 1991). Note that Todd's figure of nearly nineteen million does not differentiate between one-time and returning visitors to the fair.

9. *Panama-Pacific International Exposition, San Francisco, 1915* (official pamphlet), Panama-Pacific International Exposition Papers (hereafter PPIEP), CA 190, Carton 108, Bancroft Library (hereafter BL), University of California at Berkeley (hereafter UCB). For analyses of the fair, see Robert W. Rydell, *All*

the World's a Fair: Visions of Empire at American International Expositions, 1876–1916 (Chicago: University of Chicago Press, 1984); Burton Benedict, ed., *The Anthropology of World's Fairs: San Francisco's Panama Pacific International Exposition of 1915* (Berkeley, CA: Lowie Museum of Anthropology, 1983), 114–33; Kevin Starr, *Americans and the California Dream, 1850–1915* (New York: Oxford University Press, 1973), chap. 9; Bill Brown, "Science Fiction, the World's Fair, and the Prosthetics of Empire, 1910–1915," in *Cultures of United States Imperialism,* ed. Amy Kaplan and Donald E. Pease (Durham, NC: Duke University Press, 1993), 129–63; Keith L. Eggener, "Maybeck's Melancholy: Architecture, Empathy, Empire, and Mental Illness at the 1915 Panama-Pacific International Exposition," *Winterthur Portfolio* 29, no. 4 (1994): 211–26; and Michael L. Smith, *Pacific Visions: California Scientists and the Environment, 1850–1915* (New Haven, CT: Yale University Press, 1987), chap. 9.

10. See Elizabeth N. Armstrong, "Hercules and the Muses: Public Art and the Fair," in Benedict, *Anthropology of World's Fairs,* 114–33.

11. See Michael Worboys, "Tropical Diseases," in *Companion Encyclopedia of the History of Medicine,* ed. W.F. Bynum and Roy Porter (New York: Routledge, 1993), 1:512–36; François Delaporte, *The History of Yellow Fever: An Essay on the Birth of Tropical Medicine,* trans. Arthur Goldhammer (Cambridge, MA: MIT Press, 1991); Victoria A. Harden, *Rocky Mountain Spotted Fever: History of a Twentieth-Century Disease* (Baltimore: Johns Hopkins University Press, 1990); and Kim Pelis, "Prophet for Profit in French North Africa: Charles Nicolle and the Pasteur Institute of Tunis, 1903–1936," *Bulletin of the History of Medicine* 71, no. 4 (1997): 583–622.

12. On "upward causation," see Lily E. Kay, *The Molecular Vision of Life: Caltech, the Rockefeller Foundation, and the Rise of the New Biology* (New York: Oxford University Press, 1993).

13. For the best articulation of homologies between eugenics and public health, see Martin S. Pernick, *The Black Stork: Eugenics and the Death of "Defective" Babies in American Medicine and Motion Pictures since 1915* (New York: Oxford University Press, 1996), chap. 3, and "Eugenics and Public Health in American History," *American Journal of Public Health* 87 (1997): 1967–72. On sanitarian campaigns, see John Duffy, *The Sanitarians: A History of American Public Health* (Chicago: University of Illinois Press, 1990).

14. See William Cronon, *Nature's Metropolis: Chicago and the Great West* (New York: W.W. Norton, 1991).

15. See Brechin, *Imperial San Francisco.*

16. Ibid., chap. 3. The oldest base, the Presidio, had been built by the Spanish in 1776. The US military built Fort Mason, Fort Alcatraz, and Fort McDowell (on Angel Island) during the Civil War era and continued the militarization of the Bay Area with the establishment of Yerba Buena Naval Station, Fort Baker, Fort Funston, and Fort Miley during the Spanish-American War.

17. Ibid., 130.

18. Quoted in ibid., 136.

19. David McCullough, *The Path between the Seas: The Creation of the Panama Canal, 1870–1914* (New York: Simon and Schuster, 1977), 254–55.

20. See Michael L. Conniff, *Panama and the United States: The Forced Alliance,* 2nd ed. (Athens: University of Georgia Press, 2001); McCullough, *Path between the Seas;* John Major, *Prize Possession: The United States and the Panama Canal, 1903–1979* (New York: Cambridge University Press, 1993); and Ulrich Keller, *The Building of the Panama Canal in Historic Photographs* (New York: Dover Publications, 1983). Note that the Canal Zone, like Guam and American Samoa, was considered to be an "unorganized possession," not an "incorporated territory" like Alaska and Hawai'i or an "unincorporated territory" like the Philippines and Puerto Rico.

21. McCullough, *Path between the Seas,* 393.

22. See ibid., chap. 20, for an excellent description of the "structured and paternalistic" order imposed by Colonel Goethals in the Canal Zone, which included various moral and spatial regulations, YMCA activities, church groups, and clubs and fraternal organizations, all of which were intensely segregated by race according to a two-tiered system of "gold" and "silver" payments.

23. See Brechin, *Imperial San Francisco;* and Starr, *Americans,* chap. 9. This was not the first time Burnham had a hand in making San Francisco's image. Architect of some of the city's most prominent structures, such as the Chronicle and Mills buildings, Burnham had served as director of works at the 1893 Chicago World's Fair. The following year, when the California Midwinter International Exposition was held in Golden Gate Park, many exhibits were transported from the Midwest to the "Sunset City" via rail. See Barbara Berglund, "'The Days of Old, the Days of Gold, the Days of '49': Identity, History, and Memory at the California Midwinter International Exposition, 1894," *Public Historian* 25, no. 4 (2003): 25–49; and Rydell, *All the World's a Fair.*

24. Starr, *Americans,* 292; Marjorie M. Dobkin, "A Twenty-Five-Million-Dollar Mirage," in Benedict, *Anthropology of World's Fairs,* 66–93.

25. See Todd, *Story of the Exposition,* vol. 1. It is important to note that although Congress approved the PPIE as an international exposition it did not provide federal funding for the event. Moore demonstrated his acumen as a businessman by overseeing a successful campaign to raise the required funds through bonds, taxes, and donations.

26. Bascom Johnson, *Moral Conditions in San Francisco and at the Panama-Pacific Exposition* (New York: American Social Hygiene Association, 1915), 1. For a comparison between the San Francisco's laxity and Los Angeles's moral absolutism, see Gerald Woods, "A Penchant for Probity: California Progressives and the Disreputable Pleasures," in *California Progressivism Revisited,* ed. William Deverell and Tom Sitton (Berkeley: University of California Press, 1994), 99–113. In 1915, the American Social Hygiene Association expressed ongoing dissatisfaction with the raucous dance halls and sexually suggestive shows at the fair and the meager police force entrusted with curbing vice throughout the city. See Johnson, *Moral Conditions;* and relevant letters in PPIEP, CA 190, Carton 23, BL, UCB.

27. See Guenter B. Risse, "'A Long Pull, A Strong Pull, and All Together': San Francisco and Bubonic Plague, 1907–1908," *Bulletin of the History of Medicine* 66 (1992): 260–86.

28. See Howard Markel, *When Germs Travel: Six Major Epidemics That Have Invaded America since 1900 and the Fears They Have Unleashed* (New York: Pantheon, 2004); Nayan Shah, *Contagious Divides: Epidemics and Race in San Francisco's Chinatown* (Berkeley: University of California Press, 2001); and Alan M. Kraut, *Silent Travelers: Germs, Genes, and the "Immigrant Menace"* (Baltimore: Johns Hopkins University Press, 1995).

29. See Frank Morton Todd, *Eradicating Plague from San Francisco* (San Francisco: Press of C. A. Murdock, 1909).

30. See Risse, "'Long Pull.'"

31. Todd, *Eradicating Plague*, 84.

32. See Risse, "'Long Pull.'"

33. See Todd, *Eradicating Plague* and *Story of the Exposition*, vol. 1.

34. See 1913 correspondence between C. C. Moore and Surgeon General Rupert Blue, PPIEP, CA 190, Carton 9, BL, UCB.

35. See Todd, *Eradicating Plague*.

36. Barry, *City of Domes*, 10.

37. Ibid.; and Ardee Parsons, *A Day at the Exposition*, pamphlet, n.p., n.d.

38. Quoted in Armstrong, "Hercules and the Muses," 116.

39. Quoted in ibid., 122. Also see Brechin, *Imperial San Francisco*, 245–49.

40. See Barry, *City of Domes*, 44–50.

41. Ibid.

42. Todd, *Story of the Exposition*, 2:302.

43. Ibid., 2:324–29. On female suffrage in California, see Gayle Ann Gullett, *Becoming Citizens: The Emergence and Development of the California Women's Movement, 1880–1911* (Urbana: University of Illinois Press, 1999).

44. See "Women to Promote Permanent Peace at the Great Exposition by Margaret Wallace," press release, June 2, 1915, PPIEP, CA 190, vol. 71, BL, UCB. Also see Anna Pratt Simpson, *Problems Women Solved: Being the Story of the Woman's Board of the Panama-Pacific International Exposition; What Vision, Enthusiasm, Work and Co-operation Accomplished* (San Francisco: Woman's Board, 1915).

45. Although opinions certainly differed on the Woman's Board, it conveyed a fairly uniform antiwar and prosuffrage message throughout the PPIE.

46. See Rydell, *All the World's a Fair*; and pertinent letters in PPIEP, CA 190, Carton 23, BL, UCB.

47. See S. L. Mash, President, Colored Non-Partisan Leagues of California, to Hon. Chas. C. Moore, January 14, 1915; Secretary, PPIE, to Mr. S. L. Mash, February 6, 1915; and S. L. Mash to C. C. Moore, February 13, 1915, all in PPIEP, CA 190, Carton 23, BL, UCB.

48. Wilson and Waters to the Mayor of San Francisco, March 8, 1915, PPIEP, CA 190, Carton 23, BL, UCB.

49. J. S. Tobin to Mr. C. C. Moore, January 25, 1915, PPIEP, CA 190, Carton 23, BL, UCB.

50. See relevant letters in PPIEP, CA 190, Carton 23, BL, UCB; and Rydell, *All the World's a Fair*, 228–29.

51. Rydell, *All the World's a Fair,* chap. 8; Smithsonian Institution, *The Exhibits of the Smithsonian Institution at the Panama-Pacific International Exposition* (San Francisco: Press of H. S. Crocker, 1915).

52. Quoted in Todd, *Story of the Exposition,* 2:151.

53. See McCullough, *Path between the Seas;* and William C. Gorgas, *Sanitation in Panama* (New York: D. Appleton, 1915).

54. See Warwick Anderson, "'Where Every Prospect Pleases and Only Man Is Vile': Laboratory Medicine as Colonial Discourse," in *Discrepant Histories: Translocal Essays on Filipino Cultures,* ed. Vicente L. Rafael (Philadelphia: Temple University Press, 1995), 83–112, "Excremental Colonialism: Public Health and the Poetics of Pollution," *Critical Inquiry* 21, no. 3 (1995): 640–69, and "Immunities of Empire: Race, Disease, and the New Tropical Medicine, 1900–1920," *Bulletin of the History of Medicine* 70, no. 1 (1996): 94–118. Also see Reynaldo Ileto, "Cholera and the Origins of the American Sanitary Order in the Philippines," in Rafael, *Discrepant Histories,* 51–81; and Melbourne Tapper, "Interrogating Bodies: Medico-Racial Knowledge, Politics, and the Study of a Disease," *Comparative Studies in Society and History* 37, no. 1 (1995): 76–93.

55. See McCullough, *Path between the Seas,* 415.

56. Ibid., 418; Gorgas, *Sanitation in Panama,* chaps. 4–6.

57. McCullough, *Path between the Seas,* 415; Gorgas, *Sanitation in Panama,* chaps. 4–6.

58. Ibid. Also see Todd, *Story of the Exposition,* vol. 1; Charles Francis Adams, *The Panama Canal Zone: An Epochal Event in Sanitation* (Boston: Proceedings of the Massachusetts History Society, 1911); and James Ewing Mears, *The Triumph of American Medicine in the Construction of the Panama Canal* (Philadelphia: Wm. J. Dornan, 1911).

59. McCullough, *Path between the Seas,* 144.

60. Ibid.

61. Gorgas, *Sanitation in Panama,* 182.

62. Gorgas, *Report of the Department of Health of the Isthmian Canal Commission for the Month of January, 1906* (Washington, DC: Government Printing Office, 1906), 6–9.

63. C. Adams, *Panama Canal Zone,* 4; Todd, *Story of the Exposition,* 1:26; *Panama-Pacific International Exposition* (pamphlet).

64. James A. Buchanan and Gail Stuart, eds., *History of the Panama-Pacific International Exposition* (San Francisco: Pan-Pacific Press Association, 1916), 14.

65. See Conniff, *Panama.*

66. See C. Adams, *Panama Canal Zone,* 28. For an excellent analysis of these connections, see W. Anderson, "'Where Every Prospect Pleases.'"

67. See W. Anderson, "'Where Every Prospect Pleases,'" and "Immunities of Empire."

68. See Alexandra Minna Stern, "Yellow Fever Crusade: U.S. Colonialism, Tropical Medicine, and the International Politics of Mosquito Control, 1900–1920," in *Medicine at the Border: Disease, Globalization, and Security: 1850 to the Present,* ed. Alison Bashford (London: Palgrave, 2007), 41–59.

69. McCullough, *Path between the Seas,* 501; Michael L. Conniff, *Black Labor on a White Canal: Panama, 1904–1981* (Pittsburgh, PA: University of Pittsburgh Press, 1985).

70. "Insects Great Enemy of Mankind," *San Francisco Chronicle,* June 26, 1915.

71. See *Panama-Pacific International Exposition* (pamphlet).

72. US Public Health Service (hereafter USPHS), *Official List of Commissioned and Other Officers of the United States Public Health Service* (Washington, DC: Government Printing Office, 1914), 13; *Who Was Who in America* (Chicago: A. N. Marquis, 1950), 2:425; "Personal," *Canal Record* 7 (December 10, 1913): 143.

73. USPHS, *Annual Report of the Surgeon General of the Public Health Service of the United States* (Washington, DC: Government Printing Office, 1915), 277–82.

74. See C. C. Pierce to the Surgeon General, May 8, 1915, PPIEP, CA 190, Carton 86, BL, UCB.

75. Letter of Dr. R. M. Woodward, June 4, 1913, re: Hospital Service at Grounds, 14, PPIEP, CA 190, Carton 23, BL, UCB; USPHS, *Annual Report* (1915), 279–80; Todd, *Story of the Exposition,* 5:187–92.

76. Todd, *Story of the Exposition,* 5: 187.

77. Ibid.; USPHS, *Annual Report* (1915), 281.

78. International Jury Awards, 20–25, PPIEP, CA 190, Carton 51, BL, UCB.

79. Ibid.

80. W. C. Rucker and C. C. Pierce, *United States Public Health Service Exhibit at the Panama-Pacific International Exposition, San Francisco, 1915,* Supplement no. 27, USPHS Reports (Washington, DC: Government Printing Office, 1915), 1.

81. Ibid.

82. List of Exhibits referring to Hygiene and Sanitation—Located in Palace of Education, PPIE, Dr. J. R. Hurley, USPHS, Superintendent of Hygiene and Sanitation Exhibits, PPIEP, CA 190, Carton 131, BL, UCB.

83. Todd, *Story of the Exposition,* 5:16.

84. Manager James A. Barr to Dr. W. F. Snow, October 26, 1912, PPIEP, CA 190, Carton 66, BL, UCB.

85. See materials in PPIEP, CA 190, Carton 156, BL, UCB; and Todd, *Story of the Exposition,* vol. 5, chap. 5.

86. Todd, *Story of the Exposition,* vol. 5, chap. 5.

87. Helen Dare, "They Say We Owe the Canal to Medical Men," *San Francisco Chronicle,* June 22, 1915.

88. Untitled report of the American Society for Tropical Medicine (submitted to Todd by John W. Swan), PPIEP, CA 190, Carton 156, BL, UCB.

89. See Charles A. L. Reed, "The Relation of the Medical Profession to the Practical Panamericanism of the Twentieth Century" (presidential address to the Seventh Medical Congress, June 18, 1915), PPIEP, CA 190, Carton 156, BL, UCB.

90. See W. Anderson, "Immunities of Empire."

91. Reed, "Relation."

92. Ibid.

93. See Shah, *Contagious Divides.*

94. C. C. Pierce to D. H. Connick, December 15, 1915, PPIEP, CA 190, Carton 86, BL, UCB. Pierce left San Francisco on December 15, just eleven days after the exposition ended.

95. USPHS, *Official List of Commissioned and Other Officers of the United States Public Health Service* (Washington, DC: Government Printing Office, 1916), 27–28.

96. C. C. Pierce to Frank Morton Todd, August 8, 1917, PPIEP, CA 190, Carton 156, BL, UCB.

97. "Program of the Second International Conference on Race Betterment," August 4–8, 1915, PPIEP, CA 190, Carton 12, BL, UCB.

98. See *Official Proceedings of the Second National Conference on Race Betterment* (Battle Creek, MI: Race Betterment Foundation, 1915).

99. See relevant references to programs and schedules, PPIEP, CA 190, vol. 71, CL, UCB.

100. Todd, *Story of the Exposition,* 4:39.

101. International Jury Award 137, PPIEP, CA 190, Carton 51, BL, UCB.

102. Ibid.

103. J. H. Kellogg to Mr. Alvin E. Pope, January 26, 1915; "Introduction, Purpose, Aims, and Methods of This Exhibit," PPIEP, CA 190, Carton 51, BL, UCB.

104. "Introduction, Purpose, Aims, and Methods of This Exhibit."

105. *Official Proceedings,* 145.

106. Todd, *Story of the Exposition,* 4:38.

107. James A. Barr to David Starr Jordan, December 14, 1912, February 5, 1913, and February 21, 1913, all in PPIEP, CA 190, Carton 66, BL, UCB.

108. James A. Barr to David Starr Jordan, February 21, 1913, PPIEP, CA 190, Carton 66, BL, UCB.

109. Pope quoted in James A. Barr to Dr. W. F. Snow, August 21, 1913, PPIEP, CA 190, Carton 66, BL, UCB.

110. "Panama-Pacific International Exposition Will Display Achievements of Eugenic Societies," *Pacific Medical Journal* 56, no. 11 (November 1913): 649.

111. Ibid.; Alvin E. Pope, "Educational and Social Economic Contributions of the Panama-Pacific International Exposition to Pan-American Interests (Address Delivered January 7, 1916, to the Pan-American Scientific Congress)," PPIEP, CA 190, Carton 27, BL, UCB.

112. "Child of Genius Often a Bluffer," *San Francisco Chronicle,* August 18, 1915; "San Francisco Joint Meeting of Section H of the American Association for the Advancement of Science and the American Psychological Association" (Section H = Anthropology and Psychology), PPIEP, CA 190, Carton 157, BL, UCB.

113. "San Francisco Joint Meeting"; Henry Herbert Goddard, *The Kallikak Family: A Study in the Heredity of Feeble-Mindedness* (New York: Macmillan, 1912). For a masterful biography of Goddard, see Leila Zenderland, *Measuring Minds: Henry Herbert Goddard and the Origins of American Intelligence Testing* (New York: Cambridge University Press, 1998).

114. "Twelfth Annual Meeting of the American Genetic Association, August 2–7, 1915," PPIEP, CA 190, Carton 157, BL, UCB.

115. Ibid.

116. "Sex Topics before Purity Congress," *San Francisco Chronicle,* July 21, 1915.

117. See Charles B. Davenport to David Starr Jordan, February 11, 1913, David Starr Jordan Papers (hereafter DSJP), 86/776, Special Collections (hereafter SC), Stanford University (hereafter SU).

118. See *Official Proceedings.*

119. "Minutes of the Fourth Meeting of the Board of Trustees of the Race Betterment Foundation" (September 25, 1915), John Harvey Kellogg Papers, 117:47, Large Collection 13, University Archives and Historical Collections, Michigan State University; J.H. Kellogg to Charles B. Davenport, May 20, 1915, Charles B. Davenport Papers (hereafter CBDP), B:D27, American Philosophical Society (hereafter APS). The Race Betterment Foundation spent more than $8,000 on the PPIE. Its paid employees were Read, Stolz, Emily Robbins (the foundation's secretary), and Fannie Perrin, who spent several weeks assisting at the exhibit. See "Minutes of the Fourth Meeting" and attached "Race Betterment Foundation Statement of Income and Expenditures, Year Ending December 31, 1914," 117:45–48; "Minutes of the Fourth Meeting" (November 9, 1915), 117:55.

120. Paul Popenoe to his parents, November 18, 1914, Box 3, Paul Bowman Popenoe Papers, 1874–1991, Accession no. 4681 (4681), American Heritage Center, University of Wyoming. Since I conducted my research at the American Heritage Center, the Popenoe Papers have been recatalogued. Working with the new finding aid, I have been able to deduce the location of some of my sources; when that was not possible with accuracy, I have omitted unverifiable information, such as the box or folder title or number. Between my reconstructed citations and the new finding aid, which is organized chronologically and thematically, researchers should be able to locate all of my references.

121. Samuel G. Dixon, "Race Betterment," in *Official Proceedings,* 9.

122. "Program of the Second International Conference on Race Betterment, August 4–8, 1915," PPIEP, CA 190, Carton 12, BL, UCB; J.H. Kellogg to Charles B. Davenport, August 15, 1915, CBDP, B:D27, APS. For an astute analysis of this play, see Wendy Kline, *Building a Better Race: Gender, Sexuality, and Eugenics from the Turn of the Century to the Baby Boom* (Berkeley: University of California Press, 2001), chap. 1.

123. David Starr Jordan, "Eugenics and War," in *Official Proceedings,* 13. Jordan blamed many of American's problems following the Civil War on the dysgenic effects of that conflict, which destroyed the fittest and left young widows who did not remarry and produce more children. See David Starr Jordan and Harvey Ernest Jordan, *War's Aftermath: A Preliminary Study of the Eugenics of War* (Boston: Houghton Mifflin, 1914). For an extended discussion, see David Starr Jordan, *The Blood of the Nation: A Study of the Decay of Races through the Survival of the Unfit* (Boston: American Unitarian Association, 1910).

124. Luther Burbank, "Evolution and Variation with the Fundamental Significance of Sex," in *Official Proceedings,* 50.

125. A. W. Hoisholt, "The Commitment of the Insane," in *Official Proceedings*, 107–13.

126. Paul Popenoe, "Natural Selection in Man," in *Official Proceedings*, 54–61. See Kathy J. Cooke, "The Limits of Heredity: Nature and Nurture in American Eugenics before 1915," *Journal of the History of Biology* 31, no. 2 (1998): 263–78.

127. *Official Proceedings*, 4.

128. John Harvey Kellogg, "The Eugenics Registry," in *Official Proceedings*, 79.

129. Ibid., 79–80.

130. Ibid.; J. H. Kellogg to David Starr Jordan, June 24, 1915, DSJP, 92/822, SC, SU.

131. J. H. Kellogg to David Starr Jordan, June 24, 1915, DSJP, 92/822, SC, SU; and J. H. Kellogg to Charles B. Davenport, May 20, 1915; June 16, 1915, CBDP, B:D27, APS. Davenport told Kellogg that he was unable to attend the SNCRB because of a busy summer training field workers at the Eugenics Record Office.

132. See Cooke, "Limits of Heredity."

133. See Steven Selden, *Inheriting Shame: The Story of Eugenics and Racism in America* (New York: Teacher's College, Columbia University, 1999), chap. 1.

134. "Race Betterment Problems" (editorial), *San Francisco Chronicle*, August 15, 1915.

135. Helen Dare, "After We Are Eugenically and Otherwise Remodelled," *San Francisco Chronicle*, August 12, 1915.

136. J. H. Kellogg to Charles B. Davenport, August 15, 1915, CBDP, B:D27, APS.

137. J. H. Kellogg to David Starr Jordan, August 15, 1915, DSJP, 92/824, SC, SU.

138. Ibid.; J. H. Kellogg to David Starr Jordan, October 25, 1915, DSJP, 94/838, SC, SU. See subsequent correspondence (1915–26) for details of Kellogg's doctoring of Jordan.

139. Frank Morton Todd and George Sterling, *An Account of the Closing Ceremonies of the Panama-Pacific International Exposition, San Francisco, Dec. 4, 1915* (San Francisco: Press of the Blair-Murdock, 1915).

140. Robert W. Rydell, *World of Fairs: The Century-of-Progress Expositions* (Chicago: University of Chicago Press, 1993).

141. "San Francisco Joint Meeting," PPIEP, CA 190, Carton 157, BL, UCB.

142. "National Congress on Recreation to the Chambers of the Commerce of the Pacific Coast," PPIEP, CA 190, vol. 71, BL, UCB; *Sacramento Bee*, July 8, 1915, Charles Matthias Goethe Papers, 85F2, no. 8, SSCF 10, University Archives, California State University, Sacramento.

2. QUARANTINE AND EUGENIC GATEKEEPING ON THE US-MEXICAN BORDER

1. Telegram, Secretariat of Foreign Relations to Jesus Acuña, March 6, 1916, 17-9-204, Historical Archive of the Secretariat of Foreign Relations (hereafter HASFR), Mexico City. All translations from the Spanish are my own.

2. H. J. Hamilton to Melquiades Garcia, March 6, 1916, 17–9-204, HASFR.

3. H. J. Hamilton to Surgeon General, March 5, 1916, File 1169 (San Antonio; Laredo), Central File, 1897–1923, US Public Health Service (hereafter USPHS), Record Group 90 (hereafter RG90), National Archives and Records Administration (hereafter NARA).

4. James E. Trout to Melquiades García, March 11, 1916, 17–9-204, HASFR.

5. See Jonathan Xavier Inda, "Foreign Bodies: Migrants, Parasites, and the Pathological Nation," *Discourse* 22, no. 3 (2000): 46–62.

6. Claude C. Pierce to H. D. H. Connick, December 15, 1915, Panama-Pacific International Exposition Papers, CA 190, Carton 86, Bancroft Library, University of California, Berkeley.

7. Very similar patterns unfolded in Germany, where, starting in World War I, health authorities patrolled the borders of eastern Europe and implemented harsh delousing campaigns that medicalized and racialized Jews and created associations of Jews with lice and typhus that would play out in a harrowing fashion during the Nazi era. See Paul Weindling, *Epidemics and Genocide in Eastern Europe, 1890–1945* (New York: Oxford University Press, 2000).

8. See reports and employee files, Consejo Superior de Salubridad, Box 57, Folder 1 (Ciudad Juárez); Box 63, Folder 1 (Ciudad Juárez); Box 60, Folder 25 (Nuevo Laredo); Box 43, Folder 28 (Ciudad Porfirio Diaz/Piedras Negras), Archivo General de la Nación, Mexico City.

9. See Ann R. Gabbert, "El Paso, a Sight for Sore Eyes: Medical and Legal Aspects of Syrian Immigration, 1906–1907," *Public Historian* 65, no. 1 (2002): 15–42.

10. See Alexandra Minna Stern, "Buildings, Boundaries, and Blood: Medicalization and Nation-Building on the U.S.-Mexico Border, 1910–1930," *Hispanic American Historical Review* 79, no. 1 (1999): 41–81.

11. See, for example, "Quarantine Is Modified against Mexico," *El Paso Herald,* May 9, 1904; "Texas Quarantines Mexico," *El Paso Herald,* April 13, 1905.

12. Claude C. Pierce to Surgeon General, December 20, 1915, File 2126, USPHS, RG90, NARA.

13. Ibid.

14. "El Paso Forces Sanitary Homes for Mexicans," *El Paso Herald,* January 27–28, 1917.

15. "Close Quarantine Is Placed on Juarez to Keep the Typhus Out," *El Paso Herald Post,* January 24, 1917; Claude C. Pierce, "Mexican Border Quarantine," January 23, 1917, File 1248, Central File 1897–1923, El Paso, USPHS, RG90, NARA.

16. Kluttz fell ill in late December and died on January 2, 1917. In the local papers he was portrayed as a martyr of municipal sanitation campaigns, and his death was directly linked to valiant attempts to treat a sick Mexican family living in El Paso tenements. See "Dr. W. C. Kluttz, City Health Officer, Succumbs to Typhus," *El Paso Herald Post,* January 4, 1917; "City Physician Kluttz Gives His Life in Cause of Municipal Sanitation," *El Paso Times,* January 5, 1917. Seven days after Kluttz's death, Pierce sent a four-page letter to the surgeon

general recommending that a quarantine be immediately established. See Claude C. Pierce to Surgeon General, January 9, 1917, File 1248, USPHS, RG90, NARA.

17. See "El Paso Is a Great Health Center for the Southwest," *El Paso Herald,* January 27–28, 1917. The El Paso elite was obsessed with presenting the city as the Southwest's "Magic Mountain," a desirable area blessed with a dry and curative climate ideal for patients with respiratory ills.

18. Pershing and his troops began evacuating their encampments in Chihuahua the very weekend (January 27–28) the quarantine began. See Linda B. Hall and Don M. Coerver, *Revolution on the Border: The United States and Mexico, 1910–1920* (Albuquerque: University of New Mexico Press, 1988).

19. "Auburn-Haired Amazon at Santa Fe Street Bridge Leads Feminine Outbreak," *El Paso Times,* January 29, 1917.

20. "Quarantine Riot in Juarez, Women Lead Demonstrations against American Regulations," *New York Times,* January 29, 1917.

21. "200 Women Lead in Assault at Bridge," *El Paso Herald,* January 29, 1917.

22. For a comparison of medical inspections on the four sides of the continental United States, see Howard Markel and Alexandra Minna Stern, "Which Face? Whose Nation? Immigration, Public Health, and the Construction of Disease at America's Ports and Borders, 1891–1928," *American Behavioral Scientist* 42, no. 9 (1999): 1314–31.

23. C. C. Pierce, "Combating Typhus Fever on the Mexican Border," *Public Health Reports* 32 (March 23, 1917): 426–29. Also see S. B. Grubbs, "Destroying Lice on Typhus Fever Suspects," *Public Health Reports* 31 (October 20, 1916): 2918–23.

24. Pierce, "Combating Typhus Fever." Within the context of the bacteriological revolution, which began in earnest in the 1880s when scientists such as Robert Koch and Louis Pasteur discovered and verified that microorganisms caused infection and disease, the etiology of typhus was discerned rather late. In the early 1900s, bacteriologists believed that the typhus microbe was probably transmitted through some species of anthropod. In 1909, the French physician Charles Nicolle of the Pasteur Institute in Tunisia demonstrated that *Pediculus humanis corporis,* or the human body louse, was the principal vector of typhus. This was confirmed in 1916 by the Brazilian bacteriologist Henrique Da Roche Lima. The bacterium, *Rickettsia prowazekii,* which had eluded researchers because of its tiny size, was named after two victims of typhus fever, Howard Ricketts and Stanislaus Prowazek, who perished while trying to identify the microbe (the former, in fact, in Mexico in 1910). Carrying the deadly bacteria in its intestines, the louse attaches parasitically to a human host to consume blood and soon deposits its feces. By scratching the rash and skin irritations occasioned by lice bites, the victim eventually introduces the bacteria into her or his bloodstream. After an incubation period of from five to fifteen days, the onset of the disease is sudden. The clinical manifestations of the disease are high fever, severe headache, prostration, and chills, followed by a purplish and sienna rash that covers the body's trunk and limbs. Although no treatments existed in the early 1900s, since the introduction of broad-spectrum antibiotics in the

middle of the century typhus has become curable if diagnosed early on. See "Epidemic Typhus," in *The Cambridge World History of Human Disease,* ed. Kenneth F. Kiple (Cambridge: Cambridge University Press, 1993), 1080–84; Howard Markel, *When Germs Travel: Six Major Epidemics That Have Invaded America since 1900 and the Fears They Have Unleashed* (New York: Pantheon, 2004), chap. 4; Kim Pelis, "Prophet for Profit in French North Africa: Charles Nicolle and the Pasteur Institute of Tunis, 1903–1936," *Bulletin of the History of Medicine* 71, no. 4 (Winter 1997): 583–622; Hans Zinsser, *Rats, Lice and History: Being a Study in Biography, Which after Twelve Preliminary Chapters Indispensable for the Preparation of the Lay Reader, Deals with the Life History of Typhus Fever* (Boston: Little, Brown, 1935); and Victoria A. Harden, *Rocky Mountain Spotted Fever: History of a Twentieth-Century Disease* (Baltimore: Johns Hopkins University Press, 1990).

25. Pierce, "Combating Typhus Fever," 427.

26. Ibid., 428.

27. After passage of the Immigration Act of 1917, new booklets with itemized instructions and examples of "undesirability" were published and distributed to immigration officers in the field. See USPHS, *Regulations Governing the Medical Inspection of Aliens* (Washington, DC: Government Printing Office, 1917), and *Manual of the Mental Examination of Aliens* (Washington, DC: Government Printing Office, 1918). On the disease classifications used at the time, see USPHS, *The Control of Communicable Diseases: Report of the American Public Health Association Committee on Standard Regulations Appointed in October, 1916* (Washington, DC: Government Printing Office, 1920).

28. Pierce to the Surgeon General, January 9, 1917, File 1248, USPHS, RG90, NARA; *Public Health Reports,* February 2, 1917, 211.

29. *Public Health Reports,* June 1, 1917, 865, and June 29, 1917, 1057.

30. These figures are calculated according to the numbers reported by Pierce in *Public Health Reports* from the week ending January 12, 1917, to the week ending June 29, 1917 (twenty-one weeks total). These weekly reports are spotted with numerous inconsistencies where it appears that Pierce double-counted cases. Nonetheless, following these liberal figures shows that of thirty-one total cases in the United States during this period, twenty-five occurred in El Paso (including three fatalities), three in Laredo, one in Eagle Pass, one in Austin, and one in New York.

31. These figures are calculated according to the numbers given in *Public Health Reports* from the week ending February 2, 1917 (when the first inspection numbers during the quarantine are reported) to the week ending June 29, 1917.

32. USPHS documents and newspaper articles indicate that the Santa Fe Street station had at least two and usually three physicians on active duty during the first four months of the quarantine. These included Pierce, John W. Tappan, a USPHS assistant surgeon and El Paso's city physician for several months after Kluttz's death, and at different times either Dr. T. C. Galloway, also of the USPHS, or the local doctor Hugh White. It is likely that additional physicians took part in quarantining and vaccinating, as the city's medical community regularly collaborated with the immigration service and the US Army. Excluding

physicians and associated immigration inspectors, the El Paso quarantine station had about a dozen full-time employees running the plant by January 1917. See "Personnel of the Texas-Mexican Border Quarantine, El Paso," June 1916, File 126, USPHS, RG 90, NARA; and the correspondence between June 1916 and January 1917 from Pierce and Tappan to the Surgeon General requesting more workers for the station, Files 1248 and 126, USPHS, RG 90, NARA. Although I have calculated an estimate of 2,696 immigrants inspected daily in El Paso, it is probable that this number was actually much higher, since many estimates stress that 75 percent or more of all entries came through El Paso.

33. See Howard Markel, *Quarantine! East European Jewish Immigrants and the New York City Epidemics of 1892* (Baltimore: Johns Hopkins University Press, 1997), chaps. 6–8; and Alan M. Kraut, *Silent Travelers: Germs, Genes, and the "Immigrant Menace"* (Baltimore: Johns Hopkins University Press, 1995), 55–56.

34. This figure comes from Harlan D. Unrau, *Historic Resource Study (Historic Component): Ellis Island, Statue of Liberty National Monument, New York–New Jersey* (Washington, DC: US Department of the Interior, National Park Service, 1984), 3:734. I thank John Parascandola, retired USPHS historian, for this source and for pointing out the difficulties of calculating precise figures for this period of immigration and inspection history.

35. James J. Davis, "Memorandum for the Bureau of Immigration," November 17, 1923, Microfilm Records of the Immigration and Naturalization Service (INS), Reel 3, Series A, Part 2, casefile 52903/29.

36. Irving McNeil to J. W. Tappan, December 22, 1923, Microfilm Records of the INS, Reel 3, Series A, Part 2, casefile 52903/29. Letters and reports from Files 126, 1248, and 2126, USPHS, RG90, NARA, document that after Pierce left the border Tappan took over direction of the quarantine and continued to order equipment, deal with the daily logistics of operating the plant, and supervise personnel.

37. Will E. Soult to Supervisor, Immigration Service, El Paso, Texas, December 13, 1923, Microfilm Records of the INS, Reel 3, Series A, Part 2, casefile 52903/29.

38. John McMullen, Senior Surgeon, to the Surgeon General, January 28, 1928, NC-34, General Correspondence with Quarantine Stations, 1927–34, District #4 (El Paso), USPHS, RG90, NARA.

39. "Quarantine Operations at the Port of Laredo, Texas during the Fiscal Year Ending June 30, 1926," General Subject Files, 1924–35, Domestic Stations, Laredo, USPHS, RG90, NARA.

40. "Annual Report of Quarantine Operations at El Paso, Texas during the Fiscal Year Ended June 30, 1938," General Classified Records, Group 1, Domestic Stations, 1936–44, El Paso, USPHS, RG90, NARA.

41. See Howard Markel and Alexandra Minna Stern, "The Foreignness of Germs: The Persistent Association of Immigrants and Disease in American Society," *Milbank Quarterly* 80, no. 4 (2002): 757–88.

42. "Annual Report of Quarantine Operations at El Paso, Texas during the Fiscal Year Ended June 30, 1938," General Classified Records, Group 1, Domestic Stations, 1936–44, El Paso, USPHS, RG90, NARA.

43. R. L. Allen to the Surgeon General, November 13, 1941, General Classified Records, Group 1, Domestic Stations, 1936–44, El Paso, USPHS, RG90,
NARA. Smaller stations, such as the Presidio, Rio Grande City, and Roma
appear to have been the first to discontinue delousing in 1937, although Eagle
Pass reported 163 disinfections that same year. See P. J. Gorman, Senior Surgeon
to the Surgeon General, July 17, 1937, General Classified Records, Group 1,
Domestic Stations, 1936–1944, Laredo, USPHS, RG90, NARA; and "Quarantine Transactions at Mexican Border Stations (Eagle Pass, Texas) for the Year
Ending June 30, 1937," General Classified Records, Group 1, Domestic Stations, 1936–44, Eagle Pass, USPHS, RG90, NARA.

44. R. L. Allen to the Surgeon General, November 29, 1944, General Classified Records, Group 1, Domestic Stations 1936–44, El Paso, USPHS, RG90,
NARA.

45. "Annual Report. Medical Inspection. Aliens. Port Huron, Mich, 1928,"
NC 34 E10, General Subject File, 1924–35, USPHS, RG90, NARA.

46. J. W. Tappan, "Protective Health Measures on United States–Mexico
Border," *Journal of the American Medical Association* 87, no. 13 (1926): 1022.

47. See Nayan Shah, *Contagious Divides: Epidemics and Race in San Francisco's Chinatown* (Berkeley: University of California Press, 2001); Charles J.
McClain, *In Search of Equality: The Chinese Struggle against Discrimination in
Nineteenth-Century America* (Berkeley: University of California Press, 1994);
and Kraut, *Silent Travelers.*

48. By the mid-1920s, Johnson was both a member of the American Eugenics Society and president of its affiliated Eugenics Research Association.

49. See John Higham, *Strangers in the Land: Patterns of American Nativism,
1860–1925*, 2nd ed. (New Brunswick, NJ: Rutgers University Press, 1988); and
Mae M. Ngai, *Impossible Subjects: Illegal Aliens and the Making of Modern
America* (Princeton, NJ: Princeton University Press, 2004).

50. George J. Sánchez, *Becoming Mexican American: Ethnicity, Culture, and
Identity in Chicano Los Angeles, 1900–1945* (New York: Oxford University Press,
1993); Francisco E. Balderrama and Raymond Rodríguez, *Decade of Betrayal:
Mexican Repatriation in the 1930s* (Albuquerque: University of New Mexico
Press, 1995); Vicki L. Ruiz, *From Out of the Shadows: Mexican Women in Twentieth-Century America* (New York: Oxford University Press, 1998); Gabriela F.
Arredondo, *Mexican Chicago: Race, Ethnicity, and Gender, 1916–1939* (Urbana:
University of Illinois Press, in press). Statistics on Mexican immigration are notoriously problematic because of shifting racial and legal classifications and the circular and seasonal nature of Mexican migration patterns. Many scholars concur,
however, that at least one million and perhaps even two million Mexicans entered
the United States from 1910 to 1930, the majority from 1920 to 1930. The 1930
census offers the following statistics: 367,510 Mexicans in the United States in
1910; 700,541 in 1920; and 1,422,533 in 1930. See US Census Bureau, "Table
E-7. White Population of Mexican Origin, for the United States, Regions, Divisions, and States: 1910 to 1930," www.census.gov/population/documentation.

51. See David G. Gutiérrez, *Walls and Mirrors: Mexican Americans, Mexican Immigrants, and the Politics of Ethnicity* (Berkeley: University of California
Press, 1995), chaps. 2 and 3.

52. Goethe is listed as a council member of *Survey Graphic* beginning in 1918.

53. See chapter 4. Goethe sent Laughlin a postcard of the Arizona desert, on which he wrote: "Am down here on the Border studying the eugenic aspects of the Mexican immigration problem. One's reaction to their slums surrounding the Nordic quarters of border towns is that the latter are competing with a rabbit-type birth rate. The more one studies the peon the more one wonders: Did the Conquistadores eliminate the thinkers when he destroyed the Aztec priest and soldier?" Charles M. Goethe to Harry H. Laughlin, February 1927, Harry H. Laughlin Papers (hereafter HHLP), Box C-4-1, Special Collections (hereafter SC), Truman State University (hereafter TSU). Also cited in Randall D. Bird and Garland Allen, "The J.H.B. Archive Report: The Papers of Harry Hamilton Laughlin, Eugenicist," *Journal of the History of Biology* 14, no. 2 (1981): 339–53, which discusses the correspondence between Laughlin and Goethe.

54. C. M. Goethe, "The Influx of Mexican Amerinds," *Eugenics* 2, no. 1 (January 1929): 6–9.

55. Ibid., 6.

56. Similar language was used in depictions of the Irish domestic worker Mary Mallon, better known as "Typhoid Mary," the first confirmed "silent carrier" of typhoid. See Judith Walzer Leavitt, *Typhoid Mary: Captive to the Public's Health* (Boston: Beacon Press, 1996).

57. Harry H. Laughlin to John C. Merriman, September 24, 1929, HHLP, Box C-4-6, SC, TSU.

58. We can assume with almost complete certainty that this individual was male, given that there were few if any female physicians in El Paso in the early twentieth century.

59. "Questions Pertaining to Mexican Immigration to Be Answered by Persons Interested in Public Health," included in John C. Box to Harry H. Laughlin, January 29, 1930, HHLP, Box C-4-1, SC, TSU.

60. See "Auburn-Haired Amazon."

61. Señora X, interview by Maria Nuckolls, December 7, 1979, Tape 722, Institute of Oral History (hereafter IOH), SC, University of Texas at El Paso (hereafter UTEP).

62. The interviewee is probably referring to some cyanide compound; there is no explicit reference to cryolite in the USPHS records. José Cruz Burciaga, interview by Oscar J. Martínez, February 16, 1974, Tape 143, IOH, SC, UTEP.

63. Felix López Urdiales, interview by Oscar J. Martínez, February 22, 1974, Tape 144C, IOH, SC, UTEP.

64. "The Future of Mexican Immigration," Survey of Race Relations Collection, Box 4, Hoover Institution Archives, Stanford University.

65. Nat K. King to the Surgeon General, July 22, 1922, File 1169, USPHS, RG90, NARA.

66. "Copy of Reports of Mounted Guards Heston B. Martin and Alvis C. Taylor Beginning August 1st and Ending August 31st (1921) Inclusive," File 1169, USPHS, RG90, NARA.

67. "Daily Reports of Mounted Guards Alvis C. Taylor and Heston B. Martin Beginning September 1st and Ending September 31st (1921) Inclusive," File 1169, USPHS, RG90, NARA.

68. Ibid.; Nat K. King to the Surgeon General, July 9, 1923, File 1169, USPHS, RG90, NARA.

69. See David J. Weber, *The Spanish Frontier in North America* (New Haven, CT: Yale University, 1992); and María Teresa Koreck, "Space, Power, and Imperial Remappings of the Mexican North, 1730–1840," unpublished manuscript.

70. See David Montejano, *Anglos and Mexicans in the Making of Texas, 1836–1986* (Austin: University of Texas Press, 1987); Robert M. Utley, *The Indian Frontier of the American West, 1846–1890* (Albuquerque: University of New Mexico Press, 1984); and Elliott Young, "Remembering Catarino Garza's 1891 Revolution: An Aborted Border Insurrection," *Mexican Studies/Estudios Mexicanos* 12, no. 2 (1996): 231–72.

71. For a more recent history, see Timothy J. Dunn, *The Militarization of the U.S.-Mexico Border, 1978–1992: Low-Intensity Conflict Doctrine Comes Home* (Austin: CMAS Books, University of Texas at Austin, 1996).

72. Oliver Knight, foreword to *Six Years with the Texas Rangers, 1875–1881*, by James B. Gillett (1921; repr., Lincoln: University of Nebraska Press 1976), xiii.

73. Montejano, *Anglos and Mexicans*, 117–128; Benjamin Heber Johnson, *Revolution in Texas: How a Forgotten Rebellion and Its Bloody Suppression Turned Mexicans into Americans* (New Haven, CT: Yale University Press, 2003).

74. Montejano, *Anglos and Mexicans*, 117–28.

75. See Kelly Anne Lytle Hernández, "Entangling Bodies and Borders: Racial Profiling and the U.S. Border Patrol, 1924–1955" (PhD diss., University of California, Los Angeles, 2002).

76. US Border Patrol, "History of United States Border Patrol," 4, General Archives, US Border Patrol Museum, El Paso, TX.

77. US Department of Labor, Bureau of Immigration, "General Order No. 49," March 16, 1925, included in US House of Representatives, *Immigration Border Patrol Hearings before the United States House Committee on Immigration and Naturalization, 75th Congress, 2nd session, on January 15, 1930* (Washington, DC: Government Printing Office, 1930), 27.

78. Ibid., 4–6; I. F. Wixon, *The Mission of the Border Patrol*, US Department of Labor, INS, Lecture no. 7, March 19, 1934 (Washington, DC: Government Printing Office, 1937).

79. US House of Representatives, *To Establish a Border Patrol: Hearings before the United States House Committee on the Judiciary, Subcommittee No. 1 (Judiciary), Sixty-Ninth Congress, First Session, on Apr. 12, 19, 1926* (Washington, DC: Government Printing Office, 1926), 32.

80. Wixon, *Mission*, 2.

81. Ngai, *Impossible Subjects,* chap. 2.

82. Ibid., 60.

83. Ibid., 67.

84. For a more extensive development of this argument, see Alexandra Minna Stern, "Nationalism on the Line: Masculinity, Race, and the Creation of the Border Patrol, 1910–1940," in *Continental Crossroads: Remapping U.S.-Mexico Borderlands History,* ed. Samuel Truett and Elliott Young (Durham, NC: Duke University Press, 2004), 299–323.

85. For a persuasive exposition of this new conception of entry into the nation's interior, see Ngai, *Impossible Subjects.*

86. "Why Marfa, Texas Is Sector Headquarters for the United States Immigration Border Patrol," D87.92.12, Marfa Sector Folder, General Archives, US Border Patrol Museum, El Paso, TX.

87. Wixon, *Mission,* 8–9.

88. See, for example, Alvin Edward Moore, *Border Patrol* (Santa Fe, NM: Sunstone Press, 1988); Clement David Hellyer, *The U.S. Border Patrol* (New York: Random House, 1963); and Jack Kearney, *Tracking: A Blueprint for Learning How* (El Cajon, CA: Pathways Press, 1978).

89. Quoted in Peter Odens, *The Desert Trackers: Men of the Border Patrol* (Yuma, AZ: Southwestern Printers, 1975), chap. 3 (no page numbers).

90. Quoted in ibid. Murphy J. Steen, a Miami-based patrolman who often carried out boat patrol, also claimed that master sign-cutters could read "race" out of such clues: "The individual's color was an important means of identification, and we could usually tell whether the person who had preceded us along the trail was white or black." Murphy J. F. Steen, *Twenty-Five Years a U.S. Border Patrolman* (Dallas, TX: Royal, 1958), 11.

91. See Philip J. Deloria, *Playing Indian* (New Haven, CT: Yale University Press, 1998); and Michael Rosenthal, *The Character Factory: Baden-Powell and the Origins of the Boy Scout Movement* (New York: Pantheon, 1986).

92. US House of Representatives, *To Establish a Border Patrol,* 17–18.

93. See Gail Bederman, *Manliness and Civilization: A Cultural History of Gender and Race in the United States, 1880–1917* (Chicago: University of Chicago Press, 1995); and Matthew Basso, Laura McCall, and Dee Garceau, eds., *Across the Great Divide: Cultures of Manhood in the American West* (New York: Routledge, 2001).

94. Hellyer, *U.S. Border Patrol,* 20–21.

95. Clifford Alan Perkins, *Border Patrol: With the U.S. Immigration Service on the Mexican Boundary, 1910–54* (El Paso: Texas Western Press, University of Texas at El Paso, 1978).

96. Complaints were endemic in southwestern newspapers in the late 1920s, as the creation of the Border Patrol merged with stricter immigration laws to lead to a rapid rise in the deportation and harassment of Mexicans. For example, see "Texas Mexicans Are Told to Demand Search Warrant before Admitting Officers," *Antonio Evening News,* November 14, 1929; "Border Patrol Slays Mexican," *El Paso Herald,* September 7, 1929; "Border Citizen Protests against New Regulations," *Big Bend Sentinel,* March 7, 1929; and "Amazing Abuses of Mexicans in U.S. Is Charged in Report," *Bisbee Daily Review,* January 26, 1929, Microfilm Records of the INS, Reel 16, Series A, Part 2, casefile 55598/459D. Numerous instances of outrage are also archived in the HASFR in Mexico City. In his 1934 report, Wixon refers obliquely to this period: "There

was a period when pressure from the Department for arrests and deportations inculcated a competitive spirit in the force and led to grave abuses and invasions of the rights of both citizens and aliens." Wixon, *Mission*, 9.

97. Perkins, *Border Patrol*, 102.

98. Hellyer, *U.S. Border Patrol*, chap. 9.

99. Perkins, *Border Patrol*, 100.

100. Wixon, *Mission*, 11.

101. Ibid.

102. Quoted in US Department of Labor, Bureau of Immigration, *Annual Report of the Commissioner General of Immigration to the Secretary of Labor for the Fiscal Year Ended June 30, 1930* (Washington, DC: Government Printing Office, 1930), 42.

103. See Mary Kidder Rak, *Border Patrol* (Boston: Houghton Mifflin, 1938), and *They Guard the Gates: The Way of Life on the American Borders* (Evanston, IL: Row, Peterson, 1941).

104. See Neil Foley, *The White Scourge: Mexicans, Blacks, and Poor Whites in Texas Cotton Culture* (Berkeley: University of California Press, 1997); Grace Peña Delgado, *Making the Chinese Mexican: Global Migration, Exclusion, and Localism in the U.S.-Mexico Borderlands* (Palo Alto, CA: Stanford University Press, 2012); and Elliott Young, *Alien Nation: Chinese Migration in the Americas from the Coolie Era through World War II* (Chapel Hill: University of North Carolina Press, 2014).

105. See D. Gutiérrez, *Walls and Mirrors*.

106. On interior frontiers and intimate frontiers, see Ann Laura Stoler, "Sexual Affronts and Racial Frontiers: European Identities and the Cultural Politics of Exclusion in Colonial Southeast Asia," in *Tensions of Empire: Colonial Cultures in a Bourgeois World,* ed. Ann Laura Stoler and Frederick Cooper (Berkeley: University of California Press, 1997), 198–237.

107. Quoted in Rachel C. St. John, *Line in the Sand: A History of the Western U.S.-Mexico Border* (Princeton, NJ: Princeton University Press, 2011), 166–67, Kindle Loc 3527.

108. See Matthew Frye Jacobson, *Whiteness of a Different Color: European Immigrants and the Alchemy of Race* (Cambridge, MA: Harvard University Press, 1998).

109. Ngai, *Impossible Subjects*.

110. Kelly Lytle Hernández, *Migra! A History of the U.S. Border Patrol* (Berkeley: University of California Press, 2010).

3. INSTITUTING EUGENICS IN CALIFORNIA

1. "Fred Hogue Funeral Service Will Be Conducted Thursday," *Los Angeles Times,* July 1, 1941.

2. Fred Hogue, "Social Eugenics," *Los Angeles Times (Sunday Magazine),* February 16, 1936.

3. K. Burchardi, "Why Hitler Says: 'Sterilize the Unfit!'," *Los Angeles Times,* August 11, 1935; Tony [Anthony] Platt, *What's in a Name? Charles M. Goethe, American Eugenics, and Sacramento State University* (Sacramento, CA: T. Platt,

2004), 17; Mike Anton, "Forced Sterilization Once Seen as Path to a Better World," *Los Angeles Times,* July 16, 2003.

4. Fred Hogue, Social Eugenics, *Los Angeles Times (Sunday Magazine),* January 19, 1936.

5. Fred Hogue, Social Eugenics, *Los Angeles Times (Sunday Magazine),* March 26, 1939.

6. Fred Hogue, Social Eugenics, *Los Angeles Times (Sunday Magazine),* May 10, 1936.

7. Fred Hogue, Social Eugenics, *Los Angeles Times (Sunday Magazine),* February 23, 1941; Fred Hogue, Social Eugenics, *Los Angeles Times (Sunday Magazine),* November 17, 1940. Hogue usually referred his queries to the AIFR.

8. Fred Hogue, Social Eugenics, *Los Angeles Times (Sunday Magazine),* June 21, 1936.

9. Fred Hogue, Social Eugenics, *Los Angeles Times (Sunday Magazine),* March 5, 1939.

10. Assembly Bill no. 1607, January 26, 1935; Assembly Bill no. 2590, January 22, 1937, Folder 1, Box 3, E. S. Gosney Papers and Records of the Human Betterment Foundation Papers (hereafter ESGP-RHBF), Institute Archives (hereafter IA), California Institute of Technology (hereafter CIT).

11. Assembly Bill no. 1607, January 26, 1935, Folder 1, Box 3, ESGP-RHBF, IA, CIT.

12. Ibid.

13. The 1935 bill passed the assembly but died in the senate. See "Background Paper," in California Legislature, Senate Select Committee on Genetics, Genetic Technologies, and Public Policy, *California's Compulsory Sterilization Policies, 1909–1979, July 16, 2003, Informational Hearing* (Sacramento: California Publications, 2003), vi. On sterilization in California, see Philip R. Reilly, *The Surgical Solution: A History of Involuntary Sterilization in the United States* (Baltimore: Johns Hopkins University Press, 1991); Wendy Kline, *Building a Better Race: Gender, Sexuality, and Eugenics from the Turn of the Century to the Baby Boom* (Berkeley: University of California Press, 2001); Joel Braslow, *Mental Ills and Bodily Cures: Psychiatric Treatment in the First Half of the Twentieth Century* (Berkeley: University of California Press, 1997); Richard W. Fox, *So Far Disordered in Mind: Insanity in California, 1870–1930* (Berkeley: University of California Press, 1978); and Robert William Biller, "Defending the Last Frontier: Eugenic Thought and Action in the State of California, 1890–1941" (MA thesis, Simon Fraser University, 1993).

14. In 1941, sterilizations reached almost the same number, 818. See California State Department of Institutions, *Statistical Report of the Department of Institutions of the State of California, Year Ending June 30, 1939* (Sacramento: California State Printing Office, 1940), 26, and *Statistical Report of the Department of Institutions of the State of California, Year Ending June 30, 1940* (Sacramento: California State Printing Office, 1941), 82. These are fiscal years, not calendar years. These data have been supplemented by calculations drawn from our California eugenic sterilization data set.

15. See Reilly, *Surgical Solution.* The national figure fluctuates between 60,000 and 66,000, depending on source and citation; the California figure of

20,000 is commonly accepted. On the basis of the reports of the Department of Institutions and its predecessor (Commission in Lunacy) and successor (Department of Mental Hygiene), as well as recent statistics provided by the Departments of Mental Health and Developmental Services, I have calculated a total of 19,250. This does not, however, include sterilizations performed at the very active Patton hospital between 1951 and 1960, the small yet undetermined number of operations performed at all institutions between 1961 and 1979, or procedures at state prisons and other facilities that technically were not allowed to sterilize but did, most likely in excess of 1,000 operations. Hence, I believe that 20,000 is a fair working estimate, although probably low.

16. One of the first studies to examine a region other than the East Coast is Edward J. Larson, *Sex, Race, and Science: Eugenics in the Deep South* (Baltimore: Johns Hopkins University Press, 1995). California has much in common with Virginia. See Gregory Michael Dorr, *Segregation's Science: Hereditarian Thought in Virginia, 1785 to the Present* (Chapel Hill: University of North Carolina Press, in press); Paul A. Lombardo, "Miscegenation, Eugenics, and Racism: Historical Footnotes to *Loving v. Virginia,*" *University of California, Davis, Law Review* 21, no. 421 (1988): 421–52; and Lisa Linquist Dorr, "Arm in Arm: Gender, Eugenics, and Virginia's Racial Integrity Acts of the 1920s," *Journal of Women's History* 11, no. 1 (Spring 1999): 143–66. On North Carolina, see Johanna Schoen, *Choice and Coercion: Birth Control, Sterilization, and Abortion in Public Health and Welfare* (Chapel Hill: University of North Carolina Press, 2005). There is a growing historiography on midwestern and western states with active eugenics movements such as Minnesota, Michigan, Indiana, and Oregon (see Introduction).

17. Quoted in Steven Selden, *Inheriting Shame: The Story of Eugenics and Racism in America* (New York: Teacher's College, Columbia University, 1999), 4; Charles B. Davenport to David Starr Jordan, May 24, 1910, 62/604, David Starr Jordan Papers (hereafter DSJP), Special Collections (hereafter SC), Stanford University (hereafter SU).

18. Charles B. Davenport to David Starr Jordan, May 24, 1910, 67/645, DSJP, SC, SU.

19. Charles B. Davenport to David Starr Jordan, June 21, 1910, 68/649, DSJP, SC, SU.

20. See William Deverell, "Introduction: The Varieties of Progressive Experience," in *California Progressivism Revisited,* ed. William Deverell and Tom Sitton (Berkeley: University of California Press, 1994), 1–11.

21. On eugenics and citriculture, see Douglas Cazaux Sackman, *Orange Empire: California and the Fruits of Eden* (Berkeley: University of California Press, 2005).

22. On racism in nineteenth-century California, see Tomás Almaguer, *Racial Fault Lines: The Historical Origins of White Supremacy in California* (Berkeley: University of California Press, 1994); Lisbeth Haas, *Conquests and Historical Identities in California, 1769–1936* (Berkeley: University of California Press, 1995); Nayan Shah, *Contagious Divides: Epidemics and Race in San Francisco's Chinatown* (Berkeley: University of California Press, 2001); Charles J. McClain, *In Search of Equality: The Chinese Struggle against Discrimination*

in Nineteenth-Century America (Berkeley: University of California Press, 1994); and Elmer Clarence Sandmeyer, *The Anti-Chinese Movement in California* (1973; repr., Urbana: University of Illinois Press, 1991).

23. See the Haynes Foundation website at www.haynesfoundation.org and Tom Sitton, *John Randolph Haynes: California Progressive* (Stanford, CA: Stanford University Press, 1992), chap. 11. When designing their foundation, the Hayneses designated seven major categories of support; the fourth was the "improvement of the human race by aiding and encouraging the science of eugenics." Today, the foundation distributes up to $3 million annually, primarily for local research projects, many of which, ironically, address the racial and social inequities spawned by eugenic racism in the first half of the twentieth century.

24. See Almaguer, *Racial Fault Lines;* McClain, *In Search of Equality;* and Sandmeyer, *Anti-Chinese Movement.*

25. See Albert Camarillo, *Chicanos in a Changing Society: From Mexican Pueblos to American Barrios in Santa Barbara and Southern California, 1848–1930* (1979; repr., Cambridge, MA: Harvard University Press, 1996); and Almaguer, *Racial Fault Lines.*

26. California State Department of Institutions, *Second Biennial Report of the Department of Institutions for the Year Ending June 30, 1924* (Sacramento: California State Printing Office, 1924), 15.

27. See Fox, *So Far Disordered.*

28. California State Department of Institutions, *Second Biennial Report,* 15.

29. California State Department of Institutions, *Statistical Report of the Department of Institutions of the State of California, Year Ending June 30, 1942* (Sacramento: California State Printing Office, 1942), 18.

30. California State Board of Charities and Corrections, *Seventh Biennial Report of the State Board of Charities and Corrections of the State of California from July 1, 1914 to June 30, 1916* (Sacramento: California State Printing Office, 1916), 56.

31. Quoted in Biller, "Defending the Last Frontier," 55.

32. California State Department of Institutions, *Fourth Biennial Report of the Department of Institutions for the Year Ending June 30, 1928* (Sacramento: California State Printing Office, 1928), 18.

33. California State Department of Institutions, *Sixth Biennial Report of the Department of Institutions for the Year Ending June 30, 1932* (Sacramento: California State Printing Office, 1932), 9, *Statistical Report of the Department of Institutions of the State of California, Year Ending June 30, 1937* (Sacramento: California State Printing Office, 1937), 22, and *Statistical Report of the Department of Institutions of the State of California, Year Ending June 30, 1938* (Sacramento: California State Printing Office, 1938), 23.

34. Earl E. Jensen to Dr. Edwin Wayte, August 30, 1927, and Harry Lutgens and Charles F. Waymire to Edwin Wayte, November 1, 1937: "Property of Patients Being Deported from Norwalk State Hospital November 14, 1937," both in Department of Mental Hygiene-Norwalk, Correspondence and Reports, F408, California State Archives, Sacramento.

35. See Kevin Starr, *Endangered Dreams: The Great Depression in California* (New York: Oxford University Press, 1996), 176–77.

36. California State Department of Institutions, *Statistical Report . . . 1942*, 18.

37. This founding motto appeared on all Commonwealth Club of California (hereafter CCC) publications in the 1920s and 1930s.

38. "The Alien Land Law," *Transactions of the Commonwealth Club of California* 15, no. 4 (1920): 175–212; "Quota or Exclusion for Japanese Immigrants?" *Commonwealth* 8, no. 51 (1932): 285.

39. Samuel J. Holmes published many books related to eugenics, the most important of which were *A Bibliography of Eugenics* (Berkeley: University of California Press, 1924) and *The Trend of the Race: A Study of Present Tendencies in the Biological Development of Civilized Mankind* (New York: Harcourt, Brace, 1921). On his eugenics courses, see "The Factors of Evolution in Man," *Bulletin of the University Extension*, n.s., 4, no. 22 (January 1919), Folder: Holmes-Misc., Carton 2, Samuel J. Holmes Papers (hereafter SJHP), CB 935, Bancroft Library (hereafter BL), University of California at Berkeley (hereafter UCB), and "The University of California," *Eugenics* 2, no. 9 (1929): 26–27. On his eugenic study of college students, see Samuel J. Holmes to Dean A. O. Leuschner, February 1, 1924, Folder: Outgoing Letters L, Box 2, SJHP, CB 935, BL, UCB. On monetary incentives, see "Wants Prizes for Professors' Babies," *Syracuse Herald*, n.d., and "Bonus on Babies Urged by Savant," *San Francisco Journal*, October 19 1922, Loose Folders, Carton 4, SJHP, CB 935, BL, UCB. Holmes was a member of the American Eugenics Society, the Eugenics Research Association, and the American Association for the Advancement of Science.

40. Samuel J. Holmes, "Perils of the Mexican Invasion," *North American Review* 227, no. 5 (1929): 615–23, Carton 1, offprints, SJHP, CB 935, BL, UCB. Quotation from p. 617.

41. Ibid., 617; also see Holmes, "An Argument against Mexican Immigration," *Transactions of the Commonwealth Club of California*, part 2, 2, no. 12 (1926): 21–27.

42. "Progress Report for 1928," *Commonwealth*, Part 2, 5, no. 5 (1929): 450.

43. Reprint of Charles M. Goethe to CCC Board of Directors, August 1, 1924, included in April 20, 1933, Notes and Minutes, Eugenics Section (hereafter ES), Commonwealth Club of California (private collection) (hereafter CCC (pc)), unprocessed collection since acquired by the Hoover Institution, Stanford University.

44. Ibid.

45. Charles M. Goethe to Samuel J. Holmes, February 20, 1924, Folder: Goethe, Box 1, SJHP, CB 935, BL, UCB; "Progress Report for 1924," *Transactions of the Commonwealth Club of California* 19, no. 11 (1925): 724; "Minutes of the Board of Governors, July 21, 1924," CCC (pc). The Board of Governors' minutes indicate that Holmes accepted the chairmanship in October 1924. "Minutes of the Meeting of the Board of Governors," October 29, 1924, CCC (pc).

46. "Eugenics," *Transactions of the Commonwealth Club of California* 21, no. 4, reproduced in *Commonwealth* 2, no. 25 (1926): 153–87, quotations from 159, 182.

47. "Sterilization in California," Notes and Minutes, September 26, 1925, ES, CCC (pc).

48. "Section on Eugenics," August 9, 1928, Notes and Minutes, ES, CCC (pc).

49. "Speaker: Stuart R. Ward," August 14, 1928, Notes and Minutes, ES, CCC (pc).

50. "Commonwealth Club of California, Section on Eugenics, Minutes of May 22, 1928," Notes and Minutes, ES, CCC (pc).

51. David Starr Jordan to Charles B. Davenport, May 7, 1925, Charles B. Davenport Papers (hereafter CBDP), B:D27, American Philosophical Society (hereafter APS).

52. Charles M. Goethe, form letter, March 27, 1928, Papers of Harry H. Laughlin (hereafter HHLP), C-4-1, Special Collections (hereafter SC), Truman State University (hereafter TSU).

53. "Mexican Strays into California," *Eugenical News* 11, no. 6 (1926): 88.

54. On Proposition 187 and eugenic discourse, see Jonathan Xavier Inda, "Biopower, Reproduction, and the Migrant Woman's Body," in *In Decolonial Voices: Chicana and Chicano Cultural Studies in the 21st Century,* ed. Arturo J. Aldama and Naomi Quiñonez (Bloomington: Indiana University Press, 2002), 98–112; Dorothy Nelkin and Mark Michaels, "Biological Categories and Border Controls: The Revival of Eugenics in Anti-immigration Rhetoric," *International Journal of Sociology and Social Policy* 18, nos. 5–6 (1998): 35–63; and Daniel HoSang, *Racial Propositions: Ballot Initiatives and the Making of Postwar California* (Berkeley: University of California Press, 2010).

55. See Kent A. Ono and John M. Sloop, *Shifting Borders: Rhetoric, Immigration, and California's Proposition 187* (Philadelphia: Temple University Press, 2002). On images of Mexican immigration in the 1990s, see Leo R. Chávez, *Covering Immigration: Popular Images and the Politics of the Nation* (Berkeley: University of California Press, 2001).

56. J. Harold Williams et al., *Whittier Social Case History Manual* (Whittier, CA: California Bureau of Juvenile Research, Whittier State School, 1921), 50. See the website for the California Youth Authority (www.cya.ca.gov), which, interestingly, does not explicitly acknowledge the California Bureau of Juvenile Research.

57. Williams et al., *Whittier Social Case History Manual,* 50. The last issue of the *Journal of Juvenile Research* indicated that its publication would continue, in a different guise, as the *California Journal of Guidance.* However, I have not yet found any evidence that this journal was ever published. See "Editorial," *Journal of Juvenile Research* 22, nos. 3–4 (1938): 143–44.

58. See California State Department of Institutions, *Second Biennial Report,* and *Sixth Biennial Report,* suppl.

59. See Mary E. Odem, *Delinquent Daughters: Protecting and Policing Adolescent Female Sexuality in the United States, 1885–1920* (Chapel Hill: University of North Carolina Press, 1995).

60. See Alexandra Minna Stern and Howard Markel, eds., *Formative Years: Children's Health in the United States, 1880–2000* (Ann Arbor: University of Michigan Press, 2002).

61. See Fox, *So Far Disordered.*

62. See Stephen Jay Gould, *The Mismeasure of Man,* 2nd ed. (New York: W. W. Norton, 1996).

63. See Daniel J. Kevles, *In the Name of Eugenics: Genetics and the Uses of Human Heredity,* rev. ed. (Cambridge, MA: Harvard University Press, 1995).

64. Lewis M. Terman, *The Measurement of Intelligence: An Explanation of and a Complete Guide for the Use of the Stanford Revision and Extension of the Binet-Simon Intelligence Scale* (New York: Houghton Mifflin, 1916), 79; Paul Davis Chapman, *Schools as Sorters: Lewis M. Terman, Applied Psychology, and the Intelligence Testing Movement, 1890–1930* (New York: New York University Press, 1988).

65. Terman, *Measurement of Intelligence,* 79. His classifications were: 25 or below = idiot; 26–50 = imbecile; 51–70 = moron; 71–80 = borderline deficiency sometimes classifiable as dullness, often as feeblemindedness; 81–90 = dullness rarely classifiable as feeblemindedness; 91–110 = normal or average intelligence; 111–120 = superior intelligence; 121–140 = very superior intelligence; above 140 = "near" genius or genius. Any score of 70 or below indicated "definite feeblemindedness."

66. Ibid., 87.

67. Lewis M. Terman, "Feeble Minded Children in the School," in *Report to the 1915 Legislature Committee on Mental Deficiency and the Proposed Institution for the Care of Feeble-Minded and Epileptic Persons* (Whittier, CA: Whittier State School, Department of Printing Instruction, 1917), 45–53, contained in J. Harold Williams Papers (hereafter JHWP), Box 7, Collection 1504, Department of Special Collections (hereafter SC), University of California at Los Angeles (hereafter UCLA). On the emergence of the "menace of the feebleminded," see James W. Trent Jr., *Inventing the Feeble Mind: A History of Mental Retardation in the United States* (Berkeley: University of California Press, 1994).

68. Chapman, *Schools as Sorters,* chap. 1; J. Harold Williams, *A Study of 150 Delinquent Boys,* Bulletin 1 (Stanford, CA: Research Laboratory of the Buckel Foundation, Department of Education, Stanford University, 1915).

69. Lewis M. Terman, *Research in Mental Deviation among Children: A Statement of the Aims and Purposes of the Buckel Foundation,* Research Laboratory of the Buckel Foundation, Department of Education, Stanford University, Bulletin 2 (Stanford, CA: Stanford University, 1915), 3.

70. Williams, *Study,* 13; J. Harold Williams, "Early History of the California Bureau of Juvenile Research," *Journal of Juvenile Research* 18, no. 4 (1934): 187–214.

71. Williams, *Study,* 13. Also see Norman Fenton, *The Delinquent Boy and the Correctional School* (Claremont, CA: Claremont Colleges Guidance Center, 1935).

72. Williams, "Early History," 191. Many offprints related to the CBJR's formation are contained in JHWP, Collection 1504, SC, UCLA.

73. Williams et al., *Whittier Social Case History Manual,* 50. Also see entries on the CBJR in California State Department of Institutions, *Biennial Reports* for the years 1922–34; and Charles B. Davenport to J. Harold Williams, May 14, 1921, CBDP, B:D27, APS.

74. California State Commission in Lunacy, *Ninth Biennial Report of the State Commission in Lunacy for the Two Years Ending June 30, 1914* (Sacramento: California State Printing Office, 1914), 8–9; J. Harold Williams, *Defective, Delinquent, and Dependent Boys*, Department of Research Bulletin 1 (Whittier, CA: Whittier State School, Department of Printing Instruction, 1915).

75. Fred C. Nelles to Charles B. Davenport, July 25, 1917, CBDP, B:D27, APS; Williams, "Early History," 212–13. This is one of the most fascinating and least explored aspects of California eugenics and is preserved in voluminous case files and other documents, many on microfilm, contained in the Eugenics Record Office Papers (hereafter EROP) at the APS. Cowdery's first study using Eugenics Record Office (hereafter ERO) methods was published in 1916; see Karl M. Cowdery, "Analysis of Field Data Concerning One Hundred Delinquent Boys," *Journal of Delinquency* 1, no. 3 (1916): 129–53.

76. Williams et al., *Whittier Social Case History Manual*, 50.

77. Ibid.; J. Harold Williams to Dr. Fred Kuhlmann (Faribault, MN), November 29, 1920, CBDP, B:D27, APS; Charles B. Davenport, *The Trait Book*, ERO Bulletin 6 (Cold Spring Harbor, NY: ERO, 1912); Harry H. Laughlin with Charles B. Davenport, *How to Make a Eugenical Family Study*, ERO Bulletin 13 (Cold Spring Harbor, NY: ERO, 1915).

78. Williams also used the following symbols: *?* for probably feebleminded, *I* for insane, *N* for mentality normal, *Sx* for immoral, *TB* for tubercular, and a hand with a pointed pinkie finger to signify commitment to an institution. See J. Harold Williams, "Heredity and Juvenile Delinquency," Box 7, JHWP, 1504, SC, UCLA.

79. Williams et al., *Whittier Social Case History Manual*, 59.

80. "State of California, Bureau of Juvenile Research, Social Case History no. 351," Series 7, Box 1, EROP, APS; also see microfilm reels 1822196, Box 56; 1822577, Box 58. For how public health officials in Los Angeles represented and sought to reform Mexican maternal and infant hygiene in similar ways, see Natalia Molina, "Illustrating Cultural Authority: Medicalized Representations of Mexican Communities in Early-Twentieth-Century Los Angeles," *Aztlán* 28 (2003): 129–43.

81. Fred C. Nelles, "Changes in the Nature of the Population of Whittier State School," *Journal of Delinquency* 9, no. 6 (1925): 231.

82. See Miroslava Chávez-Garcia, *States of Delinquency: Race and Science in the Making of California's Juvenile Justice System* (Berkeley: University of California Press, 2012).

83. See Research Staff of the Whittier State School, "The Present Status of Juvenile Delinquency in California," *Journal of Delinquency* 5, no. 5 (1920): 183–89; Paul E. Bowers, "The Necessity for Sterilization," *Journal of Delinquency* 6, no. 5 (1921): 487–504; Paul Popenoe, "The Extent of Mental Disease and Defect in the American Population," *Journal of Juvenile Research* 13, no. 2 (1929): 97–103; Norman Fenton and Paul Popenoe, "Twenty-Five Years of Eugenic Sterilization," *Journal of Juvenile Research* 19, no. 4 (1935): 201–4; Norman Fenton to Lewis M. Terman, August 3, 1933, Folder 4, Box 14, Lewis M. Terman Papers, SC38, SC, SU; and Paul Popenoe and Norman Fenton, "Sterilization as a Social Measure," unpublished ms., Folder 6, Box 1, ESGP-RHBF, IA, CIT.

84. See Gilbert Gonzalez, *Chicano Education in the Era of Segregation* (Philadelphia: Balch Institute Press, 1990); Chapman, *Schools as Sorters;* Haas, *Conquests and Historical Identities,* 189–96; and Judith Rosenberg Raftery, *Land of Fair Promise: Politics and Reform in Los Angeles Schools, 1885–1941* (Stanford, CA: Stanford University Press, 1992).

85. Gonzalez, *Chicano Education,* 83; Irving G. Hendrick and Donald L. MacMillan, "Modifying the Public School Curriculum to Accommodate Mentally Retarded Students: Los Angeles in the 1920s," *Southern California Quarterly* 70, no. 4 (1988): 399–414. Raftery emphasizes that some elementary school teachers, especially those with many Mexican pupils, were highly dissatisfied with the intelligence tests recommended by the California Bureau of Juvenile Research and either translated tests into Spanish or administered alternative exams. See Raftery, *Land of Fair Promise,* chap. 5.

86. Popenoe, "Extent of Mental Disease," 99. In the mid-1910s, this district initiated testing with the Stanford-Binet; see Laura R. Bennett, "Department of Psychology in Los Angeles City Schools: A Study of the Mentally Different," *California State Journal of Medicine* 14, no. 3 (1916): 101–3.

87. See David G. Gutiérrez, "Introduction," in *Between Two Worlds: Mexican Immigrants in the United States,* ed. David G. Gutiérrez (Wilmington, DE: Scholarly Resources, 1996), xi–xxvii; and Mark Reisler, *By the Sweat of Their Brow: Mexican Immigrant Labor in the United States, 1900–1940* (Westport, CT: Greenwood Press, 1976).

88. See Douglas Monroy, *Rebirth: Mexican Los Angeles from the Great Migration to the Great Depression* (Berkeley: University of California Press, 1999), chap. 3.

89. See Charles Wollenberg, *All Deliberate Speed: Segregation and Exclusion in California Schools, 1855–1975* (Berkeley: University of California Press, 1976).

90. Ibid.; Haas, *Conquests and Historical Identities;* Robert M. Fogelson, *The Fragmented Metropolis: Los Angeles, 1850–1930* (1967; repr., Cambridge, MA: Harvard University Press, 1993).

91. Haas, *Conquests and Historical Identities,* 190; Raftery, *Land of Fair Promise,* 110–19.

92. Wollenberg, *All Deliberate Speed,* 112.

93. On vocational education in California, see Harvey A. Kantor, *Learning to Earn: School, Work, and Vocational Reform in California, 1880–1930* (Madison: University of Wisconsin Press, 1988).

94. Williams, "Early History," 195.

95. See, for example, Lewis M. Terman et al., *Intelligence Tests and School Reorganization* (Yonkers-on-Hudson, NY: World Book, 1923), in which Terman's students reported on tests that repeated these results in different parts of California. I have also arrived at this conclusion after close analysis of all volumes of the *Journal of Delinquency/Journal of Juvenile Research* from 1916 to 1938.

96. See Carl C. Brigham, *A Study of American Intelligence* (Princeton, NJ: Princeton University Press, 1923); Kimball Young, "Mental Differences in Certain Immigrant Groups," *University of Oregon Publications* 1, no. 11 (1922): 77–78.

97. Young, "Mental Differences."

98. Kate Gordon, "Report on Psychological Tests of Orphan Children," *Journal of Delinquency* 4, no. 1 (1919): 46–56, esp. 50.

99. Julia Mathews, "A Survey of 341 Delinquent Girls in California," *Journal of Delinquency* 8, nos. 3–4 (1923): 196–231.

100. William H. Sheldon, "The Intelligence of Mexican School Children," *School and Society* 19, no. 475 (1924): 139–42.

101. Thomas R. Garth, "The Intelligence of Mexican School Children," *School and Society* 27, no. 705 (1928): 791–94, quotation on 794.

102. Franklin C. Paschal and Louis R. Sullivan, *Racial Influences in the Mental and Physical Development of Mexican Children*, Comparative Psychology Monographs 3:14 (1925): 54.

103. Not surprisingly, 5,756 of these geniuses were from "Nordic areas," whereas Spain could claim only two. See Charles M. Goethe, *What Will Your Greatgrandchildren Face?* (Sacramento, CA: n.p., n.d.), 1.

104. See US House of Representatives, *Immigration from the Countries of the Western Hemisphere. Hearings before the Committee on Immigration and Naturalization, 71st Congress, March 14, 1930* (Washington, DC: Government Printing Office, 1930); and Reisler, *By the Sweat.*

105. Thomas R. Garth, "The Industrial Psychology of the Immigrant Mexican," *Industrial Psychology* 1 (1926): 183–87.

106. Don T. Delmet, "A Study of the Mental and Scholastic Abilities of Mexican Children in the Elementary School," *Journal of Juvenile Research* 14, no. 4 (1930): 279.

107. See Los Angeles Police Department, *Law Enforcement in Los Angeles* (1924; repr., New York: Arno Press, 1975).

108. Ibid., 134.

109. On the emergence of the critique of IQ testing as culturally biased and attention to the "language handicap" in the 1930s, see Carlos Kevin Blanton, "From Intellectual Deficiency to Cultural Deficiency: Mexican Americans, Testing, and Public School Policy in the American Southwest, 1920–1940," *Pacific Historical Review* 72, no. 1 (2003): 39–62.

110. See Gonzalez, *Chicano Education*, 139–40; Wollenberg, *All Deliberate Speed.*

111. See Harry H. Laughlin, *Eugenical Sterilization in the United States* (Chicago: Psychopathic Laboratory of the Municipal Court of Chicago, 1922), chap. 3.

112. Cited in ibid., 17. On Hatch, see Braslow, *Mental Ills,* 56.

113. The 1917 sterilization law provided for the sterilization, with or without consent, of any person lawfully committed to a state hospital for the insane or feebleminded, and of recidivists imprisoned at least twice for rape or other sexual crimes, or at least three times for other crimes. Consultation with state agencies and directors was always required for the latter but not necessarily for the former. The sterilization of minors, with the consent of a parent or guardian, was also included in this revision. The 1917 revision contained more administrative and legal qualifications and eugenic language than the original 1909 law. See "Sterilization in California Institutions," in California State Department of Institutions, *Sixth Biennial Report*, 146–47.

114. Laughlin, *Eugenical Sterilization,* 18–19.

115. Ibid., 19; also see Fred O. Butler, "Sterilization Procedure and Its Success in California Institutions," in California State Department of Institutions, *Third Biennial Report of the Department of Institutions of the State of California, Two Years Ending June 30, 1926* (Sacramento: California State Printing Office, 1926), 92–97. The "sexual perversion" aspect of the law was amended and clarified with a 1923 statute that applied to those "convicted of carnal abuse of a female under the age of ten years."

116. Braslow, *Mental Ills,* 56.

117. Reilly, *Surgical Solution,* chap. 4.

118. On *Buck v. Bell,* see Paul A. Lombardo, "Three Generations, No Imbeciles: New Light on *Buck v. Bell,*" *New York University Law Review* 60 (1985): 30–62.

119. Reilly, *Surgical Solution,* 97–101.

120. On Georgia's law, see Paul A. Lombardo, "From Better Babies to the Bunglers: Eugenics on Tobacco Road," in *A Century of Eugenics in America: From the Indiana Experiment to the Human Genome Era,* ed. Paul A. Lombardo (Bloomington: Indiana University Press, 2011), 45–67.

121. See John Sitton, *John Randolph Haynes;* Sitton, "John Randolph Haynes and the Left Wing of California Progressivism," in Deverell and Sitton, *California Progressivism Revisited,* 15–33; and Edward E. Harnagel, "Physician Entrepreneurs and Philanthropists in Early Los Angeles," *Southern California Quarterly* 71, nos. 2–3 (1989): 195–209.

122. John R. Haynes, "Human Society Deals with Both Eugenics and Euthenics," Box 193, Sterilization, Papers of John R. Haynes (hereafter JRHP), Collection 1241, SC, UCLA.

123. Ibid.

124. Sitton, *John Randolph Haynes,* 191.

125. On the Friday Morning Club, see Thelma Lee Hubbell and Gloria R. Lothrop, "The Friday Morning Club: A Los Angeles Legacy," *Southern California Quarterly* 50, no. 1 (1968): 59–90; and Mary Odem, "City Mothers and Delinquent Daughters: Female Juvenile Justice Reform in Early Twentieth-Century Los Angeles," in Deverell and Sitton, *California Progressivism Revisited,* 175–99. For insightful analysis of the Friday Morning Club and similar white women's voluntary organizations in Los Angeles, see Jennifer Koslow, *Cultivating Health: Los Angeles Women and Public Health Reform* (New Brunswick, NJ: Rutgers University Press, 2009).

126. J. Percy Wade to John R. Haynes, February 26, 1916, Box 193, JRHP, 1241, SC, UCLA.

127. G.A. Smith to John R. Haynes, February 21, 1916, Box 193, JRHP, 1241, SC, UCLA. Other examples include Anna M. Petersen to John R. Haynes, March 20, 1916, Box 193, JRHP, 1241, SC, UCLA, in which Petersen commented on her hope that Virginia would soon be able to successfully move a sterilization law through the legislature and applauded the operations being quietly performed at the feebleminded and epileptic colony; and Charles W. Allen to John R. Haynes, February 18, 1918, Box 193, JRHP, 1241, SC, UCLA,

in which Allen remarked that Pennsylvania had not yet authorized sterilization, although it should be a precondition for release: "All insane should be sterilized before discharge by dislocation of tubes or vasectomy, and imbeciles and degenerates by oophorectomy or castration."

128. John A. Reily to John R. Haynes, February 19, 1916, Box 193, JRHP, 1241, SC, UCLA. Reily was echoed by the medical superintendents at Mendocino and Sonoma, and by their counterparts at Whittier and Preston, who related their disappointment that the state's sterilization law did not apply to juvenile facilities. Stockton's female medical superintendent strongly endorsed sterilization in a related piece of correspondence. Margaret L. Smyth to John R. Haynes, June 3, 1916, Box 17, JRHP, 1241, SC, UCLA. One exception was Dr. Leonard Stocking, the medical superintendent at the Agnews State Hospital. Stocking was much more cautious, explaining to Haynes that he had "done very little of this work. . . . I do not think direct benefit to the patient is to be expected unless it may be in cases where the mental trouble follows and recurs with pregnancy or childbirth." Leonard Stocking to John R. Haynes, March 11, 1916, Box 193, JRHP, 1241, SC, UCLA. On Agnews, see Braslow, *Mental Ills*.

129. John R. Haynes, "Care of the Insane," in California State Board of Charities and Corrections, *Eighth Biennial Report of the State Board of Charities and Corrections of the State of California from July 1, 1916 to June 30, 1918* (Sacramento: California State Printing Office, 1918), 62.

130. See John R. Haynes, "The Sterilization of the Unfit," n.d., Box 193, JRHP, 1241, SC, UCLA. In the 1920s, Haynes wrote different versions of this article, which appears to have been published first in the *Pacific Coast Journal of Nursing* in 1922.

131. Ibid.

132. John R. Haynes, "A Moron Colony for California," n.d., Box 193, JRHP, 1241, SC, UCLA. On the "threat" of moron girls, see Kline, *Building a Better Race*.

133. California State Department of Institutions, *First Biennial Report of the Department of Institutions of the State of California for the Two Years Ending June 30, 1922* (Sacramento: California State Printing Office, 1923), 68, *Fourth Biennial Report*, 51, and *Fifth Biennial Report of the Department of Institutions of the State of California for the Two Years Ending June 30, 1930* (Sacramento: California State Printing Office, 1931), 80–90.

134. California State Commission in Lunacy, *Twelfth Biennial Report of the State Commission in Lunacy for the Two Years Ending June 30, 1920* (Sacramento: California State Printing Office, 1921), 59 (the figure offered here is 220, which appears low given the increase in sterilization at Sonoma once Fred Butler became superintendent in 1918; thus I have provided the more malleable figure of fewer than 1,000); Human Betterment Foundation, *Sterilization for Human Betterment: Some Outstanding Results of 6,000 Operations in California* (Pasadena, CA: Human Betterment Foundation), pamphlet in Box 193, JRHP, 1241, SC, UCLA.

135. See Sitton, *John Randolph Haynes*, 191. A loose document in Box 193, JRHP, 1241, SC, UCLA, suggests that Haynes managed to get five individuals—

two rabbis, another doctor, and a female reformer associated with the Friday Morning Club—to pledge contributions to this fund.

136. See "E. S. Gosney, Lawyer, Banker, Stock Raiser Established the Human Betterment Foundation," and associated documents, Folder 8, Box 3, ESGP-RHBF, IA, CIT.

137. See Sierra Madre–Lamanda Citrus Association to the Human Betterment Foundation, June 14, 1939, Folder 9, Box 3, ESGP-RHBF, IA, CIT.

138. Based on calculations in Ronald Tobey and Charles Wetherell, "The Citrus Industry and the Revolution of Corporate Capitalism in Southern California, 1887–1944," *California History* 74, no. 2 (1995): 6–19.

139. Harry H. Laughlin to E S. Gosney, December 5, 1924, Folder 2, Box 7, ESGP-RHBF, IA, CIT.

140. E. S. Gosney to Harry H. Laughlin, October 30, 1925, D-2-3, HHLP, SC, TSU.

141. Gosney sought out the advice of William F. Snow, director of the American Social Hygiene Association, and Robert L. Dickinson, a prominent gynecologist who supported sterilization and birth control. See Robert L. Dickinson to E. S. Gosney, February 5, 1926, Folder 2, Box 7; William F. Snow to E. S. Gosney, February 1, 1926, Folder 2, Box 7, ESGP-RHBF, IA, CIT. On Dickinson and sterilization, see Kline, *Building a Better Race*, 66–79.

142. See Paul Popenoe, "Origin of the Date Palm," *Journal of Heredity* 5, no. 11 (1914): 498–508.

143. "Suggestions Concerning a Tentative Program of Work for a Race Hygiene Foundation," enclosed with letter, Paul Popenoe to E. S. Gosney, January 10, 1926, Folder 2, Box 7, ESGP-RHBF, IA, CIT.

144. Ibid.

145. Laughlin congratulated Gosney on the choice of sterilization as the HBF's initial focus: "I am glad to learn that you are just now especially interested in the physiological and mental effects of sexual sterilization." Harry H. Laughlin to E. S. Gosney, February 13, 1926, D-2-3, HHLP, SC, TSU.

146. W. D. Wagner, Director of Institutions, to Medical Superintendents, February 26, 1926, Folder 2, Box 7, ESGP-RHBF, IA, CIT.

147. Paul Popenoe, "Memorandum for Mr. Gosney," October 12, 1927, Folder 2, Box 7, ESGP-RHBF, IA, CIT. For example, in 1926 Popenoe shared his views on eugenics and sterilization with the Napa Rotary Club, telling Gosney that the information he presented was "all new to them." Paul Popenoe to E. S. Gosney, July 28, 1926, Folder 2, Box 7, ESGP-RHBF, IA, CIT.

148. Paul Popenoe, "Memorandum for Mr. Gosney," October 12, 1927; Paul Popenoe to E. S. Gosney, August 31, 1926, Folder 2, Box 7, ESGP-RHBF, IA, CIT.

149. Paul Popenoe to E. S. Gosney, March 25, 1926, Folder 2, Box 7, ESGP-RHBF, IA, CIT.

150. Fred O. Butler, "Report of Medical Superintendent of the Sonoma State Home," in California State Department of Institutions, *First Biennial Report,* 80. After retirement, Butler continued to defend his views on eugenic sterilization. See interview of Fred O. Butler by Margot W. Smith, October 30, 1970,

Regional Oral History Project, BL, UCB. I thank Alex Wellerstein for bringing this interview to my attention.

151. Ezra S. Gosney and Paul Popenoe, *Sterilization for Human Betterment: A Summary of Results of 6,000 Operations in California, 1909–1929* (New York: Macmillan, 1929).

152. Ibid., ix.

153. Paul Popenoe, "Trends in Human Sterilization," *Eugenical News* 22, no. 3 (1937): 42–43.

154. Paul Popenoe and Norman Fenton, "Sterilization as a Social Measure," n.d., Folder 6, Box 1, ESGP-RHBF, IA, CIT. See Fenton and Popenoe, "Twenty-Five Years," for an abstract of this study. As with Popenoe's first study, the Department of Institutions offered "hearty cooperation." See "Annual Report of the Secretary of the Human Betterment Foundation for the Year Ending February 13th, 1934," Folder 13, Box 2, Lewis M. Terman Papers, SC38, SC, SU. A pamphlet version of this was also published, without Fenton listed as author: Paul Popenoe and E. S. Gosney, *Twenty-Eight Years of Sterilization in California* (Pasadena, CA: Human Betterment Foundation, 1938).

155. Stefan Kühl, *The Nazi Connection: Eugenics, American Racism, and German National Socialism* (Oxford: Oxford University Press, 1994), 42–48; Platt, *What's in a Name?*, 12–20. For a fascinating and detailed discussion of past and present issues related to German eugenics in Los Angeles, see Anthony Platt, *Bloodlines: Recovering Hitler's Nuremberg Laws, from Patton's Trophy to Public Memorial* (New York: Paradigm, 2005).

156. "Progress Report for 1930," *Transactions of the Commonwealth Club of California* 7, no. 14 (1931): 574.

157. "Minutes of August 26, 1930," Notes and Minutes, ES, CCC (pc) (Butler); "Minutes of May 27, 1930," ES, CCC (pc) (Smyth).

158. "Minutes of October 14, 1930," Notes and Minutes, ES, CCC (pc).

159. In a personal letter, Gosney, obviously concerned about potential legal ramifications, stated that he thought Stanley was too zealous about sterilization. In 1941, he replied to an HBF correspondent asking for information about the sterilization of criminals. He referred him to Dr. Leo Stanley, the medical superintendent at San Quentin, who had performed "some 600 or more sterilizations in that prison, by request of the patients. Dr. Stanley is our good friend and we do not wish to be quoted, but our opinion is that he is a little over-enthusiastic about the use of sterilization for prisoners. That is, we do not feel there is any ground for holding that 'criminality' is inherited." See Ezra S. Gosney to Mr. Elmo R. Smith, October 9, 1941, Folder 9, Box 6; Folder 7, Box 11ESGP-RHBF, IA, CIT. For more on Leo Stanley's sterilization of and hormonal experimentations on prisoners, see Ethan Blue, "The Strange Career of Leo Stanley: Remaking Manhood and Medicine at San Quentin State Penitentiary, 1913–1951," *Pacific Historical Review* 78:2 (2009): 210–41.

160. See Folder 5, Box 41; Folder 1, Box 42; Folder 9, Box 12; ESGP-RHBF, IA, CIT. These folders also include a substantial number of sterilization records from the Chicago Lying-In Hospital. There are a small number of voluntary vasectomy cases in Folder 1, Box 44, ESGP-RHBF, IA, CIT, from Los Angeles and other American cities.

4. "I LIKE TO KEEP MY BODY WHOLE"

1. Sterilization recommendation 114–1692. In compliance with HIPAA and patient confidentiality, only pseudonyms are used. The sterilization recommendations and data set are used in accordance with the California Committee for the Protection of Human Subjects (12–04–0166) and the University of Michigan Medical School Institutional Review Board (HUM00084931). These recommendations are categorized according to reel and document number as recorded in the digitized files.

2. I have chosen to use the term *patient* instead of *inmate* to describe individuals committed to state institutions. Although the term *inmate* is used in some of the historical records, and institutionalized individuals were committed indefinitely and often involuntarily, the term *patient* appears much more frequently in the sterilization documents; in addition, it captures the medicalized aspect of what can be understood as a form of incarceration.

3. Sterilization recommendation 114–0813.

4. Sterilization recommendations 120–0639 through 120–0641; Sterilization index card 361–2292.

5. Sterilization recommendation 125–1934.

6. Sterilization recommendation 121–0166.

7. Consent for sterilization 126–0167.

8. California Legislature, *Statutes of California, 1937* (Sacramento: California State Printing Office, 1937), 1005–6, 1154–55.

9. On institutional segregation as a eugenic strategy in Illinois, see Michael A. Rembis, *Defining Defiance: Sex, Science, and Delinquent Girls, 1890–1960* (Urbana-Champaign: University of Illinois Press, 2011). Erika Dyck offers compelling illustrative profiles of sterilizations in Alberta that followed similar patterns; see her *Facing Eugenics: Reproduction, Sterilization, and the Politics of Choice* (Toronto: University of Toronto Press, 2013). On the patriarchal aspects of sterilization in Sonoma, see Wendy Kline, *Building a Better Race: Gender, Sexuality, and Eugenics from the Turn of the Century to the Baby Boom* (Berkeley: University of California Press, 2001).

10. Johanna Schoen, *Choice and Coercion: Birth Control, Sterilization, and Abortion in Public Health and Welfare* (Chapel Hill: University of North Carolina Press, 2005).

11. For a longer discussion of diagnostic classification of psychiatric disorders during this period, see Elizabeth Lunbeck, *The Psychiatric Persuasion: Knowledge, Gender, and Power in Modern America* (Princeton, NJ: Princeton University Press, 1994), and Gerald Grob, *The Mad among Us: A History of the Care of America's Mentally Ill* (New York: Free Press, 1994).

12. Sterilization recommendation 114–0813.

13. A classic (and largely forgotten) study that explores commitments to and sterilizations in early twentieth-century California (with a focus on San Francisco Superior Court and Mendocino) is Richard W. Fox, *So Far Disordered in Mind: Insanity in California, 1870–1930* (Berkeley: University of California Press, 1978).

14. This figure is 1,471 higher than the 6,427 provided by the state in a retrospective report from 2003—suggesting a pronounced pattern of under-

counting that we will try to understand better as we analyze the data set. Not until the 1940s, when California claimed about 60 percent of all operations nationwide, did a few places, such as Delaware, North Carolina, and Virginia, begin to consistently overtake California in per capita or annual terms. See Birthright, Inc., *U.S. Maps Showing the States Having Sterilization Laws in 1910, 1920, 1930, 1940*, pamphlet, Publication 5 (Princeton, NJ: Birthright, Inc., n.d.), reprinted in California Legislature, Senate Select Committee on Genetics, Genetic Technologies, and Public Policy, *California's Compulsory Sterilization Policies, 1909–1979, July 16, 2003, Informational Hearing*, ed. Lisa M. Matocq (Sacramento: California Publications, 2003); Clarence J. Gamble, "Preventive Sterilization in 1948," *Journal of the American Medical Association* 141, no. 11 (1949): 773, and "Sterilization of the Mentally Deficient under State Laws," *American Journal of Mental Deficiency* 51, no. 2 (1946): 164–69.

15. To be true to the historical era of eugenic sterilization, I use the terms employed at the time. Today these kinds of facilities generally are referred to as developmental centers (feebleminded homes) and state hospitals (mental hospitals).

16. See Alex Wellerstein, "States of Eugenics: Institutions and Practices of Compulsory Sterilization in California," in *Reframing Rights: Bioconstitutionalism in the Genetic Age*, ed. Sheila Jasanoff (Cambridge, MA: MIT Press, 2011), 29–58.

17. See Joel T. Braslow, "In the Name of Therapeutics: The Practice of Sterilization in a California State Hospital," *Journal of the History of Medicine and Allied Sciences* 51, no. 1 (1996): 29–51; Wellerstein, "States of Eugenics."

18. California Legislature, *California's Compulsory Sterilization Policies*, table 4, "Resident Population of State Mental Hospitals, June 30, 1851–1945."

19. Joel Braslow, *Mental Ills and Bodily Cures: Psychiatric Treatment in the First Half of the Twentieth Century* (Berkeley: University of California Press, 1997), 21.

20. Ibid., 80.

21. See California State Department of Institutions, *Statistical Report of the Department of Institutions of the State of California, Year Ending June 30, 1940* (Sacramento: California Printing Office, 1940).

22. California Legislature, *California's Compulsory Sterilization Policies*, table 1, "Population, Normal Capacity, and Excess Population, All Institutions, June 30, 1950." During the 1940s, the Department of Mental Hygiene put a great deal of effort into planning for projected population increases in mental homes and hospitals, but before ground was broken on those facilities the state instead began to move toward deinstitutionalization and toward a model of developmental centers.

23. John A. Reily to John Randolph Haynes, February 19, 1916, Box 193, John Randolph Haynes Papers (hereafter JRHP), 1241, Special Collections (hereafter SC), UCLA.

24. California State Department of Institutions, *Third Biennial Report of the State Department of Institutions* (Sacramento: California State Printing Office, 1926), 83.

25. See Braslow, "In the Name of Therapeutics," and Alex Wellerstein, "States of Eugenics."

26. California State Department of Institutions, *Second Biennial Report of the Department of Institutions of the State of California, Two Years Ending June 30, 1924* (Sacramento: California State Printing Office, 1924), 101–2.

27. On Smyth, see Richard W. Rohrbacher, "Margaret Hamilton Smyth, M.D.: A Capable and Qualified 19th Century Woman," *Dogtown Territorial Quarterly* 49 (2002): 34–44.

28. Margaret H. Smyth, "Psychiatric History and Development in California," *American Journal of Psychiatry* 94 (1938): 1223–36; on Smyth's ardent support of sterilization, see Margaret H. Smyth to John Randolph Haynes, June 3, 1916, Box 17, JRHP, 1241, SC, UCLA.

29. Leonard Stocking to John Randolph Haynes, March 11, 1916, Box 193, JRHP, 1241, SC, UCLA.

30. See California Legislature, *California's Compulsory Sterilization Policies*, and Braslow, *Mental Ills, Bodily Cures*.

31. California State Department of Institutions, *Statistical Report . . . 1940*, 12.

32. For more on the sterilization of the feebleminded, see James W. Trent Jr., *Inventing the Feeble Mind: A History of Mental Retardation in the United States* (Berkeley: University of California Press, 1994); and Allison C. Carey, *On the Margins of Citizenship: Intellectual Disability and Civil Rights in 20th Century America* (Philadelphia: Temple University Press, 2009).

33. Kline, *Building a Better Race*, 52.

34. Paul Popenoe to Ezra S. Gosney, March 25, 1926, Box 7, Folder 2, Ezra S. Gosney Papers and Records of the Human Betterment Foundation, Institute Archives, California Institute of Technology.

35. Fred O. Butler, "Interview on Mental Health and Mental Retardation" (rough transcript), interview by Margot W. Smith, 1970, Regional Oral History Office, Bancroft Library, University of California, Berkeley; Fred O. Butler, "A Quarter of a Century's Experience in Sterilization of Mental Defectives in California," *American Journal of Mental Deficiency* 49, no. 4 (1945): 1–6, in California Legislature, *California's Compulsory Sterilization Policies*.

36. California Legislature, *California's Compulsory Sterilization Policies*, "Cumulative Sterilization Data, 1909–50."

37. Ibid.

38. These preliminary results were produced by combining data from the sterilization data set with 1940 US Census data from Pacific Colony. I am grateful to Nicole Novak for designing and performing this data analysis.

39. On gender and feeblemindedness, see Kline, *Building a Better Race*.

40. Natalie Lira and Alexandra Minna Stern, "Resisting Reproductive Injustice in California: Mexican Americans and Eugenic Sterilization, 1920–1950," *Aztlán* 39, no. 2 (2014): 9–34. For a thorough and compelling analysis of Pacific Colony, see Natalie Lira, "'Of Low Grade Mexican Parentage': Race, Gender, and Eugenic Sterilization in California, 1928–1950," PhD diss., University of Michigan, 2015.

41. Sterilization recommendation 123–0923.

42. Sterilization index card 361–3956.

43. See Lira and Stern, "Resisting Reproductive Injustice," and Lira, "'Of Low Grade Mexican Parentage.'"

44. Sterilization recommendations 120–1778 and 120–1779; Sterilization index card 361–1829.

45. Fred O. Butler to Mr. S, November 21, 1931, Inmate #13694, F3738:20, Inmate Records, Inmates Histories, Papers of the Preston School of Industry, California Youth Authority, California State Archives (hereafter CSA). Pseudonyms used per CSA confidentiality agreement.

46. Ibid.

47. J.C. Geiger to Fred O. Butler, November 24, 1931, Inmate #13694, F3738:20, Inmate Records, Inmates Histories, Papers of the Preston School of Industry, California Youth Authority, CSA.

48. For more on transfers from Preston, and the Whittier reformatory, to Sonoma and other institutions for sterilization, see Miroslava Chávez-García, *States of Delinquency: Race and Science in the Making of California's Juvenile Justice System* (Berkeley: University of California Press, 2012).

49. Sterilization recommendations 122–0272 through 122–0277.

50. Sterilization recommendations 124–0179 through 124–0180.

51. Sterilization index card 361–4114.

52. Cases involving allegations of medical malpractice, demands for damages, and petitions for the state to provide nontherapeutic surgical sterilizations for the indigent were heard in California's supreme and appellate courts between 1930 and 1979, but only the cases filed by Ruíz and García challenged the constitutionality of the sterilization law. I searched Lexis/Nexis Legal Academic Search for California Supreme Court and appellate court cases using the terms *sterilization, asexualization, salpingectomy, vasectomy, tubal ligation,* and *eugenics.* See *Jessin v. County of Shasta,* Civ. No. 12027, Court of Appeal of California, Third Appellate District, 274 Cal. App. 2d 737; 79 Cal. Rptr. 359; 1969 Cal. App. LEXIS 2107; 35 A.L.R.3d 1433, July 11, 1969; Kline, *Building A Better Race,* chap. 4.

53. "Girl Files Suit over Operation," *Los Angeles Times,* November 29, 1930, A8; "Arguments on Ruiz Girl's Suit Slated Today," *Los Angeles Times,* January 5, 1931, A3.

54. Sara Rosas Garcia v. State Department of Institutions of the State of California, 1939, Civ. No. 12533, CSA.

55. For more extensive analysis of the resistance of Mexican-origin families to sterilization, see Lira, "'Of Low Grade Mexican Parentage.'"

56. Sterilization recommendations 121–0763 and 121–0764.

57. Sterilization index card 361–4551.

58. On the importance of seemingly isolated pre-1960s acts of resistance in the health system, see Beatrix Hoffman, *Health Care for Some: Rights and Rationing in the United States since 1930* (Chicago: University of Chicago Press, 2012).

59. Sterilization recommendation 119–1345.

60. See Jennifer Terry, *An American Obsession: Science, Medicine, and Homosexuality in Modern Society* (Chicago: University of Chicago Press, 1999).

61. Sterilization recommendation 121–1333.

62. Sterilization recommendation 188–2153.

63. Sterilization recommendations 188–2153 and 188–2154.

64. Report of sterilization operations performed, Pacific Colony, November 1950, 188–0251.

65. G. T. to Governor Earl Warren, March 21, 1952, Earl Warren Papers—Administrative Files, Department of Mental Hygiene—Pacific Colony Hospital, 1950–53, CSA.

66. Frank F. Tallman to G. T., April 9, 1952, Earl Warren Papers—Administrative Files, Department of Mental Hygiene—Pacific Colony Hospital, 1950–53, CSA.

67. See the entry "Informed Consent," in James B. Tubbs, *Handbook of Bioethics Terms* (Washington, DC: Georgetown University Press, 2009); Tom L. Beauchamp and James F. Childress, *Principles of Biomedical Ethics,* 6th ed. (New York: Oxford University Press, 2009), chap. 4.

68. P. F. to Mrs. Vera Fowler Clayton, March 23, 1948, Earl Warren Papers—Administrative Files, Department of Mental Hygiene—Pacific Colony Hospital, 1945–1949, CSA.

69. J. W..C. to Governor Earl Warren, April 8, 1948, Earl Warren Papers—Administrative Files, Department of Mental Hygiene—Pacific Colony Hospital, 1945–1949, CSA.

70. P. H. to Mrs. Vera Fowler Clayton, March 23, 1948, Earl Warren Papers—Administrative Files, Department of Mental Hygiene—Pacific Colony Hospital, 1945–1949, CSA.

71. Sterilization recommendation 124–1617. Sterilization consent 124–1618.

72. Sterilization recommendation 119–2079. Sterilization consent 119–2080.

73. Sterilization memo 125–1936.

74. Sterilization letter 125–1890 and 125–1891.

75. Report of sterilizations performed at Patton State Hospital, 139–0609.

76. Sterilization memo 125–1936.

77. Sterilization letter 125–1938.

78. Sterilization letter 125–1933.

79. Sterilization letter 125–0278.

80. Sterilization letter 125–0277.

81. See Sarah Linsley Starks and Joel T. Braslow, "The Making of Contemporary American Psychiatry, Part 1: Patients, Treatments and Therapeutic Rationales Before and After World War II," *History of Psychology* 8, no. 2 (2005): 176–93.

82. George Tarjan to Frank F. Tallman, July 21, 1950, Earl Warren Papers—Administrative Files, Department of Mental Hygiene—Pacific Colony Hospital, 1950–1953, CSA.

83. California Citizens' Committee for Mental Hygiene, Inc., "Report on the Governor's Conference on Mental Health, Sacramento 3 and 4, 1949," Earl Warren Papers—Administrative Files, Department of Mental Hygiene Conference, March 3–4, 1949, CSA.

84. See Legislative History, Senate Bill 750, Microfilm 3:2(4); "Legislative Memorandum," April 4, 1953, Legislative History, Assembly Bill 2683, Micro-

film Reel 3:2 (10); Frank F. Tallman to Honorable Earl Warren, March 31, 1953, Legislative History, Assembly Bill 2683, Microfilm Reel 3:2(10), CSA.

85. For a discussion of Catholic opposition to sterilization, which solidified in the 1920s, see Christine Rosen, *Preaching Eugenics: Religious Leaders and the American Eugenics Movement* (New York: Oxford University Press, 2004).

86. On Earl Warren's gubernatorial administration in California, and his rise to Supreme Court justice, see Jim Newton, *Justice for All: Earl Warren and the Nation He Made* (New York: Riverhead Books, 2006).

87. "Background Paper" and "Sterilization Operations in California State Hospitals, April 26, 1909 through June 30, 1960," in California Legislature, *California's Compulsory Sterilization Policies*. Also see "History, Description, and Evaluation of the Department of Mental Hygiene" (1962), Nathan Sloate Papers, Department of Mental Hygiene Records (hereafter DMH), CSA.

88. "Sonoma State Hospital," Biennial Report, 1952–54, Sonoma State Hospital, Administrative Files, DMH, F3501, Loc D0419, Box 154, CSA.

89. See Starks and Braslow, "Making of Contemporary American Psychiatry, Part 1"; Joel T. Braslow and Sarah Linsley Starks, "The Making of Contemporary American Psychiatry, Part 2: Therapeutics and Gender before and after World War II," *History of Psychology* 8, no. 3 (2005): 271–88. These companion articles track shifts in institutional psychiatry across World War II using a rich set of sampled files from Stockton State Hospital. Also see Gerald N. Grob, "Origins of *DSM-I*: A Study in Appearance and Reality," *American Journal of Psychiatry* 148, no. 4 (1991): 421–31.

90. Sonoma State Hospital, interoffice memorandum, November 29, 1956, re: W & I Code Changes, Sonoma State Hospital, Administrative Files, DMH, F3501, Loc D0419, Box 153, CSA.

91. Pearl S. Buck, *The Child Who Never Grew* (1950; repr., Vineland, NJ: Woodbine House, 1992); Dale Evans Rogers, *Angel Unaware* (1953; repr., Westwood, NJ: Fleming H. Revell, 1953).

92. Eunice Kennedy Shriver, "Hope for Retarded Children." *Saturday Evening Post,* September 22, 1962, 71. An excellent study of Shriver's dedication to the cause of mental retardation is Edward Shorter, *The Kennedy Family and the Story of Mental Retardation* (Philadelphia: Temple University Press, 2000).

93. David J. Rothman and Sheila M. Rothman, *The Willowbrook Wars: Bringing the Mentally Disabled into the Community* (1984; repr., New Brunswick, NJ: AldineTransactions, 2005); Joel D. Howell and Rodney A. Hayward, "Writing Willowbrook, Reading Willowbrook: The Recounting of a Medical Experiment," in *Useful Bodies: Human in the Service of Medical Science in the Twentieth Century,* ed. Jordan Goodman, Anthony McElligott, and Lara Marks (Baltimore: Johns Hopkins, 2003), 190–213.

94. California Legislature, *Statutes of California, 1985–1986 Regular Session* (Sacramento: California State Printing Office, 1986), 3483.

5. CALIFORNIA'S EUGENIC LANDSCAPES

Epigraph: Joan Didion, "Girl of the Golden West," in *Vintage Didion* (New York: Vintage Books, 2004), 7–8.

1. See Gene E. Carte and Elaine H. Carte, *Police Reform in the United States: The Era of August Vollmer, 1905–1932* (Berkeley: University of California Press, 1975). Vollmer served on the advisory council of the American Eugenics Society from 1927 to 1935.

2. See Erwin G. Gudde, *California Place Names: The Origin and Etymology of Current Geographical Names* (Berkeley: University of California Press, 1960), 338; and William Bright, *1500 California Place Names: Their Origin and Meaning* (Berkeley: University of California Press, 1998).

3. See Federal Writers' Project of the Works Progress Administration for the State of California, *California: A Guide to the Golden State* (New York: Hastings House, 1939).

4. Richard E. Walpole, District Manager, East Bay Regional Park District (hereafter EBRPD), "Tenth Anniversary Report of the East Bay Regional Park District," and "Inter-office Communication," August 12, 1935, both in Folder: EBRPD, Carton 5, August Vollmer Papers (hereafter AVP), CB 403, Bancroft Library (hereafter BL), University of California at Berkeley (hereafter UCB). For those readers familiar with the EBRPD, the redesigned areas were Wildcat Canyon, Lake Chabot, and Lake Temescal.

5. "History of the Creation of the East Bay Regional Park District," Folder: EBRPD, Carton 5, AVP, C-B 403, BL, UCB. The seven cities were Berkeley, Alameda, Oakland, Piedmont, Emeryville, Albany, and San Leandro.

6. See Carte and Carte, *Police Reform*.

7. August Vollmer, *The Criminal* (Brooklyn, NY: Foundation Press, 1949), 411; see also his *The Police and Modern Society* (Berkeley: University of California Press, 1936).

8. August Vollmer to Thomas D. Eliot, October 30, 1929, Folder: Correspondence July–October 1929, Box 40, AVP, C-B 403, BL, UCB.

9. Vollmer, *Criminal*, 94, 97.

10. See Harold G. Schutt, "Advanced Police Methods in Berkeley," *National Municipal Review* 11, no. 3 (1922): 80–85; and Gerald Woods, *The Police in Los Angeles: Reform and Professionalization* (New York: Garland, 1993).

11. See Carte and Carte, *Police Reform*.

12. There are samples of these tests in Folder: Miscellaneous, Carton 6, AVP, C-B 403, BL, UCB. Vollmer did the same in Los Angeles in 1924, when he spent a year attempting to clean up and professionalize the Los Angeles Police Department. Working with the California Bureau of Juvenile Research, he gave the entire police force (1,712 men) the Army Alpha and Beta, Terman Group, and National Intelligence tests. See Grace M. Fernald and Ellen B. Sullivan, "Personnel Work with the Los Angeles Police Department," *Journal of Delinquency* 10, no. 1 (1926): 252–67. Additionally, while in Los Angeles, Vollmer sponsored a crime symposium (mentioned in chapter 3) at which hereditarian explanations of criminality and eugenic solutions for crime prevention, such as sterilization, predominated. For descriptions of the latter, see August Vollmer to Pat, May 5, 1924, Folder: Correspondence 1918–1928, Box 40, AVP, C-B 403, BL, UCB; and Los Angeles Police Department, *Law Enforcement in Los Angeles* (1924; repr., New York: Arno Press, 1975).

13. Vollmer, *Criminal*, 434.

14. Richard Walpole, "Report, District Manager, East Bay Regional Park District," 1934, Folder: EBRPD, Carton 5, AVP, C-B 403, BL, UCB.

15. Dominick Cavallo, *Muscles and Morals: Organized Playgrounds and Urban Reform, 1880–1920* (Philadelphia: University of Pennsylvania Press, 1981); American Academy of Political and Social Science, *Public Recreation Facilities* (Philadelphia: American Academy of Political and Social Science, 1910).

16. See Hal K. Rothman, *Saving the Planet: The American Response to the Environment in the Twentieth Century* (Chicago: Ivan R. Dee, 2000), 75; and Neil M. Maher, "A New Deal Body Politic: Landscape, Labor, and the Civilian Conservation Corps," *Environmental History* 7, no. 3 (2002): 435–61.

17. See Bryant Simon, "'New Men in Body and Soul': The Civilian Conservation Corps and the Transformation of Male Bodies and the Body Politic," in *Seeing Nature through Gender,* ed. Virginia J. Scharff (Lawrence: University of Kansas Press, 2003), 80–102.

18. US National Park Service, *A Study of the Park and Recreation Problem of the United States* (Washington, DC: Government Printing Office, 1941), 4. On engendering environmental history, see Scharff, *Seeing Nature through Gender.*

19. "Memorandum Regarding East Bay Park District," Folder: EBRPD, Carton 5, AVP, C-B 403, BL, UCB.

20. Ibid.

21. Barry Alan Mehler, "A History of the American Eugenics Society, 1921–1940" (PhD diss., University of Illinois at Urbana-Champaign, 1988), 435.

22. See constitutions and meeting agendas, Folder: Berkeley Inter-racial Committee, Carton 4, AVP, C-B 403, BL, UCB.

23. Carte and Carte, *Police Reform.*

24. For an excellent overview of this complex spectrum, see Robert Gottlieb, *Forcing the Spring: The Transformation of the American Environmental Movement* (Washington, DC: Island Press, 1993), chap. 1.

25. On the invisibility of labor, see Don Mitchell, *The Lie of the Land: Migrant Workers and the California Landscape* (Minneapolis: University of Minnesota Press, 1996).

26. One of the few historians to have linked environmentalism and eugenics is Gray Brechin. See "Conserving the Race: Natural Aristocracies, Eugenics, and the U.S. Conservation Movement," *Antipode* 28, no. 3 (1996): 229–45.

27. Gudde, *California Place Names,* 150.

28. A 1939 *Eugenical News* article suggested that recreation enabled young couples to socialize in a wholesome manner and encouraged the hereditarily "favored" to produce more children. In short, recreation was seen as fostering a child-centered and eugenic family life. See Weaver W. Pangburn, "Recreation and Eugenics," *Eugenical News* 24, no. 1 (1939): 53–57.

29. "Constituent Profile: Estate of C. M. Goethe," Save-the-Redwoods League, San Francisco (generously provided to me by the Save-the-Redwoods League).

30. Carolyn Merchant, *Reinventing Eden: The Fate of Nature in Western Culture* (New York: Routledge, 2004).

31. See Donald Worster, "Beyond the Agrarian Myth," in *Trails: Toward a New Western History,* ed. Patricia Nelson Limerick, Clyde A. Milner II, and Charles E. Rankin (Lawrence: University of Kansas Press, 1991), 7.

32. See Matthew Basso, Laura McCall, and Dee Garceau, eds., *Across the Great Divide: Cultures of Manhood in the American West* (New York: Routledge, 2001); and Richard Slotkin, *Gunfighter Nation: The Myth of the Frontier in Twentieth-Century America* (New York: HarperPerennial, 1993).

33. See Madison Grant, *The Conquest of a Continent; or, The Expansion of Races in America* (New York: Charles Scribner's Sons, 1933).

34. See Patricia Seed, *Ceremonies of Possession in Europe's Conquest of the New World, 1492–1640* (Cambridge: Cambridge University Press, 1995).

35. On place-naming, see George R. Stewart, *Names on the Land: A Historical Account of Place-Naming in the United States* (Boston: Houghton Mifflin, 1958); Rebecca Solnit, *Savage Dreams: A Journey into the Landscape Wars of the American West* (New York: Vintage, 1994); and Charles W. J. Withers, "Authorizing Landscape: 'Authority,' Naming, and the Ordnance Survey's Mapping of the Scottish Highlands in the Nineteenth Century," *Journal of Historical Geography* 26, no. 4 (2000): 532–54.

36. See William H. Goetzmann, *Exploration and Empire: The Explorer and the Scientist in the Winning of the American West* (New York: Alfred Knopf, 1966); and Dawn Hall, ed., *Drawing the Borderline: Artist-Explorers of the U.S.-Mexico Boundary Survey* (Albuquerque, NM: Albuquerque Museum, 1996).

37. See David Lowenthal, *The Past Is a Foreign Country* (New York: Cambridge University Press, 1985).

38. See Susan R. Schrepfer, *The Fight to Save the Redwoods: A History of Environmental Reform, 1917–1978* (Madison: University of Wisconsin Press, 1983).

39. Merriam wrote about ancient California in *The Living Past* (New York: Charles Scribner's Sons, 1930).

40. Henry Fairfield Osborn, "Preface to the New Edition," in *The Passing of the Great Race, or, The Racial Basis of European History*, by Madison Grant, 3rd ed. (New York: Charles Scribner's Sons, 1920), xi.

41. M. Grant, *Passing*, 12.

42. The first comprehensive biography of Madison Grant is Jonathan Peter Spiro, "Patrician Racist: The Evolution of Madison Grant" (PhD diss., University of California, Berkeley, 2000).

43. See Schrepfer, *Fight*; Spiro, "Patrician Racist."

44. Quoted in Schrepfer, *Fight*, 3; see her chap. 1 for an evocative description of the trio's pilgrimage.

45. Madison Grant, "Saving the Redwoods: An Account of the Movement during 1919 to Preserve the Redwoods of California," *Zoological Society Bulletin* 22, no. 5 (1919): 97. Merriam is quoted in Richard St. Barbe Baker, *The Redwoods* (London: Lindsay Drummond, 1943), 87.

46. Newton Bishop Drury, interview by Amelia Roberts Fry and Susan Schrepfer, 1972, part 1 of 4, p. 106 (transcript), Regional Oral History Project (hereafter ROHO), BL, UCB.

47. See Schrepfer, *Fight*, chap. 3.

48. Walt Whitman, "Song of the Redwood-Tree," in *Leaves of Grass* (London: G. P. Putnam's Sons, 1897), 165–69.

49. See Willie Yaryan, Denzil Verardo, and Jennie Verardo, *The Sempervirens Story: A Century of Preserving California's Ancient Redwood Forest, 1900–2000* (Los Altos, CA: Sempervirens Fund, 2000).

50. Ibid.; Schrepfer, *Fight.*

51. Yaryan et al., *Sempervirens Story,* 15–17.

52. John C. Merriam, *A Living Link in History,* pamphlet (Berkeley: Save-the-Redwoods League, [1934]), 4; John Muir, "Save the Redwoods," *Sierra Club Bulletin* 11, no. 1 (1920): 1–4.

53. Rodney Sydes Ellsworth, *The Giant Sequoia* (Oakland, CA: J.D. Berger, 1924), 107; for an astute analysis of redwoods and westward expansion, see Dana Frank, "Redwood Empires," in *Local Girl Makes History: Exploring Northern California's Kitsch Monuments* (San Francisco: City Lights Books, 2007), 1–37.

54. Madison Grant, "Saving the Redwoods," *National Geographic Magazine* 37, no. 6 (1920): 525.

55. William Cronon, "The Trouble with Wilderness; or, Getting Back to the Wrong Nature," in *Uncommon Ground: Rethinking the Human Place in Nature,* ed. William Cronon (New York: W.W. Norton, 1996), 69–90.

56. Another irony is that the automobile provided much of the access to the wilderness that advocates then sought to protect from intrusion. See Paul S. Sutter, *Driven Wild: How the Fight against Automobiles Launched the Modern Wilderness Movement* (Seattle: University of Washington Press, 2002).

57. See Solnit, *Savage Dreams.*

58. On the conflicted mission of army patrols in Yellowstone, see Karl Jacoby, *Crimes against Nature: Squatters, Poachers, Thieves, and the Hidden History of American Conservation* (Berkeley: University of California Press, 2001). Also see Solnit, *Savage Dreams,* and Cronon, "Trouble with Wilderness."

59. John Muir, *Our National Parks* (Cambridge, MA: Riverside Press, 1901), 76.

60. Joseph D. Grant, *Redwoods and Reminiscences* (San Francisco: Save-the-Redwoods League and the Menninger Foundation, 1973), 135.

61. See Gottlieb, *Forcing the Spring.*

62. See Thomas M. Shapiro, *Population Control Politics: Women, Sterilization, and Reproductive Choice* (Philadelphia: Temple University Press, 1985); Betsy Hartmann, *Reproductive Rights and Wrongs: The Global Politics of Population Control,* rev. ed. (Boston: South End Press, 1995); and Carole R. McCann, *Birth Control Politics in the United States, 1916–1945* (Ithaca, NY: Cornell University Press, 1994).

63. See Spiro, "Patrician Racist"; and File: Madison Grant Grove, Memorial Groves (hereafter MG), Save-the-Redwoods League Archives (hereafter SRLA), San Francisco (hereafter SF).

64. "Save-the-Redwoods League—Proposed Acquisition," and Save-the-Redwoods League to Mr. DeForest Grant, January 1948, File: Madison Grant Forest and Elk Refuge (hereafter MGFER), MG, SRLA, SF.

65. "To Dedicate Madison Grant Memorial Redwood Forest and Elk Refuge," 1948, MGFER, MG, SRLA, SF.

66. Save-the-Redwoods League, *Saving the Redwoods, 1948–49* (Berkeley: Save-the-Redwoods League, 1949), 6.

67. "Save-the-Redwoods League Dinner Commemorating the Establishment of the Madison Grant Forest and Elk Refuge in Prairie Creek Redwoods State Park, Humboldt County, California," July 29, 1948, MGFER, MG, SRLA, SF.

68. See, for example, language in Conservation Foundation, *In View of the Future, Annual Report of the Conservation Foundation* (New York: Conservation Foundation, 1949). Osborn and Madison Grant's brother DeForest were trustees of this foundation.

69. Gottleib, *Forcing the Spring,* 256; Paul Ehrlich, *The Population Bomb* (San Francisco: Sierra Club/Ballantine Books, 1968).

70. Gottleib, *Forcing the Spring,* 253–59; Elena Rebéca Gutiérrez, "The Racial Politics of Reproduction: The Social Construction of Mexican-Origin Women's Fertility" (PhD diss., University of Michigan, 1999); Mark Dowie, *Losing Ground: American Environmentalism at the Close of the Twentieth Century* (Cambridge, MA: MIT Press, 1995), 160–66.

71. See Linda Gordon, *Woman's Body, Woman's Right: Birth Control in America,* rev. ed. (New York: Penguin Books, 1990).

72. Gottleib, *Forcing the Spring,* 258.

73. See Dowie, *Losing Ground.*

74. See Gottleib, *Forcing the Spring;* and Eileen Maura McGurty, "From NIMBY to Civil Rights: The Origins of the Environmental Justice Movement," *Environmental History* 2, no. 3 (1997): 301–23.

75. Frank, "Imperialism," 12. Frank offers a brilliant analysis of this kind of time-making.

76. Theodore Roosevelt, transcription of remarks at Leland Stanford Jr. University, Palo Alto, CA, 68–70, pamphlets, Box 9, CA 284, the Save-the-Redwoods League Papers, BL, UCB.

77. M. Grant, "Saving the Redwoods," 519.

78. Joseph D. Grant, *Saving California's Redwoods* (Berkeley: Save-the-Redwoods League/University of California at Berkeley, 1922), 4.

79. David Starr Jordan, *The Days of Man: Being Memories of a Naturalist, Teacher, and Minor Prophet of Democracy* (Yonkers-on-Hudson, NY: World Book, 1922), 1:428.

80. Merriam, *Living Past,* 58.

81. See Frank, "Imperialism."

82. Ibid., 10–11.

83. See Mike Davis, *City of Quartz: Excavating the Future in Los Angeles* (New York: Vintage Books, 1992), 28.

84. Joseph P. Widney, *Race Life of the Aryan Peoples* (New York: Funk and Wagnalls, 1907), 2:15.

85. Joseph P. Widney, *The Three Americas: Their Racial Past and the Dominant Racial Factors of their Future* (Los Angeles: Pacific Publishing, 1935).

86. Joseph P. Widney, *The Greater City of Los Angeles: A Plan for the Development of Los Angeles City as a Great World Health Center* (Los Angeles: n.p., 1938).

87. See Peter Dreyer, *A Gardener Touched with Genius: The Life of Luther Burbank* (New York: Coward, McCann and Geoghegan, 1975).

88. Ibid.

89. See, for example, Edward J. Wickson, "Luther Burbank: The Man, His Methods, and His Achievements," which ran in four parts in *Sunset* 8, no. 2 (1901): 57–69; 8, no. 4 (1902): 145–56; 8, no. 6 (1902): 277–85; and 9, no. 2 (1902): 101–12.

90. Ray Lyman Wilbur, "Broadening Horizons: An Interview with Ray Lyman Wilbur," *Sunset* 62, no. 4 (1929): 17–19, 18.

91. Ibid., 18.

92. Dreyer, *Gardener Touched with Genius*, 215.

93. See Douglas Cazaux Sackman, "Inside the Skin of Nature: Science and the Quest for the Golden Orange," in *Science, Values, and the American West,* ed. Stephen Tchudi (Reno: Nevada Humanities Committee, 1997), 117–45.

94. Ibid.

95. Quoted in Kevin Starr, *Americans and the California Dream, 1850–1915* (New York: Oxford University Press, 1973), 429.

96. Luther Burbank, *An Architect of Nature* (London: Watts, 1939), 17, 20.

97. He explained his Lamarckian position, of environment as "the architect of heredity," as follows: "All characters which are transmitted have been acquired, not necessarily at once in a dynamic or visible form, but as an increasingly latent force ready to appear as a tangible character when by long-continued natural or artificial repetition any specific tendency has become inherent, inbred, or 'fixed,' as we call it." Luther Burbank, *The Training of the Human Plant* (New York: Century, 1922), 82.

98. Ibid., 5.

99. Ibid., 9–10.

100. Jordan, *Days of Man*, 1:226.

101. David Starr Jordan, *California and the Californians* (San Francisco: Whitaker-Ray, 1903), 13.

102. David Starr Jordan, "Eugenics and War," in *Official Proceedings of the Second National Conference on Race Betterment* (Battle Creek, MI: Race Betterment Foundation, 1915), 22.

103. Jordan, *Days of Man*, 1:434.

104. "Two University Presidents Speak for the City," *Sunset* 20, no. 6 (1908): 546.

105. Starr, *Americans*, 312.

106. Jordan, *Days of Man*, 1:369. On Jordan and the founding of Stanford, see Starr, *Americans*, chap. 10.

107. David Starr Jordan, ed., *Footnotes to Evolution: A Series of Popular Addresses on the Evolution of Life* (New York: D. Appleton, 1907).

108. Ibid., 289.

109. Ibid., 309.

110. Quoted in Starr, *Americans*, 309.

111. David Starr Jordan to Charles B. Davenport, June 1, 1925, Charles B. Davenport Papers, B:D27, American Philosophical Society.

112. "Conservationist Goethe Is Dead," *San Francisco Chronicle*, July 11, 1966, in File: Mary Glide Goethe Memorial Grove (hereafter MGGMG), MG, SRLA, SF.

113. Ibid.

114. "Dr. C.M. Goethe, 91, Philanthropist, Dies," *Sacramento Bee*, July 11, 1966, Folder 1, Box 85D, Papers of Charles Matthias Goethe (hereafter CMGP), University Archives (hereafter UA), California State University at Sacramento (hereafter CSUS). These papers have been reorganized recently, and the new corresponding box and folder numbers for the materials cited in this chapter can be located using the finding aid available through the Online Archive of California.

115. Ibid.

116. Ibid.

117. See "Conservationist Goethe Is Dead."

118. Charles M. Goethe, *Seeking to Serve* (Sacramento, CA: Keystone Press, 1949), 28.

119. Ibid.

120. Ibid., 184.

121. Ibid., 96.

122. Andrew Schauer, "Charles Matthias Goethe, 1875–1966," Foundation of the California State University Sacramento, 1976, 85A:1, CMGP, UA, CSUS.

123. Ibid., 7.

124. Ibid., 18.

125. Ibid.

126. [Rodger Bishton], *In Commemoration of the C.M. Goethe National Recognition Day on His Ninetieth Birthday, March 28, 1965*, pamphlet, CMGP, UA, CSUS.

127. Quoted in Schauer, "Charles Matthias Goethe," 35; and Charles M. Goethe, Diary, October 16, 1903, 85F:7, CMGP, UA, CSUS.

128. See untitled document that seeks to answer the question "How Much Was Goethe Actually Worth and How Did He Accrue His Extensive Estate?" 85F3:45, CMGP, UA, CSUS. For the most part, these were cheaper lots on the city's outskirts and, in the 1930s, included the Oak Park, Fruitridge, Stockton, Del Paso Heights, and Elmhurst subdivisions.

129. Ibid., 9.

130. Ibid., 12. For a thorough accounting of Goethe's estate and property, including his library, see Tony [Anthony] Platt, *What's in a Name? Charles M. Goethe, American Eugenics, and Sacramento State University* (Sacramento, CA: T. Platt, 2004).

131. Lewis M. Terman to California Historical Society, August 8, 1953; California Historical Society to Lewis M. Terman, August 17, 1953; Folder 12, Box 14, Lewis M. Terman Papers, SU 38, Special Collections (hereafter SC), Stanford University (hereafter SU).

132. See Carl Russell, "A 40th Anniversary," *Yosemite Nature Notes* 39, no. 7 (1960): 153–55.

133. James C. Mullaney to Dr. Thomas Gunn, February 2, 1967; Invoice, Sacramento State College Foundation, February 28, 1967, 85B:22, CMGP, UA, CSUS; Platt, *What's in a Name?*, 41.

134. Discussions about naming the CSUS science building after Goethe began in 1963. See Rodger Bishton to Charles M. Goethe, October 11 1963; Charles M. Goethe to Rodger Bishton, October 14, 1963; 85F3:9, CMGP, UA, CSUS.

135. "Proclamation Issued by the Mayor, City of Sacramento, Dr. Charles M. Goethe Day, March 28, 1964," 85A:2, CMGP, UA, CSUS.

136. See "Charles M. Goethe Grove," MG, SRLA, SF. The League matched $100,000 (withdrawn from Goethe's probate estate) to pay for this forty-acre grove.

137. C. M. Goethe, *What's in a Name?* (Sacramento, CA: Keystone Press, 1949), xv.

138. Ibid., xvii.

139. Ibid.

140. See Myrtle Shaw Lord, *A Sacramento Saga: Fifty Years of Achievement—Chamber of Commerce Leadership* (Sacramento, CA: Sacramento Chamber of Commerce, 1946).

141. Joanne E. Ornellas, "An Historical Study of the Playground Movement in the City of Sacramento" (MS thesis, California State University, Sacramento, 1977); "C.M. Goethe Back from Abroad, Studied Playgrounds in Many Lands," *Sacramento Union*, May 17, 1912, scrapbook SSCF A, Box 36 in the reorganized files, CMGP, UA, CSUS. The story is more complicated. There were actually two parallel groups working to establish playgrounds in Sacramento in the early 1910s, and, technically, the Goethes were second, but their playground was staffed with a supervisor, whom they had personally interviewed for the job.

142. See Charles M. Goethe, "Early Boy Scout Memories," n.d., 85D:4, CMGP, UA, CSUS.

143. Ornellas, "Historical Study," 67. Also see correspondence with David Starr Jordan regarding nature study. Charles M. Goethe to David Starr Jordan, July 10, 1917, 95/847; form letter, January 1, 1948, David Starr Jordan Papers, SC, SU.

144. Goethe, *Seeking to Serve*, 106.

145. Harold C. Bryant and Newton B. Drury, "Development of the Naturalist Program in the National Park Service," interview by Amelia B. Fry, 1964, p. 3 (transcript), ROHO, BL, UCB.

146. Carl Russell, "Revealing Parks to the People," *Sierra Club Bulletin* (1960): 4–6, C. M. Goethe Memorial Grove (hereafter CMGMG), MG, SRLA, SF; C.M. Goethe, "Nature Study in National Parks Interpretive Movement," *Yosemite Nature Notes* 39, no. 7 (1960): 156–58.

147. Goethe, "Nature Study."

148. Quoted in John Ise, *Our National Park Policy: A Critical History* (Baltimore: Resources for the Future/Johns Hopkins University Press, 1961), 194. There is disagreement among environmental historians about the nuances of the meanings of *preservation* and *conservation*. I follow the definitions offered by Gottlieb in *Forcing the Spring* and believe that my reading of this distinction works fairly well for the environmental groups and initiatives under consideration in early to midcentury California.

149. There are several renditions of this story. In one Mather received a note from Bryant and traveled across the lake in a boat to hear the lecture; in another, this encounter resulted in the invitation of the Goethes to Mather's Christmas party, where Charles pledged that he would fund the work of Bryant and Miller the following summer in Yosemite. See Goethe, "Nature Study." Also see Loye H. Miller, "The Nature Guide Movement in National Parks," *Yosemite Nature Notes* 39, no. 7 (1960): 159–60; and Harold C. Bryant, "The Beginning of Yosemite's Educational Program," *Yosemite Nature Notes* 39, no. 7 (1960): 161–65.

150. Bryant and Drury, "Development"; Don Carlos Miller, "Founder of the World's Largest Summer School," *American Forests*, September 1961, 85D:1 CMGP, UA, CSUS. Also see Ise, *National Park Policy*, 199–202.

151. D. Miller, "Founder"; see *Yosemite Nature Notes* 2, no. 1 (June 1923).

152. "A Personal Invitation," *Yosemite Nature Notes* 4, no. 1 (1925): inside front cover.

153. See Harold C. Bryant and Wallace W. Atwood Jr., *Research and Education in the National Parks* (Washington, DC: Government Printing Office, 1932).

154. See pamphlets and clippings in scrapbook SSCF-C, including Immigration Study Commission, "Your Grandchildren's America Will Be What Your Generation Makes It," and "Mexican Immigration Opposed by C. M. Goethe," *Sacramento Bee*, November 26, 1927, CMGP, UA, CSUS.

155. See Charles M. Goethe, "Racial Extinction Threatened," *Arroyo Grande* (CA) *Herald Recorder*, November 10, 1927, SSCF-C, CMGP, UA, CSUS.

156. C. M. Goethe, letter to the editor, *Santa Cruz Sentinel*, October 4, 1927, SSCF-C, CMGP, UA, CSUS.

157. Charles M. Goethe, "Field Studies on the Eugenical Aspects of Mexican Immigration," *Eugenical News* 12, no. 8 (1927): 109.

158. Charles M. Goethe to S. W. Ward, February 26, 1926, C-4-1, Harry H. Laughlin Papers, Special Collections, Truman State University.

159. I have reconstructed these correspondence networks almost entirely by reviewing the papers of the eugenicists who received numerous letters from Goethe. The Goethe collection, housed at CSUS, contains almost no letters before the 1950s. Although the story is uncorroborated, it appears that before Goethe's papers were officially donated to the University Archives they were "sanitized," perhaps by Rodger Bishton, a longtime colleague who probably wanted to protect his mentor and friend from any associations with bigotry and Nazism. In addition, in 1970, when there was growing pressure to figure out how to handle his estate, CSUS hastily arranged for the auction of Goethe's voluminous personal library (more than two thousand books, one hundred periodicals, and ephemera). It was purposely auctioned off to a wholesale dealer in Los Angeles so that it would be difficult to trace back to Sacramento. According to the gallery partner who oversaw the auction, the collection was full of disturbing racist material that seemed to him important for historical research, but "the university wanted it gone." See Platt, *What's in a Name?*, 61. Platt carried out painstaking detective work to determine why most of the Goethe col-

lection disappeared and, in addition, has sought to encourage discussion about how CSUS, a multicultural campus community, can productively reckon with Goethe's legacy.

160. "Eugenics Research Association," *Eugenical News* 20, no. 4 (1935): 59; "Eugenics Research Association," *Eugenical News* 21, no. 4 (1936): 78.

161. Charles M. Goethe, "Patriotism and Racial Standards," *Eugenical News* 21, no. 4 (1936): 66.

162. Charles M. Goethe, "Extinction of the Inca Highcastes," *Eugenical News* 22, no. 4 (1937): 57.

163. See Goethe, *Seeking to Serve*.

164. "Eugenics Society of Northern California," *Eugenical News* 23, no. 4 (1938): 76. Pitts drafted a eugenic education plan in the late 1930s, which he envisioned being launched county by county across the nation by dedicated committees who used schools, civic groups, and newspapers to disseminate their message. For his part, Pitts spread the word through local radio broadcasts, such as "The Need of at Least Four Children in the High-Powered Stocks," and "The Cost to Taxpayers of the Increased Multiplication of Social Inadequates." See Eugene H. Pitts, "Educating the Public to Eugenics," *Eugenical News* 23, no. 1 (1938): 1–3, and "Radio Lectures on Eugenics by Dr. E.H. Pitts," *Eugenical News* 23, no. 1 (1938): 3.

165. A handful of these pamphlets are contained in the Goethe Papers at CSUS. However, the most complete collection was bound at the University of Minnesota and includes three volumes of eighty-nine pamphlets. They are not dated, but my best inference is that they ran from the mid-1930s to the late 1950s. For a longer explanation of the egret, see Charles M. Goethe, *The Elfin Forest* (Sacramento, CA: Keystone Press, 1953), 70. For Goethe, the plight of the egret symbolized the dangers of "race suicide": "In pioneer days, when egrets were numerous, human families numbered 8, 10, even 14 children."

166. Schauer, "Charles Matthias Goethe," 125; also see Platt, *What's in a Name?*

167. See Charles Matthias Goethe, interview by Giles T. Brown, April 4, 1966, ROHO, BL, UCB. Goethe claimed to have sent out about seventeen thousand publications over the course of his life. If these were ever returned or rejected, Goethe became very upset. In fact, in the 1950s, Stanford University inadvertently lost out on a potentially sizable bequest when its librarian sent Goethe a letter stating, "These publications do not receive the use that would justify our continuing to impose on your generosity. Will you therefore please remove our name from your mailing list." Goethe was offended and "surprised at this letter. The constant stream of correspondence thru my desk shows that most of the universities and colleges are making very heavy use of it. . . . We are glad not to send material where it is not wanted." Terman, who had been receiving donations from Goethe for his "gifted children" study, was clearly perturbed at this forfeited opportunity. See F.S. Randall to Charles M. Goethe, March 8, 1951; Charles M. to F.S. Randall, March 12, 1951, Folder 12, Box 14, Lewis M. Terman Papers, SC 38, SC, SU.

168. His books, all apparently self-published through Sacramento's Keystone Press, included *Sierran Cabin . . . from Skyscraper: A Tale of the Sierran*

Piedmont (1943), *War Profits and Better Babies* (1946), *Geogardening* (1948), *What's in A Name?* (1949), *Seeking to Serve* (1949), *The Elfin Forest* (1953), and *Garden Philosopher* (1955).

169. See Charles M. Goethe, *War Profits and Better Babies* (Sacramento, CA: Keystone Press, 1946).

170. Quoted in William H. Schneider, *Quality and Quantity: The Quest for Biological Regeneration in Twentieth-Century France* (New York: Cambridge University Press, 1990), 124.

171. Charles M. Goethe, *Geogardening* (Sacramento, CA: Keystone Press, 1948), 9.

172. Strom Thurmond to Charles M. Goethe, March 11, 1957, 85F3:12, CMGP, UA, CSUS.

173. Charles M. Goethe to the Save-the-Redwoods League, April 12, 1948, MGGMG, MG, SRLA, SF. In this letter Goethe explained his long-term intentions: to remit the unpaid balance on his wife's grove, contribute $5,000 toward a "Bible Toter Jedediah Smith Memorial Grove," fund a hospice in the redwoods for hikers, and support a Newton and Aubrey Drury Grove.

174. Correspondence indicates that he began to support the Save-the-Redwoods League financially as early as 1922, although his first official donation of $25,000 wasn't recorded until 1948. Each year thereafter he made sizable contributions to the League and after his death the League continued to receive annual payments from the Goethe trust ranging from $1,500 to $616,000. For his earliest contributions, see "Membership Record, Sep 5, 1941," which lists a February 2, 1922, donation of two dollars, MGGMG, MG, SRLA, SF; "Constituent Profile," SRLA, SF; and Save-the-Redwoods League, *Saving the Redwoods,* 10.

175. Charles M. Goethe to Aubrey Drury, January 18, 1947, MGGMG, MGA, SRLA, SF. Goethe asked that the inscription on the plaque read: "This grove in memory of my wife Mary Glide Goethe who loved these sequoias." See also John B. Dewitt to William Allison, June 15, 1976, MGGMG, MG, SRLA, SF.

176. "Terms of Establishment of the Mary Glide Goethe Memorial Redwood Grove" (approved April 30, 1948), and financial statement, "Mary Glide Goethe Memorial Redwood Grove," MGGMG, MG, SRLA, SF.

177. Charles M. Goethe, "When Help Came from the Mountains," *Yosemite Nature Notes* 29, no. 1 (1950): 3; Gudde, *California Place Names,* 298. See Bright, *1500 California Place Names,* 144.

178. Frederick C. Gale, "Jedediah Smith Meets Indians and Vice Versa," *Pacific Historian,* 1966, in File: Jedediah Smith Memorial Grove (JSMG), MG, SRLA, SF.

179. Aubrey Drury to California State Park Commission, July 23, 1949, JSMG, MG, SRLA, SF.

180. Ibid.; Charles M. Goethe to Aubrey Drury, April 12, 1948, JSMG, MR, SRLA, SF.

181. Charles M. Goethe to Aubrey Drury, August 23, 1949, and photograph of plaque, JSMG, MG, SRLA, SF.

182. Aubrey Drury to Charles M. Goethe, March 20, 1958, JSMG, MG, SRLA, SF.

183. On plaques, memorials, and historical memory, see Lowenthal, *Past.*

184. Save-the-Redwoods League, *Saving the Redwoods;* File: Luther Burbank Memorial Grove and File: MG, SRLA, SF.

185. "C.M. Goethe Arboretum Society," June 11, 1960, 85A:2, CMGP, UA, CSUS.

186. "By-Laws of the C.M. Goethe Arboretum Society," August 17, 1960, 85A:2, CMGP, UA, CSUS.

187. Guy A. West to A.L. Delisle, March 18, 1960, 85A:2, CMGP, UA, CSUS. Goethe and Bishton corresponded regularly in the 1960s, and sometimes, in letters marked "confidential," discussed their shared belief in eugenics: "Eugenics seems to me to be such a logical and rational control for man to use if he is sincerely interested in guiding and directing the evolutionary change of man and society." Rodger Bishton to Charles M. Goethe, December 17, 1963, 85F3:9, CMGP, UA, CSUS.

188. *Sacramento Bee,* March 23, 1961, 85A; Charles M. Goethe to Guy A. West, February 26, 1959, 85A:2; A.L. Delisle to Guy A. West, March 16, 1960: Guy A. West to A.L. Delisle, March 18, 1960, Box 85A:4A, CMGP, UA, CSUS.

189. "SSC Plaque, Speakers Honor C.M. Goethe," *Sacramento Bee,* March 26, 1961, 85A:2, CMGP, UA, CSUS.

190. May Second Committee, "Sacramento State's Own Doctor Strangelove: New Multimillion Dollar Science Building at S.S.C. to Be Named after C.M. Goethe, Prominent Racist and Eugenist," ca. 1965, 85D:9, CMGP, UA, CSUS.

191. Despite the idealism behind the arboretum when it was created, by the 1970s it had fallen into disarray, was littered, and in a "deplorable" state; it had been vandalized, benches were destroyed, and the redwood marker was damaged. See A.L. Delisle to Mrs. Florence Marsh and Mr. Glen Carlson, October 10, 1971, 85A:2, CMGP, UA, CSUS. Today it suffers not so much from abuse as from neglect; the arboretum, with its wilting markers for native plant species and stolid redwood marker still intact, sits on the other side of the CSUS parking lot and, as far as one can tell, is completely ignored by the students.

192. "Julia Morgan House," 85D:9, CMGP, UA, CSUS.

193. Goethe's will was dispersed in six allotments that totaled more than twenty-four million dollars. See "Estate of Charles Matthias Goethe," CMGMG, MGA, SRLA, SF; Schauer, "Charles Matthias Goethe"; and Platt, *What's in a Name?*

194. "Estate of Charles Matthias Goethe," CMGMG, MGA, SRLA, SF; John B. Dewitt to J. Frank Frain, August 26, 1976, CMGMG, MG, SRLA, SF.

195. "Estate of Charles Matthias Goethe," CMGMG, MG, SRLA, SF.

196. See Platt, *What's in a Name?*; "Glide Goethe Memorial Fund, Balance, November 30, 1976,—by Sub-account" and "Synopsis Re: Goethe Will," 1970, 85A:16, CMGP, UA, CSUS.

197. "Glide Goethe Memorial Fund, Balance, November 30, 1976,—by Sub-Account" and "Synopsis Re: Goethe Will," 1970, 85A:16, CMGP, UA, CSUS. See Platt, *What's in a Name?*, for a discussion of CSUS's problematic handling of the Goethe estate.

198. "Dr. C.M. Goethe, 91, Philanthropist, Dies," A4, 85D: 1; [Bishton], *In Commemoration,* 85.

199. [Bishton], *In Commemoration,* 85.

200. Schauer, "Charles Matthias Goethe," 146.

201. See Maurice A. Bigelow to Paul Popenoe, October 10, 1949, Box 16, Paul Bowman Popenoe Papers, American Heritage Center, University of Wyoming.

202. See *Racing Camels . . . Japan's Longtailed Cocks . . . Galton's Gifted Families . . . California's Incest Prisoner . . .* (eugenics pamphlet, n.d., probably early to mid-1960s), 4.

203. Bryant and Drury, "Development," p. 8 (transcript).

204. Goethe, *Seeking to Serve,* 163.

6. CENTERING EUGENICS ON THE FAMILY

1. Autobiographical Statement by Mrs. C, Box 148, Papers of Paul Bowman Popenoe (hereafter PBPP), Accession no. 4681, American Heritage Center (hereafter AHC), University of Wyoming (hereafter UW). I have withheld names for reasons of confidentiality. Since I conducted my research at the American Heritage Center, the Popenoe Papers have been recatalogued. Working with the new finding aid, I have been able to deduce the location of some of my sources; when that was not possible with accuracy, I have omitted unverifiable information, such as the box or folder title or number. Between my reconstructed citations and the new finding aid, which is organized chronologically and thematically, researchers should be able to locate all of my references. For example, this case history is now most likely in Box 148 of Series V (AIFR Case Histories).

2. Ibid.

3. The initial Johnson Temperament Analysis (JTA) had 182 questions; the Taylor-Johnson Temperament Analysis Test (T-JTA) has 180. These categories are from first version of the test; they have changed in subtle but important ways since 1941.

4. Intake Form on Mr. and Mrs. C, April 18, 1945, Box 148, PBPP, AHC, UW.

5. Ibid.

6. On psychology in the Cold War era and the cult of expertise, see Ellen Herman, *The Romance of American Psychology: Political Culture in the Age of Experts* (Berkeley: University of California Press, 1995).

7. Frederick Osborn, "Eugenics and Modern Life: Retrospect and Prospect," *Eugenical News* 31, no. 3 (1946): 33.

8. See Elof Axel Carlson, *The Unfit: A History of a Bad Idea* (Cold Spring Harbor, NY: Cold Spring Harbor Laboratory Press, 2001); and Diane B. Paul, *Controlling Human Heredity: 1865 to the Present* (Atlantic Highlands, NJ: Humanities Press, 1995).

9. For an excellent analysis of population control as the antidote to underdevelopment, see Laura Briggs, *Reproducing Empire: Race, Sex, Science, and U.S. Imperialism in Puerto Rico* (Berkeley: University of California Press, 2002), chap. 4.

10. Guy Irving Burch and Elmer Pendell, *Human Breeding and Survival: Population Roads to Peace or War* (New York: Penguin, 1945).

11. See Briggs, *Reproducing Empire;* and Johanna Schoen, *Choice and Coercion: Birth Control, Sterilization, and Abortion in Public Health and Welfare* (Chapel Hill: University of North Carolina Press, 2005), chap. 4.

12. See William B. Provine, "Geneticists and Race," *American Zoologist* 26 (1986): 857–87; and L.C. Dunn and Th. Dobzhansky, *Heredity, Race, and Society* (New York: Mentor Books, 1946). On the transition from race to population, see Donna Haraway, *Modest_Witness@Second_Millennium.FemaleMan©_Meets_OncoMouse™: Feminism and Technoscience* (New York: Routledge, 1997).

13. See Linda Gordon, *Woman's Body, Woman's Right: Birth Control in America,* rev. ed. (New York: Penguin Books, 1990), chap. 13; and Thomas M. Shapiro, *Population Control Politics: Women, Sterilization, and Reproductive Choice* (Philadelphia: Temple University Press, 1985).

14. On the shift from pyramid to continuum, see Hamilton Cravens, *The Triumph of Evolution: The Heredity-Environment Controversy, 1900–1941* (Baltimore: Johns Hopkins University Press, 1988). On biotypology and constitutional medicine, see Sarah W. Tracy, "An Evolving Science of Man: The Transformation and Demise of American Constitutional Medicine, 1920–1950," in *Greater Than the Parts: Holism in Biomedicine, 1920–1950,* ed. Christopher Lawrence and George Weisz (New York: Oxford University Press, 1998), 161–88, and "George Draper and American Constitutional Medicine, 1916–1946: Reinventing the Sick Man," *Bulletin of the History of Medicine* 66, no. 1 (1992): 53–89; and Heather Munro Prescott, "I Was a Teenage Dwarf: The Social Construction of 'Normal' Adolescent Growth and Development in the United States," in *Formative Years: Children's Health in the United States, 1880–2000,* ed. Alexandra Minna Stern and Howard Markel (Ann Arbor: University of Michigan Press, 2002), 153–82. On biotypology in Germany, see Michael Hau, *The Cult of Health and Beauty in Germany: A Social History, 1890–1930* (Chicago: University of Chicago Press, 2003). On biotypology in Latin America, see Nancy Leys Stepan, *"The Hour of Eugenics": Race, Gender, and Nation in Latin America* (Ithaca, NY: Cornell University Press, 1991); and Alexandra Minna Stern, "From Mestizophilia to Biotypology: Racialization and Science in Mexico, 1920–1960," in *Race and Nation in Modern Latin America,* ed. Nancy Applebaum, Anne S. MacPherson, and Karin Alejandra Rosemblatt (Chapel Hill: University of North Carolina Press, 2003), 187–210.

15. See David Theo Goldberg, *Racial Subjects: Writing on Race in America* (New York: Routledge, 1997); Michael Omi and Howard Winant, *Racial Formation in the United States: From the 1960s to the 1990s,* 2nd ed. (New York: Routledge, 1994); and Briggs, *Reproducing Empire.*

16. See Daniel J. Kevles, *In the Name of Eugenics: Genetics and the Uses of Human Heredity,* rev. ed. (Cambridge, MA: Harvard University Press, 1995); and Wendy Kline, *Building a Better Race: Gender, Sexuality, and Eugenics from the Turn of the Century to the Baby Boom* (Berkeley: University of California Press, 2001).

17. See Schoen, *Choice and Coercion.*

18. Molly Ladd-Taylor has persuasively challenged the usefulness of the "reform" descriptor and has perceptively analyzed Popenoe and the American

Institute of Family Relations (hereafter AIFR) in this regard; see Ladd-Taylor, "Eugenics, Sterilisation and Modern Marriage in the USA: The Strange Career of Paul Popenoe," *Gender and History* 13, no. 2 (2001): 298–327.

19. Paul Popenoe, "Heredity and Education," October 29, 1948, PBPP, AHC, UW.

20. On "sexual liberalism" and its contradictions, see John D'Emilio and Estelle B. Freedman, *Intimate Matters: A History of Sexuality in America,* 2nd ed. (Chicago: University of Chicago Press, 1997); on homosexuality, see Jennifer Terry, *An American Obsession: Science, Medicine, and Homosexuality in Modern Society* (Chicago: University of Chicago Press, 1999).

21. See Elaine Tyler May, *Homeward Bound: American Families in the Cold War Era* (New York: Basic Books, 1988); Jane Gerhard, *Desiring Revolution: Second-Wave Feminism and the Rewriting of American Sexual Thought, 1920 to 1982* (New York: Columbia University Press, 2001); and Wini Breines, *Young, White, and Miserable: Growing Up Female in the Fifties* (Chicago: University of Chicago Press, 1992).

22. See Kline, *Building a Better Race,* for an analysis of eugenic pronatalism and the baby boom.

23. See Untitled Manuscript (Autobiographical) #1, Box 174, PBPP, AHC, UW.

24. Popenoe, "The Racial Effects of Alcohol," Bionomics 8, Thesis, May 1, 1908, PBPP, AHC, UW.

25. See Barbara Kimmelman, "The American Breeders' Association: Genetics and Eugenics in an Agricultural Context, 1903–13," *Social Studies of Science* 13 (1983): 163–204.

26. See Untitled Manuscript (Autobiographical) #2, PBPP, AHC, UW.

27. Paul Popenoe, *Date Growing in the Old World and the New* (Altadena, CA: West India Gardens, 1913), and "Date Growing in California and Arizona," in *Date Culture in Southern California,* by George Wharton James, Paul Popenoe, and Ralph D. Cornell (Los Angeles: Out West, 1912), 13–33.

28. Paul Popenoe to parents, October 9, 1913, Box 2, PBPP, AHC, UW.

29. See Paul Popenoe's correspondence with his parents for the years 1913–17, in which he regularly discussed date cultivation, Boxes 2–5, PBPP, AHC, UW.

30. See correspondence between Paul and Wilson during 1914–17, Boxes 3–5, PBPP, AHC, UW.

31. Paul Popenoe to parents, April 7, 1914, Box 3, PBPP, AHC, UW.

32. Paul Popenoe to parents, November 18, 1914, Box 3, PBPP, AHC, UW.

33. See Paul Popenoe, "Natural Selection in Man," in *Official Proceedings of the Second National Conference on Race Betterment* (Battle Creek, MI: Race Betterment Foundation, 1915), 60–61; and Kathy J. Cooke, "The Limits of Heredity: Nature and Nurture in American Eugenics before 1915," *Journal of the History of Biology* 31, no. 2 (1998): 263–78.

34. See Paul Popenoe and Roswell H. Johnson, *Applied Eugenics* (New York: Macmillan, 1918; 2nd ed. 1933).

35. Herbert also participated in California eugenics, through psychometric work at the California Bureau of Juvenile Research.

36. On the history of venereal disease control on the border during World War I, see Allan M. Brandt, *No Magic Bullet: A Social History of Venereal Disease in the United States since 1880* (Oxford: Oxford University Press, 1987).

37. Paul Popenoe to parents, July 31, 1920, Box 8, PBPP, AHC, UW.

38. David Popenoe, "Remembering My Father: An Intellectual Portrait of 'The Man Who Saved Marriages,'" Box 174, PBPP, AHC, UW.

39. Paul Popenoe to Betty Popenoe, July 13, 1920, Box 8, PBPP, AHC, UW.

40. Paul Popenoe to Betty Popenoe, May 3, 1920, Box 7, PBPP, AHC, UW.

41. Untitled Manuscript (Autobiographical) #2, Box 174, PBPP, AHC, UW.

42. Ibid.

43. David Popenoe, "Remembering My Father."

44. See Paul Popenoe, *The Conservation of the Family* (Baltimore: Williams and Wilkins, 1926); *Problems of Human Reproduction* (Baltimore: Williams and Wilkins, 1926); and *Modern Marriage: A Handbook for Men* (New York: Macmillan, 1925).

45. Paul Popenoe to parents, March 24, 1924, Box 9, PBPP, AHC, UW.

46. See Ezra S. Gosney and Paul Popenoe, *Sterilization for Human Betterment: A Summary of Results of 6,000 Operations in California, 1909–1929* (New York: Macmillan, 1929). See chapter 3 for a discussion of the Human Betterment Foundation.

47. Paul Popenoe to Leon Whitney, February 2, 1929, and February 11, 1929; Folders: Southern California Branch (hereafter SCB), American Eugenics Society Papers (hereafter AESP), 575.06 Am3, American Philosophical Society (hereafter APS).

48. Paul Popenoe to Leon Whitney, November 7, 1929, SCB, AESP, APS.

49. Leon Whitney to Paul Popenoe, November 26, 1929, and meeting minutes, which run from 1929 to 1936, SCB, AESP, APS.

50. See California Division newsletters in Folder: Ezra S. Gosney, Charles B. Davenport Papers, B:D27, APS.

51. Untitled Manuscript (Autobiographical) #1, Box 174, PBP, AHC, UW. Also see Paul Popenoe, "The Institute of Family Relations," *Journal of Home Economics* 22, no. 11 (1930): 906–7; AIFR, "The Institute of Family Relations" (pamphlet), Folder 8, Box 5, Ezra S. Gosney Papers and Records of the Human Betterment Foundation (hereafter ESGP-RHBF), Institute Archives (hereafter IA), California Institute of Technology (hereafter CIT).

52. Untitled Manuscript (Autobiographical) #1, Box 174, PBPP, AHC, UW. On the HBF's funding of the AIFR, at least until the mid-1930s, see Paul Popenoe to Lewis M. Terman, December 10, 1930, and the 1930–34 HBF annual reports contained in Folder 13, Box 2, Lewis M. Terman Papers, SC38, Special Collections, Stanford University.

53. Constance Chandler, "Marriage Ills Clinic Formed," *Los Angeles Times*, February 9, 1930.

54. Untitled Manuscript (Autobiographical) #1, Box 174, PBPP, AHC, UW.

55. David Popenoe, "Remembering My Father," 6.

56. See synopsis of article on Hayward and Popenoe in the tabloid *Top Secret* (1956) in which Popenoe was ridiculed as a pseudopsychologist. There

are several other relevant case histories of Hollywood stars, all protected by confidentiality stipulations, PBPP, AHC, UW.

57. AIFR, "Institute of Family Relations" (pamphlet); Ladd-Taylor, "Eugenics, Sterilisation," 311. On the German context, see Atina Grossman, *Reforming Sex: The German Movement for Birth Control and Abortion Reform, 1920–1950* (New York: Oxford University Press, 1995).

58. Paul Popenoe, "The Institute of Family Relations," *Eugenics* 3, no. 4 (1930): 134–37.

59. Paul Popenoe, "What the Marriage Counselor Should Know about Heredity," PBPP, AHC, UW. This message changed little over the forty years of the AIFR and was further informed by knowledge of the work of the country's dozen genetic counseling centers.

60. Paul Popenoe, "Eugenics and Family Relations," *Eugenical News* 25, no. 1 (1940): 74.

61. Paul Popenoe, "Problems of Heredity," chap. 14 of what was apparently a internal training manual for AIFR staff (title and date unknown), 14, PBPP, AHC, UW.

62. See, for example, Norman Fenton and Paul Popenoe, "Twenty-Five Years of Eugenic Sterilization," *Journal of Juvenile Research* 19, no. 4 (1935): 201–4.

63. Ibid., 14–16; Paul Popenoe, "Who Should *Not* Marry?" *Hygeia* (1939), offprint, PBPP, AHC, UW.

64. Paul Popenoe, "Marriage Counseling," *General Practitioner* 6, no. 4 (1952): 53–60, quotation on 55. Popenoe viewed voluntary childlessness among the middle classes as a major eugenic problem. See Paul Popenoe, "Childlessness: Voluntary or Involuntary," Box 4 (Eugenics Materials), Papers of Paul Popenoe (hereafter PPP), Special Collections, Occidental College.

65. "Chap. XIV. Problems of Heredity," 17.

66. See Stefan Kühl, *The Nazi Connection: Eugenics, American Racism, and German National Socialism* (New York: Oxford University Press, 1994).

67. Popenoe, "Eugenics and Family Relations," 74.

68. "Chap. XIV. Problems of Heredity," 14.

69. For the most part, both marriage and genetic counselors advised against interracial marriage, usually for cultural reasons, although hereditary assumptions were often tacitly implied. As Popenoe told the concerned parents of a teenage girl who was dating a Mexican boy, "She should be told that no writers in the field of dating, courtship, and marriage have any good to say for dating with those whose nationality, moral standards, religious convictions, interests, and family backgrounds are different." See Paul Popenoe to Mrs. P, April 30, 1956, Box 65, PBPP, AHC, UW. For more on the relationship of eugenics and genetic counseling, see Alexandra Minna Stern, *Telling Genes: The Story of Genetic Counseling in America* (Baltimore: Johns Hopkins University Press, 2012).

70. Kline, *Building a Better Race,* 143.

71. Popenoe, "What the Marriage Counselor Should Know"; Mrs. Helen G. Hammons to Paul Popenoe, June 15, 1956, Box 27, PBPP, AHC, UW.

72. On the history of genetic counseling, see Diane B. Paul, *The Politics of Heredity: Essays on Eugenics, Biomedicine, and the Nature-Nurture Debate*

(Albany: State University of New York Press, 1998); and Molly Ladd-Taylor, "'A Kind of Genetic Social Work': Sheldon Reed and the Origins of Genetic Counseling," in *Women, Health, and Nation: Canada and the United States since 1945*, ed. Georgina Feldberg, Molly Ladd-Taylor, Alison Li, and Kathryn McPherson (Montreal: McGill-Queen's University Press, 2003), 67–83.

73. Popenoe collected articles on heredity counseling and kept abreast of the activities of the Dight Institute at the University of Minnesota. In 1940, he felt confident enough in his understanding of human genetics and epilepsy to advise a man whose fraternal twin sister was epileptic that, in his case, "the inheritable tendency" was relatively small. See Mr. P. to Paul Popenoe, April 17, 1940; Paul Popenoe to Mr. P., April 19, 1940, Box 25, PBPP, AHC, UW.

74. Paul Popenoe, "The American Institute of Family Relations," PBPP, AHC, UW.

75. See Popenoe, "Institute of Family Relations" [*Eugenics*].

76. See Paul Popenoe, "A Family Consultation Service," *Journal of Social Hygiene* 17, no. 6 (1931): 309–21, PPP, Special Collections, Occidental College.

77. AIFR pamphlets and flyers, Folder 8, Box 5, ESGP-RHBF, IA, CIT; Popenoe, "American Institute."

78. Popenoe, "Family Consultation Service."

79. AIFR, "The First Ten Years of the American Institute of Family Relations," PBPP, AHC, UW.

80. AIFR, "News and Notes of the American Institute of Family Relations, January 1942," Folder 8, Box 5, ESGP-RHBF, CIT, IA.

81. See Paul Popenoe, "Eugenics after the War," *Eugenical News* 28 (1943): 19–20.

82. Paul Popenoe, *Be It Ever So Jumbled There's No Place Like Home* (New York: Army and Navy Department of the YMCA, 1945), 9, PBPP, AHC, UW.

83. Paul Popenoe, "Home, America's Strongest Bulwark" (advertisement), PBPP, AHC, UW.

84. On the connection between federally subsidized housing and the economic consolidation of white America after World War II, see George Lipsitz, *The Possessive Investment in Whiteness: How White People Profit from Identity Politics* (Philadelphia: Temple University Press, 1998).

85. Paul Popenoe and Dorothy Cameron Disney, *Can This Marriage Be Saved?* (New York: Macmillan, 1953), xii.

86. AIFR, "The American Institute of Family Relations" (1955 retrospective), PBPP, AHC, UW.

87. Paul Popenoe, "Forty Years of the AIFR," *Family Life* 30, no. 2 (1970): 2. Popenoe was first heard on the radio version of *Art Linkletter's House Party* and appeared regularly on radio shows in Southern California. See Kline, *Building a Better Race*, 143.

88. "Dr. Popenoe Contributes to Human Understanding through Television," *TV Time* 4, no. 14 (1951); "Divorce Hearing," KTLA, advertisement for the network's show *Divorce Hearing*, n.d., PBPP, AHC, UW.

89. Paul Popenoe to Mr. Dille, August 18, 1936, Box 12, PBPP, AHC, UW.

90. His last syndicated column was part of the series "Your Family and You," and ran on September 8, 1972. In this good-bye to his readers, he

implored Americans to protect family life and asked women, in particular, to shun feminism and to ask instead, "What will hold my family together?" PBPP, AHC, UW.

91. Kline, *Building a Better Race,* 153.

92. Popenoe and Disney, *Can This Marriage Be Saved?*

93. See Mrs. S to Paul Popenoe, April 30, 1958, Box 68, PBPP, AHC, UW.

94. Mrs. T to Paul Popenoe, January 6, 1959, Box 71, PBPP, AHC, UW.

95. Mrs. S to Paul Popenoe, January 21, 1960, Box 73, PBPP, AHC, UW.

96. See May, *Homeward Bound;* and Stephanie Coontz, *The Way We Never Were: American Families and the Nostalgia Trap* (New York: Basic Books, 1992).

97. See Paul Popenoe, "Toward an American Population Policy," *Eugenical News* 30 (1945): 20–21; Popenoe, "The Practice of Marriage Counseling," Publication 526, AIFR, PBPP, AHC, UW.

98. Popenoe, "Toward an American Population Policy," 21.

99. Paul Popenoe, "Human Genetics and Eugenics" (White House Conference on Basal Sciences and Fetal and Maternal Problems), PBPP, AHC, UW.

100. Paul Popenoe, "The Psychology of the Male Sex," chap. 4 of the internal training manual for AIFR staff cited in note 61 (title and date unknown), 4.

101. Ibid., 11.

102. Ibid., 11–12.

103. Ibid., 3–4.

104. Paul Popenoe, draft of foreword to *Marriage and You: A Sociological and Psychological Study of American Marriage and Family Life,* by Barnard J. Oliver (draft date unknown but the book was published in 1964), PBPP, AHC, UW.

105. Popenoe, "Why Are Women Like That?" 1, PBPP, AHC, UW. Also see "Why Are Men Like That?" PBPP, AHC, UW.

106. Popenoe, "Why Are Women Like That?" 2.

107. Popenoe, "Heredity and Education," 8.

108. Paul Popenoe, *Eight Cures for Man Haters,* pamphlet, 1939, PBPP, AHC, UW.

109. See Gerhard, *Desiring Revolution.*

110. Popenoe, "Why Are Women Like That?" 12.

111. Popenoe, "Marriage Counseling," 53.

112. Popenoe, "Why Are Men Like That?" 4; also see Popenoe, "Psychology of the Male Sex," 4.

113. Popenoe, "Psychology of the Male Sex," 4.

114. Paul Popenoe, *Boss Him and Lose Him,* pamphlet, 1943, PBPP, AHC, UW.

115. Popenoe, *Be It Ever So Jumbled,* 15.

116. See Paul Popenoe, "Cooperation in Family Relations," *Journal of Home Economics* 26, no. 8 (1934): 483–86; Paul Popenoe, "Should a Family Have Two Heads?" *Parents' Magazine* (repr., 1939), PBPP, AHC, UW.

117. Popenoe, *Boss Him and Lose Him;* Paul Popenoe, *Smart Wives Don't Have to Nag,* pamphlet, 1939, PBPP, AHC, UW.

118. Popenoe, "Psychology of the Male Sex," 4.

119. Popenoe, "Why Are Men Like That?" 7.

120. "AIFR Policies," n.d., PBPP, AHC. UW. In addition, these included, among others, attending staff meetings, not referring to private physicians, absolutely refraining from any physical contact, refraining from socializing with clients, and being careful about using a religious approach.

121. "Case File of H and J," PBPP, AHC, UW.

122. Paul Popenoe to Mr. R, September 6, 1940, Box 25, PBPP, AHC, UW.

123. Paul Popenoe, *Aggressiveness Can Wreck Romance*, pamphlet, 1945, PBPP, AHC, UW.

124. The sex/gender separation started in the 1950s even as "sex" was being contested by transsexuality and intersexuality; see Joanne Meyerowitz, *How Sex Changed: A History of Transsexuality in the United States* (Cambridge, MA: Harvard University Press, 2002).

125. Ibid., chap. 3.

126. Paul Popenoe, "Some Biological Foundations of Counseling," 2, and notes for "Introverts and Extraverts," PBPP, AHC, UW.

127. Paul Popenoe, "Introverts and Extraverts," *Scientific American*, October 1937, 197–200, PBPP, AHC, UW.

128. Ibid.

129. Paul Popenoe, "Special Procedures in Counseling," chap. 3 of the internal training manual for AIFR staff cited in note 61 (title and date unknown), 5, PBPP, AHC, UW.

130. Popenoe, notes for "Introverts and Extraverts."

131. Popenoe, "Introverts and Extraverts," 200.

132. Paul Popenoe, "Introverts and Extraverts—'Project'—October 9, 1971," PBPP, AHC, UW.

133. Popenoe, "Introverts and Extraverts," 200.

134. Intake form of Mr. and Mrs. K, August 31, 1945, Box 156, PBPP, AHC, UW.

135. Popenoe and Disney, *Can This Marriage Be Saved?*, xvii.

136. On Terman's rejection of his earlier beliefs about the connections between race and intelligence, see Stephen Jay Gould, *The Mismeasure of Man*, 2nd ed. (New York: W. W. Norton, 1996); and Lewis M. Terman and Catharine Cox Miles, *Sex and Personality: Studies in Masculinity and Femininity* (New York: Russell and Russell, 1936).

137. Terman and Miles, *Sex and Personality*, chap. 11. For a discussion of Terman and the M-F Test, see Kline, *Building a Better Race*, chap. 5.

138. See Roswell H. Johnson to Lewis M. Terman, April 30, 1937, and Lewis M. Terman to Roswell H. Johnson, May 5, 1937, both in Folder 7, Box 2, Lewis M. Terman Papers, SC38, Special Collections, Stanford University.

139. Kline, *Building a Better Race*, 138; Michael Kimmel, *Manhood in America: A Cultural History* (New York: Free Press, 1996).

140. "Memorandum on Tests and Measurements Used by the AIFR," PBPP, AHC, UW.

141. Roswell H. Johnson, "Temperament Factor in Marital Happiness" and "Factors Producing Temperament," both in PBPP, AHC, UW.

142. See Francesca Bordogna, "The Psychology and Physiology of Temperament: Pragmatism in Context," *Journal of the History of the Behavioral*

Sciences 37, no. 1 (2001): 3–25; and Otniel E. Dror, "Counting the Affects: Discoursing in Numbers," *Social Research* 68, no. 2 (2001): 357–78.

143. See Richard Stephen Uhrbrock, *An Analysis of the Downey Will-Temperament Tests* (New York: Teacher's College, Columbia University, 1928).

144. See George W. Stocking, *Race, Culture, and Evolution: Essays in the History of Anthropology* (Chicago: University of Chicago Press, 1982).

145. See Jennifer Terry, "Anxious Slippage between 'Us' and 'Them': A Brief History of the Scientific Search for Homosexual Bodies," in *Deviant Bodies: Critical Perspectives on Difference in Science and Popular Culture,* ed. Jennifer Terry and Jacqueline Urla (Bloomington: Indiana University Press, 1995), 129–69.

146. Popenoe, "Special Procedures in Counseling"; "Memorandum on Tests."

147. "Memorandum on Tests."

148. These questions are paraphrased (for copyright reasons) from the T-JTA because I did not find any original JTA questionnaires (in draft or printed form) in Popenoe's papers.

149. "Aids to Interpreting Johnson Temperament Analysis Profiles," PBP, AHC, UW.

150. Ibid.

151. Ibid.

152. Robert M. Taylor and Lucile P. Morrison, *Taylor-Johnson Temperament Analysis Manual* (1966; repr., Thousand Oaks, CA: Psychological Publications, 1996), 33–36.

153. "Client Will Come Back for Second Time If," PBPP, AHC, UW.

154. Leslie F. Kimmell to Dr. H, April 15, 1954, PBPP, AHC, UW. The Marriage Readiness Materials are most likely in Boxes 95 and 96 or were alphabetically interfiled into one of the twenty-one boxes of case histories.

155. Leslie F. Kimmell to Miss K, May 21, 1954, PBPP, AHC, UW.

156. Miss M to Paul Popenoe, Feb. 24, 1954, PBPP, AHC, UW.

157. Mary Jane Hungerford to Miss M, n.d. (probably April 1954), PBPP, AHC, UW.

158. Gene Benton to Miss M, July 30, 1954, PBPP, AHC, UW.

159. "Marital Counseling," case notes, June 7, 1952, and JTA, September 20, 1952, both for Mrs. P, PBPP, AHC, UW.

160. Ibid.

161. JTA of Miss H, June 9, 1954, PBPP, AHC, UW.

162. Gene Benton to Miss H, August 17, 1954, PBPP, AHC, UW.

163. "Counseling on Frigidity," AIFR information sheet, PBPP, AHC, UW. It is likely that most of the material on frigidity is in Box 153.

164. For an early articulation of Popenoe's ideas about frigidity, see Paul Popenoe, "Marital Counseling: With Special Reference to Frigidity," *Western Journal of Surgery, Obstetrics and Gynecology* (1937), PBPP, AHC. UW. In keeping with the logic that women had many more sexual problems than men and could find more ways to help themselves, Popenoe identified five kinds of frigidity: pseudo, occasional, relative, pathological, and essential. According to him, 25 percent of all women experienced one of these types of frigidity during their married life, and all but the last two, which were viewed as the most bio-

logically rooted, could be overcome with a steady program of psychological and physical exercises.

165. Paul Popenoe and Arnold H. Kegel, "New Approach to Sexual Problems," 9, and "Improvement of Technique in Sexual Intercourse," 1, both in PBPP, AHC, UW.

166. Popenoe and Kegel, "New Approach."

167. Ibid., 6; *Family Life,* 15, no. 7 (1955): 2, PBPP, AHC, UW.

168. Popenoe and Kegel, "Improvement of Technique."

169. Ibid.

170. Popenoe and Kegel, "New Approach."

171. In 1962, the trustees hired Floyd Anderson, a PhD-trained marriage counselor from Utah who proved to be a terrible manager and demoralizing leader. Moreover, he was a Mormon who let his religious affiliations dictate his plans for the institute even though he had promised when hired that he would take an ecumenical approach. See letters from 1962–63, Paul Popenoe to AIFR trustees, Box 145, PBPP, AHC, UW.

172. David Popenoe, "Remembering My Father."

173. Ibid., 3.

174. In the early 1960s, Robert M. Taylor, who replaced Johnson as counseling director, revised the JTA with Johnson's approval. After recalibrating the tests on hundreds of test subjects in Texas, Colorado, and California, it was reissued as the T-JTA in 1966. Its logic remains the same, but the wording of the questions and categories has been updated to reflect contemporary terminology. See Taylor and Morrison, *Taylor Johnson Temperament Analysis,* 33; also see H. Norman Wright, *Biblical Application for the Taylor-Johnson Temperament Analysis* (Santa Ana, CA: Christian Enrichment, 1975); and materials on the Right Start Premarital Program available at their website (www.rightstartpublications .com).

7. CONTESTING HEREDITARIANISM

1. May Second Committee, "Sacramento State's Own Doctor Strangelove: New Multimillion Dollar Science Building at S.S.C. to Be Named after C.M. Goethe, Prominent Racist and Eugenist," ca. 1965, 85D:9, Charles Matthias Goethe Papers (hereafter CMGP), University Archives (hereafter UA), California State University Sacramento (hereafter CSUS). There is a clue that Goethe was aware of the protest; in a letter dated April 9, 1965, he wrote to three science faculty, whose research he had funded, about that week's "battleaxe" incident. See Charles M. Goethe to Dr. Albert Delisle, Dr. J. Harold Severaid, and Dr. W.J. Beeson, April 9, 1965, 85F3:9, CMGP, UA, CSUS.

2. May Second Committee, "Banned at Sac State," ca. 1965, 85D:9, CMGP, UA, CSUS.

3. Ibid.

4. "Goethe Immortalized by Science Building," *State Hornet,* March 30, 1965.

5. See Tony [Anthony] Platt, *What's in a Name? Charles M. Goethe, American Eugenics, and Sacramento State University* (Sacramento, CA: T. Platt, 2004); "Estate of Charles Matthias Goethe," C.M. Goethe Memorial Grove,

Memorial Grove Archives, Save-the-Redwoods League, San Francisco; and Andrew Schauer, "Charles Matthias Goethe, 1875–1966," Foundation of the California State University Sacramento, 1976, 85A:1, CMGP, UA, CSUS.

6. Quoted in Platt, *What's in a Name?* 54. Also see "Academic Senate Agenda," October 3, 1967, 83:3:02, Academic Senate Files (hereafter ASF), UA, CSUS, where scribbles on the margin of a senate agenda intimate that this action was specifically directed at Goethe. Beside item 8, "Naming of Buildings," someone wrote, "substitute motion, naming of building, consent of Academic Senate, Goethe Bldg.—deliberate."

7. Platt, *What's in a Name?*, 54–55.

8. See Darrell J. Inabnit to Robert Thompson, November 9, 1967, 83:3:03, and "Academic Senate Minutes," November 14, 1967, 83:3:03, ASF, UA, CSUS.

9. See Terry H. Anderson, *The Movement and the Sixties: Protest in America from Greensboro to Wounded Knee* (New York: Oxford University Press, 1995); and Todd Gitlin, *The Sixties: Years of Hope, Days of Rage,* 2nd ed. (New York: Bantam Books, 1993).

10. I have borrowed the phrase "hidden in plain view" from Paul A. Lombardo; see his "Eugenics: Lessons from a History Hidden in Plain View," lecture to the California Legislature, Senate Select Committee on Genetics, Genetic Technologies, and Public Policy, March 11, 2003.

11. See Martin S. Pernick, *The Black Stork: Eugenics and the Death of "Defective" Babies in American Medicine and Motion Pictures since 1915* (New York: Oxford University Press, 1996); Diane B. Paul, *The Politics of Heredity: Essays on Eugenics, Biomedicine, and the Nature-Nurture Debate* (Albany: State University of New York Press, 1998).

12. Daniel J. Kevles, *In the Name of Eugenics: Genetics and the Uses of Human Heredity,* rev. ed. (Cambridge, MA: Harvard University Press, 1995), chaps. 8–9.

13. Steve Selden, *Inheriting Shame: The Story of Eugenics and Racism in America* (New York: Teachers College, Columbia University, 1999), 111.

14. See Leon Whitney to Paul Popenoe, February 21, 1929, Folder: Southern California Branch, Papers of the American Eugenics Society, 575.06 Am3, American Philosophical Society.

15. William H. Tucker, *The Funding of Scientific Racism: Wickliffe Draper and the Pioneer Fund* (Urbana: University of Illinois Press, 2002), 43; Paul Lombardo, "'The American Breed': Nazi Eugenics and the Origins of the Pioneer Fund," *Albany Law Review* 65, no. 3 (2002): 743–830.

16. G. Sabagh and R. B. Edgerton, "Sterilized Mental Defectives Look at Eugenic Sterilization," *Eugenics Quarterly* 9, no. 4 (1962): 213–22. Also see Robert B. Edgerton, *The Cloak of Competence,* 2nd ed. (Berkeley: University of California Press, 1993).

17. See Kevles, *In the Name;* Selden, *Inheriting Shame.*

18. Sinclair Lewis, *Arrowsmith* (1924; repr., New York: Signet Classic, 1980). Also see Howard Markel, "Prescribing Arrowsmith," *New York Times Book Review,* September 24, 2000.

19. Lewis, *Arrowsmith,* 241.

20. Stephen Jay Gould, *The Mismeasure of Man,* 2nd ed. (New York: W. W. Norton, 1996), 263.

21. See Mary Conway Kohler, interview by Gail Hornstein, November 2, 1983 (cited with permission); Dede Welles, "Mary Conway Kohler," Women's Legal History, 1997, www.stanford.edu/group/WLHP/ papers/kohler.html.

22. Quoted in Kevles, *In the Name,* 166.

23. See Elazar Barkan, *The Retreat of Scientific Racism: Changing Concepts of Race in Britain and the United States between the World Wars* (New York: Cambridge University Press, 1992).

24. M. F. Ashley Montagu, "The Concept of Race in the Human Species in Light of Genetics," *Journal of Heredity* 32, no. 8 (1941): 243–47.

25. L. C. Dunn and Th. Dobzhansky, *Heredity, Race, and Society* (New York: Mentor Books, 1946), 115.

26. See Donna J. Haraway, *Modest_Witness @ Second_Millennium.Female Man©_Meets_OncoMouse™: Feminism and Technoscience* (New York: Routledge, 1997), chap. 6.

27. United Nations Educational, Scientific and Cultural Organization (UNESCO), *The Race Concept: Results of an Inquiry* (Paris: UNESCO, 1952).

28. See Matthew Frye Jacobson, *Whiteness of a Different Color: European Immigrants and the Alchemy of Race* (Cambridge, MA: Harvard University Press, 1998); and Mae M. Ngai, *Impossible Subjects: Illegal Aliens and the Making of Modern America* (Princeton, NJ: Princeton University Press, 2004).

29. On the time lag between institutionalized racism and "race" as defined by science, see David Theo Goldberg, *Racial Subjects: Writing on Race in America* (New York: Routledge, 1997).

30. See Ronald Takaki, *Double Victory: A Multicultural History of America in World War II* (Boston: Little, Brown, 2000).

31. See Gilbert Gonzalez, *Chicano Education in the Era of Segregation* (Philadelphia: Balch Institute Press, 1990).

32. See Ed Duran Ayres, "Statistics," in NAACP, *NAACP 1940–55. General Office File. Zoot Suit Riots, 1943–44,* microfilm, Part 7, Series A, Reel 29 (Frederick, MD: University Publications of America). On the trial and its political context, see Edward J. Escobar, *Race, Police, and the Making of a Political Identity: Mexican Americans and the Los Angeles Police Department, 1900–1945* (Berkeley: University of California Press, 1999).

33. Frederick V. Field to Walter White, May 17, 1943, in NAACP, *NAACP 1940–55,* Part 7, Series A, Reel 29.

34. Emory S. Bogardus, "Gangs of Mexican-American Youth," *Sociology and Social Research* 28, no. 1 (1943): 60. See also his article "The Mexican Immigrant," *Journal of Applied Sociology* 11, no. 3 (1927): 470–88.

35. See Mario T. Garcia, *Mexican Americans: Leadership, Ideology, and Identity, 1930–1960* (New Haven, CT: Yale University Press, 1989), chap. 10; and Steven Schlossman, "Self-Evident Remedy? George I. Sanchez, Segregation, and Enduring Dilemmas in Bilingual Education," *Teachers College Board* 84, no. 4 (1983): 871–907.

36. See Gonzalez, *Chicano Education;* Nancy Leys Stepan and Sander L. Gilman, "Appropriating the Idioms of Science: The Rejection of Scientific

Racism," in *The Bounds of Race: Perspectives on Hegemony and Resistance,* ed. Dominick LaCapra (Ithaca, NY: Cornell University Press, 1991), 72–103.

37. For 1970s critiques of IQ testing in Mexican communities, see Esteban L. Olmedo, "Psychological Testing and the Chicano: A Reassessment," and John Garcia, "Intelligence Testing: Quotients, Quotas, and Quackery," in *Chicano Psychology,* ed. Joe L. Martinez Jr. (New York: Academic Press, 1977), 175–95, 197–212.

38. Editorial, *El Grito* 3, no. 2 (1970): 2.

39. Patricia Pullenza de Ortiz, "Chicano Children and Intelligence," *Aztlán* 10 (1979): 71–72; James Vásquez, "Measurement of Intelligence and Language Differences," *Aztlán* 3, no. 1 (1972): 161.

40. Ian F. Haney López, *Racism on Trial: The Chicano Fight for Justice* (Cambridge, MA: Belknap Press of Harvard University Press, 2003), 17.

41. Ibid., 21. Also see Ernesto Chávez, *"Mi Raza Primero!": Nationalism, Identity, and Insurgency in the Chicano Movement in Los Angeles, 1966–1978* (Berkeley: University of California Press, 2002).

42. See José E. Limón, "Stereotyping and Chicano Resistance: An Historical Dimension," *Aztlán* 4, no. 2 (1973): 257–70; Raul Fernández, "The Policy Economy of Stereotypes," *Aztlán* 1, no. 2 (1970): 39–45; and Nick C. Vaca, "The Mexican-American in the Social Sciences, 1912–1970, Part I (1912–1935)," *El Grito* 3, no. 3 (1970): 3–24; "Part II (1936–1970)," *El Grito* 4, no. 1 (1970): 17–51.

43. See, for example, Armando Morales, "Mental and Public Health Issues: The Case of the Mexican Americans in Los Angeles," *El Grito* 3, no. 2 (1970): 3–11, and "The Impact of Class Discrimination on the Mental Health of Mexican-Americans," in *Chicanos: Social and Psychological Perspectives,* ed. Nathaniel N. Wagner and Marsha J. Haug (St. Louis: C. V. Mosby, 1971), 257–62; Armand J. Sanchez, "The Definers and the Defined: A Mental Health Issue," *El Grito* 4, no. 4 (1971): 4–35; Ruben Zamorano-Gamez and Eveline P. Carsman, "Chicano Consumer Participation in Health Planning: Reality and Myth," *Atisbos: Journal of Chicano Research* 1 (Summer 1975): 126–39; and Luis M. Laosa, Alvin G. Burstein, and Harry W. Martin, "Mental Health Consultation in a Rural Chicano Community: Crystal City," *Aztlán* 6, no. 3 (1976): 433–53.

44. See Ramón A. Gutiérrez, "Decolonizing the Body: Kinship and the Nation," *American Archivist* 57, no. 1 (1994): 86–99.

45. See Keith Wailoo, *Dying in the City of Blues: Sickle Cell Anemia and the Politics of Race and Health* (Chapel Hill: University of North Carolina Press, 2001); and E. Chávez, *"Mi Raza Primero!"*

46. Manuel Ferran, coord., *Health Cultural Awareness Conference: "Viva la Diferencia"* (published conference proceedings) (Albuquerque: New Mexico Regional Medical Program, 1972).

47. See *NCHO Newsletters* (1971–76).

48. See Naomi Rogers, "'Caution: The AMA May Be Dangerous to Your Health': The Student Health Organizations (SHO) and American Medicine, 1965–1970," *Radical History Review* 80 (2001): 5–34.

49. See Joseph P. Shapiro, *No Pity: People with Disabilities Forging a New Civil Rights Movement* (New York: Three Rivers Press, 1993); and Paul K.

Longmore and Lauri Umansky, eds., *The New Disability History: American Perspectives* (New York: New York University Press, 2001).

50. Betty Friedan, *The Feminine Mystique* (1963; repr., New York: W. W. Norton, 1983).

51. Ibid.

52. See Jane Gerhard, *Desiring Revolution: Second-Wave Feminism and the Rewriting of American Sexual Thought, 1920 to 1982* (New York: Columbia University Press, 2001), chap. 3.

53. Paul Popenoe, "Marriage Counseling," n.d., Papers of Paul Bowman Popenoe (hereafter PBPP), American Heritage Center (hereafter AHC), University of Wyoming (hereafter UW). Since I conducted my research at the American Heritage Center, the Popenoe Papers have been recatalogued. Working with the new finding aid, I have been able to deduce the location of some of my sources; when that was not possible with accuracy, I have omitted unverifiable information, such as the box or folder title or number. Between my reconstructed citations and the new finding aid, which is organized chronologically and thematically, researchers should be able to locate all of my references.

54. Stephanie Coontz, *The Way We Never Were: American Families and the Nostalgia Trap* (New York: Basic Books, 1992), 24; Elaine Tyler May, *Homeward Bound: American Families in the Cold War Era* (New York: Basic Books, 1988), 6, 136–37.

55. For an excellent analysis of the rise of Freudian psychoanalysis in relation to middle-class women and the female body in midcentury America, see Gerhard, *Desiring Revolution*.

56. Paul Popenoe, untitled review of *The Feminine Mystique*, by Betty Friedan, n.d., PBPP, AHC, UW.

57. Susan Brownmiller, *In Our Time: Memoir of a Revolution* (New York: Dial Press, 1999), 86. They also demanded a cessation of the columns by Bruno Bettelheim and Theodore Rubin.

58. Karla Jay, *Tales of the Lavender Menace: A Memoir of Liberation* (New York: Basic Books, 1999), 114. On this action, also see Alice Echols, *Daring to Be Bad: Radical Feminism in America, 1967–1975* (Minneapolis: University of Minnesota Press, 1989).

59. Gina, "Written in Anger," *It Ain't Me Babe* 1, no. 6 (1970): 6.

60. Anne Koedt, "The Myth of the Vaginal Orgasm," in *Notes from the Second Year* (New York: Radical Feminists, 1970), 38. I thank Carol Karlsen for sharing her collection of women's liberation pamphlets with me.

61. See Gerhard, *Desiring Revolution*.

62. See Ruth Hubbard, Mary Sue Henifin, and Barbara Fried, eds., *Biological Woman—The Convenient Myth* (Cambridge, MA: Schenkman, 1982).

63. Naomi Weisstein, "Kinder, Küche, Kirche as Scientific Law: Psychology Constructs the Female," *motive: on the liberation of women* 29, nos. 6–7 (1969): 83.

64. Ibid., 80.

65. See Boston Women's Health Book Collective, *Our Bodies, Ourselves: A Book by and for Women* (New York: Simon and Schuster, 1973).

66. See Sheryl Burt Ruzek, *The Women's Health Movement: Feminist Alternatives to Medical Control* (New York: Praeger, 1978); and Sandra Morgen, *Into Our Own Hands: The Women's Health Movement in the United States, 1969–1990* (New Brunswick, NJ: Rutgers University Press, 2002).

67. Gerhard, *Desiring Revolution,* 85.

68. Roswell H. Johnson, "Homosexuality" (n.d., probably late 1940s), Box 123, PBPP, AHC, UW.

69. On the cross-fertilization of psychoanalytic and genetic theories, see Nancy Ordover, *American Eugenics: Race, Queer Anatomy, and the Science of Nationalism* (Minneapolis: University of Minnesota Press, 2003).

70. Ibid.

71. Paul Popenoe to Barry Tanner, July 27, 1972, probably Box 123, PBPP, AHC, UW.

72. See Paul Popenoe, "The Life of a Homosexual," *Family Life* 22, no. 11 (1962): 3, "Again, Homosexuality," *Family Life* 27, no. 7 (July 1967): 2, and "Quality of Family Life," New Year's Edition, 1972, loose op-ed piece from unidentifiable newspaper, p. B13, all from (probably) Box 123, PBPP, AHC, UW.

73. Ronald Bayer, *Homosexuality and American Psychiatry: The Politics of Diagnosis* (Princeton, NJ: Princeton University Press, 1987).

74. On the Kinsey spectrum, see Jennifer Terry, "Anxious Slippage between 'Us' and 'Them': A Brief History of the Scientific Search for Homosexual Bodies," in *Deviant Bodies: Critical Perspectives on Difference in Science and Popular Culture,* ed. Jennifer Terry and Jacqueline Urla (Bloomington: Indiana University Press, 1995), 129–69.

75. AIFR, "One Minute and 48 Seconds on Homosexuality," and Don Page, "KABC Special on Homosexuality," November 14, 1971, both in (probably) Box 123, PBPP, AHC, UW.

76. Craig Alfred Hanson to Paul Popenoe, November 20, 1971, (probably) Box 123, PBPP, AHC, UW.

77. See Jennifer Terry, *An American Obsession: Science, Medicine, and Homosexuality in Modern Society* (Chicago: University of Chicago Press, 1999); Bayer, *Homosexuality and American Psychiatry.*

78. Art Torres to Edmund G. Brown Jr., September 7, 1979, Legislative History, Assembly Bill 1204, Microfilm 3:3 (57), California State Archives (hereafter CSA).

79. "Enrolled Bill Report," August 31, 1979, Legislative History, Assembly Bill 1204, Microfilm 3:3 (57), CSA. Also see California Legislature, Senate Select Committee on Genetics, Genetic Technologies, and Public Policy, *California's Compulsory Sterilization Policies, 1909–1979, July 16, 2003, Informational Hearing,* ed. Lisa M. Matocq (Sacramento: California Publications, 2003).

80. Art Torres, interview by author, November 17, 2003, San Francisco.

81. See Johanna Schoen, *Choice and Coercion: Birth Control, Sterilization, and Abortion in Public Health and Welfare* (Chapel Hill: University of North Carolina Press, 2005), chaps. 2 and 3; and Leslie J. Reagan, *When Abortion Was a Crime: Women, Medicine, and Law in the United States, 1867–1973* (Berkeley: University of California Press, 1997).

82. See Elena R. Gutiérrez, "Policing 'Pregnant Pilgrims': Situating the Sterilization Abuse of Mexican-Origin Women in Los Angeles County," in *Women, Health, and Nation: Canada and the United States since 1945*, ed. Georgina Feldberg, Molly Ladd-Taylor, Alison Li, and Kathryn McPherson (Montreal: McGill-Queen's University Press, 2003), 381.

83. See Thomas M. Shapiro, *Population Control Politics: Women, Sterilization, and Reproductive Choice* (Philadelphia: Temple University Press, 1985), 87.

84. Ibid., 113.

85. E. Gutiérrez, "Policing 'Pregnant Pilgrims,'" 381.

86. T. Shapiro, *Population Control Politics*, 115.

87. See Simone M. Caron, "Birth Control and the Black Community in the 1960s: Genocide or Power Politics," *Journal of Social History* 31, no. 3 (1998): 545–69.

88. See Linda Gordon, *Woman's Body, Woman's Right: Birth Control in America*, rev. ed. (New York: Penguin Books, 1990).

89. On abortion and mainstream feminism, see Ruth Rosen, *The World Split Open: How the Modern Women's Movement Changed America* (New York: Viking, 2000).

90. See L. Gordon, *Woman's Body, Woman's Right.*

91. See Angela Y. Davis, *Women, Race, and Class* (New York: Vintage Books, 1981), chap. 12; Jack Slater, "Sterilization: Newest Threat to the Poor," *Ebony*, October 1973, 150–56.

92. T. Shapiro, *Population Control Politics;* Ordover, *American Eugenics.*

93. Quoted in T. Shapiro, *Population Control Politics*, 5.

94. Ibid.

95. Helen Rodrigues-Triaz, "Sterilization Abuse," in Hubbard, Henifin, and Fried, *Biological Woman*, 149.

96. Sally J. Torpy, "Native American Women and Coerced Sterilization: On the Trail of Tears in the 1970s," *American Indian Culture and Research Journal* 24, no. 2 (2000): 5.

97. Ibid.; Ordover, *American Eugenics*, 171–72.

98. See Laura Briggs, *Reproducing Empire: Race, Sex, Science, and U.S. Imperialism in Puerto Rico* (Berkeley: University of California Press, 2002); Iris Lopez, "Agency and Constraint: Sterilization and Reproductive Freedom among Puerto Rican Women in New York City," *Urban Anthropology* 22, nos. 3–4 (1993): 299–323; and Rodrigues-Triaz, "Sterilization Abuse."

99. Jennifer A. Nelson, "'Abortions under Community Control': Feminism, Nationalism, and the Politics of Reproduction among New York City's Young Lords," *Journal of Women's History* 13, no. 1 (2001): 157–80.

100. See Julius Paul, "The Return of Punitive Sterilization Proposals: Current Attacks on Illegitimacy and the AFDC Program," *Law and Society Review* 3, no. 1 (1968): 88–92; and Katherine Castles, "Quiet Eugenics: Sterilization in North Carolina's Institutions for the Mentally Retarded, 1945–1965," *Journal of Southern History* 68, no. 4 (2002): 849–78.

101. See Philip R. Reilly, *The Surgical Solution: A History of Involuntary Sterilization in the United States* (Baltimore: Johns Hopkins University

Press, 1991); Ordover, *American Eugenics;* and T. Shapiro, *Population Control Politics.*

102. See Ordover, *American Eugenics*; J. Paul, "Return of Punitive Sterilization"; and Rickie Solinger, *Wake Up Little Susie: Single Pregnancy and Race before Roe v. Wade,* 2nd ed. (New York: Routledge, 2002).

103. See Schoen, *Choice and Coercion;* and Slater, "Sterilization."

104. See J. Paul, "Return of Punitive Sterilization."

105. Student Nonviolent Coordinating Committee (SNCC), *Genocide in Mississippi* (Atlanta, GA: SNCC, 1964).

106. J. Paul, "Return of Punitive Sterilization," 91.

107. See Dorothy Roberts, *Killing the Black Body: Race, Reproduction, and the Meaning of Liberty* (New York: Vintage Books, 1997); J. Paul, "Return of Punitive Sterilization."

108. Health Research Group, *A Health Research Group Study on Surgical Sterilization: Present Abuses and Proposed Regulations* (Washington, DC: Health Research Group, 1973), 1.

109. Ibid., 2.

110. Ibid., 7.

111. Diane Ainsworth, "Mother No More," *Reader: Los Angeles' Free Weekly,* January 26, 1979, 4.

112. See Virginia Espino, "'Woman Sterilized as Gives Birth': Forced Sterilization and the Chicana Resistance in the 1970s," in *Las Obreras: Chicana Politics of Work and Family,* ed. Vicki L. Ruiz and Chon Noriega (Los Angeles: UCLA Chicano Studies Research Center Publications, 2000), 65–82.

113. Committee to Stop Forced Sterilization, *Stop Forced Sterilization Now!* (Los Angeles: n.p., n.d.), 3. Also see Patti Garcia, "Forced Sterilization of Third World Women," *La Razón Mestiza,* Summer 1975, n.p.

114. For more on the *Andrade* case, see Virginia Rose Espino, "Women Sterilized as They Give Birth: Population Control, Eugenics, and Social Protest in the Twentieth-Century United States," PhD diss., Arizona State University, 2007.

115. For a penetrating analysis of *Madrigal v. Quilligan,* see Elena Rebéca Gutiérrez, "The Racial Politics of Reproduction: The Social Construction of Mexican-Origin Women's Fertility" (PhD diss., University of Michigan, 1999), chap. 5, and "Policing 'Pregnant Pilgrims.'" Also see Espino, "'Woman Sterilized as Gives Birth'"; Claudia Dreifus, "Sterilizing the Poor," in *Seizing Our Bodies: The Politics of Women's Health,* ed. Claudia Dreifus (New York: Vintage Books, 1977), 105–20; Adelaida R. Del Castillo, "Sterilization: An Overview," in *Mexican American Women in the United States: Struggles Past and Present,* ed. Madgalena Mora and Adelaida R. Del Castillo, Occasional Paper 2 (Los Angeles: UCLA Chicano Studies Research Center Publications, 1980), 65–70, 71–94; Carlos G. Vélez-Ibañez, "Se Me Acabó la Canción: An Ethnography of Nonconsenting Sterilizations among Mexican American Women in Los Angeles," in Mora and Del Castillo, *Mexican American Women,* 71–94; and Antonia Hernández, "Chicanas and the Issue of Involuntary Sterilization: Reforms Needed to Protect Informed Consent," *Chicano Law Review* 3 (1976): 3–37. Primary materials and court transcripts related to the case can be found in Carlos G. Vélez-Ibañez Papers (hereafter CGVIP), Sterilization Archive (here-

after SA), Collection 5, Chicano Studies Research Library (hereafter CSL), University of California at Los Angeles (hereafter UCLA).

116. "Madrigal v. Quilligan," CV 74-2057-JWC, Report's Transcript of Proceedings, Tuesday, May 30, 1978, SA 230–240, CGVIP, SA, 5, CSL, UCLA.

117. Ibid., 12.

118. Ibid., 19.

119. Ibid., 12.

120. Affidavit of DG, SA 110, CGVIP, SA, 5, CSL, UCLA. For confidentiality reasons, I have protected the names of the women who offered supporting affidavits.

121. Affidavit of VA, SA 132, CGVIP, SA, 5, CSL, UCLA.

122. Affidavit of MC, SA 135, CGVIP, SA, 5, CSL, UCLA.

123. "Madrigal v. Quilligan," CV 74-2057-JWC, Report's Transcript of Proceedings, Tuesday, May 30, 1978, SA 230–240, CGVIP, SA, 5, CSL, UCLA, p. 802.

124. Ibid., 797.

125. E. Gutiérrez, "Racial Politics of Reproduction"; Ordover, *American Eugenics.*

126. Quoted in "Plaintiffs Lose Suit over 10 Sterilizations," *Los Angeles Times,* July 1, 1978, Part 2, SA 40, clipping in CGVIP, SA, 5, CSL, UCLA; also quoted in E. Gutiérrez, "Racial Politics of Reproduction," 212.

127. Quoted in E. Gutiérrez, "Racial Politics of Reproduction," 213, and in Ainsworth, "Mother No More," 5.

128. Quoted in E. Gutiérrez, "Racial Politics of Reproduction," 208.

129. "For Immediate Release," Los Angeles Center for Law and Justice, July 10, 1978, SA 80, CGVIP, SA, CSL, UCLA.

130. See E. Gutiérrez, "Policing 'Pregnant Pilgrims,'" for an excellent explanation of this.

131. T. Shapiro, *Population Control Politics,* 137; Chicago Committee to End Sterilization Abuse, *Sterilization Abuse: A Task for the Women's Movement,* January 1977, Chicago Women's Liberation Union Herstory Archive, www.cwluherstory.com/ CWLUArchive/cesa.html. The Washington, D.C.–based Health Research Group (affiliated with Ralph Nader's organization Public Citizen) conducted the studies that catalyzed much of the guidelines formulation process, producing a total of four reports. The last, published in 1981, asserted that many states and hospitals were not complying with HEW regulations. See Daniel W. Sigelman, *Sterilization Abuse of the Nation's Poor under Medicaid and Other Federal Programs* (Washington, DC: Health Research Group, 1981).

132. Charles M. Goethe, press release, March 21, 1935, Harry H. Laughlin Papers, C-4–6, Special Collections, Truman State University.

133. In 1935, the less controversial Home Problems Section quietly absorbed the Commonwealth Club of California's Eugenics Section. Given the long tradition of debate at the Club, it is likely that eugenicists such as Goethe, who were adamant about mass sterilization in California, began to be challenged by members more interested in a softer eugenics based on public hygiene, not invasive surgery.

134. See Peter Novick, *The Holocaust in American Life* (Boston: Houghton Mifflin, 1999). For an example of this, see Herbert Aptheker, "Sterilization, Experimentation and Imperialism," *Political Affairs* 53 (1974): 37–48.

135. See Michelle Mitchell, *Righteous Propagation: African Americans and the Politics of Racial Destiny after Reconstruction* (Chapel Hill: University of North Carolina Press, 2004); and Gregory Michael Dorr, *Segregation's Science: Hereditarian Thought in Virginia, 1785 to the Present* (Chapel Hill: University of North Carolina Press, in press).

CONCLUSION

1. Gary Robertson, "Virginia Lawmakers OK Payout to Forced Sterilization Survivors," Reuters, February 26, 2015, www.reuters.com/article/2015/02/26 /us-usa-virginia-sterilization-idUSKBN0LU2D420150226.

2. Peter L. Hardin and Paul A. Lombardo, "Compensate Virginia's Sterilization Survivors," *Richmond Times-Dispatch*, February 25, 2014, A11. This budget package can compensate up to sixteen sterilization victims. It seems likely that more victims will come forward and that the Virginia legislature will need to revisit this issue in the near future.

3. Scott Neuman, "North Carolina Set to Compensate Forced Sterilization Victims," NPR, July 25, 2013, www.npr.org/blogs/thetwo-way/2013/07/25 /205547272/north-carolina-set-to-compensate-forced-sterilization-victims.

4. Eric Mennel, "Payments Start for N.C. Eugenics Victims, But Many Won't Qualify," NPR, October 31, 2014, www.npr.org/blogs/health/2014/10/31 /360355784/payments-start-for-n-c-eugenics-victims-but-many-wont-qualify.

5. See Alexandra Minna Stern, "Eugenics and Historical Memory in America," Viewpoints Section, *History Compass* 3, no. 1 (2005): 1–11.

6. Kevin Begos, Danielle Deaver, John Railey, and Scott Sexton, *Against Their Will: North Carolina's Sterilization Program* (Apalachicola, FL: Gray Oak Books, 2012). The original series appeared as "Against Their Will: North Carolina's Sterilization Program," *Winston-Salem Journal*, December 8–12, 2002.

7. See Paul A. Lombardo, ed., *A Century of Eugenics in America: From the Indiana Experiment to the Human Genome Era* (Bloomington: Indiana University Press, 2010); Alexandra Minna Stern, "We Cannot Make a Silk Purse Out of a Sow's Ear: Eugenics in the Hoosier Heartland, 1900–1960," *Indiana History Magazine* 103, no. 1 (2007): 3–38; and Alexandra Minna Stern, ed., "Improving Hoosiers: Indiana and the Wide Scope of American Eugenics," special issue, *Indiana Magazine of History* 106, no. 3 (2010), which includes my introduction and three essays on different dimensions of eugenics in Indiana.

8. For more information on Indiana's historical plaque recognizing sterilization victims, see Indiana University–Purdue University Indianapolis, Medical Humanities-Health Studies Program "Historical Marker," Indiana Eugenics: History and Legacy, 1907–2007, n.d., www.iupui.edu/~eugenics/events _Marker.htm; and Indiana Historical Bureau, "1907 Indiana Eugenics Law," Historical Markers, n.d., www.in.gov/history/markers/524.htm.

9. See the website of the Living Archives on Eugenics at http://eugenicsarchive.ca.

10. See Carl Ingram, "State Issues Apology for Policy of Sterilization," *Los Angeles Times,* March 12, 2003.

11. Senate Resolution No. 20, Senate, California Legislature, 2003–4 Regular Session.

12. In 2012 the Center for Genetics and Society (CGS) collaborated with scholars and activists on a one-day symposium that launched the Network to Address California's Eugenics History. Held at Boalt Law School at the University of California at Berkeley, the public portion of this event attracted a crowd of over two hundred people. See a video of the symposium, *Eugenics in California: A Legacy of the Past?*, YouTube, August 29, 2012, https://www.youtube.com/watch?v=BrF1QoG4g5o. The following year CGS, the Living Archives of Eugenics, Facing History and Ourselves, and this author organized another well-attended conference on November 1, 2013, hosted by the Paul K. Longmore Institute on Disability at San Francisco State University on the intersections of eugenics and disability. For the video of this conference, see *Future Past: Eugenics, Disability, and Brave New Worlds*, 2013, http://longmoreinstitute.sfsu.edu/futurepast.

13. See Aaron Zitner, "Davis' Apology Sheds No Light on Sterilization," *Los Angeles Times,* March 16, 2003.

14. Emil Guillermo, "Sterilization Victim First to Break Silence," *Stockton Record*, August 5, 2003; "No Money to Bury Man Sterilized by Force," *The Chart*, CNN, April 11, 2012, http://thechart.blogs.cnn.com/2012/04/11/no-money-to-bury-man-sterilized-by-force/.

15. See Mike Anton, "Forced Sterilization Once Seen as a Path to a Better World," *Los Angeles Times,* July 16, 2003; Robert B. Edgerton, *The Cloak of Competence*, 2nd ed. (Berkeley: University of California Press, 1993); Robert B. Edgerton, e-mail to author, January 27, 2004.

16. Erika Dyck's recent book on eugenic sterilization in Alberta benefits from and contributes to the Living Archives project. See Erika Dyck, *Facing Eugenics: Reproduction, Sterilization, and the Politics of Choice* (Toronto: University of Toronto Press, 2013).

17. "Jerry Brown Signs Bill Requiring Schools to Teach Gay History," *Sacramento Bee,* July 14, 2011, http://blogs.sacbee.com/capitolalertlatest/2011/07/jerry-brown-schools-gay-history-senate-bill-48.html. Facing History and Ourselves, an international educational organization with offices in Los Angeles and San Francisco that develops thoughtful and provocative curricula on racism, prejudice, and anti-Semitism, has played an important role in engaging high school teachers and students in the history of eugenics in California. One of their hallmark resource books is *Race and Membership in American History: The Eugenics Movement*. See their website at https://www.facinghistory.org/.

18. See Peter Schrag, *Not Fit for Our Society: Nativism and Immigration* (Berkeley: University of California Press, 2010); Leo R. Chavez, *The Latino Threat: Constructing Immigrants, Citizens, and the Nation* (Stanford, CA: Stanford University Press, 2008).

19. See Robert G. Resta, "Historical Aspects of Genetic Counseling: Why Was Maternal Age 35 Chosen as the Cut-Off for Offering Amniocentesis," *Medicina nei Secoli Arte e Scienza* 14, no. 3 (2002): 793–811.

20. See Campbell K. Brasington, "What I Wish I Knew Then . . . Reflections from Personal Experiences in Counseling about Down Syndrome," *Journal of Genetic Counseling* 16, no. 6 (2007): 731–34.

21. See, for example, Anne C. Madeo et al., "The Relationship between the Genetic Counseling Profession and the Disability Community: A Commentary," *American Journal of Medical Genetics* Part A 155, no. 8 (2011): 1777–85; Jan Hodgson and Jon Weil, "Commentary: How Individual and Profession-Level Factors Influence Discussion of Disability in Prenatal Genetic Counseling," *Journal of Genetic Counseling* 25, no. 21 (2012): 24–26.

22. Victor K. McElheny, *Drawing the Map of Life: Inside the Human Genome Project* (New York: Basic Books, 2010).

23. NICHD National Registry for Amniocentesis Study Group, "Midtrimester Amniocentesis for Prenatal Diagnosis," *Journal of the American Medical Association* 236, no. 13 (1976): 1475.

24. See Keith Wailoo and Stephen Pemberton, *The Troubled Dream of Genetic Medicine:* Ethnicity and Innovation in Tay-Sachs, Cystic Fibrosis, and Sickle Cell Disease (Baltimore: Johns Hopkins University Press, 2006), and Alondra Nelson, *Body and Soul: The Black Panther Party and the Fight against Medical Discrimination* (Minneapolis: University of Minnesota Press, 2011).

25. See Katie Stoll, "NIPS Is Not Diagnostic: Convincing Our Patients and Convincing Ourselves," *The DNA Exchange* (blog), July 11, 2013, http://thednaexchange.com/2013/07/11/guest-post-nips-is-not-diagnostic-convincing-our-patients-and-convincing-ourselves/.

26. Beth Daley and New England Center for Investigative Reporting, "Oversold and Misunderstood: Prenatal Screening Tests Prompt Abortion," New England Center for Investigative Reporting, December 14, 2014, http://features.necir.org/prenatal-testing.

27. Heather D. Boonstra and Elizabeth Nash, "A Surge of State Abortion Restrictions Puts Providers—and the Women They Service—in the Crosshairs," *Guttmacher Policy Review* 17, no. 1 (2014), www.guttmacher.org/pubs/gpr/17/1/gpr170109.html.

28. Chrissie Thompson, "Bill Would Ban Abortion after Down Syndrome Diagnosis," Cincinnati.com, February 10, 2015, www.cincinnati.com/story/news/2015/02/10/ohio-anti-abortion-group-lays-legislative-agenda/23171035/. On North Dakota, see RH Reality Check, "North Dakota Abortion Ban for Sex Selection and Genetic Abnormalities," RCHC Data, December 25, 2014, http://data.rhrealitycheck.org/law/north-dakota-abortion-ban-for-sex-selection-and-genetic-abnormalities-hb-1305/.

29. Nathaniel Comfort, *The Science of Human Perfection: How Genes Became the Heart of American Medicine* (Baltimore: Johns Hopkins University Press, 2012).

30. Nicholas Wade repackages arguments about the racial and biological basis of intelligence in his recent book *A Troublesome History: Genes, Race, and Human History* (New York: Penguin, 2014); for a trenchant critique of

Wade's arguments and assumptions, see Nathaniel Comfort, "Genetics: Under the Skin," *Nature* 513 (2014): 306–7.

31. Troy Duster identified this dynamic in his groundbreaking *Backdoor to Eugenics* (New York: Routledge, 2003).

32. Dorothy Roberts, *Fatal Invention: How Science, Politics, and Big Business Re-create Race in the Twenty-First Century* (New York: New Press, 2012).

Bibliography

ARCHIVES

California

Institute Archives, California Institute of Technology
  Ezra S. Gosney Papers and Records of the Human Betterment Foundation
California State Archives, Sacramento
  Legislative Histories (microfilm)
  Eugenic Sterilization Data Set, created by Alexandra Minna Stern and team
    using microfilmed records from the California Department of State Hos-
    pitals (1921–53).
University Archives, California State University, Sacramento
  Academic Senate Papers
  Charles M. Goethe Papers
Commonwealth Club of California (private collection). Since acquired by the
  Hoover Institution, Stanford University
Special Collections, Occidental College
  Paul Popenoe Papers
Save-the-Redwoods League Archives, San Francisco
Special Collections, Stanford University
  David Starr Jordan Papers
  Lewis M. Terman Papers
Hoover Institution, Stanford University
  David Starr Jordan Papers
  Survey of Race Relations Papers
Special Collections, University of California at Los Angeles
  John Randolph Haynes Papers
  J. Harold Williams Papers

Chicano Studies Library, University of California at Los Angeles
    Carlos G. Vélez-Ibañez Papers
Bancroft Library, University of California at Berkeley
    Samuel J. Holmes Papers
    Panama-Pacific International Exposition Papers
    Regional Oral History Office, Oral History Transcripts
    Save-the-Redwoods League Papers
    August Vollmer Papers

Texas

Special Collections, University of Texas at El Paso
    Institute of Oral History
U.S. Border Patrol Museum
    General Administrative Files

East Coast

Archives, American Philosophical Society Library, Philadelphia
    American Eugenics Society Papers
    Charles B. Davenport Papers
    Eugenics Record Office Papers
National Archives and Records Administration
    Record Group 85, Records of the Immigration and Naturalization Service
    Record Group 90, Records of the US Public Health Service

Other US Sites

American Heritage Center, University of Wyoming
    Paul Bowman Popenoe Papers
Special Collections, Truman State University, Kirksville, Missouri
    Harry H. Laughlin Papers
University Archives and Historical Collections, Michigan State University
    John Harvey Kellogg Papers
Bentley Library, University of Michigan
    John Harvey Kellogg Papers
    Clarence C. Little Papers

Mexico City

Archivo Histórico de la Secretaria de Relaciones Exteriores (Historical Archive
    of the Secretariat of Foreign Relations)
Archivo General de la Nación (National Archives)
    Ramo: Consejo Superior de Salubridad (Section: Superior Council of Health)

JOURNALS AND NEWSPAPERS

American Journal of Mental Delinquency
American Journal of School Hygiene

Aztlán
California and Western Medicine (California State Journal of Medicine)
Canal Record
Commonwealth/Transactions of the Commonwealth Club of California
El Grito
El Paso Herald
El Paso Times
Eugenical News/Eugenics Quarterly/Social Biology
Eugenics
Eugenics Society of Northern California (pamphlets)
Industrial Psychology
Journal of Applied Psychology
Journal of Educational Psychology
Journal of Experimental Psychology
Journal of Heredity
Journal of Juvenile Research/Journal of Delinquency
Journal of the American Medical Association
Los Angeles Times
National Parks Bulletin
NCHO Newsletter
Pacific Surgery and Medicine
Public Health Reports
San Francisco Chronicle
School and Society
School Hygiene
Scientific Monthly
Sexology
Southern California Practitioner
Southwest Medicine
Southwest Quarterly
Sunset
Survey Graphic
Transactions of the Commonwealth Club of California
USPHS Reports
Yosemite Nature Notes

PRIMARY SOURCES

Adams, Charles Francis. *The Panama Canal Zone: An Epochal Event in Sanitation.* Boston: Proceedings of the Massachusetts History Society, 1911.
"Against Their Will: North Carolina's Sterilization Program." *Winston-Salem Journal,* December 8–12, 2002.
Ainsworth, Diane. "Mother No More." *Reader: Los Angeles' Free Weekly,* January 26, 1979, 1, 4–5.
American Academy of Political and Social Science. *Public Recreation Facilities.* Philadelphia: American Academy of Political and Social Science, 1910.

Anton, Mike. "Forced Sterilization Once Seen as a Path to a Better World." *Los Angeles Times,* July 16, 2003.

Aptheker, Herbert. "Sterilization, Experimentation, and Imperialism." *Political Affairs* 53 (1974): 37–48.

Baker, Richard St. Barbe. *The Redwoods.* London: Lindsay Drummond, 1943.

Barry, John D. *The City of Domes.* San Francisco: John J. Newbegin, 1915.

Begos, Kevin, Danielle Deaver, John Railey, and Scott Sexton. "Against Their Will: North Carolina's Sterilization Program." *Winston-Salem Journal,* December 8–12, 2002.

Bennett, Laura R. "Department of Psychology in Los Angeles City Schools: A Study of the Mentally Different." *California State Journal of Medicine* 14, no. 3 (1916): 101–3.

Bjornstad, Randi. "Sterilization Apology Offered in Oregon." *Register-Guard* (Salem, OR), December 3, 2002.

Bogardus, Emory S. "Gangs of Mexican-American Youth." *Sociology and Social Research* 28, no. 1 (1943): 55–66.

———. "The Mexican Immigrant." *Journal of Applied Sociology* 11, no. 3 (1927): 470–88.

Boston Women's Health Book Collective. *Our Bodies, Ourselves: A Book by and for Women.* New York: Simon and Schuster, 1973.

Bowers, Paul E. "The Necessity for Sterilization." *Journal of Delinquency* 6, no. 5 (1921): 487–504.

Branigin, William. "Virginia Apologizes to the Victims of Sterilizations." *Washington Post,* May 3, 2002.

Brigham, Carl C. *A Study of American Intelligence.* Princeton, NJ: Princeton University Press, 1923.

Bryant, Harold C. "The Beginning of Yosemite's Educational Program." *Yosemite Nature Notes* 39, no. 7 (1960): 161–65.

Bryant, Harold C., and Wallace W. Atwood Jr. *Research and Education in the National Parks.* Washington, DC: Government Printing Office, 1932.

Buchanan, James A., and Gail Stuart, eds. *History of the Panama-Pacific International Exposition.* San Francisco: Pan-Pacific Press Association, 1916.

Buck, Pearl S. *The Child Who Never Grew.* 1950. Reprint, Vineland, NJ: Woodbine House, 1992.

Burbank, Luther. *An Architect of Nature.* London: Watts, 1939.

———. "Evolution and Variation with the Fundamental Significance of Sex." In *Official Proceedings of the Second National Conference on Race Betterment,* 50. Battle Creek, MI: Race Betterment Foundation, 1915.

———. *The Training of the Human Plant.* New York: Century, 1922.

Burch, Guy Irving, and Elmer Pendell. *Human Breeding and Survival: Population Roads to Peace or War.* New York: Penguin, 1945.

Butler, Fred O. "A Quarter of a Century's Experience in Sterilization of Mental Defectives in California." *American Journal of Mental Deficiency* 49, no. 4 (1945): 1–6. In California Legislature, *California's Compulsory Sterilization Policies.*

————. "Report of Medical Superintendent of the Sonoma State Home." In California State Department of Institutions, *First Biennial Report of the Department of Institutions of the State of California for the Two Years Ending June 30, 1922*, 80. Sacramento: California State Printing Office, 1923.

————. "Sterilization Procedure and Its Success in California Institutions." In California State Department of Institutions, *Third Biennial Report of the Department of Institutions of the State of California, Two Years Ending June 30, 1926*, 92–97. Sacramento: California State Printing Office, 1926.

Butler, Fred O., and Clarence J. Gamble. "Sterilization in a California School for the Mentally Deficient." *American Journal of Mental Deficiency* 51, no. 4 (1947): 745–47.

California Coalition for Women Prisoners. "Critical Statistics." Updated March 2007. Accessed February 13, 2015. www.womenprisoners.org/resources/critical_statistics.html.

"California Governor Signs Inmate Sterilization Ban." Reuters, September 25, 2014. www.reuters.com/article/2014/09/26/us-usa-california-prisons-idUSKC-NoHL07720140926. History of SB 1135. http://leginfo.legislature.ca.gov/faces/billNavClient.xhtml;jsessionid=2ccf804451d89d5c5834f82b9c3a.

California Legislature. *Report of 1915 Legislature Committee on Mental Deficiency and the Proposed Institution for the Care of Feeble-Minded and Epileptic Persons*. Whittier, CA: Whittier State School, Department of Printing Instruction, 1917.

————. *Statutes of California*. Sacramento: California State Printing Office.

California Legislature. Senate Select Committee on Genetics, Genetic Technologies, and Public Policy. *California's Compulsory Sterilization Policies, 1909–1979, July 16, 2003, Informational Hearing*. Ed. Lisa M. Matocq. Sacramento: California Publications, 2003.

California State Auditor. "Sterilization of Female Inmates: Some Inmates Were Sterilized Unlawfully, and the Safeguards Designed to Limit Occurrence of the Procedure Failed." Report 2013–120. June 2014. Sacramento, CA.

California State Board of Charities and Corrections. *Biennial Reports*. Sacramento: California State Printing Office, 1903–22.

California State Commission in Lunacy. *Biennial Reports*. Sacramento: California State Printing Office, 1896–1920.

California State Department of Institutions. *Biennial Reports*. Sacramento: California State Printing Office, 1920–45.

————. *Statistical Reports*. Sacramento: California State Printing Office, 1920–45.

California State Department of Mental Hygiene. *Statistical Reports*. Sacramento: California State Printing Office, 1946–54.

Center for Genetics and Society. "Assessment of the California Stem Cell Research and Cures Act." September 15, 2004 (revised September 22, 2004). www.genetics-and-society.org/policies/california/assessment.html.

Chicago Committee to End Sterilization Abuse. *Sterilization Abuse: A Task for the Women's Movement.* January 1977. Chicago Women's Liberation Union Herstory Archive. www.cwluherstory.com/ CWLUArchive/cesa.html.

Committee to Stop Forced Sterilization. *Stop Forced Sterilization Now!* Los Angeles: n.p., n.d.

Conservation Foundation. *In View of the Future, Annual Report of the Conservation Foundation.* New York: Conservation Foundation, 1949.

Cowdery, Karl M. "Analysis of Field Data Concerning One Hundred Delinquent Boys." *Journal of Delinquency* 1, no. 3 (1916): 129–53.

Cruz, Laurence M. "Eugenics Yields Dark Past." *Statesman Journal* (Salem, OR), December 1, 2002.

———. "Governor Apologizes for Eugenics." *Statesman Journal* (Salem, OR), December 3, 2002.

Daley, Beth, and New England Center for Investigative Reporting. "Oversold and Misunderstood: Prenatal Screening Tests Prompt Abortion." New England Center for Investigative Reporting, December 14, 2014. http://features .necir.org/prenatal-testing.

Davenport, Charles B. *Heredity in Relation to Eugenics.* New York: Henry Holt, 1911.

———. *The Trait Book.* ERO Bulletin 6. Cold Spring Harbor, NY: Eugenics Record Office, 1912.

Davenport, Charles B., Clyde E. Keeler, Maude Slye, and Madge Thurlow Macklin. *Medical Genetics and Eugenics.* Philadelphia: Women's Medical College of Pennsylvania, 1940.

Delmet, Don T. "A Study of the Mental and Scholastic Abilities of Mexican Children in the Elementary School." *Journal of Juvenile Research* 14, no. 4 (1930): 267–79.

Dixon, Samuel G. "Race Betterment." In *Official Proceedings of the Second National Conference on Race Betterment*, 9. Battle Creek, MI: Race Betterment Foundation, 1915.

Dugdale, Richard L. *The Jukes: A Study in Crime, Pauperism, Disease, and Heredity.* New York: G.P. Putnam's Sons, 1877.

Dunn, L.C., and Th. Dobzhansky. *Heredity, Race, and Society.* New York: Mentor Books, 1946.

Ehrlich, Paul. *The Population Bomb.* San Francisco: Sierra Club/Ballantine Books, 1968.

Ellsworth, Rodney Sydes. *The Giant Sequoia.* Oakland, CA: J.D. Berger, 1924.

Estabrook, Arthur. *The Jukes in 1915.* Washington, DC: Carnegie Institution of Washington, 1916.

Federal Writers' Project of the Works Progress Administration for the State of California. *California: A Guide to the Golden State.* New York: Hastings House, 1939.

Feist, Paul. "Davis Apologizes for State's Sterilization Program." *San Francisco Chronicle,* March 12, 2003.

Fenton, Norman. *The Delinquent Boy and the Correctional School.* Claremont, CA: Claremont Colleges Guidance Center, 1935.

Fenton, Norman, and Paul Popenoe. "Twenty-Five Years of Eugenic Sterilization." *Journal of Juvenile Research* 19, no. 4 (1935): 201–4.

Fernald, Grace M., and Ellen B. Sullivan. "Personnel Work with the Los Angeles Police Department." *Journal of Delinquency* 10, no. 1 (1926): 252–67.

Fernández, Raul. "The Policy Economy of Stereotypes." *Aztlán* 1, no. 2 (1970):
39–45.

Ferran, Manuel, coord. *Health Cultural Awareness Conference: "Viva la Diferencia."* Published conference proceedings. Albuquerque: New Mexico
Regional Medical Program, 1972.

Friedan, Betty. *The Feminine Mystique.* 1963. Reprint, New York: W. W. Norton, 1983.

"Full Text of State's Apology Regarding Eugenics." *Statesman Journal* (Salem,
OR), December 3, 2002.

Galton, Francis. *Essays in Eugenics.* London: Eugenics Education Society, 1909.

Gamble, Clarence J. "Preventive Sterilization in 1948." *Journal of the American Medical Association* 141, no. 11 (1949): 773.

———. "Sterilization of the Mentally Deficient under State Laws." *American
Journal of Mental Deficiency* 51, no. 2 (1946): 164–69.

Garcia, John. "Intelligence Testing: Quotients, Quotas, and Quackery." In *Chicano Psychology,* ed. Joe L. Martinez Jr., 197–212. New York: Academic
Press, 1977.

Garcia, Patti. "Forced Sterilization of Third World Women." *La Razón Mestiza,* Summer 1975, n.p.

Garth, Thomas R. "The Industrial Psychology of the Immigrant Mexican."
Industrial Psychology 1 (1926): 183–87.

———. "The Intelligence of Mexican School Children." *School and Society* 27,
no. 705 (1928): 791–94.

Gillett, James B. *Six Years with the Texas Rangers, 1875–1881.* 1921. Reprint,
Lincoln: University of Nebraska Press, 1976.

Gina. "Written in Anger." *It Ain't Me Babe,* April 28, 1970, 6.

Goddard, Henry Herbert. *The Kallikak Family: A Study in the Heredity of
Feeble-Mindedness.* New York: Macmillan, 1912.

Goethe, Charles M. *The Elfin Forest.* Sacramento, CA: Keystone Press, 1953.

———. "Extinction of the Inca Highcastes." *Eugenical News* 22, no. 4 (1937):
53–57.

———. "Field Studies on the Eugenical Aspects of Mexican Immigration."
Eugenical News 12, no. 8 (1927): 109.

———. *Garden Philosopher.* Sacramento, CA: Keystone Press, 1955.

———. *Geogardening.* Sacramento, CA: Keystone Press, 1948.

———. "The Influx of Mexican Amerinds." *Eugenics* 2, no. 1 (January 1929):
6–9.

———. *Mother Lode Gold Mining Stories.* Natural History Series No. 1. Sacramento, CA: Sacramento State College Publications, 1950.

———. "Nature Study in National Parks Interpretive Movement." *Yosemite
Nature Notes* 39, no. 7 (1960): 156–58.

———. "Patriotism and Racial Standards." *Eugenical News* 21, no. 4 (1936):
65–69.

———. *Seeking to Serve.* Sacramento, CA: Keystone Press, 1949.

———. *Sierran Cabin . . . from Skyscraper: A Tale of the Sierran Piedmont.* Sacramento, CA: Keystone Press, 1943.

———. *War Profits and Better Babies.* Sacramento, CA: Keystone Press, 1946.

———. *What Will Your Greatgrandchildren Face?* Sacramento, CA: n.p., n.d.

———. *What's in a Name?* Sacramento, CA: Keystone Press, 1949.

———. "When Help Came from the Mountains." *Yosemite Nature Notes* 29, no. 1 (1950): 3.

Gordon, Kate. "Report on Psychological Tests of Orphan Children." *Journal of Delinquency* 4, no. 1 (1919): 46–56.

Gorgas, William C. *Report of the Department of Health of the Isthmian Canal Commission for the Month of January, 1906.* Washington, DC: Government Printing Office, 1906.

———. *Sanitation in Panama.* New York: D. Appleton, 1915.

Gosney, Ezra S., and Paul Popenoe. *Sterilization for Human Betterment: A Summary of Results of 6,000 Operations in California, 1909–1929.* New York: Macmillan, 1929.

Grant, Joseph D. *Redwoods and Reminiscences.* San Francisco: Save-the-Redwoods League and Menninger Foundation, 1973.

———. *Saving California's Redwoods.* Berkeley: Save-the-Redwoods League/ University of California at Berkeley, 1922.

Grant, Madison. *The Conquest of a Continent; or, The Expansion of Races in America.* New York: Charles Scribner's Sons, 1933.

———. *The Passing of the Great Race; or, The Racial Basis of European History.* 3rd ed. New York: Charles Scribner's Sons, 1920.

———. "Saving the Redwoods." *National Geographic Magazine* 37, no. 6 (1920): 519–36.

———. "Saving the Redwoods: An Account of the Movement during 1919 to Preserve the Redwoods of California." *Zoological Society Bulletin* 22, no. 5 (1919): 91–118.

Grubbs, S.B. "Destroying Lice on Typhus Fever Suspects." *Public Health Reports* 31 (October 20, 1916): 2918–23.

Guillermo, Emil. "Sterilization Victim First to Break Silence." *Stockton Record,* August 5, 2003.

Guttmacher, Alan F. "The Place of Sterilization." In *The Population Crisis: Implications and Plans for Action,* ed. Larry K.Y. Ng and Stuart Mudd, 201–6. Bloomington: Indiana University Press, 1965.

Hardin, Peter. "Apology for Eugenics Set: Warner Action Makes Virginia First State to Denounce Movement." *Richmond Times-Dispatch,* May 2, 2002.

Hardin, Peter L., and Paul A. Lombardo. "Compensate Virginia's Sterilization Survivors." *Richmond Times-Dispatch,* February 25, 2014, A11.

Haynes, John R. "Care of the Insane." In California State Board of Charities and Corrections, *Eighth Biennial Report of the State Board of Charities and Corrections of the State of California from July 1, 1916 to June 30, 1918,* 62. Sacramento: California State Printing Office, 1918.

Health Research Group. *A Health Research Group Study on Surgical Sterilization: Present Abuses and Proposed Regulations.* Washington, DC: Health
Research Group, 1973.

Hellyer, Clement David. *The U.S. Border Patrol.* New York: Random House,
1963.

Hernández, Antonia. "Chicanas and the Issue of Involuntary Sterilization: Reforms
Needed to Protect Informed Consent." *Chicano Law Review* 3 (1976): 3–37.

"History of Oregon Eugenics Law." *Oregonian,* June 30, 2002.

Hoisholt, A. W. "The Commitment of the Insane." In *Official Proceedings of
the Second National Conference on Race Betterment,* 107–13. Battle Creek,
MI: Race Betterment Foundation, 1915.

Holmes, Samuel J. "An Argument against Mexican Immigration." *Transactions
of the Commonwealth Club of California,* part 2, 2, no. 12 (1926): 21–27.

———. *A Bibliography of Eugenics.* Berkeley: University of California Press,
1924.

———. *The Trend of the Race: A Study of Present Tendencies in the Biological
Development of Civilized Mankind.* New York: Harcourt, Brace, 1921.

Human Betterment Foundation. *Collected Papers on Eugenic Sterilization in
California: A Critical Study of Results in 6000 Cases.* Pasadena, CA: Human
Betterment Foundation, 1930.

Indiana Historical Bureau. "1907 Indiana Eugenics Law." Historical Markers,
n.d. www.in.gov/history/markers/524.htm.

Indiana University–Purdue University Indianapolis, Medical Humanities-
Health Studies Program. "Historical Marker." Indiana Eugenics: History
and Legacy, 1907–2007, n.d. www.iupui.edu/~eugenics/events_Marker.htm.

Ingram, Carl. "State Issues Apology for Policy of Sterilization." *Los Angeles
Times,* March 12, 2003.

Jay, Karla. *Tales of the Lavender Menace: A Memoir of Liberation.* New York:
Basic Books, 1999.

"Jerry Brown Signs Bill Requiring Schools to Teach Gay History." *Sacramento
Bee,* July 14, 2011. http://blogs.sacbee.com/capitolalertlatest/2011/07/jerry
-brown-schools-gay-history-senate-bill-48.html.

Johnson, Bascom. *Moral Conditions in San Francisco and at the Panama Pacific
Exposition.* New York: American Social Hygiene Association, 1915.

Johnson, Corey G. "Calif. Prison Doctor Linked to Sterilizations No Stranger
to Controversy." Center for Investigative Reporting, February 13, 2014.
http://cironline.org/reports/calif-prison-doctor-linked-sterilizations-no-
stranger-controversy-5859.

———. "Female Inmates Sterilized in California Prisons without Approval."
Center for Investigative Reporting, July 7, 2013. http://cironline.org/reports
/female-inmates-sterilized-california-prisons-without-approval-4917.

———. "Lawmakers Call for Investigation into Sterilization of Female
Inmates." Center for Investigative Reporting, July 10, 2013. http://cironline
.org/reports/lawmakers-call-investigation-sterilization-female-inmates-4961.

Joint Committee on Recreational Survey of Federal Lands. *Recreation Resources
of Federal Lands.* Washington, DC: National Conference on Outdoor Recreation, 1928.

Jordan, David Starr. *The Blood of the Nation: A Study of the Decay of Races through the Survival of the Unfit.* Boston: American Unitarian Association, 1910.

———. *California and the Californians.* San Francisco: Whitaker-Ray, 1903.

———. *The Days of Man: Being Memories of a Naturalist, Teacher, and Minor Prophet of Democracy.* 2 vols. Yonkers-on-Hudson, NY: World Book, 1922.

———. "Eugenics and War." In *Official Proceedings of the Second National Conference on Race Betterment,* 13, Battle Creek, MI: Race Betterment Foundation, 1915.

———, ed. *Footnotes to Evolution: A Series of Popular Addresses on the Evolution of Life.* New York: D. Appleton, 1907.

Jordan, David Starr, and Harvey Ernest Jordan. *War's Aftermath: A Preliminary Study of the Eugenics of War.* Boston: Houghton Mifflin, 1914.

Jordan, David Starr, and Sarah Louise Kimball. *Your Family Tree.* New York: D. Appleton, 1929.

Kearney, Jack. *Tracking: A Blueprint for Learning How.* El Cajon, CA: Pathways Press, 1978.

Kellogg, J.H. "The Eugenics Registry." In *Official Proceedings of the Second National Conference on Race Betterment,* 79. Battle Creek, MI: Race Betterment Foundation, 1915.

Knight, Oliver. Foreword to *Six Years with the Texas Rangers, 1875–1881,* by James B. Gillett. 1921. Reprint, Lincoln: University of Nebraska Press 1976.

Koedt, Anne. "The Myth of the Vaginal Orgasm." In *Notes from the Second Year,* ed. Shulamith Firestone, 37–41. New York: Radical Feminists, 1970.

Laosa, Luis M., Alvin G. Burstein, and Harry W. Martin. "Mental Health Consultation in a Rural Chicano Community: Crystal City." *Aztlán* 6, no. 3 (1976): 433–53.

Laughlin, Harry H. *Eugenical Sterilization in the United States.* Chicago: Psychopathic Laboratory of the Municipal Court of Chicago, 1922.

Laughlin, Harry H., with Charles B. Davenport. *How to Make a Eugenical Family Study.* ERO Bulletin 13. Cold Spring Harbor, NY: Eugenics Record Office, 1915.

Lewis, Sinclair. *Arrowsmith.* 1924. Reprint, New York: Signet Classic, 1980.

Limón, José E. "Stereotyping and Chicano Resistance: An Historical Dimension." *Aztlán* 4, no. 2 (1973): 257–70.

Lord, Myrtle Shaw. *A Sacramento Saga: Fifty Years of Achievement—Chamber of Commerce Leadership.* Sacramento, CA: Sacramento Chamber of Commerce, 1946.

Los Angeles Police Department. *Law Enforcement in Los Angeles.* 1924. Reprint, New York: Arno Press, 1975.

Mathews, Julia. "A Survey of 341 Delinquent Girls in California." *Journal of Delinquency* 8, nos. 3–4 (1923): 196–231.

Mears, James Ewing. *The Triumph of American Medicine in the Construction of the Panama Canal.* Philadelphia: Wm. J. Dornan, 1911.

Mendel, Gregor. "Experiments in Plant Hybridization." In *Classic Papers in Genetics,* ed. James Peters, 1–20. Englewood Cliffs, NJ: Prentice Hall, 1959.

Mennel, Eric. "Payments Start for N.C. Eugenics Victims, But Many Won't Qualify." NPR, October 31, 2014. www.npr.org/blogs/health/2014/10/31/360355784/payments-start-for-n-c-eugenics-victims-but-many-wont-qualify.

Merriam, John C. *A Living Link in History.* Pamphlet. Berkeley: Save-the-Redwoods League, [1934].

———. *The Living Past.* New York: Charles Scribner's Sons, 1930.

Miller, Loye H. "The Nature Guide Movement in National Parks." *Yosemite Nature Notes* 39, no. 7 (1960): 159–60.

Montagu, M. F. Ashley. "The Concept of Race in the Human Species in Light of Genetics." *Journal of Heredity* 32, no. 8 (1941): 243–47.

Morales, Armando. "The Impact of Class Discrimination on the Mental Health of Mexican-Americans." In *Chicanos: Social and Psychological Perspectives,* ed. Nathaniel N. Wagner and Marsha J. Haug, 257–62. St. Louis, MO: C. V. Mosby, 1971.

———. "Mental and Public Health Issues: The Case of the Mexican Americans in Los Angeles." *El Grito* 3, no. 2 (1970): 3–11.

Muir, John. *Our National Parks.* Cambridge, MA: Riverside Press, 1901.

———. "Save the Redwoods." *Sierra Club Bulletin* 11, no. 1 (1920): 1–4.

Muller, Hermann J. "Better Genes for Tomorrow." In *The Population Crisis: Implications and Plans for Action,* ed. Larry K. Y. Ng and Stuart Mudd, 223–47. Bloomington: Indiana University Press, 1965.

National Association for the Advancement of Colored People (NAACP). *NAACP 1940–55. General Office File. Zoot Suit Riots, 1943–44.* Microfilm, part 7, series A, reel 29. Frederick, MD: University Publications of America.

Nelles, Fred C. "Changes in the Nature of the Population of Whittier State School." *Journal of Delinquency* 9, no. 6 (1925): 231–32.

Neuman, Scott. "North Carolina Set to Compensate Forced Sterilization Victims." NPR, July 25, 2013. www.npr.org/blogs/thetwo-way/2013/07/25/205547272/north-carolina-set-to-compensate-forced-sterilization-victims.

Ng, Larry K. Y., and Stuart Mudd, eds. *The Population Crisis: Implications and Plans for Action.* Bloomington: Indiana University Press, 1965.

"No Money to Bury Man Sterilized by Force." *The Chart,* CNN, April 11, 2012. http://thechart.blogs.cnn.com/2012/04/11/no-money-to-bury-man-sterilized-by-force/.

Odens, Peter. *The Desert Trackers: Men of the Border Patrol.* Yuma, AZ: Southwestern Printers, 1975.

Official Proceedings of the Second National Conference on Race Betterment. Battle Creek, MI: Race Betterment Foundation, 1915.

Olmedo, Esteban L. "Psychological Testing and the Chicano: A Reassessment." In *Chicano Psychology,* ed. Joe L. Martinez Jr., 175–95. New York: Academic Press, 1977.

Osborn, Fairfield. *Our Plundered Planet.* Boston: Little, Brown, 1948.

Osborn, Frederick. "Eugenics and Modern Life: Retrospect and Prospect." *Eugenical News* 31, no. 3 (1946): 33–35.

———. *The Future of Human Heredity: An Introduction to Eugenics in Modern Society.* New York: Weybright and Talley, 1968.

———. *Preface to Eugenics.* Rev. ed. New York: Harper, 1951.

———. "The Protection and Improvement of Man's Genetic Inheritance." In *The Population Crisis: Implications and Plans for Action,* ed. Larry K. Y. Ng and Stuart Mudd, 215–22. Bloomington: Indiana University Press, 1965.

"Panama-Pacific International Exposition Will Display Achievements of Eugenic Societies." *Pacific Medical Journal* 56, no. 11 (November 1913): 649.

Pangburn, Weaver W. "Recreation and Eugenics." *Eugenical News* 24, no. 1 (1939): 53–57.

Parsons, Ardee. *A Day at the Exposition.* Pamphlet. N.p., n.d.

Paschal, Franklin C., and Louis R. Sullivan. *Racial Influences in the Mental and Physical Development of Mexican Children.* Comparative Psychology Monographs 3:14. San Francisco: R and E Research Associates, 1925.

Perkins, Clifford Alan. *Border Patrol: With the U.S. Immigration Service on the Mexican Boundary, 1910–54.* El Paso: Texas Western Press, University of Texas at El Paso, 1978.

Pierce, C. C. "Combating Typhus Fever on the Mexican Border." *Public Health Reports* 32 (March 23, 1917): 426–29.

Pitts, Eugene H. "Educating the Public to Eugenics." *Eugenical News* 23, no. 1 (1938): 1–3.

———. "Radio Lectures on Eugenics by Dr. E. H. Pitts." *Eugenical News* 23, no. 1 (1938): 3.

Popenoe, Paul. *Be It Ever So Jumbled There's No Place Like Home.* New York: Army and Navy Department of the YMCA, 1945.

———. *The Conservation of the Family.* Baltimore: Williams and Wilkins, 1926.

———. "Cooperation in Family Relations." *Journal of Home Economics* 26, no. 8 (1934): 483–86.

———. "Date Growing in California and Arizona." In *Date Culture in Southern California,* by George Wharton James, Paul Popenoe, and Ralph D. Cornell, 13–33. Los Angeles: Out West, 1912.

———. *Date Growing in the Old World and the New.* Altadena, CA: West India Gardens, 1913.

———. "Eugenics after the War." *Eugenical News* 28 (1943): 19–20.

———. "Eugenics and Family Relations." *Eugenical News* 25, no. 1 (1940): 70–74.

———. "The Extent of Mental Disease and Defect in the American Population." *Journal of Juvenile Research* 13, no. 2 (1929): 97–103.

———. "A Family Consultation Service." *Journal of Social Hygiene* 17, no. 6 (1931): 309–21.

———. "Forty Years of the AIFR." *Family Life* 30, no. 2 (1970): 1–4.

———. "The Institute of Family Relations." *Eugenics* 3, no. 4 (1930): 134–37.

———. "The Institute of Family Relations." *Journal of Home Economics* 22, no. 11 (1930): 906–7.

———. "Introverts and Extroverts." *Scientific American,* October 1937, 197–200.

———. "Marriage Counseling." *General Practitioner* 6, no. 4 (1952): 53–60.

———. *Marriage Is What You Make It.* New York: Macmillan, 1950.

———. *Modern Marriage: A Handbook for Men.* New York: Macmillan, 1925.

———. "Natural Selection in Man." In *Official Proceedings of the Second National Conference on Race Betterment*, 54–61. Battle Creek, MI: Race Betterment Foundation, 1915.

———. "Origin of the Date Palm." *Journal of Heredity* 5, no. 11 (1914): 498–508.

———. *Practical Applications of Heredity*. Baltimore: Williams and Wilkins, 1930.

———. *Problems of Human Reproduction*. Baltimore: Williams and Wilkins, 1926.

———. "Toward an American Population Policy." *Eugenical News* 30 (1945): 20–21.

———. "Trends in Human Sterilization." *Eugenical News* 22, no. 3 (1937): 42–43.

Popenoe, Paul, and Dorothy Cameron Disney. *Can This Marriage Be Saved?* New York: Macmillan, 1953.

Popenoe, Paul, and E. S. Gosney. *Twenty-Eight Years of Sterilization in California*. Pasadena, CA: Human Betterment Foundation, 1938.

Popenoe, Paul, and Roswell H. Johnson. *Applied Eugenics*. New York: Macmillan, 1918; 2nd ed., 1933.

Pullenza de Ortiz, Patricia. "Chicano Children and Intelligence." *Aztlán* 10 (1979): 69–83.

Race Betterment Foundation. *Race Betterment Exhibit*. Battle Creek, MI: n.p., 1915.

Rak, Mary Kidder. *Border Patrol*. Boston: Houghton Mifflin, 1938.

———. *They Guard the Gates: The Way of Life on the American Borders*. Evanston, IL: Row, Peterson, 1941.

Reid, Deborah. "Reproductive Justice Advocates: Don't Roll Back Sterilization Consent Rules." RH Reality Check, April 2, 2014. http://rhrealitycheck.org/article/2014/04/02/reproductive-justice-advocates-dont-roll-back-sterilization-consent-rules/.

Research Staff of Whittier State School. "The Present Status of Juvenile Delinquency in California." *Journal of Delinquency* 5, no. 5 (1920): 183–89.

RH Reality Check. "North Dakota Abortion Ban for Sex Selection and Genetic Abnormalities." RCHC Data, December 25, 2014. http://data.rhreality-check.org/law/north-dakota-abortion-ban-for-sex-selection-and-genetic-abnormalities-hb-1305/.

Robertson, Gary. "Virginia Lawmakers OK Payout to Forced Sterilization Survivors." Reuters, February 26, 2015. www.reuters.com/article/2015/02/26/us-usa-virginia-sterilization-idUSKBN0LU2D420150226.

Rodrigues-Triaz, Helen. "Sterilization Abuse." In *Biological Woman—The Convenient Myth*, ed. Ruth Hubbard, Mary Sue Henifin, and Barbara Fried, 147–60. Cambridge, MA: Schenkman, 1982.

———. *Women and the Health Care System; Sterilization Abuse*. New York: Barnard College Women's Center, 1978. Two lectures given at Barnard College in 1976.

Rogers, Dale Evans. *Angel Unaware*. 1953. Reprint, Westwood, NJ: Fleming H. Revell, 1953.

Rucker, W. C., and C. C. Pierce. *United States Public Health Service Exhibit at the Panama-Pacific International Exposition, San Francisco, 1915.* Suppl. no. 27, USPHS Reports. Washington, DC: Government Printing Office, 1915.

Russell, Carl. "A 40th Anniversary." *Yosemite Nature Notes* 39, no. 7 (1960): 153–55.

———. "Revealing Parks to the People." *Sierra Club Bulletin* (1960): 4–6.

Sabagh, G., and R. B. Edgerton. "Sterilized Mental Defectives Look at Eugenic Sterilization." *Eugenics Quarterly* 9, no. 4 (1962): 213–22.

Sanchez, Armand J. "The Definers and the Defined: A Mental Health Issue." *El Grito* 4, no. 4 (1971): 4–35.

Save-the-Redwoods League. *Saving the Redwoods, 1948–49.* Berkeley: Save-the-Redwoods League, 1949.

Schutt, Harold G. "Advanced Police Methods in Berkeley." *National Municipal Review* 11, no. 3 (1922): 80–85.

Sheldon, William H. "The Intelligence of Mexican School Children." *School and Society* 19, no. 475 (1924): 139–42.

Sigelman, Daniel W. *Sterilization Abuse of the Nation's Poor under Medicaid and Other Federal Programs.* Washington, DC: Health Research Group, 1981.

Simpson, Anna Pratt. *Problems Women Solved: Being the Story of the Woman's Board of the Panama-Pacific International Exposition; What Vision, Enthusiasm, Work and Co-operation Accomplished.* San Francisco: Woman's Board, 1915.

Slater, Jack. "Sterilization: Newest Threat to the Poor." *Ebony,* October 1973, 150–56.

Smithsonian Institution. *The Exhibits of the Smithsonian Institution at the Panama-Pacific International Exposition.* San Francisco: Press of H. S. Crocker, 1915.

Smyth, Margaret H. "Psychiatric History and Development in California." *American Journal of Psychiatry* 94 (1938): 1223–36.

Society for the Study of Social Biology. "A New Name—Society for the Study of Social Biology (formerly the American Eugenics Society)." *Social Biology* 20, no. 1 (1973): 1.

Steen, Murphy J. F. *Twenty-Five Years a U.S. Border Patrolman.* Dallas, TX: Royal, 1958.

Stelloh, Tim. "California's Great Prison Experiment." *Nation,* July 5, 2013. www.thenation.com/article/174680/californias-great-prison-experiment#.

"Sterilization Program Targeted Women, Blacks in Later Years." *Associated Press,* December 9, 2002.

Stoll, Katie. "NIPS Is Not Diagnostic: Convincing Our Patients and Convincing Ourselves." *The DNA Exchange* (blog), July 11, 2013. http://thednaexchange.com/2013/07/11/guest-post-nips-is-not-diagnostic-convincing-our-patients-and-convincing-ourselves/.

Student Nonviolent Coordinating Committee. *Genocide in Mississippi.* Atlanta, GA: Student Nonviolent Coordinating Committee, 1964.

Tansey, Bernadette. "Proposition 71: Stem Cell Initiative Aids State." *San Francisco Chronicle,* November 4, 2004.

Tappan, J. W. "Protective Health Measures on United States–Mexico Border." *Journal of the American Medical Association* 87, no. 13 (1926): 1022–26.

Taylor, Robert M., and Lucile P. Morrison. *Taylor-Johnson Temperament Analysis Manual*. 1966. Reprint, Thousand Oaks, CA: Psychological Publications, 1996.

Terman, Lewis M. *The Measurement of Intelligence: An Explanation of and a Complete Guide for the Use of the Stanford Revision and Extension of the Binet-Simon Intelligence Scale*. New York: Houghton Mifflin, 1916.

———. *Research in Mental Deviation among Children: A Statement of the Aims and Purposes of the Buckel Foundation*. Research Laboratory of the Buckel Foundation, Department of Education, Bulletin No. 2. Stanford, CA: Stanford University, 1915.

Terman, Lewis M., Virgil E. Dickson, A. H. Sutherland, Raymond H. Franzen, C. R. Tupper, and Grace Fernald. *Intelligence Tests and School Reorganization*. Yonkers-on-Hudson, NY: World Book, 1923.

Terman, Lewis M., and Catharine Cox Miles. *Sex and Personality: Studies in Masculinity and Femininity*. New York: Russell and Russell, 1936.

Thompson, Chrissie. "Bill Would Ban Abortion after Down Syndrome Diagnosis." Cincinnati.com, February 10, 2015. www.cincinnati.com/story/news/2015/02/10/ohio-anti-abortion-group-lays-legislative-agenda/23171035/.

Todd, Frank Morton. *Eradicating Plague from San Francisco*. San Francisco: Press of C. A. Murdock, 1909.

———. *The Story of the Exposition: Being the Official History of the International Celebration Held at San Francisco in 1915 to Commemorate the Discovery of the Pacific Ocean and the Construction of the Panama Canal*. 5 vols. New York: G. P. Putnam's Sons, 1921.

Todd, Frank Morton, and George Sterling. *An Account of the Closing Ceremonies of the Panama-Pacific International Exposition, San Francisco, Dec. 4, 1915*. San Francisco: Blair-Murdock, 1915.

Uhrbrock, Richard Stephen. *An Analysis of the Downey Will-Temperament Tests*. New York: Teacher's College, Columbia University, 1928.

United Nations Educational, Scientific, and Cultural Organization (UNESCO). *The Race Concept: Results of an Inquiry*. Paris: UNESCO, 1952.

Unrau, Harlan D. *Historic Resource Study (Historic Component): Ellis Island, Statue of Liberty National Monument, New York–New Jersey*. Vol. 3. Washington, DC: US Department of the Interior, National Park Service, 1984.

US Bureau of the Census. "Table E-7. White Population of Mexican Origin, for the United States, Regions, Divisions, and States: 1910 to 1930." www.census.gov/population/documentation.

US Department of Labor and Bureau of Immigration. *Annual Report of the Commissioner General of Immigration to the Secretary of Labor for the Fiscal Year Ended June 30, 1930*. Washington, DC: Government Printing Office, 1930.

US House of Representatives. *Immigration Border Patrol Hearings before the United States House Committee on Immigration and Naturalization, 75th Congress, 2nd Session, on January 15, 1930*. Washington, DC: Government Printing Office, 1930.

———. *Immigration from the Countries of the Western Hemisphere. Hearings before the Committee on Immigration and Naturalization, 71st Congress, March 14, 1930*. Washington, DC: Government Printing Office, 1930.

———. *Seasonal Agricultural Laborers from Mexico*. Washington, DC: Government Printing Office, 1926.

———. *To Establish a Border Patrol: Hearings before the United States House Committee on the Judiciary, Subcommittee No. 1 (Judiciary), Sixty-Ninth Congress, First Session, on Apr. 12, 19, 1926*. Washington, DC: Government Printing Office, 1926.

US Marine-Hospital Service. *Annual Reports of the Surgeon General of the Marine-Hospital Service of the United States*. Washington, DC: Government Printing Office, fiscal years 1891–1901.

US National Park Service. *A Study of the Park and Recreation Problem of the United States*. Washington, DC: Government Printing Office, 1941.

US Public Health Service. *Annual Reports of the Surgeon General of the Public Health Service of the United States*. Washington, DC: Government Printing Office, fiscal years 1912–30.

———. *The Control of Communicable Diseases: Report of the American Public Health Association Committee on Standard Regulations Appointed in October, 1916*. Miscellaneous Publication no. 24. Washington, DC: Government Printing Office, 1920.

———. *Manual of the Mental Examination of Aliens*. Miscellaneous Publication no. 18. Washington, DC: Government Printing Office, 1918.

———. *Official List of Commissioned and Other Officers of the United States Public Health Service*. Washington, DC: Government Printing Office, 1914–16.

———. *Regulations Governing the Medical Inspection of Aliens*. Miscellaneous Publication no. 5. Washington, DC: Government Printing Office, 1917.

US Public Health Service and Marine-Hospital Service. *Annual Reports of the Surgeon General of the Public Health and Marine-Hospital Service of the United States*. Washington, DC: Government Printing Office, fiscal years 1902–11.

Vaca, Nick C. "The Mexican-American in the Social Sciences, 1912–1970, Part I (1912–1935)," *El Grito* 3, no. 3 (1970): 3–24; "Part II (1936–1970)," *El Grito* 4, no. 1 (1970): 17–51.

Vásquez, James. "Measurement of Intelligence and Language Differences." *Aztlán* 3, no. 1 (1972): 155–61.

Vollmer, August. *The Criminal*. Brooklyn: Foundation Press, 1949.

———. *The Police and Modern Society*. Berkeley: University of California Press, 1936.

Watson, James D. *The Double Helix: A Personal Account of the Discovery of the Structure of DNA*. New York: Atheneum, 1968.

Weisstein, Naomi. "Kinder, Küche, Kirche as Scientific Law: Psychology Constructs the Female." *motive: on the liberation of women* 29, nos. 6–7 (1969): 78–85.

Whitman, Walt. *Leaves of Grass*. London: G. P. Putnam's Sons, 1897.

Wickson, Edward J. "Luther Burbank: The Man, His Methods, and His Achievements." *Sunset* 8, no. 2 (1901): 57–69; 8, no. 4 (1902): 145–56; 8, no. 6 (1902): 277–85; and 9, no. 2 (1902): 101–12.

Widney, Joseph P. *The Greater City of Los Angeles: A Plan for the Development of Los Angeles City as a Great World Health Center.* Los Angeles: n.p., 1938.

———. *Race Life of the Aryan Peoples.* 2 vols. New York: Funk and Wagnalls, 1907.

———. *The Three Americas: Their Racial Past and the Dominant Racial Factors of Their Future.* Los Angeles: Pacific Publishing, 1935.

Wilbur, Ray Lyman. "Broadening Horizons: An Interview with Ray Lyman Wilbur." *Sunset* 62, no. 4 (1929): 17–19.

Williams, J. Harold. *Defective, Delinquent, and Dependent Boys.* Department of Research, Bulletin 1. Whittier, CA: Whittier State School, Department of Printing Instruction, 1915.

———. "Early History of the California Bureau of Juvenile Research." *Journal of Juvenile Research* 18, no. 4 (1934): 187–214.

———. *A Study of 150 Delinquent Boys.* Bulletin 1. Stanford, CA: Research Laboratory of the Buckel Foundation, Department of Education, Stanford University, 1915.

Williams, J. Harold, Millis W. Clark, Mildred S. Covert, and Edythe K. Bryant. *Whittier Social Case History Manual.* Whittier, CA: California Bureau of Juvenile Research, Whittier State School, 1921.

Wixon, I. F. *The Mission of the Border Patrol.* US Department of Labor, Immigration and Naturalization Service, Lecture no. 7, March 19, 1934. Washington, DC: Government Printing Office, 1937.

Woods, Gerald. *The Police in Los Angeles: Reform and Professionalization.* New York: Garland, 1993.

Young, Kimball. "Mental Differences in Certain Immigrant Groups." *University of Oregon Publications* 1, no. 11 (1922): 77–78.

Zamorano-Gamez, Ruben, and Eveline P. Carsman. "Chicano Consumer Participation in Health Planning: Reality and Myth." *Atisbos: Journal of Chicano Research* 1 (1975): 126–39.

Zitner, Aaron. "Davis' Apology Sheds No Light on Sterilization." *Los Angeles Times,* March 16, 2003.

SECONDARY SOURCES

Adams, Mark B., ed. *The Wellborn Science: Eugenics in Germany, France, Brazil, and Russia.* New York: Oxford University Press, 1990.

Allen, Garland E. "The Double-Edged Sword of Genetic Determinism: Social and Political Agendas in Genetic Studies of Homosexuality, 1940–1994." In *Science and Homosexualities,* ed. Vernon A. Rosario, 242–70. New York: Routledge, 1997.

———. "The Eugenics Record Office at Cold Spring Harbor, 1910–1940." *Osiris,* 2nd ser., 2 (1986): 225–64.

———. "The Misuse of Biological Hierarchies: The American Eugenics Movement, 1900–1940." *History and Philosophy of the Life Sciences* 5, no. 2 (1983): 105–28.

Almaguer, Tomás. *Racial Fault Lines: The Historical Origins of White Supremacy in California.* Berkeley: University of California Press, 1994.

Anderson, Terry H. *The Movement and the Sixties: Protest in America from Greensboro to Wounded Knee.* New York: Oxford University Press, 1995.

Anderson, Warwick. "Excremental Colonialism: Public Health and the Poetics of Pollution." *Critical Inquiry* 21, no. 3 (1995): 640–69.

———. "Immunities of Empire: Race, Disease, and the New Tropical Medicine, 1900–1920." *Bulletin of the History of Medicine* 70, no. 1 (1996): 94–118.

———. "'Where Every Prospect Pleases and Only Man Is Vile': Laboratory Medicine as Colonial Discourse." In *Discrepant Histories: Translocal Essays on Filipino Cultures,* ed. Vicente L. Rafael, 83–112. Philadelphia: Temple University Press, 1995.

Arendt, Hannah. *The Origins of Totalitarianism.* 1951. Reprint, New York: Harcourt, Brace, 1973.

Armstrong, Elizabeth N. "Hercules and the Muses: Public Art and the Fair." In *The Anthropology of World's Fairs: San Francisco's Panama Pacific International Exposition of 1915,* ed. Burton Benedict, 114–33. Berkeley, CA: Lowie Museum of Anthropology, 1983.

Arredondo, Gabriela F. *Mexican Chicago: Race, Ethnicity, and Gender, 1916–1939.* Urbana: University of Illinois Press, in press.

Balderrama, Francisco E., and Raymond Rodríguez. *Decade of Betrayal: Mexican Repatriation in the 1930s.* Albuquerque: University of New Mexico Press, 1995.

Barkan, Elazar. *The Guilt of Nations: Restitution and Negotiating Historical Injustices.* Baltimore: Johns Hopkins University Press, 2001.

———. *The Retreat of Scientific Racism: Changing Concepts of Race in Britain and the United States between the World Wars.* New York: Cambridge University Press, 1992.

Basso, Matthew, Laura McCall, and Dee Garceau, eds. *Across the Great Divide: Cultures of Manhood in the American West.* New York: Routledge, 2001.

Bayer, Ronald. *Homosexuality and American Psychiatry: The Politics of Diagnosis.* Princeton, NJ: Princeton University Press, 1987.

Beauchamp, Tom L., and James F. Childress. *Principles of Biomedical Ethics.* 6th ed. New York: Oxford University Press, 2009.

Bederman, Gail. *Manliness and Civilization: A Cultural History of Gender and Race in the United States, 1880–1917.* Chicago: University of Chicago Press, 1995.

Begos, Kevin, Danielle Deaver, John Railey, and Scott Sexton. *Against Their Will: North Carolina's Sterilization Program.* Apalachicola, FL: Gray Oak Books, 2012.

Benedict, Burton, ed. *The Anthropology of World's Fairs: San Francisco's Panama Pacific International Exposition of 1915.* Berkeley, CA: Lowie Museum of Anthropology, 1983.

Berglund, Barbara. "'The Days of Old, the Days of Gold, the Days of '49': Identity, History, and Memory at the California Midwinter International Exposition, 1894." *Public Historian* 25, no. 4 (2003): 25–49.

Biller, Robert William. "Defending the Last Frontier: Eugenic Thought and Action in the State of California, 1890–1941." MA thesis, Simon Fraser University, 1993.

Bird, Randall D., and Garland Allen. "The J.H.B. Archive Report: The Papers of Harry Hamilton Laughlin, Eugenicist." *Journal of the History of Biology* 14, no. 2 (1981): 339–53.

Birthright, Inc. *U.S. Maps Showing the States Having Sterilization Laws in 1910, 1920, 1930, 1940.* Pamphlet. Publication 5. Princeton, NJ: Birthright, Inc., n.d. In California Legislature, *California's Compulsory Sterilization Policies.*

Black, Edwin. *War against the Weak: Eugenics and America's Campaign to Create a Master Race.* New York: Four Walls Eight Windows, 2003.

Blanton, Carlos Kevin. "From Intellectual Deficiency to Cultural Deficiency: Mexican Americans, Testing, and Public School Policy in the American Southwest, 1920–1940." *Pacific Historical Review* 72, no. 1 (2003): 39–62.

Blue, Ethan. "The Strange Career of Leo Stanley: Remaking Manhood and Medicine at San Quentin State Penitentiary, 1913–1951." *Pacific Historical Review* 78:2 (2009): 210–41.

Boag, Peter. *Same-Sex Affairs: Constructing and Controlling Homosexuality in the Pacific Northwest.* Berkeley: University of California Press, 2003.

Boonstra, Heather D., and Elizabeth Nash. "A Surge of State Abortion Restrictions Puts Providers—and the Women They Service—in the Crosshairs." *Guttmacher Policy Review* 17, no. 1 (2014). www.guttmacher.org/pubs /gpr/17/1/gpr170109.html.

Bordogna, Francesca. "The Psychology and Physiology of Temperament: Pragmatism in Context." *Journal of the History of the Behavioral Sciences* 37, no. 1 (2001): 3–25.

Borrero, Sonya, Nikki Zite, and Mitchell D. Creinin. "Federally Funded Sterilization: Time to Rethink Policy?" *American Journal of Public Health* 102, no. 10 (2012): 1822–25.

Bowler, Peter J. *The Eclipse of Darwinism: Anti-Darwinian Evolution Theories in the Decades around 1900.* Baltimore: Johns Hopkins University Press, 1983.

Brandt, Allan M. *No Magic Bullet: A Social History of Venereal Disease in the United States since 1880.* Oxford: Oxford University Press, 1987.

Brasington, Campbell K. "What I Wish I Knew Then . . . Reflections from Personal Experiences in Counseling about Down Syndrome." *Journal of Genetic Counseling* 16, no. 6 (2007): 731–34.

Braslow, Joel. "In the Name of Therapeutics: The Practice of Sterilization in a California State Hospital." *Journal of the History of Medicine and Allied Sciences* 51, no. 1 (1996): 29–51.

———. *Mental Ills and Bodily Cures: Psychiatric Treatment in the First Half of the Twentieth Century.* Berkeley: University of California Press, 1997.

Braslow, Joel, and Sarah Lindsay Starks. "The Making of Contemporary American Psychiatry, Part 2: Therapeutics and Gender before and after World War II." *History of Psychology* 8, no. 3 (2005): 271–88.

Brechin, Gray. "Conserving the Race: Natural Aristocracies, Eugenics, and the U.S. Conservation Movement." *Antipode* 28, no. 3 (1996): 229–45.

———. *Imperial San Francisco: Urban Power, Earthly Ruin.* Berkeley: University of California Press, 1999.

Breines, Wini. *Young, White, and Miserable: Growing Up Female in the Fifties.* Chicago: University of Chicago Press, 1992.

Breman, Jan, ed. *Imperial Monkey Business: Racial Supremacy in Social Darwinist Theory and Colonial Practice.* Amsterdam: V.U. University Press, 1990.

Briggs, Laura. *Reproducing Empire: Race, Sex, Science, and U.S. Imperialism in Puerto Rico.* Berkeley: University of California Press, 2002.

Bright, William. *1500 California Place Names: Their Origin and Meaning.* Berkeley: University of California Press, 1998.

Broberg, Gunnar, and Nils Roll-Hansen. *Eugenics and the Welfare State: Sterilization Policy in Denmark, Sweden, Norway and Finland.* East Lansing: Michigan State University Press, 1996.

Brown, Bill. "Science Fiction, the World's Fair, and the Prosthetics of Empire, 1910–1915." In *Cultures of United States Imperialism,* ed. Amy Kaplan and Donald E. Pease, 129–63. Durham, NC: Duke University Press, 1993.

Browner, C.H., H. Mabel Preloran, Maria Christina Casado, Harold N. Bass, and Ann P. Walker. "Genetic Counseling Gone Awry: Miscommunication between Prenatal Genetic Service Providers and Mexican-Origin Clients." *Social Science and Medicine* 56 (2003): 1933–46.

Brownmiller, Susan. *In Our Time: Memoir of a Revolution.* New York: Dial Press, 1999.

Camarillo, Alberto. *Chicanos in a Changing Society: From Mexican Pueblos to American Barrios in Santa Barbara and Southern California, 1848–1930.* 1979. Reprint, Cambridge, MA: Harvard University Press, 1996.

Carey, Allison C. *On the Margins of Citizenship: Intellectual Disability and Civil Rights in 20th Century America.* Philadelphia: Temple University Press, 2009.

Carlson, Elof Axel. *The Unfit: A History of a Bad Idea.* Cold Spring Harbor, NY: Cold Spring Harbor Laboratory Press, 2001.

Caron, Simone M. "Birth Control and the Black Community in the 1960s: Genocide or Power Politics." *Journal of Social History* 31, no. 3 (1998): 545–69.

Carte, Gene E., and Elaine H. Carte. *Police Reform in the United States: The Era of August Vollmer, 1905–1932.* Berkeley: University of California Press, 1975.

Castles, Katherine. "Quiet Eugenics: Sterilization in North Carolina's Institutions for the Mentally Retarded, 1945–1965." *Journal of Southern History* 68, no. 4 (2002): 849–78.

Cavallo, Dominick. *Muscles and Morals: Organized Playgrounds and Urban Reform, 1880–1920.* Philadelphia: University of Pennsylvania Press, 1981.

Chamberlain, J. Edward, and Sander L. Gilman, eds. *Degeneration: The Dark Side of Progress.* New York: Columbia University Press, 1985.

Chan, Sucheng, ed. *Entry Denied: Exclusion and the Chinese Community in America, 1882–1943.* Philadelphia: Temple University Press, 1991.

Chandler, Cynthia. "The Gender-Responsive Prison Expansion Movement." In *Interrupted Life: Experiences of Incarcerated Women in the United States,* ed. Rickie Solinger, Paula C. Johnson, Martha L. Raimon, Tina Reynolds, and Ruby C. Tapia, 332–37. Berkeley: University of California Press, 2010.

Chapman, Paul Davis. *Schools as Sorters: Lewis M. Terman, Applied Psychology, and the Intelligence Testing Movement, 1890–1930.* New York: New York University Press, 1988.

Chávez, Ernesto. *"Mi Raza Primero!": Nationalism, Identity, and Insurgency in the Chicano Movement in Los Angeles, 1966–1978.* Berkeley: University of California Press, 2002.

Chavez, Leo R. *Covering Immigration: Popular Images and the Politics of the Nation.* Berkeley: University of California Press, 2001.

———. *The Latino Threat: Constructing Immigrants, Citizens, and the Nation.* Stanford, CA: Stanford University Press, 2008.

Chávez, Marisela R. "'We Lived and Breathed and Worked the Movement': The Contradictions and Rewards of Chicana/Mexicana Activism in el Centro de Acción Social Autónomo–Hermandad General de Trabajadores (CASA-HGT), Los Angeles, 1975–1978." In *Las Obreras: Chicana Politics of Work and Family,* ed. Vicki L. Ruiz and Chon Noriega, 83–105. Los Angeles: UCLA Chicano Studies Research Center Publications, 2000.

Chavez-Garcia, Miroslava. *States of Delinquency: Race and Science in the Making of California's Juvenile Justice System.* Berkeley: University of California Press, 2012.

Clarke, Adele E. *Disciplining Reproduction: Modernity, American Life Sciences, and "the Problems of Sex."* Berkeley: University of California Press, 1998.

Cleminson, Richard. "Eugenics by Names or by Nature? The Spanish Anarchist Sex Reform of the 1930s." *History of European Ideas* 18, no. 5 (1994): 729–40.

Comfort, Nathaniel. "Genetics: Under the Skin." *Nature* 513 (2014): 306–7.

———. *The Science of Human Perfection: How Genes Became the Heart of American Medicine.* Baltimore: Johns Hopkins University Press, 2012.

Condit, Celeste Michelle. *The Meanings of the Gene: Public Debates about Human Heredity.* Madison: University of Wisconsin Press, 1999.

Conniff, Michael L. *Black Labor on a White Canal: Panama, 1904–1981.* Pittsburgh, PA: University of Pittsburgh Press, 1985.

———. *Panama and the United States: The Forced Alliance.* 2nd ed. Athens: University of Georgia Press, 2001.

Cooke, Kathy J. "The Limits of Heredity: Nature and Nurture in American Eugenics before 1915." *Journal of the History of Biology* 31, no. 2 (1998): 263–78.

Coontz, Stephanie. *The Way We Never Were: American Families and the Nostalgia Trap.* New York: Basic Books, 1992.

Cooper, Frederick, and Ann Laura Stoler, eds. *Tensions of Empire: Colonial Cultures in a Bourgeois World.* Berkeley: University of California Press, 1997.

Cravens, Hamilton. *The Triumph of Evolution: The Heredity-Environment Controversy, 1900–1941.* Baltimore: Johns Hopkins University Press, 1988.

Cronon, William. *Nature's Metropolis: Chicago and the Great West.* New York: W. W. Norton, 1991.

———. "The Trouble with Wilderness; or, Getting Back to the Wrong Nature." In *Uncommon Ground: Rethinking the Human Place in Nature,* ed. William Cronon, 69–90. New York: W. W. Norton, 1996.

Cronon, William, George Miles, and Jay Gitlin, eds. *Under an Open Sky: Rethinking America's Western Past.* New York: W. W. Norton, 1992.

Daniels, Cynthia R., and Janet Golden. "Procreative Compounds: Popular Eugenics, Artificial Insemination and the Rise of the American Sperm Banking Industry." *Journal of Social History* 38, no. 1 (2004): 5–27.

Davis, Angela Y. *Women, Race, and Class.* New York: Vintage Books, 1981.

Davis, Mike. *City of Quartz: Excavating the Future in Los Angeles.* New York: Vintage Books, 1992.

Delaporte, François. *The History of Yellow Fever: An Essay on the Birth of Tropical Medicine.* Translated by Arthur Goldhammer. Cambridge, MA: MIT Press, 1991.

Del Castillo, Adelaida R. "Sterilization: An Overview." In *Mexican American Women in the United States: Struggles Past and Present,* ed. Madgalena Mora and Adelaida R. Del Castillo, 65–70. Occasional Paper 2. Los Angeles: UCLA Chicano Studies Research Center Publications, 1980.

Delgado, Grace Peña. *Making the Chinese Mexican: Global Migration, Exclusion, and Localism in the U.S.-Mexico Borderlands.* Palo Alto, CA: Stanford University Press, 2012.

Deloria, Philip J. *Playing Indian.* New Haven, CT: Yale University Press, 1998.

D'Emilio, John, and Estelle B. Freedman. *Intimate Matters: A History of Sexuality in America.* 2nd ed. Chicago: University of Chicago Press, 1997.

Deutsch, Sarah. "Landscape of Enclaves: Race Relations in the West, 1865–1990." In *Under an Open Sky: Rethinking America's Western Past,* ed. William Cronon, George Miles, and Jay Gitlin, 110–31. New York: W. W. Norton, 1992.

———. *No Separate Refuge: Culture, Class, and Gender on an Anglo-Hispanic Frontier in the American Southwest, 1880–1940.* New York: Oxford University Press, 1989.

Deverell, William. "Introduction: The Varieties of Progressive Experience." In *California Progressivism Revisited,* ed. William Deverell and Tom Sitton, 1–11. Berkeley: University of California Press, 1994.

———. "Plague in Los Angeles, 1924: Ethnicity and Typicality." In *Over the Edge: Remapping the American West,* ed. Valerie J. Matsumoto and Blake Allmendinger, 172–200. Berkeley: University of California Press, 1999.

Deverell, William, and Tom Sitton, eds. *California Progressivism Revisited.* Berkeley: University of California Press, 1994.

Dewitt, John B. *California Redwood Parks and Preserves.* San Francisco: Save-the-Redwoods League, 1993.

Didion, Joan. *Vintage Didion.* New York: Vintage Books, 2004.

Dikötter, Frank. *Imperfect Conceptions: Medical Knowledge, Birth Defects, and Eugenics in China*. New York: Columbia University Press, 1998.

———. "Race Culture: Recent Perspectives on the History of Eugenics." *American Historical Review* 103, no. 2 (1998): 467–78.

Dobkin, Marjorie M. "A Twenty-Five-Million-Dollar Mirage." In *The Anthropology of World's Fairs: San Francisco's Panama Pacific International Exposition of 1915*, ed. Burton Benedict, 66–93. Berkeley, CA: Lowie Museum of Anthropology, 1983.

Dorr, Gregory Michael. *Segregation's Science: Hereditarian Thought in Virginia, 1785 to the Present*. Chapel Hill: University of North Carolina Press, in press.

Dorr, Lisa Linquist. "Arm in Arm: Gender, Eugenics, and Virginia's Racial Integrity Acts of the 1920s." *Journal of Women's History* 11, no. 1 (1999): 143–66.

Dowbiggin, Ian Robert. *Keeping America Sane: Psychiatry and Eugenics in the United States and Canada, 1880–1940*. Ithaca, NY: Cornell University Press, 1997.

Dowie, Mark. *Losing Ground: American Environmentalism at the Close of the Twentieth Century*. Cambridge, MA: MIT Press, 1995.

Dreifus, Claudia. "Sterilizing the Poor." In *Seizing Our Bodies: The Politics of Women's Health*, ed. Claudia Dreifus, 105–20. New York: Vintage Books, 1977.

Dreyer, Peter. *A Gardener Touched with Genius: The Life of Luther Burbank*. New York: Coward, McCann and Geoghegan, 1975.

Dror, Otniel E. "Counting the Affects: Discoursing in Numbers." *Social Research* 68, no. 2 (2001): 357–78.

Duffy, John. *The Sanitarians: A History of American Public Health*. Urbana: University of Illinois Press, 1990.

Dunn, Timothy J. *The Militarization of the U.S.-Mexico Border, 1978–1992: Low-Intensity Conflict Doctrine Comes Home*. Austin: CMAS Books, University of Texas at Austin, 1996.

Duster, Troy. *Backdoor to Eugenics*. New York: Routledge, 2003.

Dyck, Erika. *Facing Eugenics: Reproduction, Sterilization, and the Politics of Choice*. Toronto: University of Toronto Press, 2013.

Echols, Alice. *Daring to Be Bad: Radical Feminism in America, 1967–1975*. Minneapolis: University of Minnesota Press, 1989.

Edgerton, Robert B. *The Cloak of Competence*. 2nd ed. Berkeley: University of California Press, 1993.

Eggener, Keith L. "Maybeck's Melancholy: Architecture, Empathy, Empire, and Mental Illness at the 1915 Panama-Pacific International Exposition." *Winterthur Portfolio* 29, no. 4 (1994): 211–26.

Escobar, Edward J. *Race, Police, and the Making of a Political Identity: Mexican Americans and the Los Angeles Police Department, 1900–1945*. Berkeley: University of California Press, 1999.

Espino, Virginia. "'Woman Sterilized as Gives Birth': Forced Sterilization and the Chicana Resistance in the 1970s." In *Las Obreras: Chicana Politics of Work and Family*, ed. Vicki L. Ruiz and Chon Noriega, 65–82. Los Angeles: UCLA Chicano Studies Research Center Publications, 2000.

———. "Women Sterilized as They Give Birth: Population Control, Eugenics, and Social Protest in the Twentieth-Century United States." PhD diss., Arizona State University, 2007.

Ewald, Donna, and Peter Clute. *San Francisco Invites the World: The Panama-Pacific International Exposition of 1915.* San Francisco: Chronicle Books, 1991.

Facing History and Ourselves. *Race and Membership in American History: The Eugenics Movement.* Brookline, MA: Facing History and Ourselves National Foundation, 2002.

Fernlund, Kevin, ed. *The Cold War American West, 1945–1989.* Albuquerque: University of New Mexico Press, 1998.

Fogelson, Robert M. *The Fragmented Metropolis: Los Angeles, 1850–1930.* 1967. Reprint, Cambridge, MA: Harvard University Press, 1993.

Foley, Neil. *The White Scourge: Mexicans, Blacks, and Poor Whites in Texas Cotton Culture.* Berkeley: University of California Press, 1997.

Fox, Richard W. *So Far Disordered in Mind: Insanity in California, 1870–1930.* Berkeley: University of California Press, 1978.

Frank, Dana. "Redwood Empires." In *Local Girl Makes History: Exploring Northern California's Kitsch Monuments,* 1–37. San Francisco: City Lights Books, 2007.

Gabbert, Ann R. "El Paso, a Sight for Sore Eyes: Medical and Legal Aspects of Syrian Immigration, 1906–1907." *Public Historian* 65, no. 1 (2002): 15–42.

Gallagher, Nancy L. *Breeding Better Vermonters: The Eugenics Project in the Green Mountain State.* Hanover, NH: University Press of New England, 1999.

Garcia, Mario T. *Mexican Americans: Leadership, Ideology, and Identity, 1930–1960.* New Haven, CT: Yale University Press, 1989.

Garcia, Matt. *A World of Its Own: Race, Labor, and Citrus in the Making of Greater Los Angeles, 1900–1970.* Chapel Hill: University of North Carolina Press, 2002.

Gerhard, Jane. *Desiring Revolution: Second-Wave Feminism and the Rewriting of American Sexual Thought, 1920 to 1982.* New York: Columbia University Press, 2001.

Gilmore, Ruth Wilson. *Golden Gulag: Prisons, Surplus, Crisis, and Opposition in Globalizing California.* Berkeley: University of California Press, 2007.

Gitlin, Todd. *The Sixties: Years of Hope, Days of Rage.* 2nd ed. New York: Bantam Books, 1993.

Goetzmann, William H. *Exploration and Empire: The Explorer and the Scientist in the Winning of the American West.* New York: Alfred Knopf, 1966.

Goldberg, David Theo. *Racial Subjects: Writing on Race in America.* New York: Routledge, 1997.

Gonzalez, Gilbert. *Chicano Education in the Era of Segregation.* Philadelphia: Balch Institute Press, 1990.

Gordon, Linda. *The Great Arizona Orphan Abduction.* Cambridge, MA: Harvard University Press, 1999.

———. *Woman's Body, Woman's Right: Birth Control in America*. Rev. ed. New York: Penguin Books, 1990.

Gottlieb, Robert. *Forcing the Spring: The Transformation of the American Environmental Movement*. Washington, DC: Island Press, 1993.

Gould, Stephen Jay. *The Mismeasure of Man*. 2nd ed. New York: W. W. Norton, 1996.

Greenhalgh, Paul. *Ephemeral Visions: The Expositions Universelles, Great Exhibitions and World's Fairs, 1851–1939*. Manchester: Manchester University Press, 1988.

Grob, Gerald. *The Mad among Us: A History of the Care of America's Mentally Ill*. New York: Free Press, 1994.

———. "Origins of *DSM-I*: A Study in Appearance and Reality." *American Journal of Psychiatry* 148, no. 4 (1991): 421–31.

Grossman, Atina. *Reforming Sex: The German Movement for Birth Control and Abortion Reform, 1920–1950*. New York: Oxford University Press, 1995.

Gudde, Erwin G. *California Place Names: The Origin and Etymology of Current Geographical Names*. Berkeley: University of California Press, 1960.

Gullett, Gayle Ann. *Becoming Citizens: The Emergence and Development of the California Women's Movement, 1880–1911*. Urbana: University of Illinois Press, 2000.

Gutiérrez, David G. Introduction to *Between Two Worlds: Mexican Immigrants in the United States*, ed. David G. Gutiérrez, xi–xxvii. Wilmington, Del.: Scholarly Resources, 1996.

———. "Significant to Whom? Mexican Americans and the History of the American West." *Western Historical Quarterly* 24, no. 4 (1993): 519–37.

———. *Walls and Mirrors: Mexican Americans, Mexican Immigrants, and the Politics of Ethnicity*. Berkeley: University of California Press, 1995.

Gutiérrez, Elena Rebéca. *Fertile Matters: The Politics of Mexican-Origin Women's Reproduction*. Austin: University of Texas Press, 2008.

———. "Policing 'Pregnant Pilgrims': Situating the Sterilization Abuse of Mexican-Origin Women in Los Angeles County." In *Women, Health, and Nation: Canada and the United States since 1945*, ed. Georgina Feldberg, Molly Ladd-Taylor, Alison Li, and Kathryn McPherson, 379–403. Montreal: McGill-Queen's University Press, 2003.

———. "The Racial Politics of Reproduction: The Social Construction of Mexican-Origin Women's Fertility." PhD diss., University of Michigan, 1999.

Gutiérrez, Ramón A. "Community, Patriarchy and Individualism: The Politics of Chicano History and the Dream of Equality." *American Quarterly* 45, no. 1 (1993): 44–72.

———. "Decolonizing the Body: Kinship and the Nation." *American Archivist* 57, no. 1 (1994): 86–99.

Haas, Lisbeth. *Conquests and Historical Identities in California, 1769–1936*. Berkeley: University of California Press, 1995.

Hall, Dawn, ed. *Drawing the Borderline: Artist-Explorers of the U.S.-Mexico Boundary Survey*. Albuquerque, NM: Albuquerque Museum, 1996.

Hall, Linda B., and Don M. Coerver. *Revolution on the Border: The United States and Mexico, 1910–1920*. Albuquerque: University of New Mexico Press, 1988.

Haller, Mark H. *Eugenics: Hereditarian Attitudes in American Thought*. New Brunswick, NJ: Rutgers University Press, 1963.

Haraway, Donna J. *Modest_Witness@Second_Millennium.FemaleMan©_Meets_OncoMouse™: Feminism and Technoscience*. New York: Routledge, 1997.

Harcourt, Bernard. "An Institutionalization Effect: The Impact of Mental Hospitalization and Imprisonment on Homicide in the United States, 1934–2001." Data set, ICPSR34986-v1, Inter-university Consortium for Political and Social Research, Ann Arbor, MI.

Harden, Victoria A. *Rocky Mountain Spotted Fever: History of a Twentieth-Century Disease*. Baltimore: Johns Hopkins University Press, 1990.

Harnagel, Edward E. "Physician Entrepreneurs and Philanthropists in Early Los Angeles." *Southern California Quarterly* 71, nos. 2–3 (1989): 195–209.

Hartmann, Betsy. *Reproductive Rights and Wrongs: The Global Politics of Population Control*. Rev. ed. Boston: South End Press, 1995.

Hau, Michael. *The Cult of Health and Beauty in Germany: A Social History, 1890–1930*. Chicago: University of Chicago Press, 2003.

Hendrick, Irving G., and Donald L. MacMillan. "Modifying the Public School Curriculum to Accommodate Mentally Retarded Students: Los Angeles in the 1920s." *Southern California Quarterly* 70, no. 4 (1988): 399–414.

Henig, Robin Marantz. *Pandora's Baby: How the First Test Tube Babies Sparked the Reproductive Revolution*. Boston: Houghton Mifflin, 2004.

Herman, Ellen. *The Romance of American Psychology: Political Culture in the Age of Experts*. Berkeley: University of California Press, 1995.

Hernández, Kelly Anne Lytle. "Entangling Bodies and Borders: Racial Profiling and the U.S. Border Patrol, 1924–1955." PhD diss., University of California, Los Angeles, 2002.

———. *Migra! A History of the U.S. Border Patrol*. Berkeley: University of California Press, 2010.

Herrnstein, Richard J., and Charles Murray. *The Bell Curve: Intelligence and Class Structure in American Life*. New York: Free Press, 1994.

Higham, John. *Strangers in the Land: Patterns of American Nativism, 1860–1925*. 2nd ed. New Brunswick, NJ: Rutgers University Press, 1988.

Hodgson, Jan, and Jon Weil. "Commentary: How Individual and Profession-Level Factors Influence Discussion of Disability in Prenatal Genetic Counseling." *Journal of Genetic Counseling* 25, no. 21 (2012): 24–26.

Hoffman, Beatrix. *Health Care for Some: Rights and Rationing in the United States since 1930*. Chicago: University of Chicago Press, 2012.

HoSang, Daniel. *Racial Propositions: Ballot Initiatives and the Making of Postwar California*. Berkeley: University of California Press, 2010.

Howell, Joel D., and Rodney A. Hayward. "Writing Willowbrook, Reading Willowbrook: The Recounting of a Medical Experiment." In *Useful Bodies: Human in the Service of Medical Science in the Twentieth Century*, ed. Jordan Goodman, Anthony McElligott, and Lara Marks, 190–213. Baltimore: Johns Hopkins, 2003.

Huang, Priscilla. "Anchor Babies, Over-breeders, the Population Bomb: The Reemergence of Nativism and Anti-population Control in Anti-immigration Policies." *Harvard Law and Policy Review* 2 (2008): 385–406.

Hubbard, Ruth, Mary Sue Henifin, and Barbara Fried, eds. *Biological Woman— The Convenient Myth*. Cambridge, MA: Schenkman, 1982.

Hubbell, Thelma Lee, and Gloria R. Lothrop. "The Friday Morning Club: A Los Angeles Legacy." *Southern California Quarterly* 50, no. 1 (1968): 59–90.

Ileto, Reynaldo. "Cholera and the Origins of the American Sanitary Order in the Philippines." In *Discrepant Histories: Translocal Essays on Filipino Cultures*, ed. Vicente L. Rafael, 51–81. Philadelphia: Temple University Press, 1995.

Inda, Jonathan Xavier. "Biopower, Reproduction, and the Migrant Woman's Body." In *In Decolonial Voices: Chicana and Chicano Cultural Studies in the 21st Century*, ed. Arturo J. Aldama and Naomi Quiñonez, 98–112. Bloomington: Indiana University Press, 2002.

———. "Foreign Bodies: Migrants, Parasites, and the Pathological Nation." *Discourse* 22, no. 3 (2000): 46–62.

Ise, John. *Our National Park Policy: A Critical History*. Baltimore: Resources for the Future/Johns Hopkins University Press, 1961.

Jacobson, Matthew Frye. *Whiteness of a Different Color: European Immigrants and the Alchemy of Race*. Cambridge, MA: Harvard University Press, 1998.

Jacoby, Karl. *Crimes against Nature: Squatters, Poachers, Thieves, and the Hidden History of American Conservation*. Berkeley: University of California Press, 2001.

Jameson, Elizabeth, and Susan Armitage, eds. *Writing the Range: Race, Class, and Culture in the Women's West*. Norman: University of Oklahoma Press, 1997.

Jay, Karla. *Tales of the Lavender Menace: A Memoir of Liberation*. New York: Basic Books, 1999.

Johnson, Benjamin Heber. *Revolution in Texas: How a Forgotten Rebellion and Its Bloody Suppression Turned Mexicans into Americans*. New Haven, CT: Yale University Press, 2003.

Jones, James H. *Bad Blood: The Tuskegee Syphilis Experiment*. Rev. ed. New York: Free Press, 1992.

Kantor, Harvey A. *Learning to Earn: School, Work, and Vocational Reform in California, 1880–1930*. Madison: University of Wisconsin Press, 1988.

Kay, Lily E. *The Molecular Vision of Life: Caltech, the Rockefeller Foundation, and the Rise of the New Biology*. New York: Oxford University Press, 1993.

Kearney, Jack. *Tracking: A Blueprint for Learning How*. El Cajon, CA: Pathways Press, 1978.

Keller, Ulrich. *The Building of the Panama Canal in Historic Photographs*. New York: Dover Publications, 1983.

Kevles, Daniel J. *In the Name of Eugenics: Genetics and the Uses of Human Heredity*. Rev. ed. Cambridge, MA: Harvard University Press, 1995.

Kimmel, Michael. *Manhood in America: A Cultural History*. New York: Free Press, 1996.

Kimmelman, Barbara. "The American Breeders' Association: Genetics and Eugenics in an Agricultural Context, 1903–13." *Social Studies of Science* 13 (1983): 163–204.

Kiple, Kenneth F., ed. *The Cambridge World History of Human Disease.* Cambridge: Cambridge University Press, 1993.

Klein, Kerwin Lee. *Frontiers of Historical Imagination: Narrating the European Conquest of Native America, 1890–1990.* Berkeley: University of California Press, 1997.

Kline, Wendy. *Building a Better Race: Gender, Sexuality, and Eugenics from the Turn of the Century to the Baby Boom.* Berkeley: University of California Press, 2001.

Koreck, María Teresa. "Space, Power, and Imperial Remappings of the Mexican North, 1730–1840." University of Chicago. Unpublished manuscript.

Koslow, Jennifer. *Cultivating Health: Los Angeles Women and Public Health Reform.* New Brunswick, NJ: Rutgers University Press, 2009.

Kraut, Alan M. *Silent Travelers: Germs, Genes, and the "Immigrant Menace."* Baltimore: Johns Hopkins University Press, 1995.

Kühl, Stefan. *The Nazi Connection: Eugenics, American Racism, and German National Socialism.* Oxford: Oxford University Press, 1994.

Ladd-Taylor, Molly. "Eugenics, Sterilisation and Modern Marriage in the USA: The Strange Career of Paul Popenoe." *Gender and History* 13, no. 2 (2001): 298–327.

———. "'A Kind of Genetic Social Work': Sheldon Reed and the Origins of Genetic Counseling." In *Women, Health, and Nation: Canada and the United States since 1945,* ed. Georgina Feldberg, Molly Ladd-Taylor, Alison Li, and Kathryn McPherson, 67–83. Montreal: McGill-Queen's University Press, 2003.

———. *Mother-Work: Women, Child Welfare, and the State, 1890–1930.* Chicago: University of Chicago Press, 1994.

———. "Saving Babies and Sterilizing Mothers: Eugenics and Welfare Politics in the Interwar United States." *Social Politics* 4 (1997): 136–53.

———. "The 'Sociological Advantages' of Sterilization: Fiscal Policies and Feeble-Minded Women in Interwar Minnesota." In *Mental Retardation in America: A Historical Reader,* ed. Steven Noll and James W. Trent Jr., 281–99. New York: New York University Press, 2004.

Largent, Mark A. "'The Greatest Curse of the Race': Eugenic Sterilization in Oregon, 1909–1983." *Oregon Historical Quarterly* 103, no. 2 (2002): 188–209.

Larson, Edward J. *Sex, Race, and Science: Eugenics in the Deep South.* Baltimore: Johns Hopkins University Press, 1995.

Leavitt, Judith Walzer. *Typhoid Mary: Captive to the Public's Health.* Boston: Beacon Press, 1996.

Limerick, Patricia Nelson. *The Legacy of Conquest: The Unbroken Past of the American West.* New York: W.W. Norton, 1987.

Limerick, Patricia Nelson, Clyde A. Milner II, and Charles E. Rankin, eds. *Trails: Toward a New Western History.* Lawrence: University of Kansas Press, 1991.

Lipsitz, George. *The Possessive Investment in Whiteness: How White People Profit from Identity Politics.* Philadelphia: Temple University Press, 1998.

Lira, Natalie. "'Of Low Grade Mexican Parentage': Race, Gender, and Eugenic Sterilization in California, 1928–1950." PhD diss., University of Michigan, 2015.

Lira, Natalie, and Alexandra Minna Stern. "Resisting Reproductive Injustice in California: Mexican Americans and Eugenic Sterilization, 1920–1950." *Aztlán* 39, no. 2 (2014): 9–34.

Lombardo, Paul A. "'The American Breed': Nazi Eugenics and the Origins of the Pioneer Fund." *Albany Law Review* 65, no. 3 (2002): 743–830.

———, ed. *A Century of Eugenics in America: From the Indiana Experiment to the Human Genome Era.* Bloomington: Indiana University Press, 2010.

———. "Eugenics: Lessons from a History Hidden in Plain View." Lecture to the California Legislature, Senate Select Committee on Genetics, Genetic Technologies, and Public Policy. March 11, 2003.

———. "From Better Babies to the Bunglers: Eugenics on Tobacco Road." In *A Century of Eugenics in America: From the Indiana Experiment to the Human Genome Era*, ed. Paul A. Lombardo, 45–67. Bloomington: Indiana University Press, 2011.

———. "Miscegenation, Eugenics, and Racism: Historical Footnotes to *Loving v. Virginia*." *University of California, Davis Law Review* 21, no. 421 (1988): 421–52.

———. "Three Generations, No Imbeciles: New Light on *Buck v. Bell*." *New York University Law Review* 60 (1985): 30–62.

Longmore, Paul K., and Lauri Umansky, eds. *The New Disability History: American Perspectives.* New York: New York University Press, 2001.

López, Ian F. Haney. *Racism on Trial: The Chicano Fight for Justice.* Cambridge, MA: Belknap Press of Harvard University Press, 2003.

———. *White by Law: The Legal Construction of Race.* New York: New York University Press, 1996.

Lopez, Iris. "Agency and Constraint: Sterilization and Reproductive Freedom among Puerto Rican Women in New York City." *Urban Anthropology* 22, nos. 3–4 (1993): 299–323.

Lowen, Rebecca S. *Creating the Cold War University: The Transformation of Stanford.* Berkeley: University of California Press, 1997.

Lowenthal, David. *The Past Is a Foreign Country.* New York: Cambridge University Press, 1985.

Ludmerer, Kenneth M. *Genetics and American Society: A Historical Appraisal.* Baltimore: Johns Hopkins University Press, 1972.

Lugo-Lugo, Carmen R., and Mary K. Bloodsworth-Lugo. "'Anchor/Terror Babies' and Latina Bodies: Immigration Rhetoric in the 21st Century and the Feminization of Terrorism." *Journal of Interdisciplinary Feminist Thought* 8, no. 1 (2014). http://digitalcommons.salve.edu/jift/vol8/iss1/1/?utm_source= digitalcommons.salve.edu%2Fjift%2Fvol8%2Fiss1%2F1&utm_medium= PDF&utm_campaign=PDFCoverPages.

Lunbeck, Elizabeth. *The Psychiatric Persuasion: Knowledge, Gender, and Power in Modern America.* Princeton, NJ: Princeton University Press, 1994.

Lutz, Tom. *American Nervousness, 1903: An Anecdotal History.* Ithaca, NY: Cornell University Press, 1991.

Macleod, Roy, and Milton Lewis, eds. *Disease, Medicine, and Empire: Perspectives on Western Medicine and the Experiences of European Expansion.* London: Routledge, 1988.

Madeo, Anne C., Barbara B. Biesecker, Campbell Brasington, Lori H. Erby, and Kathryn F. Peters. "The Relationship between the Genetic Counseling Profession and the Disability Community: A Commentary." *American Journal of Medical Genetics* Part A 155, no. 8 (2011): 1777–85.

Maher, Neil M. "A New Deal Body Politic: Landscape, Labor, and the Civilian Conservation Corps." *Environmental History* 7, no. 3 (2002): 435–61.

Major, John. *Prize Possession: The United States and the Panama Canal, 1903–1979.* New York: Cambridge University Press, 1993.

Markel, Howard. "Prescribing Arrowsmith." *New York Times Book Review,* Bookend essay, September 24, 2000.

———. *Quarantine! East European Jewish Immigrants and the New York City Epidemics of 1892.* Baltimore: Johns Hopkins University Press, 1997.

———. *When Germs Travel: Six Major Epidemics That Have Invaded America since 1900 and the Fears They Have Unleashed.* New York: Pantheon, 2004.

Markel, Howard, and Alexandra Minna Stern. "The Foreignness of Germs: The Persistent Association of Immigrants and Disease in American Society." *Milbank Quarterly* 80, no. 4 (2002): 757–88.

———. "Which Face? Whose Nation? Immigration, Public Health, and the Construction of Disease at America's Ports and Borders, 1891–1928." *American Behavioral Scientist* 42, no. 9 (1999): 1314–31.

May, Elaine Tyler. *Homeward Bound: American Families in the Cold War Era.* New York: Basic Books, 1988.

McCann, Carole R. "Birth Control, Eugenics, and the Foundations of Demography." Unpublished manuscript. University of Maryland, Baltimore County.

———. *Birth Control Politics in the United States, 1916–1945.* Ithaca, NY: Cornell University Press, 1994.

McClain, Charles J. *In Search of Equality: The Chinese Struggle against Discrimination in Nineteenth-Century America.* Berkeley: University of California Press, 1994.

McCullough, David. *The Path between the Seas: The Creation of the Panama Canal, 1870–1914.* New York: Simon and Schuster, 1977.

McElheny, Victor K. *Drawing the Map of Life: Inside the Human Genome Project.* New York: Basic Books, 2010.

McGurty, Eileen Maura. "From NIMBY to Civil Rights: The Origins of the Environmental Justice Movement." *Environmental History* 2, no. 3 (1997): 301–23.

McLaren, Angus. *Our Own Master Race: Eugenics in Canada, 1885–1945.* Toronto: McClelland and Stewart, 1990.

Mehler, Barry Alan. "A History of the American Eugenics Society, 1921–1940." PhD diss., University of Illinois at Urbana-Champaign, 1988.

Merchant, Carolyn. *Reinventing Eden: The Fate of Nature in Western Culture.* New York: Routledge, 2004.

Meyerowitz, Joanne. *How Sex Changed: A History of Transsexuality in the United States.* Cambridge, MA: Harvard University Press, 2002.

Mitchell, Don. *The Lie of the Land: Migrant Workers and the California Landscape.* Minneapolis: University of Minnesota Press, 1996.

Mitchell, Michele. *Righteous Propagation: African Americans and the Politics of Racial Destiny after Reconstruction.* Chapel Hill: University of North Carolina Press, 2004.

Mittman, Ilana, William R. Crombleholme, James R. Green, and Mitchell S. Golbus. "Reproductive Genetic Counseling to Asian-Pacific and Latin American Immigrants." *Journal of Genetic Counseling* 7, no. 1 (1998): 49–70.

Molina, Natalia. "Illustrating Cultural Authority: Medicalized Representations of Mexican Communities in Early-Twentieth-Century Los Angeles." *Aztlán* 28 (2003): 129–43.

Monroy, Douglas. *Rebirth: Mexican Los Angeles from the Great Migration to the Great Depression.* Berkeley: University of California Press, 1999.

Montejano, David. *Anglos and Mexicans in the Making of Texas, 1836–1986.* Austin: University of Texas Press, 1987.

Moore, Alvin Edward. *Border Patrol.* Santa Fe, NM: Sunstone Press, 1988.

Morgen, Sandra. *Into Our Own Hands: The Women's Health Movement in the United States, 1969–1990.* New Brunswick, NJ: Rutgers University Press, 2002.

Nelkin, Dorothy, and Mark Michaels. "Biological Categories and Border Controls: The Revival of Eugenics in Anti-immigration Rhetoric." *International Journal of Sociology and Social Policy* 18, nos. 5–6 (1998): 35–63.

Nelson, Alondra. *Body and Soul: The Black Panther Party and the Fight against Medical Discrimination.* Minneapolis: University of Minnesota Press, 2011.

Nelson, Jennifer A. "'Abortions under Community Control': Feminism, Nationalism, and the Politics of Reproduction among New York City's Young Lords." *Journal of Women's History* 13, no. 1 (Spring 2001): 157–80.

Newton, Jim. *Justice for All: Earl Warren and the Nation He Made.* New York: Riverhead Books, 2006.

Ngai, Mae M. *Impossible Subjects: Illegal Aliens and the Making of Modern America.* Princeton, NJ: Princeton University Press, 2004.

NICHD National Registry for Amniocentesis Study Group. "Midtrimester Amniocentesis for Prenatal Diagnosis." *Journal of the American Medical Association* 236, no. 13 (1976): 1475.

Novick, Peter. *The Holocaust in American Life.* Boston: Houghton Mifflin, 1999.

Nye, Robert A. "The Rise and Fall of the Eugenics Empire: Recent Perspectives on the Impact of Biomedical Thought on Modern Society." *Historical Journal* 36, no. 3 (1993): 687–700.

Odem, Mary E. "City Mothers and Delinquent Daughters: Female Juvenile Justice Reform in Early Twentieth-Century Los Angeles." In *California Progressivism Revisited,* ed. William Deverell and Tom Sitton, 175–99. Berkeley: University of California Press, 1994.

———. *Delinquent Daughters: Protecting and Policing Adolescent Female Sexuality in the United States, 1885–1920*. Chapel Hill: University of North Carolina Press, 1995.

Omi, Michael, and Howard Winant. *Racial Formation in the United States: From the 1960s to the 1990s*. 2nd ed. New York: Routledge, 1994.

Ono, Kent A., and John M. Sloop. *Shifting Borders: Rhetoric, Immigration, and California's Proposition 187*. Philadelphia: Temple University Press, 2002.

Ordover, Nancy. *American Eugenics: Race, Queer Anatomy, and the Science of Nationalism*. Minneapolis: University of Minnesota Press, 2003.

Ornellas, Joanne E. "An Historical Study of the Playground Movement in the City of Sacramento." MS thesis, California State University, Sacramento, 1977.

Pagan, Eduardo Obregon. *Murder at the Sleepy Lagoon: Zoot Suits, Race, and Riot in Wartime L.A.* Chapel Hill: University of North Carolina Press, 2003.

Parens, Erik, and Adrienne Asch. "The Disability Rights Critique of Prenatal Testing." *Hastings Center Report* 29, suppl. (1999): 1–22.

———, eds. *Prenatal Testing and Disability Rights*. Washington, DC: Georgetown University Press, 2000.

Pascoe, Peggy. "Democracy, Citizenship, and Race: The West in the Twentieth Century." In *Perspectives on Modern America: Making Sense of the Twentieth Century*, ed. Harvard Sitkoff, 227–46. New York: Oxford University Press, 2001.

———. "Miscegenation Law, Court Cases, and Ideologies of 'Race' in Twentieth-Century America." *Journal of American History* 83, no. 1 (1996): 44–69.

———. "Race, Gender, and the Privileges of Property: On the Significance of Miscegenation Law in the U.S. West." In *Over the Edge: Remapping the American West*, ed. Valerie J. Matsumoto and Blake Allmendinger, 215–30. Berkeley: University of California Press, 1999.

———. *Relations of Rescue: The Search for Female Moral Authority in the American West, 1874–1939*. New York: Oxford University Press, 1990.

———. *What Comes Naturally: Miscegenation Law and the Making of Race in America*. Oxford: Oxford University Press, 2009.

Paul, Diane B. *Controlling Human Heredity: 1865 to the Present*. Atlantic Highlands, NJ: Humanities Press, 1995.

———. *The Politics of Heredity: Essays on Eugenics, Biomedicine, and the Nature-Nurture Debate*. Albany: State University of New York Press, 1998.

Paul, Julius. "The Return of Punitive Sterilization Proposals: Current Attacks on Illegitimacy and the AFDC Program." *Law and Society Review* 3, no. 1 (1968): 77–106.

Pauly, Philip J. "Essay Review: The Eugenics Industry—Growth or Restructuring?" *Journal of the History of Biology* 26, no. 1 (Spring 1993): 131–45.

Pelis, Kim. "Prophet for Profit in French North Africa: Charles Nicolle and the Pasteur Institute of Tunis, 1903–1936." *Bulletin of the History of Medicine* 71, no. 4 (1997): 583–622.

Pernick, Martin S. *The Black Stork: Eugenics and the Death of "Defective" Babies in American Medicine and Motion Pictures since 1915*. New York: Oxford University Press, 1996.

———. "Eugenics and Public Health in American History." *American Journal of Public Health* 87 (1997): 1767–72.

Pick, Daniel. *Faces of Degeneration: A European Disorder, c. 1848–1918.* Cambridge: Cambridge University Press, 1989.

Platt, Anthony. *Bloodlines: Recovering Hitler's Nuremberg Laws, from Patton's Trophy to Public Memorial.* New York: Paradigm, 2005.

——— [Tony]. *What's in a Name? Charles M. Goethe, American Eugenics, and Sacramento State University.* Sacramento, CA: T. Platt, 2004.

Potter, Joseph E., Kari White, Kristine Hopkins, Sarah McKinnon, Michele G. Shedin, Jon Amastae, and Daniel Grossman. "Frustrated Demand for Sterilization among Low-Income Latinas in El Paso, Texas." *Perspectives on Sexual and Reproductive Health* 44, no. 4 (2012): 228–35.

Prescott, Heather Munro. "'I Was a Teenage Dwarf: The Social Construction of 'Normal' Adolescent Growth and Development in the United States." In *Formative Years: Children's Health in the United States, 1880–2000.* ed. Alexandra Minna Stern and Howard Markel, 153–82. Ann Arbor: University of Michigan Press, 2002.

Press, Nancy, and Carol H. Browner. "Why Women Say Yes to Prenatal Diagnosis." *Social Science and Medicine* 45, no. 7 (1997): 979–89.

Proctor, Robert. *Racial Hygiene: Medicine under the Nazis.* Cambridge, MA: Harvard University Press, 1988.

Provine, William B. "Geneticists and Race." *American Zoologist* 26 (1986): 857–87.

Rafter, Nicole Hahn, ed. *White Trash: The Eugenic Family Studies, 1877–1919.* Boston: Northeastern University Press, 1988.

Raftery, Judith Rosenberg. *Land of Fair Promise: Politics and Reform in Los Angeles Schools, 1885–1941.* Stanford, CA: Stanford University Press, 1992.

Rapp, Rayna. *Testing Women, Testing the Fetus: The Social Impact of Amniocentesis in America.* New York: Routledge, 1999.

Reagan, Leslie J. *When Abortion Was a Crime: Women, Medicine, and Law in the United States, 1867–1973.* Berkeley: University of California Press, 1997.

Reilly, Philip R. *The Surgical Solution: A History of Involuntary Sterilization in the United States.* Baltimore: Johns Hopkins University Press, 1991.

Reisler, Mark. *By the Sweat of Their Brow: Mexican Immigrant Labor in the United States, 1900–1940.* Westport, CT: Greenwood Press, 1976.

Rembis, Michael A. *Defining Defiance: Sex, Science, and Delinquent Girls, 1890–1960.* Urbana-Champaign: University of Illinois Press, 2011.

———. "The New Asylums: Madness and Mass Incarceration in the Neoliberal Era," in *Disability Incarcerated: Imprisonment and Disability in the United States and Canada,* ed. Liat-Ben Moshe, Chris Chapman, and Allison C. Carey, 139–59. New York: Palgrave Macmillan, 2014.

Resta, Robert G. "Historical Aspects of Genetic Counseling: Why Was Maternal Age 35 Chosen as the Cut-Off for Offering Amniocentesis." *Medicina nei Secoli Arte e Scienza* 14, no. 3 (2002): 793–811.

Reverby, Susan M., ed. *Tuskegee's Truths: Rethinking the Tuskegee Syphilis Study.* Chapel Hill: University of North Carolina Press, 2000.

Risse, Guenter B. "'A Long Pull, A Strong Pull, and All Together': San Francisco and Bubonic Plague, 1907–1908." *Bulletin of the History of Medicine* 66 (1992): 260–86.

Roberts, Dorothy. *Fatal Invention: How Science, Politics, and Big Business Recreate Race in the Twenty-First Century.* New York: New Press, 2012.

———. *Killing the Black Body: Race, Reproduction, and the Meaning of Liberty.* New York: Vintage Books, 1997.

Robertson, Jennifer. "Japan's First Cyborg? Miss Nippon, Eugenics, and Wartime Technologies of Beauty, Body, and Blood." *Body and Society* 7, no. 1 (2001): 1–34.

Rogers, Naomi. "'Caution: The AMA May Be Dangerous to Your Health': The Student Health Organizations (SHO) and American Medicine, 1965–1970." *Radical History Review* 80 (2001): 5–34.

Rohrbacher, Richard W. "Margaret Hamilton Smyth, M.D.: A Capable and Qualified 19th Century Woman." *Dogtown Territorial Quarterly* 49 (2002): 34–44.

Rosemblatt, Karin Alejandra. "Sexuality and Biopower in Chile and Latin America." *Political Power and Social Theory* 15 (2001): 315–72.

Rosen, Christine. *Preaching Eugenics: Religious Leaders and the American Eugenics Movement.* New York: Oxford University Press, 2004.

Rosen, Ruth. *The World Split Open: How the Modern Women's Movement Changed America.* New York: Viking, 2000.

Rosenthal, Michael. *The Character Factory: Baden-Powell and the Origins of the Boy Scout Movement.* New York: Pantheon, 1986.

Ross, Dorothy. *The Origins of American Social Science.* New York: Cambridge University Press, 1991.

Roth, Rachel, and Sara L. Ainsworth. "'If They Hand You a Paper, You Sign It': A Call to End the Sterilization of Women in Prison." *Hastings Women's Law Journal* 26, no. 7 (Winter 2015). https://litigation-essentials.lexisnexis.com /webcd/app?action=DocumentDisplay&crawlid=1&doctype=cite&docid=2 6+Hastings+Women%27s+L.J.+7&srctype=smi&srcid=3B15&key=7ff277 94b45b9a4a98ef8086ef3a9a64.

Rothman, Barbara Katz. *The Tentative Pregnancy: How Amniocentesis Changes the Experience of Motherhood.* New York: W. W. Norton, 1993.

———. *The Tentative Pregnancy: Prenatal Diagnosis and the Future of Motherhood.* New York: Penguin, 1987.

Rothman, David J., and Sheila M. Rothman. *The Willowbrook Wars: Bringing the Mentally Disabled into the Community.* 1984. Reprint, New Brunswick, NJ: AldineTransactions, 2005.

Rothman, Hal K. *Saving the Planet: The American Response to the Environment in the Twentieth Century.* Chicago: Ivan R. Dee, 2000.

Rothman, Sheila M. *Living in the Shadow of Death: Tuberculosis and the Social Experience of Illness in America.* Baltimore: Johns Hopkins University Press, 1995.

Ruiz, Vicki L. *From Out of the Shadows: Mexican Women in Twentieth-Century America.* New York: Oxford University Press, 1998.

Ruzek, Sheryl Burt. *The Women's Health Movement: Feminist Alternatives to Medical Control.* New York: Praeger, 1978.

Rydell, Robert W. *All the World's a Fair: Visions of Empire at American International Expositions, 1876–1916.* Chicago: University of Chicago Press, 1984.
———. *World of Fairs: The Century-of-Progress Expositions.* Chicago: University of Chicago Press, 1993.
Sackman, Douglas Cazaux. "Inside the Skin of Nature: Science and the Quest for the Golden Orange." In *Science, Values, and the American West,* ed. Stephen Tchudi, 117–45. Reno: Nevada Humanities Committee, 1997.
———. *Orange Empire: California and the Fruits of Eden.* Berkeley: University of California Press, 2005.
Sánchez, George J. *Becoming Mexican American: Ethnicity, Culture, and Identity in Chicano Los Angeles, 1900–1945.* New York: Oxford University Press, 1993.
Sandmeyer, Elmer Clarence. *The Anti-Chinese Movement in California.* 1973. Reprint, Urbana: University of Illinois Press, 1991.
Sapp, Jan. "The Struggle for Authority in the Field of Heredity, 1900–1932: New Perspectives on the Rise of Genetics." *Journal of the History of Biology* 16, no. 3 (1983): 311–42.
Scharff, Virginia J., ed. *Seeing Nature through Gender.* Lawrence: University of Kansas Press, 2003.
Schlossman, Steven. "Self-Evident Remedy? George I. Sanchez, Segregation, and Enduring Dilemmas in Bilingual Education." *Teachers College Board* 84, no. 4 (1983): 871–907.
Schneider, William H. *Quality and Quantity: The Quest for Biological Regeneration in Twentieth-Century France.* New York: Cambridge University Press, 1990.
Schoen, Johanna. "Between Choice and Coercion: Women and the Politics of Sterilization in North Carolina, 1929–1975." *Journal of Women's History* 13, no. 1 (2001): 132–56.
———. *Choice and Coercion: Birth Control, Sterilization, and Abortion in Public Health and Welfare.* Chapel Hill: University of North Carolina Press, 2005.
Schrag, Peter. *Not Fit for Our Society: Nativism and Immigration.* Berkeley: University of California Press, 2010.
Schrepfer, Susan R. *The Fight to Save the Redwoods: A History of Environmental Reform, 1917–1978.* Madison: University of Wisconsin Press, 1983.
Seed, Patricia. *Ceremonies of Possession in Europe's Conquest of the New World, 1492–1640.* Cambridge: Cambridge University Press, 1995.
Selden, Steven. *Inheriting Shame: The Story of Eugenics and Racism in America.* New York: Teacher's College, Columbia University, 1999.
Shah, Nayan. *Contagious Divides: Epidemics and Race in San Francisco's Chinatown.* Berkeley: University of California Press, 2001.
Shapiro, Joseph P. *No Pity: People with Disabilities Forging a New Civil Rights Movement.* New York: Three Rivers Press, 1993.
Shapiro, Thomas M. *Population Control Politics: Women, Sterilization, and Reproductive Choice.* Philadelphia: Temple University Press, 1985.
Shorter, Edward. *The Kennedy Family and the Story of Mental Retardation.* Philadelphia: Temple University Press, 2000.

Silver, Lee M. *Remaking Eden: How Genetic Engineering and Cloning Will Transform the American Family*. New York: Avon Books, 1997.

Simon, Bryant. "'New Men in Body and Soul': The Civilian Conservation Corps and the Transformation of Male Bodies and the Body Politic." In *Seeing Nature through Gender*, ed. Virginia J. Scharff, 80–102. Lawrence: University of Kansas Press, 2003.

Sisti, Dominic A., Andrea G. Segal, and Ezekiel J. Emanuel. "Improving Long-Term Psychiatric Care: Bring Back the Asylum." *Journal of the American Medical Association* 313, no. 3 (2015): 243–44.

Sitton, Tom. *John Randolph Haynes: California Progressive*. Stanford, CA: Stanford University Press, 1992.

———. "John Randolph Haynes and the Left Wing of California Progressivism." In *California Progressivism Revisited*, ed. William Deverell and Tom Sitton, 15–33. Berkeley: University of California Press, 1994.

———. "'Promoting the Well-Being of Mankind': The John Randolph Haynes and Dora Haynes Foundation." *Southern California Quarterly* 70, no. 1 (1988): 97–106.

Slotkin, Richard. *Gunfighter Nation: The Myth of the Frontier in Twentieth-Century America*. New York: HarperPerennial, 1993.

Smith, Michael L. *Pacific Visions: California Scientists and the Environment, 1850–1915*. New Haven, CT: Yale University Press, 1987.

Solinger, Rickie. *Wake Up Little Susie: Single Pregnancy and Race before Roe v. Wade*. 2nd ed. New York: Routledge, 2000.

Solnit, Rebecca. *Savage Dreams: A Journey into the Landscape Wars of the American West*. New York: Vintage, 1994.

Spiro, Jonathan Peter. "Patrician Racist: The Evolution of Madison Grant." PhD diss., University of California, Berkeley, 2000.

St. John, Rachel C. *Line in the Sand: A History of the Western U.S.-Mexico Border*. Princeton, NJ: Princeton University Press, 2011.

Starr, Kevin. *Americans and the California Dream, 1850–1915*. New York: Oxford University Press, 1973.

———. *Endangered Dreams: The Great Depression in California*. New York: Oxford University Press, 1996.

Stepan, Nancy Leys. *"The Hour of Eugenics": Race, Gender, and Nation in Latin America*. Ithaca, NY: Cornell University Press, 1991.

Stepan, Nancy Leys, and Sander L. Gilman. "Appropriating the Idioms of Science: The Rejection of Scientific Racism." In *The Bounds of Race: Perspectives on Hegemony and Resistance*, ed. Dominick LaCapra, 72–103. Ithaca, NY: Cornell University Press, 1991.

Stern, Alexandra Minna. "Buildings, Boundaries, and Blood: Medicalization and Nation-Building on the U.S.-Mexico Border, 1910–1930." *Hispanic American Historical Review* 79, no. 1 (1999): 41–81.

———. "Eugenics and Historical Memory in America." Viewpoints Section. *History Compass* 3, no. 1 (2005): 1–11.

———. "From Mestizophilia to Biotypology: Racialization and Science in Mexico, 1920–1960." In *Race and Nation in Modern Latin America*, ed. Nancy

Applebaum, Anne S. MacPherson, and Karin Alejandra Rosemblatt, 187–210. Chapel Hill: University of North Carolina Press, 2003.

———, ed. "Improving Hoosiers: Indiana and the Wide Scope of American Eugenics." Special issue, *Indiana Magazine of History* 106, no. 3 (2010).

———. "Making Better Babies: Public Health and Race Betterment in Indiana, 1920–1935." *American Journal of Public Health* 92, no. 5 (2002): 742–52.

———. "Nationalism on the Line: Masculinity, Race, and the Creation of the Border Patrol, 1910–1940." In *Continental Crossroads: Remapping U.S.-Mexico Borderlands History,* ed. Samuel Truett and Elliott Young, 299–323. Durham, NC: Duke University Press, 2004.

———. *Telling Genes: The Story of Genetic Counseling in America.* Baltimore: Johns Hopkins University Press, 2012.

———. "We Cannot Make a Silk Purse Out of a Sow's Ear: Eugenics in the Hoosier Heartland, 1900–1960." *Indiana History Magazine* 103, no. 1 (2007): 3–38.

———. "Yellow Fever Crusade: U.S. Colonialism, Tropical Medicine, and the International Politics of Mosquito Control, 1900–1920." In *Medicine at the Border: Disease, Globalization, and Security: 1850 to the Present,* ed. Alison Bashford, 41–59. London: Palgrave, 2007.

Stern, Alexandra Minna, and Howard Markel, eds. *Formative Years: Children's Health in the United States, 1880–2000.* Ann Arbor: University of Michigan Press, 2002.

Stewart, George R. *Names on the Land: A Historical Account of Place-Naming in the United States.* Boston: Houghton Mifflin, 1958.

Stocking, George W. *Race, Culture, and Evolution: Essays in the History of Anthropology.* Chicago: University of Chicago Press, 1982.

Stoler, Ann Laura. "Sexual Affronts and Racial Frontiers: European Identities and the Cultural Politics of Exclusion in Colonial Southeast Asia." In *Tensions of Empire: Colonial Cultures in a Bourgeois World,* ed. Ann Laura Stoler and Frederick Cooper, 198–237. Berkeley: University of California Press, 1997.

———, ed. *Tense and Tender Ties.* Durham, NC: Duke University Press, in press.

Stoll, Steven. *The Fruits of Natural Advantage: Making the Industrial Countryside in California.* Berkeley: University of California Press, 1998.

Sutter, Paul S. *Driven Wild: How the Fight against Automobiles Launched the Modern Wilderness Movement.* Seattle: University of Washington Press, 2002.

Takaki, Ronald. *Double Victory: A Multicultural History of America in World War II.* Boston: Little, Brown, 2000.

Tapper, Melbourne. "Interrogating Bodies: Medico-Racial Knowledge, Politics, and the Study of a Disease." *Comparative Studies in Society and History* 37, no. 1 (1995): 76–93.

Tchudi, Stephen, ed. *Science, Values, and the American West.* Reno: Nevada Humanities Committee, 1997.

Terry, Jennifer. *An American Obsession: Science, Medicine, and Homosexuality in Modern Society.* Chicago: University of Chicago Press, 1999.

———. "Anxious Slippage between 'Us' and 'Them': A Brief History of the Scientific Search for Homosexual Bodies." In *Deviant Bodies: Critical Perspectives on Difference in Science and Popular Culture,* ed. Jennifer Terry and Jacqueline Urla, 129–69. Bloomington: Indiana University Press, 1995.

Thompson, Heather Ann. "Why Mass Incarceration Matters: Rethinking Crisis, Decline, and Transformation in Postwar American History." *Journal of American History* 97, no. 3 (2010): 703–34.

Tobey, Ronald, and Charles Wetherell. "The Citrus Industry and the Revolution of Corporate Capitalism in Southern California, 1887–1944." *California History* 74, no. 2 (1995): 6–19.

Torpy, Sally J. "Native American Women and Coerced Sterilization: On the Trail of Tears in the 1970s." *American Indian Culture and Research Journal* 24, no. 2 (2000): 1–22.

Tracy, Sarah W. "An Evolving Science of Man: The Transformation and Demise of American Constitutional Medicine, 1920–1950." In *Greater Than the Parts: Holism in Biomedicine, 1920–1950,* ed. Christopher Lawrence and George Weisz, 161–88. New York: Oxford University Press, 1998.

———. "George Draper and American Constitutional Medicine, 1916–1946: Reinventing the Sick Man." *Bulletin of the History of Medicine* 66, no. 1 (Spring 1992): 53–89.

Trent, James W., Jr. *Inventing the Feeble Mind: A History of Mental Retardation in the United States.* Berkeley: University of California Press, 1994.

Tubbs, James B. *Handbook of Bioethics Terms.* Washington, DC: Georgetown University Press, 2009.

Tucker, William H. *The Funding of Scientific Racism: Wickliffe Draper and the Pioneer Fund.* Urbana: University of Illinois Press, 2002.

Utley, Robert M. *The Indian Frontier of the American West, 1846–1890.* Albuquerque: University of New Mexico Press, 1984.

Vélez-Ibáñez, Carlos G. "Se Me Acabó La Canción: An Ethnography of Nonconsenting Sterilizations among Mexican American Women in Los Angeles." In *Mexican American Women in the United States: Struggles Past and Present,* ed. Madgalena Mora and Adelaida R. Del Castillo, 71–94. Occasional Paper No. 2. Los Angeles: UCLA Chicano Studies Research Center Publications, 1980.

Wade, Nicholas. *A Troublesome History: Genes, Race, and Human History.* New York: Penguin, 2014.

Wailoo, Keith. *Dying in the City of Blues: Sickle Cell Anemia and the Politics of Race and Health.* Chapel Hill: University of North Carolina Press, 2001.

Wailoo, Keith, and Stephen Pemberton. *The Troubled Dream of Genetic Medicine: Ethnicity and Innovation in Tay-Sachs, Cystic Fibrosis, and Sickle Cell Disease.* Baltimore: Johns Hopkins University Press, 2006.

Weber, David J. *The Spanish Frontier in North America.* New Haven, CT: Yale University Press, 1992.

Weil, Jon. "Psychosocial Genetic Counseling in the Post-Nondirective Era: A Point of View." *Journal of Genetic Counseling* 12, no. 3 (2003): 199–211.

Weindling, Paul. *Epidemics and Genocide in Eastern Europe, 1890–1945.* New York: Oxford University Press, 2000.

———. *Health, Race, and German Politics between National Unification and Nazism, 1870–1945.* Cambridge: Cambridge University Press, 1989.

Weir, Robert F., Susan C. Lawrence, and Evan Fales, eds. *Genes and Human Self-Knowledge: Historical and Philosophical Reflections on Modern Genetics.* Iowa City: University of Iowa Press, 1994.

Wellerstein, Alex. "States of Eugenics: Institutions and Practices of Compulsory Sterilization in California." In *Reframing Rights: Bioconstitutionalism in the Genetic Age,* ed. Sheila Jasanoff, 29–58. Cambridge, MA: MIT Press, 2011.

Welles, Dede. "Mary Conway Kohler." Women's Legal History, 1997. www.stanford.edu/group/WLHP/papers/kohler.html.

White, Karl, Kristine Hopkins, Joseph E. Potter, and Daniel Grossman. "Knowledge and Attitudes about Long-Acting Reversible Contraception among Latina Women Who Desire Sterilization." *Women's Health Issues* 23, no. 4 (2014): 257–63.

Who Was Who in America. Vol. 2. Chicago: A. N. Marquis, 1950.

Wilson, Brian C. *Dr. John Harvey Kellogg and the Religion of Biologic Living.* Bloomington: Indiana University Press, 2014.

Withers, Charles W. J. "Authorizing Landscape: 'Authority,' Naming, and the Ordnance Survey's Mapping of the Scottish Highlands in the Nineteenth Century." *Journal of Historical Geography* 26, no. 4 (2000): 532–54.

Wollenberg, Charles. *All Deliberate Speed: Segregation and Exclusion in California Schools, 1855–1975.* Berkeley: University of California Press, 1976.

Woods, Gerald. "A Penchant for Probity: California Progressives and the Disreputable Pleasures." In *California Progressivism Revisited,* ed. William Deverell and Tom Sitton, 99–113. Berkeley: University of California Press, 1994.

———. *The Police in Los Angeles: Reform and Professionalization.* New York: Garland, 1993.

Worboys, Michael. "Tropical Diseases." In *Companion Encyclopedia of the History of Medicine,* ed. W. F. Bynum and Roy Porter, 1:512–36. New York: Routledge, 1993.

Worster, Donald. "Beyond the Agrarian Myth." In *Trails: Toward a New Western History,* ed. Patricia Nelson Limerick, Clyde A. Milner II, and Charles E. Rankin, 3–25. Lawrence: University of Kansas Press, 1991.

Wright, H. Norman. *Biblical Application for the Taylor-Johnson Temperament Analysis.* Santa Ana, CA: Christian Marriage Enrichment, 1975.

Wyatt, David. *The Fall into Eden: Landscape and the Imagination in California.* New York: Cambridge University Press, 1986.

Yaryan, Willie, Denzil Verardo, and Jennie Verardo. *The Sempervirens Story: A Century of Preserving California's Ancient Redwood Forest, 1900–2000.* Los Altos, CA: Sempervirens Fund, 2000.

Young, Elliott. *Alien Nation: Chinese Migration in the Americas from the Coolie Era through World War II.* Chapel Hill: University of North Carolina Press, 2014.

———. "Remembering Catarino Garza's 1891 Revolution: An Aborted Border Insurrection." *Mexican Studies/Estudios Mexicanos* 12, no. 2 (1996): 231–72.

Young, Robert J. C. *Colonial Desire: Hybridity in Theory, Culture, and Race.* New York: Routledge, 1995.

Yung, Judy. *Unbound Feet: A Social History of Chinese Women in San Francisco.* Berkeley: University of California Press, 1995.

Zenderland, Leila. *Measuring Minds: Henry Herbert Goddard and the Origins of American Intelligence Testing.* New York: Cambridge University Press, 1998.

Zinsser, Hans. *Rats, Lice and History: Being a Study in Biography, Which after Twelve Preliminary Chapters Indispensable for the Preparation of the Lay Reader, Deals with the Life History of Typhus Fever.* Boston: Little, Brown, 1935.

FILM AND VIDEO

The Border, directed by Tony Richardson, 1982, 107 min.

Eugenics in California: A Legacy of the Past? Video of conference, Center for Genetics and Society. YouTube, August 29, 2012. https://www.youtube.com/watch?v=BrF1QoG4g5o.

Future Past: Eugenics, Disability, and Brave New Worlds. Video of conference proceedings, Paul K. Longmore Institute on Disability, November 2013. http://longmoreinstitute.sfsu.edu/futurepast.

Acknowledgments

A book is a planned itinerary that yields unexpected journeys and much serendipity. That is certainly the case with this project, which began in a different form as a dissertation at the University of Chicago, where I was very fortunate to have the learned and inspiring guidance of George Chauncey, Friedrich Katz, Sander Gilman, and, from afar, Patricia Seed. Since that formative period, I have traveled to many places to conduct further research and moved across the country twice.

A knowledgeable archivist can be a historian's greatest ally, and I thank all those who assisted me with the research for this book. In particular, I would like to acknowledge Claudia Rivers of the University of Texas at El Paso, Roy Goodman of the American Philosophical Society, Georgiana White and Sheila O'Neill of the California State University at Sacramento, Carol Bowers and Leslie Shores at the American Heritage Center at the University of Wyoming, Marian L. Smith of the Immigration and Naturalization Service, Jim Coplan of the Commonwealth Club of California, and Theresa Salazar and Walter Brem of the Bancroft Library at the University of California at Berkeley for their generosity, hospitality, and expertise.

Friends and colleagues have enriched my life enormously during the preparation of this book. They have challenged me to pursue new questions, provided solace in difficult times, and brought much joy and laughter. Tony Platt, Beth Haas, Johanna Schoen, Molly Ladd-Taylor, and Vicki Ruiz read the manuscript in its entirety; I am indebted to them for their incisive comments. Peggy Pascoe has been a stellar series editor and has nurtured this project from the beginning. Howard Markel readmultiple versions of every chapter and always provided constructive criticism.Many other people have taken time to read parts of this book or helped me along in the writing process. They include Carol Karlsen, Rob Buffington, Ann Stoler, Laura Briggs, Nayan Shah, George Lipsitz, Anne-Emanuelle Birn, Steven Palmer, Penny Von Eschen, Gina Morantz- Sanchez, Gabriela Arredondo, Ernie Chavez, Marty Pernick, John Carson, Diane Paul, Sam Truett, Terri Koreck, Elliott Young, Emma Pérez, Dana Frank, Maria Montoya, Nancy Chen, Ellen Herman, Mary Joe Gilpin, John Gilpin, Mary Parsons, Mary Lou Stern, Andrew Stern, Barbara Berglund, Jennifer Robertson, Ilona Katzew, Paul Kramer, and Paul Lombardo.

The Center for the History of Medicine at the University of Michigan Medical School has been the ideal environment for thinking about the implications of the history explored in this book. I thank Allen Lichter, David Bloom, Howard Markel, and Tim Johnson for their commitment to medical humanities and history. I have also benefited greatly from the intellectual engagement of colleagues in the American Culture program and the Science, Technology, and Society program. I would like to acknowledge the excellent research assistance of José Amador and Shawn Kimmel, as well as the top-notch administrative skills of Jeff Clevenger. Finally, many thanks to the supportive scholars and friends at the University of California at Santa Cruz, especially those affiliated with the Chicano Latino Research Center.

Envisioning and enacting the transformation of manuscript into book would not have been possible without the dynamism and professionalism of my editor, Monica McCormick, and her editorial assistant, Randy Heyman. It was a pleasure to work closely with both of them. John Thompson, of Biomedical Communications at the University of Michigan, applied his digital and design skills to optimize the images in this book.

Grants and fellowships enabled me to conduct much of the research for this project. These included an American Heritage Center travel grant, two University of California Committee on Research grants, a Social Science Research Council International Migration Fellowship, an Albert J. Beveridge Grant from the American Historical Association, a Mellon travel grant from the University of Chicago, and a Fulbright Hays / U.S. Department of Education fellowship. Finally, my deepest gratitude is to my parents, Andrew and Mary Lou Stern, whose unconditional love and support has sustained me for almost forty years, and to my life partner, Terri Koreck, who every day manages to bring magic out of the mundane.

Portions of earlier versions of chapter 2 appeared in "Nationalism on the Line: Masculinity, Race, and the Creation of the Border Patrol, 1910–1940," in Samuel Truett and Elliott Young, eds., *Continental Crossroads: Remapping U.S.-Mexico Borderlands History* (Durham, NC: Duke University Press, 2004), 299–323, and "Buildings, Boundaries, and Blood: Medicalization and Nation-Building on the U.S.-Mexico Border," *Hispanic American Historical Review* 79, no. 1 (1999): 41–81. Both are used courtesy of Duke University Press. The production of this book was supported by a Publication Subvention Award from the Office of the Vice President for Research at the University of Michigan.

Index

AMERICAN CROSSROADS

Edited by Earl Lewis, George Lipsitz, George Sánchez, Dana Takagi, Laura Briggs, and Nikhil Pal Singh

Milton Keynes UK
Ingram Content Group UK Ltd.
UKHW030648080924
447992UK00001B/56